The Uses of the Dead

Studies in Medieval and Early Modern Canon Law

Kenneth Pennington, General Editor

Editorial Advisory Board

Uta-Renate Blumenthal, The Catholic University of America

Giles Constable, Institute for Advanced Study

Richard Helmholz, University of Chicago

John E. Lynch, The Catholic University of America

Robert Somerville, Columbia University

Brian Tierney, Cornell University

Studies in Medieval and Early Modern Canon Law

VOLUME 16

The Uses of the Dead
The Early Modern Development of Cy-Près Doctrine

Caroline R. Sherman

The Catholic University of America Press
Washington, D.C.

Copyright © 2018
The Catholic University of America Press
All rights reserved

Design and composition by Kachergis Book Design

Library of Congress Cataloging-in-Publication Data
Names: Sherman, Caroline R., 1976– author.
Title: The uses of the dead : the early modern development of Cy-près doctrine / Caroline R. Sherman.
Description: Washington, D.C. : The Catholic University of America Press, 2018. | Series: Studies in medieval and early modern canon law ; Volume 16 | Includes bibliographical references and index.
Identifiers: LCCN 2017009724 | ISBN 9780813236346 (pbk : alk. paper)
Subjects: LCSH: Charitable uses, trusts, and foundations. | Cy-près doctrine—History. | Wills.
Classification: LCC K797 .S44 2018 | DDC 346/.0642—dc23
LC record available at https://lccn.loc.gov/2017009724

remembered with a grant
Figure Foundation
intersecting serious

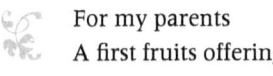 For my parents
A first fruits offering

Contents

	Acknowledgments	xi
	Abbreviations	xv
	Introduction	1
1.	Posthumous Gifts and the Soul	24
2.	Patronage Rights and Consensus in Medieval Gift Culture	61
3.	Use in the *Ius Commune*	117
4.	Humanist Influences	168
5.	Gifts in the Continental Reformations	218
6.	Charitable Uses in the English Reformation	262
7.	A Doctrine Is Born	341
	Epilogue	389
	Bibliography	401
	Index	437

Acknowledgments

This work owes its existence to my employment at the Catholic University of America, where truly distinguished medievalists and scholars of early Christianity have been my colleagues. Every early modernist should be so lucky as to have Philip Rousseau down the hall to help with Latin obscurities; Kate Jansen willing to explain what we do and do not know about feudalism while also chairing the department; Jennifer Davis available to suggest a book or two or three; Jennifer Paxton gamely answering apparently random questions about monastic property; Larry Poos on call to discuss ecclesiastical courts and their records—and to decode some truly odd legal maxims; Bill Klingshirn ready to chat about Roman wills; or Uta-Renate Blumenthal holding forth at a dinner party hosted by Ken Pennington. As for Ken himself, there is no possible way to describe the good fortune of inadvertently winding up as a junior colleague to Ken Pennington, except to say that in an ideal world, this would happen to every newly minted Ph.D.

Without the seminars and workshops, idle chatter and serious conversation, and coursework and dissertation work largely on medieval topics, I would never have begun to question the mythology of the canon law origins of cy-près, which I was happily and unreflectively parroting in my course on the history of law. One day, though, in the midst of a lecture, I asked myself: "Why would theologians and jurists give credit for works done with property that the testator no longer needed?" It was only with the patient help of my colleagues that I could begin looking for an answer to that question. And while the Catholic University of America is particularly known for medieval history, my colleagues in other fields have all also been a source of inspiration, support, and engaging debate. I offer heartfelt thanks to Ron Calinger, raconteur for whom nothing human is foreign; Tom Cohen, for his support and sage advice; Michael Kimmage, for invigorating conversation; Arpad von Klimo, who encouraged this project and others; Laura Mayhall, guardian angel in human form; Timothy Meagher, for his kindness and sense of perspective; Nelson Minnich, who gave invaluable suggestions on what to read; Jerry Z. Muller, mentor and friend; James Riley, my first chair, who read everything his colleagues wrote; Jason Sharples, now at Florida Atlantic University but certainly missed; Leslie Woodcock Tentler and her husband Thomas Tentler, who between them can answer nearly any question on Catholic history; Lev Weitz, a happy new addition to the department; Steve West, redoubtable chair of the executive council; and Julia Young, comrade.

More broadly, the resources and support of the Catholic University of America, its faculty and students, and its library and library staff were vital, as were the resources of the Library of Congress and, although I am loathe to admit it, Google Books. My mother-in-law, Maria Skladany, and Shea-Mikal Green both made it possible for me to find quiet time for working.

The anonymous reviewers for this project gave remarkable, detailed, invaluable comments that tried mightily to save me from my own worst tendencies. As I worked through their comments I came to see just how charitable the peer review process is, with so much effort spent so selflessly trying to snatch the author out of the fire. Neither reviewer can be held accountable for the argument of the book, with which they do not necessarily agree, but both gave it a fair and considered response and transformed it with their responses. Neil Jones generously shared the results of his meticulous research in the Chancery archives. Peter Gohn provided research assistance and edited an early draft of this work. Trevor Lipscombe, Theresa Walker, and the staff at CUA Press were unstinting in their wise advice, patience, and help. The book benefitted enormously from the editorial and copyediting work of Susan Needham.

Mark Kishlansky, who died as I was working on this project, was a mentor to me, and to so many others, during my undergraduate studies. In addition to his many other endearing qualities, he was a remarkable and generous teacher. There are other mentors and teachers who are owed thanks for their patient help along the way, including Ann Blair, Anthony Grafton, James Hankins, Louis Miller, and Theodore Rabb. They have all made me cognizant of infinite debts, never repaid.

My family supported this project unstintingly, particularly my mother, Laurel Price Jones, who helped me edit some of the most challenging sections. My father, Thomas Sherman, and my sister, Claire Sherman, both offered encouragement at the right moments. My beloved children, Beatrice, Pascal, and Theodora, have grown up with this book, moving from diapers to noisy scholastic disputations on the topics they set for themselves, such as "Did God make God?" and the slightly less elevated but more testable "Do gingerbread men actually run?"—a question they answered with careful scientific experimentation. My husband, Martin, a legal scholar in his own right—with, blessedly, a side interest in wills and trusts—was willing to talk endlessly about this project with me. He is a man who hates praise, so in lieu of proper credit for everything he did, I'll just say that without him this book would be nothing more than a fond thing, vainly invented, and grounded upon no warrant. To the extent that it remains in that state after these years, the fault is all my own.

Abbreviations

References to Roman Law

Code 1.1.1	*Corpus iuris civilis,* Code
Codex Theodosianus 1.1	Theodosian Code
Digest 1.1.1.1	*Corpus iuris civilis,* Digest
Institutes 1.1.1	*Corpus iuris civilis,* Institutes
Nov. 1.1	*Corpus iuris civilis,* Novels

References to Canon Law

C.1 q.1 c.1	Gratian's *Decretum,* Causae
Clem. 1.1.1	*Constitutiones Clementinae*
D.1 c.1	Gratian's *Decretum,* Distinctiones
De poen. D.1 c.1	Gratian's *Decretum,* Tractatus de Poenitentia
Extrav. Jo. XXII	*Extravagantes Joannis XII*
Gl. Ord. ad	Ordinary Gloss on a text
VI 1.1.1	*Liber sextus*
X 1.1.1	*Liber extra*

References to the English Reports Series

2 Freem.	Freeman's Reports, Chancery
Amb.	Ambler's Reports, Chancery
Beav.	Beavan's Reports, Rolls Court
Bro. C.C.	Brown's Chancery Cases
Bulst.	Bulstrode's Reports, King's Bench

Abbreviations

Co. Rep.	Coke's Reports, King's Bench
Cro. Eliz.	Croke's Reports, Elizabeth's reign, King's Bench
Eq. Ca. Abr.	Equity Cases Abridged, Chancery
Finch	Finch's Precedents in Chancery
Jenk. Cent.	Jenkins's Reports, Exchequer
Jones, W.	William Jones's Reports, King's Bench
Lane	Lane's Reports, Exchequer
Moo. K.B.	Moore's Reports, King's Bench
P. Wms	Peere Williams's Reports, Chancery
Ph.	Phillips's Reports, Chancery
Plowden	Plowden's Reports, King's Bench
Pop.	Popham's Reports, King's Bench
Show. K.B.	Shower's Reports, King's Bench
Toth.	Tothill's Reports, Chancery
Vern.	Vernon's Reports, Chancery
Ves.	Vesey Junior's Reports, Chancery
Ves. Jr.	Vesey Junior's Reports, Chancery
Ves. Sen.	Vesey Senior's Reports, Chancery
Wilm.	Wilmot's Notes of Cases, King's Bench

Miscellaneous

2–4 Inst.	Coke, *Institutes of the Lawes of England*, parts 2–4
21 Hen. 8 c.5	Statute of Henry VIII, regnal year 21, chapter 5
A.2d	Atlantic Reporter, Second Series
All E.R.	All England Law Reports
Allen	Allen's Reports of Massachusetts
Co. Litt.	Coke on Littleton
Conn.	Connecticut Reports
Duke	Duke, *Law of Charitable Uses*
Duke (Moore)	Moore's *Reading on the Statute of Charitable Uses* in Duke, *Law of Charitable Uses*

Gray	Gray's Massachusetts Supreme Judicial Court Reports
Herne	Herne, *Law of Charitable Uses*
LF	Libri Feudorum
Mass.	Massachusetts Reports
N.E.	North Eastern Reporter
PG	J.-P. Migne, ed., Patrologia Graeca
PL	J.-P. Migne, ed., Patrologia Latina
PRO	Public Record Office
Ritchie	Ritchie, *Reports of Cases Decided by Francis Bacon*
S.P. Dom.	State Papers Domestic, National Archives
U.S.	United States Reports of the Supreme Court
Watts	Watts Reports of Pennsylvania
Westminster 2	Statute of Westminster 2
Y. B.	Year Book

Introduction

> But tho' this piety to the deceased and regard to the will of the testator inclines us to dispose of his goods and obey his will for some time after his death, yet we do not naturally imagine that this regard is to last for ever. In a few years, often in a few months, our respect for the will of (the) testator is altogether worn off.
> Adam Smith, *Lectures on Jurisprudence*,
> Report of 1762–63, section 155

In the 1620s, Puritans began buying the rights for tithes and placements in the Anglican Church.[1] These Puritans were the "Feoffees for Impropriations," and their goal was to control the placement of ministers, preaching ministers, and schoolmasters. When this practice—or plot—was discovered, the crown claimed the property was forfeit to be used *ad opus nostrum*. In the 1633 *Feoffees for Impropriations Case (Attorney-General v. Gouge)*, the lord high treasurer, Richard, Lord Weston, earl of Portland, gave the king's explanation of what would be done with the forfeited goods. He quoted the king: "(to use his own words)… he would not poison his treasurers with anything so ill gotten." Instead, "he would yet use it according to the intent of the donors as near as might be."[2] The goods were forfeit and "ill got-

---

1. They purchased impropriations, the right for a lay person or lay institution to collect tithes from ecclesiastical property, and advowsons, the right to "present," or nominate, a candidate to fill an ecclesiastical vacancy.

2. W. H. Bryson, ed., *Cases Concerning Equity and the Courts of Equity 1550–1660*, vol. 2 (London: Selden Society, 2001), 657.

ten"—but the king would still honor donor intent. And yet nothing could have been further from the original intent of the Puritans than the use that Charles I announced was the next closest thing. He gave the property to the supervision of Archbishop Laud, archenemy of the Puritans. This is prerogative cy-près, created by the Reformation and evidenced in early seventeenth-century cases like this one. This book explains how cy-près power and its attendant doctrine developed in the early modern period and why Charles I made, in probable sincerity, a statement that appears to us to be absurd.

Prerogative cy-près is one of two forms of cy-près doctrine; it governs the power to take gifts that have been given for one purpose and turn them to a new purpose that approximates the old. The label "prerogative cy-près" refers most often to non-conforming (superstitious or dissenting) religious gifts that were altered to support the Established Church, although it is also associated with changes to charitable gifts made on the basis of the king's authority and prerogative, through his Sign Manual, that is, his signature.[3] The other form is equitable, or judicial, cy-près, which we also find in early modern cases in Chancery, the court of equity under the supervision of the lord chancellor. Equitable cy-près rescues a charitable trust whose purpose is failing by redirecting it to a new, similar purpose. The Restatement (Third) of Trusts offers an oft-cited definition of cy-près:

Unless the terms of the trust provide otherwise, where property is placed in trust to be applied to a designated charitable purpose and it is or becomes unlawful, impossible, or impracticable to carry out that purpose, or to the extent that it is or becomes wasteful to apply all of the property to the designated purpose, the charitable trust will not fail but the court will direct application of the property or appropriate portion thereof to a charitable purpose that reasonably approximates the designated purpose.[4]

---

3. I do not attempt to define superstition in this book; rather I report where superstition is perceived in the eye of the beholder.
4. Restatements are summaries of law produced by the American Law Institute. The third restatement of trust law was promulgated in 2001 and continues to be updated: *Restatement (Third) of Trusts* (St. Paul, Minn.: American Law Institute, 2003–) § 67.

For example, if a testator left money in a trust for a London lazar house, a judge might invoke cy-près doctrine to turn the trust over to a hospital or medical research facility, on the grounds that there are so few, if any, lepers left in contemporary London. In the modern world, cy-près has similarly been used to alter trusts for the redemption of nonexistent British slaves held in Turkey or Barbary, for the maintenance of smallpox hospitals after the creation of the vaccine, and for the purpose of converting Native Americans near William and Mary College after they had all been driven out of the region.[5] This remarkable power has given judges wide latitude to redirect charitable gifts, from object to object and purpose to purpose. The Third Restatement follows a broader common law trend in setting the judge free from an earlier requirement in cy-près that the settlor must have been found to have "manifested a more general intention to devote the property to charitable purposes" before cy-près power would be employed.[6] These were the original grounds for cy-près: that, in honor of a general charitable intention, donor intent might be approximated so that it might not fail.

To go along with this remarkable power, cy-près has had an equally striking origin story bestowed upon it. As this origin story goes, the Catholic Church considered gifts made on the deathbed by *verba novissima* or through the last will and testament to be potentially essential to the donor's salvation, which meant that their fulfillment was critical to his or her eternal life.[7] To be sure, medieval canon law allowed last wills and testaments to be given orally, literally on the deathbed, to a confessor priest, who might then act as executor in carrying out these precious last intentions, which provided "the means whereby the Christian might perform the charitable acts that

---

5. *Attorney-General v. Ironmongers' Company*, 2 Beav. 316; *Attorney-General v. Kell*, 2 Beav. 578; *Attorney-General v. Oglander*, 3 Bro. C.C. 166; *Case of Robert Boyle's Charity*, 3 Bro. C.C. 171 and 1 Ves. Jr. 243. In the Boyle's case, "for want of objects ... the charity, therefore, must be applied *de novo*."

6. *Restatement (Second) of Trusts* § 399 (St. Paul, Minn.: American Law Institute Publishers, 1959).

7. Frederick Pollock and Frederic William Maitland, *The History of English Law Before the Time of Edward I*, vol. 1 (Cambridge: Cambridge University Press, 1968), 314.

4   Introduction

were required of him."⁸ Consequently, "the welfare of the decedent's soul" could seem to be "at stake in every bequest."⁹ If one holds with this interpretation of Catholic soteriology, then the term "cy-près" appears to refer to the necessity of carrying out the testator's wishes as closely as possible (*aussi près que possible*), because of the eternal consequences attached to the performance of the legacies, or alternatively it could mean that the terms of the donations should be changed, but only slightly, if they could not be implemented perfectly. Since canon law asserted that salvation was held to be the highest purpose of the law, other legal principles or forms might equitably be mitigated in order to save souls. If a bishop rescued a failed charitable gift, approximating its original terms, he might thereby be considered to have snatched souls out of the fire by making good their last charitable intentions.

This book argues, in opposition to this origin story, that cy-près is better understood as an early modern development in English law, not even necessarily directly descended from *ius commune* treatment of impossible gifts, which also changed from the fourteenth century on as a consequence of some of the same pressures that would help to produce cy-près, but which always retained a number of concerns and norms that were antithetical to cy-près power as exercised in England. In fact, cy-près rulings are first documented only in seventeenth-century cases, and there are many good reasons to doubt that cy-près can be traced back to concerns over salvation and to locate its emergence, instead, in the seizure of ecclesiastical endowments. After all, the doctrine is not attested before the seventeenth century, not even in Francis Moore's 1607 reading upon the 1601 statute of charitable uses.¹⁰ Seventeenth- and eighteenth-century

---

8. Michael Sheehan, *The Will in Medieval England: From the Conversion of the Anglo-Saxons to the End of the Thirteenth Century* (Toronto: Pontifical Institute of Mediaeval Studies, 1963), 303.

9. Harold J. Berman, *Law and Revolution: The Formation of the Western Legal Tradition* (Cambridge, Mass.: Harvard University Press, 1983), 236–37.

10. Gareth Jones, "Francis Moore's Reading on the Statute of Charitable Uses," *The Cambridge Law Journal* 25 (1967): 224–38. Moore argues that an heir must give consent to the changing of a condition, and he does not allow the chancellor to deviate from one charitable use to another: "A Case from Frances

sources are ambivalent and uncertain about the concept: it is unevenly applied or at times ignored altogether. Although the presumption, resting on the legend of cy-près origins, has been that prerogative cy-près derived from an older, existing judicial cy-près, in fact both arose within the early modern context, and the correct order of events may have been the reverse of the order that has been assumed. Prerogative cy-près, originating as it did in the secularization of church property, may have helped to set the stage for the less far-reaching judicial cy-près to develop.[11] The origin story of cy-près makes it seem as if the power to alter gifts rests on the doctrine: the moral and equitable impulse to honor the charitable intentions of the dead prompted the creation of a power to do so. But it is also possible to imagine that judges developed the doctrine to tame the unilateral power to take and redirect gifts that had been asserted in the Reformation. This unilateral power had been a repudiation of the earlier *ius commune* preference to arrive at consensus among all of the interested parties to a failing gift, including the heirs, the beneficiaries, and the trustees.

The memorable origin story of cy-près has caused it to be seen as a paradigmatic example of the influence of the medieval *ius commune* on modern common law, and indeed the broad *ius commune* roots of English testamentary law are undeniable.[12] As Michael Sheehan

---

Moore's Reading," Appendix G, in Gareth Jones, *History of the Law of Charity, 1532–1827* (Cambridge: Cambridge University Press, 1969), 249. Cambridge University Library MS Hh. III 2(c); an abridged copy is published in George Duke, *Law of Charitable Uses* (London: Henry Twyford, 1676).

11. This is not to deny that prerogative cy-près had important legal antecedents, such as civil forfeiture, deodands, resumption, and the treatment of surpluses. Moreover, the legal struggles over the secularization or alteration of church property certainly began before the Reformation.

12. R. H. Helmholz, *The Oxford History of the Laws of England*, vol. 1: *The Canon Law and Ecclesiastical Jurisdiction from 597 to the 1640s* (Oxford: Oxford University Press, 2004), 417–18; R. H. Helmholz, "The Law of Charity and the English Ecclesiastical Courts," in *The Foundations of Medieval English Ecclesiastical History* (Woodbridge, England: Boydell Press, 2005), 111–23; Herbert Felix Jolowicz, *Roman Foundations of Modern Law* (Oxford: Clarendon Press, 1957), 139; Harold J. Berman, *Law and Revolution*, 236–37; Reinhard Zimmermann, "Cy-près," in *Iuris Professio: Festgabe für Max Kaser zum 80. Geburtstag*, ed. Hans-Peter Benöhr et al. (Vienna: Böhlau, 1986), 395–415; Joseph Willard, "Illustrations of the Origin of 'cy

has shown, the medieval English will was derived from the "theory of bequest, drawn from Roman civil law, and the simplified canonical requirements for validity."[13] Suggestively, English probate was even more solicitous toward the testator than canon law officially required, which could be taken as evidence that English courts were particularly focused on the observation of the last wishes of the testator, even if the form in which they were conveyed was imperfect.[14] Since medieval English ecclesiastical courts had simultaneous supervision over testaments and over the care of the poor, both of which relate to cy-près, the belief that cy-près derived from canon law was reasonable, particularly given that cy-près has also been attributed to the other half of the *ius commune*, that is, to pre-Christian Roman law.[15] H. F. Jolowicz asserted this connection in his unfinished *Roman Foundations of Modern Law*, citing the "preferential treatment given charitable legacies which is also at the root of the English *cy-près* doctrine."[16] One opinion from the Digest in particular has been used to argue that Romans had cy-près powers to redirect bequests to new purposes.[17]

The *ius commune* had two primary terms to describe changes in gifts. The first, commutation, was a power that bishops could exercise to moderate the terms of a gift with respect to time, place, frequency, mode, or kind, ideally with the consent of the interested parties. The second was conversion, which changed the use, or purpose, of a gift and ordinarily required a dispensation from the pope, who also normally demanded the consent of all interested parties

---

près,'" *Harvard Law Review* 8 (1894): 69–92; Edith L. Fisch, "The Cy Pres Doctrine and Changing Philosophies," *Michigan Law Review* 51 (1953): 375–88; George Bogert, *Trusts and Trustees* § 431 (St. Paul, Minn.: West Publishing, 1935).

13. Michael Sheehan, "Canon Law and English Institutions: Some Notes on Current Research," in *Marriage, Family, and Law in Medieval Europe: Collected Studies*, ed. James K. Farge (Toronto: University of Toronto Press, 1997), 32. See also Sheehan, *The Will in Medieval England*.

14. R. H. Helmholz, *Roman Canon Law in Reformation England* (Cambridge: Cambridge University Press, 1990), 7.

15. Sheehan, "Canon Law and English Institutions," in *Marriage, Family, and Law*, 32.

16. H. F. Jolowicz, *Roman Foundations*, 139.

17. Digest 33.2.16.

to the change. In Anglo-American common law, deviation is similar to commutation because it allows that, when a trust cannot be fulfilled according to the exact specifications, some modification may be made in order to maintain the purpose of the gift. Thus, if an endowment was supposed to support ten poor scholars but was sufficient for the support of only five, the principle of deviation, or *ius commune* commutation, might allow the terms of the trust to be modified to support the five.[18] However, neither deviation nor commutation changed the purpose, as cy-près does, and in modern common law deviation is available to charitable and non-charitable trusts alike, which means that it is not necessarily related to the privileges of charity, although it is easiest to apply to charitable trusts, in part because the broader power of cy-près to alter the purpose makes deviation appear relatively insignificant in comparison.[19] The availability of both deviation and cy-près for charitable trust adjustment has also made the line between the two powers less obvious, particularly because under cy-près treatment of trusts, "purpose" has lost the earlier, more abstract sense of *usus*, a legal category with many resonances, and has often been treated as if it referred to the specific terms of the gift. This change in the understanding of purpose obscures the history of cy-près, because if the property of a medieval hospital was applied to another hospital, it might be understood today as a similar purpose rather than the same purpose, as it would have been understood at the time. Thus a medieval commutation might appear to us to change the purpose of the gift and thereby incorrectly seem to be an early example of cy-près.

Roman and canon testamentary law have their differences—for example, Roman law is less flexible about form and accordingly more

---

18. The phrase "as close as possible" could easily be used to describe the allowable deviation. For example, in this case the closest approximation would be to support all five scholars, not three with the remainder of the money to be used in some other way. I do not believe that this limitation placed on the operation of deviation is the origin point for cy-près, but it does reinforce cy-près as a principle and confuse the issue.

19. Modern common law, for example, struggles over the distinction between administrative terms, which are fairly easily deviated from, and dispositive terms, which have stricter rules applied to them.

prone to break the whole will if one part is not perfectly made.[20] The fact that despite these differences cy-près had apparent support from both sides of the *ius commune* seems compelling, and when eighteenth-century jurists linked it to the *ius commune* and to benighted medieval traditions more generally, they did so on the basis of an already constructed early modern idea of the "Middle Ages."[21] So convincing was this story of cy-près—whose origins were hyperbolically described as "striking with deepest root into the soil of mediaeval society from the earliest period"—that for a time it was thought that perhaps cy-près ought to be discarded in a new, more rational age.[22] When cy-près revived in force in the Progressive era— in America under the legal reasoning of Oliver Wendell Holmes Jr.— it did so on the grounds of utility and in order to suit new, ever expanding, purposes.[23]

Since a major form of cy-près application was the redistribution, to charitable purposes, of gifts made for "superstitious" purposes, it is odd that judges who were making cy-près distributions should have drawn on a law that they derived from these superstitions, as if superstition could drive out superstition—and dissenting belief too. It is also strange that a doctrine so supposedly linked to Catholic soteriology—or at least to a caricature of Catholic soteriology—should

20. James Brundage has described the difference as follows: "canon law favoured flexible disposition by testament, while civil law tended to prefer succession according to fixed rules." *Medieval Canon Law* (London: Longman, 1995), 97.
21. J. G. A. Pocock, *The Ancient Constitution and the Feudal Law: A Study of English Historical Thought in the Seventeenth Century: A Reissue with a Retrospect* (Cambridge: Cambridge University Press, 1987); R. J. Smith, *The Gothic Bequest: Medieval Institutions in British Thought, 1688–1863* (Cambridge: Cambridge University Press, 1987); May McKisack, *Medieval History in the Tudor Age* (Oxford: Clarendon Press, 1971).
22. Willard, "Illustrations," 69. Alternatively: "originally conceived in its present form in the eleventh century," Eric G. Pearson, "Reforming the Reform of the Cy Pres Doctrine: A Proposal to Protect Testator Intent," *Marquette Law Review* 90 (2006): 127, citing Marion Fremont-Smith, *Governing Nonprofit Organizations* (Cambridge, Mass.: Belknap Press, 2004), 173; or "derived exclusively from [the *Corpus Iuris Civilis*]," William Robert Augustus Boyle, *A Practical Treatise on the Law of Charities* (London: Saunders and Benning, 1837), v–vi.
23. Rachael P. Mulheron, *The Modern Cy-près Doctrine: Applications and Implications* (London: Cavendish Publishing, 2006).

have flourished in the aftermath of a Reformation that emphatically denied the utility of works even in life, much less after death. But the civil law could be a foil to common law for the most uncomfortable part of the ruling, the loss of the rights of the heirs to property whose purpose was being diverted.[24] This use of Roman-canon law as an apparent precedent could in fact mitigate two misgivings about the doctrine: first, that it violated the specific stated intentions of the testator, and second, that it kept the failed charitable portion of the estate out of the hands of the heirs. Early modern judges who applied cy-près sometimes relieved their consciences by noting that the testator had settled other property on his or her heirs, or they directed that a portion of the new charitable scheme should go to any relations of the testator who qualified as poor, even against the express intentions of the testator.

At first glance the component parts of cy-près do seem ubiquitous in medieval testamentary law. Cy-près appears to be anticipated wherever there is a mention of following a testator's wishes or an example of modifying the terms of a gift. Approximation can represent two different motions—either to permit imperfect performance as good enough or to allow an intentional departure from a standard—and either could be considered an example of a "near enough is good enough" principle. Cy-près connects to many legal themes that are not distinctive to it, including the privileges of charity, the duty to execute the will of the testator exactly and promptly, remedies for a gift that is insufficient to its stated purposes, the replacement of faithless trustees, and the sacredness of a testator's intentions.

That a last will should be scrupulously observed can be traced back through Gregory the Great and into Roman law, but cy-près sits uncomfortably with that principle, because it claims to follow the donor's intentions by modifying them.[25] The intentions are honored

---

24. In the *Venables Case* of 1607 and 1608, the heirs were warned that civil law, which forfeited illegal gifts, would prevent the return of the property in question. Civil law also appears as a foil in *White v. White*, 1 Bro. C.C. 15, and *Attorney-General v. Downing*, Wilm. 33.

25. C.18 q.8 c.4; Code 1.2.1.

in their very breach. Cy-près doctrine is implicitly paradoxical and polysemic; it approaches the status of a contranym, a word with two opposing meanings, such as "cleave." After all, at times the legal application of cy-près doctrine has arrived at purposes that are notoriously at odds with the original intentions of the settlor. In 1754 *Da Costa v. De Pas* took money that had been left to create a center for Jewish study and education and used it instead to pay for a Christian preacher in a foundling hospital.[26] Similarly, at the turn of the millennium, the repeated cy-près revisions and equitable deviations to the Barnes Foundation trust were made in flagrant violation of the donor's stated intentions: a significant collection of impressionist art left in a trust to serve as the study materials for a school for fine art, whose premises they were never to leave, instead became a museum that sent the art out on global tour and eventually decamped for Philadelphia.[27] These cases are exceptional, but they speak to the tension inherent in cy-près, which gives the judiciary the power to make a better charitable use out of property while trying to make the testator's intentions justify the shift. As it turns out, the dead are exceptionally agreeable to the perspectives of the living: it is not uncommon to find a judge who first criticizes the wisdom of the donor's plans but then explains that the donor, despite his or her limitations, would have agreed with the judge's ultimate ruling.[28]

This focus on donor intent, however convoluted, seems to be the fundamental characteristic of cy-près; it is also an obvious connection to the *ius commune*, which emphasized the *voluntatem fundatorum*. But the purpose of testamentary law is to allow the wishes of the testator to be honored if they are both legal and possible. If a legal culture gives the right to testate, that is, to make a will, then any statement that a testator's wishes should be followed as closely as possible could be a virtual tautology, nearly equivalent to an observation that the law ought to be followed as closely as possible. Since,

26. Amb. 228 (1754).
27. Neil L. Rudenstine, *The House of Barnes: The Man, the Collection, and the Controversy*, Memoirs of the American Philosophical Society, vol. 266 (Philadelphia: American Philosophical Society, 2012).
28. For example, *Attorney-General v. Tyndall* (1764), Amb. 614.

at times, some donations will inevitably be illegal, impractical, or not feasible, all testamentary law will wrestle with whether in these circumstances a bequest should be amended or returned to the estate. An impossible gift cannot be implemented; the bequest will necessarily change in some way. This problem is magnified in the case of trusts, since the attempt to dictate perpetual terms to govern an uncertain future makes the likelihood of failure even greater. Cy-près is not distinctive in claiming to honor a donor's will or intentions, nor is cy-près equivalent to any permitted legal deviation or allowance of imperfect performance. And so the focus on intentions is deceiving: neither adherence to intentions nor deviations from intentions is necessarily connected to the emergence of cy-près, because cy-près has its own characteristic logic.

This logic is not found in the canonical privileges of charity, even though they are frequently cited in cy-près rulings. Chancery claimed, from *ius commune* origins, the right to distribute imperfect charitable gifts, particularly if the object was uncertain or if the form of the gift was defective. A bequest "to the poor" or "to charity" could be directed by Chancery, which stepped into the role of the ordinary, who had normally been empowered since late antiquity to distribute alms that were given to him for a general charitable purpose as he saw fit.[29] After all, the equitable jurisdiction of Chancery over charity has been derived from the power of the ordinary, from transferred principles of ecclesiastical courts, or from the king's role as *parens patriae*.[30] But the connection between this privilege of uncertainty and cy-près doctrine is much less obvious than it might seem. For one thing, as cy-près doctrine developed, it sometimes circumscribed these traditional

29. Jerome Daniel Hannan, "The Canon Law of Wills: An Historical Synopsis and Commentary" (J.C.D. dissertation, The Catholic University of America, 1934), 419.
30. Timothy S. Haskett, "The Medieval English Court of Chancery," *Law and History Review* 14 (1996): 245–313; Mark Fortier, *The Culture of Equity in Early Modern England* (Aldershot, England: Ashgate, 2005). John Fortescue, "In Praise of the Laws of England," in *On the Laws and Governance of England*, ed. Shelley Lockwood (Cambridge: Cambridge University Press, 1997), 78. Canon lawyers also gave the church and the king joint jurisdiction over the poor: Gl. Ord. ad C.24 q.3 c.21.

privileges and required definite trusts within specific charitable parameters, rather than open-ended trusts expressing only a broad eleemosynary intent that would have been honored in canon law. That is, English judges deliberately refused some of the powers of the ordinary in relationship to charitable trusts, even if that meant that a charitable intention would fail.

More significantly, it was broad, undefined gifts "to the poor" that, to use anachronistic language, manifested a true general charitable intent. The donor issued only a bare order to give alms. Any additional stipulation on the part of the donor appears, on the face of it, to reduce the "generalizability" of the charitable intent. Cy-près looks past the particular, stated wishes of the donor and finds instead a generalized intent that justifies new, specific purposes. But the fact that general gifts give a general power to executors is neither a legal nor a logical antecedent to a development whereby judicial supervisors of specific gifts can divert those gifts to other specific ends. Lord Eldon acknowledged that the power to provide a specific destination for a general gift is distinct from cy-près power in *Mills v. Farmer* (1815):

> Where the Court has acted upon an intention to give to charity generally, it is because it has found, or thinks it has found, that *general* but *perfect* intention. Where it has decreed a performance *cy pres*, it is because the testator has in like manner manifested a *perfect* intention, although, that intention being specific and incapable of being carried specifically into effect, the Court has imagined that it is more nearly executed by finding a purpose bearing some affinity to that which the testator himself has pointed out than by letting the property go as it would have gone if no disposition whatever had been attempted to be made of it.[31]

Cy-près remedies a specific purpose by substituting a different specific purpose.

The most obvious alternative to the redistribution of failed gifts would be to have the property revert to the original estate or be held by the people who had been entrusted with carrying out a failed pious purpose. In medieval practice it was not uncommon for an impossible gift to return to the heirs of the donor, be kept by the trust-

31. 19 Ves. 607.

ee, or, alternatively, for all interested parties to be asked to consent to a transition of use. These various options are what cy-près prevents: if the donor is found to have had a general charitable intent, then that intent is honored in a new way, as determined by an impartial judge who is supposed to prioritize the approximation of donor intent above other factors or claims.

This continuity of a generalized charitable intent at the expense of the heirs has had profound effects on the practice of charitable trust law and on the legal relationship between heirs and the donation. For example, in 2002 the Robertson family, the heirs of Marie Robertson, sued Princeton University's Woodrow Wilson School of Public and International Affairs and alleged that Princeton had failed to use the $35 million Marie Robertson had given in 1961 to support public service as she had intended. They claimed that the money, now grown considerably through investment, had been diverted to support other university endeavors, but they did not seek to have the money simply restored to them. After all, the influence of cy-près would probably have prevented the return of the donation to the estate, and abuse or misuse by trustees is not usually considered grounds for the return of the gift, a principle that is derived from the *ius commune*. More significantly, Princeton alleged in response that only the heirs who were trustees to the donation had standing to sue.[32] Cy-près has effectively instituted the principle that charitable donations permanently exclude heirs even from an interest in the supervision of the property.[33]

So there are two distinctive and essential features to the development of cy-près doctrine: first, that a generalized charitable intent can be derived from a specific charitable intent and that this generalized intent justifies the shifting of property from one use to another; and second, that the generalized intent of the donor can eliminate presumed reversionary interests or the right by heirs, trustees, or beneficiaries to consent to alterations of use. These two features

---

32. Doug White, *Abusing Donor Intent: The Robertson Family's Epic Lawsuit Against Princeton University* (St. Paul, Minn.: Cambridge University Press, 2014).
33. Edith Fisch et al., *Charities and Charitable Foundations* (Pomona, N.Y.: Lond Publications, 1974), 525–26.

do not, as will be shown, fit well with *ius commune* treatment of gifts or with broader medieval priorities. The rights of heirs to retrieve failed bequests for purposes through writs of *cessavit, cessavit de cantaria,* and *faciendo stare rationabilem divisam;* the statutes of mortmain to limit perpetual trusts; the distrust of deathbed disherision; the desire to have all interested parties approve of changes in the use of a gift; the belief that gifts set up ongoing relationships between the donor, recipient, and the gift itself; and the general inflexibility of medieval common law, especially in relationship to trusts and uses: all these seem antithetical to a legal culture that would support cy-près.[34]

Moreover, common law treatment of bequests is also not overly protective of the testator's intentions. If a specific gift was no longer in the testator's estate at the time of his death, the doctrine of ademption generally eliminated the bequest, which meant that the testator's intention to give a legacy was not held to be important enough to attempt to make up the bequest in another fashion. This is particularly telling because the three great threats to the soul of the medieval testator, attested in sermons, folklore, and popular songs, were unpaid tithes, debts, and "restitution"—that is, anything that was owed for wrongs committed against one's fellow man, whether through usury, theft, gambling, or other illicit profits or takings. In all of these cases the repayment needed to be specifically made to the offended person or church; the diversion of money to other charitable purposes was not believed to help.[35] Meanwhile, Catholic theology offered a sure reward only for gifts made in life,

---

34. Pollock and Maitland, *The History of English Law,* vol. 2, 372. Helmholz, "Legitim in English Legal History," *University of Illinois Law Review* (1984), 659–74; Sheehan, "The Bequest of Land in England in the High Middle Ages: Testaments and the Law," in *Marriage, Family, and Law,* 311; T. F. T. Plucknett, *A Concise History of the Common Law,* 5th ed. (London: Butterworth, 1956), 735; Francis Bacon, *The Learned Reading of Sir Francis Bacon, one of Her Majesties learned counsell at law, upon the statute of uses* (London: Mathew Walbancke and Laurence Chapman, 1642), 34. Henrici de Bracton, *De Legibus et Consuetudinibus Angliae,* trans. Samuel E. Thorne, vol. 2 (Cambridge, Mass.: Harvard University Press, 1968), pp. 178 and 181.

35. Canon law was more merciful on this point than was popular folklore, but it was essential that the dying man attempt to make specific restitution if he wished to be saved.

not for those made on the deathbed or through a will. The testator needed to make specific amends to those he had wronged, and canon law provided only limited, particular ways for the dead to be helped; thus it was never the case in medieval theology or law that if the "paramount object [was] salvation, [then] the means were immaterial."[36] Moreover, although the *ius commune* was more protective of bequests than the common law, it was still possible for a legacy to fail. If the origin story of cy-près doctrine were correct, then one would expect that since any bequest might have been restitution or a form of settlement for an informal debt, then all bequests ought to have been eligible for approximation, including perhaps even bare gifts to a particular person *pro anima*. But this was not the case.

R. H. Helmholz has shown that the supervision of uses, especially if the feoffor to uses was dead, fell into the ecclesiastical courts of Canterbury and Rochester before the emergence of Chancery. These courts claimed jurisdiction over the poor and over anything relating to the state of the soul. They supervised probate and had, at least in theoretical agreement, jurisdiction over testaments of personal property, but they were also willing to adjudicate land uses, because common law courts could do little with them if the feoffor was no longer available to sue.[37] However, most of these cases for uses related to "contradictory instructions from the original feoffor," not situations in which the wishes of the feoffor to uses were impossible or impractical.[38] Certainly the ecclesiastical courts were sometimes involved in changes to the use of a gift, but a coercive cy-près power that took away the rights of the heirs to consent to alterations would have been unlikely to develop there, given the restrictions placed on these courts not to violate the laws of England. Also, their inability legally to effect a change in the title to land would have placed a cy-près order for any significant donation outside the realm of possibility for them.[39] Although ecclesiastical courts did have canonical powers of equity, these were used to

36. Willard, "Illustrations," 91.
37. Helmholz, *Roman Canon Law*, 14.
38. R. H. Helmholz, "The Early Enforcement of Uses," *Columbia Law Review* 79 (1979): 1503–13.
39. Ralph Houlbrooke, *Church Courts and the People During the English Reformation 1520–1570* (Oxford: Oxford University Press, 1979).

"soften judgments with mercy" or to find just resolutions to difficult cases, not to injure the rights of interested parties.[40]

Chancery, which emerged in the late fourteenth century, allowed equity and sat under the supervision of the lord chancellor, who was usually an ecclesiastic and could well have imported some of the equitable principles and procedures of Roman-canon law.[41] Chancery also had jurisdictions over trusts and their earlier form, uses, and was willing to perfect trusts (especially to find a new trustee) even though, according to the equitable maxim, it was unwilling to complete an imperfect gift. By 1465, Helmholz argues, uses had passed definitively over to Chancery, where, as Sheehan indicates, "the will is advanced as evidence as to the true intent of the feoffor/testator, and the chancellor is asked to enforce it."[42] Chancery had the power of injunction and the power to compel specific performance; this additional factor could suggest that cy-près power began there, since judges were enabled to redirect property according to their best judgment and to require charitable institutions to restructure their work according to the judge's dictates. If cy-près had begun as a canon law principle, it would have jumped over to Chancery in the fifteenth century when the jurisdiction of uses moved. But the phrase "cy-près" clearly derives from Law French, the peculiar patois used in common law courts and the discussions on the readings and moots at the Third University through the seventeenth century, rather than from the Latin used in ecclesiastical courts.[43] Other Latin phrases from the *ius commune* survived and even blossomed in common law usage, and if there had been a distinct Latin legal term for cy-près, it would easily have made the transition.

Lord Eldon, baffled by the origins of cy-près, alluded to but dismissed its supposed *ius commune* connections in the 1803 case *Mog-*

---

40. Richard Wunderli, *London Church Courts and Society on the Eve of the Reformation* (Cambridge, Mass.: The Medieval Academy of America, 1981), 59.
41. Y. B. 4 Hen. 7, fol. 4, Hil., pl 8 (Ch.1489).
42. Sheehan, "English Wills and the Records of the Ecclesiastical and Civil Jurisdictions," in *Marriage, Family, and Law*, 210.
43. J. H. Baker, *The Law's Two Bodies: Some Evidential Problems in English Legal History* (Oxford: Oxford University Press, 2001). He observes that 'cy-près' is not found in early sources.

gridge v. Thackwell: "In what the doctrine originated, whether, as supposed by Lord Thurlow in *White v. White* (1 Bro. C.C. 12), in the principles of the Civil Law, as applied to charities, or in the religious notions entertained formerly in this country, I know not."[44] When, through the force of precedent he regretfully applied cy-près, he added: "If this decision is wrong, and if this strange doctrine, as I should have called it, if I had sat here two centuries ago, that you can find a charitable purpose in a purpose, that is to fail altogether, can be shaken, I can do no more than allow them to go to a higher tribunal."[45] It was a profound note of skepticism to suggest that at the beginning of the seventeenth century cy-près doctrine would have appeared to Chancery to be "strange," and Eldon has not been alone in finding the origins of cy-près to be "obscure," as Gareth Jones called it in his study of the early modern law of charity, in which he questioned some of the more florid descriptions of cy-près links to medieval canon law.[46] John Baker likewise noted that "the cy pres doctrine postdates most law Fr[ench] texts."[47]

In fact, the development of cy-près doctrine seems to offer a case study for Baker's argument that there was a humanist transformation of common law in the early modern period.[48] Cy-près doctrine served several humanist concerns: to avoid wasteful uses of property, to promote utility and convenience, to limit the costs of superstition, to supply relief for the poor, and to find a balance between private and communal visions of property. Indeed, the cultural presumptions that support cy-près doctrine are all early modern in their outlook, reinforcing the priorities of humanism, the Reformation, and an expansive state power.

To begin with, cy-près relies on an early modern definition of "charity." As Bossy explains:

---

44. *Moggridge v. Thackwell* (1803), 7 Ves. 69.
45. Ibid., 87.
46. Jones, *History of the Law of Charity*, 73 and 74n.
47. J. H. Baker, *Manual of Law French*, 2d ed. (Burlington, Vt.: Ashgate, 1990), 83.
48. J. H. Baker, *The Oxford History of the Laws of England*, vol. 6: 1483–1558 (Oxford: Oxford University Press, 2003), 15–18.

18 Introduction

"Charity" in 1400 meant the state of Christian love or simple affection which one was in or out of regarding one's fellows; an occasion or body of people seeking to embody that state; the love of God, in both directions. In 1700 it meant an optimistic judgment about the good intentions of others; an act of benevolence towards the poor or needy; an institution erected as a result of such an act. In the second case the plural was possible from about 1600, in the third from about 1700.[49]

Bossy may have slightly overstated how late this change was and underestimated the role played by the secularization of property in creating the new understanding of charity. In 1529 Thomas More captured the moment when the competing definitions of charity conflicted with each other in his *Supplication of Souls*, in which he suggested that the suffering souls in purgatory were desperate for "charity" from the living, but that those who would plunder church resources to turn them over to the poor were falsely putting on a "veneer of charity."[50] During the 1530s, propaganda sponsored by Thomas Cromwell referred to "charitable uses" as a category to which church property might be applied. The English Reformation, drawing on Protestant concepts of gratuitous gifts, marked a transition from one idea of charity to another, in which charity became a material gift made freely without expectation of return. It was this later understanding of charity that would be drawn upon in cy-près, which justifies transitions of uses in order to defend the donor's "charitable intent" and according to which no part of a charitable gift remains with the family of the donor.

More specifically, having a "charitable intent" can only anachronistically be applied to the late medieval testator. To die "in charity" was essential: this meant to be securely in the bonds of Christian love with one's family and fellow humans, in which state, through prayer, one could perform loving charity without giving away anything at all.[51] On the other hand, if a man had material goods, he could not die in charity without providing from his belongings for

---

49. John Bossy, *Christianity in the West, 1400–1700* (Oxford: Oxford University Press, 2004), 168.
50. Thomas More, *The Supplication of Souls*, in *The Four Last Things, The Supplication of Souls, A Dialogue on Conscience*, ed. Mary Gottschalk (New York: Scepter Publishers, 2002), 69, 77, 102, and 106.
51. D.45 c.13.

his family.⁵² Someone like the nineteenth-century American industrial baron Wellington R. Burt, who gave considerably to benevolent causes but stretched the Rule Against Perpetuities to its limits in order to prevent his children and grandchildren from inheriting his wealth, would never have been considered charitable in the fifteenth-century sense of the word, even though in contemporary news reports he was described as both a philanthropist and a spiteful old man. In the late Middle Ages, by contrast, pious donations on the deathbed did not reveal the personality, virtues, or philanthropy of the donor. They demonstrated piety and secured additional prayers and masses to help speed a soul through purgatory.

In fact, what made the deathbed dreadful was precisely the awareness that a man could no longer perform acts of charity but could only receive them—at least until he was fully sanctified by purgation.⁵³ Thus, while a man ought to die "in charity," it would not have suited the fifteenth century to suggest that once he was dead his charitable intention would live on. Rather, he had now become a beggar of prayers from the living. Late medieval pardon brasses plead for the prayerful charity of passersby.⁵⁴ Late medieval tombs likewise emphasized the pathetic impotence of the dead, in order to motivate others to pity them with prayers.⁵⁵ By contrast, in the seventeenth century, a new culture of memorialization portrayed the dead as triumphantly leaving behind a legacy of works by which they would be remembered.⁵⁶ These philanthropists could be said to have had a

52. Ralph Houlbrooke, *Death, Religion and the Family in England, 1480–1750* (Oxford: Oxford University Press, 2000), 91.
53. Although some theologians held that the souls in purgatory could pray for the living, it was not usually believed that they could benefit themselves by those prayers in the way that living Christians could help themselves by helping others.
54. Peter Marshall cites one that tried to offer an exchange: "Ye shall not lose your charitable devotion; xii cardinals have granted you xii days of pardon," *Beliefs and the Dead in Reformation England* (Oxford: Oxford University Press, 2004), 31. Eamon Duffy, in *Saints, Sacrilege and Sedition: Religion and Conflict in the Tudor Reformations* (London: Bloomsbury Academic, 2012), 66, quotes one example: "some such of my Evencristianes as shall see and loke upon it wull of ther charite pray for or soulys."
55. Marshall, *Beliefs and the Dead*, 22.
56. Keith Thomas, *The Ends of Life: Roads to Fulfillment in Early Modern England* (Oxford: Oxford University Press, 2010); Nigel Llewellyn, *The Art of Death: Visual*

"charitable intent" in the exclusively benevolent sense that cy-près rulings have sought.

There are other distinctively early modern aspects to the doctrine. By cutting off a donor's heirs from reversionary interests in the property, cy-près might be expected to discourage charitable giving. Indeed, in an age that anticipated restrained social mobility and limited wealth, it was considered impious and uncharitable for a testator to send too much of his fortune outside of the family, even to pious causes.[57] For all of these reasons, the edifice of charitable giving, particularly once cy-près doctrine was available, depended in part on a dynamic economy in which the testator could imagine that in the future there would be wealth to be made, not simply lost.[58]

Similarly, freehold ownership would be a likely condition for the development of a regular cy-près power, since cy-près depends on and affirms the clear, singular ownership of property—or at the very least on the judge being willing to overlook competing claims of ownership in order to assign charitable property to a new purpose, perhaps with the justification of the king's ultimate dominion over all lands and his right to resume property. In the second half of the sixteenth century, "various legal restrictions on the freedom to dispose of property by will or testament were removed." This transition supported the treatment of property as belonging fully and sole-

---

Culture in the English Death Ritual c. 1500–c. 1800 (London: Reaktion Books, 1991); Lorraine C. Attreed, "Preparation for Death in Sixteenth Century Northern England," *The Sixteenth Century Journal* 13 (1982): 63–65.

57. Lorenzo Valla used the ridiculousness of casual disherision in his critique of the fraudulent Donation of Constantine. What terrible anger the sons of Constantine would have had toward him and toward the Catholic Church if he had actually given half of his—soon to be their—empire to the papacy: "Father, do you really deprive, disinherit, and cast off your sons, you who loved very much until now? ... You are transferring it to others at our expense and to our disgrace.... You can indeed do what you want with your empire and even with us, with one exception, which we will fiercely uphold unto death ... if you do bestow [the empire on Sylvester], we will not only refuse to become Christians, but you will cause the very name of Christian to be hated, loathed, and cursed by us." Valla, *On the Donation of Constantine,* trans. G. W. Bowersock (Cambridge, Mass.: Harvard University Press, 2008), 9–11.

58. On "pure" gifts in modern capitalist systems, see Johnathan Parry, "*The Gift,* the Indian Gift and the 'Indian Gift,'" *Man* 21 (1986): 453–73.

Introduction 21

ly to the donor.[59] On the other hand, Robert W. Gordon noted that even in the eighteenth century, "in the midst of such a lush flowering of absolute dominion talk in theoretical and political discourse ... English and colonial social practices contained so many property relations that actually seemed to traduce the ideal of absolute individual rights."[60] Cy-près doctrine sits neatly within the "paradox" of private property that Gordon describes: it depended on a claim to absolute ownership, according to which the donated property had no attachments except the intent given to it by the testator, and yet it also served to transmit donations to causes that would better serve a common good, even while ostensibly signaling the testator's supposed ability to control the charitable direction of his gift. In all of these ways cy-près doctrine appears acutely early modern: it simultaneously affirms and undermines singular control over property, and it seems to emphasize the rights of the testator, yet permits judges to redirect his property to serve the commonwealth. Considerable early modern social critique focused on how much property was transferred out of the commons; cy-près was a way to return property to the commons without raising the specter of Anabaptism—and while offending no one other than the dead and the heirs whom they themselves had deprived.

Just as no legal system could ever be perfectly consistent, it is also possible for law to move in two opposing directions at the same time. Ken Pennington has shown that an increased focus on individual rights tended to be cultivated by medieval jurists alongside their theories of absolutism.[61] Susan Reynolds observed that in the nineteenth and twentieth centuries, at the time when expropriations for the common good were most necessary and utilized, the legal discussion of them fell silent in favor of an increased emphasis on individual property rights, just as William Blackstone upheld the inviolability of property law while also acknowledging the right of the

59. Houlbrooke, *Death, Religion, and the Family,* 83–84.
60. Robert W. Gordon, "Paradoxical Property," in *Early Modern Conceptions of Property,* ed. John Brewer and Susan Staves (New York: Routledge, 1996), 96.
61. Kenneth Pennington, *The Prince and the Law, 1200–1600: Sovereignty and Rights in the Western Legal Tradition* (Berkeley: University of California Press, 1993).

legislature to force an exchange of property if it was for the common good.[62] A tendency in one direction may provoke a reaction in the opposite direction, as a compensation or safeguard. In the case of cy-près, two contradictory impulses—to reinforce both private control and centralized supervision—can reach an accommodation within one legal doctrine.

In 1529 Henry VIII claimed the right to control probate fees and mortuaries. This alteration was one of the first moves against canon law during the English Reformation, and yet historians have found that he changed nothing of the basic structure or spirit of medieval testamentary law.[63] Helmholz has shown that during the Reformation there was little move in general to dissociate the law from the *ius commune* and that this immobility "gave cause for grievance or alarm to those who thought that the English Church should have put its 'popish' past behind it."[64] Indeed, research by John Witte and others has revealed that, despite the initial enthusiasm of many Reformers to overthrow canon law, the primary legal effect of the Reformation turned out to be the transfer of jurisdiction and authority from the church to the state, rather than the obsolescence of old laws and the construction of new. But in at least one aspect, through the ultimate creation of cy-près doctrine, the English Reformation may have been quietly legally transformative.

Still, despite questioning whether cy-près doctrine originates directly from the *ius commune*, this book nonetheless demonstrates the saturation of *ius commune* principles in the legal and cultural world of the late Middle Ages. The Reformation was a profoundly innovative moment that argued with the *ius commune* in its terms and used many of its norms. Pennington has observed that many of the most important principles in law are not named or even necessarily artic-

---

62. Susan Reynolds, *Before Eminent Domain: Toward a History of Expropriation of Land for the Common Good* (Chapel Hill: University of North Carolina Press, 2010), 102–3 and 138–39.

63. The Probate and Mortuaries Act of 1529, 21 Hen. 8 cc. 5–6. See Helmholz, *Roman Canon Law*, 39–41; John Witte Jr., *Law and Protestantism: The Legal Teachings of the Lutheran Reformation* (Cambridge: Cambridge University Press, 2002).

64. Helmholz, *Roman Canon Law*, 167–68.

ulated.[65] In this case, the unspoken principle that runs throughout many of the centuries covered in this book is not cy-près doctrine but rather an anti–cy-près doctrine: that the purpose of a gift—its use or its end—should not be changed. Property was marked by the purposes given to it. This does not mean that the purposes of gifts were never changed, but rather that the principle was not shaken when they were, not even when jurists wrote consilia on how an impossible gift might legitimately be altered or when dispensations derogated from canon law without setting a precedent for the future. Even as a doctrine to permit regular change was formulated in the seventeenth and eighteenth centuries in England, there was an ongoing attempt to avoid the outright denial of this principle of perpetual and unalterable purpose, by making only a small change or by changing only the "mode" of the gift. Some aspects of canon law were kept—but put to a truly new use.

A Note on Translations

Since I have no talent for the art of translation, I have used (and very rarely emended) reliable translations in the main text whenever possible, with attribution given in the notes. Readers can be tempted to skim long block quotations, so I have, for English-language sources, sometimes drawn on editions that use modernized English, to entice the reader to give a passage the attention it deserves. The effect may seem odd at times, though, since I have usually left shorter passages in the original.

65. Pennington, *The Prince and the Law*, 63.

1

Posthumous Gifts and the Soul

"Give your goods while they are yours, for after death they aren't yours anymore" (*Da tua dum tua sunt, quia post mortem tua non sunt*).[1] This anonymous piece of medieval verse became an English legal maxim used to assert the transfer of ownership upon death of the testator, but in its origins it attests the pressing medieval belief that the benefits of almsgiving were available only to the living. Canon law agreed that man should give in the present because a testament tried to give what was no longer his, for it would have been strange if either Catholic law or theology had endorsed the tenet that posthumous almsgiving, after the testator truly had no more need for the property, would be beneficial to his eternal state, as the legend of cy-près origins suggests. The dying man who saved his almsgiving for his executors to distribute sacrificed nothing at all; he simply removed assets from the estate he handed on to his heirs. It bears resemblance to a slave-owner who frees his slaves at his death, having used them for as long as was convenient to him.[2]

Medieval and early modern wills and testaments are undeni-

---

1. Alternatively: "Da tua dum tua sunt, post mortem tunc tua non sunt." Thomas Branch, *Principia legis et aequitatis* (London: Henry Lintot, 1753), 18; 3 Bulst. 18; 1 Plowden 280.

2. Giambattista Impallomeni, *Le manomissioni mortis causa: Studi sulle fonti autoritative romane* (Padua: CEDAM, 1963).

ably religious documents. Some scholars have argued that the entire purpose of the medieval will was the opportunity it offered for "pious bequests."[3] That pre-modern testators were concerned about the state of their souls in their will-making is indisputable: the language of gifts made *pro anima* is pervasive. The soul itself could be left as a bequest to God or the saints; imprecatory warnings sometimes threatened those who did not honor the stipulations of the will; fears of sacrilege, impiety, or the wrath of God may have affected the care with which executors and heirs treated them. Medieval law codes in their turn claimed that the wishes of the testator are sacred.[4] Of course, the fact that wills were religious documents did not prevent them from serving other functions. Ariès has noted the ways in which they allowed testators to run their hands over their goods in one last appreciation of what was being left behind, and their commemorative and memorial roles have been broadly studied. Gifts with a purpose also comforted the dying, who could imagine that they themselves would have some further effect on the world after they were gone.

Because religion is so obvious and powerful a motivator in human affairs, especially in relationship to death, particularly careful treatment is required to avoid the reduction of a complicated set of competing pressures to the single motive of attaining salvation. This chapter will show—in a most cursory fashion—that ambivalence about the salvific benefit of deathbed gifts was a frequent theme from late antiquity on. At best, deathbed gifts might be accepted as almsgiving in the same manner that deathbed confessions could remit sins without the performance of penance—although some penalty might remain even there. This was hardly fertile ground for the development of a legal doctrine to permit the redirection of property in a propitiatory offering on behalf of the deceased. Canon law, meanwhile, strictly limited the kinds of help that could be given the dead, and it required specific, not indiscriminate, restitution for wrongs.

---

3. Philippe Ariès, *The Hour of Our Death*, trans. Helen Weaver (New York: Vintage, 1981), 190; Sheehan, *Will in Medieval England*, 3 and 303.

4. *The Coutumes de Beauvaisis of Philippe de Beaumanoir*, trans. F. R. P. Akehurst (Philadelphia: University of Pennsylvania Press, 1992), 133.

Evidence suggests that the uncertainty about deathbed giving was well understood by donors, as was the tension between providing for one's family and securing one's eternal life. These pressures of the economy of salvation helped to create a legal culture that mitigated these dilemmas in ways that would have been hostile to the development of cy-près doctrine, which could only emerge with a soteriological model that emphasized the indifference of all works.

Almsgiving was a prominent theme in patristic writings, grounded on the promise that it built up a treasury in heaven.[5] The Bible instructs the Christian who would be perfect to sell all that he has and give the money to the poor, which will "redeem [his] sins with alms."[6] If almsgiving or other acts of mercy were frustrated, the man would still be saved by the attempt (1 Corinthians 3:12–15). Clement of Alexandria, whose *Quis dives salvetur* reassured the wealthy that they could be saved without total divestment of their worldly goods, posited that alms were the way to love both God and neighbor. Cyprian of Carthage phrased it more negatively in *De opera et eleemosynis*—alms were a necessary and perpetual penance.[7] They both used the language of a spiritualized commerce, in which heaven could be bought, and in which, as Cyprian suggested, man lent money to God through his alms.[8]

Although the church fathers taught that alms were essential to the Christian life, they were not so clear that almsgiving could extend into death. Cyprian cited Luke 12:20: the soul of the rich man might be demanded of him tonight, and then to whom would his riches belong? Many patristic sources were reluctant to reassure the living that they might help themselves after death with bequests. Basil of Caesarea warned:

Yet you say, "I will enjoy all these things during my life, but after my death I will leave my goods to the poor, making them beneficiaries of

---

5. Gary A. Anderson, "Redeem Your Sins by the Giving of Alms: Sin, Debt, and the 'Treasury of Merit' in Early Jewish and Christian Tradition," *Letter and Spirit* 3 (2007): 39–69.
6. Matthew 19:16–21; Mark 10:17–21; Luke 18:18–22; Daniel 4:24.
7. Helen Rhee, *Loving the Poor, Saving the Rich: Wealth, Poverty, and Early Christian Formation* (Grand Rapids, Mich.: Baker Academic, 2012).
8. Cyprian, *De opere et eleemosynis*, PL, vol. 4, col. 614.

my will and granting them all my possessions." When you are no longer among your fellow human beings, then you will become a philanthropist! When I see you dead, then I will call you a lover of your brothers and sisters! You deserve great thanks for your magnanimity, since you became so generous and noble-hearted after you were laid in the grave and your body had dissolved in the earth. Tell me, however, from what period you intend to seek your reward: the time of your life, or that which comes after your departure? When you were still alive, squandering your years in luxury and wasting them on frivolous pursuits, you never bothered to consider the plight of the needy. What exchange is possible now that you are dead? What reward of your labor is due to you? Show your works and seek your recompense. No one transacts business after the end of the festival, nor is anyone who arrives after the close of the games crowned, nor does anyone who comes after the war perform deeds of valor. It is thus apparent that no one can perform good works after the conclusion of life.... Why then do you deceive yourself? You wickedly dispose of your wealth now for selfish gratification, while making promises for the future concerning things of which you will no longer be master.[9]

Similarly, Augustine's 86th sermon on the New Testament covered Matthew 19:21, on selling everything one has and giving it to the poor.[10] Augustine rejected both avarice, which saves for the future, and extravagance, which indulges oneself. Augustine urged instead a new form of ascetic extravagance, in which a man would spend unashamedly on himself by giving his money away long before death could overtake him.

Ambrose's *De excessu fratris Satyri*, written on the occasion of the death of his brother Satyrus in 376, offers a model of deathbed giving.[11] Satyrus declined to write a will to distribute his goods, saying that he left all decisions up to his brother and sister, "not, however, forgetting the poor, but only asking that so much should be giv-

9. Basil the Great, Homily 7, PG, vol. 31, cols. 277C–304C; trans. C. Paul Schroeder, *On Social Justice* (Crestwood, N.Y.: St. Vladimir's Seminary Press, 2009), 55–56.

10. Augustine, *Sermons*, vol. 3, trans. Edmund Hill (Brooklyn, N.Y.: New City Press, 1991), 396–406.

11. Peter Brown argues that at precisely the same moment, the church began to accumulate wealth through donations; see his *Through the Eye of a Needle: Wealth, the Fall of Rome, and the Making of Christianity in the West, 350–550 AD* (Princeton, N.J.: Princeton University Press, 2012), xxii. See also Sheehan, *Will in Medieval England*, 8.

en to them as should seem just to us." But, Ambrose concluded, this meant that "he left them not a little, but the whole. For this is the total sum of justice, to sell what one has and give to the poor.... So he left us as stewards, not heirs."[12] Satyrus's indifference to the distribution indicates that he understood his goods were irrelevant to him in every sense. Satyrus was modeling the good death, dying as he had lived, with care for the poor and dispassion for the world, and even symbolically disinheriting his relatives for their own good. Many patristic authors, most notably Chrysostom, chastised the wealthy for believing that their goods had been legitimated by being inherited rather than earned.[13] The corruption of wealth could be inherited like original sin; generous pious bequests could protect heirs from the trap of riches that had ensnared the donor.

The first notable legal reference to the value of testamentary bequests comes from the fifth-century Fourth Council of Carthage, which decreed that those who interfere with bequests to the church are to be excommunicated as *egentium necatores*, murderers of the poor.[14] There was no mention of spiritual consequences to the donor.[15] Only the Council of Vaison, ten years after the Fourth Council of Carthage, raised concern for the testator, and even there it was distinctly not suggested that the testator would suffer spiritually because of interference in his last wishes, but rather that both the testator and the poor would be defrauded, the testator of the "plenitude" of his vows (*votorum plenitudine*) and the poor of sustenance.[16] The Council of Ag-

12. Book I.59–60: "Denique et oratus et obsecratus a nobis, nihil tamen condendum putavit: non oblitus tamen pauperum, sed tantum obsecrans esse tribuendum, quantum nobis justum videretur.... et postulando quod justum est, non exiguum, sed totum reliquit, haec enim est summa justitiae, vendere quae habeas, et conferre pauperibus.... Ergo dispensatores nos, non haeredes reliquit; nam haereditas successori quaeritur, dispensatio pauperibus obligatur." PL, vol. 16, col. 1309. In *Ambrose: Select Works and Letters*, trans. H. de Romestin, Nicene and Post-Nicene Fathers, Series II, vol. 10 (Grand Rapids, Mich.: Wm. B. Eerdmans, 1979), 170.

13. Charles Avila, *Ownership: Early Christian Teaching* (Eugene, Ore.: Wipf and Stock, 2004), 84, 89, 94, and 136.

14. C. Munier, ed., *Concilia Africae A. 345–A. 525*, Corpus Christianorum Series Latina (hereafter CCSL), vol. 149 (Turnhout: Brepols 1974), 352; C.18 q.2 c.9.

15. Peter Brown, *The Ransom of the Soul* (Cambridge, Mass.: Harvard University Press, 2015), 173.

16. C.13 q.2 c.10. *Concilia Galliae A. 345–A. 352*, CCSL, vol. 148, 97–98.

atha that followed in the early sixth century agreed that the withholding of donations was tantamount to murdering the poor but did not address its effect on the testator's soul.[17] In the collected canonical texts that accumulated on the topic from these and other sources, there were repeated urges to honor the wishes of the testator exactly, including those stipulations that were totally irrelevant to the soul.[18]

Peter Brown argues that the development of the testamentary bequest was part of a "series of compromises" that "worldly-wise bishops offered the average rich Christian."[19] One compromise had been to encourage repeated small donations, almsgiving throughout life, to affirm the attitude of constant repentance while allowing for practical necessities.[20] This theme would carry on through the centuries, with the practice of routine, or even daily, almsgiving to add treasure regularly to heaven without ruining the household economy on earth.[21] Regular alms were *fructus digni poenitentia* (fruits worthy of penance) and a method of maintaining penitence. Deathbed alms were another compromise: in the context of economic decline, Salvian's fifth-century *Ad Ecclesiam* advocated giving to the church above all else, and Brown notes that until this text the salvific function of almsgiving, whether in life or as a legacy, was deliberately left unclear.[22] Indeed, the largely uncelebrated afterlife of Salvian reveals some ecclesiastical reluctance to endorse his text.

Salvian acknowledged the tension between providing for one's family and seeking salvation, and he drew an analogy with the church. An increase in converts had decreased fervor: "You, the Church, have become weaker as your fertility has progressed."[23] Weak Christians

17. C.13 q.2 c.11.
18. C.16 q.1 c.14; X 3.26.3.
19. Brown, *Through the Eye*, xxiv.
20. Brown, *Ransom of the Soul*, 100ff.
21. Hilda Johnstone, "Poor Relief in the Royal Households of Thirteenth-Century England," *Speculum* 4 (1929): 149–67; Paul Webster, *King John and Religion* (Woodbridge, England: Boydell Press, 2015).
22. Brown, *Through the Eye*; Brown, *The Ransom of the Soul*, 117–19.
23. Salvian, "The Four Books of Timothy to the Church," in *The Writings of Salvian, the Presbyter*, trans. Jeremiah F. O'Sullivan (New York: Cima Publishing, 1947), 270: "factaque es, ecclesia, profectu tuae fecunditatis infirmior." Corpus Scriptorum Ecclesiasticorum Latinorum (hereafter CSEL), vol. 8 (Vienna: C. Geroldus, 1883), 225.

store up their wealth: they "hide baneful treasures in the earth which will bring a brief joy to their heirs and a long lament to their begetters."[24] They do not distribute riches as they receive them, but rather they are "driven to seek money and acquire tremendous wealth out of preoccupation for their offspring and an all but violent love for their children."[25] But all this parental getting and begetting weighed the children down: "almost all children succeed as much to the vices as to the patrimony of their parents."[26] If a parent could not bear to disinherit his or her children, then he or she should tailor the inheritance to the child, giving the most to any children who had renounced the world. God should always be given the bulk of the estate, lest God take second place to men. Testaments jeopardized the soul by keeping it attached to this world, encouraging it to ignore the seriousness of death in favor of fantasizing about how much the heirs would appreciate their inheritance.[27] Worse, "the prayers of such people [who grasp for legacies] are of no avail whatsoever with God."[28]

God had given to man as usufructory tenants by *precarium*, with the intention that man should give it back to God through Christ, the poor man.[29] Men who tried to "alienate from the donor the ownership of the thing given" by using it in some other way refused to acknowledge the rights of God as the ultimate owner.[30] Any men who died with wealth were "already guilty by the very fact that they have

---

24. Salvian, *Writings*, 271; CSEL, vol. 8, 226: "mandantes terrae thesauros luctuosos heredibus breve gaudium auctoribus longum maerorem adlaturos."
25. Salvian, *Writings*, 273; CSEL, vol. 8, 227–28: "qui ad quaerendas pecunias et ampliandas latissime opes conpelli se pignorum cura et quasi violento filiorum amore causantur."
26. Salvian, *Writings*, 274; CSEL, vol. 8, 228: "et hinc est, quod pene omnes parentibus suis filii non magis in patrimonia quam in vitia succedunt."
27. Salvian, *Writings*, 357 and 350–51; CSEL, vol. 8, 304 and 298–99.
28. Salvian, *Writings*, 351; CSEL, vol. 8, 298: "nihil omnino apud deum vota talium praevalere."
29. Salvian, *Writings*, 278 and 361; CSEL, vol. 8, 232 and 307.
30. Salvian, *Writings*, 278; CSEL, vol. 8, 232: "si enim usus rerum aliquarum cuipiam homini alterius hominis beneficio ac largitate tribuatur isque inmemor illius, a quo fructum rerum indeptus est, avertere ab eo ipso proprietatem praestitae rei atque alienare conetur, nonne ingratissimus omnium atque infidelissimus iudicetur, qui oblitus scilicet hominis benefici ac liberalissimi spoliare illum iure dominii sui velit."

kept possession of all they have up to the very moment of death."[31] The dead could not do penance for themselves—works done with the money left behind were irrelevant—but the deathbed did offer, as Brown noted, "one slight hope as an asylum for fleeing eternal fire."[32] In these final moments a man should prove his faith and repentance by returning his goods to God.[33] This would work only if the man "shall have previously renounced his sins and cast away that sordid and dirty garment of his crimes and shall have received the new robe of conversion and holiness."[34] Absent this total repentance, bequests would do nothing. The testator was already "all the more indebted" because he did this only when he was "dying or on the very point of death," so it would be madness for him not to give everything to God, as a last effort to save himself, to "leave nothing untried when dying," although in return he would receive only "hope," not "surety."[35] Moreover, alms should be given not out of love for man, a worldly charitable intent, but "out of love for God."[36]

The emergence of pious bequests is indicative of a larger transition in the function of the Christian deathbed. Frederick Paxton has shown that the earliest Christian deathbed rites were triumphalist. They assumed that the dying man, having already fought the good fight, was in the process of being received by God. These rites emphasized neither confession nor the distribution of a man's estate, and often did not even give instructions for them. This suggests that

31. Salvian, *Writings*, 281; CSEL, vol. 8, 234: "ergo, ut supra diximus, quo modo se quidam reos omnino non putant, si nec in morte sibimet per dispensationem substantiae consuluerint, cum etiam ex hoc rei sint, quod usque ad mortem cuncta servaverint?"
32. Salvian, *Writings*, 339 and 348; CSEL, vol. 8, 286–87 and 296: "cui unum tantummodo superest inter suprema perfugium una effugiendi aeterni ignis specula datur."
33. Salvian, *Writings*, 348–49; CSEL, vol. 8, 296–97.
34. Salvian, *Writings*, 284; CSEL, 237: "nisi antea et peccatis renuntiaverit et sordidam illam criminum tunicam lutulentamque proiecerit et novam conversionis ac sanctimoniae vestem de manu apostoli praedicantis acceperit."
35. Salvian, *Writings*, 291 and 293; CSEL, vol. 8, 244–45: "tu autem tanto plus pro te debes, quod haec vel moriens facis vel iam iamque moriturus"; "si id non fecerit, ne quid saltim moriens inexpertum"; "spem indicat, non fiduciam pollicetur."
36. Salvian, *Writings*, 325; CSEL, vol. 8, 274: "religionis faciat affectu."

early Christianity was not particularly welcoming of last-minute donations unless necessitated by a sudden conversion.[37] Only over centuries did the deathbed rites come to express instead that the dying man was in serious need of help, which might encourage the expending of various resources to help navigate this fraught final battle.[38] But before the rituals changed, deathbed repentance had already been scrutinized for a number of reasons, including the criticism that Christianity allowed all sin to be discarded as long as one managed to repent at precisely the right time.[39] Too much emphasis on mercy, for the eleventh-hour worker or the Prodigal Son, seemed unjust. As a result, many early theologians, most famously Clement of Alexandria and Augustine, held that though deathbed repentance could save, there would still be some temporal punishment to follow.[40] Penitential theory generally did not allow a sinner to simply make a confession and then escape all temporal punishment.[41]

The deathbed had become a privileged zone, but these privileges could not remedy all of the consequences of a misspent life.[42] As Thomas Tentler points out, "by the early middle ages, private penance had confirmed the practice of deathbed reconciliation, in which a Christian 'received' penance rather than performed it," but to give a legacy of alms from the deathbed as a confirmation of the sincerity of repentance was a natural response much encouraged by the church.[43] Since almsgiving had been linked to baptism, as a second washing away of sins, the gesture might help to restore baptismal purity.[44] The last-minute deathbed donation became, then, a char-

---

37. Frederick S. Paxton, *Christianizing Death: The Creation of a Ritual Process in Early Medieval Europe* (Ithaca, N.Y.: Cornell University Press, 1990), 87.
38. Paxton, *Christianizing Death*, 68.
39. Ibid., 35, 73–74, and 95.
40. Houlbrooke, *Death, Religion, and the Family*, 34.
41. G. R. Evans, *Law and Theology in the Middle Ages* (London: Routledge, 2002), 168.
42. Leo the Great, Letter CVIII, to Theodore, Bishop of Forum Julii, PL, vol. 54, col. 1012A–1014A.
43. Sheehan, *Will in Medieval England*, 11; Thomas Tentler, *Sin and Confession on the Eve of the Reformation* (Princeton, N.J.: Princeton University Press, 1977), 295.
44. Maximus of Turin, Sermon 22A, in *Sermons of Maximus of Turin*, trans. Boniface Ramsey (Mahwah, N.J.: Paulist Press, 1989), 55–57.

ity offered by the church to the dying sinner, since repentance normally required acts of penitence performed by the sinner, which the church waived for confessions made *in extremis*. Similarly, the church could exert its influence on behalf of the dying by offering that testamentary bequests might "count" as an act done in life. But this was no sure thing, certainly not a guaranteed method to gain access to heaven, and it did not lay the ground for an embrace of deathbed alms as salvific.[45]

Once the custom of giving alms after confessing sins as a token of repentance had taken hold, then it was reinforced by the fact that suspicion began to attach if a dying man, after being shriven, would not give alms. Nonetheless, the essential issue for the dying remained, as Salvian had suggested, in the attempt to give, not in the ultimate performance of the donation. Gratian's *Tractatus De Penitentia* began by weighing intention against performance in its first distinction on the necessity of confession, and the treatise concluded in the seventh distinction by warning, with passages drawn from Cyprian and Augustine, about the insecurity of deathbed repentance.[46] The jurists thus certainly understood that it was perilous to leave repentance to the end, even for those who had recourse to all of the church's sacramental help in their last moments.[47]

On the other hand, long before the formal rise of the doctrine of purgatory, it appeared that the living could help the dead with alms and prayers offered on their behalf, because Christ had conquered death.[48] The New Testament itself offers mixed evidence: the rich man in the parable about Lazarus suffers an apparently hopeless fate, but in the second epistle to Timothy, Paul offered prayers for Onesiphorus. Augustine reported approvingly in his *Confessions* that

45. See Sheehan's discussion, *Will in Medieval England*, 12–13, of the attribution to the *Penitential of Theodore* in C.26 q.7 c.1.
46. Gratian, *Tractatus de Penitentia: A New Latin Edition with English Translation*, ed. and trans. by Atria Larson (Washington, D.C.: The Catholic University of America Press, 2016).
47. Ibid., 277.
48. Robert James Edmund Boggis, *Praying for the Dead: An Historical Review of the Practice* (New York: Longmans, Green, 1913), chapters 4–5; Jacques Le Goff, *The Birth of Purgatory*, trans. Arthur Goldhammer (Chicago: University of Chicago Press, 1984), 11 and 45.

his mother had asked for him to commemorate her name at the altar after her death.[49] A strong propensity to pray for the dead developed, along with other experimental remedies for those who had run out of time. The councils at Carthage and Auxerre rebuked those who wished to give *viaticum*—the Eucharist for the dying, named for the pagan custom of putting money in the mouths of the dead to help them on their way—posthumously, as if it would help the recently deceased.[50] Still, there was a legitimate way to send a man's money after him. The receipt of a legacy was an opportunity for those left behind to help the dead with the property they had received, as John Chrysostom suggested:

> For if barbarians are wont to burn men's goods together with their dead bodies, much more is it right for you to dispatch the deceased's goods with him: not with the object of reducing them to ashes, as in the former case, but in order that they may enhance the man's glory. And if the departed was a sinner, this is done to obtain forgiveness of his sins; if a righteous man, that his recompense and reward may be increased.[51]

Heirs and legatees could give an inheritance to charity on behalf of the dead, which would allow the departed to obtain the fullest possible salvific value for his former goods. But this was their choice to make, and it was almsgiving inspired by the dead, not commanded by them in a will. Chrysostom warned that no one should rely on this generosity or depend on anyone else for spiritual aid: "a man should practice charity while alive and not wait for his relatives to distribute philanthropies after his death on his behalf."[52] Augustine added in *De cura pro mortuis gerenda* that the only things a person could do to affect his salvation were acts done "by the body," a claim supported by 2 Corinthians 5:10. Alms done by the living on behalf of the dead could have an effect on the souls of the dead—but only on those who had merited this effect, through repentance or their

---

49. Augustine of Hippo, *Confessiones*, in CSEL, vol. 33, 219.
50. R. C. Finucane, *Appearances of the Dead: A Cultural History of Ghosts* (Buffalo, N.Y.: Prometheus Press, 1984), 31–32; Paxton, *Christianizing Death*, 32–36.
51. Quoted in Boggis, *Praying for the Dead*, 52.
52. Demetrios J. Constantelos, *Byzantine Philanthropy and Social Welfare* (New Brunswick, N.J.: Rutgers, 1968), 22; John Chrysostom, *On Wealth and Poverty* (Crestwood, N.Y.: St. Vladimir's Seminary Press, 1981), 80 and 111.

own good deeds in life. The testamentary bequest of alms, by contrast, was neither an act done by the body nor an act done on behalf of the dead.

The mass was another work that the living could perform to help the dead, despite the skepticism of early Christian Irish monks, who responded to the innovation of masses for the dead by asking why performing the Eucharist on behalf of the dead was helpful, if the dead had not communed in their lifetime.[53] The *Dialogues* of Gregory the Great, whose authenticity would be questioned early in the Reformation, lent support to the idea: Justus was set free from punishment in the afterlife after thirty masses (later known as a trental) commissioned on his behalf by Gregory.[54] Exactly how the afterlife worked was ambiguous, although several early texts, starting with the third-century *Acts of Perpetua*, suggested works by the living could deliver the dead out of some very unhappy fates. This belief that the dead could be helped remained strong in Greek Orthodox Christianity. Byzantine wills usually contained pious bequests, and the Kneeling Prayers at Pentecost were offered on behalf of the denizens of hell.[55] And yet Greek theologians rejected purgatory as false hope: "do good during your lifetime, for everything is inert after death."[56] For the Greeks, then, the judgment at death was severe—saved or damned—but the living might be able to pull a man out of hell. This would be such an extraordinary and exhausting spiritual feat, attributed to rare saints, that there was much less focus than in Latin Christianity on repeated long-term commemoration once the forty days after death had passed and the soul had settled into its new home.

In the western tradition, however, hell was hopeless, but most souls were bound for purgatory, where they could be easily helped by ordinary Christians. An eighth-century letter from Pope Gregory II to Boniface clarified that there were only four means for helping the dead—masses, prayers, alms, and fasting—and the *Decretum* would

---

53. Boggis, *Praying for the Dead*, 113; Edward Warren, *The Liturgy and Ritual of the Celtic Church* (Oxford: Clarendon Press, 1891).
54. Gregory the Great, *Dialogues*, trans. Odo John Zimmerman (Washington, D.C.: The Catholic University of America Press, 1959), Book 4, 269.
55. Constantelos, *Byzantine Philanthropy*, 119–22, 132, 139–44, and 165.
56. Quoted in Le Goff, *Birth of Purgatory*, 287.

subsequently affirm these four means.[57] But the alms were those offered by friends in memory of the good works of the dead, not those given by the dead themselves. For the dead to leave bequests of alms in order to inspire prayers from the recipients was a circumnavigation around these canonical terms, and within the logic of this loophole, then, the performance of the bequest suddenly mattered, since if no alms were distributed, then no prayers would be offered.

That suspicions might attach to the church for her willingness to trade prayers for the dead in return for money was obvious early on and would remain a long-running theme. Cyril of Alexandria addressed the problem directly: "Why then do [our critics] impiously attribute to us a base love of gain, knowing nothing of such matters, as though we were disturbing the heavenly repose of those who have fallen asleep in the faith? But when we offer for them the holy and mystic sacrifice, we obtain mercy for them."[58] It was in part for this reason that priests and bishops were originally forbidden to act as executors.[59] And so it is not surprising that canon law never affirmed that testamentary bequests were salvific and that it sought to find a moderate way for man to provide for himself, his eternal life, and the welfare of his family all at the same time, while limiting, in some respects, the ability of the church to interfere with the will as given by the testator. In particular, canon law reminded the testator that there could be no charity without a loving disposition, and that, alternatively, there could be charity without giving away anything material at all.[60]

An additional complication was the ongoing tension between saving oneself and providing for one's household. Although the Bible commands almsgiving in life and detachment from earthly provisions, it also demands care for the family (1 Timothy 5:8) and that no one person should feel burdened to give alms beyond their capacity (2 Corinthians 8:13–14). Basil reported that the rich would complain

---

57. C.13 q.2 c.22: "Animae defunctorum quatuor modis solvuntur, aut oblationibus sacerdotum, aut precibus sanctorum, aut karorum elemosinis, aut ieiunio cognatorum."
58. PG, vol. 76, col. 1425C. Trans. and quoted in Boggis, *Praying for the Dead*, 59.
59. Sheehan, *Will in Medieval England*, 124–26.
60. D.45 c.13.

that they could not give alms because they had a family, to which he answered, "[Your children] have their own Master who cares for their needs.... Is not your own soul more intimately related to you than any child?... Give to your soul first in the order of inheritance."[61] Cyprian offered a different solution: the more children you have, the harder you should work in order to be able to give more, so that your prayers for them will be more efficacious. The problem was even more difficult for women, who had less property with which to give alms; it was a trope of the hagiographies of married female saints that they endured criticism or worse from husbands who believed their generosity to the poor destabilized the household's finances.[62] Augustine reproved the eager convert Ecdicia, who not only sentenced her husband to an unwanted celibacy but also gave away the family fortune to two passing monks, destroying her family in her zealousness.[63]

Patristic theologians responded by linking gifts to the church with the need to provide for one's family. In an epistle defending deathbed bequests to the clergy, Jerome did not argue that they could save the giver, but he explained instead that nothing could be more natural than to leave money to the church, which was one's own mother.[64] Augustine influentially suggested that men should consider Christ to be one of their sons, so if they had four sons, then Christ would be their fifth: "what you give to your Lord will be to the advantage of both yourself and your children; but what you save up, avariciously, for your children will be to both your and their disadvantage."[65] This prescription was later incorporated into canon law as advice on will-making, as a moderate way to balance the needs of the family and the needs of the church.[66] Gratian believed that

61. Basil, *Social Justice*, 54.
62. Constantelos, *Byzantine Philanthropy*, 100 and 106, on Saint Maria the Younger and Saint Thomaïs of Lesbos.
63. *St. Augustine on Marriage and Sexuality*, ed. Elizabeth Clark (Washington, D.C.: The Catholic University of America Press, 1996), 24–31.
64. Jerome, epistle 52.6, to Nepotian, PL, vol. 22, col. 533.
65. Augustine, *Sermons*, 403; similarly, see Valerianus of Cimiez, Homily 4, PL, vol. 52, col. 703B–706A.
66. Mario Falco, *Le Disposizioni 'pro Animo' fondamenti dottrinali e forme giurdiche* (Turin: Fratelli Bocca, 1911), and Eberhard Bruck, *Kirchenväter und soziales Erbrecht* (Berlin: Springer-Verlag, 1956).

Augustine, in giving a son's share to the church, was placing an upper limit on how much should be used for pious bequests and burial costs. The church should not be willing to take more than that sum.[67] The glossators generally rejected Gratian's interpretation, reserving the Falcidian fourth to the heir and allowing all of the rest to be given away to pious causes.[68] The tension between caring for the family and giving to the church or to the poor was real, and delaying donations to the deathbed did not resolve the conflict.[69]

A solution came from Cicero and Ambrose, who conceptualized a man's responsibilities as being greatest to those who were closest to him. He stood in the center of concentric circles of duty. Aquinas later endorsed this model and limited the extent of almsgiving even in life, maintaining in his *Summa Theologica* that man had many duties to himself, his station in life, his family, and his nation and his church, all of which needed to be discharged before alms could be given from his "superfluities."[70] The most important scholastic theologian thereby discouraged the ideal of a radically unworldly life for those who lived in the world, and this was in agreement with the *Decretum*. One's first charitable duty was to family and immediate relatives, to whom were owed sustenance but not inordinate wealth. For donations beyond the closest kin, discrimination should be employed to give to the worthiest.[71] This compromise, which acknowledged a moral obligation to care for family first, could satisfy the competing demands of salvation and family. As will be seen, the presumed right of return for failed gifts, which protected the interests of the heirs, also made it easier to give.

But this was a profoundly Roman solution, centered on the spiritual dilemmas of the head of the household and dependent on wealth

---

67. C.13 q.2 c.8.
68. Sheehan, *Will in Medieval England*, 127–28.
69. Jack Goody observes how unusual the Christian pattern of pious gifts was: *Death, Property and the Ancestors: A Study of the Mortuary Customs of the LoDagaa of West Africa* (Stanford, Calif.: Stanford University Press, 1962), 11.
70. Aquinas, *Summa Theologica*, in *Opera Omnia*, vol. 8 (Rome: Polyglotta, 1895), II-II, q. 32, pp. 249–61; Gl. Ord. ad C.12 q.1 c.11; Gl. Ord. ad D.42 c.2. Even Salvian agreed with this distinction: Salvian, *Writings*, 314; CSEL, 264.
71. Brian Tierney, "The Decretists and the 'Deserving Poor,'" *Comparative Studies in Society and History* 1 (1959): 360–73.

that he owned outright. It could not translate easily to a "Barbarian" context, in which all family members had a strong legal claim to property and in which it was difficult for a dying man to give away anything of significant value. It is true that astonished Romans, like Tacitus in his *Germania,* may have exaggerated this limitation in contrast to their own relative freedom of testation. Still, the systems were different. Although the emphasis on property as familial seems to have weakened over time, it is notable that Gregory of Tours recorded successful attempts by families to prevent, or demand the return of, pious donations to the church.[72] Even in the eleventh and twelfth centuries, because of the strength of the continuing connection between the family and its land, monasteries frequently asked family members to sign their consent to a gift when it was made in a *laudatio parentum*.[73]

A legal solution was to allow each man a part of his chattel or personal property to be distributed at death. Scholars have observed that as Germanic tribes Christianized, they transitioned from burying a man with some of his personal treasure, presumably to go with him into the next world, to giving some of his personal property on his behalf to monasteries.[74] In English custom this was generally a third, the "soul's part," which would be spent, even for the intestate, on the funeral, masses, and alms to the poor, who would be expected to pray for the deceased in return.[75] In that sense a dying man could choose what to do with what was truly his.[76]

---

72. For an early legal effort to prevent the resumption of gifts by heirs, see the *Leges Alamannorum* I.2 in *Leges Nationum Germanicarum,* vol. 5, part 1 (Hanover: Hahn, 1888), 64–65.

73. Stephen D. White, *Custom, Kinship, and Gifts to Saints: The 'Laudatio Parentum' in Western France, 1050–1150* (Chapel Hill: The University of North Carolina Press, 1988).

74. Georges Duby, *The Early Growth of the European Economy: Warriors and Peasants from the Seventh to the Twelfth Century,* trans. Howard B. Clarke (Ithaca, N.Y.: Cornell University Press, 1973); Lester K. Little, *Religious Poverty and the Profit Economy in Medieval Europe* (Ithaca, N.Y.: Cornell University Press, 1978), 5–6.

75. Hannan, *Canon Law of Wills,* 29–30. Generally neither common nor canon lawyers wanted to take credit for this allocation of a "soul's part," which—despite the attestation in Glanvill and Bracton—did not seem commendable. Innocent IV had fewer scruples and declared that a third of the intestate's movable belongings were owed to the church in his *Commentaria* on X 5.3.42.

76. Pollock and Maitland, *History of English Law,* vol. 2, 356.

Even if Pollock and Maitland were right to be skeptical about the strength of the concept of "family ownership" of property in the early Middle Ages, the fact that one's property was not fully one's own meant, conversely, that the whole family was bound up in the problem of everyone's individual salvation.[77] Anselm of Canterbury drew on this paradigm when he related Christ's atonement for the sins of mankind to this understanding that the entire family was tied in to the payment of each others' sins. As Bossy explained it, Christ "offer[ed] spontaneously to the Father the death to which he was not subject in due satisfaction for the offence of his kin" in an "axiom of kinship," in which family members "inherit the breach of relations with the party offended, and the debt of satisfaction which is owed to him" but in which they may "substitute themselves for the offending party in offering satisfaction."[78] Kin could pay the debts of a man if they so chose.

However, the axiom could work the other way; it could push beyond the payment of debt and into the accumulation of a spiritual storehouse. The medieval saints who cast off all family ties in order to pursue the ascetic life not only contributed to their family's spiritual welfare from afar through prayer and fasting but also allowed the remaining members of the family to use for themselves what resources the ascetics would have had. In a more ordinary household, families could save themselves collectively if they could accumulate spiritual treasure together. The rules of medieval gift culture, which are elaborated upon in the next chapter, allowed a family to do good works in life, largely through gifts to the church, while avoiding either a material or a spiritual disinheritance, because the family's connection to the gift would not be sundered by the donation. Prayers would be made on behalf of the whole family, and descendants would have the right not only to the return of the property if the purpose of the gift failed, but also to other possible material interests in the property even when it was functioning properly. In this way gifts, made in life or after death, were a service to the whole family, as the countess Ermessend, who had made 64 bequests in her

77. Ibid., 267–68.
78. Bossy, *Christianity in the West*, 4–5.

will, observed when she included a note, perhaps defensively, to her grandson Count Ramon Berenguer I to let him know that "I did this for you."[79] Cy-près, in which the donation might be turned to a new purpose and its material and spiritual connection to the heirs severed, is entirely antithetical to this scheme and would have corroded the new compromise that had been struck.

The ambiguity of deathbed alms appeared early in England. The canons of Clovesho in 747 urged almsgiving upon the faithful, but only that done in life out of licit income. Illicit income needed to be restored to the man who had been defrauded, for if it was given in alms it would arouse the anger of God. The canons warned that God promised forgiveness but not more time. The synods at Chelsea in 787, later picked up in the Lutheran ecclesiastical history *Magdeburg Centuries,* were reported to have denied postmortem prayers for those who died without confession. Sheehan observed an Anglo-Saxon preference for works done by the living, where "the sacrifice was greater and freedom from the attraction of wealth was more firmly established." The pressure for bequests on the deathbed as a sign of repentance after confession—which Sheehan associates in particular with Caesarius of Arles—was less notable in England than elsewhere, emerging only in 1000 when, "in spite of the manifest preference for alms given during life, the bequest for pious causes was also recommended."[80]

For example, the tenth-century Blickling homilies gave no hope that it was possible for a man to earn heaven after death: in life a man must give a tenth of his wealth to the church, give another tenth to the poor, and also let them have the scraps from his table and his old clothing, along with anything else that was superfluous. This would guarantee entry to heaven—but if the poor died around him while he did nothing, then only hell could await him. True, the living might petition God on behalf of the dead, but if a man has been negligent in his own salvation, how could he expect other men to be more assiduous?[81] A man could do good for himself only while

---

79. Nathaniel Lane Taylor, "The Will and Society in Medieval Catalonia and Languedoc, 800–1200," (Ph.D. diss., Harvard University, 1995), 164.

80. Sheehan, *Will in Medieval England*, 11–13.

81. "The Third Sunday in Lent," *The Blickling Homilies of the Tenth Century,* ed. R. Morris (London: Early English Text Society, 1880), 38–53.

alive: "let us redeem our souls the while we have life and price at our command, lest that death come and we lose at once life and price."[82] Indeed, at the moment of death, all of one's possessions turn into an occasion for mourning. The only solution was for a man to "distribute the best portion to God for himself whilst he is alive here."[83]

Although the dispersal of property on the deathbed for the good of the soul is attested early in English documents, the sources also reveal the ambiguity of deathbed bequests. *The Life of Saint Wilfrid*, an eighth-century hagiography, makes clear that despite the many good works of Bishop Wilfrid in life, he still gave to the poor on his deathbed, along with other donations for secular purposes, including riches to be used to bribe temporal leaders.[84] Wilfrid had been given advance warning of his death, and most of the property that he distributed was to other monks, who would supervise the monastic lands he had ruled. Wilfrid had accumulated gifts that he intended to take to Rome on a pilgrimage, for his soul (*pro anima mea*), but when he realized he was dying instead, he left a quarter of his estate to the poor for the redemption of his soul (*pro redemptione animae meae*).[85] Gifts made in health would improve the quality of the soul itself, while gifts made after death could merely aid its redemption, paying off any debts it had accumulated. Abbot Acca then commemorated Wilfrid and gave to the poor after his death, using the goods that Wilfrid had left for him, "for himself and for the soul of his bishop (*pro se et pro anima episcopi*) and always in his name."[86]

Despite this precedent, the *Life of Wilfrid* is unusual among hagiographies of the period in mentioning deathbed gifts to the poor for the redemption of the testator's soul, which is why it tends to appear prominently in accounts of Anglo-Saxon deathbed gifts. Other contemporary hagiographies do not. Bede's *Life of Cuthbert* revealed the great anxiety the saint felt whenever anyone gave him a gift, lest he

---

82. "Soul's Need," *Blickling Homilies*, 100.
83. "A Fragment," *Blickling Homilies*, 194.
84. The reliability of the text has been questioned; e.g., B. W. Wells, "Eddius' Life of Wilfrid," *English Historical Review* 6 (1891): 535–50.
85. Eddius Stephanus, *The Life of Bishop Wilfrid by Eddius Stephanus*, trans. Bertram Colgrave (Cambridge: Cambridge University Press 1985), 136.
86. Ibid., 180–81.

not be able to return it before he died, but at the deathbed of Cuthbert there was no last-minute distribution of alms. Similarly, in Bede's account of the *Lives of the Abbots of Wearmouth and Jarrow,* none of the abbots gave alms on their deathbed, only instruction and consolation. In the anonymous *Voyage of Saint Brendan,* the saint did no more than finish up loose ends before taking the sacraments and dying, and Abbot Ceolfrith's deathbed went entirely unrecorded in his hagiography.

Bede provides an instructive case, because he, like other Anglo-Saxon theologians, saw deathbed alms as somewhat disreputable, since there was, as Sheehan notes, "a rather unpleasant hint of the bribing of divine justice" in them.[87] When he wrote his lives of saints, Bede did not mention any deathbed distributions—perhaps in deliberate contrast to the account of the death of Saint Wilfrid, whom he did not like. In discussing the life of Saint Fursa, who was chastised by a demon for taking a gift from a dying man who was subsequently damned, Bede upheld that gifts to the poor from a deathbed penance must be distributed, and that a man who refuses to do penance at death should not be allowed to give alms. But a priest should not take anything for himself from a dying man who has been living in great sin. Bede upheld the connection between confession, penance, and alms on the deathbed without praising the distribution of alms at death as inherently meritorious.[88] At his own death, Bede gave gifts—but not specifically alms—and asked the recipients for their prayers.[89] This was the problem of saintly deathbeds: saints could not give away too much at death, but even monastic saints had goods at the end of their lives that, as a token of affection or good will, they offered before their death, asking for prayers in return that would help their soul. Deathbed gifts were valid only if they partook of repentance or served as the prudential arrangement of material goods, and while these gifts by *verba novissima* were apparently frequent and popular, their precise meaning is not clear.[90] Still, because of the bonds of reciprocal giving, it appears that the living understood that they in-

87. Sheehan, *Will in Medieval England,* 68.
88. Ibid., 14–15.
89. Ibid., 28 and 34.
90. Ibid., 33–34.

curred a debt of prayers in return for the gifts received: the Frankish noblewoman Dhuoda, in her ninth-century instruction manual for her son, advised him to calibrate his prayers so that he prayed the most for those who had left him the most property.[91]

By the time of the Anglo-Saxon wills (or, records of gifts *causa mortis*) of tenth- and eleventh-century England, it had become customary to make gifts explicitly "for the good of my soul." This included gifts made outright to the church and gifts made to relatives with the request that the relative then pray for the testator. Since these gifts were at least theoretically irrevocable (but not transferred until death), they did involve some sacrifice while the donor was still alive because the donor was not supposed to change his or her mind and give them to someone else.[92] They were also considered contractual, so they laid out expectations for the donation, with the exchange of prayers for property.[93] The donation obliged the recipient to return a gift of prayers. For example, the will of Aelfgar proclaimed: "I grant to my daughter Aethelflaed the estates at Cockfield and Ditton and that at Lavenham after my death on condition that she be the more zealous for the welfare of my soul and of her mother's soul and of her brother's soul and of her own." Aelfgar's provisions of his property carried on in this vein, making the care of his soul a condition of the distribution of his property. At the end of his will he begged that no one alter his will "for my soul's sake" but then went one step further, hurling imprecatory curses at those who might try: "if anyone alter it, may he have to account for it with God and the holy saints to whom I have bequeathed my property, so that he who shall alter this will may never repent it except in the torment of hell, unless I myself alter it before my death."[94] These Anglo-Saxon wills, then, carry the formulaic assertion that gifts were made for the good of the soul,

---

91. Dhuoda, *Manuel pour mon fils*, ed. Pierre Riché, in Sources Chrétiennes, vol. 225 (Paris: Editions du Cerf, 1975), 8.14.320.
92. Pollock and Maitland, *History of English Law*, vol. 2, 352; Sheehan, *Will in Medieval England*, 38.
93. *Anglo-Saxon Wills*, trans. Dorothy Whitelock (Cambridge: Cambridge University Press, 1930), x–xi and xx, and xxvi; Sheehan, *Will in Medieval England*, 27–29.
94. *Anglo-Saxon Wills*, 7–9.

Posthumous Gifts and the Soul 45

but the conditions and petitions laid upon the heirs suggests that the testators believed that it was the gratitude of the recipient, who then became more likely to persevere in prayer, that would make the difference.

Many of the complicated legal forms for donations, such as irrevocable gifts *causa mortis*, that developed in the Middle Ages seem explainable in part by the continuing tension between the need to provide for one's family, both now and in the future, and the need to take spiritual care of oneself, which required making some sacrifice in life and ensuring targeted postmortem help. It was possible to create life interests in property that would revert to the church upon the death of the heirs; to give money (the fruits) while keeping the land for the family; or to give land to the church that would conditionally revert to the family if more heirs appeared. *Post obit* gifts, in which transfer was made after death, might appear to have been the most avaricious of arrangements and the least sensitive to the need to give now, but because they were supposed to be irrevocable as they were made, they entailed a firm resolution in life and the sacrifice of the right of disposal. Moreover, as Pollock and Maitland point out, "occasionally in such cases it was thought well that the donor should put himself under the obligation of paying a small rent to the abbey while he lived."[95] This was another means to delay the gift but profit spiritually from it by bringing some cost forward into the donor's lifetime. Had deathbed gifts not been treated with suspicion, this otherwise odd arrangement of paying rent on a future donation would not have developed.

After the Norman Conquest in 1066 the canonical will was adopted in England, subject to the rules of canon law.[96] Following Roman law, canonical wills were revocable, as were all deathbed gifts if a man recovered.[97] This represented a major shift from Anglo-Saxon *post obit* gifts.[98] Gratian, and most of the canonists who followed him,

95. Pollock and Maitland, *History of English Law*, vol. 2, 339. See also Plucknett, *Concise History of the Common Law*, 733; Sheehan, *Will in Medieval England*, 25 and 59.
96. Sheehan, *Will in Medieval England*, 119–47.
97. But not a benefice renounced by a priest to become a monk: C.17 q.4 c.4.
98. Sheehan, *Will in Medieval England*, 28 and 140.

upheld that gifts made *in extremis* should be returned if the giver recovered, especially if he went on to have a child.[99] Similarly, the *Decretals* allowed the ill to offer only moderate alms, not to donate excessively when in fear of death.[100] Moreover, if senility prior to death could be proved, then the will would be thrown out, because the testator was not in his right mind.[101]

This canonical scrupulousness presented a new problem, because revocable penitence did not seem sincere. This is not to suggest that irrevocability was desirable in itself, since donors conceived of themselves as giving not free gifts but rather gifts with specific countergifts attached, without which the donor would be defrauded. In response to the canonical will, ways were found to create irrevocable gifts that still gave the donor the use of the property while living, such as the *donatio post obitum* with a re-grant.[102] Moreover, the bulk of medieval evidence suggests that many of the most important gifts were made in life, a trend that accelerated with the statutes of mortmain, which required a license in order to give property to the church. The process of obtaining and setting up a suitable property and then purchasing the license was so time-consuming that it was best to begin while in good health.[103]

A further shift occurred with the emergence of a formal doctrine of purgatory in 1274 at the Council of Lyon. The theory of purgatory, which allows that the confession of sin removes the threat of hell but not the need for sanctification, meant that "while one might certainly make a start by good works in life, the process could be completed (and might, indeed, be wholly satisfied) in purgatory."[104] Purgato-

---

99. C.17 q.2 c.1; C.17 q.4. c.43; Sheehan, *Will in Medieval England*, 124 and 137.

100. X 3.25.8.

101. X 3.27.3. Brandon T. Parlopiano, "Madmen and Lawyers: The Development and Practice of the Jurisprudence of Insanity in the Middle Ages" (Ph.D. diss., The Catholic University of America, 2013).

102. Sheehan, *Will in Medieval England*, 114.

103. Raban, *Mortmain Legislation and the English Church 1279–1500* (Cambridge: Cambridge University Press), 51. On the earlier preference to give in life, see White, *Custom, Kinship, and Gifts*, 31.

104. Clive Burgess, "'Longing to be prayed for': death and commemoration in an English parish in the later Middle Ages," in *The Place of the Dead: Death and*

ry had the effect of closing the door on hell: the church was limited to helping pull a sinner out of purgatory faster, and it was generally agreed that no number of masses could deliver the damned. Purgatory also moved the concept of time into the afterlife, trying to get the eternal to meet the temporal. Since purgatory would stop at the end of time, there was no knowing what would happen to the sinners left there if the end of the world occurred before they had finished their penances. Happily, perhaps, the torments of purgatory felt eternal, and thousands of purgatorial years fit into one earthly day. The testamentary escalation of commemorative masses—dozens, or hundreds, or occasionally thousands and into perpetuity—suggests that the dying were worried. Purgatory promised, according to some, pains as terrible as those of hell, meaning that the suffering of this world would be followed by something unimaginably worse before access to heaven was granted.[105] How distant from Paxton's description of the triumphant late antique death scene this is, if for the dying man the *valle lacrimarum* lay ahead, not behind. If the common man took purgatory seriously, then death for most Christians promised not rest or a beatific vision but a frightful and excruciating interlude.

Scholastic philosophers like Aquinas and canon lawyers like Alessandro Lombardo explored the concept of purgatory, but Le Goff argues that "canon law played ... a small role in the inception of Purgatory" due to unfavorable passages in the *Decretum*.[106] Indeed, Le Goff calls the canon lawyers "backwards" with regard to the development of purgatory, citing the author of the *Summa coloniensis*, a commentary on Gratian, who wrote that on the treatment of the dead by the living, "I never discussed the question, which is of interest to theologians more than canonists."[107] Later canonists offered

---

Remembrance in Late Medieval and Early Modern Europe, ed. Bruce Gordon and Peter Marshall (Cambridge: Cambridge University Press, 2000), 49.

105. Alan Kreider, *English Chantries: The Road to Dissolution* (Cambridge, Mass.: Harvard University Press, 1979), 41, and Eamon Duffy, *The Stripping of the Altars: Traditional Religion in England, c. 1400–c. 1580* (New Haven, Conn.: Yale University Press, 1992), 338–39 and 344.

106. Le Goff, *Birth of Purgatory*, 148.

107. Ibid., 173.

increasingly elaborate discussions of guilt (*culpa*) that picked apart the purpose of masses said for the dead, as categorized by their moral status.[108] A central problem was the understanding by some canonists that a man who had started penance for his sins in his lifetime was in a spiritually superior state to the man who had not.[109] Purgatory did not necessarily lessen the strain between justice and mercy. Moreover, canonists had difficulty with the jurisdiction of purgatory; Le Goff indicates that the church appears to have decided that it had coseigniory with God over purgatory, meaning that its services could help the suffering souls but could never bypass the judgment of God.[110] Still, when canonists like the thirteenth-century Franciscan Alexander of Hales wrestled with the question of how it was that the church could help the dead, they did not suggest that the impotent dead could fund their own salvation through bequests.[111] Canon lawyers, far from advocating for indiscriminate works on behalf of the dead, pushed back against the novelty. Moreover, they refused gifts made by those who had oppressed the poor (*Eorum, qui pauperes obprimunt, dona a sacerdotibus sunt refutanda*) and encouraged restitution to the wounded party first, if possible.[112] The church kept the patrimony of the poor, but not at their expense.

Purgatory functioned as part of a culture of increasing soteriological precision. Le Goff has shown how concern for the perfect justice of God required the creation of this institution where painful sanctification for one's sins was precisely meted out, so that exactly one's due was received. The treasury of merits also began to keep better accounts. Sixtus IV's *Salvator noster* of 1476 offered plenary remission for the souls in purgatory related to any donors who contributed, over a period of ten years, at targeted levels of giving. But generally the wealthy were required to give more in order to receive the same effect that the less wealthy could receive for smaller donations: Al-

---

108. Stephan Kuttner, *Kanonistische Schuldlehre von Gratian bis auf die Dekretalen Gregors IV: Systematisch auf Grund der handschriftlichen Quellen dargestellt*, Studi e testi, vol. 64 (Vatican City: Biblioteca Apostolica Vaticana, 1935).
109. Le Goff, *Birth of Purgatory*, 222–23.
110. Ibid., 248–49.
111. Ibid., 249.
112. X 1.15.8.

bert of Mainz's 1515 *Instructio summaria* gave specific assessments for the money necessary for plenary remission for each social class, and he suggested that prayers offered by the ill ought to be said before an image to concentrate the mind on God and not on oneself. Because the material gifts of a sick or dying man were not worth as much as they would have been in health, they required pious support to multiply their effect. Precise calculations of relative value are also evidenced in pastoral care: one priest, visiting an ill man, urged him "to give a penny to each of five people, telling him that 'oon peny now gyven was better then xx after.'"[113] Archbishop John Peckham, in his 1281 constitutions issued at Lambeth, tried to explain why many people could not be as well served by being simultaneously—rather than individually—commemorated in one mass. Ultimately, he admitted that canon law would allow one mass to serve all, but "God doth work in such mysteries under a certain distribution of His fulness, which He hath knit unto them with a law that cannot be expressed."[114] Pushed too far, precision threatened to collapse into obscurity.

But as Caroline Walker Bynum has shown, precision could be "an assertion of personal religious agency," rather than evidence of superstitious panic.[115] The rise of the chantry allowed for greater precision on the other side of the exchange too—as well as greater donor control. K. L. Wood-Legh notes a single eleventh-century foundation of a chantry in Britain, but they became prominent in Britain and continental Europe in the twelfth century, reaching an apex in the thirteenth through fifteenth centuries.[116] The endowments that established chantries paid for masses, sometimes in perpetuity, for the

113. Quoted in Houlbrooke, *Death, Religion, and the Family*, 96.
114. The translation is from *Constitutions provincialles and of Otho and Octhobone translated in to Englyshe* (1534). The original Latin can be found in Lyndwood's *Provinciale* (Oxford: Richard Davis, 1679) III.23.2: "Operatur enim in huiusmodi Mysteriis, distributione certa suae plenitudinis, quam ipse eisdem Lege ineffabili alligavit."
115. Caroline Walker Bynum, *Christian Materiality: An Essay on Religion in Late Medieval Europe* (New York: Zone Books, 2011), 269.
116. K. L. Wood-Legh, *Perpetual Chantries in Britain* (Cambridge: Cambridge University Press, 1965), 4; Howard Colvin, "The Origin of Chantries," *Journal of Medieval History* 26 (2000): 164.

soul of their founder and his or her family. They allowed the donor to be especially particular in the foundation and for the heirs to oversee whether the donor's specifications were being observed—and demand the return of the property if they were not. Responding to the emphasis on the effectiveness of the mass, chantries were highly efficient in meeting the spiritual and familial needs of the donor. The donor demonstrated a perceptive understanding of exactly what would help him and his family, and the family in turn could monitor and appoint the chaplain with little ecclesiastical intervention.

In earlier arrangements, frankalmoin (or, "free alms") tenure in relationship to monasteries had offered none of these advantages. Frankalmoin tenure had no military or other services attached, although prayers and masses were normally an expected countergift, and they were free from royal jurisdiction. It was difficult to retrieve property in these agreements except in the case of total alienation, so what materialized in the late Middle Ages was actually a move toward greater accountability for the donor's stipulations, with legal reversion to the heirs if the foundation documents were not observed specifically. Additionally, while patronage relationships with monasteries tended to involve repeated donations over the centuries, chantries were theoretically a one-time foundation. They promised to liberate future generations from the obligation of further donations, while still bestowing on them all of the benefits of intercessory prayer. This was a significant part of their appeal, although in point of fact many decayed endowments in the age of inflation would require help from the heirs in order to continue.

The foundation documents for chantries were complex, and Wood-Legh discovered that many were established during the founder's lifetime and began offering prayers while the founder was still alive, so that the good works started in life itself. A foundation in life also allowed the founder to seek out the mortmain license on his own, since no one else would be as motivated to pursue the license as the original donor, and he or she could then be sure that the chantry was operating and would thereby prevent fraud and embezzlement.[117] Even

---

117. Wood-Legh, *Perpetual Chantries*, 32.

in late medieval England, the spiraling number of masses commanded by wealthy testators was evidence that they understood both that their earthly wealth was a problem (since they had used it to their last days) and that masses were a relatively secure recompense, because the church was considered reliable about delivering on agreements to perform private masses and because masses were sanctioned by canon law as one of the limited means of helping the dead. Attempts by founders to ensure their chantries would not fall vacant similarly acknowledged the postmortem utility of each mass actually said, not the work of founding the chantry itself.[118] While many chantries had charitable functions—including alms, care for the sick, or education—their foundations usually required that the recipients of their postmortem alms be reminded both of their names and of the need for the recipient to pray on behalf of the donor's soul in return for the gifts. Guests in almshouses might have to attend liturgical services to pray for the donor as a condition of their stay. This indicates a good understanding that it was not the postmortem alms themselves that could help, but the prayerful petitions of the poor who received them.[119]

A move toward these new forms of intercessory institutions has also been observed elsewhere in Europe in the late Middle Ages, and it marked a decline in the relationship to a community of saints through monastic patronage.[120] Chantries marshaled spiritual resources for the family and its chaplain alone, depending not on the quality of intercession but on the repetition of masses, however said. Proximity to the saints and to a community of pious monks was devalued.[121] While the relationship to a "profit economy" seems real,

118. Ibid., 69.
119. Marjorie Kenston McIntosh, *Poor Relief in England, 1350–1600* (Cambridge: Cambridge University Press, 2012), chapter 3. Count Theobald of Champagne liked to give alms personally in order to improve the frequency and intensity of the poor's prayers: Paul Webster, *King John and Religion*, 130.
120. Maureen Miller, "Donors, Their Gifts, and Religious Innovation in Medieval Verona," *Speculum* 66 (1991): 27–42.
121. Megan McLaughlin, *Consorting with Saints: Prayer for the Dead in Early Medieval France* (Ithaca, N.Y.: Cornell University Press, 1994); Barbara H. Rosenwein, *To Be the Neighbor of Saint Peter: The Social Meaning of Cluny's Property, 909–1049* (Ithaca, N.Y.: Cornell University Press, 1989); Benjamin Thompson, "Monasteries

52　Posthumous Gifts and the Soul

this transition perhaps marked an acknowledgment of canon law limits on how to help the dead. The new system was more focused on the goal than the earlier system had been. It trusted less in the prayers of righteous men and more on the efficacy of the mass.[122]

For those who could not afford to fund a chantry, a variety of lesser options included obits (an annual mass), lights (perpetual candles placed in front of images, which were a kind of prayer in themselves and might prompt both the saint being honored and those who saw the light to pray for the deceased), or guilds (in which a brotherhood would fund communal prayers for its dead). Even modest donations could earn a testator a spot on the bede-roll of his parish church, while a more prominent family could ensure that their coat of arms would be displayed. The middling sort could join a guild that would offer posthumous prayers for their members and would also serve as an insurance venture: members who fell on hard times might be eligible for alms, a provision that echoed the patronage rights granted to the members of the families of wealthy donors to the church.[123] Often these commemorative institutions included the distribution of alms or some other charitable aspect "devoted to provide for poor people, who were called beadsmen or beadswomen, and whose duty it was to attend the services and pray for the souls of their benefactors."[124]

Gifts could multiply their spiritual benefits, which distinguished the gift economy from the commercial economy. Money, considered as a limited commodity, could not make more money—and money should not even try to do so. It was therefore possible to justify the disinheriting of children through gifts to the church as a form of wise investment, in which the gifts became an ever-growing spiritual currency of *caritas* that ran throughout the Christian community and to the heirs themselves. Just as this system was about to collapse in

---

and Their Patrons at Foundation and Dissolution," *Transactions of the Royal Historical Society,* Sixth Series, 4 (1994): 103–25.

122. B. J. Kidd, *The Later Medieval Doctrine of the Eucharistic Sacrifice* (London: SPCK, 1958); Miri Rubin, *Corpus Christi: The Eucharist in Late Medieval Culture* (Cambridge: Cambridge University Press, 1992).

123. Timothy G. Fehler, *Poor Relief and Protestantism: The Evolution of Social Welfare in Sixteenth-Century Emden* (Aldershot, England: Ashgate, 1999), 43–44.

124. Boggis, *Praying for the Dead,* 152.

the English Reformation, Thomas More imagined what the suffering souls of purgatory would say about it:

Send here your prayer; send here your alms before you. So we will find ease, and so will you too find it. For just as when you light a candle for someone else, you have no less light for yourself, and when you blow on a fire to warm someone else, you also warm yourself with it, so, good friends, surely the good that you send here before you both greatly refreshes us and still is wholly preserved here for you, with our prayers added to it for your further advantage.[125]

More suggested that the priest as an intermediary multiplied these effects even faster. The donor, the priest, and the suffering soul in purgatory all combined their prayers for each other, earning merits from God as they did so, and lifted each other up to heaven so surely that this world and the next abounded with the effects of charitable prayer.[126] This was a joyful and exponential mathematics.

But some of the new remedies for this late medieval culture of precision undermined the accommodations that had already been made. Chantries, hospitals, almshouses, guilds, and donations of treasure recorded on the bede-rolls were all lasting gifts whose connection to their family of origin was culturally and legally enforced. They offered local services that could be seen and monitored; they were concrete and visible. Meanwhile, the mendicant orders, which were strongly associated with the cultivation of purgatory, were less tied to the locality. In fact, the closer they remained to their ideal of voluntary poverty, the more deracinated they appeared, collecting alms that disappeared into their coffers, it seemed, or were sent abroad.[127] Worse, the mendicants were prominently connected to indulgences, which had migrated from their tenth-century origins as approved substitutions for penances to what increasingly appeared to be a commercial system of straightforward purchase.[128] This system threatened

---

125. More, *Four Last Things*, 184.
126. Ibid., 168.
127. Geoffrey Dipple, *Antifraternalism and Anticlericalism in the German Reformation* (Aldershot, England: Ashgate, 1996).
128. R. N. Swanson, ed., *Promissory Notes on the Treasury of Merits: Indulgences in Late Medieval Europe* (Leiden: Brill, 2006); R. N. Swanson, *Indulgences in Late Medieval England: Passports to Paradise?* (Cambridge: Cambridge University Press, 2007).

the economy of salvation in several ways. Indulgences were sometimes obtained on behalf of only one person, which upset the balance between the individual and the family. They were much less tangible than other intercessory institutions, since they offered nothing obvious in return for the donation besides the assurance that a spiritual countergift had been conveyed and a piece of paper backed by the full faith and credit of the Apostolic See at a time when anticlerical sentiment was strong and trust in the ecclesiastical hierarchy weak. Finally, with an indulgence there was no lingering connection or residual property rights between the gift and the family. The gift was made, the soul was sprung, and the money was gone.

The period of increasingly precise spiritual accounting also went hand-in-hand with the entrapping growth of economic practices that seemed both usurious and inescapable. There was little hope for the usurer, whose sin mounted as relentlessly as the interest he charged and who needed to attempt precise restitution with ill-gotten goods that were probably insufficient.[129] Neither the debtor nor the usurer could keep up with the debts they incurred. The early fifteenth-century poem *The Child of Bristowe* demonstrates the popular awareness of the limited means for helping the dead and the familial anxiety in a tightening economy of salvation. In the poem, a merchant has devoted himself to amassing wealth through usury out of love for his son, who also wants make his career in trade—although without recourse to charging interest. On the father's deathbed he repents of his ways and is shriven. His son then spends his father's estate on prayers and alms. After two weeks the father's spirit, wrapped in burning chains, appears to the boy and announces that without restitution for his usurious wrongs, the father cannot be freed. The boy borrows against his own portion of the estate to pay back anyone from whom his father had taken interest, but his father's spirit then appears again, in purgatorial pain and apparently rescued from hell. He tells his son that unpaid tithes and offerings are now keeping him from heaven. The son sells himself into bondage and donates the proceeds to all of the churches his father had neglected. When the son runs out of money,

---

129. Jacques Le Goff, *Your Money or Your Life: Economy and Religion in the Middle Ages*, trans. Patricia Ranum (New York: Zone Books, 1998).

he gives away his clothes to a creditor who had neglected to ask his father for his debt, and he goes to his dead father's bedchamber to pray. There he sees a vision of his father being received into heaven. Joyfully he returns to the master to whom he had sold his liberty, who, impressed with the boy's fidelity, takes him on as his own heir, and so the boy ends up rich in this life both materially and spiritually.

The effect on the listeners may not have been as encouraging as the author intended. The boy had to expend all possible resources to rescue his father, even selling his own future, to make up for his father's sins. The man who lent him money to pay for the return of his father's ill-gotten gains was probably, by doing so, wrapping himself in the chains that had bound the father. Were it not for the fortuitous rescue by his new master, the son would have spent his life destitute—and would have had no money with which to atone for his own sins. Sin, especially usurious sin, was an alarming threat to the family finances, and the problem was not necessarily only fictional. Jacques Heers has argued that the dispersal of fortunes to pious causes was an economically destabilizing force in the late Middle Ages.[130] Although the poem's representation of the afterlife was not officially sanctioned, it did emphasize the specificity of restitution above all else. For the son to give money to any poor person would not have helped—it was the poor that his father had individually hurt that he needed to find. In popular understanding, then, cy-près would have been useless to him. Medieval English ghost stories told the same tale: the dead begged for suffrages, for specific restitution to be made on their behalf, or even for the living to arrange absolution for them over in the earthly world where sins could be forgiven.[131] No ghost asked for general philanthropy on their behalf.

The specificity endorsed by the poem was a distorted echo from

---

130. Ariès, *The Hour of Our Death*, 192, citing Jacques Heers, *L'Occident aux XIVe et XVe siècles* (Paris: Presses Universitaires de France, 1966), 96. V. Gordon Childe argued that wealthier societies give proportionally fewer resources to the dead: "Directional Changes in Funerary Practices during 50,000 Years," *Man: A Record of Anthropological Science* 45 (1945): 13–19.

131. M. R. James, "Twelve Medieval Ghost-Stories," *The English Historical Review* 37 (July 1922): 413–22; H. E. D. Blakiston, "Two More Medieval Ghost Stories," *The English Historical Review* 38 (1923): 85–87.

canon law, which asked that an offender attempt to make specific, not general, restitution. A thief, usurer, or simoniac could not make up for his sins by giving the appropriated goods to the poor while avoiding restitution to those he had wronged.[132] Specific wrongs should be undone in their particular form. Still, the attempt at restitution was essential, but if it could not be performed there were alternatives: "No thief, dying, can be saved unless he gives back the property whence it came. If those from whom it was taken cannot be found, then he should bestow it upon a church or the poor."[133] This sat uncomfortably with canon law texts that forbade the church to take illicit goods, of course, but it was a dispensation in view of the exigencies of the deathbed. It was not an invitation to divert donations from one use to another, and it was not even a suggestion that a thief would necessarily be saved by his last-minute efforts.

Two striking contrasts between Catholic and Protestant theology were the treatment of the dead and the possibility that works could help one's spiritual condition. It is not surprising, then, to find that in the sixteenth and seventeenth centuries, in the midst of confessional disputes, the two issues might have become conflated in the popular imagination, belying the earlier, subtler treatment of postmortem gifts. Carlos Eire has found testaments in Counter-Reformation Spain that offer a hope that bequests could "extinguish the flames of the fires of hell" or "evade the fires of hell."[134] Even priests sometimes allowed this language to slip into their wills. Juan de Talavera Salazar asked that the wealth he had amassed as a canon and hospital administrator be counted not as money that ought to have been already given away, but rather as a credit to his work, since "it is fitting that my soul ... should now enjoy the fruits of this labor, and that my earnings all be spent in masses and sacrifices, so that through these devotions and through His mercy, God my redeemer may desist from damning me, and save me."[135] Eire found a con-

132. C.1 q.1 c.27; C.14 q.5 c.1; C.14 q.5 c.3; Cf. Gl. Ord. ad D. 35 c.1.
133. C.14 q.5 c.4: "Nemo, qui rapit, moriens, si habet unde reddat, salvatur. Si eos, quorum fuit, invenire non poterit, ecclesiae vel pauperibus tribuat."
134. Carlos M. N. Eire, *From Madrid to Purgatory: The Art and Craft of Dying in Sixteenth-Century Spain* (Cambridge: Cambridge University Press, 1995), 233.
135. Ibid., 194.

sistent inflationary pressure on the number of posthumous masses ordered across seventeenth-century Spain as well as a genuine fear about the horrors that awaited during the purgatorial sentence. Purgatory had exacerbated the sense of God as a demanding accountant, not releasing man from jail until he had paid the last penny of his debt. It is understandable that the psychological pressures of this system might have appeared to Protestants in the seventeenth and eighteenth centuries as an obviously fertile ground in which cy-près doctrine could have grown.

Nonetheless, medieval cautiousness about what counted for salvation was taken seriously by donors and led to distinct patterns of giving, both in life and in death: "bequests to the indigent were far less numerous than ones to the parish church or to priests ... [and] the most ambitious charitable foundations, such as almshouses, were often established during benefactors' lives, rather than by will."[136] Over the centuries, testators had proven remarkably canny about the efficient use of resources for their salvation, and at no point had they behaved as though indiscriminate charity would rescue the dead. If this had been clear to the donors themselves, how much more clear must it have been to the canon lawyers, who had a particularly sober assessment of bequests. When the potential superstitiousness of bequests came under particular assault in the Reformation, the critique was not new: "That alms given during a person's lifetime were more meritorious than those bequeathed by will was a theme inherited from the Middle Ages. A lifetime gift, unlike a testamentary bequest, involved an immediate sacrifice."[137] And yet it was this long-running cautiousness about gifts made on the deathbed that had led to what appeared to Protestants to be a lamentable disregard for posthumous alms, in favor of more sure remedies. The necessity of almsgiving in life had sparked the original quest to reconcile competing spiritual, familial, and temporal demands, but it had resulted in a system that could elevate other means, besides alms, to help the dead to make up for their failures to give sufficient alms in life. The central impor-

---

136. Houlbrooke, *Death, Religion, and the Family*, 114–15; Ariès, *The Hour of Our Death*, 303.
137. Houlbrooke, *Death, Religion, and the Family*, 63.

tance of alms in life had paradoxically led to the promotion of masses, not alms, after death.

When in the early sixteenth century Simon Fish proposed that all the money spent on the dead ought to go to better uses for the living, Thomas More replied, in his *Supplication of Souls,* with the protest that this would defraud the dead. The moderate evangelical, Christopher Saint German, responded that "because great riches have come to the Church for praying for souls in purgatory, [they] have by words affirmed that there is no purgatory."[138] God would not be tricked by spiritual simony. But Thomas More, trying to save the system, suggested that postmortem works offered hope:

> Surely, since we could and should have done it ourselves, and because of a filthy affection for our goods could not find it in our heart to part with any part of them, if our executors now play us false and do no more for us than we did for ourselves, our Lord would do us no wrong if he gave us no credit for any of our whole last will and testament, but imputed the frustration and nonperformance of it to our own fault.... We who have so died have found that the goods disposed of after our departure get our executors great credit and are toward us accounted before God as much less than half our own.[139]

This was the most powerful statement on behalf of testamentary bequests yet made; it was also riddled with ambivalence. It seems improbable that such a grudging nod to bequests, made in the context of a bid to turn them over to new purposes, could have underlain a legal doctrine to redirect property for the sake of suffering souls.

Moreover, a man on his deathbed who made oral charitable bequests, witnessed by a priest who was hearing his last confession, was understood to be doing something rather different than a man who made a will ahead of time, planning posthumous philanthropy deliberately. Across the centuries, there is evidence that the preference was to make significant donations while living if this was financially possible, so that the donor could observe the foundation and receive full salvific credit for a gift done in the safety of life. However, the deathbed remained an arena for the combat of faith against

---

138. Quoted in Alan Kreider, *English Chantries,* 101.
139. More, *Four Last Things,* 188.

despair well into the seventeenth century. In many ways this lingering emphasis on the good death was, as Wunderli and Broce note, a rebellion of popular culture against a theology of predestination.[140] But it also meant that to give charitable bequests from the deathbed was part of the ritual of a good death, demonstrating piety and giving the dying something to do that would keep morale up and reveal a repentant spirit. A will made in advance might lack the emotional intensity—the purity of repentance—that was the only redemptive aspect of deathbed bequests, despite the late hour at which they were made.

And so, despite the push from above to encourage testators to plan ahead, well past the Reformation the deathbed remained the predominant arena for will making. The prudent planning of one's estate was the pastoral solution offered time and again as a means to encourage the living to face death now, and yet the vast majority of last wills and testaments that remain are dated within days of the testator's death, even into the seventeenth century.[141] Psychological resistance and the difficulty of producing a legal document may not entirely account for this fact, because it was understood that to write a will beforehand that included charitable gifts was an unavoidable demonstration that the testator was postponing good works. But while it was dangerous to rely solely on deathbed giving, it was also dangerous not to give on the deathbed, since that could suggest a defiant, not a penitential, attitude at the critical point of spiritual transition. For those who took the standard advice of clergymen and wrote wills before death, codicils could help solve the dilemma by serving to reinforce the penitential spirit of the testator. The legendarily avaricious Cardinal Henry Beaufort, for example, assembled a will in January of 1446 but then wrote two codicils during his extended, ultimately fatal illness in April of 1447. Each codicil gave away personal items and also remitted debt, gave alms, and paid for more masses. A

---

140. Richard Wunderli and Gerald Broce, "The Final Moment Before Death in Early Modern England," *The Sixteenth Century Journal* 20 (1989): 259–75. Tessa Watt has also shown that anxiety about works and deathbed repentance continued to be striking themes well into the seventeenth century. Tessa Watt, *Cheap Print and Popular Piety 1550–1640* (Cambridge: Cambridge University Press, 1991).

141. Houlbrooke, *Death, Religion, and the Family*, 377.

prolonged deathbed could require repeated acts of giving, much like the daily almsgiving recommended by the early church.

Neither canon law nor Catholic theology approved of indiscriminate gifts after death as a means to save the dead, and both, until the Reformation, sought reasonable limits to the pressures for pious bequests. The greater focus on control and specificity that emerged over time was antithetical to cy-près doctrine, as was the emphasis on rectifying the concrete wrongs one had committed. To whatever extent the desire to direct endowments to new ends was a theme of the late Middle Ages, it was driven not by concerns for salvation but by concerns of this world. After all, as Duby notes, the pagans took wealth with them into the afterlife, and pre-Christian treasure hoards were treated by contemporaries with great reverence, rarely disturbed or dug up despite the wealth contained in the grave. In the Middle Ages, legacies would become "fruitful" rather than "sterile," used to build churches or feed the poor rather than lying in the ground with the dead.[142] Cy-près would be a further step along the trajectory of making gifts more abundant in their secular fruits.

142. Duby, *Early Growth*, 55.

2

Patronage Rights and Consensus in Medieval Gift Culture

Augustine was for centuries the model bishop. His biographer Possidius reported approvingly that he made no will on his deathbed because he had nothing to give.[1] He used church property to care for the poor, and he, like Ambrose, melted down church plate in order to ransom captives and alleviate poverty.[2] According to Possidius, Augustine observed that legacies were the easiest way for the church to receive gifts, because the dying were more generous than the living. Despite this, Augustine treated gifts on a case-by-case basis. He sometimes returned legacies to the family, even though he acknowledged that this was against the will of the testator.[3] Likewise, Augustine reverted gifts back to the donor if the donor changed his or her mind. This is one form of equity in action. A doctrine, such as cy-près, need not be the highest form of equity; indeed it has long been recognized that equitable solutions to particularly difficult cas-

---

1. Possidius, "Sancti Augustini Vita scripta a Possidio episcopo," ed. Herbert T. Weiskotten (Ph.D. diss., Princeton University, 1919), 142.
2. Ibid., 94–100.
3. Ibid., 96. On Augustine and disputed inheritances, see Peter Brown, *Augustine of Hippo: A Biography*, new ed. (Berkeley: University of California Press, 2000), 222.

es should not be generalized into principle. Equity could offer flexibility in the administration of law, fitting solutions to circumstances through a Lesbian rule, in order to better serve justice by "rendering to each his due."[4]

Augustine's actions indicate that he recognized multiple interests in a gift, and the medieval gift culture within which the *ius commune* subsequently flourished was one in which gift-giving entailed a lasting relationship between the donor, his or her heirs, the gift, and the recipient. When conditions changed, these perpetual gifts sometimes needed alterations to the terms of the donation, ideally made by the consent of all interested parties and with injury to the rights of none. However, there was an effort to honor the purpose of the gift above all other stipulations, such as the location of the gift or the trustees who supervised it. Consequently, even during times of unscrupulous abuse of donations or calls for radical reform, two cultural ideals were generally upheld: that multiple parties held ongoing rights in the gift and that the use of the gift ought to be preserved. Through the thirteenth century, learned laws largely reflected these broader cultural norms. After all, the *ius commune* included the *Libri feudorum* as part of the texts available for study and consultation (the *ius commune feudorum*), and it also allowed that custom had some weight in legal understanding, even where custom might limit the applicability of learned laws. As Accursius explained in the Ordinary Gloss to the *Libri feudorum*, "[T]he authority of the Roman laws is not negligible, but they do not extend their force to the point at which they overcome custom or usage."[5] The learned laws that governed gifts to the church were not arcane principles unknown to the rest of society, and they were not at war with cultural perceptions of justice.

---

4. Peter Landau, "'Aequitas' in the 'Corpus Iuris Canonici,'" *Syracuse Journal of International Law and Commerce* 20 (1994): 95–104.

5. Cited in Magnus Ryan, "Succession to Fiefs: A Ius Commune Feudorum?" in *The Creation of the Ius Commune: From Casus to Regula* (Edinburgh: Edinburgh University Press, 2010), 146: "Legum Romanarum non vilis est auctoritas, non tamen usque adeo vim suam extendunt, ut consuetudinem vincant, aut mores ut." Glos. Ord. ad LF 1.1.3. On the legal validity of custom and its relationship to the consent of the people, see also Digest 1.3.32.1, Institutes 1.2.9, affirmed in D.12 c.6, and C.9 q.3 c.8.

Medieval Gift Culture

Marcel Mauss argued that in most primitive societies a gift is a reciprocated act: a gift (in medieval Latin, *munus*) is matched with a countergift (*remuneratio*) by the recipient in the expected exchange. Medievalists, most famously Georges Duby, embraced Mauss's reconceptualization of the economy of the gift, which illuminates social norms that demanded that receiving always be matched or improved upon, both up and down the social scale.[6] Sometimes the countergift was explicitly spelled out in the original donation; "free" gifts, made without an expectation of a countergift, were a rarity. Instead, as Patrick Geary summarizes, "a donor keeps eternal rights in the gift and hence in the recipient," making the return of a countergift, to which the second donor would keep rights as well, an essential act of reciprocity.[7] Geary, writing on the exchange relationship between the living and the dead in the Middle Ages, points out that "the gifts the living had received from the dead [life itself, property, and personal identity] were so great as to threaten the receivers unless balanced by equally worthy countergifts."[8] A solution was to involve the church, which could hold property in a kind of permanent trust for "the living, the dead, and the future," performing spiritual services on behalf of generations of the donor family while also allowing the family to maintain an interest in the property such that the heirs were not entirely cut off from the land if they fell on hard times.[9]

The norms of medieval gift relationships can appear in unexpected ways. For example, the donation of a saint's relics to a church was a specific and intimate gift, understood, as Geary notes, as a "*pignora*, literally, the security deposits left by the saints upon their deaths as guarantees of their continuing interest in the earthly community."[10] Where these relics were legitimately attached to a loca-

---

6. Duby, *Early Growth*, 48–57.
7. Patrick J. Geary, *Living with the Dead in the Middle Ages* (Ithaca, N.Y.: Cornell University Press, 1994), 78.
8. Ibid.
9. Ibid., 79.
10. Ibid., 202.

tion—either through the directive of the lawful custodian of the relics or because the saint had requested burial in a specific place—they were bequests for a purpose that might nonetheless be commuted by transport from one church to another via gifts, thefts, or, more rarely, commerce.[11] In a remarkable attestation to the fundamental importance of purpose above all else, the theft of relics could be considered better than buying and selling them as long as the purpose of the theft was pious, because the relics would be put to the same use, but in a different location.[12] As Patrick Geary has shown, the "will" of the saints was used to justify the successful theft (or transfer) of relics from one place to another, and the essence of the "will" was the purpose, not the terms.[13] Of course, theoretically the donor's will was always honored in the case of relics, because the saint could call upon God for immediate revenge upon those who violated his will. Silence was consent.

Child oblation also highlights the assumptions of medieval gift culture, because it tried to thwart them. As Mayke De Jong has shown, the donation of a child to a monastery by his or her parents was a widespread Carolingian practice.[14] The child was presented, with his hand wrapped in an altar cloth and bearing a gift, at the altar, where he was symbolically transformed into a holocaust, a burnt offering. But the rights of the donor that the child's parents might have expected to enjoy for any other kind of donation to the church were nullified in the case of the oblate because the child was a sacrifice to God. As such, he or she could never be returned to the world.[15]

11. Ibid., 208.
12. Robert Bartlett, *Why Can the Dead Do Such Great Things?: Saints and Worshippers from the Martyrs to the Reformation* (Princeton, N.J.: Princeton University Press, 2013), 311; Cf. Codex Theodosianus 9.17 and 9.17.7.
13. Patrick J. Geary, *Furta Sacra: Theft of Relics in the Central Middle Ages*, rev. ed. (Princeton, N.J.: Princeton University Press, 2011), chapter six, drawing on Heinrich Fichtenau and Klaus Schreiner.
14. Mayke de Jong, *In Samuel's Image: Child Oblation in the Early Medieval West* (Leiden: Brill, 1996). On Anglo-Saxon links to Carolingian culture: Joanna Story, *Carolingian Connections: Anglo-Saxon England and Carolingian Francia, c. 750–870* (Aldershot, England: Ashgate, 2003); James T. Palmer, *Anglo-Saxons in a Frankish World, 690–900* (Turnhout: Brepols, 2009); Wilhelm Levison, *England and the Continent in the Eighth Century* (Oxford: Clarendon Press, 1946).
15. De Jong, *In Samuel's Image*, 7. For those who could not make such an

The oblate had to be completely disinherited from the family, with no claim to any of its property, and so, in theory at least, cut off from all worldly ties.[16] This distinction was not always clear to either the parents or the child: there are instances in which the family or the adult oblate attempted to petition for the oblate to be set free or to receive a governing interest in family property, but these petitions were almost always unsuccessful. Unlike other monastics, oblates could not even be expelled for bad behavior.[17] Gifts could be returned; sacrifices could not.

When parents gave their children, with their accompanying offering that represented what would have been the child's inheritance, to the monastery, the names of the parents themselves were entered into the commemoration lists.[18] The language of *pro remedio animae* faded over time, but as votive masses and commemorations developed in ninth-century monasteries, gifts could increasingly function penitentially, being donated at the offertory of the mass, and "alms could now be converted into the celebration of votive masses."[19] Gifts flowed in all directions: a gift and sacrifice by the donor could make possible the celebration of the mass, which was itself a gift and a sacrifice, and "in exchange for which the donor could expect a reward (*remuneratio*)."[20] When medieval gift culture encountered the mass, the effects of the ongoing exchange multiplied.

As a result, the monasteries' "ensuing obligation of commemoration" for the donors of the child effectively produced "an enduring link between the donor and the community, which was sufficiently tenacious to last for centuries."[21] Thus the hope of creating perpetual links to a monastery and its commemorations remained after the decline of child oblation, although it became necessary to be clear-

---

irrevocable sacrifice, Benedict suggested that donors might create more flexible arrangements with land donations, reserving some of the rights of the land to themselves. Ibid., 26. Benedict, *Regula*, PL, vol. 66, col. 839–40.

16. De Jong, *In Samuel's Image*, 28.
17. Ibid., 77, 91, and 142.
18. Ibid., 100, 116, 118, and 121.
19. Ibid., 174–75.
20. Ibid., 176.
21. Ibid., 123 and 288.

er about what was expected in return for gifts. Indeed, the pattern of "keeping-while-giving," a term adopted from Annette Weiner, seems to have been a strong tendency in medieval gifts that was supported, not thwarted, by the laws.[22] As Ilana Silber has explained, donations to monasteries carried with them "a fully explicit insistence on reciprocity" that "was perceived as fully legitimate, and not at all contradictory to either the other-worldly, spiritual motive or the very idea of giving itself." Silber finds that the "element of reciprocity became in fact even more salient in time," not diminishing at the end of the Middle Ages but instead maintaining the rights of the donor and his or her family over the gift.[23] As covered in the last chapter, the rise of the chantry was appealing in part because of the unprecedented levels of donor control that it offered, from the foundation that laid out the donor's particular stipulations, to the chaplain's oath to honor the foundation, to (in England) the right of the donor's heirs to ensure the functioning of the chantry according to its establishment or else sue in common law courts for its return.[24] The right of the donor to dictate terms of the gift, as Wood-Legh notes, was understood as a natural consequence of the donation. As one founder explained: "[I]t is just and consonant with reason that he who provides the emoluments should impose what form he wishes."[25] A *ius commune* jurist might have put it: *cuius est dare eius est disponere* (whose it is to give, it is his to dispose—that is, the donor, as owner of the property, sets the terms of the gift).

Running parallel to "keeping-while-giving" was a pattern of "taking-while-leaving," in which secular leaders could avail themselves of church property while avoiding outright seizure. Precarial grants, in which "the church could make grants of property and yet retain its rights," could be a form of either "keeping-while-giving" or "taking-while-leaving," depending on whose idea the grant had been

22. Annette B. Weiner, *Inalienable Possessions: The Paradox of Keeping-While-Giving* (Berkeley: University of California Press, 1992).
23. Ilana F. Silber, "Gift-giving in the Great Traditions: The Case of Donations to Monasteries in the Medieval West," *Archives Européennes de Sociologie* 36 (1995): 215–16.
24. Wood-Legh, *Perpetual Chantries*, 303.
25. Quoted in Wood-Legh, *Perpetual Chantries*, 304.

and how compulsory it was.²⁶ Either way it created temporary, overlapping claims to property, such as usufructuary interest in church property. Charles Martel used these kinds of exchanges, in which precarial grants of church land were made with the promise that the church would eventually—at least in theory—regain its land in full. Paul Fouracre has shown that it was the excessive use of precarial grants that led Hincmar to accuse Charles Martel of sacrilege, perhaps because Charles failed to observe the carefully balanced norms of these transactions and tried to treat church property and its gifts as his to manipulate as needed.²⁷ This illustrates an ongoing medieval struggle that De Jong has called "the question of who controlled the gifts."²⁸ The problem was that any singular control exercised over gifts would destroy the balance of relationships that they were intended to guarantee.

Considerations in Canon Law

As a consequence, although canon law did reserve unto the Apostolic See the right, through dispensation, to make unilateral dispositions of ecclesiastical property for the good of the church, the more ordinary and equitable function of canon law would be to recognize that there were many interested parties to any failing gift, including the family of the donor, the trustees, and the beneficiaries, and to bring them all, if possible, to a consensus, such that gifts were not unilaterally controlled by any one party. Canon law did recognize that both the prince and the pope had the legal power to expropriate property for cause (*ex causa*), which often meant circumstances of pressing need, during which time church plate might be sold to remedy a famine, to ransom Christian captives, or to defend the realm.²⁹ Invasion, danger, plague, or famine could all demand relief;

26. Paul Fouracre, *The Age of Charles Martel* (Harlow, England: Pearson, 2000), 138.
27. Ibid., 121–26 and 137–45.
28. De Jong, *In Samuel's Image*, 278–79.
29. Most famously, Gregory the Great and Ambrose permitted church plate to be sold in emergencies. X 3.13.12; C.12 q.2 cc.13, 19–20; D.86 c.18. Aristotle had argued that all things returned to the common state in times of need; Aquinas

these were external motivations that did not evaluate the purpose of the gift itself. This is opposite to the rationale of cy-près, which operates only when the purpose of the gift has a problem, and not because there is a more exigent need elsewhere. In the first case, under canon law, a diversion ameliorates a bad circumstance; in the second case, under cy-près, a diversion fixes a bad purpose. The canon law alienation of property in an emergency was allowable not only because of the exigencies of the circumstance, but also because canon law recognized that all property was liable to be shared in a time of need, since all people had an equal claim to property under natural law.[30] This natural law claim was not subsequently used as a rationale for cy-près, which was justified in terms of donor intent alone.

In fact, late medieval canon law texts were not friendly to cy-près doctrine and contained relatively little on succession law in general—at least in comparison to civil law.[31] Canon law specified that it was not ordinarily possible to deviate from the use of a gift left by a donor; that a founder's terms ought to be followed exactly; and that the donor and his heirs maintained an ongoing relationship to the property given, including, according to the Ordinary Gloss, the right to give approval if a change in the use of a donation was sought—even from one religious use to another, such as changing the use from a church to a monastery, and even if the alteration would be an improvement.[32] The fourteenth-century Parisian canon lawyer Henricus Bohic, also the author of a treatise on patronage, considered the question of the transfer of use in his *Distinctiones in libros V Decretalium* to ask whether money given for the poor could be diverted to repairs for the church. His answer was effectively no, it was not possible to transfer donations from one use to another. The only exception he could think of was if there was a plausible way to turn the repair of the church into a gift for the poor, thereby maintaining the given use. The diversion

---

agreed, and so did the Ordinary Gloss. Christopher Pierson, *Just Property: A History in the Latin West* (Oxford: Oxford University Press, 2013).

30. Gl. Ord. ad X 2.20.8.
31. Helmholz, *Oxford History of the Laws of England*, vol. 1, 389.
32. Ord. Glo. ad C.16 q.7 c.33. Quoted in Jörn Sieglerschmidt, *Territorialstaat und Kirchenregiment* (Cologne: Böhlau, 1987), 112. On the strict maintenance of the gift as given, see C.16 q.7 c.34.

of funds could be permitted if the church was so decrepit that divine services could not be held, which prevented the collection of alms within the church, and there was no other possible way to repair the church, and also the local poor were not in any immediate need of the donation. This loaned the donation to the repair of the church in order to be able to resume the collection of alms that would repay the loan and ultimately benefit the poor.[33]

Nonetheless, canon law sometimes allowed for the alteration of the specific terms, through commutation within the same category of use and ideally with the consent of interested parties. The demand for consent to alteration seems to be a holdover from an earlier medieval preference for the law (and the bishop) to operate as peacemakers seeking compromises between disputing parties.[34] Indeed, even the right to change terms other than the use of the gift with the consent of all may not originally have belonged to the bishop: the epistles of Gregory the Great indicate that he personally gave permission to bishops to allow the location of an impossible gift to be altered or to discern what to do in the case of insufficiency of the gift.[35] When one of these instructions later entered into a collection of decretals, it became more universally applicable, allowing bishops to commute the location of an otherwise impossible gift where before they may have believed themselves to be bound to ask for papal permission first.[36]

33. Henricus Bohic, *In Quinque Decretalium Libros Commentaria* (Venice: Hieronymous Scotus, 1576), vol. 5, p. 170; quoted in Brian Tierney, *Medieval Poor Law: A Sketch of Canonical Theory and Its Application in England* (Berkeley: University of California Press, 1959), 88–89.

34. White, *Custom, Kinship, and Gifts*, 47–50, 70–78, and 149; Stephen D. White, "Inheritances and Legal Arguments in Western France, 1050–1150," *Traditio* 43 (1987): 65–70 and 101; Arnoud-Jan Bijsterveld, *Do ut des: Gift Giving, Memoria, and Conflict Management in the Medieval Low Countries* (Hilversum: Verloren, 2007), chapter 8; Stephen D. White, "'Pactum ... Legem Vincit et Amor Judicium'—The Settlement of Disputes by Compromise in Eleventh-Century Western France," *American Journal of Legal History* 22.4 (1978): 281–308; Richard L. Keyser, "'Agreement Supersedes Law, and Love Judgment': Legal Flexibility and Amicable Settlement in Anglo-Norman England," *Law and History Review* 30.1 (2012): 37–88.

35. Gregory I, *Registri epistolarum*, PL, vol. 77, col. 620, 674, 684, 1135, and 1280. See Hannan, *Canon Law of Wills*, 473.

36. X 3.26.3.

The pope could always, through dispensation and for cause, arrange for property to be transferred from one use to another, although this power by its nature fell outside of the regular function of canon law, and in practice the pope often required the consent of interested parties to the change as well—as Cardinal Wolsey would discover to his frustration. Even inalienable church property, might, in times of necessity, be sold.[37] Moreover, the church adopted the Roman procedure of *restitutio in integrum*, to restore someone to integrity, and developed it into a principle of canon law that could be widely applied, including to heirs who were wrongfully dispossessed of their inheritance by testators who impulsively sold off or donated excessive amounts of property on the deathbed.[38]

As Helmholz notes, some jurists—including Hostiensis and Innocent IV, as remarked upon by Lyndwood—suggested that all legacies might be considered pious.[39] This interpretation makes the absence of any jurisprudence to prevent ordinary legacies from failing more notable. However, "pious uses"—alternatively "pious causes"—was a protected category.[40] That is, all gifts might be pious, but gifts given to be used in pious ways—such as building a church or feeding the poor—were supposed to be given extra attention by bishops, who should supervise local pious uses to make sure that they were going to their intended purpose (*ad usum destinatum*).[41] Canon law forbade gifts offered to pious uses from being turned to other uses, although the thrust of the relevant decretal and its gloss was to maintain the donation strictly (*fideliter et plenarie in usus praedictos*).[42] This decre-

---

37. Brundage, *Medieval Canon Law*, 87. On the nonalienation of church property, see X 3.13.5–6.
38. On the remedy and its broad application, see R. H. Helmholz, *The Spirit of Classical Canon Law* (Athens: University of Georgia Press, 1996), 88–115.
39. Helmholz, *Oxford History of the Laws of England*, vol. 1, 396.
40. X 3.26.3; X 3.26.11.
41. X 3.36.3. Helmholz notes that in administrative practice there is evidence of separate record keeping for pious gifts: *History of the Laws of England*, vol. 1, 399 and 417.
42. X 3.26.17: "Tua nobis fraternitas intimavit, quod nunnulli tam religiosi, quam clerici seculares et laici, pecuniam et alia bona, quae per manus eorum ex testamentis decedentium debent in usus pios expendi, non dubitant aliis usibus applicare."

tal emphasized that the last wishes of the testator should be carried out precisely; it did not give room for bishops to swap one pious use for another.[43] A hospital was a religious house and so could not be transformed to a worldly use (*ad mundanos usus redire non debet*); instead, alienations of its property would be managed "undoubtedly according to ancient customs" (*antiqua consuetudo indubitanter*) with the approval of the pope.[44] This probably meant that if a hospital failed, known donors could retrieve their gifts if they wanted them, while the rest of the property would be given to another hospital, thereby maintaining the same, not a similar, use if possible, or seeking the consent of all to transfer the use if it was not. "Ancient customs" lumped all of these possibilities together. If there had been a standard to divert the use as closely as possible, which would have been a conveniently brief way to express how a gift could be altered, then surely that would have been said instead. These passages did not affirm that goods could be maneuvered from one pious use to another, but they did appear to draw a boundary around goods for a pious purpose, as belonging to their own category.

Meanwhile, although the mind (*mens*) of the donor was important to the interpretation of the gift, and the pious intention was vital to any potential salvific return on the gift—for as theologians argued, good works done without right faith were irrelevant to salvation—there is little evidence that intent was used (as it later would be in common law) as a method to override the will itself or that the specific interests of the donor were given priority in dealing with a difficult gift. If a reasonable man would have wanted to change his will for circumstances that were unknown to him at the point of his death, such as the imminent destitution of the family or the birth of an unknown child, then the redirection of the will should be effected. But this is not the same thing as an attempt to assess the motives of a donation. A gift given to pious causes (*ad pias causas*) was presumed to have been given for pious reasons, and a gift could even honor piety itself (*pietatis intuitu*). In conversations about the internal

---

43. X 3.26.19. On the strictness of the observance of last wishes, see X 3.26.10, X 3.26.17, C.13 q.2 c.4.

44. X 3.36.4.

forum, confessors and penitents may have dealt with motivations for donations with more nuance, but unlike modern cy-près law, which has had to create jurisprudence to figure out when a "general charitable intent" can be found, under the *ius commune* the destination *ad pias causas* spoke for itself. These pious motivations were not cause to reorient gifts to any pious destination, but there was little discussion about the extent to which the specific instructions for the treatment of a gift interacted with the pious motivations. On the other hand, the pious motivations of a donor were constantly used to reproach those who attempted to obstruct the gift.

Canon law acknowledged that a gift could be revoked if the recipient was ungrateful, a concept drawn from civil law and reinforced by Gregory IX.[45] If the donor was silent about the ingratitude, then his heirs could not press the case, but if the donor was unaware of the ingratitude, if he had protested the ingratitude in his lifetime, or if the ingratitude arose after the death of the donor, then the heirs were allowed to recover. The practice of sometimes returning gifts to unhappy heirs for a variety of reasons is attested, sporadically, from Augustine to the Council of Trent and beyond. Certainly it was not universal that if an heir asked for property back that he or she would receive it, and family members were criticized for trying if their motives were suspect. But requests were frequent enough that it is notable that such events were not singled out as examples of sacrilege, secularization, or alienation. After all, the living, who cared deeply about the property in question and were still at risk of damnation, had a higher claim than the dead, who were either beyond hope, safely being sanctified, or enjoying the beatific vision. Given that the church had an ongoing interest in both the salvation of the living and the cultivation of future donations, it is unsurprising that it sometimes determined that returning the gift was the right choice— not simply prudent or pragmatic, but even justified by a higher good and the care of souls.

The entangled nature of gifts to the church is best observed in the development of the rights of patronage (*ius patronatus*) out of

---

45. X 3.24.10.

the proprietary churches (*Eigenkirche*) attacked by Gregory VII in the context of prolonged and multifaceted struggle over lay control of churches during the Investiture Controversy.[46] Ultimately ownership did not vest entirely in the church or with the patron.[47] Alexander III placed patronage rights within neither the temporal law nor the spiritual law of the church but rather as annexed to the spiritual law while still subject to the civil laws on property of a nation—an admission of the peculiar mixture of financial interest, donation, insurance, property rights, and divine service that went into the creation of the patronage system.[48]

The story of this transformation, whose legal complications are detailed by Landau, is not straightforward, but by the end of the thirteenth century there was a coherent patronage structure that had maintained some of the older proprietary rights.[49] Simply put, a founder of a benefice, or more precisely someone who founded, endowed, or built a church (*fundatio, dotatio, constructio,* or *aedificatio*), was given the right of patronage by the church, which granted to him and his descendants certain rights. These included the right to nominate the priest who would hold the benefice (the *ius praesentandi*), affirmed by the Novels in the sixth century, along with the right to prayers and assorted other spiritual goods associated with the benefice, and the maintenance of a kind of financial claim to the property, including the right to hospitality.[50] If the descendants of the founder became destitute, they would receive any surplus from

---

46. Uta-Renate Blumenthal, *The Investiture Controversy: Church and Monarchy from the Ninth to the Twelfth Century* (Philadelphia: University of Pennsylvania Press, 1988); Susan Wood, *The Proprietary Church in the Medieval West* (Oxford: Oxford University Press, 2006).

47. Pollock and Maitland, *History of English Law*, vol. 1, 524.

48. X 2.1.3; X 3.1.2; Hostiensis, *Commentaria* X 1.6.28, cited in Harold J. Berman, "The Spiritualization of the Secular Law: The Impact of the Lutheran Reformation," *Journal of Law and Religion* 14 (1999): 315.

49. Peter Landau, *Ius Patronatus: Studien zur Entwicklung des Patronats im Dekretalenrecht und der Kanonistik des 12. Und 13. Jahrhunderts* (Cologne-Vienna: Böhlau, 1975).

50. Nov. 57.2; Nov. 123.18; Gl. Ord. ad C.23 q.7 c.26; Clem. 3.12.2; Norman P. Tanner, ed., *Decrees of the Ecumenical Councils*, vol. 2 (London: Sheed and Ward, 1990), Trent, XIV, c. 12 de Ref. and XXV, c. 9 de Ref.

the endowment, according to the *iura utilia*.[51] Patrons had to consent to the alienation of their property, just as a gift that was to be turned to a new purpose needed the consent of the founder or his or her heirs. Patronage also often entailed the right to allow or forbid changes to the property, which essentially enabled the current patron to speak on behalf of the founder when revisions to a donation were necessary. This right included making decisions about repairs, sales, or reductions in the number of masses said.[52] Nonetheless, these rights were not absolute: if a patron became a heretic or committed other ecclesiastical crimes, he would lose his patronage, just as if he deliberately nominated inappropriate people to the benefice.[53] Furthermore, patronage carried with it the responsibility to help a floundering donation, if possible, which might require that an heir "refound" the foundation, becoming a second founder to it. Patronage was, in its ideal form, an enduring tie between the founder, his family, and the donation, entirely unlike modern court-ordered cy-près schemes.

It was obvious in the Middle Ages that patronage rights could be troublesome. The selling of patronage rights was widely criticized, as was the abuse of the right to present. The Cluniac reform began in the tenth century with a foundation by William of Aquitaine in which he explicitly renounced, for himself and his family, all patronage rights over the monastery of Cluny, in order to protect it from temporal control.[54] Still, even in writing his foundation, William of Aquitaine laid down expectations that he believed would be perpetually honored, just as, in a fictional example, Rabelais's Gargantua did in founding and endowing the abbey of Thélème, where the fundamental rule was that the religious should do as they wanted, but to which he added stipulations, including that there should be no walls or clocks and that the abbey would admit only attractive monks and nuns. Gargantua could not subsequently stop himself from engaging

51. X 3.38.25.
52. Wood-Legh, *Perpetual Chantries*, 74–77.
53. A heretic could not become a patron in the first place, no matter how much property he gave to the church. VI 1.3.1.
54. Auguste Bernard and Alexandre Bruel, ed., *Recueil des chartes de l'abbaye de Cluny*, vol. 1 (Paris: Imprimerie nationale, 1876), 124–28.

in his right to reform his foundation to make the dress more beautiful and pleasing, in violation of his original foundation, according to which the inhabitants could wear whatever they wanted. Patrons could never entirely set their gifts free, even when they tried, and changes to the foundation inevitably belonged to them and their heirs. Indeed the childless William of Aquitaine would have been chagrined to discover that after his death his wife's relatives did not honor his desire for Cluny to remain without interference.[55] Thus the priorities of the current patron and the intentions of the original donor could often come into conflict, particularly if the patron was attempting to keep for himself the revenues from a vacant benefice. This potential bifurcation between original founder and current patron would be heightened and exploited during the Reformation.

Of course, patronage is a larger concept than the relationship between a church and its founder. The Roman law of patronage had included the requirement of mutual financial help between patron and client, depending on need, and it is likely that canon law, insofar as it considered itself to be Roman, drew on this ideal of mutual aid and dependence. Indeed, the right of presentation, which was to become so onerous to the church, may originally have been only a personal right that adhered to the founder himself, whereas very early on the material relationship between the patron's family and the patronal church was transmissible through the family line, suggesting that these property links were the more essential aspect to patronage as originally conceived.[56] Additionally, other forms of patronage that are evident in medieval and early modern society, including magnate patronage and artistic patronage, had a similar understanding of property exchange in which the gifts that were given were never completely gone but instead helped to hold the social tie in place as material conduits between the two parties. Canon law did not reject that understanding.

In addition, medieval England would have been a particularly hostile place for any cy-près principle to have developed in oppo-

---

55. Constance Britton Bouchard, *Those of My Blood: Creating Noble Families in Medieval Francia* (Philadelphia: University of Pennsylvania Press, 2001), 94.
56. C.16 q.7 c.31.

sition to patronage rights. English donors had their rights over their gifts protected by both spiritual and temporal powers, since the king claimed, as part of his jurisdiction over patronage, the right to adjudicate issues of alienation or of failure to uphold the spiritual works of a benefice, which after two years of neglect could be grounds for a writ of *cessavit de cantaria* to return the gift to the donor or the heirs.[57] This potential revocability of gifts—demonstrated on high with royal resumptions and grants of confirmation, each of which affirmed the principle in a different way—and the cultural sense of the perpetual ties between donor, gift, and donee both help to explain why donations were sometimes accompanied by solemn oaths, binding the parties in order to fix the terms permanently and set the donation outside of the normal operations of gift-giving. Henry II, in the 1164 Constitutions of Clarendon, declared that presentations and advowsons could be litigated in royal courts, which set up centuries of jurisdictional disputes on the topic while affirming the royal right to intervene on behalf of the supervision of the use of donations. Henry II also used the threat of royal resumptions to keep the religious compliant with his demands, as when he warned the Cistercians that he would impoverish them for protecting Thomas Becket.[58] Similarly, Ayton's gloss on the *Constitutiones,* title "cum patrono," affirmed the ongoing right of patronage by which any patron had rights of oversight over an ancestor's gift.[59] In England it was common for the advowson rights to be transferred or sold by the patron or his descendants, a fact that illustrated the difference between the church, which limited its own ability to alienate, and the patron, who maintained the power to alienate his own patronage rights. Consequently, only the donor or his representative could change the use for which a gift was made. Moreover, in England the role of advocate,

---

57. William Blackstone, *Commentaries on the Laws of England.* A Facsimile of the First Edition of 1765–1769 (Chicago: University of Chicago Press, 1979), III.15, 232. As Plucknett points out, there were *ius commune* origins for the *cessavit*, which protected reversionary interests. Plucknett, *Concise History of the Common Law,* 298.

58. Bartlett, *Why Can the Dead Do Such Great Things?* 194.

59. John Ayton, *Constitutiones legitime seu legatine regionis Anglicane cum subtilissima interpretatione domini Johannis de Athon* (Paris: 1504).

known elsewhere as conservator, gained particular power.[60] The advocate defended the right of a benefice and could sometimes come to assume the role of patron. Canon law regarded this as an abuse of the role, but it was also a confirmation of the ways in which medieval English culture presumed that gifts or service to the church entailed reciprocated, ongoing property interests that were not purely spiritual suffrages.

Thirteenth-Century Examples

Through the thirteenth century there is no evidence that bishops could exercise an ordinary and unilateral power to change the use of a gift. Bracton's contemporary *De legibus et consuetudinibus Angliae* offers a glimpse into what thirteenth-century English norms for gifts might have been, reflecting both local and some developing *ius commune* influences. Bracton, following Azo, tried to keep modes ("ut"—a gift in order that something be done), conditions ("si"—a gift if something was done), and causes ("quia"—a gift because of something) distinct in their treatment. Notably, causes gave very little latitude for the gift to be controlled by the donor unless he added conditions to them; in the later English development of cy-près, charitable gifts would consequently be treated as given to a cause, not with a condition.

On the other hand, modes and conditions offered no room for alterations without consent. Bracton wrote that even an illegal mode attached to a gift ought to be observed, as long as it did not harm anyone else, and that donors could attach any condition or requirement that they wanted to their donations.[61] Bracton held that it was possible for a man to relinquish his own rights in things and the rights of his heirs, but he could not relinquish the rights that others held in property or benefits due to them.[62] Consequently, gifts of-

---

60. John A. Godfrey, *The Right of Patronage According to the Code of Canon Law* (Ph.D. diss., The Catholic University of America, 1924), 43.

61. Henrici de Bracton, *De legibus et consuetudinibus Angliae*, trans. Samuel E. Thorne, vol. 2 (Cambridge, Mass.: Harvard University Press, 1968), folios 68 and 106.

62. Ibid., vol. 2, f. 74.

ten involved the consent of many interested parties, at the very least the consent of the donor and the donee, but frequently, Bracton observed, more than that. Meanwhile, if the parties that had consented to the formation of an interest in property, such as a servitude, then reached consensus to dissolve it, it was within their power to do so and convert it "to another use" through a new consensus.[63] In general, Bracton treated gifts with conditions as being void if the condition was not satisfied, and so a gift with an impossible condition attached to it was not valid.[64] However, where the condition was impossible to implement because a third party prevented it—as in the example of property given for the building of a priory that the bishop forbade—then the donation remained good and the condition vanished. Bracton did not suggest that this condition, a pious one, needed to be fulfilled in another, similar manner or with any other pious work.[65] The issue at stake appears to have been what had been bound: a recipient who could not perform an impossible but pious condition could be released from it without having the condition bind him to a new, but alternate, pious act in order to receive the property. On the other hand, property that had been given to a pious cause itself was then bound to it. Bracton did not address this second issue, but he did explain the concept of property being perpetually attached to whatever had been laid on it by the donor: "because agreements, conditions, pacts and limitations of various kinds, if at once put into them become parts of gifts, they impose a law upon the gift, shape it, give an exception to the donor, bind the persons of the contracting parties, burden the thing given and accompany it as it passes from person to person."[66] Bracton also highlighted the ea-

63. Ibid., vol. 3, f. 178.
64. Ibid., vol. 2, f. 71.
65. Ibid., vol. 2, f. 72: "Si quis dederit alicui advocationem alicujus ecclesiae, ut ibi faciat prioratum et illum in proprios usus convertat, hoc sine voluntate episcopi vel alterius ordinarii adimpleri non poterit, et si illi consentire noluerint, non erit hoc imputandum donatorio, quod conditio non extiterit, et tenebit donatio, maxime cum donatorius ad hoc diligentiam adhibuerit, pro posse suo, efficacem."
66. Ibid., vol. 2, f. 64: "Item quia conventiones, condiciones, et pacta, et modi diversi donationum incidunt in donationibus, si incontinenti apponantur legem dant donationi et donationem informant et dant exceptionem donatori, et ligant

gerness of the law to facilitate gifts in general: "[N]othing is more in accord with natural equity than to make effective the will of a lord wishing to transfer his property to another."[67] Bracton famously did not consider gifts to pious causes as their own category within his treatment of gifts, including gifts of free alms, which had no service attached, but this may simply tell us that he did not believe that royal law regarded them differently; it cannot be taken as evidence of ecclesiastical practice. Still, Bracton did not hold that pious intentions necessarily cured all defects: an incomplete gift of land to the church was not perfected if the donor died while seised of it unless his heir was willing to give his consent.[68]

But Bracton's treatment of gifts and property in general, such as his emphasis on the power of the mutual consent of interested parties both to effect and to change the disposition of property, as well as his concern that rights not be infringed by third parties, aligns well with *ius commune* norms. Bracton described things given in pure alms, things that belonged to the fisc, or state treasury, and things attached to the common good as quasi-sacred—they could not be given or sold and could be transferred only by a justice of the king.[69] Gifts that serve the common good have a special status, but Bracton was not arguing that gifts to the common good with specific conditions attached can be stripped of those conditions in the name of a charitable intent. There is potential for development here, but only pure alms or things that are in the commons are set aside.

That was in England. In Spain *Las siete partidas* can also be taken as evidence that the civil law, as understood in the mid-thirteenth century, did not support a doctrine for the alteration of use. Conversion of use was not listed in the code as one of the rights or duties of the bishop, although he did have rights of exchange (with consent of others) and supervision. There was no distinction made in the treatment of gifts to pious causes with respect to how to manage

---

personas contrahentium, et obligant ipsam rem datam, et transeunt cum ipsa re de persona in personam."

67. Ibid., vol. 2, f. 67: "nihil tam conveniens est naturali aequitati, quam voluntatem domini, volentis rem suam in alium transferre, ratam haberi."

68. Ibid., vol. 2, f. 94.

69. Ibid., vol. 2, f. 59.

them if they were impossible. Rather, the expected Roman rules applied: a legacy written with an impossible condition had the condition dropped, as if it had not been written.[70] If an heir received an estate that carried a condition with which he could not comply, as to free a slave who had died, then the condition would disappear and the heir could inherit with no mention of any ongoing burden to perform an alternate pious use.[71] This solution was similar to that proposed by Bracton.

Guillelmus Durantis likewise did not affirm the ability of bishops to convert gifts to new uses in his *Speculum iudiciale*, written and revised at the end of the thirteenth century. He served in the papal Rota and wrote a commentary on the Second Council of Lyon, so he was well aware of the debates that were emerging at the end of the thirteenth century over the control of property and its use. He did not suggest the indifference of pious causes, and he reiterated some rules of interpretation and peace-making.[72] Canon law demanded the "benign" interpretation of testaments, which would include a consideration of the *mens testatoris* in relationship to the most likely scenarios that would disrupt the implementation of a will, such as recalcitrant heirs, failure to get all of the parties necessary to a transaction to agree, or the death of one of the men who had been charged with overseeing the pious work. Citing "nos quidem" from the *Liber extra*, Durantis offered that if it was not possible to build a hospital where the testator had wanted it, then it could be built elsewhere.[73] When a pious gift was delayed because of conflict, Durantis indicated that the

70. *Las siete partidas*, trans. Samuel Parsons Scott, vol. 5 (Philadelphia: University of Pennsylvania Press, 2001), Part VI, Tit. IV, Laws 3–4, p. 1204.

71. Ibid., vol. 5, Part VI, Tit. IV, Law 14, p. 1208. See Bartolus's commentary on Digest 33.1.13.pr.

72. For example: "Si vero iussit fundari monasterium, vel aliquod pium opus fieri, tunc omnium consensus debet requiri, qui si discordent, vel differant, tunc etiam ad unius eorum instantiam eos episcopus coget. Nec debet tunc episcopus alium substituere, altero eorum mortuo, cum alii possint id fideliter exequi, non enim fuit mens testatoris, ut altero eorum decedente, alii non possint exequi sed e contra. Et in testamentis benigna est interpretatio facienda, extra de donatio cum dilectus ut voluntas defuncti impleatur." *Speculum iuris* (Venice: n.p., 1585), Book II, Part II, *De Instrumentorum editione*, § 13, p. 697.

73. Ibid., § 13, 64, p. 713: "Sed si hospitale fieri non potest ubi testator fieri iussit, fiat alibi."

bishop should serve "as judge or arbiter for the consensus of the parties."[74] No broader cy-près principle or power was suggested.

Similarly the thirteenth-century canonist Hostiensis, in his *Summa*, gave more latitude for gifts to the church to be revoked than with perfected gifts to private use, which could be revoked only for ingratitude—although the failure to use a gift for its specified purpose could be considered ingratitude. In this wider set of conditions for revocability, Hostiensis included gifts that were too large, gifts made by an angry father seeking to disinherit his son, gifts that did not belong to the giver (in which case there was no need to honor the intention with property that did belong to the giver), gifts with a defect in form, and gifts that turned out to be excessive to the need they were intended to fulfill.[75] Hostensius clarified that the grounds for the revocability of gifts extended to those made *causa mortis*.[76] Although it was customary that gifts *causa mortis* could be revoked if they were made in anticipation of death but recovery followed, Hostiensis added that these gifts *causa mortis* could also fail if a condition or cause of the gift was deficient.[77] This sense of the potential revocability of gifts to the church, evidenced both in the writings of canonists and in the relationships between patrons, princes, and prelates, would have been a factor for the judge to consider in thinking about difficult gifts and how to resolve them equitably. Hostiensis was firm that a bishop should not act unilaterally when the rights of others were involved: he carefully elaborated, for example, on the cases in which a bishop needed to seek the consent of others, including the consent of the chapter or of a city, the patron, and the pope for alienation of property.[78] Moreover, because gifts of benevolence were so important, partaking of natural law (*naturali iure primaevo*), they should not be tainted, or taint the recipients, with fraud, de-

---

74. Ibid., § 13, 74, p. 716: "Sicut potest episcopus esse iudex, vel arbiter partium consensu."
75. Hostiensis, *Summa* (Venice: Melchior Sessa, 1570), Book III, *De Donationibus*, § 8, f. 267.
76. Ibid., Book III, *De Donationibus causa mortis*, § 7, f. 268.
77. Ibid.
78. Ibid., Book III, *De his quae fiunt ab Episcopo sine consensu capituli*, § 1, f. 235v–236.

ception, turpitude, or other deficits. Far from opening the door to pious gifts, Hostensius, like many other (but not all) canonists, was limiting them—for example, a gift to a good cause could not necessarily redeem its bad origins.[79] The bishop did have powers of supervision and reconciliation between warring parties who were inhibiting the last will of the testator from being implemented.[80] He should attempt to bring them to a peaceful and just resolution, not impose new terms on the basis of his own authority.

The Temptation of Endowments

Ilana Silber observes that wealth tended to "pool" and become "immobilized" in medieval monasteries, unlike in many other gift-systems, in part because of the canonical rules governing gifts.[81] The specter of an endowed church raised questions about the donations, their effects on the church and the state, their purposes, and the possibility of transforming them in some way. In England, Edward I moved against perpetual endowments for an already endowed church with his two statutes of mortmain (1279 and 1290). In the midst of war with France, he also initiated the first wave of confiscations of alien priories that would continue, and at times reverse, throughout the fourteenth century. More generally, parties who all had some claim to the property of the church tried to assert a larger, even unilateral, claim to obstruct the consensus model in some way, exploiting the fact that consent conveys power.

For example, in the struggle between Boniface VIII and Philip IV some stark lines over the disposition of property were laid out, with exaggerated claims to unitary authority made by both sides, each of which declared themselves to be defenders of the true use of donat-

---

79. Ibid., Book III, *De donationibus*, § 10, f. 267–267v. The English had a particular constitution, *Cordis dolere*, concerning the return of fraudulent gifts. See Helmholz, *Oxford History of the Laws of England*, vol. 1, 413–14.

80. Hostiensis, *Summa*, Book III, *De testamentis et ultimis voluntatibus*, § 23, f. 274v–275v.

81. Ilana F. Silber, "Gift-giving in the Great Traditions: The Case of Donations to Monasteries in the Medieval West," *Archives Européennes de Sociologie* 36 (1995): 222.

ed property. One of Philip's publicists supported his claims with the 1297 *Disputatio inter clericum et militem,* which spread in manuscript form across Europe and was translated into English on the orders of Cromwell in the early 1530s.[82] The text denied the pope's temporal powers and authorized kings to turn the superfluous property of the church to better purposes. On behalf of the rights of the prince the knight cited the precedent of King Joash (IV Kings 12), who took money from the priests of the temple. The priest retorted that Joash used the money to repair the temple itself, returning it to religious use. But the knight replied that religious purposes could mean succor for the poor and sick or the defense of the realm. The king could take this property on his own authority and without any intention to make restitution later. Indeed, the knight wanted to use church property for military purposes on an ongoing basis, not just in times of war, and for the overall good of the commonwealth, whatever that might entail.

The priest warned against encouraging kings to resume their gifts: "If things once given can be taken back, then every vow can be broken."[83] The knight disagreed because the purpose (*usus*) was the same:

I don't mean to take back things given to God, but rather to apply them to the purpose for which they were given. For whatever is given to God is thereby meant for pious and holy uses. And, in fact, what could be more holy than the Christian people's welfare, and what more precious to the Lord than to keep enemies and ravenous murderers away from the Christian people and to win peace for His faithful subjects? Thus when the Church's goods are spent in this way, they are indeed expended for the uses to which they were dedicated.[84]

---

82. Norma N. Erickson, "A Dispute between a Priest and a Knight," *Proceedings of the American Philosophical Society* 111 (1967): 288–309.

83. Ibid., 307 and 299: "Si possunt revocari que semel sunt donata, ergo irritari possunt omnia vota."

84. Ibid.: "Hoc non est ea que data sunt Deo revocare, sed eis usibus quibus data sunt applicare. Que enim sunt Deo data eo ipso sunt piis et sanctis usibus dedicata. Quid enim potest esse sanctius, quam Christiani populi salus, et quid pretiosius Domino quam hostes et rapaces interfectores arcere a populo Christiano, et quam pacem subiectis et fidelibus emere? Cum ergo in his bona ecclesiae expenduntur, vere usibus quibus fuerant dedicata redduntur."

84   Patronage Rights and Consensus

The original donor—God—would have consented to the change, since He had given everything in the world for the benefit of His people, and pious donors would have aligned their will with His. The rule on the maintenance of a gift for the purpose for which it was given held fast, even in the midst of a propaganda war with Boniface VIII. But the knight did give one very striking and novel justification for his proposals, as he claimed that every man kept an interest in his own soul, and so had a perpetual interest in the right use of his donations:

> Haven't our temporalities been given you by our ancestors, and given abundantly, to be used wholly in divine worship? But, really, you don't use them for this purpose, but apply to your own needs all those things which you should use in alms and in works of charity to feed the poor. Isn't it necessary that the dead be cleansed and the living saved by such holy works? When you use these goods wrongly, consume them in excess, and squander them, contrary to the intentions (*contra intencionem*) of the donors and also, as it were, of the recipients, by using them badly don't you hurt the dead and the living, and damnably rob them? Doesn't a man who refuses to fight rightly forfeit his wages? And certainly a vassal who doesn't render his service justly loses his fief.[85]

The dead were cleansed by alms and charity, and since the knight was proposing the transition of the gifts of the dead to military and commonwealth causes, he was suggesting that these works would also be useful to the dead. The author was proposing a cy-près power that should reside with secular authority for the good of the souls of the donors, who would be served by the application of their gifts to ends that more closely approximated their intentions. It was a line of argument that would be used later to explain cy-près's origins in

---

85. Ibid., 305 and 297: "Et nonne vobis a parentibus nostris, ad hoc sunt nostra temporalia data et vobis copiosissime ministrata ut in cultum Dei totaliter expendantur? Sed certe nihil inde facitis, sed omnia vestris necessitatibus applicatis que per eleemosynas et opera caritatis in visceribus pauperum claudere debetis. Nonne est necesse ut per huiusmodi sanctissima opera mortui innarentur et slavuarentur vivi? Nonne cum ea perperam expenditis superflueque consumitis et ea contra intencionem dancium et etiam quodammodo accipiencium disperditis, male utendo vivos et mortuos leditis, et vivis et mortuis damnabiliter derogatis? Nonne ei qui non vult militare auferetur digne stipendium? Et certe vassalus non implens servicium merito perdit feodum."

ecclesiastical law, but here it clearly serves as a pretext for the secular ambitions of the French king. In a culture still deeply entangled in gift networks, where everything had been given or inherited with implied purposes attached, it was too threatening for any but the most radical or the most dispossessed to advocate for a principle of changing uses. Even the humanists, who could imagine so many better uses for property, would find that their courage faltered on this point. Still, policy motivations pushed against the boundaries of use and will, looking for a way to honor the donor while doing something else with the property he had left behind.

In fact, any desirable end could prompt arguments on why monastic wealth might be better used toward it; the Crusades, which required vast resources, were one such tempting purpose. Humbert of Romans, a Dominican who had studied canon law, suggested turning dissolute monasteries over to the crusade in his *Opus tripartitum* for the Second Council of Lyon in 1274:

What would be the harm if the Church sold its superfluous ornaments in each diocese, ornaments which waste with age? What would be the harm if in the cathedral churches and other rich chapters containing many canons, the number of offices should be reduced and the returns of the prebends applied to the crusade? What would be the harm if the livings of some of the innumerable priors, whose dissolute lives are the scandal of the world, should be used for the crusade? Incomes from monasteries destroyed because they are beyond hope of reform could be put to the same use. Why not apply vacant and fat benefices to the same use? ... Thus perpetual returns can be obtained from movable goods and assigned to the holy war in perpetuity: all incomes so assigned would be defended and protected by the Church. But since worldly wisdom may fear that as time goes on this income might be transferred to other uses by the Roman Church and since financial aid might be hindered by this objection, it is necessary that an adequate remedy be found for this possible abuse.... And if by chance a permanent remedy against abuse cannot be found, at least one that would serve for a long time could be devised.[86]

---

86. Quoted in Palmer A. Throop, *Criticism of the Crusade: A Study of Public Opinion and Crusade Propaganda* (Amsterdam: N.V. Swets and Zeitlinger, 1940), 198–99, from Humbert of Romans, *Opus tripartitum*, in Edward Brown, *Appendix ad fasciculum rerum expetendarum et fugiendarum, prout ab Orthvino Gratio* (London: Richard Chiswell, 1690), I.26, p. 205: "Quod iterum damnum esset si in cathedralibus Ecclesiis et aliis capitulis divitibus, in quibus sunt multi canonici, minueretur

Anthony Leopold has shown that although several theorists tried to raise more money for the crusades through bequests, none of them suggested the method of diverting bequests.[87] Humbert of Romans came the closest to that proposal, on the grounds of superfluity, vacancy, and misemployment, but even he made it clear that this was only for the defense of Christendom, a legitimate use of the church property, not an invitation to other changes to use, since he acknowledged that it was an abuse if the church transferred uses.

At the Second Council of Lyon, to which representatives from the beleaguered Byzantine empire came, bringing with them hopes for the reunification of the church, Gregory X declined all of the radical proposals that were put forward by Humbert and others. While he criticized those "patrons" and "advocates" who claimed feudal lordship over church properties in *De rebus ecclesiae non alienandis,* he upheld the principle that property should be used strictly for its intended purpose. The only property that he allowed to be turned to a new use was that which had been given to the mendicants (*De religiosis domibus, ut episcopo sint subiectae*), because mendicant orders were not supposed to possess property, even collectively. Consequently, anything they had was, by extension, probably in violation of the terms (whether stated or unstated) by which the donor had given it,

---

in aliquo numerus eorum, et redditus praebendarum sic minutarum isti usui sic applicarentur? Quod malum iterum esset si de prioratibus religiosorum, qui sunt innumerabiles per mundum, in quibus religiosi multum dissolute viventes sunt scandalum mundo, multi applicarentur ad eosdem usus? Et idem fieret etiam de abbatiis destructis, de quibus non habetur spes, quod unquam valeant reformari? Quod etiam damnum esset si de beneficiis vacantibus et pinguibus pars aliqua per annum unum vel plures ad hoc idem applicaretur? Sunt autem et alia multa circa personas ecclesiasticas et personas laicas, quae sapientia secularis sciret melius adinvenire, quae ultra humanam aestimationem ascenderent, si perducerentur ad effectum, et perpetuo possent valere negotio. Et de mobilibus quibusdam ad haec pertinentibus, possent emi redditus perpetui, ad hoc perpetuo deputati, et omnia haec deputata, gratiis et defensione ecclesiastica munirentur. Sed quia sapientia mundi multum formidare potest, ne ista tempore procedente ad usus alios per Romanam Ecclesiam transferrentur, ne occasione hâc impediantur processus huiusmodi, expedit contra hoc competens remedium invenire ... Et si forte non possint remedia perpetua procurari, saltem ad tempus longum, prout fieri poterit, procurentur."

87. Antony Leopold, *How to Recover the Holy Land: Crusade Proposals in the Late Thirteenth and Early Fourteenth Centuries* (Aldershot, England: Ashgate, 2000), 79.

since the donor did not expect the property to accumulate but rather to support their immediate needs. The pope pointed out that their property had been collected through begging, so it was impossible to return the donations or consult with the unknown donors for any deviation or alteration in use. And so: "We reserve these possessions for the disposal of the apostolic see, to be used for aid to the Holy Land or for the poor or to be turned to other pious uses through local ordinaries or others commissioned by the apostolic see."[88] This power to change the purpose was reserved to the Apostolic See, which might commission bishops or others to act on its behalf.

Gregory X also rejected proposals to merge the Hospitallers and the Templars in order that they might work more effectively, but then the 1291 defeat at Acre increased the pressure to find novel ways to take back the Holy Land, which prompted new calls for the union of the two orders.[89] The lawyer Pierre Dubois suggested this merger in his 1306 *De recuperatione Terre Sancte* as part of sweeping reforms by which he would convince the church to put its property into trusts administered by laymen to protect them from corruption, bring true peace to Christendom through political unity, exile all who disturbed the peace to the Holy Land, marry well educated Christian girls to the Saracens to convert their husbands and all of their husbands' wives, and rationalize legal procedure to eliminate most legal fees. Dubois proposed true legal change: he repeated many times a paraphrase from the Digest that what mattered was not what was done in Rome but what ought to be done in Rome, and he claimed all laws could be changed to benefit society.[90] He had no objection to changing customs and even to altering the purpose of a law for the greater good.[91] Reform and legal innovation had to

---

88. Tanner, ed., *Decrees of the Ecumenical Councils*, vol. 1, 326: "Nos enim ea dispositioni sedis apostolicae reservamus, in Terrae sanctae subsidium vel pauperum aut alios pios usus per locorum ordinarios vel eos quibus sedes ipsa commiserit, convertenda."

89. Malcolm Barber, *The Trial of the Templars*, 2d ed. (Cambridge: Cambridge University Press, 2012); Leopold, *How to Recover the Holy Land*.

90. Digest 44.1.20; Pierre Dubois, *The Recovery of the Holy Land*, trans. and ed. Walther Brandt (New York: Columbia University Press, 1956), Part I, 48 [XXIX–XXX], pp. 106–7.

91. Dubois, *Recovery of the Holy Land*, Part I, 97 [LVII], p. 146.

be embraced because old laws and customs did not always suit new times.[92]

Despite this, even Dubois framed his arguments in relationship to the purposes for which things had been given, citing the popular saying that "gifts accepted bind."[93] God was the "Supreme Founder" and had given the Holy Land to the Christians, who were required to put it back to this original purpose.[94] The church had been given money in order to pray for the world, but it could not return to its spiritual duties unless it was reformed by putting its property into trusts ruled by laymen.[95] The military orders had been given property in Europe to support the Holy Land, but they misappropriated these western European lands for their own use, which is why Dubois proposed that the military orders should be forced to live in Cyprus and the Holy Land itself, while the donations that had been given to them should fund both a crusade and schools to teach the necessary languages, sciences, and crafts to conquer the Holy Land and convert its residents. These schools "would be better suited to the purpose" of recovering the Holy Land than Hospitaller or Templar priories.[96]

Gifts ought to be maintained for their original purpose, and donors should receive the intended recompense of prayers and masses. Corrupt gifts should be banned, as should future gifts to the church, except for simple gifts to mendicants and donations to a common treasury and foundation that should be established to supervise the gifts and determine the best possible use for the endowment.[97] Once it was clear to the common man how little good the legacies to the Holy Land had done, Dubois thought, only the assurance of this treasure chest, kept in each cathedral and carefully monitored,

---

92. *Summaria brevis et compendiosa doctrina felicis expedicionis et abreviacionis guerrarum ac litium regni Francorum*, BNF Cod. Lat. 6222C, fol. 31r; printed in *Quellen zur Geistesgeschichte des Mittelalters und der Renaissance*, vol. 4, ed. Hellmut Kämpf (Leipzig: Teubner, 1936), 52; used by Brandt in Dubois, *Recovery of the Holy Land*, 108n.

93. Dubois, *Recovery of the Holy Land*, Part I, 35 [XVIII], p. 95.

94. Ibid., Part I, 46 [XXVII] and 47 [XXVIII], p. 104.

95. Ibid., Part I, 3 [IV], p. 74.

96. Ibid., Part I, 60 [XXXVII], p. 117.

97. Ibid., Part I, 102 [LXI], p. 153, and 107 [LXV], p. 158.

would permit gifts to resume, and in greater number and value than before.⁹⁸ This ideal of a centrally controlled endowment that would prevent the whims of future donors from interfering with rational plans and good order would resonate amongst humanists and reformers alike. And yet, while it was not good that donors could do whatever they wanted, it was still necessary, Dubois thought, to honor the terms of their gifts.

In his eagerness to accumulate this endowment, Dubois listed a number of potential sources, including the property of intestate clergy and abandoned property—anything that could be taken "without prejudice to anyone" (*absque alieno prejudicio*), which included heirs. He put in this category "all lapsed legacies left to uncertain persons or indistinctly left" (*omnia legata caduca incertis personis et indistincte relicta*).⁹⁹ These failed gifts had been left without a home, and they could be taken, presumably instead of returning to the estate. But neither as a current legal fact nor as a potential legal innovation did Dubois suggest that failed pious gifts could be sent to the fund. Given his concern to send over only property with no other claim on it, even the wildly ambitious Dubois implicitly recognized the rights of heirs and was unaware of any cy-près doctrine that could have served his larger goal of transforming the Holy Land and Christendom itself. To his suggestion that small non-conventual priories should be dissolved, their monks sent to larger abbeys, and their property divided up between the support of the relocated monks and his fund for the Holy Land, Dubois offered no legal precedent— even though he had scattered *ius commune* references throughout his text—except to claim that these small priories wasted their endowments and had thereby lost their rights to administer them.

But still, the "whole residue belongs to the poor and is for them."¹⁰⁰ This would be a persistent theme from the fourteenth century onward to help the poor distantly rather than immediately; church property would be allowed first to help someone else and then subsequently, indirectly, to help the poor. A council could be called to

98. Ibid., Part I, 107 [LXV], pp. 158–59.
99. Ibid., Part I, 44 [XXV], p. 103.
100. Ibid., Part I, 57 [XXXIV], p. 113.

90   Patronage Rights and Consensus

authorize that the money of the dissolved priories should be sent to the Holy Land, which will "tend to reform and truly unite the whole commonwealth of Catholics." The economic opening up of the Holy Land to trade with the west would then ameliorate poverty better than simple distributions. Dubois thereby solved his dilemma by reconciling his plans with the ultimate reservation of church property to the poor, without citing any charitable intentions of the donors.[101]

He later added an appendix to reassure Philip the Fair that by selling Templar property the king would "apply [the property] to the original purpose" and would not "revert [it] to secular uses" but would rather serve "the common good of the whole world" and protect "the commonwealth."[102] Dubois argued in the appendix that "the greater part of the property of deceased persons" should also be applied to the same cause.[103] He was reaching for cy-près power, but he did not have it to draw upon, and in many respects he remained wedded to ideals about the maintenance of purpose and founders' rights.[104] He claimed that he would uphold the rights of old founders in the new endowment he would build, maintaining prayers, masses, and the right to dictate some of the curricula used in the new schools.[105] He acknowledged that founders would have to give their consent to his scheme to restrict convents to thirteen nuns and to turn their surpluses over to his new endowment.[106] Founders' rights could even justify his plans, since the prince was the "patron and the founder and donor of the whole patrimony of the Church" and thus had rights of supervision, resumption, and reform.[107]

Nothing came of Dubois's ideas, but the far more influential Raymond Lull offered a similar proposal to rationalize efforts in the Holy

101. Ibid., Part I, 67 [XLII], p. 123. Raymond Lull had also argued that funding the study of oriental languages would ultimately benefit the poor, by increasing compassion for them.
102. Ibid., pp. 200–201 and 204.
103. Ibid., Part I, 57 [XXXIV], p. 114.
104. Ibid., Part I, 102 [LX], p. 151. But Dubois did not support the right of patrons to appoint prioresses, which he thought led to corruption.
105. Ibid., Part I, 65–66 [XLI], p. 123, and 72 [LXVI], p. 128, and 84 [LII], p. 138.
106. Ibid., Part I, 102 [LX], pp. 150–51.
107. Ibid., Part II, 118 [LXXIII], p. 180.

Land through the unification of the Templars and Hospitallers, and in 1306 Clement V asked Jacques de Molay to comment on the suggested merger. De Molay defended their separation as inherent in their foundations. The two had distinct purposes, the one order centered on war and the other on hospitality; it would be an affront to the donors and a spiritual threat to those who had taken vows to each respective order to treat them indifferently.[108] Still, de Molay conceded, it would save enormous sums of money (*maxima allevatio expensarum*) to unify them, and they would be more effective in protecting themselves from those who wanted to plunder their resources if they joined, since they lived in an age when the "people who want to take from the monks are more numerous than those who want to give to them."[109] Given the overwhelming desirability of mutual defense and financial savings, it is telling that de Molay trusted that the argument from purposes would convince the pope.

Philip the Fair proved de Molay right in one regard when in 1307 he turned on the Knights Templar, to whom he owed money, and extracted confessions of heresy from them under torture. He pressed Clement V to disband the order, and although the council summoned to deal with the issue refused to find the Templars guilty of heresy, Clement bowed to the pressure and at the Council of Vienne in 1311–12 ordered the transfer of all of the assets that had belonged to the Templars to the Knights Hospitallers. It was an ugly affair in which Philip's mercenary motives were as obvious as the illegality of the executions of Templars who had recanted their confessions. Nothing about it partook of the consensus model—and yet the ideal of the maintenance of use was upheld throughout the endeavor.

Philip had set his propagandists and jurists to work on the problem from the start. One, Guillaume de Nogaret, tried to pacify public opinion by suggesting that some of the property of the Templars might be used to fund a new Crusade. This partial maintenance of

---

108. *Le Dossier de l'affaire des Templiers*, ed. Georges Lizerand, 4th ed. (Paris: Les Belles Lettres, 2007), 4 and 6.
109. Ibid., 12: "Quia plurimi reperiuntur velle auferre religiosis quam dare." *The Templars: Selected Sources*, trans. Malcolm Barber and Keith Bate (Manchester, England: Manchester University Press, 2002), 237–38.

use utterly failed to convince the king's critics. Anthony Leopold points out that Nogaret cut from a second draft of his proposal his original argument that superfluous funds of monasteries could be deviated to the crusades on the grounds that the founders had already provided sufficiently for the establishments.[110] This was too extreme to be supported, and in these early sorties, Philip's propagandists discovered that the principle of use was broadly held to be inviolable, not divertible to similar purposes.[111]

In 1308 Philip the Fair appealed to the masters of theology at the University of Paris for their opinions on a number of questions relating to the Templars, including the disposition of their goods. He asked: should the goods "be confiscated for the profit of the prince in whose jurisdiction they are situated, or should [they] rather be used for that of the Church or the Holy Land, in consideration of which these goods were given to them or sought by them elsewhere?" If, "perchance by law or the devotion of the princes," they should be reserved for their original purpose, then the subsequent questions were "to whom should their distribution, regulation and administration belong" and was there any claim for the prince to supervise them?[112]

The vocabulary of the theologians' response was philosophical rather than legal, as they discussed a final intention and an end, rather than a will and a purpose, but scholasticism and canon law worked nicely together. An emphasis on natural essences that honored fundamental teleologies, with a particular attunement to causes and ends, easily supported the maintenance of all rightly ordered use:

[S]ince the goods of the Temple were not given to the Templars as principal, as if they were lords, but rather as agents for the defense of the faith and aid for the Holy Land, and this was the final intention (*finalis intentio*) of those giving these goods; and those goods given to an end (*ad finem*),

---

110. Leopold, *How to Recover the Holy Land*, 76 and 78.

111. Sophia Menache, "Contemporary Attitudes Concerning the Templars' Affair: Propaganda's Fiasco?" *Journal of Medieval History* 8 (1982): 135–47.

112. Barber and Bate, trans., *Templars*, 259–60; Lizerand, ed., *Le Dossier*, 60–62: "Septimo, si forsan ex iure vel devocione principum Terre Sancte negocio applicentur, ad quem disposicio, regimen bonorum talium vel administracio, debeat pertinere: an ad ecclesiam, an ad principes, maxime in regno Francie, ubi omnia bona Templariorum ab antiquo in speciali domini regis et predecessorum suorum garda et custodia fuisse noscuntur?"

for a reason or a need, should be allotted to that end; since the said end still exists, and the agents are failing, the said goods ought to be faithfully collected and conserved for the said end.[113]

The Templars could be replaced as trustees with the use maintained; the king was not the only donor, so he could not resume their property. The only consolation for Philip was that the masters suggested that on the question of supervision, "they ought to be collected in the way that will best serve the said end."[114] It was plausible that a warrior king might be better situated to lead the next crusade with these goods in hand than the church.

Philip had already resumed all royal grants given to the Templars since 1258, when Louis IX had confirmed their possessions. Still, the strategy of both king and pope in the dispute was to agree that the use of the property would be maintained by transferring it to an equivalent order. Then the patrons and kings could take extractions as the cost of their work in transferring the property. Neither side would give up their claim: secular rulers would claim that they could resume if they liked but were too pious to do so, while the pope would reply that if he wanted to he could transfer the property to the Hospitallers without their consent. After decades of struggle between king and pope, neither side wanted to acknowledge formally the usual rights of the other.

John of Burgundy, the ambassador, demonstrated this standoff when he wrote to James II of Aragon to summarize Guillaume de Plaisians's speech on behalf of Philip in May of 1308. Plaisians explained that the king did not renounce his potential legal right to the property but gave a pious motivation for its transfer to the Hospi-

113. Barber and Bate, trans., *Templars*, 262; Lizerand, ed., *Le Dossier*, 68: "Dicimus quod, cum bona Templi non fuerint data Templariis principaliter et ut dominis, sed pocius ut ministris ad deffensionem fidei et subsidium Terre Sancte, et hoc fuerit finalis intentio dancium illa bona, et ea que sunt ad finem, rationem et necessitatem sortiantur ex fine, cum predictus finis adhuc remaneat, ipsis deficientibus, debent dicta bona ad dictum finem ordinari fideliter et servari." On *usus* and its relationship to will in Aquinas's theory of action, see Stephen L. Brock, "What is the Use of *Usus* in Aquinas' Psychology of Action?" in *Moral and Political Philosophies in the Middle Ages*, ed. B. Carlos Bazán et al., vol. 2 (Ottawa: Legas, 1995), 654–64.
114. Barber and Bate, trans., *Templars*, 262; Lizerand, *Le Dossier*, 68: "De gardia autem nobis videtur ordinandum secundum quod magis expedit dicto fini."

tallers: "It is possibly the case that he could confiscate them for himself in all legality, but this was not his wish, since the intention (*intentio*) of his ancestors who gave them in consideration for the Holy Land, would be frustrated; instead he wanted them to be used for this purpose."[115] If the report is accurate, Plaisians had made an important shift: it was not the will (*voluntas*) of the donors that was being upheld but rather a broader intent, whose moral, but not legal, weight the king recognized. This was an innovation that was not in his earlier draft of the text, and Lizerand points out that in the speech as delivered, Plaisians increased the implicit threats to the pope, including, it seems, this assertion that the king could resume all of the gifts to the Templars.[116] Plaisians presented material to support resumption, claiming that the Templars had worked against the cause for which they had been endowed, that they squandered and embezzled church wealth, and that they refused to give alms. And ultimately in his 1312 letter ordering that the goods of the Templars be sent on to the Hospitallers, minus costs, Philip indicated that he, as an interested party, was giving his consent to the transfer, a consent that his patronage rights (held both mediately and immediately) made essential to the operation and which could, presumably, have been withheld if he had preferred.[117] But in the circumstances of extended disputes between king and pope, Philip did not seek a truly consensual agreement about the property, nor would Clement V have been inclined to find one, since he was not going to yield any ground to kings who were abusing their authority to go after the wealthiest orders. On Philip's side, as the instigator of the crackdown on the order, Philip would suffer too much damage to his credibility if he were to take the goods of the Templars directly, even if he might have some claim to them through the rights of the founders. An appearance of plausible legality mattered.

115. Barber and Bate, trans, *Templars*, 265; Heinrich Finke, *Papsttum und Untergang des Templerordens*, vol. 2 (Münster: Druck und Verlag der Aschendorffschen, 1907), 143: "Licet enim ipse forte de iure posset ea sibi confiscare, non vult tamen, quod intentio suorum progenitorum, qui ea dederunt contemplatione Terre Sancte, frustraretur, sed quod in illo negotio expendantur."
116. Finke, *Papsttum und Untergang*, vol. 2, 135–40; Lizerand, ed., *Le Dossier*, 110–25.
117. Lizerand, ed., *Le Dossier*, 200.

The actual disposition of Templar property in England followed a pattern similar to that used in France. The papal bull of 1312 commanding the transfer of property to the Hospitallers was sent accompanied by special pleas to the king, archbishops, bishops, and nobles to aid in the process. The king in Parliament made a legal response with *De terris Templar,* in which it was asserted that "by the Law of the Realm" the lands should escheat to the king and "other Lords of the Fees."[118] But while this was legal, the king and the nobles in Parliament had determined according to "Conscience" that goods of the Templars should instead be transferred to the Hospitallers in accordance with the will (*voluntatem*) of the donors, since the purposes of "the Defense of Christians, and the Holy Land against Pagans and Sarazens, and other Enemies of Christ and Christians, and the Universal Holy Church" would be the same. These purposes were pious, because the lands had been given *in pios usus,* and the Hospitallers were called upon to maintain the same activities of "relieving of the Poor, in Hospitalities, in celebrating divine Service, Defense of the Holy Land, and by all other Charges and Services before time due, by whatsoever Names they be called." This was done to honor the "pious and salubrious will" (*pia et saluberrima voluntas*) of the donors, but not to help their souls. Parliament declared that their restraint in refusing to exercise their rights according to the law of the realm was so that they should not condemn themselves spiritually: "for the Health of their Souls and Discharge of their Consciences." In the end, of course, the statute was not perfectly upheld; the king kept some property, including, most famously, the London Temple. It is telling that in all of the maneuvers to prevent the Temple from falling into the hands of the Hospitallers—dividing it into Inner, Outer, and Middle sections in response to claims made against it—the kings never had their chancellors make a cy-près argument to defend the undeniable transfer of use that had occurred with the Temple under the king's authority. They rested their claims instead on the right to resume the failed gift.

A number of issues relevant to the origins of cy-près are raised by the fall of the Templars in England. Both the Parliament and the

118. 17 Ed. 2 Stat 2.

pope agreed that there would be continuity of use in the transition, in accordance with the will of the founders. There was no discussion of intent, because the will itself was performed intact, with a deviation in terms but not in use. Both sides expressed that the will of the donor, being pious, should be honored, and Parliament acknowledged that in conscience, if not in law, they felt themselves bound to preserve that will. As a consequence, Parliament used the statute to prohibit recovery by interested parties in this instance, overriding what was acknowledged to be the law of the realm, and pushing back against the king's reluctance to transfer property to the Hospitallers.

In Aragon, meanwhile, James II wanted to follow the usual consensus model in which potential failure of a gift was grounds for renegotiation by interested parties, and he was surprised to discover that the pope was unwilling to accede to equitable negotiations. The king protested through his ambassadors that the property to the Templars had been given by his ancestors and others in *feudum*, with an oath of fealty, and so could be transferred to someone else only with the will and assent (*voluntate et assensu*) of the king.[119] Clement V replied formally that this was wrong in both fact and law, specifically because he knew that neither the king nor his ancestors had received any rights or services from the Templars except for the *cens*, a tax that they had extracted against the protests of the Templars.[120] This did not fully respond to the issue, and Cardinal Berenguer Fredol approached the king's ambassadors secretly, presumably with the blessing of the pope, to concede that their request was reasonable and just, since they would lose the use of the property. But, he told them, the church could neither afford to give way on the issue nor stop them from doing as they wanted.[121] Implicitly the suggestion was that they, like other rulers, make a show of compliance but take what they wanted in the transfer, a solution that did not appeal to James II. Only after the death of Clement V was the problem resolved, by John XXII, who made concessions. The king succeeded

119. Finke, *Papsttum und Untergang*, vol. 2, 214.
120. Ibid., 221.
121. Ibid., 218–19.

in some of his demands that property go to the Calatrava order and to monasteries of royal foundation that had no purpose in defending the Holy Land. Here consensus won out, against the attempt by Clement V to avoid giving any formal acknowledgment of the right of donors to consent to deviations of their gifts.

Ultimately, then, everyone agreed in theory to a transfer of Templar property within use; theoretical accommodations were made to previous rights or particular circumstances, and in practice things sorted out in a way that could make it plausible that the legal settlement was being followed, even though secular leaders took advantage of the transition to appropriate property. This resolution helps to highlight the fact that with large donations to pious causes, no one had the power to transfer within use without negotiations with all of the involved parties. Even commutations without the change of use were contested and required negotiation. And while each interested party was perfectly willing to divert parts of gifts into their own treasuries with the transfer—such that it has been suggested that the Hospitallers may have lost more money than they gained—there was at least rhetorical agreement that gifts given for purposes were to be conserved to that purpose.[122] None of the antagonists in the Templar affair suggested anything else, and all upheld the conservation of use as a moral principle.

More striking, however, is the fact that virtually everyone agreed that the use would in fact be maintained in the transfer. Many parties were eager to profit from the dissolution of the Templars, but there were no voices of rebuttal. In the negotiations, despite the obvious angling for advantage, there was no significant dissent, such as that of de Molay in 1306, which had argued that the Hospitallers had a fundamentally different purpose than the Templars. When Clement V enforced the transfer of property on an unwilling council—for if the report of the Aragonese ambassadors is correct, many of the attendees at the council would have preferred to create a new order—his insistence on the continuity of use was presumably all the more important, since one good reason to create a new order was that it

122. Andreas Beck, *Der Untergang der Templer. Grösster Justizmord des Mittelalters?* (Freiburg im Breisgau: Herder, 1993).

could be made to conform exactly to the Templars, which the Hospitallers, having their own independent foundation documents, could not. If approximation of purpose had been a principle, this would have been a good place for the pope to employ it in explaining why the Hospitallers were a good enough destination for the property, even if they were somewhat different from the Templars. But he did not suggest this: the use was, instead, held to be identical. This silence and lack of objection to the Hospitallers as a comparable equivalent to the Templars may be due to uncertainty: what would the consequence be if the purpose were altered, even just a little? Everyone understood that the church would not stand by and watch the entirety of the Templar wealth be dissipated into national treasuries; no one was either completely bound by the will of donors or, alternatively, willing to simply abandon the protections of gifts for purposes, which served them all.

The documents issued by the pope at the Council of Vienne were constructed with an eye toward their legal ramifications and would subsequently be included in the Clementine constitutions.[123] They make clear what the law ought to be, absent manifest political pressures. Thus Philip was improbably praised because "he was not moved by greed. He had no intention of claiming or appropriating for himself anything from the Templars' property; rather, in his own kingdom he abandoned such claim and thereafter released entirely his hold on their goods."[124] The Templars had been "convicted of such heresies, errors and crimes through their spontaneous confessions ... which render the order very suspect, and the infamy and suspicion render it detestable."[125] This air of suspicion was the grounds on which the pope disbanded the order, which could not be effective if

123. Sophia Menache, *Clement V* (Cambridge: Cambridge University Press, 2003), 279–305.
124. Council of Vienne I.1, in Tanner, ed., *Decrees of the Ecumenical Councils*, vol. 1, 337: "Cui eadem fuerant facinora nunciati, non typo avaritiae—cum de bonis Templariorum nihil sibi vindicare aut appropriare intenderit, immo ea in regno suo dimisit, manum suam exinde totaliter amovendo."
125. Ibid., 341: "per eorum confessiones spontaneas de praedictis haeresibus, erroribus et sceleribus sunt convictae, quia etiam ipsae confessiones dictum ordinem reddunt valde suspectum, et quia infamia et suspicio praelibatae dictum ordinem reddunt ... abominabilem."

it was not trusted. Since these conditions of distrust "would lead in all probability to the total loss, destruction and dilapidation of the Templars' property [which] has for long been given, bequeathed, and granted by the faithful for the aid of the holy land and to oppose the enemies of the Christian faith," the pope was obligated to intervene.[126]

In this framing, the will of the donors was paramount: property had been given to the Templars for a purpose that would be frustrated because of the disrepute attached to the Templars. It fell to the pope to pension off the remaining members of the order, so that their rights were not violated, and to transfer the order's property to the Hospitallers, who would apply "the property to the use for which it was intended."[127] Clement emphasized in his bulls this claim that he was obliged "by apostolic provision and ordinance" to act quickly in order to preserve the property of the Templars, which had been given by the faithful to defend the Holy Land.[128] Failure to act on his part would cause the property to be lost and the intentions of the donors to be violated:

Afterwards we took care lest the said property, which over a long period had been given, bequeathed, granted and acquired from the worshippers of Christ for the help of the holy Land and to assail the enemies of the Christian faith, should be left without management and perish as belonging to nobody or be used in ways other than those intended by the pious devotion of the faithful. There was the further danger that tardiness in our arrangements and dispositions might lead to destruction or dilapidation.[129]

---

126. Ibid., 342: "bonorum Templi quae dudum a subsidium Terrae sanctae et impugnationem inimicorum fidei christianae a Christi fidelibus data, legata, et concessa fuerunt, totalis amissio, destructio et dilapidatio, ut probabiliter creditur, sequeretur."
127. Ibid., 342: "bona ad usum, ad quem deputata fuerant." This maintenance of the use, but not the trustee, was affirmed in England with 17 Ed. 2 Stat 2.
128. Ibid., 348: "per viam provisionis et ordinationis apostolicae."
129. Ibid., Council of Vienne, I.2, "Ad perpetuam rei memoriam," 344: "Ac postmodum ne dicta bona quae dudum ad subsidium Terrae sanctae et impugnationem inimicorum fidei christianae a Christi cultoribus data, legata, concessa et acquisita fuerunt, debita gubernatione carentia tamquam vacantia deperirent vel converterentur in usus alios quam in illos ad quos fuerant pia devotione fidelium deputata, vel propter tarditatem ordinationis et dispositionis huiusmodi eorum destructio vel dilapidatio sequeretur."

Although Clement cited the intentions of the pious donors as the reason to preserve the property for its original use, he did not suggest that the fate of the dead rested on the continued use of their property in some pious way. Rather, the anxiety expressed in the text was that the frustration of purpose could lead to outright resumption or confiscation. There was no legal doctrine cited that would govern the redirection of a gift when its charitable purpose was frustrated.

The decrees of the Council of Vienne elaborated on donor intentions and the continuity of use, especially *Quia contingit*, which would remain an important legal text for charitable donations and hospital administration. The decree began by lamenting that charitable institutions had been misemployed, embezzled, and destroyed: "that which has been given by the faithful for a certain purpose should, except by authority of the apostolic see, be applied to that purpose and no other."[130] The intended purpose of the gift must be maintained. Johannes Andreae's Ordinary Gloss on the text affirmed this and did not add other qualifications. The will of the donor limited the use to which a gift could be put, and only the Apostolic See could give a dispensation to a change in purpose. By explicitly reserving the right to give a dispensation of use to the Apostolic See, *Quia contingit* demonstrated that this right was not part of the ordinary powers of the bishop. Similarly, Guillaume Le Maire, Bishop of Angers, who submitted an opinion on the Templar property to Clement V, argued that the Holy See should destroy the order and take the property right away, without troubling with legal procedures but using instead the plenitude of papal power. Le Maire did not consider whether or not the use would change, but he did appear to believe that bishops did not have the power to redirect donations given to the Templars in their own diocese.[131]

The dissolution of the order of the Templars would seem to have been one of the best opportunities for cy-près to be expressed. If cy-près had been an acknowledged doctrine, it could have come into

---

130. Ibid., Council of Vienne II, d. 17, "Quia contingit," 374–75: "quae ad certum usum largitione sunt destinata fidelium, ad illum debeant non ad alium, salva quidem sedis apostolicae auctoritate, converti." Clem. 3.11.2.

131. Barber and Bate, trans., *Templars*, 240.

play here, and yet most participants on all sides, despite their conflicts with each other, made an effort not to conceptualize the problem as one in which the purpose would be changing. This reluctance may well relate not just to scruples about interfering with pious donations but also to the understanding of the legal treatment of gifts made with a purpose attached. There was a deep sense that the purpose of a gift was—at least in theory—inviolable by the law. We know that this was not necessarily a superstitious taboo: plenty of executors, legatees, heirs, and donees tried to violate the terms of gifts, and property did get shuffled off to new uses. Nonetheless, despite the violations of the principle, the legal transfer of a gift for purposes to a new purpose was a rhetorically impossible argument. This demonstrates a teleological mentality, a worldview in which almost everything had a purpose assigned to it, by God or more immediately by the donor. The individual could find good, private reasons to ignore these purposes in particular cases, but he or she could not advocate for a legal principle of changing purpose. That idea would have been too destabilizing. Indeed, Le Maire, who wished to transfer the Templar property without legal proceedings, arrived at many of the same justifications and analogies that would reappear in the Reformation: the initial donations might have been well done, or at least seemed so in the time when they were made, but since they now appeared "superstitious," they should be destroyed immediately by the governing powers in the model of Hezekiah, who destroyed Moses' brazen serpent.[132] God had commanded it to be made; He then subsequently commanded it to be demolished because it was being worshipped.[133] For Le Maire, the fiction of destruction was better than the explicit articulation of a new use applied to donated property.

Additionally, a consensual model of equity, by which ecclesiastical law tried to get all interested parties to consent to even small changes to a gift, is an echo, in small form, of larger operations, such as the political demands for consent—that parliaments consent to loans or to changes in taxation or that the king consent to honor privileges and customs—that are apparent across late medieval Europe. It is easy

132. Ibid., 240.
133. IV Kings 18:4.

from a modern perspective to imagine that these displays were *pro forma* or that they were important only in establishing the principle of the necessity of consent. But consent was a gift, expressed as such in most European languages, and, as Erasmus pointed out in *Dulce bellum inexpertis*, the gift of consent could be revoked. Because consent was a gift, with ongoing ties between the giver and receiver of the consent, the gift of consent could be employed only for its intended purpose, as one had consented to one thing and not another. This understanding of the gift of consent makes clear the stakes of honoring purpose, for everything from property dispositions to the ceremonies of government. The solicitation of consent and the maintenance of purpose were two key factors in making the world just and nonarbitrary.

Poverty, Property, and Patronage

Another pressing issue that emerged in the Council of Vienne and would carry over into the fourteenth century was the growing popularity of the friars. The decrees of the council encouraged the friars not to accept all gifts, so that their churches would not be so ornate. They should not accept inheritances—not even inheritances only for the use of something—since, in an anticipation of the debate that would break out in the 1320s, the council declared that they should have neither "possessions [n]or even their use."[134] This debate over voluntary poverty, its meaning and legitimacy, would center around the issue of use. Was it possible to have a *usus pauper*, a spiritual poverty maintained even while deriving sustenance from material goods, or alternatively, was it was heretical to reject property and thereby threaten the longstanding compromise on property that the church offered the faithful, as John XXII would charge?[135]

---

134. Council of Vienne, in Tanner, ed., *Decrees of the Ecumenical Councils*, Vol. 1, II, d. 38, p. 398: "sicut et possessiones vel eorum etiam usum, cum eis non reperiatur concessus."

135. Giorgio Agamben, *The Highest Poverty: Monastic Rules and Form-of-Life*, trans. Adam Kotsko (Stanford, Calif.: Stanford University Press, 2013), 123–43; Virpi Mäkinen, *Property Rights in the Late Medieval Discussion on Franciscan Poverty* (Leuven: Peeters, 2001).

After all, to divest all property and throw oneself, penniless, into the desert, the monastery, or the streets in order to follow Christ without worldly attachments was neither practical nor even appealing to those who felt bound by ties of obligation to their household.[136] The periodic display of radical movements of poverty in the Middle Ages—the Franciscans, the Spiritual Franciscans, or the third order of the Humiliati, among others—demonstrated an anxiety that the demands of Christian life were total, a fear that was supported by the increasingly precise accounting of the afterlife.[137] The *vita apostolica* tried to reconcile life in the world with an embrace of at least spiritual poverty, but it was difficult to attain true purity without also being dependent upon the goodwill of others. The desire of some female medieval saints to feed others without having to be fed, except by God in the Eucharist, as described by Caroline Walker Bynum, speaks to a similar problem in medieval Christian social ethics.[138] This psychological tension felt by an individual between the total, radical demand of an apparently pure Christianity and the need to function in the world was what the Reformation would attempt to cast off, which is why a Reformation that began with deterministic visions of justification and avowals of the futility of works would be greeted by some with such a sense of relief, as a liberation from one's continual failure to be fully or perfectly Christian.

This is one of the reasons why the mendicants would be bitterly targeted in Reformation polemics. They had responded to the wealth of the church with a solution that—for all of its apparent apostolic purity—threatened the sense of reasonable compromise that the Thomists and canon lawyers had offered to reconcile care for the poor with care for one's family.[139] Consequently they remained a source of contention no matter how faithful to their foundation documents they were. MacCulloch has pointed out that "in regions as

---

136. Nor was it necessarily biblical: 2 Corinthians 8:13–14.
137. Little, *Religious Poverty*.
138. Caroline Walker Bynum, *Holy Feast, Holy Fast: The Religious Significance of Food to Medieval Women* (Berkeley: University of California Press, 1987).
139. Gl. Ord. ad D.86 c.18. On jurists and private property in a changing late medieval economy, see John F. McGovern, "The Rise of New Economic Attitudes in Canon and Civil Law, A.D. 1200–1550," *The Jurist* 32 (1972): 39–50.

widely separated as Germany and Scotland" statues of Saint Francis were particularly targeted in Reformation iconoclastic frenzies.[140] Since Francis himself was rarely accused of any of the crimes of his followers, this is difficult to understand except through the tensions his example provoked. Furthermore, most mendicants were manifestly not saints but men who claimed that their dependency on others was the source of their moral superiority to the ordinary Christians who supported them.[141] In opposition to the idea of conserving wealth within the family in order to be able to help the poor continuously, the Franciscans and other mendicant orders, including the Dominicans, offered a model that could not be generalized to everyone.[142]

The history of the Franciscan order itself demonstrates many of the problems of reconciling property and Christianity. Francis had left, in addition to the Rule, a Testament, which he said should be honored exactly and without deviation. This testament charged Francis's spiritual heirs with the obligation, among others, to avoid the accumulation of property in their name—to be always as poor pilgrims. By calling this a testament Francis may have intended to give it greater weight than the rule itself, since a testament carried burdens of performance with it. But in the disputes over the Franciscans that would follow, the Testament would be held up by some, including Gregory IX, as less binding than the Rule, in part, ironically, because a testament that did not pass on property could not bind the inheritors, and so Francis, being poor, could not enforce his will on the living after his death.[143]

But it was extremely difficult to make this Testament align with the great popularity of the Franciscans anyway, since they were desired by the world precisely because of their otherworldliness. The

140. Diarmaid MacCulloch, *The Reformation: A History* (New York: Penguin, 2003), 155.
141. Dipple, *Antifraternalism and Anticlericalism*; Martin Greschat, *Martin Bucer: A Reformer and his Times*, trans. Stephen E. Buckwalter (Louisville, Ky.: Westminster John Knox Press, 2004), 50.
142. Gl. Ord. ad C.12 q.1 c.7.
143. David Burr, *The Spiritual Franciscans: From Protest to Persecution in the Century after Saint Francis* (University Park: Pennsylvania State University Press, 2001), 4.

Franciscans consequently faced almost immediate pressure to accommodate themselves, but when they adhered to their original rule, they implicitly criticized the apparently tempered Christianity that had endowed the church, and when they advanced in the world they appeared emblematic of a false piety. As David Burr writes, "A number of mendicants thought that their orders ought to engage in activities like preaching, pastoral work, and teaching because these activities needed to be performed by competent, holy men, and the friars were just that. They should be bishops and cardinals for the same reason."[144] Even the "spiritual" Franciscans, in rebellion against their superiors but claiming perfect fidelity to Francis's Testament, would take property to restore it to a better use, as when in 1317 they seized control of the Franciscan houses in Narbonne and Béziers.[145]

The more successful that the Franciscans were, the more disruptive they were to established compromises on property and salvation. As exemplars of apostolic poverty, they provoked frustration. They were the poor in Christ and consequently the obvious recipients of the charity of ordinary Christians, who knew that the poor could receive even ill-gotten property without sin. But due to the Franciscan rule, the friars could not serve as uncomplicated recipients of any property, much less cleanse problematic property through its receipt and offer prayers in return. Moreover, the debates over use tended to clarify how impossible it was to live in the world but not lay claim to things, even if only in consumption, and the more scrupulous the adherence to the rules, the more apparent it was that strict Franciscans simply pushed necessary duties off onto an array of helpers: men to collect gifts; men to touch money; men to litigate in their name and to own property on their behalf. The Franciscan proposal that the friars might honor their rule by living only through the fiction of expropriation (*expropriatio*), as though they were innocents in the Garden of Eden collecting the fruits that had grown without any cultivation, demonstrated the problem.[146]

144. Ibid., 9.
145. Ibid., 1.
146. Ibid., 142.

106   Patronage Rights and Consensus

Nicholas III, in his 1279 *Exiit qui seminat*, attempted to sort out how the Franciscan Rule could be reconciled with both the world and the law. If a donation was made to fulfill a specific need for the friars and the money turned out to be excessive, the donor should be asked whether the remainder could be used for an alternate purpose, and if he did not give consent, then the money should be returned to him.[147] Similarly, if a donation was made through a testament that the friars could not take, then it should be refused. Nicholas III did not suggest, then, that this legacy should be turned to another, similar pious use. He did, however, recommend that gifts to the friars be general and that donations should be understood as licit if they did not violate the rule.[148]

Still, the Franciscans would open up the specter of the expected conversion of gifts, at first only so that they would be in a form that they could licitly use.[149] Because they were considered to be the poor in Christ, goods that were given for their use in one kind could be converted to something else. In one sense the use did not change: the Franciscans or other poor would have the use, as the donor had intended. But many legal intricacies emerged from their attempt simultaneously not to own property or touch money but to be able to use things and receive legacies. This situation forced the issue of conversion and exchange into the foreground and paved the way for alterations of difficult donations to become normal. At the 1329 Council of Tarragona, bishops were required to consult with heirs regarding illicit gifts to the Franciscans so that either the masses and anniversaries might be celebrated somewhere else or alternate pious works performed.[150] Meanwhile, the frequency of the appearance of

---

147. *Exiit qui seminat* § 14, in J. Gay, ed., *Les Registres de Nicholas III (1277–1280)* (Paris: Albert Fontemoing, 1904), document 564, 232–41. Bartolus would concede this but insist that if the donor was dead, the excess would stay with the friars. Anna T. Sheedy, *Bartolus on Social Conditions in the Fourteenth Century* (New York: Columbia University Press, 1942), 204.

148. *Exiit qui seminat* § 15, in Gay, ed., *Registres*.

149. Bartolus, *Liber minoricarum decisionum*, Liber 1, Dist. 4, Cap. 1, 108ra, on the question of conversion "in usum pauperum," from *Opera omnia* (Venice: Iuntas, 1590).

150. Giovanni Domenico Mansi, *Sacrorum conciliorum*, vol. 25 (Venice: Antonius Zatta, 1782), 866: "convertere studeant cum heredum defunctorum, qui

problematic legacies and trusts for the benefit of the friars in the consilia of contemporary jurists makes it clear how significant the Franciscans were for the development of jurisprudence on the problem of failing pious gifts.

As the example of the friars indicates, property was at the heart of many pre-Reformation movements for reform, both in their theoretical conception and in their popular execution. Many of these critiques ultimately rested on the question of the nature of gifts to the church and their effect. Many of them also relied on pulling apart the balance of interests in the gift and vesting ultimate power in one party in the cause of reform. And yet all of these attempts to undermine the consensus model, even radical critiques of the wealth of the church, still usually attempted to explain their actions in terms of some broader continuity of purpose and higher intentions of the donors. Dead donors almost always approved of the proposed new disposition of their gifts, as they would continue to do under cy-près.

For instance, John Wyclif wanted to strengthen the claims of patronage, even though he believed that to found a monastery or give money to the church was a sin. Simony, which Wyclif defined broadly, was a spiritual leprosy, spread through the ranks of the church across time, as an inheritance that destroyed the integrity of the heir—just as laymen passed sin on to their heirs by giving them property that was held while in a state of sin.[151] No one could hold property justly unless he or she were in the grace of God, and kings had the duty to dispossess sinners. Wyclif suggested a series of solutions to these problems that depended on the rights of patrons, despite the fact that the founders had erred in their original donations. Patrons should exercise their rights to repossess if the recipient of the gift fell from grace. The laity, likewise, could take their alms and apply them

---

praedicta dederint, assignaverint, seu legaverint, consilio, in anniversaria in aliis locis facienda, vel missas celebrandas, vel alia pietatis opera voluntates ipsorum defunctorum, in quibus observari commode poterunt, observando."

151. Johannes Wyclif, *Tractatus de simonia*, ed. Herzberg-Fränkel and Michael Henry Dziewicki (London: Trübner, 1898), 7; John Wyclif, *On Simony*, trans. Terrence A. McVeigh (New York: Fordham University Press, 1992), 35.

to the poor when their priests sinned. The church should never have perpetual endowments, because the sinner ought to be deprived of his property.[152] It was the king's duty to ensure that property not fall into "dead hands," to prevent the recurrence of this problem.[153] As William Farr points out, Wyclif effectively made all endowments, especially to the church, "conditional," and he tried with some success to use common law to support resumption.[154]

In this sense Wyclif inverted Giles of Rome, who in the early fourteenth century had argued in his *De ecclesiastica potestate* that it was the pope who had permanent *dominium* over all property, with temporary *dominium* granted to kings, lords, and men only as long as they were in communion with the church. Giles explained away the existence of pious donations by noting that they simply gave a secondary *dominium* to the church for property over which it already had primary and permanent *dominium*.[155] Although the church should not be hasty to strip property from those who fell away from the faith, since Christian mercy required the attempt to persuade them back into the fold, the church had both the right and the duty to take property away from those who should not have it, in accordance with justice.[156] Indeed, despite what Giles acknowledged was the justice of succession as a means of property distribution, he argued that no man could lawfully inherit property from his father unless both men had been baptized by the church, as a purely carnal man had no claim to lawful *dominium*.[157]

Thus both Wyclif and Giles of Rome imagined concentrating power in the hands of one man with the right to redistribute property from those who ought not to have it to those who ought. They both hoped to clarify the complicated property relationships of the medie-

---

152. Wyclif, *On Simony*, trans. McVeigh, 9. Wyclif himself was supported by the income of two endowments.
153. John Wyclif, *Trialogus*, trans. Stephen E. Lahey (Cambridge: Cambridge University Press, 2013), IV.19, p. 249.
154. William Farr, *John Wyclif as Legal Reformer* (Leiden: Brill, 1974), chapter 6.
155. Giles of Rome, *On Ecclesiastical Power*, trans. R. W. Dyson (New York: Columbia University Press, 2004), xxv and III.11, pp. 379–80.
156. Ibid., II.12, pp. 188–211.
157. Ibid., II.7, pp. 130–41.

val world, in which few *de facto* examples of pure *dominium* could be found. Indeed, the burgeoning claims of the nation-state in the early modern period would subsequently represent an attempt to reify these extreme claims of medieval political theory in the hope that unilateral power would bring reform and good order. For both Giles and Wyclif, the problem was not simply that the wrong jurisdiction claimed *dominium* and that the wrong people held property uncorrected, but additionally that the holding of sinful property heaped sin on the heads of the already damned.[158]

For Wyclif, the donor, however humble, had certain responsibilities in making a gift. To give to a sinful priest out of anxiety for one's soul was, in itself, sinful, but to resume a gift was not.[159] A donor was required to discriminate and judge. In arguing for the role of the laity in using their claims to property to enforce reform, Wyclif drew on the canonical duty of patrons to supervise the churches they had founded.[160] Even a good Christian could have dirty hands by failing to scrutinize the gifts he had given in apparent good faith. Nor did Wyclif assume that the donor had good faith when he endowed the church, since donations were the result of Satan's machinations, particularly Constantine's donation, which, although Wyclif was reluctant to affirm its authenticity, had poisoned the church by giving it things. In the *Trialogus*, Wyclif pointed out that Constantine should not be forgiven for his gift just because he thought he was being pious.[161] In his memorable phrase, the monasteries, or "castles of CAYN [Carmelites, Augustinians, Jacobites, and Minorites]," were built by temporal lords who hoped for nothing less than to frustrate Christ's purposes on earth. The conclusion that others might draw from this argument was left unsaid: patrons like these deserved no protection or legal recognition, for they had given with the understanding that they would ruin the mission of the church. Because of the reciprocal nature of gifts, they expected that they would contin-

158. Ibid., II.4, p. 91.
159. Wyclif, *Tractatus de officio pastorali*, ed. Gotthardus Victor Lechler (Leipzig: A. Edelmannum, 1863), I.8, pp. 15–16.
160. C.16 q.7 cc.30–31.
161. Wyclif, *Trialogus* IV.18, 243–46.

ue to reap profits from their donations too. Donors of chantries were particularly in error, and their intentions had no ethical imperative, because by their donation they had shown that they were unworthy of their property. They damned themselves and those who tried to carry out their intentions: "alle thes feden the world, and done no profit to the soule; as thei harmen men lyvynge, so thei done harm to the soul."[162] Citing the command to "Go and sin no more," Wyclif urged priests to cast off the burden of property that had been thrust upon them.[163] The simoniac could receive forgiveness for his sin only through restitution, and, according to Wyclif, there were three possibilities for this: the money might be returned to the donor; the king, the patron of all lands in his realm, might legitimately receive it; or, the poor could be the beneficiaries. These would be the three main contenders for church endowments during the expropriations of the Reformation.

If the priests would not dispossess themselves, then the king or other secular lords ought to dispossess them. Wyclif simultaneously supported the rights of patrons and the ultimate title of the king over all land.[164] Wherever patrons had used or sold the right of appointing priests for their own material advantage, they had become heretics themselves and lost their patronage rights, so the king clearly had the better claim. Wyclif claimed that patronage would be transformed by the dispossession of the church, "changing from an irreligious, material heritage to a spiritual patronage," which will be "happy and meritorious" for patrons because "such a state without property would be a broader and more exalted way to attain salvation."[165] Patrons would benefit spiritually from a transforma-

---

162. P. Arnold, ed., *Select English Works of John Wyclif* (Oxford: Clarendon Press, 1869), vol. 2, 213; quoted in Wood-Legh, *Perpetual Chantries*, 305n.

163. Wyclif, *Tractatus de officio pastorali*, II.11, p. 45; see also his *Trialogus*.

164. Wyclif, *Tractatus de simonia*, 31; Wyclif, *On Simony*, trans. McVeigh, 69.

165. Wyclif, *Tractatus de simonia*, 37; Wyclif, *On Simony*, trans. McVeigh, 74: "Hic dico quod utile foret et honorificum ecclesie multas eius dotaciones dissolvere, nec in hoc destruitur patronatus, sed melioratur ab irreligiosa temporali tradicione ad spiritualem patronatum conversus. Sed felix et meritoria patronis foret talis mutacio, quia non dubium, quin Christus omnipotens et omnisciens et omnivolens ordinavit et aptavit vitam et statum sponse sue competenciorem pro

tion of the church's relationship to property, even where it threatened their endowments. Violating their intentions might purify their souls. Moreover, no one would suffer even if unjustly deprived of their property, Wyclif wrote, because God would always make good the insult: "he will not lose brotherly charity because of some possible wrongdoing of his brother. If injustice occurs, it is clear that the doer of the injustice does no damage, but by an invincible law works to the advantage of God's servant."[166] Neither the living nor the dead had anything to fear.

When the king gave to the church, Wyclif wrote, he "reserves for himself the chief ownership because otherwise he would destroy his kingdom."[167] Patronage should always be held by the laity, not transferred to monasteries, so that the church would have lay supervision. In the case of charitable donations, the donors and their heirs ought likewise to maintain their rights to supervise or even to take the gift back if it was badly managed.[168] And so Wyclif himself hoped to uphold simultaneously the rights of the king, the patron, and the poor.[169] It was the current mismanagement of property, particularly in the exchange of corrodies, that threatened the stipulations of the original gift:

It betrays the founders and the poor. The founders because where religious men had mandated that the poor subsist on their alms, the rich of the world sacrilegiously consume these alms in a pleasure-loving, irreligious manner; nor is there any doubt that the diminution of such goods

---

beatitudine acquirenda ... ergo status talis exproprietarius foret apercior et alcior pro beatitudine acquirenda."

166. John Wyclif, *Tractatus de civili dominio liber primus*, ed. Reginald Lane Poole (London: Trübner, 1885), 60–61; John Wyclif, "On Civil Lordship," in *The Cambridge Translations of Medieval Philosophical Texts*, ed. Arthur Stephen McGrade, et al., vol. 2 (Cambridge: Cambridge University Press, 2001), I.9, p. 639: "nec excidet a fraterna caritate propter aliquam iniuriacionem possibilem fratris sui; que si assit, patet quod iniurians non dampnificat, sed lege invincibili cooperatur in comodum servi Dei."

167. Wyclif, *Tractatus de simonia*, 33: "quod alias extingueret regnum suum"; Wyclif, *On Simony*, trans. McVeigh, 71.

168. Wyclif, *Tractatus de simonia*, 34–35; Wyclif, *On Simony*, trans. McVeigh, 72.

169. Margaret Aston, "Lollardy and the Reformation: Survival or Revival?" in *Lollards and Reformers: Images and Literacy in Late Medieval Religion* (London: Hambledon Press, 1984), 219–42.

defrauds the poor.... Nor can a great distortion of founders' intentions be prevented with regard to the nature of the endowment and its obligation.[170]

Here Wyclif gestured back toward his point that endowments led inevitably to simony and, apparently thereby, to a violation of the donor's intentions. Although the thrust of his argument opposed upholding donor intentions, he still used intentions as a justification for action, recounting in *De ecclesia* that he was a warden during the transition in 1366 at Canterbury College from supporting the secular clergy to supporting monastics, against its original establishment.[171] Colleges, therefore, also ought to be dispossessed, since they were not good guardians of the donations made to them.

The Lollards, however inspired by Wyclif, lacked his appreciation for patronage rights. Their *Twelve Conclusions* suggested that only a hundred almshouses were needed, and that the king might take the rest of them to prevent idleness. The Lollards pointed out that most of the founders of chantries, who gave money for their "venomous dotacion" (that is, poisonous endowments), had gone "the broad way" to hell. To pray for their souls was thus offensive to God because they were damned. The donor, having entrapped the living into performing a blasphemous prayer that displeased God, was then dragging the living down into hell after him through the performance of his last wishes.[172] The Lollards concluded that "all houses of alms in England have been wrongly founded." The purposes of the donors could certainly be ignored. But this was an unusual stance, renouncing as it did both the rights of patrons and the continuity of use.

By contrast, in William Langland's *Piers Plowman,* the narrator, Will, begins by searching for Do-Well, which is a surer route to sal-

---

170. Wyclif, *Tractatus de simonia,* 85; Wyclif, *On Simony,* trans. McVeigh, 133: "prodit fundatores et pauperes. Fundatores, quia ubi religiosi ordinarunt pauperes vivere de suis elemosinis, mundi divites voluptuose et irreligiose consumunt ipsas sacrilege; nec dubium quin talium bonorum substraccio de tanto defraudat pauperes.... Nec evadi potest quin de oracionibus fundatorum secundum formam donacionis et obligacionis de tanto subtrahitur."

171. Wyclif, *On Simony,* trans. McVeigh, 147n.

172. "The Twelve Conclusions of the Lollards," *English Historical Review* 22 (1907): 292–304.

vation than superstitious helps (Passus VII and XI). But in Passus XV, Anima persuades him that even better is to search for the spirit of charity, described as a universal love and benevolence that is concerned not so much with particular actions as with the overall disposition with which a Christian man should live. Endowments failed to cultivate this spirit of love in their trustees and consequently were not charitable but corrupting. The laity ought to provide daily for needs of the religious but should not make big gifts to them. Instead they should "take the money back where they'd got it from," that is, return it to the local economy, rather than exploiting the poor in order to accumulate money to give to the friars.[173] Langland bemoaned the stripping away of inheritances for such a ridiculous purpose, when the monks already had enough to fulfill their original purpose of prayer:

It's a great pity, my noble friends, that you listened to such bad advice and alienated from your own descendants the property that your ancestors left you! To get them to pray for you, you gave money to those who are already rich—orders that were founded, endowed even, for no purpose except to pray for others![174]

Since this purpose was sufficiently taken care of already, anything additional would be a surplus that would not really fulfill the purpose for which it was given, and, in keeping goods from the poor, the donors and the monks who received their gifts were committing sacrilege.[175] Purpose was paramount and could be maintained by taking the gifts back and making smaller, regular alms. Langland, like Wyclif, could hope to maintain donor's rights and use, even in radical reform.

Following Wyclif on the critique of simony, Jan Hus similarly concluded that endowments and foundations erred in their nature: "It is best, therefore, that a man give alms while still alive, without aspiring to leave behind him a perpetual charity trust. For nowhere in the Scriptures is it stated that men should establish perpetual chari-

---

173. William Langland, *Piers Plowman,* trans. A. V. C. Schmidt (Oxford: Oxford University Press, 1992), Passus XV, p. 177.
174. Ibid.
175. Ibid., 178.

ty endowments ... A faithful lover of God gives the poor, while he is alive, whatever he can."[176] To delay a gift, especially up to the point of death, is stingy, and, moreover, why should the poor suffer longer than necessary in order to conserve a trust that has been established? By creating a trust, the donor put other people, the managers of the endowment, in a position to sin themselves, since they would live off the endowment and conserve it, instead of giving it all to the poor. A trust compounded the sin and spread it from the donor to the trustees, in perpetuity.[177] The intentions of a settlor were not charitable or admirable at all:

> They are likewise fools who save well-earned money in order to establish similar trusts, and seeing those in need, do not aid them; for thereby they sin gravely, mortally.... The many quarrels, litigations, and murders as well as other sins which result from those perpetual charity trusts who can describe? For one assumes a great responsibility—the management of the trust—and retains it for his use till his death, and then wills it to another, with the intention that his successor perform the stipulation of the trust. But the latter likewise retains it for his own use till his death; and so it goes on until nothing remains of the endowment. Miserable people! How lacking in sense they are, desiring that others should do for them what they themselves, although able to do it, fail to do.... For the Lord Jesus, his apostles, and other saints, have not established perpetual charity trusts.[178]

The fictional person of the trust refused to behold the fowls of the air but always sought its own, immortal preservation, instead of spending itself into extinction through an Augustinian extravagance of almsgiving.

And yet, Hus, like Wyclif, did not protest against the principle of patronage itself. Patronage rights were spiritual, not material. Even the canonical property claims of the donor and his family against the donation did not trouble Hus, who instead chastised monks for failing to give back to impoverished donors.[179] True, patrons could

---

176. Jan Hus, "On Simony," in *Advocates of Reform: From Wyclif to Erasmus*, ed. by Matthew Spinka (Louisville, Ky.: Westminster Knox Press, 1953), 260.
177. Ibid., 259–60.
178. Ibid., 260.
179. Ibid., 258.

commit simony by selling or exchanging their rights or using the *ius praestandi* for material benefits.[180] But on whole he was in favor of the principle that the laity maintained some rights over their donations unless they attempted to capitalize unjustly on them. In this he followed Wyclif, who desired that "the entire enterprise of patronage should be managed by the laity."[181] The theoretical and political attacks on endowments aimed to eradicate the consensus model of seeking the consent of all interested parties, but they tried to uphold the continuity of use and the rights of the donors. It was, tellingly, consensus that was under silent attack and that would ultimately be lost in cy-près rulings, which would preserve only the importance of the intent of the original donor out of all of the multifaceted medieval considerations about gifts.

Even radical criticisms of the use of property and the role of donors in the late Middle Ages featured the poor themselves as only a minor theme and mostly honored the rights of patrons. Attention focused on the problem that the wrong people had property and were using it in the wrong way, but the issue of poverty did not drive discontent with the endowed church. Brian Tierney has noted that the canon lawyers of the fourteenth and fifteenth centuries focused on scholastically elaborating upon, without substantively diverging from, the thirteenth-century canon law of the poor. He argued that, in the midst of economic upheaval, this was a mistake, particularly since canon law's emphasis on local care for the poor did not address the pressing issue of vagrancy. Tierney concluded: "[A] theory of poor relief, to be effective, must be flexible, not fossilized, continuously adapted in its practical applications to changes in the social and economic environment within which it operates."[182] This flexibility in responding to contemporary policy interests is precisely what cy-près would eventually offer. But as we shall see in the next chapter, there was some subtle flexibility being exercised in the fourteenth- and fifteenth-century *ius commune*, not on behalf of the poor, but to preserve the rights of the poor in Christ and pious

180. Ibid., 236–37.
181. Wyclif, *On Simony*, trans. McVeigh, 11.
182. Tierney, *Medieval Poor Law*, 133.

gifts more generally, as they were so obviously under threat from all sides. In this jurisprudence of the fourteenth and fifteenth centuries, however, the ideal of consensus for change was not lost, as the *ius commune* remained attached to consent and to honoring the rights of all interested parties even as the political landscape continued to shift. In this regard the *ius commune* would reject the unilateral redirection of gifts that would come to characterize cy-près.

3

Use in the *Ius Commune*

In England *usus* would have many meanings: the purpose for which property was donated, a trust that held property for a purpose, and usages, that is, customary law. In the Middle Ages, these multiple meanings of *usus* may have mutually reinforced each other. New uses were no more thinkable than a new custom. A use had to be honored because the user did not have the right, or the title, to change it, and the right that the user did have was grounded on the agreement to not change the use. *Usus* was an equally rich term in Roman law, where it was possible to hold the *usus* of property without having *dominium*, as in usufruct, which gave both use and fruits, or the servitude *usus*. The terms of *usus* were narrowly enforced: if property had been loaned for one use, the holder could not use it in some other way. If he did so believing that he was "acting contrary to the owner's will," then he had committed theft (*furtum usus*).[1] The overlap in the meanings of *usus* may have influenced legal perceptions about how flexible, or not, the *usus* of a donation could be.[2]

---

1. Digest 47.2.77(76)pr., trans. Alan Watson, *The Digest of Justinian*, vol. 4 (Philadelphia: University of Pennsylvania Press, 1985), 270; Alan Watson, "D.47.2.52.20: The Jackass, the Mares and 'Furtum,'" in *Studies in Roman Private Law* (London: Hambledon Press, 1991), 303–7.

2. The use was bound up in the nature of the gift, which explains why the pope's approval would be necessary to change the use of a gift, since jurists ac-

Cy-près and its power to vary the use has sometimes been traced back to Roman law from before the Christianization of the empire. Bequests and trusts for charitable purposes were rare; those for public purposes, although more common, did not have a settled jurisprudence.[3] In the Code of Justinian, under apparent Christian inspiration, gifts to charity were given some privileges over other legacies, a principle that left a lasting influence on the *ius commune*. For example, under certain circumstances, charitable estates could evade the rules on the Falcidian portion, that is, the quarter of the estate that was reserved to the heir. The local hospital could administer generic or uncertain gifts to the poor, and if there was no hospital, then the bishop could supervise the distribution and could make them certain by determining who would receive them. However, specific gifts to particular poor people or institutions were to be honored exactly, given to them only, and returned if they failed.[4] The presumption was that if the gift failed, it would be treated like any other failed bequest.[5] Suetonius informs us that at times even an attempt by an emperor to redirect a bequest given for a specific purpose could fail because of the inviolability of the legator's will, as happened when Tiberius tried unsuccessfully to redirect money left for a theater to road construction.[6]

In classical Roman culture, gifts predominantly functioned for social exchange, and the bulk of legal and literary evidence revolves

---

knowledged that he had the power to change "the substance, the quantity, or the nature of things" (substantiam, qualitatem, sive naturam): Goffredus da Trani, gloss to X 1.7.3, quoted in Pennington, *Pope and Bishops*, 29.

3. David Johnston, "Munificience and Municipia: Bequests to Towns in Classical Roman Law," *The Journal of Roman Studies* 75 (1985): 105–25; Giuseppe Grosso, *I legati nel diritto romano*, 2d ed. (Rome: Giappichelli, 1962); F. Messina Vitrano, "La convertiblità del modo eretto su legato o fedecommesso nel diritto romano classico e giustinianeo," *Studi Riccobono* 3 (1936): 97–110. Champlin points out that the Digest "includes fewer than twenty references to bequests to or for the community." Edward Champlin, *Final Judgments: Duty and Emotion in Roman Wills 200 B.C.–A.D. 250* (Berkeley: University of California Press, 1991), 156.

4. Code 1.3.48(49).

5. Digest 33.2.17, although in this case the testator had explicitly called for the return of the gift if the town did not perform the purpose for which the gift was given.

6. Suetonius, *Lives of the Caesars*, trans. J. C. Rolfe, vol. 1 (Cambridge, Mass.: Harvard University Press, 1914), 338–39.

around gifts made not for public benefit but to solidify relationships of friendship and patronage. A truly liberal man would give wisely and without apparently counting the cost—although he would also be sure always to repay or exceed the value of gifts he had received from others. If a gift was made for an explicit purpose but was converted by the recipient to a new use, this might be ingratitude, which legally could be used to force the return of a gift. For personal gifts such a question rarely emerged. Seneca did not even consider gifts for any specific purpose in *De beneficiis*, where the only problem with a wasted gift was that the giver was so miserly of spirit as to have noticed the waste.[7] For Seneca, the gift should be evaluated by the spirit in which it was given (*animus*), not by its size or its effect.[8]

There were principles and opinions in Roman law that would seem to have hindered a cy-près rule. For instance, the fisc, or state treasury, had a claim to gifts to the unworthy or other illegal or problematic dispositions.[9] Property held by an illicit *collegium* (many of which had religious or fraternal purposes) would be divided amongst the members when the *collegium* was dissolved—not given to a similar, licit *collegium* or turned to a new, similar, licit purpose.[10] The rights of the contributors were acknowledged, even though their venture was illegal. Jolowicz observes that the Ordinary Gloss assumes that members of a legal *collegium* could do the same if it failed.[11]

However, there was one opinion, by Modestinus, that allowed for an alteration within a trust (*fideicommissum*) in order that the memory of the testator be preserved.[12] This was the passage that would later be most frequently cited to assert the Roman origins of cy-près doctrine, and it did explicitly keep the gift from the heirs. What it did not necessarily do was allow a change of use (*usus*) rather than of kind (*genus*):

---

7. Seneca, *On Benefits*, I.6 in *Moral Essays*, vol. 3, trans. John W. Basore (Cambridge, Mass.: Harvard University Press, 1958), 521–25.
8. Ibid., 23: "Beneficium non in eo quod fit aut datur consistit sed in ipso dantis aut facientis animo."
9. Code 6.35, Digest 34.9.10, Digest 34.9.1, or Digest 34.9.9.1.
10. Digest 47.22.3pr.
11. Jolowicz, *Roman Foundations*, 138.
12. Digest 33.2.16.

A legacy was left to a town, so that from the revenues each year a spectacle should be celebrated in that town to keep alive the memory of the deceased, but it was not permitted to celebrate it there; I ask what you think about the legacy. He replied that since the testator wanted a spectacle to be celebrated in the town, but of such a kind as could not legally be celebrated there, it was unfair that the sum which the deceased had intended for the spectacle should fall to the profit of the heirs. Therefore the heirs and the chief men of the town should be summoned to discuss how the *fideicommissum* could be transformed (*in quam rem converti*) so that the testator's memory would be celebrated in some other legal way (*alio et licito genere celebretur*).[13]

In this opinion, the alteration to the gift might be read as a change within a use, *alio et licito genere*, "by means of another, licit kind," that is, from one kind of spectacle to another, with the use itself holding steady. It might be a different proposition to transfer gifts *in alios usus*, to another use, although the boundaries of use were not clearly demarcated.[14] An emperor could authorize the transition of one work to another, whereas a municipality could not, but these opinions avoided the concept of use entirely, focusing instead on *opus* (work). On the other hand, the Digest specified in another opinion that the transfer from the work of buildings to the work of repairs was permitted if the community did not need any new buildings and had no money to repair the ones that it had.[15] David Johnston, summariz-

13. Ibid.: "Legatum civitati relictum est, ut ex reditibus quotannis in ea civitate memoriae conservandae defuncti gratia spectaculum celebretur, quod illic celebrari non licet: quaero, quid de legato existimes. respondit, cum testator spectaculum edi voluerit in civitate, sed tale, quod ibi celebrari non licet, iniquum esse hanc quantitatem, quam in spectaculum defunctus destinaverit, lucro heredum cedere: igitur adhibitis heredibus et primoribus civitatis dispiciendum est, in quam rem converti debeat fideicommissum, ut memoria testatoris alio et licito genere celebretur." Trans. Watson.

14. Digest 50.8.1: "Quod ad certam speciem civitatis relinquitur, in alios usus convertere non licet." Some editions give instead "Quod ad certam speciem *civitati* relinquitur, in alios usus convertere non licet," which is a stronger statement in support of the maintenance of use. See also Digest 50.8.6(4): "Legatam municipio pecuniam in aliam rem quam defunctus voluit convertere citra principis auctoritatem non licet." The latter opinion does allow for a narrowing of purpose if necessary. Alternatively, Digest 50.8.7.1 warns "Nisi ad opus novum pecunia specialiter legata sit, vetera ex hac reficienda sunt." Some have suggested that "nova" is interpolated; others that the second opinion is universal and the first only a deviation from it. Johnston, "Munificence and *Municipia*," 123.

15. Digest 50.10.7pr.: "Pecuniam, quae in opera nova legata est, potius

ing the divergent opinions on the extent to which the terms of a gift might be modified, observes that there was a general move over time toward greater flexibility, which he terms "variation"; that the emperor had greater powers to authorize change than the municipality; and that necessity (especially after the introduction of the Falcidian fourth) was the most commonly accepted reason for these transitions.[16] Deviations, or modifications within a use, might be necessary if, for example, the funds left were insufficient to the purpose.

The Modestinus opinion did not indicate that all illegal or impossible gifts should be redeemed. It is tempting to consider illegal gifts as a subsection of impossible gifts more broadly, but this is not always a reliable heuristic. Conditional legacies with an initial impossibility were usually voided and given to the heir as long as the impossibility was not "impossible in the nature of things"; those that became impossible after the death of the testator were often given to the legatee without the condition attached. Many illegal or impossible conditions to a bequest were simply struck out in Roman law, treated as if they had not been written, which allowed the legacy to go forward unencumbered by the condition.[17] This was similar to the rule proposed by Scaevola, which Peter Stein has listed as one of the general rules of Roman law: that "those things which are written in a will in such a way that they cannot be understood are as if they were not written."[18] Perhaps Modestinus was suggesting the elimination only of the words that specified an illegal variant, leaving instead a general command for a spectacle, which would then be decided in consultation between

---

in tutelam eorum operum quae sunt convertendam, quam ad inchoandum opus erogandam divus pius rescripsit: scilicet si satis operum civitas habeat et non facile ad reficienda ea pecunia inveniatur."

16. Johnston, "Munificience and *Municipia*." On the rarity of Roman endowments and the difficulty of assessing the evidence of the practice of licit conversion of use in late antique practice, see Julia Hillner, "Families, Patronage, and the Titular Churches of Rome, c. 300–c. 600," in Kate Cooper and Julia Hillner, eds., *Religion, Dynasty, and Patronage in Early Christian Rome, 300–900* (Cambridge: Cambridge University Press, 2007), 225–61.

17. Digest 35.1.7.

18. Digest 50.17.73.3. Trans. Watson: "Quae in testamento ita sunt scripta, ut intellegi non possint, perinde sunt, ac si scripta non essent." Peter Stein, *Regulae Iuris: From Juristic Rules to Legal Maxims* (Edinburgh: Edinburgh University Press, 1966), 37–38.

the heirs and the city. The opinion did allow the interpreter to choose the meaning: it could be read as a shift from one spectacle to another, or from a spectacle to something else. Anything that preserved the memory of the testator appeared to honor the ultimate purpose of the gift. The city and heirs should discuss what alternative spectacle—or perhaps some other commemorative thing—would be a good choice. Moreover, anyone charged with a *fideicommissum* was required to have benefitted in some way from the will and so was either the heir or a legatee. These trustees, to use an anachronistic term, would sometimes become the beneficiary if the trust failed or was voided. Given that Gaius had observed that municipalities were *privatorum loco*, it is possible, although not certain, that Modestinus may have anticipated that the city could have a claim to be the default recipient to the gift, if the purpose failed, which would eliminate the rights of the heirs to recover the property. So the Modestinus opinion could be treated narrowly or expansively, and tracing the interpretation of Digest 33.2.16 allows us to follow the meaning it would have in other contexts. Until the fourteenth century it was not a particularly important opinion, as there was little need for a solution to a relatively limited problem of illegal bequests that could be transformed easily into legal bequests. The Ordinary Gloss on the passage reflected the lack of interest in it and merely clarified the meaning of three words (that *legatum* could mean *fundi,* that *reditibus* could mean *dicti legati,* and that *quotannis* signified *singulis annis*). A comment from Rogerius was added to the gloss to the effect that this stripping away of "illicit conditions or modes" was a privilege granted not simply to the state but to all. This meant that churches, other institutions, or private citizens could use the law to drop illegal conditions added to gifts.[19]

Vivianus Tuscus's *casus,* which put the opinion into contemporary terms for thirteenth-century Bologna, suggested that the equivalent would be for a spectacle that was "against the statutes of brother John."[20] The solution was that "another, licit spectacle" should be

---

19. "Nullo igitur privilegio utetur hic respublica, quoniam omnibus quibus illicitae conditiones aut modi apponuntur, hoc in commune conceditur, ut multis exemplis ostenditur."

20. "non licet propter statutum fratris Ioann."

decided upon by the heirs, the elites, and the merchants of the city.[21] The *casus*, then, anticipated commutation made with the advice (*cum consilio*) of the relevant parties in order to transform the gift within a single category of use (the public spectacle) from a spectacle that was illicit to one that was licit. But the potential was there to use the Modestinus opinion more aggressively in order to permit changes in use.

Still, Roman law, as noted above, usually regarded impossible or illegal conditions to a legacy as if they were not written (*pro non scripto*), which might preserve the gift for the legatee but eliminate the impossible part.[22] Thus a key difference between the *ius commune* treatment of legacies and trusts and the later English cases in charitable trusts is that the *ius commune* began from the general assumption that impossible conditions would be erased, leaving the gift behind. The legatee or trustee might still take.[23] Often, then, it would be those who held the trust who might be most tempted to argue that it was impossible to carry out, which is one reason why across medieval and early modern Europe we can find stipulations to replace the trustee, especially in cases of misemployment.[24] Nonetheless, *ius commune* jurists understood that the recipient had a strong claim to the property, even though some burden of performance might remain. Consequently, the *ius commune* could at times mitigate the erasure of the impossible condition somewhat rather than regarding a legacy with an impossible condition as an outright gift without expec-

21. "potestas Bononiae debet in alio licito spectaculo expendere eam in memoriam mei testatoris cum consilio heredum meorum, et ancianorum populi, et mercatorum."

22. This would tend to be the case with conditions both precedent and subsequent. Gaius, Institutes 3.98, describes the debate between Sabinians (who wanted the condition to be *pro non scripto*, that is, as if it were not written) and Proculians (who wanted the entire legacy to be void). Justinian upheld the Sabinian rule.

23. *Consilia Jo. Cal. et Gas. eius filii et Dominici de Sancto Geminiano* (Milan: Ulderic Scinzenzeler, 1497), consilium 343, 43r–v.

24. See, for example, the custumal of Godmanchester (1324), in which a misemployed perpetuity is maintained but entrusted to someone new, with the approval of the community: James Ambrose Raftis, *A Small Town in Late Medieval England: Godmanchester, 1278–1400* (Toronto: Pontifical Institute of Mediaeval Studies, 1982), 433–34.

tations. By contrast, seventeenth- and eighteenth-century English trust law would consider more strongly the rights of the heirs, since trustees had little claim. The two legal systems would be working from different starting points.

However, while Roman legacies or trusts with an impossible condition would tend to maintain the gift but void the condition, legacies *sub modo*—in which the money was given in order that something be done but which vested immediately, before the performance of the commanded act—were more difficult and not well supervised. Even though Justinian had declared that there was no difference between trusts and legacies, there was still a sense, even in Code 6.51, that burdens could remain.[25] Moreover, since *ius commune* practice was to regard the will (*voluntas*), not the words (*verba*), especially for pious gifts, strict distinctions about how a legacy for purposes was set up were unlikely to matter in its disposition, with the result that when a legacy for purposes had a problem, there was no easy resolution.[26] A noncompliant recipient could cause a legacy or trust to lapse, but pious trusts, such as to free a slave, would not lose their burden of performance, which would pass with the property to the new trustee. This was particularly difficult because when a lapse occurred (called *caducum*), the rules on who could receive the property, and with what burdens of performance attached, were in dispute.[27] In the third century, the emperor Caracalla had limited the recipients of lapses to children and parents who were the heirs of the testator; if there was no one that met those criteria, then Caracalla sent the lapsed property to the fisc.

Although Justinian revoked this limitation, it was certainly clear in the late Middle Ages that the fisc was a serious threat to failing trusts—

---

25. Accursius disagreed with Justinian: Glo. Ord. ad Digest 30.1. Accursius disagreed with Justinian: Glo. Ord. ad Digest 30.1.

26. Durantis, *Speculum iuris*, Book II, Part. II, *De instrumentorum edit*. § 13, 54: "In fideicommissis autem magis spectatur voluntas testatoris, quam verba: nec est vis in verbis." Institutes 2.20.2. On *verba* and *voluntas*, see Reinherd Zimmerman, *The Law of Obligations: Roman Foundations of the Civilian Tradition* (Oxford: Oxford University Press, 1996), 622–37.

27. Jacobus Buttigrarius, *Lectura supra codice* (Paris: n.p., 1516), Book Six, "De caducis tollendis," 34v.

most notably if the trust was given to or for the benefit of someone who was considered unworthy and the donor left no heirs.[28] After the dissolution of the Templars and in the midst of ongoing struggles between princes and popes that were soon to be joined by the problem of the Great Schism and the placing of assorted regimes under interdicts that forbade the sacraments, unworthiness was not an insignificant issue. A prince's treasury should not benefit from the fact that the prince was persecuting pious causes and causing their trusts to lapse, nor, given that interdicts were intended to punish collective guilt, should a sanctioned community be able to collect lapsed trusts into its coffers just because the interdict had frustrated the purposes of these trusts.[29] An alternative solution to a frustrated or impossible bequest for purposes, rather than returning it to an heir or allowing it to escheat to the fisc, might be to allow the property to become the personal property of the trustee, likely a priest, prelate, or a procurator, which was not a desirable outcome either, especially not in the midst of disputes over the wealth of the church.[30] Moreover, almost none of the impossible situations that concerned fourteenth-century jurists were impossible in the way that Roman law had primarily thought about impossibility—that is, impossible in the nature of things. Quite the opposite: it should never be impossible to give a pious gift, for such a gift partakes of natural law. When circumstances impeded pious gifts, as they would do with some frequency in the fourteenth century, then new compromises would have to be sought. After all, donors were increasingly specific during a period when social dislocations made exact fulfillment more difficult.[31]

---

28. For example, Code 6.35.

29. Peter D. Clarke, *The Interdict in the Thirteenth Century: A Question of Collective Guilt* (Oxford: Oxford University Press, 2007).

30. Late medieval jurists generally supported the fisc, but not by any means. John F. McGovern, "The Rise of New Economic Attitudes in Canon and Civil Law, A.D. 1200–1550," *Jurist* 32 (1972): 49–50.

31. Samuel K. Cohn Jr., *The Cult of Remembrance and the Black Death: Six Renaissance Cities in Central Italy* (Baltimore: Johns Hopkins University Press, 1992). On English legal transformation as a consequence of Black Death, see Robert C. Palmer, *English Law in the Age of the Black Death, 1348–1381* (Chapel Hill: University of North Carolina Press, 1993).

Bartolus and New Uses

The debate over Franciscan poverty and property in the early fourteenth century was only one of several events that complicated the fulfillment of pious legacies, but it in particular focused attention on the meanings of *usus* and the treatment of gifts. Those like John XXII, who, in Jonathan Robinson's elegant distillation, insisted that it was not legitimate to use property without having some legal right to the property, would help to prepare the way for unilateral authority over gifts, despite the fact that John XXII's immediate goal was to reject papal *dominium* over Franciscan property. In making his argument, John XXII tended to minimize emphasis on the community of goods in the natural state in favor of concrete and discrete property rights. Similarly, he generally described gift-giving as a straightforward process that conveyed simple rights, rather than a multi-faceted and enduring relationship with many rights. On the other side, the supporters of the Spiritual Franciscans, most famously William of Ockham, who wished to be able to use property without having legal rights to it, would inadvertently help to whittle away at the rights of trustees or beneficiaries in charitable donations by insisting on their own lack of rights and the revocability of their license to use and consume.[32] Both sides, then, were moving toward a narrowed understanding of how gifts functioned in society.[33]

---

32. See Jonathan Robinson, *William of Ockham's Early Theory of Property Rights in Context* (Leiden: Brill, 2013).

33. This took place against the background of a renewed focus on the will, on which see Bonnie Kent, *Virtues of the Will: The Transformation of Ethics in the Late Thirteenth Century* (Washington, D.C.: The Catholic University of America Press, 1995). Ockham, in his work both before and after the controversy, would prefigure changes that would make cy-près possible, from his account of virtue grounded in a human will whose operations were highly interior, individual, free, not teleological nor necessarily directed toward the ultimate good but tending at times toward a variety of potential intermediate ends, and guided in part by an understanding that was liable to err (especially in a world of particular objects rather than universals). Given Ockham's stance in his early work, it is not surprising that in his later work he would emphasize the role of learned judges to correct human failings, with property law vested under human control such that appropriations should be conducted by secular power. Ockham's emphasis that merit lies in intentions, not acts, would seem to be hostile to the focus of cy-près

Meanwhile, those who sought to preserve pious gifts in the midst of the political, social, and religious tumults of the age would find that commutation and alteration were not always enough. Bartolus and other jurists of the fourteenth century ultimately responded to the times by advocating for use to be allowed to change, although ideally with the consent of interested parties. Bartolus thus retained consensus as the safeguard against unilateral expropriation. There were probably two reasons for this. First, most of the legal issues around the Franciscan debate centered on kinds of use, so if it became possible to change use in order to preserve the bequest better, then many legal difficulties would thereby be eliminated. Second, it was not possible to accommodate everything else that Bartolus wished to honor (particularly the rights of all interested parties to a difficult gift) unless use was allowed to change. By preserving the consent of the heirs and all interested parties, the modification of impossible gifts could be done without injury, as had already happened in practice. Oldradus de Ponte, Bartolus's teacher, had emphasized that even the rights of the bishop to make a gift certain were constrained by the fact that no one should suffer an injury through the narrowing or lose rights as a consequence.[34] Bartolus would hold this principle of not doing injury to be a more important norm than either the preservation or the approximation of donor intent.

And so Bartolus read the Modestinus opinion to permit the alteration of use for legacies left for impossible purposes, whether impossible in fact or law. This reading is not immediately clear in his summary of the law: "Something left for an illicit work ought to be converted to a licit work with the consent of the relevant parties: but

---

on the rehabilitation of failing actions, but his contention cuts both ways, since it also limits the apparent offense of judicial acts to correct illegal or impossible gifts as long as the legal intention was good. On Ockham's political philosophy, see Arthur Stephen McGrade, *The Political Thought of William of Ockham: Personal and Institutional Principals* (Cambridge: Cambridge University Press, 1974).

34. Oldradus de Ponte, *Consilia, seu responsa, et quaestiones aureae* (Venice: Franciscus Zilettus, 1571), consilium 61, 22. He also insisted that if a gift was made certain by the bishop but turned out to be useless, then the bishop could make it certain to a new end, but only if no one who had benefited as a consequence of the first disposition would be harmed.

not if the gift is for a licit work."[35] But Bartolus did not specify how close the work (*opus*) had to be to the original work, and he permitted the interested parties to remake the failed gift, *in alium opus, in alium usum,* or *in alium usum pium*. Where Vivianus Tuscus had suggested that the advice of the heirs was necessary to commute the kind of spectacle, Bartolus demanded instead their consent (*de consensu partium*) because he allowed for the more significant change, conversion of use.[36] If the parties could not reach consensus on how to change the gifts with the help of the bishop, then a judge as *medius* would find the equitable solution.

Not all impossible situations demanded conversion, however. Bartolus allowed that a monastery that could not be built in its intended location could be moved to a new location, with the consultation of the heirs.[37] Legacies that had an initial impossibility had to be considered very carefully, since the claim to simple return of the gift was strongest in that situation. An impossible condition that was assigned to a "licit and honest purpose" (*finem licitum et honestum*) should not defeat the purpose.[38] So if money was left for masses that were forbidden or for a monastery that was not allowed, then they could be converted, with consent, to a new use. What this use

---

35. "Relictum ad opus illicitum debet converti ad opus licitum de consensu partium: secus si ad opus licitum fuerit relictum." Bartolus de Saxoferrato, *In secundam Infor. partem commentaria* in *Opera omnia* (Turin: Nicolai Bevilaquae, 1577), 71. Denis Godefroy used this quote to summarize the entire Modestinus opinion in his edition of the *Corpus iuris civilis*. In England, *opus* may have resonated with *usus*: Maitland, "The Origin of Uses," *Harvard Law Review* 8 (1894): 127–37.

36. On consent as a broader principle in the *ius commune*, see Arthur P. Monahan, *Consent, Coercion, and Limit: The Medieval Origins of Parliamentary Democracy* (Kingston, Canada: McGill-Queen's University Press, 1987); Francis Oakley, *Natural Law, Conciliarism and Consent in the Late Middle Ages: Studies in Ecclesiastical and Intellectual History* (London: Variorum, 1984); Joseph Canning, "Law, Sovereignty and Corporation Theory, 1300–1450," in *The Cambridge History of Medieval Political Thought, c. 350–1450*, ed. by J. H. Burns (Cambridge: Cambridge University Press, 1988), 470; Brian Tierney, "Hierarchy, Consent, and the 'Western Tradition,'" *Political Theory* 15 (1987): 646–52.

37. Bartolus de Saxoferrato, *Opera omnia*, vol. 10 (Venice: Iuntas, 1602), f. 65, consilium 57; vol. 4 (Venice: Iuntas, 1596), f. 66v, on Digest 33.2.16. Still, Bartolus required that if the monastery could not be immediately built, an alternate house ought to be used in the interim in order to honor the donation.

38. Bartolus de Saxoferrato, *Opera omnia*, vol. 3 (Venice: Iuntas, 1596), f. 136.

might be was left open, not approximated. Insufficiency of the gift to the assigned purpose also opened the possibility for a new use, with consent.

If conditions were attached to the gift that were partly possible and partly impossible, then only the possible part should be upheld. Conditions that were impossible in fact, which included conditions that were *maior difficultas,* eliminated the legacy; later jurists would reject this interpretation.[39] Where money for masses was given to an order of preachers who were forbidden in that city, Bartolus recommended that the masses be held in another place. This does not seem entirely consistent with his interpretation of the Modestinus opinion, but the situations were not perfectly identical. In the first case, a gift was left to the city so that something illegal could be done in order to honor the testator's memory; the city and the heirs could then agree on a new way to serve the same purpose. In the second case, the gift was left to an order of preachers to say mass in a city that had forbidden them to do it; they could honor the gift elsewhere, maintaining the given purpose. The city itself had effectively declined the legacy, so its consent would not be necessary to move the gift.

On the other hand, some forms of difficulty could not be overcome. If a testator instituted an heir with the requirement that the heir build a church in his house, and the bishop refused to license this, then the heir was still instituted and did not need to make up the pious intention in some other fashion. Like Bracton, who followed Roman practice, Bartolus found that third-party impossibility could erase a burden. Similarly, if the testator asked the heirs to build a hospital and the bishop refused, then the heirs should not be penalized. If another bishop would allow it in a different location, then the heirs should do it there, or it might also be possible to fulfill the condition in another mode, or perhaps to use an empty house to receive poor men while building a hospital. On the other hand, if goods were given to build a home for minor friars, and it could not be done either in law or in fact, then "that clause is to be considered as not having been."[40] This end could be considered an honest one,

39. Ibid., § 7, f. 136.
40. Ibid., f. 19v.

to a pious but impossible cause, but the heirs were not required in this case to fulfill the condition in another way. The examples are not entirely clear about when a burden disappears and when it does not, but Bartolus is consistent that justice might be best served in some of these instances by allowing use to be converted with consent.

Digest 50.8.1 forbade a city to convert property given for one particular purpose to another purpose. Bartolus left this passage almost untouched in his commentary but looked at the elaboration of what he termed "Lex V" within the title, today Digest 50.8.6(4), in which the emperor (for Bartolus, the Princeps, a term with a wide range of meaning) could authorize a change in use of money left to a city for a purpose in the case of insufficiency due to the Falcidian fourth. In the original text, if the gift was for one building and there was not enough money, the emperor could authorize a change to whatever the city thought would be most necessary to it. If the gift was for multiple buildings, then it could be reduced to one. But Bartolus offered a different read. He argued, if the purpose was licit and the money was sufficient, only the Princeps could change the use of a gift to a city; if the money was insufficient, then the authority of the Princeps was not necessary. The original text spoke of things and works; Bartolus instead wrote about use. He was extending the ability to convert from use to use, and in cases of insufficiency he was limiting the external approval that it would be necessary to obtain for the conversion, particularly given that Bartolus allowed the city to stand in as the prince (*civitas sibi princeps*).[41] The original text had minimized the change, offering a deviation from many buildings to one, except in the case in which the gift was for only one building and so no part of the original gift could be maintained. Bartolus widened the scope of the law, making no restrictions on the new uses that would be found, as long as there was the consent of the interested parties.

Bartolus was willing to embrace the power of the commune to make new laws, in part because of his understanding, encapsulated here in a failed gift, of the power of consent to make new settle-

---

41. Bartolus de Saxoferrato, *In primam Digesti novi partem* (Lyon: Compagnie des libraires, 1581), 225v.

ments from below.[42] The Modestinus passage was particularly useful to this perspective because it, unlike some other opinions from the *Corpus iuris civilis*, did not require the permission of the emperor to change the gift but allowed the town to settle it amongst themselves. But Bartolus must also have remembered that his teacher Cinus da Pistoia had regarded the local law with distrust because it was particularly prone to tyranny.[43] Learned laws could legitimately give way to custom, but the *ius proprium* should not be permitted to thwart pious gifts, which fell under the jurisdiction of canon law and partook of the highest justice for their participation in restoring property to its natural, communal origins.[44] Moreover, as Ambrose had claimed, everyone had a duty to perform acts of mercy—a saying that had entered into *ius commune* jurisprudence.[45] The *ius commune* allowed for and protected private property, which began in natural law but soon moved into the domain of private law, but efforts to return property to the highest natural state—that of being held in common, or for the common good—needed protection, lest they become easy prey for the unscrupulous.[46] No legal or factual barriers should be al-

42. Manlio Bellomo, *The Common Legal Past of Europe: 1000–1800* (Washington, D.C.: The Catholic University of America Press, 1995), 190–95; Joseph Canning, *The Political Thought of Baldus de Ubaldis* (Cambridge: Cambridge University Press, 1987), 100–113; Magnus Ryan, "Bartolus of Sassoferrato and Free Cities," *Transactions of the Royal Historical Society* 10 (2000): 65–89; Floriano Jonas Cesar, "Popular Autonomy and Imperial Power in Bartolus of Saxoferrato: An Intrinsic Connection," *Journal of the History of Ideas* 65 (2004): 369–81; Cecil Nathan Sidney Woolf, *Bartolus of Sassoferrato: His Position in the History of Medieval Political Thought* (Cambridge: Cambridge University Press, 1913). On the development of the right to expropriate at will, see J. P. Canning, "Italian Juristic Thought and the Realities of Power in the Fourteenth Century," in *Political Thought and the Realities of Power in the Middle Ages*, ed. Joseph Canning and Otto Gerhard Oexle (Göttingen: Vandenhoeck and Ruprecht, 1998), 229–39.

43. James Q. Whitman, "The Lawyers Discover the Fall of Rome," *Law and History Review* 9 (1991): 191–220; Bellomo, *Common Legal Past*, 189; J. P. Canning, "Law, Sovereignty and Corporation Theory," 469–73.

44. See Bartolus's commentary on Code 1.2.1.

45. Durantis, *Speculum iuris*, Book II, Part. II, § 13, 70: "misericordia enim est communis usus" (mercy is indeed a common practice). Ambrose used the phrase in his *Expositio evangelii secundum Lucam*, Book Two, § 77, PL, vol. 15, col. 1580C. Gratian's Decretum incorporated the phrase: D.86 c.19.

46. D.1. c.7, including the more conflicted gloss, which denies that divine law gives private ownership, since "nothing belongs to a person by divine law."

lowed to prevent this transfer back into the commons. After all, most of the ways in which pious gifts could be thwarted were the result of human sin: wars, interdicts, and struggles between and around religious orders. The civil law should not allow this sin to triumph over gifts for the common good, nor should these situations be permitted to obstruct the ability of the donor to give in accordance with natural law. If a city was placed under interdict, why should a legacy for masses made by an innocent testator no longer benefit the commons in any way?

Bartolus aspired toward justice but was well aware of reality: his treatise *De tyranno* emphasized the contemporary increase in tyrants and tyrannical servitude, including a new kind of hidden tyrant, who masked his illegitimacy. All tyrants sought to divide and impoverish their people.[47] It should not be legally possible for a king like Philip IV to outlaw the recipients of trusts for pious causes and then take the property, claiming that the goods were now *caduca* and eligible for the fisc, nor should pure gifts for the use of the friars be destroyed or disputed during controversies over poverty. Bartolus, a well-known friend to the Franciscans, began his treatise on the legal issues surrounding donations to the Franciscans by acknowledging that it was difficult to reconcile the Franciscan way of life with the body of civil law (*corpore iuris civilis*), with the consequence that "many doubts arise" (*multa dubia oriuntur*).[48] He had little sympathy for heirs who clogged the courts to contest pious legacies on dubious grounds even though the living themselves almost never regretted their donations to the friars.[49] If the Franciscans, and other pious recipients, had better legal protections for gifts "to the poor of Christ," then they would not be torn between the need to protect pious do-

---

Gratian, *The Treatise on the Laws (Decretum DD. 1–20)*, trans. Augustine Thompson and James Gordley (Washington, D.C.: The Catholic University of America Press, 1993), 6.

47. Bartolus of Saxoferrato, in *Politica e diritto nel Trecento italiano. Il 'De tyranno' di Bartolo da Sassoferrato (1314–1357) con l'edizione critica dei trattati 'De guelphis et gebellinis,' De regimine civitatis' e 'De tyranno,'* ed. Diego Quaglioni (Florence: Leo S. Olschiki, 1983), 175–213.

48. *Liber minoricarum decisionum*, in *Opera omnia*, vol. 10 (Venice: Iuntas, 1590), Book I, Dist. I, Cap. 1, 106vb.

49. Ibid., Prooemium, 106vb.

nations and the strict observance of their rule, which forbade disputing and seeking the return of goods.

Despite this partiality, in his treatise on the Franciscans Bartolus upheld the rights of everyone, donors, heirs, and Franciscans alike. If a testator made the Franciscans into his heirs, for which they lacked capacity, then the will would be broken and treated as if the testator were intestate.[50] Whether or not the subsequent heirs then had any residual obligations to the Franciscans in the forum of conscience Bartolus considered at length, but there was no legal obligation left, and no requirement to satisfy a pious gift in another way. The same would hold for annuities, which would violate their rule and so were void. Similarly, if the testator instituted an heir to give the estate to the Franciscans in trust, which *Exiit qui seminat* had forbidden, then Bartolus thought the heir should give to the Franciscans a moderate portion of the estate (*quantitate moderata*), which they were allowed to receive. He did not then indicate that there was any remaining legal or moral obligation on the heir to give away the rest to other, licit pious causes.[51]

A pious cause was resilient: if the friars were made heirs so that they would distribute the property to pious causes, and the friars could not take because they lacked capacity, then while their institution as heirs would be treated *pro non scripto,* the cause would remain, and the whole city would have an interest in its performance.[52] The burden to perform would pass with the property. Bartolus also offered the distinction that if property was left to the friars in a mode that they could not take, the mode could be changed (*transmutari*), which was in accordance with *Exiit qui seminat*.[53] Alternatively, if money was left to the friars to build a house—for which they needed a license from the pope—where they might celebrate mass, Bartolus counted this as impossible by law (*impossibile de iure*). In this situation, Bartolus argued, it should be "transferred to another cause" (*in aliam causam transferatur*) in order to serve "the memory and health of

---

50. Ibid., Book I, Dist. I, Cap. 1, 106vb.
51. Ibid., Book I, Dist. II, Cap. 2, 107rb.
52. Ibid., Book I, Dist. V, Cap. 1, 108rb.
53. Ibid., Book II, Dist. II, Cap. 1, 109rb, citing Digest 33.2.16.

the soul of the deceased" (*ut memoria et salus animae defuncti servetur*).[54] The "consent of both parties" (*consensu utriusque partis*) was necessary for this transfer, meaning the heirs and the custodian or procurator for the friars, but Bartolus deliberated on whether the permission of the prince or pope was also necessary for this transition. The friars were unusual because they were mendicants, and so it would seem that a change in location could be made more easily than with other gifts to pious causes in which the city would be an interested party, as they were for gifts to their poor.[55] Here again Bartolus was far more interested in protecting the rights of those to whom property was left than in safeguarding the intent of the donor. The one guideline for these cases that Bartolus offered was entirely different from cy-près: "For the judge should favor more the will of him to whom the legacy was left rather than the will of he who left it."[56]

Bartolus also brought up the possibility of moving from one pious use to another in discussing whether pious *fideicommissa* could become *caduca*.[57] He was not the first to suggest that they could not, because they could be transferred from one trustee to another, but he suggested that they could be remedied by changing use as well. He drew this point from D32.38.5, which is telling but not apt, because the opinion regards a complicated case in which freedmen were determined to have followed the will (*voluntatem*) of the testator to provide them with joint shares in property. Shares of the land were to have fallen to the city if the freedmen violated the terms of the trust to keep the property out of the hands of strangers, which some of them seemed to have done by appointing strangers as heirs.[58]

---

54. Ibid., Book II, Dist. II, Cap. 2, 109rb.

55. Ibid., Book I, Dist. V, Cap. 3, 109va and Book II, Dist. IV, Cap. 2, 110ra.

56. Ibid., Book II, Dist. II, Cap. 3, 109va: "Quia iudex magis favebit voluntati eius, cui relinquitur, quam eius a quo relictum est."

57. Bartolus de Saxoferrato, *Commentaria in secundum Infortiati* (Lyon: Mathias Bonhomme, 1557), f. 64.

58. The case may have responded to the problem of how many transactions the testatrix could control or whether she could determine the choice of heir or place conditions on heirs that were not her own with the threat to remove the property if the heirs did not comply. The first transaction applied to the property (selling shares from one freedman to another) complied with her stipulations, which may have ended the duty of the freedmen.

The case specifically regarded, then, the keeping of property out of the hands of the town, and its fisc, but preserving it for its original purpose. Bartolus did not cite other authorities for this possibility that one pious use could be substituted for another, beyond Roman law and the right given to bishops in the *Liber extra* to intervene on behalf of pious causes when heirs were delaying their implementation ("Nos quidem").[59] He was probably referring to the gloss on the text, in which it was debated what should be done if the place in which the monastery to be built was uncertain, whether there was no obligation, whether it would become *caducum,* or whether it should be built in the place where the testament was written. The solution presented in the gloss, or at least the last and seemingly final option, was not to let it become *caducum,* because wills should be interpreted *largissime.* From this Bartolus extracted a much larger rule indeed, and in subsequent quotations, some jurists after Bartolus ignored the context of his comment and turned it into an even more potent ideal, citing him as the originator of a norm of pious continuity against the threat of all potential lapses.

But as Bartolus conceived of this, it was for the purest gifts, to which very few (if any, given that they were threatened with falling into *caduca*) individuals had a claim. These were gifts that had been directed toward a cause, sent toward an abstraction. Although this distinction would not always hold in future discussions of gifts *ad pias causas,* Bartolus was conceiving of them as sent to a cause itself, not a donation to a specific person or institution, no matter how pious or religious it might be. The question was: who had a claim to failing gifts sent to an abstract good cause? The answer was: everyone and no one. Bartolus was suggesting that for these gifts, the claim of the common good was stronger than that of the fisc or that of the heirs. There were already calls to shift property from one purpose to another; Bartolus was countering by proposing a line within which pious gifts had to be kept. This seems to have drawn on the difficulty, obvious within the civil law tradition, of eliminating a burden attached to property. Still, Bartolus clarified that even a

59. X 3.26.3.

gift that listed the recipient and then the cause could fail if the recipient failed. For example, a gift to a particular poor maiden so she could get married would appear to give evidence of the donor's intention, but no alternate poor maiden would be sought out if the specific maiden could not receive the legacy. A gift that was listed as given to a cause and then to a recipient fell into a doubtful category, Bartolus wrote, which should probably be weighed in favor of the cause because of the privileges of religion. Bartolus gave specific, contextual examples to support deviations or changes of use for instances of impossibility or illegality, but he did not supply any examples to support his point that gifts for pious causes, if given to the cause alone, ought to be given to new pious causes rather than falling *caduca*. Indeed, ordinary examples of an impossible gift to a pious cause alone are difficult to imagine. In the pre-modern world, pious causes seemed inexhaustibly able to receive.

Bartolus did not discuss the consent of the heirs in relationship to Digest 32.38.5, but he did lay out the distinction between gifts to people and gifts to causes that d'Ancarano would follow later, word for word. Bartolus argued that a gift to a *collegium* could fail if it was given with "a greater contemplation of the person than the cause."[60] This meant that if it was given to the college alone or primarily to the college and only secondarily to the cause, then it could fail without assigning the property to a new, similar *collegium*; modern cy-près, by contrast, has often been used precisely in cases in which the failing gift was to the institution alone. Bartolus seems to have appreciated that these cases were difficult, but because his interest was first and foremost to honor all of the interests of the parties and not to reap the greatest possible benefit for the soul of the testator, his decision makes sense. Although his comments on the matter are linked to Digest 32.38.5, he may have had in mind Digest 32.38.6 as well, which followed immediately:

A testator charged a *fideicommissum* on a man to whom he had bequeathed two thousand in these words: "I ask you, Petronius, to restore (*reddas*) these two thousand solidi to the priestly *collegium* of a certain temple."

60. Bartolus, *Commentaria in secundum Infortiati*, f. 64: "magis contemplatione personae, quam causae."

The question was whether, since this *collegium* had subsequently been dissolved, the legacy should belong to Petronius or remain with the heir. He replied that Petronius could rightly claim it, as it had not in any case been in his power to obey the wish of the deceased.[61]

This gift was pious, but it appeared to pertain only to the particular *collegium*, and so it was given, without any burden attached, to the one who had been burdened with the task of completing it. The substitution of a trustee, or *gravatus*, to complete a trust was common and vital, but a trust to benefit a specific person or institution would not need to be transferred to another one, no matter how pious that institution was.

After Bartolus

Canonists came to embrace Bartolus's reasoning and expanded it somewhat, but in the jurisprudence that subsequently developed on impossible pious bequests there are a range of factors and no straightforward rules.[62] Both conciliar and humanist ideals can be found in many of the opinions, which is not surprising. Bartolus has been considered a proto-humanist, and Bartolus's students were recruited to teach law in Florence. As Myron Gilmore reminds us, jurists were essential to the formation of the early Renaissance; many humanists used and appreciated Bartolus despite their criticisms of his style and method.[63] Cosimo de' Medici included *ius commune* texts in his library.[64] Bartolus's efforts to protect the common

61. Trans. Watson: "Fidei commisit eius, cui duo milia legavit, in haec verba: 'a te, petroni, peto, uti ea duo milia solidorum reddas collegio cuiusdam templi.' quaesitum est, cum id collegium postea dissolutum sit, utrum legatum ad petronium pertineat an vero apud heredem remanere debeat. respondit petronium iure petere, utique si per eum non stetit parere defuncti voluntati."

62. On the twelfth- and thirteenth-century background to the question of how independent the bishops could be, see Kenneth Pennington, *Pope and Bishops: The Papal Monarchy in the Twelfth and Thirteenth Centuries* (Philadelphia: University of Pennsylvania Press, 1984).

63. Myron Gilmore, *Humanists and Jurists: Six Studies in the Renaissance* (Cambridge, Mass.: Harvard University Press, 1963).

64. Hans Baron considered that "the great Guelph jurisprudence of the fourteenth century," by which he meant predominantly the jurisprudence of Baldus and Bartolus, upheld "many of the politico-social ideas entertained by the

138   Use in the *Ius Commune*

good and allow some shifts in use would naturally appeal to the humanist impulse. Pietro d'Ancarano drew heavily on Bartolus in commenting on *Quia contingit*, for example.[65]

It might seem that if jurists discussed how impossible gifts could be commuted or converted, then this must have meant this was the normal practice; that is, that when consensus failed, a judge would automatically choose conversion because Bartolus had suggested it as a possibility. But the fact that it could be done did not mean that it should or needed to be done. The discussions within the *ius commune*, even the consilia that they offered, did not necessitate particular legal outcomes. To take two familiar examples, the *ius commune* could discuss when torture could be employed without actually favoring its employment, and it could consider what pleases the prince without suggesting that the prince could do anything he wanted.[66]

Federicus Petruccius de Senis, a contemporary of Bartolus and teacher of Baldus, offered an answer to a question on the case of a donation made just before *Exivi de paradiso* was issued. The gift was left to an existing monastery to build a church for twelve Franciscans. Given that this could not be done by law or fact, the question was whether the gift should be revoked without a burden or left as a free gift to the monastery itself, as if the condition attached to the donation had not been added. The key issue seems to have been that the gift was not impossible when it was made, but it only suffered from a supervening impossibility, which would tend to make the gift pass to the recipient without the condition. Federicus first considered a commutation of place, which did not seem to be a possible solution, given the legal issues facing the Franciscan order as a whole, although he clearly considered having a chapel built elsewhere to be a preferable solution. Then Federicus raised conversion to another licit use,

---

citizens ... long before humanism adopted them." "Franciscan Poverty and Civic Wealth as Factors in the Rise of Humanistic Thought," *Speculum* 13 (1938): 17.

65. Pietro d'Ancarano, *Super Clementinis facundissima commentaria* (Bologna: Societatis Typographiae Bononiae, 1580), *De religiosis domibus*, "Quia contingit," § 4, 204: "usum rei non alterandum: sed utendum, ad quem destinata est."

66. Kenneth Pennington, "Torture and Fear: Enemies of Justice," *Rivista internazionale di diritto comune* 19 (2008): 203–42; Brian Tierney, "'The Prince Is Not Bound by Law': Accursius and the Origins of the Modern State," *Comparative Studies in Society and History* 5 (1963): 378–400; Pennington, *The Prince and the Law*.

marking the "words and mind of the donor" (*verbis et mente donatoris*) as well as the possibility of converting it "to any similar and proximate use to that designated by the donor" (*ad aliquem usum similem et propinquum usui designato a donatore*). Federicus left it open whether the monastery could find that use itself; his concern was that the monastery seemed to have a right to the gift free and clear and that at least the divine office and masses that the donor had wanted should be celebrated.[67] But he offered no norm and no definitive rule. Bartolus's take on the reconciliation of interests would prove to be more immediately influential, but Federicus's analysis points to a general rule that would develop later: the more focused the jurist was on the testator alone in relationship to the failing gift, the more that approximation of intent was likely to appear as a consideration. In this case, the heirs do not feature at all in the response, not even to give advice or consent to the changes. It is unclear whether there were particular circumstances to the situation that left them entirely out of the discussion, such as the entire estate being left to pious causes, or whether Federicus was drawing a strict line on the basis of the supervening impossibility. Either way, his response bears the closest resemblance to cy-près in the jurisprudence of his time.

However, Federicus's response was also an outlier, not widely cited, and Bartolus's interpretation would have far more influence. For example, Petrus de Ubaldis cautiously followed Bartolus. Petrus de Ubaldis did allow that the health of the soul of the testator should be considered in interpreting the will.[68] Use was protected: "That which has been left to a certain use, ought not to be converted to another use, nor another cause, from which the use can be implemented."[69] Petrus de Ubaldis also emphasized, in writing about legacies, that no one's rights should be abridged without consent.[70] He was

---

67. Federicus Petruccius de Senis, *Consilia, sive mavis responsa, questiones, et placita* (Venice: Antonius Betranus, 1576), questio 175, 84.

68. Petrus de Ubaldus, *Tractatus super canonia episcopali, et parochiali* in *Tractatus universi iuris*, Tome XV, Pars II (Venice: Francesco Zilletti, 1584), Chapter 7, § 56: "interpretatio debet fieri pro salute animae legantis."

69. Ibid., § 33: "Item quae relinquuntur ad certum usum, non debent nec possunt converti ad alium usum, vel ad aliam causam, ex quo potest impleri usus."

70. Ibid., § 33: "Item omnium illorum consensus requiritur de quorum iure detrahitur."

frequently cited by others on the rights of heirs to consent to changes in gifts, but he also argued, as had Bartolus, that the beneficiaries ought to consent as well, which was not always possible. This was one of the reasons why money left to feed the poor should not be turned over for construction or some other useful purpose, because the poor could not consent to the transition.

Thus for Petrus de Ubaldis, something that was possible by law and by fact could not have its use changed, unless by the pope. If the impossibility was because of fact—for a monastery to be built in an area with massive wars (*guerras ingentes*) or because the money was insufficient to the stated use—then it could be converted to a new use.[71] Petrus gave no indication of what this use might be. Other jurists would suggest that a monastery that could not be built in one location should be built in a different location instead. Petrus de Ubaldis did not; the reason might be because the gift could be used in that same area, which had an interest in the gift, in some other way. If the money was given to the city and was insufficient, then the city could choose the new use with the consent of the heirs.[72] On the other hand, if the testator left the money to a church for a chapel, but it already had as many chapels as it needed, then Petrus de Ubaldis suggested the chapel could be constructed in another place.[73] Petrus de Ubaldis did allow that money for a pilgrimage might be used *ad similem locum* if the original destination was impossible, although money to succor the Holy Land ought to be kept and await the possibility of its use there.[74]

If the gift was impossible by law, and it did not have an honest end (*nullum finem honestum*), then it was entirely void. An honest use that was illegal, however, should be converted to another honest use. Petrus de Ubaldis gave two familiar examples: a forbidden house for mendicants or money for masses in a place that was excommunicated. The question was, Petrus de Ubaldis added, who was required to consent to the change. He noted that there were many opinions on this: he suggested that the church to which the money

71. Ibid., § 35.
72. Ibid., § 38.
73. Ibid., § 36.
74. Ibid., § 36.

was left (or, in the case of money left to the city, then the city) and the heirs should both give consent. If they could not find consensus, then the bishop alone could decide whether to change the use or the location—although in the case of a change of use, the bishop would presumably need the consent of the pope as well.[75] Still, Petrus de Ubaldis pointed out that the bishop could not infringe on the patronage rights of the heirs.[76] If the testator included a clause that forbade the legacy to be moved to another place or put to another use, then it would revert to the heirs.[77] On the other hand, the intentions of the testator were not necessarily paramount: if the gift had been left for a purpose that was possible in both fact and law, but the heirs were simply negligent in doing it, then the bishop could apply it to another use, Petrus de Ubaldis suggested, adding that this was useful to know—a threat to encourage the parties to find a resolution.[78]

Bartolus's student Baldus de Ubaldis also treated problematic legacies in consilia, although he did so in a way that implies he had not gathered a concrete rule on transferring pious causes to a new use from his teacher. If a legacy was left to a city that destroyed its intended object, then the city had no claim to it. If the gift had been to the church, on the other hand, a change could be made only *de plenitudine potestatis* of the highest authority.[79] In another consilium Baldus considered whether canonical portions could be taken from various legacies to pious causes and pious gifts, and he ended by observing that gifts to pious uses could not be converted to another use.[80]

In the early fifteenth century, Panormitanus offered a consilium on the case of a woman who had left her house to her heirs to live in

75. Ibid., § 39.
76. Ibid., §§ 39–40.
77. Ibid., §§ 41–42.
78. Ibid., § 43: "de uno usu ad alium."
79. Baldus de Ubaldis, *Consiliorum, sive responsorum*, vol. 4 (Venice: Hieronymus Polus, 1575), consilium 178, 60.
80. This consilium was subsequently read to mean that gifts to free captives could not be changed to another use, but the passage implies that Baldus was discussing the general principle of not changing uses, along with other protections to pious uses. See, for example, vol. 5, consilium 131, 34: "secus esset in eo, quod relinqueret ad redemptionem captivorum: quia hoc est simile, quod legatur locis ad pios usus et qui non possunt converti in alios usus, de quibus episcopus non debet habere quartam, nec sacerdos parochialis."

with the condition that they sell it to designated buyers and then use 100 florins for projected new restorations to a specific local church, and, failing that, for repairs to the same church.[81] After many years had gone by, the church complained that it had not been given the money and that it wanted to use the legacy for the fabric of the church (which would not necessarily be a very significant difference in the use) or if not that, some other pious use. The heirs replied that there were no plans to restore or repair the church and that the testator had no "tacit or expressed will" (*voluntate tacita vel expressa*) to convert the donation to another use.

Panormitanus replied that if the gift had been insufficient to repairs or restoration, which he took to be the same use repeated twice, then it could be converted to a new pious use, as long as the heirs were summoned. Fabric would seem to be relatively close to repairs; it would have been possible to construe it as being the same use, but Panormitanus did not do this, nor did he even consider closeness of use as an issue. Gifts to pious causes should not become *caduca*, on which Panormitanus cited Bartolus on Tusculum, and Panormitanus understood that this referred to gifts given to the cause alone. He offered only one relevant rule (*regula*), which permitted an action to have as much effect as it could: "If what I do has not effect in the way I do it; let it have as much effect as it can" (*si non valet, quod ago, ut ago; valeat, ut potest valere*).[82] But although Panormitanus acknowledged that the *dominium* of the gift had passed to the church when the testator died, he also emphasized that it was not a pure gift but one with a suspensive condition—in fact, a condition that was repeated. It seemed that the donor had not given a pure gift, in "contemplation of pious causes." Hence, the gift was not eligible to be commuted or turned to a new use and should be returned. He also pointed out that while the church should be favored, this favor could not extend to the injury of others.

---

81. Panormitanus, *Consilia tractatus, quaestiones, et practica* (Venice: n.p., 1571), consilium 27, 19v.

82. Frequently associated with Code 4.38.3. Alternatively: "Quando quod ago non valet ut ago, valeat quantum valere potest." My thanks to Larry Poos for helping me with this twister of a regula.

Panormitanus added a more extended meditation on the conversion of pious gifts in a consilium in which money had been left to Lucas, a Franciscan, to pay every year for books and other necessities for theological study throughout his life. The problem began with the capacity of the Franciscan to take, although Lucas had applied for and received a special license from the pope for what was effectively an annuity. Additional difficulties included the dilemma that scholastic studies would not normally extend over an entire life and that the testatrix made clear in her testament that the gift was to support Lucas himself, not the order of friars. Panormitanus argued that the money could still be used to support Lucas even if he did not need books at the moment, in part because the gift could support Lucas's studies, and in part because a gift for theological study could be broadly understood as a gift to support divine worship (*ad divinum cultum*). The testatrix had specified in her testament that the gift was "for the health of her soul and the remission of her sins" (*pro salute animae suae, et remissione peccatorum suorum*), which meant that it was a gift to pious causes.[83] Panormitanus emphasized the fact that this motivation had been explicitly stated in her will, and he posited that gifts made *pro anima*, if their intended use could not be honored, were eligible to be converted to a new pious use.[84] In these cases, the higher cause could allow a change in use. Attention needed to be paid to the exact setting out of the gift, which could reveal the intention (*mentem*) behind it. It appears that Panormitanus was suggesting that if the gift included the phrase *pro anima* or *ad pias causas* in addition to a specific use, then it could be eligible for conversion if the given use was impossible. This is similar to cy-près in the operation that it performs out of respect for a higher purpose than the one stated.

On the other hand, in this case Panormitanus did not seem to believe that a new use would be made out of the gift, in part because he read a higher category of use out of the specific terms. He was concerned with the mind of the testator—as is usual in the jurisprudence of testaments—but he looked for signals within the original document to show that the gift could stay with the Franciscan.

83. Panormitanus, *Consilia*, consilium 63, 147.
84. Ibid., 147v.

If the Franciscan had been incapable of taking, then the gift would have failed utterly. Moreover, the long opinion showed Panormitanus's inability to draw on a norm or rule to explain why it would be just to let the Franciscan keep the gift even if he was no longer engaged in direct scholastic study. Panormitanus was reaching for a cyprès doctrine, and perhaps he was preparing the way for it. But he did not have it already at hand, and in fact his decision changed very little about the gift. Lucas could continue to receive the money, as the testatrix had stipulated, throughout his life, so that he could buy books, study, and improve divine worship. The yearly gift would be a reminder to him to pray for her soul. The particular affection that the testatrix had for Lucas would be honored by maintaining the gift, and there would be no obvious injury to anyone, since Lucas had already been given the pension for life.

One of the first works written on gifts *ad pias causas* as such was by Ludovicus Pontanus, the humanist and conciliarist.[85] For Pontanus, a pious legacy did not defeat the rights that others had in the property, and a gift made without the consent of all of the parties—including, often, that of the prince—had no effect. He rejected the possibility that heirs could lose out entirely to pious gifts. Pontanus did not treat pious causes as indefectible but pointed out their limits as well as their privileges. He allowed them at times to fail. He considered them within a range of relationships, including their relationship to the prince. Many gifts involved more than just the soul of the deceased.[86] Legacies to pious causes, in fact, fell into a particularly complicated jurisdictional area, and Pontanus was concerned with the many parties that were affected by them.

Pontanus, like other humanist jurists, was attuned to a new problem as well. In late medieval discussions of the transition of gifts, the insufficiency of a gift was a common refrain. The opposite problem, of surplusage, was more rare. A gift for a chapel to a church that could not add another one was one example mentioned in the me-

---

85. Bellomo, *Common Legal Past*, 209.
86. Ludovicus Pontanus, *Repetitio de relictis ad pias causas* (Rome: Georg Lauer and Leonhard Pflugl, 1472), 13: "legata que concernunt non solum favorem anime defuncti sed etiam alterium ut puta legata facta piis locis."

dieval *ius commune*, but it was an isolated example of abundance and impossibility coinciding. In the early modern period, the problem of wastefulness, surplusage, appears with greater frequency than it had. Pontanus considered the question of whether a bishop could commute a gift for a chalice or for the repair of the church if there was no need for it (*si ecclesia non habet opus*), in a phrase that aligns surplusage with impossibility. Digest 50.10.7pr. could be drawn upon to justify a change in use if there was another need within the church. The idea was repeated by Silvester Prierias at the start of the sixteenth century in his *Summa summarum*.[87] This is indicative of what must have been an increasing problem: it was an age in which there was a growing specificity of donations to churches that were already well provisioned. Some particularly popular donations, such as the chalice, were also durable.[88] Moreover, the rules on alienation of moveable property did not prevent an exchange of property for the better or for need, which could have provided a means for the circumnavigation of a testator's wishes—if he wished to give money to furnish a chalice, but the church needed something else, Ludovicus was effectively (but not explicitly) proposing that the middle step (buying and then exchanging an unnecessary chalice) could be skipped.[89] This was not a universally accepted proposal: certainly many jurists prior to Ludovicus had rejected the idea that a will could be commuted just for the sake of convenience or to do something better with the money—not even, necessarily, with the consent of the heirs.[90]

But it was an idea that was well in keeping with the priorities of the fifteenth century, improving the flexibility and rationality of donations. Still, there was no pretense, here, that the change would be made to honor the donor's intent or even to closely approximate it. The problem was that donors would be increasingly unlikely to do-

---

87. Silvester Prierias, *Summae, nitori suo restitutae, pars secunda* (Lyon: Mauricium Roy and Ludovicus Pefnot, 1555), Legatum IV, question 12, 122.

88. Thomas F. X. Noble, "Paradoxes and Possibilities in the Sources for Roman Society in the Early Middle Ages," in *Medieval Rome and the Christian West: Essays in Honor of Donald A. Bullough*, ed. Julia M. H. Smith (Leiden: Brill, 2000), 76–77.

89. On exchange, see Nov. 131 c.12.

90. Restrictions on alienation derived part of their legal force from the fact that the items had been left to the church and that heirs had an ongoing interest in their intended use: X 3.26.5.

nate if this possibility of immediate alienation and exchange was too openly or frequently used. Even if all gifts fail in the end, it is indelicate to flaunt a quick transition of use—a general rule of thumb seems to have been that an attempt to transition a small gift before the rights to it would have been earned through prescription would tend to offend.[91]

Johannes de Imola, commenting on *Quia contingit,* considered what it meant that only the pope could change the use of a gift. Drawing on Hostensius and others, Imola pointed out that property given to a hospital could be used to provide food and clothing for its poor without that being an alteration of use. He noted that although it might appear that the bishop could change the use of a gift with the consent of the heirs, he rejected that, because "this does not concern the good of the heirs which they could renounce, but the will of the deceased."[92] This meant not that Imola rejected the necessity of the consent of the heirs or of the patron to a change in use as part of the process, but only that the pope stood in as a representative of the deceased's will, which neither the bishop nor the heirs could do. This may be indicative of a hardening of lines, in which the heirs were losing their ability to represent the testator in difficult situations. Étienne Aufréri, Président of the Parlement in Toulouse, followed Imola to insist that the heirs could not renounce the will of the testator on his behalf. Although the consent of heirs to commutations was still necessary, heirs' ability to stand in the place of the donor would be limited.[93] The *ius commune* was shifting a little, in response to an increasingly individualistic understanding of legacies.

---

91. A period of twenty-five to thirty-five years is frequently suggested as an appropriate interval to follow the terms of a charitable donation strictly: John Sare, "Art for Whose Sake? An Analysis of Restricted Gifts to Museums," *Columbia–VLA Journal of Law and the Arts* 13 (1988): 387, 392; Lewis M. Simes, *Public Policy and the Dead Hand: Five Lectures* (Ann Arbor: University of Michigan Law School, 1955), 139; *Report of the Committee on the Law and Practice Relating to Charitable Trusts* (Nathan Committee Report), Cmd 8710 (London: H.M.S.O., 1952), 365.

92. Joannes de Imola, *Super Clementinis* (Lyon: Joannes Moylin, 1525), *De religiosis domibus,* "Quia contingit," § 9, 113v: "quia hic non agitur de utilitate heredis cui possit renunciare sed de voluntate defuncti servanda."

93. Étienne Aufréri, *Decisiones Capellae Tholosanae* (Frankfurt: Nicolas Bassaeius, 1575), Question 26, 16.

As these varied responses to impossible gifts suggest, the *ius commune* offered examples of how an impossible gift might be commuted or converted, but the ultimate decision would rest on too many factors to be formed into a firm rule. The judge could investigate how the gift was made, why it was being thwarted, which interested parties to the gift were obstructing it, whether the gift fell within the soul's part or was a larger portion of the estate, and whether the donation had been well made out of the family's superfluities or not. A range of law could matter for the judge's decision: considerations on the revocability of a gift; the requirement that the pope give approval for any change in use; rules on alienation, exchanges, and patronage. Certainly, there were many competing norms and rights within the *ius commune* that could suggest at least a potential cy-près doctrine, including the protections of pious gifts as a separate class or the value of public utility over private utility.[94] Gifts *ad pias causas* were not necessarily the same as gifts to God: Boniface VIII's rule—once a gift was dedicated to God it could not be transferred back to human use (*semel deo dicatum non est ad usos humanos ulterius transferendum*)— did not necessarily apply to all benevolent works, but pious causes were increasingly treated as their own distinct category.[95] On the other hand, there were norms that would have tended to resist the transformation of use, such as the requirements to obtain consent and not to infringe on rights. There was no short phrase that would demand the transition of a gift—although Bartolus's easily misread comment on gifts to pious causes not falling caduca could have become one—but there were a number of maxims that would have given a judge pause: *cuius est dare, eius est disponere; cessante causa, cessat effectus; impossibilium nulla est obligatio;* or *quod omnes tangit ab omnibus debet approbari*.[96] As a consequence, even though the *ius commune* discussed what to do with impossible and illegal gifts, it did not come

---

94. Jacobus Buttigrarius, *Lectura supra codice* (Paris: n.p., 1516), 35v. See also Code 6.51.14a. Pennington, *Prince and the Law*; Ennio Cortese, *La norma giuridica: Spunti teorici nel diritto comune classico*, vol. 1 (Milan: Giuffrè, 1962); Jean Gaudemet, "Utilitas publica," *Revue historique de droit français et étranger* 29 (1951): 465–99.

95. VI 5.[13].51.

96. His whose it is to give, it is his to dispose; if the cause ceases, so must the effect; the impossible cannot bind; that which touches all must be approved by all.

up with a norm or a rule like cy-près, for if it had done, then the norm would surely have been exploited by an age that was eager to find ways to explain the application of property to new uses.

Perhaps it is not a surprise, then, that on the eve of the Council of Trent, reform-minded cardinals might complain that too many gifts to pious causes were returned to the heirs, above all, but not exclusively, for reasons of poverty, including the distinctive poverty of the well-born with which the early modern period tended to be sympathetic. Canon law had long been aware that heirs were particularly likely to obstruct pious legacies in favor of the estate; it was also clear that the immediate diversion of a pious gift was likely to provoke the heirs and thus dry up their donations and alienate their affections. Given that late medieval ecclesiastical courts prioritized reconciliation, compromise, peace, and the salvation of all souls, concern for the unhappy heirs would remain an ongoing pastoral issue, one not casually set aside. Although the pope did have the right to alter the use of property unilaterally, through dispensation, it was common that dispensations came with the stipulation that the other interested parties had to give consent first; even papal privileges often tried not to cause unnecessary diminishment of the rights of others.[97] Secular courts, on the other hand, would be less likely to bend to the apparent greed of the heirs, whose salvation and future donations were of no concern to the court.

In ecclesiastical court records, legal reasoning is often not made manifest. If we assume that cy-près was a contemporary principle,

97. Similarly, Helmholz points to the diminishment of third-party harm as a rule of interpretation in privileges: "When there was a question of interpretation involved, privileges were always to be read so as not to diminish the rights of a third party.... As Hostiensis put it, 'Where it prejudices the right of another, [the privilege] is reduced to the *ius commune* if it can be.'" Helmholz, *Spirit of Classical Canon Law*, 328, citing Hostiensis, *Lectura,* ad X 2.1.12, nos. 4–7. See, for example, the case of the prior of Sele, who had spent his abbey into destitution but whose right to delay the annexation of his priory—to which he would not give consent—was defended by the pope, who allowed the priory to be turned over to Waynflete for Magdalen only after the death of the prior. Virginia Davis, *William Waynflete: Bishop and Educationalist* (Woodbridge, England: Boydell Press, 1993), 149. This is not to suggest that popes never infringed on rights. For one example, see Geoffrey Barraclough, *Papal Provisions: Aspects of Church History, Constitutional, Legal, and Administrative in the Later Middle Ages* (Oxford: Blackwell, 1935).

the cases may well seem to employ it, since many alterations to a gift could appear to have been made to approximate the donor's intent. But where we can find an authorized canonical reason other than cy-près to explain these cases, then that reason should be considered the justification for the transition.[98] A pithy doctrine is unlikely to sum up the many factors that may have been considered, as a court used its powers of inquest and discovery to look into the exact terms of a gift, the particular difficulties that attended it, and the situation of the "trustee," the beneficiaries, the locality, and the heirs. If a consensus was not possible, then external justifications of necessity might be used to defend a transition of use, or the gift could always be safely sent to the poor or returned to the heirs. The chief interest of the deceased would be understood to be the prayers and masses that he was to have received in return; an approximation of nearest charitable use to his particular preferences would have been, in fact, the least likely interest to have been considered. Commutation, to avoid entanglements with Rome, would have been the most likely result.

For example, a fifteenth-century Rochester case that "authorized a change of a bequest for repair of a church's bell tower to one for repair of the parish church itself, because of an immediate danger to the latter," does involve the changing of a bequest for purposes, but the extremity of the situation was, in canon law, a just cause that on its own permitted the change.[99] The bell tower would not survive if the church itself did not stand, and the gift would be made fully good in the future. The repairs to the bell tower were simply delayed. Additionally, a shift from the repair of one thing to the repair of another was arguably only a deviation within a purpose, rather than a shift in purpose. It is possible that the churchwardens presented this particular bequest rather than any other recent bequest to the ecclesiastical courts exactly because the shift would be so small and not a change in purpose or use. Alternatively, the testator may have solicited the

---

98. Helmholz acknowledges that "the surviving records discovered so far have only produced a few such cases" and that "the subject deserves further exploration." *Oxford History of the Laws of England*, vol. 1, 418–19.

99. Ibid., 418.

opinion of the churchwardens on what gift would be most helpful to them; once repairs to the bell tower were started, however, it may have become clear that repairs were more desperately needed for the walls. Here was another principle that could be brought in: anything unknown to the testator that would have changed the will when it was made could be used to do so posthumously.

Sometimes the problem was nonperformance of a bequest that had imposed a significant duty as the condition, such as the case of *ex officio v. Kyng,* in which John Kyng had been left money to go on a pilgrimage to Santiago de Compostella on behalf of the deceased.[100] He could not and did not want to do it, so the court turned the money over to other men to make the same pilgrimage. This was deviation: the purpose was maintained, but the mode or method of execution was changed. This case also shows how sensitive the churchwardens were to the strictness with which bequests for purposes were to be treated. It would have been less onerous to take the money given to John Kyng and turn it to other purposes, such as masses or a pilgrimage to a local site, but the judges made an effort not to do that.

It would be satisfying and useful to offer a phrase that could be used to describe the varied and complicated treatment of impossible late medieval legacies and gifts. One of the reasons that the term cy-près has been used to describe the modification of gifts is that it encapsulates the relaxation of strict terms of donation. It is hard to sum up alternative conceptions of equity in one phrase as easily as *aussi près que possible* has done. Cinus da Pistoia grasped the dilemma: "equity is not a norm."[101] There was no settled rule, no one norm, to be used to solve difficult gifts, and the equitable decision would have to be suited to the case. Cy-près, by contrast, *is* a rule for decisions; it emerges exactly where the *ius commune* fell silent.

---

100. L. S. Poos, ed., *Lower Ecclesiastical Jurisdiction in Late-Medieval England: The Courts of the Dean and Chapter of Lincoln, 1336–1349, and the Deanery of Wisbech, 1458–1484* (Oxford: Oxford University Press, 2001), 90.

101. "Potest dici quod equitas non est preceptum." Cinus of Pistoia, *Lectura* on Code 1.14.1, quoted in Bellomo, *Common Legal Past,* 188.

Canon Law's Cy-Près Moment

The secularization of property in the Reformation meant that the church's supervision over many gifts was lost—irretrievably for most, despite litigation in the imperial court. Although the basic principles of the treatment of bequests were upheld in the decrees of the Council of Trent, accommodations had to be made to the new situation to allow a shift of use when bequests were frustrated by political and religious transformations. Canon law came to push back against patronage rights, which had often served the cause of reform as newly Protestant patrons leveraged their rights over their properties, and as a consequence the sense that the heirs were connected to the bequest was weakened but not lost.

At the Council of Trent the principle of the exact observance of the testator's stipulations was repeated. It was admitted that a "just and necessary cause" might permit a change, or commutation, to a bequest, although in general "alterations of last testaments ... ought not to be made," and if a change was proposed, the Apostolic See ought to be involved to verify that "nothing is stated in the petition which conceals the truth or suggests falsehood, before such commutations are put into execution."[102] On the matter in which the consequences to the soul were clearest—in the funding of masses—the Council of Trent followed the earlier tradition that permitted abbots, generals, and bishops to reduce the number of masses said for the dead if they could not be accomplished with the funds given. This was necessary because otherwise it would be impossible to find anyone to offer the masses, which would lead to a situation in which "the pious provisions of testators (*piae testantium voluntates*) are neglected and the consciences of those concerned with these duties are burdened."[103] Deviation was equitable to everyone in this case. In

---

102. Tanner, ed., *Decrees of the Ecumenical Councils*, vol. 2, Trent, XXII, c. 6 de Ref., 739: "In commutationibus ultimarum voluntatum, quae nonnisi ex iusta et necessaria causa fieri debent, episcopi tamquam delegati sedis apostolicae summarie et extraiudicialiter cognoscant, nihil in precibus tacita veritate vel suggesta falsitate fuisse narratum, priusque commutationes praedictae exsecutioni demandentur."

103. Ibid., XXV, c. 4 de Ref., 786: "unde depereunt piae testantium voluntates, et eorum conscientias, ad quos praedicta spectant, onerandi occasio datur."

finding a resolution, which could involve failing to celebrate on the days that the testators wanted, the church would choose a solution "as seems best to promote the honour and worship of God and the advantage of the churches, but only so that some commemoration is always made of those of the dead who have left sums for the salvation of souls and for pious purposes."[104] The testator would get what he had wanted, but perhaps not in the quantity that he had desired (even though the quantity was vitally important by late medieval reckoning), and the alteration would not be made with an approximation of his preferences.[105] In the decree on purgatory, the Council of Trent affirmed both its existence and the traditional utility of prayers and masses said for the suffering souls there.[106] The decree affirmed the duty to perform these and other pious bequests diligently and accurately (*diligenter et accurate*).[107]

The requirement that church property, including almshouses, hospitals, and schools, must be used for its intended purpose was reinforced at Trent, in part because of the criticism that the church had received on these grounds and in part to rebut the claim made by evangelicals that they could take church property because it was no longer being used as intended.[108] The council affirmed that distributions to the poor ought to be made from church property and that this property ought not to be alienated or wasted.[109] Furthermore, since many monastic properties had been seized by their newly evangelical patrons, the Council of Trent attempted to limit lay influence on church property, to verify claims to patronage rights carefully, and to prevent the sale of patronage rights.[110] Any patron who attempted to take control of church lands not only would be

104. Ibid., XXV, c. 4 de Ref., 787: "quidquid magis ad Dei honorem et cultum atque ecclesiarum utilitatem viderint expedire, ita tamen, ut eorum semper defunctorum commemoratio fiat, qui pro suarum animarum salute legata ea ad pios usus reliquerunt."
105. Wood-Legh, *Perpetual Chantries*, 313; Kidd, *Later Medieval Doctrine*.
106. Tanner, ed., *Decrees of the Ecumenical Councils*, vol. 2, Trent, XXV, *Decretum de purgatorio*, 774.
107. Ibid.
108. Ibid., XXII, c. 11 de Ref., 741, and c. 9 de Ref., 740.
109. Ibid., XXV, c. 1 de Ref., 784–85.
110. Ibid., XIV, c. 12 de Ref., 718.

excommunicated but also would lose his patronage rights.[111] Patrons were forbidden to interfere with "the receipt of incomes, revenues or subsidies of any benefices, even if their right of patronage is legally established by foundation or endowment."[112] But the council admitted that the question of patronage rights was delicate: "It would not be right to remove the legitimate rights of patronage and to ride roughshod over the pious desires (*voluntates*) of the faithful in making foundations. At the same time, ecclesiastical benefices cannot be allowed to be reduced to servitude because of this claim, as in fact happens at the hands of many shameless persons."[113] The council acknowledged that the pious desires of the donors had included the receipt of patronage rights.

As a consequence, the complicated overlapping rights created between lay and religious, the family of the donor and the receiving institution, had to be treated with care. The council proposed that in cases in which patronage had recently—since the Reformation—been established, even with approval through the Apostolic See, but not "legitimately established for the quite evident need of the church," the property should be returned to the patron and the benefice set free.[114] This affirmed that it was not sacrilege to return pious gifts to the donor or his family. Because it was important not to violate the rights of the patrons, it would be simpler to avoid the problem of patronage in the first place, if possible. At this point, patronage rights had been a source of problems for centuries.

Since the intentions of the testator had been a legal point with some traction even among Protestants, the Council of Trent mentioned them frequently. The will of the donor affirmed the use to which property ought to be put, maintained the legitimacy of prop-

111. Ibid., XXII, c. 11 de Ref., 741.
112. Ibid., XXV, c. 9 de Ref., 790: "in perceptione fructuum, proventuum, obventionum quorumcumque beneficiorum, etiam si vere de iure patronatus ipsorum ex fundatione et dotatione essent."
113. Ibid., XXV, c. 9 de Ref., 789: "Sicuti legitima patronatuum iura tollere piasque fidelium voluntates in eorum institutione violare, aequum non est: sic etiam, ut hoc colore beneficia ecclesiastica in servitutem, quod a multis impudenter fit, redigantur, non est permittendum."
114. Ibid., XXV, c. 9 de Ref., 791: "ob maxime evidentem ecclesiae vel beneficii seu dignitatis necessitatem legitime constitutos esse."

erty held by the church, necessitated the upkeep of endowments for posthumous masses, and rebutted the presumptions of letters conservatory. Letters conservatory had originally been created to offer protection to institutions that appeared to be threatened: a letter conservatory gave to the conservator the charge of defending, and often managing, the institution. But in the disturbance of the Reformation, some conservators attempted to act as patrons and then would, in the words of the Council of Trent, "twist letters of that kind in many respects to a meaning which is false and contrary to the intention of the donor."[115] These letters could be used as justification to divert property, and so the Council of Trent decreed that in the future they would have no effect, with the exception of specified institutions (notably hospitals and colleges), where their use was an integral part of the operations of the institution.

In all of these ways, the political context this period must be kept in mind when reading these decrees. From the perspective of the church, endowments that had been left, often by testamentary bequest, to fund the saying of masses on behalf of the dead had been seized, both on the continent and in England, and appropriated by governments or, at times, by private citizens. The cause that might require alterations to be made to a bequest was often the Reformation itself. In particular, the council decreed, in its chapter on reducing the number of masses for an endowment, that decisions ought to be made both for the good of the church and to follow the intentions of the testator. Donor intent was not, as in eighteenth-century cyprès, the singular consideration. Endowments that were tied up with church property lost to the evangelicals ought to be returned or recompensed, so that the church could fulfill the intentions of the testators either in the original location—restoring the traditional connection between the benefactors associated with the land and the prayers offered there on their behalf—or, if necessary, elsewhere. A shift in location is only a deviation within a purpose, but it was a serious and unusual commutation in canon law, attested in canon law before

---

115. Ibid., XIV, c. 5 de Ref., 716: "eiusmodi literas in plerisque contra concedentis mentem in reprobum sensum detorqueant."

the Reformation, but brought to the fore in the sixteenth century.[116]

The section on the administration of hospitals and pilgrimage hostels highlighted the central issue of location, since the demand for these services had been greatly altered by the Reformation. Many traditional shrines were no longer in operation: "[I]f hospices were founded to receive a particular kind of pilgrims or sick or other persons, and such persons are not to be found in the locality where the hospices are situated, or very few of them, the council nevertheless orders that their revenues should be diverted to another pious purpose (*in alium pium usum*) as close to the original one as possible (*proximior*), and a more beneficial (*utilior*) one in view of the time and place."[117] Moreover, the bishop could do this on his own authority and with the advice, but not consent, of two of the members of the institution, without any consultation with the heirs of the donor.[118] It is significant that approximation was suggested here, where the heirs and consent were cut away from consideration.

The papal curia does not seem to have believed that Trent had opened to bishops broader powers in the change of use. This power could be granted in particular circumstances—such as to Jesuits in the New World—but it was still believed to be held by the Apostolic See. The Sacred Congregation of the Clergy would generally uphold this understanding.[119] This chapter from the Council of Trent did not

---

116. X 3.26.3; Panormitanus, *Abbatis Panormitani commentaria in tertium decretalium librum*, vol. 6 (Venice: Iuntas, 1588), 174.

117. If the donor had listed an alternative disposition in the case of failure, then the bishop was to follow that use instead, if possible.

118. Tanner, ed., *Decrees of the Ecumenical Councils*, vol. 2, Trent XXV, c. 8 de Ref., 789: "Quodsi hospitalia haec ad certum peregrinorum aut infirmorum aut aliarum personarum genus suscipiendum fuerint instituta, nec in loco, ubi sunt dicta hospitalia, similes personae, aut perpaucae, reperiantur: mandat adhuc, ut fructus illorum in alium pium usum, qui eorum institutioni proximior sit ac, pro loco et tempore, convertantur"; "etiam in hunc eventum, in eorum fundatione aut institutione fuerit expressum, quo casu, quod ordinatum fuit, observari curet episcopus."

119. Pietro Gasparri, *Codicis iuris canonici fontes*, vol. 3 (Rome: Polyglottis Vaticanis, 1930), 177. Curia Romana, S. C. C., Arriminen., 29 Aug. 1595, case 2291, 184: "congregatio concilii censuit debere quidem Episcopum ab administratoribus Confraternitatis et Hospitalium laicorum rationem administrationis exigere, sed non posse iubere, ut magis in unum, quam in alium usum pium redditus

overstep the theoretical legal rights of the church as it understood them, but it was a challenge to the normal practice that the church employed in its treatment of donations. The apparatus to the text offered no citations to previous law to explain the possibility of changing the purpose of a gift or to suggest that this power belonged to the ordinary without the permission of the Apostolic See. Additionally, the chapter limited the application of this power to hospices, even though it had begun by a consideration of many kinds of pious institutions, whose purpose, it said, should be strictly maintained. On this point, by contrast, the strictness of use, the apparatus did give references to earlier canon law. Taken as a whole, then, the chapter tends to suggest that this permission to change uses was not normally practiced by bishops.

In short, the upheavals of the Reformation, and the frank desire of both sides to keep the wealth associated with the church, meant that there was a new push to honor the testator with some new arrangement. Commutations or conversions might be necessary to allow the church to receive as much property back as possible, or its equivalent value, and to restore endowments for pious causes, albeit relocated, on new terms, or perhaps even turned over for a new purpose. Early modern Catholic jurists, following the mood and conditions of the times, wrestled with the possibilities. In particular, with the reduced emphasis on patronage came a decline in the relationship to the heirs, whose consent would still generally be sought for commutations but whose lasting relationship to the gift was effectively severed. By contrast, the rights of the donor would be highlighted—not least because the religious convictions of the heirs were no longer necessarily and reliably Catholic. Thus, in the sixteenth and seventeenth centuries, canon law increasingly formulated transitions of impossible gifts in terms of the intentions and soul of the testator. Henri Pirhing, the seventeenth-century German Jesuit, offered that the transition to "another pious use" for an impossible gift was made to "satisfy" the "principle intentions" of the testator

---

impendant, nisi piis testantium, qui bona reliquissent, voluntatibus aliter cautum esset, tunc enim eas ad unguem observari opotere."

and was done for his "honor and health of soul."[120] The heirs were asked to consent, but if they refused without just cause, then the bishop was empowered to proceed on his own. The role of the judge to find equity when there was no consensus had disappeared, as a consequence of the new and unpredictable legal settlements across seventeenth-century Europe.

Tomás Sanchez, the Jesuit casuist, died in 1610, and his *Consilia moralia* were published posthumously. Sanchez explained that an impossible gift should be altered in ways that were close to the testator's intentions. He drew on Trent's use of *proximior* as well as the Modestinus opinion to explain this priority. Approximation was becoming a prominent theme in the *ius commune* treatment of impossible bequests in the same time period that it emerged in England with the Venables case. Still, there were differences between Sanchez's suggestion that approximation of intent was one consideration when altering a gift and the operation of cy-près as it would appear in England. For one, Sanchez was using approximation as a way to choose among the range of options that commutation (not conversion) offered. Sanchez used the gloss to the Modestinus passage to emphasize that the bequest would be altered "to another licit spectacle" (*in alio licito spectaculo*), not to any other use at all.[121] That is, the deceased's intentions should be used "in a similar mode" (*alio modo simili*).[122] Sanchez affirmed that it was most likely that only the pope could change the use of a gift, but he upheld the right of the bishop to commute a gift with the consensus of the heirs and the recipient of the gift (or if consen-

120. Henri Pirhing, *Jus canonicum nova methodo explicatum*, vol. 3 (Venice: Remondiniana, 1759), Book III, Titulus XXVI, Section IV, CXXIII, 210: "Ratio est, quia per talem commutationem principali intentioni Testatoris satisfit, quae est honor, et salus animae, non potest autem fieri ab Episcopo talis commutatio, sine consensu haeredis, vel aliorum executorum, nisi hi sine iusta causa recusent consentire, tum enim Episcopus, etiam iis invitis, procedere potest."

121. Tomás Sanchez, *Consilia, seu opuscula moralia tomus posterior* (Lyon: Jacobus and Petrus Prost, 1635), Book IV, Cap. II, Dub. VI, 61.

122. Toschi, writing at about the same time, agreed: if possible a legacy "should be had in another similar pious cause" (debet fieri in aliam causam piam similem). Alternatively, he described this as commuting it "to another use close to the will of the testator" (in alium usum proximum voluntati testatoris). Domenico Toschi, *Practicarum conclusionum*, vol. 5 (Rome: Stephanus Paulinus, 1606), 106.

sus could not be reached, with a judge) or on his own authority for reasons of necessity.[123] Sanchez took surplusage as an example of a factual impossibility.[124] He weighed whether it was possible to change a pious gift into a better (*melius*) use and presented the sources for and against (the older sources opposed it).[125] Sanchez did not indicate which opinion he thought was more likely to be correct, probably because his loyalties were divided—he preferred that better uses be made out of gifts, but his conceptualization of donations was primarily centered around the testator, not around the competing interests in a gift. In writing about a legacy that was given to an end that was impossible in fact or law but not an inherently bad end, Sanchez considered the transition of the gift in terms of the intentions of the testator, the fate of his soul, and his explicit desire not to give the property to his heirs.[126] Still, he admitted the necessity of the consensus of the heirs of the testator and, in cases of patronage, the consent of the heirs of the original patron as well to any change in a gift.[127] He also upheld the principle that a gift that was to specific people, or to a specific class of people, or even for the advancement of a pious end, would normally fail and return to the heirs if there were no recipients. It would not be turned to a new pious end.[128]

Trent thus opened the door to increased alterations of uses in several ways: by acknowledging the necessity of change, by authorizing bishops to make changes in use in some circumstances, and by using the language of a "just and necessary cause," which could tend to

123. Sanchez, *Consilia*, Book IV, Cap. II, Dub. V, 61.
124. Ibid.
125. Ibid., Book IV, Cap. II, Dub. III, 60.
126. Ibid., Book IV, Cap. II, Dub. IV, 60: "Si impossibilitas implendi legata sit de facto, vel de iure secundo modo, nempe non quia usus sit in se malus, sed quia tantum iure prohibetur, legatum non efficitur caducum, nec in eo succedet haeres, sed convertetur in alium honestum, et licitum usum. Ratio, quia iam testator voluit illo legato privare haeredem, et id in usum honestum cedere: ergo si is, in quem testator intendit, non sit possibilis, convertetur in alium usum possibilem. Item, quia testator principaliter voluit animae suae saluti consulere, expendendo legatum in opere pio, et secundario in illo quod signavit: ergo quando in illo non potest, expendetur in alio."
127. Ibid., Book IV, Cap. II, Dub. VII, 62.
128. Ibid., Book IV, Cap. II, Dub. XXI, 70.

expand. Agostinho Barbosa's *Pastoralis solicitudinis, sive de officio, et potestate episcopi* surveyed the law on the altering of bequests.[129] He began his *allegatio* on when a bishop could commute pious gifts by asserting that only the pope had this power, citing *Quia contingit*.[130] For a chantry that could not keep up with its masses, Barbosa pointed out that bishops did have the right to reduce these masses—but they should do so not on their own but with the heir or executor.[131]

Barbosa then turned to the Council of Trent, which had delegated to bishops some rights to commute gifts that were left to one use and turn them to another use for a just and reasonable cause. Given this, he asked, was it possible for the bishop to do this on his own authority?[132] The doctors of law, he said, required the heirs to consent.[133] If the heirs refused to consent, then Barbosa laid out the learned opinions on how to proceed, whether the bishop (as empowered by Trent) could do it on his own authority or needed additional agreement from the church. Barbosa then indicated just causes that the bishop could use to commute a gift, including: if the money was insufficient; if a monastery could not be built in a given location, in which case the location should be moved; if necessity (to repair a church or to feed the poor) gave a serious reason (*ex gravissima causa*); if the donor had not specified a recipient or a cause; if the designated church was not honoring the terms of the gift, in which case the bishop could transfer the gift to another church; or for a reason of another urgent necessity.

Barbosa argued, based largely but not entirely on authorities post-Trent, that some gifts could be commuted on the grounds of impossibility, whether impossible in law or in fact.[134] If there was a temporal impediment that would later be removed, then the bishop

129. Agostinho Barbosa, *Pastoralis solicitudinis, sive de officio, et potestate episcopi*, vol. 2 (Lyon: Durand, 1628), Pars III, Allegatio LXXXIII, 265–69.
130. Ibid., § 1, 265: "Soli Romano Pontif. pias defunctorum voluntates rationabili ex causa commutare licet."
131. Ibid., § 4, 266.
132. Ibid., § 5–6, 266.
133. Ibid., § 6, 266: "in qua quaestione tenent Doctores requiri haeredis consensum."
134. Ibid., § 8, 266.

160   Use in the *Ius Commune*

should wait to see if the impediment would later disappear. If a gift was made to an "honest" use that was impossible, then it could be changed. A gift to a use that was not honest, however, was void and could not be commuted. Barbosa led the reader through the possibilities and limitations placed on bishops in dealing with difficult gifts but did not offer a broad principle for the change of use. There were many different rules and situations, and there was no one guideline for the adjustment.

Ludovico Engel, the seventeenth-century Benedictine, summarized Barbosa's careful work with a little less precision, suggesting that Barbosa had allowed that if money was left for something that was not necessary but could be put to a more useful object, that it could be shifted.[135] The example Engel gave could, in fact, have been justified by necessity, for Engel described money left to paint a church that was in ruins, but Engel pushed the example from a case of necessity to a case of utility, in which a more useful end could be favored, which was certainly not the interpretation of the strictness of use given by earlier jurists. Engel was then cited, often verbatim, in countless repetitive disputations on legacies to pious causes; it was affirmed that although pious gifts could not ordinarily be altered, they might be on the grounds of utility. Certainly the trend in sixteenth- and seventeenth-century canon law was toward an expansion of episcopal power to turn property to new uses, and to justify these transitions in the name of inextinguishable pious causes. Indeed, Engel did not mention any role for the heirs or consideration of them.

After Trent, strict distinctions between commutation and conversion started to drop away, such that some jurists, like Barbosa, began to write about a change in use as a mere commutation rather than conversion.[136] This transition may have been influenced in part by the humanist revival of a latent meaning in the Latin verb *convertere*,

---

135. Ludovicus Engel, *Collegium universi iuris canonici* (Venice: Bartholomaeus Giavarina, 1723), Title 26, Quaeritur XIX, 279: "si usus non sit necessarius, et possit res utilius applicari."

136. Toschi, *Practicarum conclusionum*, vol. 5, conclusions 105–6, 110, and 113–14; Alphonsus de Liguori, *Compendium theologiae moralis* (Ratisbon, Germany: G. Joseph Manz, 1851), Tractatus 16, *De contractibus*, Cap. II, Art. 3, Q. 16–19, 292–93.

which could, in fact, mean turning around and returning to an original purpose rather than applying property to a new purpose.[137] The change in post-Tridentine jurisprudence certainly indicates a greater casualness with regard to the change in use that went along with the increasing sense that the heirs were more estranged from the gift than they had been. However, it is still the case that even in the seventeenth century, Toschi, who allowed for a "commutation" of use, would hold that with the consent of the interested parties, no higher authentication for a change in use would be necessary.[138] This was not universally held amongst *ius commune* jurists, some of whom had conceived of the pope as protecting the will of the testator in this matter. As a general rule, Catholic jurists continued to consider the heirs in questions of the alteration of gifts, but they gave them less weight than they had two centuries before, whereas Protestant jurists were far more likely to leave them out.

The 1624 *Tractatus de communitatibus ultimarum voluntatum* by Johannes Petrus Moneta is the first significant treatise on commutation and as such is indicative of the increased need in the early modern period for jurisprudence on the subject.[139] Moneta cited *Quia contingit* to limit changes in use to the Apostolic See, and so he did not affirm that this was a power of the ordinary. Bishops could, however, work with interested parties to arrange deviations within use that were modifications of "kind, mode, place, time, or person" (*genus, modus, locus, tempus, vel persona*). These potential commutations were an appropriate response to impossibility, just as they had been in earli-

---

137. See Erasmus's description of the conversion of holy days back to their original purpose in "Ignavis semper feriae sunt," in *Opera omnia Desiderii Erasmi Roterodami*, vol. II-4 (Amsterdam: Huygens Instituut/Brill, 1987), II vi 12. On the other hand, Erasmus could at times describe the spoiling of the Egyptians as a theft, transfer, or a conversion: see Kathy Eden, *Friends Hold All Things in Common: Tradition, Intellectual Property, and the Adages of Erasmus* (New Haven, Conn.: Yale University Press, 2001), 21–23; Erasmus, *Enchiridion*, in *Opera omnia*, vol. V-8, 174: "Aegyptias opes ad Dominici templi honestamentum convertere." Erasmus, *Collected Works of Erasmus*, trans. Charles Fantazzi, vol. 66 (Toronto: University of Toronto Press, 1988), 62: "convert the riches of Egypt into the adornment of the Lord's temple."

138. Toschi, *Practicarum conclusionum*, vol. 5, conclusions 106 and 114.

139. Helmholz, *Oxford History of the Laws of England*, vol. 1, 418.

er canon law.[140] Moneta emphasized that impossible gifts were not binding: executors, heirs, and bishops should not be faulted for failing to perform the impossible.[141] Moreover, the reverence due to last wishes did not mean that unreasonable, impossible, or even very difficult (*valde difficile*) demands should be enforced by law on the living.[142] On the other hand, Moneta resisted some humanist ideals, since inconvenience or imprudence were not good reasons to deviate a will, and if a gift was only temporarily impossible, then it should be fulfilled when it became possible to do so, although this would be aggravating to the executors, no doubt, and wasteful by humanist reasoning.[143] Impossible gifts fell into a middling area in which they could be nullified (and returned to the estate) or they could be commuted.[144] Moneta suggested that the nullification of impossible legacies was better supported by the laws but that it was not required, and so commutation remained an option.[145] The heirs remained, throughout Moneta's account, interested parties to the dispositions of the testators; no exception was made for special kinds of legacies or gifts. For example, if an heir had been charged to buy specific land for a church or a hospital, but the lord refused to sell the land to him, then the heir would retain the goods that had been given to him for that purpose (*bona remanebunt heredi*).[146] There was no direction to fulfill the pious intent in some other way.

With some exceptions, early modern Catholic jurists expressed relatively little concern for the soul of the testator. Luis Molina and Francesco a Mostazo are two of the only commentators to treat explicitly the question of the testator's soul in relationship to his legacy—although Mostazo's ambivalence about the salvific utility of a *post obit* gift can be seen in the fact that he overwhelmingly paid at-

---

140. Johannes Petrus Moneta, *Tractatus de commutationibus ultimarum voluntatum* (Lyon: Cardon and Cavellat, 1624), 91 and 134.
141. Ibid., 133.
142. Ibid.
143. Ibid., 135.
144. Ibid., 134: "Ultimae voluntates circa rem de facto impossibilem, regulariter nullae sunt: aliquando tamen commutari possunt."
145. Ibid.
146. Ibid., 136.

tention to *inter vivos* gifts.¹⁴⁷ Other commentators, including the Bavarian Jesuit Francis Schmalzgrueber, even suggested that testamentary dispositions were governed by positive law and bore no relationship to salvation.¹⁴⁸

Most early modern jurists, like Barbosa and Sanchez, recognized that the heirs were interested parties in the dispersal of an estate, upheld the consensus model, and urged that the approval of the heirs was necessary before a change to a will could be made.¹⁴⁹ Schmalzgrueber and Ballerini argued that revisions to a legacy could be in keeping with the intentions of the testator, and Schmalzgrueber in particular valued utility as grounds for commuting a will.¹⁵⁰ Some of the willingness on the part of jurists to revise impossible legacies even in the face of recalcitrant heirs—as was suggested by Anacletus Reiffenstuel and Alphonsus de Liguori—appears to have been motivated by a new aggressiveness in the midst of the Catholic Reformation, when families were often divided by religion.¹⁵¹ Certainly Schmalzgrueber's extraordinary flexibility with wills can be explained not just by Jesuit casuistry but also by his experience in Bavaria, where a militant and expansive Tridentine Catholicism was confronted with a sizable Protestant minority. Not all responses to the Reformation on the Catholic side tended toward increasing flexibility and power, however. Antoine Favre reported from the Savoyard court that it was not possible to change a pious use, not even with the consent of all interested parties, unless the pope gave permission.¹⁵²

---

147. Luis Molina, *De iustitia et iure*, vol. 1 (Cologne: Tournes, 1759), disputation 249, n. 1, p. 583; Francesco a Mostazo, *De causis piis* (Lyon: Arnaud, 1686).

148. Giovanni Battista de Luca, *Theatrum veritatis et iustitiae* (Venice: Typographia Balleoniana, 1734), vol. 9, part 1, discussion 72, pp. 112–13; Antonio Ballerini, *Opus theologicum morale* (Rome: Libraria Giachetti, 1890), 3:840; Francis X. Schmalzgrueber, *Ius ecclesiasticum universum* (Rome: Camera Apostolicae, 1844).

149. Juan de Lugo, *De iustitia et iure* (Lyon: Arnaud, 1670); John Francis Lahey, "Faithful Fulfillment of the Pious Will: A Fundamental Principle of Church Law as Found in the 1983 Code of Canon Law" (J.C.D. dissertation, The Catholic University of America, 1987), 89–93.

150. Schmalzgrueber, *Ius ecclesiasticum*, n. 220.

151. Anacletus Reiffenstuel, *Ius canonicum universum*, vol. 6 (Paris: Vivès, 1868), n. 809; Lahey, *Faithful Fulfillment*, 93.

152. Antoine Favre, *Codex Fabrianus Definitionum Forensium* (Leipzig: Thomas

164   Use in the *Ius Commune*

It also remained possible for the Sacred Congregation of the Clergy (SCC) to return money to the heirs, especially if it was determined that their poverty was not known by the testator.[153] The SCC was concerned not about the fate of the testator but rather about the effects, spiritual and temporal, on the remaining members of the family, should their patrimony disappear into the church when they still had need of it. In fact, the SCC elaborated pragmatic, rather than spiritual, reasons why wills ought to be only carefully amended: because of respect for the testator and because of the concern that the laity have that their gifts not be diverted from their intended use.[154] When the salvation of souls was a given as a motive by the SCC for revisions, only the souls of the living were considered, not the soul of the testator.[155]

Meanwhile, patronage never entirely recovered from the shock of the Reformation. As John Godfrey put it, "Ever since the Council of Trent, it was the mind of the Church to limit the right of patronage as much as possible."[156] Conversely, in the era of burgeoning nation-states with absolutist ambitions, kings were eager to claim for themselves the title of patron over all lands in their realm—and sometimes, in the manner of the eighteenth-century Holy Roman Emperor Joseph II, to use this right of patronage in order to interfere with church administration and property. There had been similar movements in the past, as was demonstrated by both the Investiture Controversy and Lateran V's attempt to crack down on secular

---

Fritsch, 1706), Book I, Title 2, Definition 71, p. 47: "Quod in usus pios certos et specialiter destinatum est, non potest in alium usum quantumvis pium converti, nec consentientibus etiam iis omnibus, quorum interest; Nisi consulto prius et auctoritatem praestante Episcopo, tametsi iusta commutandi causa subsit. Adeoque licet de ipsius Episcopi iure et praeiudicio non agatur. Soletque in eam necessaria esse auctoritas summi Pontificis. Quinimo placuit nec summum Pontificem hoc facere posse sine causa, si ordinariam duntaxat potestatem exerceat, sed ita demum si absolutam. Sed etsi commutationem illam pii usus in alium Episcopus, non tam solemni auctoritate in ipso negotio interposita, quam facto adprobasset, Placuit non idcirco prohiberi cum postea improbare, si velit, Multoque magis non debere eam rem nocere successori, si pristino Episcopatus sui iure utendum putet."

153. See the many cases cited by Lahey, *Pious Fulfillment*, 76–80.
154. Ibid., 83.
155. Ibid., 86.
156. Godfrey, *Right of Patronage*, 142.

princes' claims of being patron of all.[157] In retrospect it was clear that patronage had created as many problems as it had solved.

And so, canon 1450 of the 1917 *Code of Canon Law* forbade any new patronage rights.[158] Canon 1451 encouraged bishops to suggest to those who would, in the past, have qualified for patronage, that instead they and their family could receive spiritual benefits like prayers and masses, even perhaps perpetually. If not, they could have the right to present the first holder of the benefice—and no more. Contemporary patrons were at liberty to renounce their rights, but they and their descendants would still be eligible for the traditional right to sustenance in hard times (canon 1455). In areas where patronage was collectively held, which allowed for an entire community to elect their next priest, the code stipulated that they must choose from three candidates that the bishop, limiting their choices, would select for them (canon 1452). The code sought to eradicate patronage when possible (canon 1449). The selling of patronage rights was forbidden again and described as simony; severe penalties were attached. The church was clearly eager to dismantle the patronage system, but it could not outright abolish it—not because the church did not reserve to itself the right to eliminate patronage, but because it was not equitable to do so without the consent of interested parties.[159] Thus canon 1470 carefully elaborated the actions that could destroy patronage rights but also acknowledged that the privileges of patronage were to be observed strictly as they had been originally established.[160] Canon 1469 spelled out the duties of the patron clearly and with stiff consequences: patrons who did not provide aid and advice to their patronal church, including rebuilding a church that was destroyed, repairing a church, or providing funds to keep a church going, would lose their patronage rights, at least until they made good the debt created by the duty.[161] This move in the begin-

---

157. Tanner, ed., *Decrees of the Ecumenical Councils*, vol. 1, Lateran V, Session 10.
158. *The 1917 or Pio-Benedictine Code of Canon Law: in English Translation*, trans. Edward N. Peters (San Francisco: Ignatius Press, 2001).
159. Tanner, ed., *Decrees of the Ecumenical Councils*, vol. 2, Trent, XXV, c. 9 de Ref., 789–91.
160. Godfrey, *Right of Patronage*, 50.
161. Tanner, ed., *Decrees of the Ecumenical Councils*, vol. 2, Trent, XXV, c. 7 de Ref., 788; *1917 Code of Canon Law*, canon 1459.

ning of the twentieth century to prevent new patronage had already been put in place in some lands: patronage had not been permitted in the United States, despite agitation for it by the laity at the first and second councils of Baltimore.[162] Notably, the church had tended to allow patronage rights in Catholic and civil law colonies.[163]

Contemporary canon law, as defined by the 1983 code, has no discussion of patronage at all. However, in eliminating patronage, the church did not then move closer to cy-près doctrine. In fact, just the opposite occurred. Pious donations, whether *inter vivos* or *mortis causa*, are to be precisely fulfilled, unless stipulations are attached that violate canon law, in which case the gift must not be accepted.[164] Both heirs and the church have an obligation to fulfill the "intention" of the testator, and wills "are to be fulfilled most diligently even regarding the manner of administration and distribution of goods."[165] When this is impossible or impractical, the gift is to be refused, not altered.[166] A church executor of a pious bequest can only "reduce, moderate, or commute the wills of the faithful for pious causes if the founder has expressly entrusted this power to him."[167]

Moreover, the only situation in which the Catholic church does consider itself empowered to modify bequests is that of pious foundations in support of prayers, for which the Apostolic See or bishops are allowed to reduce the number of masses offered if revenues no longer support the original foundation, or to change the masses in

---

162. Godfrey, *Right of Patronage*, 141–42.
163. Roberto Di Stefano, "Lay Patronage and the Development of Ecclesiastical Property in Spanish America: The Case of Buenos Aires, 1700–1900," *Hispanic American Historical Review* 93 (2013): 67–98.
164. *Code of Canon Law: Latin-English Edition* (Washington, D.C.: Canon Law Society of America, 1999), Title IV, Pious Wills in General and Pious Foundations, canons 1299–1310.
165. Ibid., canon 1300.
166. On the other hand, it is possible for church goods (which were presumably all received by donation at some point) to be alienated, as long as it is done for "a just cause," not "for a price less than that indicated in the appraisal," and the value received is then "invested carefully for the advantage of the Church or … expended prudently according to the purposes of the alienation." Ibid., canons 1293 and 1294.
167. Ibid., canon 1310.

some other way, such as altering the location of their offering.[168] In other words, to this day the Catholic Church reserves to itself, as it had done since the Middle Ages, the power to reduce, for cause, the one kind of posthumous obligation that is considered efficacious for the dead. In all other respects, the political and religious settlements of the nineteenth and twentieth centuries had obviated any tendency toward cy-près in modern canon law. In return for eliminating patronage, with its ongoing connection between the donor's family and the gift, the jurists renounced almost entirely the powers of deviation. It was an equitable exchange.

168. Ibid., canons 1308–9.

4

Humanist Influences

Although debates over property were endemic to late medieval reform efforts, humanists of the fifteenth and sixteenth centuries would emphasize in particular the better uses that could be made of property as a vehicle for and affirmation of moral reformation. For many humanists, wealth did not need to be a problem, nor was it an inherently corrupting force, as long as it was used well. Correctly used, money was perfectly safe; badly used, it could ruin everything. It was the disposition of things, their arrangement and management, that was the issue. The humanist emphasis on anachronism, corruption, and rebirth indirectly criticized the maintenance of things for their current uses, which should either be purified and put to their ancient uses or be set to new, contemporary, better uses. Even the city of Rome itself, the center of so much reformist and humanist attention, was evidence of the changing uses of things: some of the changes were considered good, some were not. As antiquarian efforts to reconstruct ancient Rome—like Flavio Biondo's *Roma instaurata*—made clear, the materials of ancient Rome had been set to one purpose and then, with the Christianization of Rome, transferred to another. In the ages of barbarism and decay, materials were again taken privately and reused in the making of new things. Rome was an abject lesson, as Poggio Bracciolini showed, in the ways that circumstances might sanction a change in purpose. Inheritances from the past required prudent trustees. Meanwhile, the poor, who as Michel Mollat demonstrated had been the subject of increasing hostility since the fourteenth century, appeared to require prudential reform, which prompted the humanists to think about how property could serve the commonwealth and thereby aid the poor, although not necessarily directly.[1]

Most humanists believed that the community—especially a community of friends or of Christians—should treat property so that it would be beneficial for everyone and should honor the theoretical claims of the commons even on property held individually.[2] This meant that the humanists could welcome the prospect of a wise change in use, just as the Israelites had taken the household goods of the Egyptians for their own purposes (a metaphor often applied by humanists, following Origen and Augustine, to the use of classical, pagan learning). After all, Augustine had approved of the taking of Donatist property for Catholic use.[3] There was a balancing of interests weighed by prudence and humanist predispositions, which would demand on the one hand that the follies of one rich man should not outweigh the good of all, but on the other hand that the follies of many common men should not impinge on the self-determinism of the elite few who did use their property judiciously. Private property, used well, might benefit all.

In 1440 Lorenzo Valla wrote an unpublished dialogue entitled *De professione religiosorum* in which he sharply reproved the idea that it was better to do good works after a monastic vow than of one's own free will. Monasteries, he wrote, were remedial programs for those who lacked constancy and needed to be motivated by the threat of punishment. Because of this, monks would receive a lesser reward than those who could remain in the Christian virtues without the benefit of a vow. Valla's interlocutor Laurentius challenged the vows

---

1. Michel Mollat, *Les pauvres au moyen âge* (Paris: Hachette, 1978).
2. Jonathan A. Arnold, "Profit and Piety: Thomas More, John Colet and the London Mercery," *Reformation and Renaissance Review* 12 (2010): 127–53.
3. Eden, *Friends Hold All Things in Common*, chapter one. Erasmus discussed converting pagan learning to pious uses in many places, including *Dulce bellum inexpertis*, in *Opera omnia*, vol. II-7, 28.

themselves: "It is a virtue to endure poverty, but also to distribute wealth. Chastity is good, but so is marriage. Obedience is a virtue, but so is ruling wisely."[4] Each of these conflicting virtues was good, but, in Valla's view, impossible to be sustained together with its opposing virtue in one person. Moreover, the mendicant orders lived in the gentlest form of poverty, since they were continually provided for without labor and without fear: "how great your poverty is: you are guaranteed food, clothing, a bed, and so forth, without even risking the possibility of losing them!"[5] By contrast, Laurentius defended a comfortable, but not extravagant, life in the world: "If I am able to live most blamelessly with riches, why do I need to embrace poverty?"[6] For his vocation as a scholar, "I really need my books and a considerable amount of money as well."[7] Inordinate giving indicated that "you are a fool and you do not love yourself as your neighbour" but rather "do yourself harm."[8] A monk who renounced money simply "take[s] for [him]self what belongs to others,"[9] whereas the men who live in the world and earn money to support themselves and others can provide for an uncertain future, for "how can I know what will befall me tomorrow, what I shall have to do or endure?"[10] Valla was stretching the traditional definition of acceptable wealth by asking men to consider not just what they needed now,

---

4. Lorenzo Valla, *The Profession of the Religious and Selections from the Falsely-Believed and Forged Donation of Constantine*, trans. Olga Zorzi Pugliese (Toronto: Center for Reformation and Renaissance Studies, 1985), 25; Valla, *De professione religiosorum* (Padua: Antenoreis, 1986), 22: "Est virtus paupertatis tolerande? Sed et dispensandarum opum. Est virtus continentie? Sed et coniugii. Est virtus obedientie? Sed et sapienter imperandi."

5. Valla, *Profession*, trans. Pugliese, 45; *Professione*, 52: "O quanta est vestra paupertas, quibus incolumis est, ita ut nunquam perire possit, virtus, vestitus, lectus, domus, et cetera."

6. Valla, *Profession*, trans. Pugliese, 44; *Professione*, 50: "Nam quid necesse mihi est, si cum divitiis innocentissime possum vivere, amplecti paupertatem?"

7. Valla, *Profession*, trans. Pugliese, 44; *Professione*, 51: "Mihi vero codices necessarii sunt et pecunie, eeque non pauce, unde codices plurimos ac cetera vite presidia coemam."

8. Valla, *Profession*, trans. Pugliese, 45; *Professione*, 52: "stultus sis, qui non te ut proximum amas."

9. Ibid.: "Tu cum tuis rebus te exuis, ne nescias, aliena tibi induis."

10. Valla, *Profession*, trans. Pugliese, 47; *Professione*, 55: "Unde scio, quid mihi cras eventurum sit, quid me facere, quid me pati oporteat?"

but prudently to gather into barns in order to protect against the future too. There was no penalty attached to keeping material goods rather than distributing them as alms: "I deserve a large remuneration for the alms I have given, but no punishment for those I have not donated."[11] Valla did not reject an endowed church *per se*, as long as it did good things with the money that it had. Care of temporal things was inherent to the work of the church: "pontiffs and priests ... have the task of distributing goods and riches, as is shown by the ministry and name of 'deacons.'"[12] And so, Valla summarized, "the Church possesses riches and is not condemned for owning or using them, but for tightfistedness and wastefulness in handling them."[13] Endowments were fine if they were used well.

Valla was extreme, but more tempered humanists agreed that it was better to use property well than to renounce it. Still, in seeking an apparent compromise with the world, humanists were unwilling to accommodate the imperfect, the wasteful, and the irrational in either property arrangements or personal conduct. They confronted their readers with the unchristian and unreasonable paradoxes of human behavior. Many of these critiques picked up on patristic themes. Erasmus contended that deathbed baptisms—if done from a desire to sin right up until the last possible moment—were of dubious efficacy, and he pointed out that many prayers for a good death were little more than a plea to be permitted to carry on living badly.[14] Last-minute renunciations of the world meant nothing: "Do you think it is important if you are transported to the grave with your head wrapped in the cowl of Francis? Likeness of habit will be of no profit to you when you are dead if your morals were unlike his

11. Valla, *Profession*, trans. Pugliese, 50; *Professione*, 60: "ex eleemosynis factis multum ego mereor premiorum, ex omissis vero nihil penarum."

12. Valla, *Profession*, trans. Pugliese, 46; *Professione*, 53: "pontificibus ac sacerdotibus, quibus etiam opum divitiarumque commendata est dispensatio, quod ipsum diaconum ministerium nomenque declarat?"

13. Valla, *Profession*, trans. Pugliese, 46; *Professione*, 53: "Habet ergo et Ecclesia thesauros, nec eorum possessio aut usus, sed tenacitas atque abusus reprehenditur."

14. Erasmus, *De immensa misericordia Dei concio*, in *Opera omnia*, vol. V-7, 1–98. See also canon quartus of the *Enchiridion Militis Christiani*, in *Opera omnia*, vol. V-8, 170–80.

in life."[15] Almsgiving should be done steadily throughout life to the worthy poor so that at death the estate would pass only to the heir, without any bequests.[16] Erasmus pointed out the burden placed on the living when the dying took advantage of their special status to bind the living to a "sacred" duty to perform the actions that the dying had meant—but failed—to do, or to make the receipt of their inheritance contingent upon performance of religious obligations to help the deceased.[17]

Erasmus similarly preserved many medieval ideas about property and gifts but changed their tone. In his 1524 sermon *De immensa misericordia Dei*, Erasmus observed that giving leads to being given to, mercy leads to mercy. Humanist friendships involved the reciprocal exchange of gifts, and the humanists did not suggest that the ownership of property was impossible to reconcile with the Christian life, since what mattered was indifference to material goods, a willingness to lose them or do without, but not, ideally, to live in poverty or squalor.[18] As Erasmus argued in the *Enchiridion*, "Suppose money comes your way; if it does not pose a hindrance to your [peace of mind], [direct it and] make friends for yourself of the mammon of iniquity. But if you are afraid of losing your [peace of mind], despise filthy lucre, and in emulation of Crates the Theban hurl your troublesome burden into the sea."[19] But, Erasmus acknowledged later in the *Enchiridion*,

---

15. Erasmus, *Collected Works*, vol. 66, trans. Charles Fantazzi, 72; Erasmus, *Enchiridion*, in *Opera omnia*, vol. V-8, 196: "Magnum quiddam putas, si Francisci cucullo obvolutus, sepulchro inferaris. Nihil proderit vestis similis mortuo tibi, si mores fuerunt dissimiles vivo."

16. See his colloquy *Funus*, in *Opera omnia*, vol. I-3, 537–51.

17. Erasmus, *Peregrinatio religionis ergo*, in *Opera omnia*, vol. I-3, 470–94, and *Funus* in *Opera omnia*, vol. I-3, 537–51.

18. See, for instance, Thomas More's *Utopia*, in *The Complete Works of St. Thomas More*, vol. 4, ed. Edward Surtz and J. H. Hexter (New Haven, Conn.: Yale University Press, 1965), or Erasmus's *Convivium religiosum*, in *Opera omnia*, vol. I-3, 221–22 and 231–66, or *Enchiridion* in *Opera omnia*, vol. V-8.

19. Erasmus, *Collected Works*, vol. 66, trans. Charles Fantazzi, 62. Translation modified slightly to avoid confusion. Erasmus, canon quartus of the *Enchiridion*, in *Opera omnia*, vol. V-8, 174: "Obvenit pecunia, si nihil obstat ad bonam mentem, administra para tibi amicos de mammona iniquitatis. Sin bonae mentis times dispendium, contemne damnosum lucrum, et vel Cratem illum Thebanum imitare, molestam sarcinam in mare potius praecipita."

although one could use property privately, one should not actually believe property to be your own, since Christians should regard their property as belonging to all.[20] There were many ways to use property incorrectly: it was neither good to accumulate money in order to care only for one's family or to give away everything and then end up begging.[21] The humanist solution echoed the patristic ideal of an interior detachment from money even while using it.

And yet the humanist, unlike the early Christian, should be detached from worldly goods that were also exceptionally well appointed. The inhabitants of More's *Utopia,* for example, were indifferent to the material abundance they produced—and which they continued producing, for no reason other than good social order.[22] Erasmus's ideal humanists, exemplified in his 1522 colloquy *Convivium religiosum,* used property well: tastefully, liberally, and with appreciation but not passion. They, like Dürer's Jerome, worked in beautiful libraries with rich collections. They served banquets of refreshingly simple fare, complete with plates of vegetables grown by their servants in their own gardens. These were men who knew just what presents to give their friends.

But much religious use of property, conversely, did not seem tasteful to the humanists, and the critical edge of humanism found some popular manifestations of medieval piety to be tacky, wasteful, and superstitious. Amid Erasmus's meditations in *Convivium religiosum* on the right use of property, he argued that many bequests for purposes should be put to a better use than the one the donor had intended. He wrote of a particularly opulent Carthusian monastery, "they have a legacy of three thousand ducats a year to spend on construction of the monastery. And some people think it a crime to divert that money, contrary to the testator's intentions, to pious uses."[23] His observation that this proposed redirection was considered

20. Erasmus, *Enchiridion,* in *Opera omnia,* vol. V-8, 236.
21. Erasmus, "Avaritia," in *Enchiridion,* in *Opera omnia,* vol. V-8.
22. Lisa Jardine, *Worldly Goods: A New History of the Renaissance* (London: Macmillan, 1996).
23. Desiderius Erasmus, "A Godly Feast," trans. Craig R. Thompson, in *Collected Works,* vol. 39, 199; *Convivium religiosum,* in *Opera omnia,* vol. I-3, 257: "illis legata in singulos annos tria milia ducatorum in structuram monasterii. Et sunt

a crime indicates the growing controversy over the inviolability of the testator's intentions. Erasmus posted that most ostentatious donations were given not as a mark of charity but for the glory of the donor, and the money ought to be redeemed by being used for true charity. Similarly, in his *Peregrinatio religionis ergo*, Erasmus warned that church property should never be stolen—and yet, he was sure that the saints, who helped the poor while they were alive, would prefer it if the gifts made in their honor were given to the poor instead. Here Erasmus approached the problem of the redirection of a gift from the perspective not of the donor and his heirs but rather of the apparently unwilling recipient, the saint.

Erasmus did not abandon the idea of a society held together by gifts in favor of a world of things that were either taken or bought. He still imagined a world in which everything had been given—and always, in a theological and metaphysical sense, given for a purpose. An abuse of this purpose was not merely an offense but even ingratitude and delegitimizing. Thus Erasmus explained pacifism with the metaphor of gifts in his *Dulce bellum inexpertis*. Each animal was given certain weapons, but only man was born helpless and unable to defend himself. This circumstance was nature's demonstration that man's purpose was *caritas,* not war, which was why man had been blessed with the gifts of reason, persuasiveness, and sociability, all of which should serve peace. But men had increasingly turned their gifts toward unintended ends. They applied their intelligence toward war. They followed Aristotle in rejecting the commonality of goods. They used money exclusively for themselves instead of helping the poor.

All gifts were revocable, though, Erasmus argued. Specifically, the power given to sovereigns by their subjects could be taken back if it was abused, as through needless wars that destroyed the population for the honor of the ruler. Political arrangements were an exchange of gifts, and the abuse of a gift ruined the rights of the recipient to it. To those princes who made war against other Christians for their own dynastic purposes, Erasmus warned, "What power and soveraynte so

---

qui putent esse nefas, eam pecuniam in pios usus avertere, praeter mentem testatoris."

ever you have, you have it by the consente of the people. And if I be not deceived, he that hath auctorite to gyve, hath auctoritie to take awaye ageyne."[24] A modern reading of this text would tend to emphasize the consent alone, but the fact that this consent was a gift was an equally important part of the meaning. The humanists were annoyed by the unreasonable uses of materials: the wasteful, imprudent, superstitious, or, in this case, bloody and destructive. But they were not ready to abandon entirely the idea that gifts should be preserved for their given purpose, if that purpose was good.

Indeed, the language of patronage remained vital for them. Coluccio Salutati argued in his *De seculo et religione* that the poor were the true patrons of all cities and institutions, "establishing, augmenting, and preserving" them through their labor, which meant that efforts to reform the commonwealth would implicitly serve its true patrons, to whom the city thus owed certain rights of hospitality.[25] Erasmus likewise drew on echoes of patronage to explain how horrific it was that the church of Christ had embraced war: "as though the church of Christ was begun, augmented, and stablished (*orta, provecta, constabilita*) with warres and slaughters, and not rather in spillynge of the bloude of martirs, sufferance, and despisynge of this lyfe."[26] This tripartite phrase echoed three canon law duties of the patron, recast in the language of cultivation and growth rather than *fundatio, dotatio,*

---

24. The translation is from the 1534 English translation published by Thomas Berthelet, *Bellum Erasmi* (London: Thomas Bellum, 1534), 29. Denis L. Drysdell translated it as: "This same 'right' that you have was given by the consent of the people, and the same people who gave it, if I am not mistaken, have the power to take it away." Erasmus, Adage 3001 IV.i.I, in *Collected Works*, vol. 35, 428. In the original, from *Opera omnia*, vol. II-7, 36: "Hoc ipsum ius, quod habes, populi consensus dedit. Eiusdem autem, ni fallor, est tollere, qui contulit." Erasmus used the same idea of the people giving consent to their rule in *Sileni Alcibiadis*.

25. Coluccio Salutati, *On the World and Religious Life*, trans. Tina Marshall (Cambridge, Mass.: Harvard University Press, 2014), Book II.9.38, 278–79: "Ad hanc terrenam civitatem instituendam, augendam, atque conservandam pauperes divitibus prestitisse."

26. *Bellum Erasmi*, 34; *Opera omnia*, vol. I-3, 38: "quasi bellis ac stragibus orta, provecta, constabilita sit Ecclesia, ac non potius sanguine, tolerantia, vitaeque contemptu!" *Collected Works*, vol. 35, 431: "as if the Church had originated, grown, and become established by means of wars and slaughter instead of by the blood of the martyrs, by their tolerance, and by their scorn for life."

and *aedificatio*. Christ was the first founder, but true Christians had rights in the church because they had given to it with their suffering, which in turn gave them rights to demand its correct usage. Patronage was too useful to the project of reform to be abandoned.

Another humanist, Juan Luis Vives, who had spent time as a fellow at Fox's Corpus Christi under the patronage of Wolsey, was willing to be more precise in his 1526 *De subventione pauperum*. This has been called the first social welfare treatise, as it offered a plan for the city of Bruges to mitigate poverty. Vives began with the Fall, which was the origin of the delusion, or, as he called it, the custom, of private property. Really, he argued, "what is life, but a slow death"—a man was effectively always on his deathbed and never the real possessor of anything.[27] Nor could he be, given that all people were mutually dependent upon each other, upon the bonds of love that joined society, and upon the natural bounty of the world, which belonged to everyone as a gift from God. But it was not, in Vives's view, simple greed that created poverty, although avarice certainly played a role. Rather, "lazy people demanded to be fed by the work of others."[28] The commons was divided up so that the lazy would not exploit it. Both rich and poor had failed, and the unworthiness of many of the poor wrongly stopped the rich from giving, which is why when Vives considered the ideal municipal policy, he made state support unpleasant to receive.

But there was great cause for optimism, because people were naturally charitable and good, even in the fallen world. Stinginess could stem from good motives, since "we think that we may be doing wrong to those we love, such as our children, our parents and our friends."[29] On the other hand, Vives was outraged by the refus-

27. Juan Luis Vives, *The Origins of Modern Welfare: Juan Luis Vives, De subventione pauperum, and City of Ypres, Forma subventionis pauperum*, trans. Paul Spicker (Bern: Peter Lang, 2010), 9. *Joannis Lodovici Vivis Valentini De subventione pauperum libri II* (Lyon: Melchioris and Treschel, 1532), I.2: "Nam quid aliud est haec vita, quam continua quaedam mors?"

28. Vives, *Origins*, trans. Spicker, 11; Vives, *De subventione*, I.2: "alii inertes, de alienis operibus victum postularent."

29. Vives, *Origins*, trans. Spicker, 22; Vives, *De subventione*, I.5: "liberis, propinquis, necessariis."

al of the dead to release their grasp of the goods that they had never really owned and had unjustly kept back from the poor: "in death, greed continues to live," through the erection of monuments, tombs, churches and chapels, decorated with one's coat of arms "perhaps to conquer heaven itself if necessary," and "as for the thefts and spoliations that are committed against poor people, as for the riches which are unjustly acquired and kept, even though they are no longer ours, we ask that psalms are sung for us and that masses are said."[30] Vives was trying to close the testamentary loophole and return to a strict interpretation of Augustine, according to which the dead could be helped only by those who were sincerely inspired by love and care for them, not by those who had been paid to pray.

Moreover, Vives pointed out that "posterity has no end: what limits could one place on the accumulation of wealth? What are you doing? Do you want to protect your descendants from all care? Do you want to leave them with nothing to do, with no way to improve themselves?"[31] One man could never become wealthy enough to take care of all of his descendants, and, in fact, an inheritance was not very good for the heirs: "someone who has not worked to get things has not learned how to keep them ... [and so] in trying by every means to enrich their children, the father has left them nothing but the means to be foolish and badly behaved."[32] This was a necessary step towards cy-près doctrine, to assert that the heirs did not need or were unworthy of receiving a failed charitable bequest. Vives explained that money should go to those who would know how to use it: if sons lived badly then their fathers should place their

30. Vives, *Origins*, trans. Spicker, 33; Vives, *De subventione*, I.7: "ut etiam avaritia vivat in mortuo," "vel caelum expugnet armatus," and "Ex praeda et spoliis pauperum et divitiis inique vel quaesitis vel retentis, etiam quum iam amplius nostrae non sunt, iubemus cani nobis nescio quot psalmos, et missas dici."

31. Vives, *Origins*, trans. Spicker, 40; Vives, *De subventione*, I.8: "At posteritatem cogitat quis, id profecto infinitum est, quis tandem erit cumulandi modus? Quid ipsis nullam ne vis curam relinquere? Nihil quod agant? In quo se exerceant?"

32. Vives, *Origins*, trans. Spicker, 41; Vives, *De subventione*, I.8: "Num quod conservare nescit, qui laborem non adhibuit in quaerendo. Aliorum filii sine divitiis fuissent optimi, in divitiis sunt pessimi, ut instrumentum videatur flagitiorum ac scelerum is pater reliquisse." Vives echoed Salvian on this point, probably inadvertently.

inheritances into trusts, with reversionary interests to the poor as restitution if the sons did not reform.[33]

It would be possible to rationalize the use of property only if testaments were better made. Vives exemplified the ambivalence of his time: it was unjust, he wrote, to redistribute property, and yet a rich man needed to know that "he possesses these things by the consent, will, intention and disposition of nature itself" and that if he did not honor the natural rights of the poor, then he was "nothing but a thief, a monopolist, convicted and condemned by natural law."[34] Here Vives placed something higher than the intentions of the testator: the intentions of nature herself. Since a thief had no right under the law to give away his stolen goods, his intentions in making a donation were, by extension, void. He repeated the theme in decrying waste:

> Everyone is guilty of theft and diversion, I repeat, if they waste money by gambling, if they hoard it in chests at home, spend it in feasts and banquets, spend it on precious clothing or on furniture full of diverse gold and silver vessels; whoever has clothing rotting in their house, whoever consumes their wealth by buying excessive or useless things.[35]

Vives was moving to a model of charity as a free gift, without any expectation of return here on earth, neither masses nor prayers nor gratitude from the destitute. Indeed, Vives tried to make this clear by calling charity a "sacrifice," moving it out of the gift-countergift exchange, although Christ would still offer a return in the next life.[36] Vives cautioned that since there was never any security in this world, the Christian should not worry about his future. And yet he could

---

33. Vives, *De subventione*, I.8.
34. Vives, *Origins*, trans. Spicker, 47; Vives, *De subventione*, I.9: "Quapropter sciat quisquis naturae munera possidet, si cum egeno fratre communicet, iure possidere, et ex naturae voluntate ac instituto. Sin secus, furem et raptorem esse naturae lege convictum et damnatum, quum occupet et detineat, quae natura non ipsi uni procrearat."
35. Vives, *Origins*, trans. Spicker, 48; Vives, *De subventione*, I.9: "Fur inquam est et raptor, quisquis pecuniam in aleam prodigit, qui domi in arcis coactam detinet, qui in ludos effundit aut epulas, qui in preciosas admodum vestes, aut instructissimum vario argento atque auro abacum, cui vestimenta domi computrescunt, qui emptitandis rebus supervacuis, aut inutilibus, pecuniam expendunt, qui in vanas superstructiones."
36. Vives, *Origins*, trans. Spicker, 43; Vives, *De subventione*, I.8: "sacrificium."

not resist the suggestion that charity was a kind of secular insurance too: "what you give will come back to you with interest, even in goods in this life."[37] Because so few could manage to give wholeheartedly and without expectation of return, charity failed to have its intended effect: "We make them ungrateful by relieving them halfheartedly, with coldness or malice, not with pure intentions. We have other aims than charity and grace; we outrage the poor person by the benefit itself, by the reminders, by our faces or by the annoyance we show."[38]

Although money was the least part of charity, and poverty itself was a gift, Vives also claimed that the poor were the causes of crime, insurrection, disease, prostitution, and sorcery in the commonwealth. Money mattered, then, for moral reform. He hoped to create a municipal system that would simultaneously draw on a tax base for poor relief and also inspire donations from the wealthy into the poor boxes of the parish. Vives acknowledged that "if true charity dwelt in us ... it would hold all things in common."[39] Since this was not the case, secular authorities should take responsibility for the poor; this was their jurisdiction. But in their zeal to establish a municipal system for the poor, Vives cautioned those authorities not to violate the donors' intentions in existing institutions and endowments:

No one may circumvent the founders' stipulations (*de legibus conditorum*) in setting up these institutions; these must remain inviolable. With these one should interpret not merely the words but attend primarily to their jurisdiction (as in deeds of trust) and will (*voluntas*) (as in testaments). On this point, no doubt it was the donors' desire that the funds left by them should be distributed to the best possible purposes and used in the worthiest places; they were not so much concerned by whom this should be done, or how, as that it should be done.[40]

---

37. Vives, *Origins*, trans. Spicker, 40; Vives, *De subventione*, I.8: "quod tanto cum foenore recepturus es, etiam in bonis vitae huius."
38. Vives, *Origins*, trans. Spicker, 34; Vives, *De subventione*, I.8.
39. Juan Luis Vives, *On Assistance to the Poor*, trans. Alice Tobriner (Toronto: University of Toronto Press, 1999), 37; Vives, *De subventione*, II.2: "Si quid in nobis Charitas valeret, ipsa esset nobis lex, quae amanti non est posita, ea faceret omnia communia."
40. Vives, *On Assistance*, trans. Tobriner, translation modified, 38; Vives, *De subventione*, II.2: "Nemo de legibus conditorum causificetur: inviolatae perdurabunt;

This was exactly the logic of cy-près, articulated by a humanist in a bestselling book that was sold around Europe and in England. On the one hand, the intentions should not be violated, but on the other hand, any donor would have wanted the best possible use for his or her money, and so the redirection of gifts was in fact exactly what he or she would have wanted. Vives drew this principle not from the law—which he admitted he did not know—but from common sense and humanist philanthropy. Paul Spicker, in translating this passage, found it puzzling:

> This is confusingly written in the original. Three other interpreters have seized on part of the phrase, that the wishes of the founders should remain inviolate.... I have taken it in the opposite sense, partly because Vives is dismissing the idea as an excuse, but also because I think that is the only way it can be read consistently with what comes before and after it. Vives seems here to be anticipating an objection, and this may indeed have been one of the key objections to removing the management of alms from established charitable foundations to the city.[41]

Although Spicker erred in retranslating the passage as "let no-one make the pretext that the rules of the founders remain inviolate," he did so for excellent reasons, noticing not just the apparent contradiction in Vives but indeed the tension at the heart of cy-près.[42] Spicker also correctly observed how central the problem of donor's rights and intentions were to municipal poor relief plans.

Vives further asserted the fundamental right of the state to control the property within its geographical domain by making the state the patron of its citizens: "Everyone has acquired his property with the help of the state, as if it were a gift, and can keep and hold his wealth only through the state."[43] Still, it would be easiest to redirect

---

verba in his expendenda non sunt, sed aequitas, ut in contractibus bonae fidei, et voluntas, ut in testamentis, de qua dubium non est, quin ea fuerit ut in usus, quam fieri posset optimos, relictae a se facultates distribuerentur, et dignissimo consumerentur loco; per quos, aut quemadmodum fieret, non tam solliciti, quam ut fieret."

41. Vives, *Origins*, trans. Spicker, 70n.
42. Ibid., 70.
43. Vives, *On Assistance*, trans. Tobriner, 38; Vives, *De subventione*, II.2: "Praesertim quum quisque fortunas suas beneficio civitatis tamquam munus acquisierit, ac eiusdem ope conservet, atque retineat."

foundations by first depleting them of purpose: forbid begging, offer work to the indigent, and empty out the hospitals of everyone who was not completely helpless, including the administrators who were attracted to the ease of life that a rich endowment provided. Vives proposed simplifying these institutions, eliminating all traces of luxury, and then dispensing minimal but adequate care. But Vives acknowledged that some of those who were attached to almshouses would have to be allowed to stay, including "those who have a right to stay there, such as those who have a blood right, because their ancestors made provision in exchange for the good they were doing with the hospital, or by giving a large enough part of their fortune."[44] It was common for medieval donors to include a clause stipulating that poor family members would always have a first claim on the resources of the donation, and Vives did not want to overturn these property arrangements.[45] Notably, however, it was in these concrete arrangements that humanists saw the rights of heirs; the broader sense that a donor's family had a continuing relationship to the gift and even oversight of it was gone. The donor had disinherited his heirs from that part of his estate when he made the gift.

Vives was suspicious of the accumulation of money, which attracted evil men. In an inadvertent echo of Hus, Vives suggested that the goal should be instead to give money away immediately and to prevent any men from dying of hunger while charitable trustees accumulated funds for something else.[46] Indeed, Vives specifically forbade charities to buy land, which would delay the distribution of charity and promote corruption.[47] Vives anticipated that both the indigent poor and the current trustees of endowments would fight

---

44. Vives, *Origins*, trans. Spicker, 75; Vives, *De subventione*, II.3: "In hospitalibus, qui validi sunt, et illic haerent (a) tamquam fuci fruentes alienis sudoribus, exeant, et ad opus mittantur, nisi iure aliquo illic eos manere oporteat, (b) velut gentilitio, ut quibus hoc munus relictum est beneficio suorum maiorum, aut qui de facultatibus suis illi domui impartiti fuerint."

45. Fehler, *Poor Relief and Protestantism*, 49.

46. Since legally *usus* preserved the substance of the property and did not permit any alteration, this radical proposal to rework charity faced significant structural inhibitions.

47. Vives, *De subventione*, II.6.

182 Humanist Influences

back, saying: "The stipulations of founders should not be changed."[48] But it would be possible, he repeated, to alter these endowments while better honoring the intentions of the donors:

> To these we reply: ... "If nothing is to be changed, why have they themselves gradually altered the first regulations established by the founders of an institution to such a degree that those in force today run counter to the original?" Let the records be opened, let the memories of old men be questioned. It will be discovered how much the present administration differs from that when the institution was new, and while the founder was still alive or only recently deceased. Here we have them on a crucial matter. We do not wish to change the original organization; we will not tolerate the violation of the founder's intent, for in every will this is the first—or, rather, the only—issue. The original intent can be discovered from records and the memory of many individuals. As for the will of the founder, who does not understand that these men left their money and endowments, not that the rich might be sated but that the poor might be supported, even as they pray for their deceased benefactors that they might be forgiven their sins and be received by God into His heavenly dwelling?[49]

In other words, the easiest resolution to objections would be to connect reform to the duty of society to fulfill the true intentions of the will, perhaps at the expense of the particular stipulations of the foundation, a modification partly justified by the fact that the foundations had altered over time.

Vives's readers understood that this proposal was radically innovative. In his letters, Alice Tobriner points out, he displayed an

---

48. Vives, *On Assistance*, trans. Tobriner, 52; Vives, *De subventione*, II.8: "statuta conditorum non mutanda."

49. Vives, *On Assistance*, trans. Tobriner, 53; Vives, *De subventione*, II.8: "Quibus nos opponemus ... iam si nihil est mutandum, cur ipsi primos a conditoribus relictos mores paulatim adeo immutarunt, ut hos pugnare cum illis appareat? Evolvantur acta, interrogetur senum memoria, reperietur quantum haec administrandi ratio ab illa distet, quae erat novo opere, vivente adhuc conditore, aut paullum ante vita functo; nos hic eos tenemus medios; nolumus mutari primam institutionem; non patimur institutoris voluntatem irritam fieri, quae in testamento omni prima, immo sola spectatur; de prima constitutione constat ex actis, et memoria multorum; at de voluntate, quis non videt viros illos pecunias et annuos reditus legasse, quibus non explerentur divites, sed sustentarentur pauperes, oraturi pro anima defuncti ut a peccatis vitae soluta et pura in sedes illas coelestes a Deo recipiatur?"

unusual anxiety about this text: he was reluctant to discuss it with anyone, because of the controversy that it would cause, and he was particularly worried about its relationship to existing laws.[50] The bishop of Sarepta condemned it as heretical.[51] Ole Peter Grell notes that comparable plans in Lyon were criticized by Catholic hierarchs as injurious to piety, largely because of the issue of the diversion of endowments.[52] Thirty years later, Lorenzo de Villavicencio responded to Vives with *De oeconomia sacra circa pauperum curam*, where he not only accused Vives of heresy but again raised the problem of the inviolability of the intentions of the donors. Vives's claim that he was protecting the intentions of the donors was not universally believed.

Vives's proposal was apparently inspired by the systems of poor relief erected in evangelical German cities, but there were Catholic precedents for the creation of a municipal poor box, such as the one that had flourished in Douai since the fourteenth century. Michel Mollat has shown that cities endowed about a quarter of their hospitals in the late Middle Ages in the Holy Roman Empire and had taken over the management of even more than that.[53] Jacques Chiffoleau found a struggle between the commune and the church for control of charitable endowments beginning in the thirteenth century in Avignon.[54] Natalie Zemon Davis observed that the Hôtel-Dieu passed into municipal administration at the end of the fifteenth century.[55] Similarly, cities in the Low Countries were innovating with common chests. Thus the desire to reform and be reformed was manifest before the Reformation, as, for example, in the Regensburg Poor Law Statutes (1515). Catholic cities of the Low Countries, such as Mons, soon erected their own poor relief municipal systems, al-

50. Vives, *On Assistance*, trans. Tobriner, 17–18.
51. Ibid., 18.
52. Ole Peter Grell, "The Protestant Imperative of Christian Care and Neighbourly Love," in *Health Care and Poor Relief in Protestant Europe, 1500–1700*, ed. Andrew Cunningham and Ole Peter Grell (London: Routledge, 1997), 45–46.
53. Mollat, *Les pauvres*.
54. Jacques Chiffoleau, *La Comptabilité de l'au-delà: Les hommes, la mort et la religion dans la région d'Avignon à la fin du Moyen Âge* (Paris: Albin Michel, 2011), 331.
55. Natalie Zemon Davis, "Poor Relief, Humanism, and Heresy," in *Society and Culture in Early Modern France* (Stanford, Calif.: Stanford University Press, 1965), 38.

184 Humanist Influences

though not without criticism. Ypres, where the project for social reform became a city ordinance, required that future almsgiving and future endowments for the poor were to be placed in the common chest. Of gifts already made, only the portions that had been specifically designated "to the poor" or that were "not bequeathed but left to an uncertain use" should be turned over to the common chest, while the rest was to be maintained for the purposes for which they had been donated, "faithfully bestowed according to the ordinance and will of the founders."[56] Moreover, Ypres did not, like Protestant cities, ban private charities or hope to turn all charitable works over to a centralized structure.[57] Consequently, it maintained a number of medieval hospitals and poor relief institutions and urged all people to continue with personalized, private giving too.[58]

The Ypres policy was sent to the faculty of Theology at the Sorbonne in 1531 for their approval. The faculty largely received the policy as "hard but useful ... pious and salutary," but they could not agree with some aspects: relief was denied to outsiders; begging was banned, especially by mendicant monks; and the selfish focus on their own city ignored their dependence on the surrounding countryside. The Sorbonne urged them to continue to permit private charity, not to force the collection of alms, and to be careful not to violate the endowments already in place: "[T]he secular Magistrates should not under the pretext of piety, or of relieving those without means, presume to commit sacrilege or to sequester the tithes and goods of the church. This would not be (the act) of virtuous and faithful Catholics, but of impious heretics, Waldensians, Wycliffites, or Lutherans."[59]

---

56. Vives, *Origins*, trans. Spicker, 119. *Forma subventionis pauperum quae apud Hyperas Flandrorum urbem viget, universae Reipublicae Christianae longe utilissima* (Antwerp: Martin Caesar, 1531): "rebus in vagum usum a testatoribus derelicta, ad communem pauperum crumenam transferretur: caeteris ubique partibus (quibus ex ordinatione fundatoris debentur) fideliter applicatis."

57. Vives, *Origins*, trans. Spicker, 129–30 and 134.

58. J. Nolf, *La réforme de la bienfaisance publique à Ypres au XVIe siècle* (Ghent: E. van Goethem, 1915).

59. "The Response of the Censors of the School of Theology in Paris," in Vives, *Origins*, trans. Spicker, 142. In *Forma subventionis pauperum*: "rem quidem arduam, sed utilem censemus: piam ac salutarem.... Ad haec caveant seculares

Although Catholic states helped themselves to church property as needed throughout the sixteenth, seventeenth, and eighteenth centuries, they tended not, in the creation of municipal systems, to violate donor intent, even while individual Catholic humanists entertained the idea. Natalie Zemon Davis pointed to humanism, not Protestantism, as the central inspiration for social welfare innovation, particularly in the vesting of control in lay hands, a process that had begun in the late Middle Ages.[60] Examining Lyon, she found that most of the participants in the project of the Aumône-Générale were Catholic, not Protestant. For example, the humanist priest Jean de Vauzelles urged that money given for masses for the dead be put into poor relief. This was a proposal that never had a real chance of success, and Lyon did not follow the suggestion. Instead, in the creation of its poor relief system, it handed over to the secular authorities endowments that were already earmarked for alms, transferring their supervision but not subverting donor intent.[61] This was typical of sixteenth-century Catholic social welfare programs. Even Venice, which had a strained relationship with Rome and a heightened concern for the loss of lands in perpetuity, did not divert ecclesiastical endowments when it created a poor relief system in 1529.[62]

For most Catholic humanist hierarchs, donor intent thus supplied an already good purpose that could be relied upon to meet contemporary needs. Gasparo Contarini, the Catholic humanist and reformer, argued in his *De officio viri boni et probi episcopi* that the bishop was a "procurator" of goods that had been given for two purposes: to care for the poor and provide for divine service.[63] Contarini urged bishops

---

Magistratus ne sub pietatis praetextu, aut sublevandorum inopum, ausu sacrilego ecclesiarum sive ecclesiasticorum proventus et bona quaecumque surripere attractareve praesumant: id quod non catholicorum est virorum fidelium: sed impiorum hereticorum Valdensium, Viclemstarum, ac Lutheranorum."

60. Davis, "Poor Relief, Humanism, and Heresy," in *Society and Culture*, 17–64. See also Miri Rubin, *Charity and Community in Medieval Cambridge* (Cambridge: Cambridge University Press, 1987).
61. Davis, "Poor Relief, Humanism, and Heresy," in *Society and Culture*, 54–55.
62. Brian Pullan, *Rich and Poor in Renaissance Venice: The Social Institutions of a Catholic State, to 1620* (Oxford: Basil Blackwell, 1971), 135 and 253.
63. Gasparo Contarini, *The Office of a Bishop*, trans. John Patrick Donnelly (Milwaukee: Marquette University Press, 2002), 118–19. On Contarini, see Elisabeth

to remember the intentions of the donors: "[W]hat is more improper than lavishing the income of the bishopric, which upright men once bequeathed to enrich divine worship and relieve the poverty of the needy, on a great array of dinners and the gluttony of the palate?"[64] Contarini recommended that the bishop should ignore the fourfold canon law regulation on how a bishop's income should be distributed in favor of a more expansive vision of charity, in order that he might behave as a Christian and not as "a person who thinks that he should enter into litigation with God, as if in a lawcourt."[65] The claim of the poor to the property of the church was so great that "normal" (*de more*) expenses of divine worship could be curtailed if necessary to save the lives of the poor.[66] Meanwhile, the intentions (*mens*) of the donors were to be honored even in ways that those donors had not explicitly stipulated: a man who had given property to the bishopric had intended that it would be used for the care of the poor who lived within the bishop's jurisdiction, not beyond it, and so the bishop should care only for the local poor, following the example of Pietro Barozzi, the bishop of Padua, who had made this same argument on the basis of donor intent.[67]

New Opportunities

Despite the ongoing concern for the donor's will, however, humanism emerged at a time when many endowments required some kind of intervention because they had decayed due to the inflationary pressures that followed the Black Death and were now insufficient to their designated purpose. Trustees were required to raise new funds, merge institutions, or reduce the services offered, and so

---

Gleason, *Gasparo Contarini: Venice, Rome, and Reform* (Berkeley: University of California Press, 1993).

64. Contarini, *Office*, 88–89: "Praeterea quid magis indecens, quam reditus Episcopatus, quos probi viri olim legarunt ad divinum cultum augendum et ad levandam inopiam, in magis coenarum apparatibus atque gulae ingluvie profundi?"

65. Ibid., 118–19: "qui tanquam in foro sibi cum Deo litigandum esse putet."

66. Ibid., 120–21.

67. Ibid., 120–23.

the endowments, and the dead that they served, encumbered the resources of the living.[68] Since any addition to a chantry's endowment usually required a new license and the payment of a new fine, these requirements were burdensome for those who tried to prevent chantries from failing.[69] Heirs were called in to consult on how to rescue the endowment, since their consent was necessary to revisions and diversions, but they often retrieved what was left of floundering endowments and then applied them to a new use as they saw fit.

Across Europe decayed foundations were tempting to secular lords, since the endowments still had some wealth, even if they were apparently no longer able to fulfill the founder's intentions. If the gift was old and there was no heir to be found, decayed endowments might be rolled into new, ambitious projects, constructed by bishops or municipalities. Many late medieval universities, both in England and on the Continent, received these endowments, sometimes maintaining parts of the original foundation, including prayers for the donor and the distribution of alms. In England, revisions to chantries and other similar bequests were supposed to be done by papal dispensation until 1533, when a Faculty Office was established in England. In fact, modifications were sometimes made on the ground without appealing to the pope—by heirs, priests, municipalities, bishops, and, in one famous case, Parliament.[70] Financial exigencies were the easiest grounds for obtaining the pope's consent to the eradication of some portion of the original purpose of the foundation, as when the pope agreed in 1423 to eliminate the choral services attached to Tormarton collegiate college, thereby abolishing the stipends for one chaplain, a deacon, a subdeacon, and three choristers, while leaving a warden and three chaplains to maintain the prescribed divine services.[71]

68. Samuel Cohn Jr., "Renaissance Attachment to Things: Material Culture in Last Wills and Testaments," *The Economic History Review* 65 (2012): 984–1004. Some scholars have looked at the rate of failure and speculated that property was being diverted or mismanaged by lazy clerics. Wood-Legh, *Perpetual Chantries;* Nicholas Orme and Margaret Webster, *The English Hospital 1070–1570* (New Haven, Conn.: Yale University Press, 1995), 127–46.
69. Raban, *Mortmain Legislation*, 61.
70. Kreider, *English Chantries*, 32.
71. Nicholas Orme, *Education in the West of England 1066–1548* (Exeter: University of Exeter, 1976), 213.

A. G. Dickens pointed out that in Yorkshire, of the 94 hospitals and almshouses that had been founded during the Middle Ages, 55 had disappeared by 1500 and 17 had been converted into private, noncharitable property, in some cases under the control of the heirs.[72] Moreover, the frequency with which heirs were able to have even healthy chantry endowments returned to them rather than devoted to new pious causes is a significant problem for the idea that cy-près doctrine was grounded in late medieval practice, given that local ecclesiastics would have been aware of these procedures.[73] Indeed, by the time that the chantries were dissolved in 1547, Dickens notes, many had been converted to new uses in the fourteenth and fifteenth centuries.[74] York's municipal government successfully took over chantry assets in 1536 during a "period of acute financial stringency"—a canonically justifiable diversion of use, although, as R. W. Hoyle finds, the only chantries seized "were those where the founder had no living descendant" who could protest on the basis of his or her rights to the property.[75] Dickens suggests that the "prosaic and utilitarian spirit of the Tudor citizen"[76] naturally sought a better use for the endowments due to a "lack of all scruple and superstition"[77]—but York was scrupulous enough to make provision for the priests involved to receive a pension in return for the continued observance of a reduced schedule of commemorative masses.[78] An act of Parliament was obtained to affirm the town's right to take over the failing endowments. This was not, then, quite a free-for-all, but

72. A. G. Dickens, *The English Reformation,* 2d ed. (University Park: Pennsylvania State University Press, 1989), 234.
73. Kreider, *English Chantries,* 155. The multiple gift-overs attached to chantries in wills, noted by Gareth Jones from Sharpe's collection of wills in the Court of Husting, demonstrate that donors had no expectation that a failing chantry would be transferred to a new, close use. Rather, they knew it would return to heirs who might not honor the use. Jones, *History of the Law of Charity,* 10n.
74. Dickens, *English Reformation,* 71.
75. A. G. Dickens, "A Municipal Dissolution of Chantries at York, 1536," in *Reformation Studies* (London: Hambledon Press, 1982), 47; R. W. Hoyle, "The Origins of the Dissolution of the Monasteries," *The Historical Journal* 38.2 (1995), 282.
76. Dickens, "Municipal Dissolution," 47.
77. Ibid., 51.
78. Ibid., 50.

rather a move that sought legal grounding and maintained some aspect of intercessory prayers for the donors.

But what is notable is that there was no sure legal precedent available for managing chantries that were unable to sustain themselves if there was no heir supervising them. It would have been convenient to employ cy-près doctrine to deal with them. But that was not yet possible, although the idea that there could be better uses for these endowments was clearly flourishing well before the Reformation, given that throughout the fourteenth and fifteenth centuries, petitions were repeatedly advanced to dissolve the chantries and distribute their endowments to the general populace.[79] Instead, it was the many interested parties to the gift, including the locality, that contended for failing properties without a sure legal guide.

All of these failing endowments were especially tempting for the cause of education, hailed by humanists as beneficial for both the commonwealth and Christendom. The question was whether schools and colleges could be built out of failing property given to the church for a non-educational purpose. Was the use the same, such that the transfer could be described as a deviation? A number of prominent bishops wanted to claim that it was, and they became increasingly adventurous in their efforts to build college and grammar school endowments. Many college foundations included an almshouse and bedesmen along with provisions for liturgical services, so that bishops could take the old uses of prayer and hospitality that had been attached to their properties and simply add a new purpose, education, to them. In other cases a transition "from an essentially religious foundation to one where education was of prime importance" could be managed by the founder of the college endowment himself, as Bishop Waynflete would do in the fifteenth century: once the monastic lands had been turned over to his foundation, he could use his powers as their "founder" (since the term could apply to the current patron), in order to revise their use.[80]

The quest to create college endowments out of monastic proper-

---

79. Raban, *Mortmain Legislation*, 137–39.
80. Davis, *William Waynflete*, 46.

ty took place against a broader background of monastic transformations. The repeated seizures of the alien priories beginning in 1294 were justified by the conditions of war and were always, until the start of the fifteenth century, eventually repented of, with a show made about the restoration—never total—of property. By the end of the fourteenth century, many of the foreign motherhouses were understandably interested in selling off these troublesome properties; the sale would be framed as an exchange, without a transfer of use. But in the end a resumption followed by a redirection occurred in most cases, at times against the protests of the abbots, who believed, with good reason, that their consent was necessary to the transfer. One of them, the abbot of Saint Evroux, wrote bitterly to Sheen Priory, which was benefiting from the transfer, to complain that if patrons were allowed to resume their gifts at will, then no gift would ever be safe.[81] Not even the pope had the power to do such a thing (in this case, merely transfer it from one monastic holder to another) to a gift unless it were in order to improve the gift, not destroy it (*in aedificationem, non in destructionem*), the abbot added.

And yet Benjamin Thompson has shown how powerful the idea of resumption was in the fifteenth century, propped up by the church itself.[82] The potential for resumption was a practical fact, and one to which the church's response was generally to insist on the absolute inviolability of the terms of the original donation, as written, affirming the status of the will, the *voluntas,* as expressed. Where this failed, a deviation to do the same thing in a lesser form was a possibility, or, extraordinarily, a dispensation whose practical resolutions often acknowledged the competing rights of interested parties. In none of this was there an alternative for the redirection of gifts as either a doctrinal principle or as an ordinary remedy to a political, legal, or economic problem. The strongest resemblance between cyprès and the treatment of problematic gifts lies in dispensations, but

---

81. Martène and Durand, *Thesaurus novus anecdotorum,* vol. 1 (Paris: Delaulne, 1717), 1748, as found in Benjamin Thompson, "Prelates and the Alien Priories," in *The Prelate in England and Europe, 1300–1560,* ed. Martin Heale (Rochester, N.Y.: Medieval Press, 2014), 57–58.

82. Thompson, "Prelates and the Alien Priories," 57–58.

even in the indults granted, the motivations cited for the transfer of use are not those of a failed purpose nor the honoring of a charitable intent. Moreover, the interests of relevant parties were not cut off, since the consent of abbots and patrons was demanded, which could be inconvenient to those who were ambitious to enforce change.

Examining the ultimate fate of the alien priories, Thompson points out that the redistribution of their property "to old and new English ecclesiastical foundations" was driven by laymen, not just kings but "nobles and gentry, as well as aspiring middling sorts."[83] While these transitions could appear like a cy-près action, they bear little relationship to it. The founders, demonstrating a striking "lay determination to exercise judgment over the right use of the Church's goods,"[84] took back their property and chose a new direction for it. Thompson has also shown that many bishops were involved in facilitating these transfers, often for their own purposes in building up endowments for pet projects, such as the educational foundations that emerged out of property of the alien priories. Wykeham's foundations (New College, Oxford, and Winchester) were made in part out of alien priories: one apparent motivation for the license given to him was to tidy up this persistent problem in an age of unceasing war with France, and he was not alone. Henry VI famously built up Eton and King's College, Cambridge, through the property of alien priories, notably those taken in 1414 by an act of Parliament for their failure to get charters of denization. Henry VI then added the Hospital of St. James in the Fields at Westminster to Eton in 1449, another significant transition of use.[85] Thompson posits these proceedings as an acknowledgment of the threat of resumption: English prelates chose to interfere and help redirect property to new uses in service of the church—although not always toward monastic uses *per se*—rather than having it fall into purely secular uses. Doubtless Thompson is correct on this, and the process, which did set a cultural precedent for other schemes to redirect monastic property, encouraged the very phenomenon that the prelates may have hoped to

83. Ibid., 50.
84. Ibid., 58.
85. Davis, *William Waynflete*, 42n and 43.

thwart. But the prelates knew of no other possible means to transfer from one pious use to another; they facilitated a complicated process requiring the consent of priors, patrons, and the pope rather than drawing on a precedent of cy-près unilateral transfer. Virginia Davis has examined the report produced by a commission of four lawyers who were asked by Bishop Waynflete in 1456 to determine how the transition of use of the Hospital of St. John the Baptist in Oxford to his college might be lawfully done. They concluded that the hospital could be turned over to the college if Waynflete had the consent of the patron and the pope (the king's consent was presumed), and, additionally, if "worship and hospitality were not diminished" and "the remaining members of the community were adequately provided for."[86] This was not the answer that Waynflete wanted.

In some sense the college and the monasteries could be considered to be of the same use, although a shift toward focusing exclusively on education was notable in colleges of the fifteenth century.[87] Monasteries had often educated children or run schools, and orders of preachers had set up colleges to train their own members. The provision of lessons for choristers, especially in cathedrals, had also tended to meld the religious and the educational. But the very demand to put the endowments to educational colleges made it clear that the use was not precisely the same, since otherwise why would the transition be desirable? Even Merton, a pioneer of college endowments in England, had insisted on *nemo religiosus* in his college, straining the idea that the college was no different from a monastery dedicated to learning, although for Merton this choice was in part governed by the deeds of conveyance for the property he had received from Richard de Clare, who forbade the property to be applied to religious foundations.[88] Moreover, education was not, in itself, necessarily considered to be alms—Stephen Gardiner was not alone in thinking that scholarships to study were not quite the same thing as food for the hungry, although Lyndwood had allowed in

86. Ibid., 61.
87. Ibid., 46.
88. Edward Wedlake Brayley, *A Topographical History of Surrey*, vol. 3 (London: G. Willis, 1850), 161.

his gloss in the *Provinciale* that money for poor scholars was eleemosynary and Merton had described his college as offering alms to the scholars it would support.[89] But education had near universal appeal amongst the educated classes, who judged that it would improve the quality of the clergy and strengthen the commonwealth. Humanists and scholastics might quarrel over curriculum and control, but they agreed that more money should be devoted to universities.

As James Clark has shown, the greatest push to construct educational endowments came from the bishops, many of whom were seeking, as part of a larger reform effort, to produce better-educated priests.[90] But the creation of these foundations required considerable wealth, planning, and legal expertise. Royal foundations were, naturally, the easiest to use, if the king wanted to support the project. But the difficulties endured by other prominent founders as they put together endowments for educational colleges shows that there was neither a straightforward cy-près power available to "make good" the "charitable intentions" of the founder nor any notable attention paid to trying to match the founder's intentions "as closely as possible." The bishops would work their way toward a claim of cy-près power as they struggled to get around the cumbersome aspects of the consensus model, in which so many parties had an interest in the use of the land.

Virginia Davis has pointed out that monastic lands were particularly enticing for these bishops because they had already been amortized and because monastic lands were usually safe from disputes over title.[91] But, Davis notes, the position of executor could offer another method of assurance: if consensus could be reached about the transition of a property to the new educational use, then title was clear. Thus Waynflete, she points out, found 34 percent of his en-

---

89. Lyndwood, *Provinciale*, III.19.6, p. 209; James Halliwell, ed., *Foundation Documents of Merton College Collected by James Heywood* (London: William Pickering, 1843), 20.
90. James G. Clark, "Monasteries and Secular Education in Late Medieval England," in *Monasteries and Society in the British Isles in the Later Middle Ages*, ed. Janet Burton and Karen Stöber (Woodbridge, England: Boydell Press, 2008), 165.
91. Davis, *William Waynflete*, 126.

dowment for Magdalen from "his role as executor for two wealthy magnates, Sir John Fastolf and Ralph, Lord Cromwell."[92] In both situations Waynflete would seek recourse to the testator's "intentions" in order to resolve disputes and justify a transition from the exact terms of the will; the deeds of reconveyance that he obtained—such as the one in 1476 for the manor of Stainswick, which allowed "any charitable use" of the property that had been given specifically for Winchester College—came through common law courts that had some, albeit at times disputed, recourse to equity.[93]

In England the first ostensible use of monastic lands to found a college was by Walter de Merton. He defiantly described the endowments he put together for Merton College as "my" lands (*in meo solo proprio, meis laboribus acquisito*), and it was on those grounds that the 1280 papal bull granted him the right to his foundation.[94] The only anxiety Merton described about the propriety of his endowment was the extent to which he was stripping away resources from his nephews, which is why he emphasized the rights of the "Founder's Kin" to have extended recourse to the college.[95] Some of the lands that accumulated to the endowment of Merton College came from benefactors, such as Richard de Clare, Earl of Gloucester, who in 1262 gave manors to the foundation with the stipulation that he and his heirs would maintain their patronage rights in them and would have "free and full power over [the trustees]" and the power "to compel [the trustees] by the secular authority to observe the ordinance."[96] Impropriations and appropriations were another source of revenue for Merton College. Merton prevailed on the prior of Merton, with the "advice and consent" (*de consilio et consensu*) of the bishop of Winchester, to appropriate the possessions of the church of Maldon to

92. Ibid.
93. Ibid., 129.
94. Ibid., 35.
95. Ibid., 14, 20, 37, and 53.
96. Edward France Percival, ed., *The Foundation Statutes of Merton College, Oxford* (London: William Pickering, 1847), 2; Halliwell, ed., *Foundation Documents*, 2: "Qui etiam supra ipsos ad quos dicta maneria ex ordinatione supradicta devenerint, liberam et plenam habeant potestatem ipsos compellandi per potestatem secularem ad observationem ordinationis praedictae et exhibitionis sustentationis memoratae."

the use of the college as well as to hand over the advowson to the church.[97] The church of Elham was similarly appropriated to the college.[98] Still, the system of impropriations and appropriations that was used in the late medieval period to redirect the use of property quietly—without having to seek papal consent—was controversial and would remain a perpetual irritant, for it was considered an abuse by many reformers. It was also limited. The recipient of an appropriation could not do just anything with the property and was required by law to maintain services and upkeep of the church.

Bishops would also seek the actual suppression of monastic properties, which could then be turned over with fewer limitations. And so it was that bishops compiled an impressive number of educational endowments. William Wykeham, bishop of Winchester, founded New College, Oxford, in 1379; Richard Fleming, bishop of Lincoln, founded Lincoln College, Oxford, in 1427; Henry Chichele, archbishop of Canterbury, founded All Souls College, Oxford in 1437; William Waynflete, bishop of Winchester, founded Magdalen Hall in Oxford, in 1448 and refounded it as Magdalen College in 1458; John Fisher, bishop of Rochester, and Lady Margaret Beaufort founded St. John's College at Cambridge in 1511; Richard Fox, bishop of Winchester, founded Corpus Christi, Oxford, in 1517. In the fifteenth and sixteenth centuries, many of these bishops had humanist connections and received praise from humanists for their work.[99] Many of them had also, at one point, held the position of chancellor. Sometimes the endowment was created in the aftermath of a tumultuous political career, not in the midst of it, although it was wise for a would-be founder to apply for the mortmain license while the king's favor shone upon him.[100] During their tenures as chancellor, these founders had built up financial resources, political connections, and legal awareness of the particular difficulties in these endowments. Their foundation charters and other legal documents were carefully made, as were the negotiations that brought them to a successful endow-

97. Halliwell, ed., *Foundation Documents*, 6–7.
98. Ibid., 10–11.
99. Ibid.
100. Ibid., 32.

ment. The expectation that ecclesiastical lands would be used toward the endowments was firm. For example, the 1516 charter from Henry VIII for Corpus Christi in Oxford gave to Richard Fox, keeper of the Privy Seal, not only the right to turn all kinds of secular possessions to the foundation but also to "give, grant, appropriate, consolidate, annex, and unite any priories, hospitals, free chapels, ecclesiastical, parochial, and other ecclesiastical benefices whatever, and likewise any pensions, portions, corodies, and annuities, ecclesiastical and spiritual whatever."[101] It was a list of everything that might be targeted by the king and the bishop. The process, which took years and could be easily thwarted—by death, stubborn patrons, political setback, or a failure to obtain a mortmain license in time, among other possibilities—was a frustrating one that manifested to all who engaged in it just how difficult it was to do lasting good and how many obstacles there were in the way of transitioning property from one use to another.

In order to put these endowments together, the bishops hunted for eligible properties—largely those that, they claimed, belonged to small and decayed houses that were barely able to sustain themselves and keep up liturgical services. Evidence of corrupt living was also a nice touch in pleading the case to the pope for his dispensation to convert the use, especially since the permission of a completely disgraced abbot might not be necessary. But the pope always required in turn the consent of the king and the patron, so bishops, before approaching the pope, first tried to become the patron of the properties that they wished to convert.[102] As patrons, bishops who wanted to endow a college were not always operating with the best interests of the monastic property at heart. Virginia Davis has found evidence, for example, that Waynflete helped to push one desirable property into a condition of suitable decay by appointing a prior known to be a spendthrift and by avoiding any interference with the monastery's mounting debt.[103] Davis describes a "similar tale" with Waynflete's annexation of Sel-

---

101. G. R. M. Ward, ed., *The Foundation Statutes of Bishop Fox for Corpus Christi College in the University of Oxford* (London: Longman, Brown, Green, and Longmans, 1843), xlv–xlvi.
102. Davis, *William Waynflete*, 146.
103. Ibid., 147.

borne Priory, over which, as patron to the property, Waynflete was able to serve, Davis notes, as "both plaintiff and judge" before a diocesan commission.[104] He pleaded the lengths to which he had gone, without success, to preserve the monastery. Unsurprisingly, Waynflete as judge was convinced by his own argument as plaintiff.

But this process of accumulating properties was slow going, and the right of patrons to resist the schemes, to drag out negotiations, and to demand better compensation for the loss of their patronage rights, was a major hindrance. The bishops were pushing forward into what they imagined would be an era of centralized, rationalized use of resources for the betterment of Christendom and the commonwealth, but legally they were stuck with remnants of an age of arbitration and consent-seeking, which could be frankly exploited by those who had an "interest" in the case, including co-executors to a will, who could quarrel amongst themselves, delay implementation until the will was entirely thwarted, and then receive a payoff to cease their obstruction. King Henry VI used his last will and testament to try to forestall this possibility by granting a strong executive role to William Waynflete as one of his executors and ultimate arbiter of all disputes:

If it befall that there be any diverse opinions, variance, or discord, betwixt my said feoffees and mine executours, in or for any execution of the performing of my said will or any part thereof, I give then and graunt to the said bishop of Winchester, by these presents, plain power and auctorite; and finally, I will that he, as umpire in that behalfe, have at all times power and auctoritie for to call and take unto him such discreet persons of my said feoffees as unto him for the accomplishment of my will seeme most disposed; and that after their advise heard, do make the finall conclusion in that part.[105]

In this context it becomes clear how the bishops came to think of themselves as defenders of the donor himself. Such a bishop would be understood not as standing in the place of the founder in order to

---

104. Davis, *William Waynflete*, 147–48; W. M. Macray, ed., *Calendar of Charters and Documents Relating to Selborne and Its Priory Preserved in the Muniment Room of Magdalen College Oxford* (London: Simpkin and Co., 1891), 119–34.

105. *A Collection of the Wills, Now Known to be Extant, of the Kings and Queens of England* (London: J. Nichols, 1780), 313–14.

represent him, but rather as the only man with a vision for the disbursement of the donor's wealth, a vision that no one else would protect. Here the bishops could conceive that they were preserving the "intentions" of the testator even as they thwarted his manifest will.

After prolonged negotiations over many years, Waynflete would describe his foundation out of the estate of Sir John Fastolf thus: it preserved the "wille and entent" of the man, whose will had ordered many "pitueux and charitable dedes," among them the endowment of seven priests and seven poor men to pray for the souls of members of his family.[106] Fastolf had tried to get a mortmain license to found this chantry at Caister Castle, but he had failed. At his death in 1459 he asked his executors, Waynflete among them, to obtain the license and found the chantry at Caister in his stead, but the executors and administrators of the estate threw up difficulties. In 1470, as a consequence, Waynflete was appointed sole administrator in the place of William Yelverton by Thomas Bourgchier, archbishop of Canterbury. In this role Waynflete advocated for a compromise, whereby all of the interested parties would receive some recompense for their agreement to the use of the Fastolf estate in funding a university endowment instead. John Paston II, writing to his son about a potential solution to the extended disputes that had kept the estate immobilized, asked his son to convey his wishes to Yelverton "that suche a tretye is hadd be-twen hym and me, and that ye preye God make an ende between us, and than schall we all be goode felawez ageyn."[107] The subsequent indenture recorded that the "grete variance" between the parties to the estate had caused it to "be wasted, decaied, and spent," leaving the will not executed and "never likely in tyme cummyng to be executed."[108] Waynflete described his "pité and compassion that of so blessed and charitable entent of the seiz John Fastolf no commendable effect shuld ensue, remembryng the singuler trust which the same John Fastolf to hym had."[109] The

---

106. Norman Davis, ed., *Paston Letters and Papers of the Fifteenth Century*, Part I (Oxford: Clarendon Press, 1971), 419.
107. Ibid., 414.
108. Ibid., 420.
109. Ibid.

purpose was frustrated and the trust was impossible because the relevant parties were making it so; the unusual role of the executors had, in a sense, created a new kind of third-party impossibility. Having found an agreement by which the parties could be brought to consensus through concessions, the bishop would then take the bulk of the estate for his college in Oxford, where he would keep "vii prestys and vii poore scolers to praye for the sowles of the seid John Fastolf and of Dame Milicent his wife, his frendys and benefactoures."[110] The use was similar, although now "pore scolars" were supported instead of poor men, making it seem much like a mere deviation, or relocation, from the will, and the bishop "is aggreed att his owne charge to obteyne of the Pope a sufficient dispensacion for chaungyng of the place and fundacion of the seid perpetuel prestes and poore folkes from the seid maner of Castre."[111]

Virginia Davis has shown that this settlement was bent to the interests of Waynflete in some unsavory ways and that, as a consequence, he wrote or commissioned a report to explain why the change in use was justified.[112] He relates several problems. For one, John Paston I had obtained a mortmain license for the desired chantry in Caister in 1464, but the arguments among the other interested parties had prevented it from being used. Davis shows that, in justifying his transition, Waynflete did not mention the existence of this license. Moreover, Fastolf had listed in his will the alternative uses to which he wanted his property to be put if the Caister College did not work out—largely, the maintenance of priests in established monasteries. These alternatives were ignored, even though they were feasible. In his own argument, Waynflete, or his advocate, claimed that "the charge of founding a college had been laid by Fastolf on Paston personally," not on the lands and not on Waynflete either.[113] The writer also asserted that it was only the suggestion of the college that could bring peace among the disputing interested parties, perhaps because, as the writer argued, there was "more mer-

110. Ibid., 424.
111. Ibid.
112. Davis, *William Waynflete*, 136–37; Davis, ed., *Paston Letters*, 914.
113. Davis, *William Waynflete*, 136.

it [to Oxford endowments] than many other deeds of piety," which, as Davis points out, was certainly not Fastolf's belief.[114] Indeed, she argues that the settlement "paid little regard to the observance of John Fastolf's wishes."[115] But Waynflete was willing to argue that the "charitable intent" of Fastolf could justify ignoring his "wish that he might be commemorated and prayed for locally in Norfolk by chantry priests."[116]

So there were two challenges to the old model that had developed. The first was that a consensus model of estate settlement could allow difficult executors, heirs, and administrators to thwart the execution of the will. The second was that there were new goals, and the bishops who were deeply involved in the settlements of estates had their own priorities—to found colleges and to find ways to justify transitions of uses. If there had been a settled doctrine that they could have called upon in these circumstances, it would surely have appeared in their arguments and actions. Waynflete would not have let the dispute drag on for so long if an easier recourse had been available. Further, Davis estimates that Waynflete spent more than a thousand pounds in paying off "twelve separate claimants,"[117] but he would not have depleted the resources of the foundation unless those payments had been necessary for him to obtain consensus. Moreover, deviation was obviously the most likely solution to a difficult gift, and this was largely what Waynflete proposed, that the money would serve the same purpose in Oxford that it would have in Caister, but with some additional benefits to the college. In a sense, Waynflete tried to make it appear that he had simply expanded the purpose, made the resources stretch further, rather than altered it. However, in the future, if the funds were not sufficient to maintain the priests and "pore scolars" as well as the needs of the college, then it was entirely conceivable that cuts would be made to the number of priests and poor scholars. The attempt to do more laid out a path to future deviation and diminishment of the found-

114. Ibid., 137.
115. Ibid., 138.
116. Ibid.
117. Ibid.

er's will. Nicholas Orme has found that bishops were not alone in trying to add educational purposes to commemorative gifts, noting that churchwardens and feoffees began to insist in the mid-fifteenth century that chantry priests also provide elementary lessons, trying to make the gift serve a broader common good.[118] But Waynflete was pioneering something bolder, a method of turning gifts for one purpose to another in the name of thwarted intentions.

Not only did intentions provide more flexibility than the will (*voluntas*) of the donor, but they spoke more directly to the category of purpose to which the particular stipulations of a will were laid out. To cite "intentions" could be a means to make the disparate come together. In 1444 four educational foundations (Eton, Kings College, Winchester, and New College) signed the *Amicabilis concordia* as a pact for mutual defense and assistance, in which they asserted their relationship to each other not in terms of purpose alone but rather in "the intentions of the founders" (*in fundatorum intentione*) and the "fruits of their work" (*operis fructu*).[119] A focus on "intentions" could also permit any necessary deviations from exact terms over the course of an institution: the new colleges revised their statutes repeatedly, at the behest of or with the permission of the founder and his heirs or designated administrators. But the equitable principle of deviation, which recognized the "intentions" or general purpose of the gift while changing the terms of its implementation was a necessary help, especially in an age of inflation, resumption, and insecurity. So colleges became used to referring, not to the will of the founder, which was almost certainly not being implemented as written, but to his intentions, whose spirit was honored through the ages in some sense or another, even as some of the aspects of his statutes were dropped that had, in their writing, probably been most essential to him. Merton's statutes were revised by ordinances of Peckham, Chichele, Parker, and Laud. At times these ordinances, like those of Peckham, criticized the college for its failure to uphold the founder's intentions, while at other times the ordinances

118. Orme, *Education in the West of England*, 18.
119. Cited and translated in Davis, *William Waynflete*, 45: "nec in fundatorum intentione nec operis fructu discrepare."

directed the college to make alterations to the rules and practices set down by the founder, also in the name of his intentions. The spirit of the founder's intentions could prevail over the letter of the founder's documents.

This practical change, spearheaded by the bishops, can be seen in the contrast between the expectations of Merton, constructing his college in the thirteenth century, and those of Waynflete, putting his together in the fifteenth. In Merton's 1270 refoundation, he attempted to limit the college to exactly the "the forms and conditions below written ... observed henceforth for ever."[120] And yet in the accompanying 1270 statute, he permitted the warden and eight members of Merton to enact new statutes in response to new situations, which he clarified was his "will." He further stipulated that necessary changes in location—an easily anticipated issue in an age of civil unrest—would not cause the house to lose the rights to its possessions as long as it kept the form and name; also, he drew on the pious donations that had been given to the foundation as a reason to allow it to survive any necessary relocations.[121] Merton believed that a deviation—that is, a transition within use—of location could be justified by the piety of the donors, but he was not relying on it to intervene. Merton was most concerned to make sure that the foundation would be able to adapt and survive, even claiming that future alterations should constitute his "will," so that the foundation would not be destroyed unnecessarily and so that failure to perform his will exactly would not result in the college being suppressed and its wealth sent in new directions. Merton did not anticipate that either a deviation or a cyprès intervention would save his charitable intentions, nor should he have. Two centuries later, Waynflete, well aware both of the limits to which he had stretched the law in constructing Magdalen and of how his work might be similarly undone in the future, required the president and fellows of his college to swear an oath not to change his statutes.[122] The one founder, living in a time of relative strictness in the observance of the terms of the will, sought to provide flexibility;

120. Percival, ed., *Foundation Statutes*, 13.
121. Ibid., 35–36.
122. Davis, *William Waynflete*, 151.

the other, who had innovated at the edges of the law to use "intentions" to advance his endowment, looked for protection against the alterations to which he had himself had provided precedent.

After all, the flexibility that was being employed by bishops to compile college endowments could work against them too. Edward IV, in his successful petition to Pius II in 1463 for permission to use the lands of Eton to support St. George's Chapel, claimed that the revenues received by Eton were insufficient to sustain the intentions of its founders.[123] In the end, the merger was not necessary, but the threat to suppress Eton, like Edward IV's resumptions in 1462, was a warning that college endowments were not necessarily safe, despite their popularity. This lesson was relearned by Oxford and Cambridge colleges during the Henrician Reformation, since they were apparently surprised to discover that the king believed that the secularization of property might apply to them too.

Smaller estates could be drawn into educational endowments for grammar schools as well. An example of the attempt to cut the Gordian knot that had been established through the consensus model of transitions of use is offered by the foundation of the Winchcombe grammar school.[124] Lady Joan Huddleston had been married to Sir Miles Stapleton and then Sir John Huddleston, and she had sons from each marriage. Her second husband had pushed her to turn her own lands over to their son, which he repented of on his deathbed, asking their son to return them to her and asking also that Joan should have a life interest in Temple Guiting, which was to be sold off to pay for prayers for their souls upon her death or remarriage. Joan then sold her life interest in Temple Guiting to Bishop Richard Fox for his Corpus Christi foundation, and one of the executors, Urswick, sold the reversionary interest to Fox with the agreement that masses would be offered there for the Huddlestons in perpetuity, honoring the condition that Sir John Huddleston had attached to the property.

---

123. Ibid., 52.
124. Orme, *Education in the West of England*, 186–90; Orme and Webster, *English Hospital*, 85; C. R. Hudleston, "Sir John Hudleston, Constable of Sudeley," in *The Transactions of the Bristol and Gloucestershire Archaeological Society* 48 (1926): 117–32.

The younger John Huddleston, son of Sir John and Joan, then sued with the support of another executor to the will, even though Urswick had taken less than the full value for the reversionary interest in order to guarantee the prayers for the Huddlestons' souls.

Joan Huddleston died in 1519, leaving behind a will made the year before with two executors: Richard Kidderminster and William Tracy.[125] In it she requested that an almshouse for thirteen people be constructed in Winchcombe, but she clarified that while her gift was for "that purpose," she permitted her executor to include additional charitable works in the project "by hym to be done." She also left money for a trental of 30 masses for her soul, but she did not include any specifications about prayer in the almshouse. As it turned out, she had picked two distinctive executors. Kidderminster was the abbot of Winchcombe monastery, renowned for his interest in education and his humanist connections.[126] The other executor, William Tracy, would subsequently be posthumously burnt for his evangelical last will and testament. Both men certainly had ulterior motives with regard to Joan's will, although Kidderminster seems to have been the moving force. He declared that her estate was insufficient to the cause of the almshouse. Rather than joining the money to another existing almshouse, as a deviation from the strict terms but in keeping with the purpose, Kidderminster decided to try to apply the money to the creation of a school at his abbey with maintenance for six choristers.[127] He added somewhat to the funds, effectively serving as a "second founder" to her gift by increasing it. He seems to have used the Court of Exchequer to ratify the change. The Exchequer was also a court of equity, and they were persuaded by Kidderminster's argument, repeated in the indenture to the school, that he had received the approval of both canon and common lawyers as well as that of the ordinary.[128] Kidderminster left out the normal requirement to obtain the permission of the pope.

Although the phrase was not used, the procedure was what might

125. Public Records Office, Prob 11/19.
126. David Knowles, *The Religious Orders in England*, vol. 3 (Cambridge: Cambridge University Press, 1959), 91–95.
127. Orme, *Education in the West of England*, 186–90.
128. Public Records Office, Exchequer Land Revenue, LR 6/29/2.

later be called cy-près, although the purpose to which Joan Huddleston had left her money was neither impossible nor impractical (for other almshouses could certainly have used the money, even including her name as a second founder for that reason) and there is no evidence that Joan Huddleston had any interest in education, which meant that the alteration of the purpose was certainly not "as close as possible" to her intentions. Still, the legal maneuvers involved were an acknowledgment that it was increasingly possible to change the uses of conditional gifts. Viewed in this light, modern cy-près appears to be restrained by its concern for the testator's intentions and interests and its requirement that the original purpose be impossible.

This case demonstrates that the insufficiency of the funds could be used as a pretext to shift a gift to a purpose that seemed better, and the force of the Court of the Exchequer and learned opinion was marshaled, along with the permission of the bishop, to effect the transition. Although the bishops approved of this transition of use, this does not mean they did so from canonical equitable principles. The fact that the transitions in land usage for the Huddleston estate and others had to be certified by common law courts is highly suggestive and brings to mind the probably related issue that the term "cy-près" derives from Law French rather than ecclesiastical Latin. Common lawyers were already interested in the concept of equity as a remedy for the strictness of common law, and the interest was starting to manifest in the Court of Exchequer, which was becoming a court of equity itself, but which was not at this point open to all comers.[129] The transaction costs built into the consensus model, which were inhibiting new ventures and reducing the endowments before they could even be put into place, were a powerful motivation for bishops to innovate in the law. And in the case of Winchcombe, the bishop involved was Richard Fox, previously the chancellor of Cambridge and master of Pembroke at that university, who only two years before had founded Corpus Christi

---

129. On equity in common law in the late Middle Ages, see P. Brand, "The Equity of the Common Law Courts," in *Law and Equity: Approaches in Roman Law and Common Law*, ed. E. Koops and W. J. Zwalve (Leiden: Martinus Nijhoff, 2014), 39–53.

College, Oxford, out of former monastic properties.[130] This latter fact eluded Erasmus, who, in his famous panegyric to the college sent to John Claymond, its first president, claimed that Fox had built the college entirely from his own property. Fox himself, unlike Merton, did not make this claim, but in the first chapter of the statutes instead wrote that the foundation had been built "out of the means which God of his bounty hath bestowed on us."[131]

Fox is reputed to have founded Corpus Christi as a secular college rather than a monastic college—even though it would have been easier to transition monastic lands into a monastic college—because Hugh Oldham, the bishop of Exeter, had warned him that monasticism was about to fall. The comment by Oldham seems too prescient, but Oldham had indeed annexed multiple monastic lands, contributed to the Corpus Christi endowment, and served as an adviser to Lady Margaret Beaufort, herself an endower of universities. Not only was Oldham a force for the redeployment of property toward new uses, but he had struggled with Archbishop Warham over his own right to supervise probate within his own jurisdiction. Moreover, Fox, who was committed to the concept of reform at all levels and particularly with reference to property, wrote that "the primitive simplicity of the clergy (especially of the monastic state) [is] perverted, either by indulgences or corruptions, or else become obsolete and exploded by the iniquity of the times."[132] He called on Wolsey to "restore the whole estate of the English clergy and of the monasteries to their primitive rules and dignity, and enact laws for their preservation and lasting establishment."[133] Wolsey ultimately disappointed

130. Although Corpus Christi was a notable humanist institution, Jonathan Woolfson has made a convincing argument that it was also, not contradictorily, focused on obedience to authority: "Bishop Fox's Bees and the Early English Renaissance," *Reformation and Renaissance Review* 5 (2003): 7–26.
131. Ward., ed. *Foundation Statutes*, 2.
132. Translated by G. R. M. Ward, in *Foundation Statutes*, xxviii, from a letter to Wolsey. Richard Fox, *Letters of Richard Fox 1486–1527*, ed. P. S. and H. M. Allen (Oxford: Clarendon Press, 1929), 115: "ubi, quod prius non putassem, depr<e>hendi et animadverti omnia quae ad antiquam cleri et praecipue monachiae integritatem spectant, adeo vel licentiis et corruptelis depravata vel temporum malignitate et diuturnitate abolita et corrupta."
133. *Foundation Statutes*, trans. Ward, xxx; Fox, *Letters*, 116: "Quum universum

Fox, but by all evidence from Fox's life, the sentiments he expressed were truly felt. He called for a reform that would be extensive and transformative, that would seek a return to the primitive simplicity from which the monastics in particular had fallen, and that would surely necessitate, for good reasons, transformations in property, no matter how the property had arrived in the hands of the monastics nor what the will of the donor might have been. It is no wonder that Fox would approve the transition of use for Huddleston's estate.

As we have seen, "intent" usually entered the legal discussion when the plain "will" (*voluntas*) was not enough. In documents that emphasized the strictness with which the last will and testament ought to be followed, only the will of the testator was mentioned. This distinction can be found in the common law. Coke on Littleton summarized the point: "The will of the donor, manifestly expressed in his deed of gift, is to be observed" (*Voluntas donatoris in charta doni sui manifeste expressa observetur*).[134] It was possible to treat this will generously when interpreting it, as indicated by the maxim "the will of the testator has a broad and benignant interpretation" (*Voluntas testatoris habet interpretationem latam et benignam*).[135] But Coke suggested in his commentary on Littleton that a maxim of common law was to consider the will in the light of the intent: "The last will of a testator is to be followed according to his true intention" (*Voluntas ultima testatoris est perimplenda secundum veram intentionem suam*).[136] This common law tendency to treat difficult wills by trying to cast them in the light of the true intentions was probably cultivated as bishops tried to use courts of equity in England to effect transformations in property. Common law had an increasing interest in conscience as a remedy to its notorious inflexibility, and it must have listened attentively as the humanist bishops described their equitable powers to honor intent—drawn, they said, from the learned law.

Angliae clerum et monachiam suae integritati et dignitati restituerit, et leges ad eam tuendam et inconcusse servandam condiderit."

134. Co. Litt. 21.

135. Jenk. Cent. 260, where it is explicitly tied to *voluntas donatoris* as well. Digest 50.17.12.

136. Co. Litt. 322.

Humanist Influences on the Law

The previous chapter traced some humanist developments within the *ius commune*, including the treatment of surplus donations and an increasing concern to protect the donor. These shifts likely had an effect on practice. One example Helmholz has found of what he describes as a cy-près action is from the diocese of Ely in the 1460s in which "a bequest for the purpose of erecting a cross in the parish church of Leverington was varied in favour of what the record described as 'a more convenient use' at the petition of the church wardens."[137] The description does not suggest that an external cause of immediate need was the motivation for the transition. The executors were called in by the court to give an account of the matter, and it is not possible to tell from the record what information the court received or how it arrived at its decision. Whether consensus was reached among the interested parties as a part of the process is unknown, but it seems unlikely. The records do not always indicate the position of the heirs, who would have had some claim to recover the money if they had wanted. This is certainly an example of a transition of use, and one made for no apparent reason other than convenience.

More such late medieval cases authorizing an actual transition of use will presumably be found as more research is done in the records of the ecclesiastical courts. It seems likely that the flexibility demonstrated by this example would have become particularly noticeable in the fifteenth century under humanist ideals. Bishops who claimed to the Court of the Exchequer that they had the right to transfer use would surely also have applied this understanding within the ecclesiastical courts that they supervised. At the time of the Leverington case, the bishop of Ely was William Grey, who served in this position from 1454 to 1478. Grey was a noted humanist who had studied in Italy with the eminent humanist pedagogue Guarino da Verona; he had also briefly been chancellor of Oxford in the early 1440s.

---

137. Helmholz, "Law of Charity," 119–20; Helmholz, *Oxford History of the Laws of England*, 418.

He remained dedicated to humanist study throughout his life and left an extensive manuscript collection to Balliol. After the settling of the Ely case, he would serve a brief term (1469–70) as lord high treasurer. Grey would have had ample motivation, given his humanist sympathies, to encourage greater convenience of use in church property. He would also have observed the procedures employed by Waynflete at the time. Moreover, as James Brundage has shown, the ecclesiastical courts of Ely had particularly close relationships with the canon law faculty in Cambridge, who could have advised on the recent tendency to consider unnecessary gifts as a category of the impossible.[138] Perhaps the church did not need another cross. Technically the Ely case should have cited the need for something else instead, but just as inconvenience could shade into impossibility, so could convenience shade into necessity.

Elsewhere, in treating the Modestinus opinion, humanists tended to use it as a means to serve public utility and weaken the demand for consent. The sixteenth-century humanist Jacques Cujas strengthened the Modestinus passage as much as he could: the heirs were summoned but no consent was mentioned, and the illicit kind of celebration (such as, he suggested, games or a spectacle) could make way for an entirely new use, ideally one that was necessary to the state, but which was irrelevant except that it celebrated the memory of the testator.[139] Cujas commended Melanchthon's understanding that the Modestinus opinion authorized the use of church property for schools and other common uses. This was, he said, the interpretation best suited to the times *(ad nostra tempora)*.[140] Denis Godefroy, the Calvinist compiler of the 1583 *Corpus iuris civilis*, was a little more cautious. He kept Bartolus's demand for the consensus of the heirs and added a gloss to clarify that either the state or private citi-

---

138. James A. Brundage, "The Cambridge Faculty of Canon Law and the Ecclesiastical Courts of Ely," in *Medieval Cambridge: Essays on the Pre-Reformation University*, ed. Patrick Zutshi (Woodbridge, England: Boydell and Brewer, 1993), 21–46.

139. Jacques Cujas, *Opera omnia in decem tomo*, vol. 7 (Naples: Aloysius Mutius, 1722), 1352.

140. Ibid.: "Legatur quaeso Epitome Philosophiae moralis Philippi Melanchtonis, in qua perquam apte accommodat hanc leg. ad nostra tempora."

zens could use this privilege, signaling thereby that illegal conditions attached to a bequest did not make them forfeit to the fisc and that the original recipient could still be allowed to receive the bequest, so long as the illegal condition was not followed.

The sixteenth-century humanist jurist André Tiraqueau, most famous as Rabelais's friend and legal expert, put together several novel collections of citations gathered around themes that interested him: justifications for women's legal subjection, the "law" of primogeniture, and the privileges attached to pious causes.[141] This last work, the *Tractatus de privilegiis piae causae*, comes the closest of any work up until that point to making gifts to pious causes virtually inextinguishable: such gifts survive an array of errors, uncertainties, defects, and conditions. This was, perhaps, an extension of his earlier assertion, in his treatise on the legal saying *Cessante causa, cessat effectus*, that the regula did not apply to last wills and testaments.[142] It is small wonder that his text on pious causes has been held up as an example of cy-près in the *ius commune*, although none of the privileges in fact address whether a pious cause can be converted to another pious cause except for the uncontroversial point that church property could be alienated to ransom captives or for alms for the poor (Privilege 103).[143] An impossible condition placed on a pious gift would not destroy the gift if the donor had thought the condition was possible, but this was not a rule about what to do if the purpose of the gift itself had become impossible, nor did the sources cited to support the privilege actually tend to uphold the rule as stated (Privilege 75).[144] A broad principle of alteration was not included in the text, nor did Tiraqueau explain what the privileges meant in practice; these were theoretical privileges, not an assessment of how to manage diffi-

---

141. Jacques Brejon, *Un jurisconsulte de la Renaissance: André Tiraqueau (1488–1558)* (Paris: Librairie du Recueil Sirey, 1937); Giovanni Rossi, *Incunaboli della modernità: Scienza giuridica e cultura umanistica in André Tiraqueau (1488–1558)* (Turin: Giappichelli, 2007).

142. André Tiraqueau, *Tractatus* (Lyon: Gulielmum Rouillium, 1559), 47 and 57–58 on pious causes.

143. André Tiraqueau, *De privilegiis piae causae tractatus* (Venice: Franciscus Laurentinus, 1561), 139.

144. Ibid., 107–8. Digest 35.1.72pr. and Digest 45.1.7.

cult gifts. Although Tiraqueau included the possibility of weakening the terms (Privilege 83), fulfilling a condition only in part (Privilege 166), or moving the location (Privilege 41 and 43), he also argued that gifts to pious causes were more protected from alterations of use by the prince than other gifts (Privilege 135).[145] The closest approximation to cy-près in the text was the contention that, unlike regular legacies, gifts to a pious cause did not fail if they became *caduca*. Tiraqueau, though, did not give a rule for their rescue, and the citations for the law did not exactly prove the point, as in Digest 35.1.101pr., in which a farm left to a daughter in trust if she married Aelius Philippus was left to Philippus alone if she did not marry him (Privilege 38).[146] The daughter died before she was of age, creating a supervening impossibility to the condition, and so Papinian set aside the condition and gave the farm to Philippus rather than to any other heirs to the original estate or heirs to the daughter's estate.[147] Papinian did so on the grounds that Philippus was effectively the beneficiary of the trust regardless, but the decision was in keeping with the normal treatment of supervening impossibilities and of trusts. Tiraqueau was on stronger ground with the resilience of grants of fideicommissary freedom, even if the legacy to which they were attached was void.[148] He cited Pietro d'Ancarano's commentary on *Quia contingit*, which was a fairly subtle sorting through of when a gift could be altered and when it could not, but Tiraqueau used it only as evidence for a principle that d'Ancarano had not articulated, for d'Ancarano had said that when the testator cared primarily about the motive of piety, then a gift left to no one in particular but rather to any (*aliquem*) pious use could not fail, but would be shifted to a new pious use.[149] This was not the same as saying that any pious specific gift could not fail (which d'Ancarano did not hold), nor even necessarily that a gift to an impossible but pious cause would not fail, since

---

145. Tiraqueau, *Privilegiis*, 119, 190, 81, 82, and 164.
146. Ibid., 78.
147. See the use made of this by Bartolus de Saxoferrato, *In secundam Infor. partem commentaria* in *Opera omnia* (Turin: Nicolai Bevilaquae, 1577), 128, on Pater Severinam, listed as Law 100, not 101.
148. Digest 40.5.26pr. and Digest 40.5.26.6.
149. Read in context, d'Ancarano seems to be using "causa" to mean purpose:

he gave examples of gifts to pious causes that failed and returned to the heirs.[150] In short, Tiraqueau categorized as many possible privileges for pious causes as he could, and his treatment of the topic is indicative of the humanist desire to rescue gifts for good causes, but even he did not find cy-près *tout court*.

As Myron Gilmore noted, many humanist jurists had tendencies toward absolutism rather than conciliarism. In the aftermath of the Reformation it became increasingly possible for secular powers to take religious property and turn it to secular ends with humanist approval. For example, when the Jesuits, under suspicion of encouraging regicide, were exiled from France in 1594, parliament decreed the seizure of their property and its use for new, non-religious purposes. Étienne Pasquier reported, in his 1602 *Catéchisme des Jesuites*, a speech given by Pierre du Coignet for the debate at the University of Paris over Clermont, the Jesuit college. Coignet explained why parliament could demand the confiscation of the entire property of the Jesuit order. They had been treacherous, which condemned them. Through their treachery they had forced the king into wars, which had required him to alienate crown lands, and those lands needed to be redeemed. Moreover, Coignet referred to the requirement in Roman law (presumably the Modestinus opinion, interpreted broadly) that if a gift was made to a college of which the magistrate did not approve, then it would be transferred to a different college.[151] Thus, Coignet asserted, all of the alms the Jesuits had collected should be put "to another use, for the convenience of the public."[152]

Jean Domat, the seventeenth-century humanist and friend to Jansenists, also supported extending the Modestinus opinion well beyond

---

a gift to specific poor people would fail if they were dead; a gift to a cause without a recipient listed could be shifted from one use to another use (in this case, it seems, from one user to another user); a gift that listed the recipient and then the cause would fail if the recipient was no longer able to take; while a gift that was listed to the cause (purpose) and then to the person fell in a doubtful category. This schema followed that of Bartolus.

150. d'Ancarano, *Super Clementinis, De religiosis domibus*, "Quia contingit," § 3, 203.

151. Étienne Pasquier, *Le Catéchisme des Jesuites: ou Examen de leur doctrine* (Villefranche: Guillaume Grenier, 1602), 299v.

152. Ibid.: "à autre usage, pour la commodité du public."

its original bounds—and his 1689 *Lois civiles dans leur ordre naturel* was translated into English by William Strahan in 1722, appearing just as cy-près was becoming a contentious issue and shortly before judges began considering Roman or canon law precedents to this new power. The work omitted any reference to the advice or consent of the heirs at all. Rather than being an opinion on a slight modification made to a trust because of illegality, the Modestinus passage now permitted transitions on the grounds of a gift being unnecessary and more useful in some other way:

> If a pious legacy were destined to some use which could not have its effect, as if a testator had left a legacy for building a church for a parish, or an apartment in a hospital, and it happened, either that before his death the said church or the said apartment had been built out of some other fund, or that it was noways necessary or useful, the legacy would not for all that remain without any use; but it would be laid out on other works of piety for that parish, or for that hospital, according to the directions that should be given in this matter by the persons to whom this function should belong.

Domat admitted that the original law did not relate to pious uses, "yet the rule that results from it is with much more reason very just in legacies to pious uses."[153] The privileges accorded to pious uses "have a double favor, both that of their motive for holy and pious uses, and that of their utility for the public good."[154]

---

153. Jean Domat, *The Civil Law in Its Natural Order*, trans. William Strahan, vol. 2 (Boston: Charles C. Little and James Brown, 1850), Part II, Book IV, Chapter VI, 3590.5, 537; Jean Domat, *Les Loix civiles dans leur ordre naturel*, vol. 1 (Paris: Durand, 1777), 397: "Si un legs pieux étoit destiné à quelque usage qui ne put avoir son effet, comme si un testateur avoit légué pour faire une Eglise pour une Paroisse, ou un bâtiment dans un Hôpital, et qu'il arrivât ou qu'avant sa mort cette Eglise ou ce bâtiment eût été fait de quelque autre fonds, ou qu'il n'y en eût point de nécessite ni d'utilité, le legs ne demeureroit pas pour cela sans aucun usage; mais il seroit employé à d'autres oeuvres de piété pour cette Paroisse ou pour cet Hôpital, selon les destinations qu'en feroient les personnes que cette fonction pourroit regarder" and "Quoique ce texte regarde un autre sorte de disposition, la règle qui en résulte est à plus forte raison très-juste pour des legs pieux."

154. Domat, *Civil Law*, trans. Strahan, vol. 2, Part II, Book IV, Chapter VI, 3591, p. 538. Domat, *Loix civiles*, 1, 397: "Comme les legs pour des oeuvres de piété ont la double faveur, et de leur motif pour de saints usages, et de leur utilité pour le bien public, ils sont considérés comme privilégiés dans l'esprit des lois."

Wolsey and the Conscience of Common Law

The demand for smoother and easier transitions of property was clear. With the formal approval of the pope, Wolsey closed down twenty-nine monasteries in the 1520s and put their endowments to use for schools and colleges.[155] The scale was different from the eight hundred that would be shut down a few years later, but the idea of taking a donation and putting it to better use was there.[156] Still, there were significant legal difficulties that confronted Wolsey in this enterprise. Hall's *Chronicle* claimed that Wolsey "founde the kyng founder, wher other men wer founders" in order to effect the transitions.[157] In 1528 he prevailed upon the pope to get permission to merge some monasteries that had been founded, it was asserted, by the king's ancestors without the consent of their monks.[158] Wolsey's campaign at the papal court to get the necessary power to create his new foundations out of old monasteries drew accusations of repeated misrepresentations and deceptions, perhaps necessary, in his view, in order to "conver[t the properties] to a far better use," as he wrote to the king.[159] Wolsey's suppressions and visitations would feature in the complaints about him at his fall, shortly before which Henry VIII wrote to him with an interesting distinction:

As touching the help of religious houses to the building of your colleges, I would it would more, so it were lawfully; for my intent is none but that it should appear so to all the world, and the occasion of all their mumbling might be secluded and put away.... One thing more I perceive by your letter, which a little, methinks, toucheth conscience, and that is that you

---

155. For a list of Wolsey's suppressed houses, see Knowles, *Religious Orders*, vol. 3, 470.

156. G. R. Elton, *Reform and Reformation England, 1509–1558* (Cambridge, Mass.: Harvard University Press, 1977), 235.

157. Edward Hall, *The Lives of the Kings: Henry VIII*, vol. 2 (London: T. C. & E. C. Jack, 1904), 32.

158. *Letters and Papers of the Reign of Henry VIII*, ed. J. S. Brewer et al. (London: Stationery Office, 1875), doc. 4920, p. 2136.

159. Francis Aidan Gasquet, *Henry VIII and the English Monasteries*, vol. 1 (London: John Hodges, 1889), 87. On some of the irregularities, see pp. 82, 96, 101, 106, and 98, in which Strype reports that the pope believed that some of the proposed changes would be no more than "commutations and alterations" that would preserve and augment the use of the old foundations.

have received money of the exempts for having their old visitors. Surely this can hardly be with good conscience. For if they were good why should you take money? And if they were ill it were a sinful act. Howbeit, your legateship herein might peradventure *apud homines* be a cloak, but not *apud Deum*.[160]

Henry here indicated that he wanted the actions to appear legal to all men, but that in matters of conscience Wolsey must appear righteous before God as well. Wolsey naturally protested in reply that his actions were both legal and in good conscience.[161] Soon thereafter he received from a beleaguered pope the right to merge monasteries without the consent of interested parties, a permission granted with the warning that Wolsey's conscience should bear the results.[162] Conscience was being called upon to hold the line as law gave way.

The fall of Wolsey and the use of *praemunire* to take his possessions, including his endowments, entailed property complications. Despite his own efforts to circumvent legal norms, Wolsey was shocked by Henry's claim that York Place, which belonged to the bishopric of York, was forfeit to the king. According to George Cavendish, his servant and biographer, Wolsey, having been told by William Shelley that the law demanded the forfeiture of the property to "the King and his successors," replied that conscience would demand the mitigation of this action:

When ye tell him "this is the law" it were well done ye should tell him also that "although this be the law, yet this is conscience." For law without conscience is not good to be given unto a King in counsel to use for a lawful right, but always to have a respect to conscience before the rigor of the common law, for *"laus est facere quod decet, non quod licet."* The King ought of his royal dignity and prerogative to mitigate the rigor of the law where conscience hath the most force.... Therefore I say to you in this case, although you and other of your profession perceive by your learning that the King may by an order of your laws lawfully do that thing which ye demand of me—how say you, Master Shelley, may I do it with justice

---

160. Ibid., 92.
161. Ibid., 93.
162. In the end, Wolsey did not have the time to use this new power. Ibid., 106–7. Thomas Rymer, *Rymer's Foedera* (Hague: Joannes Neulme, 1741), vol. 6, part 2, 116.

and conscience, to give that thing away from me and my successors which is none of mine?[163]

Shelley protested that conscience in fact would authorize the shift: "there is some conscience in this case; but having regard to the King's high power, and to be employed to a better use and purpose, it may be the better be suffered with conscience."[164] Shelley was suggesting that the common law tradition would allow conscience to transition property from one use to a better one. Shelley added that twice the value of the property would be given to the church of York, suggesting an extremely profitable exchange. But Wolsey pointed out that such an exchange had been "neither promised ne agreed"; there had been rather "only a bare and simple departure with another's right forever. And if every bishop may do the like, then might every prelate give away the patrimony of their churches, which is none of theirs, and so in the process of time leave nothing for their successors to maintain their dignities." The exchange, according to Cavendish, ended with Wolsey asking Shelley to convey to Henry "that there is both heaven and hell."[165] If conscience could defend or even promote the exploitation of an already battered law, then what beyond the threat of hellfire was left to place limits on the king's actions?

The issue of York Place bore mostly on the question of alienation from the church, but the right to divert uses, to new and better purposes, was also at play, along with Shelley's contention that such a diversion was a matter of conscience, which struck Wolsey, with all of his legal, ecclesiastical, and frankly predatory experience with monastic properties as nonetheless an enormous leap. Wolsey was not excessively scrupulous; he had refused to honor the legacies that Bishop Fox had left from his estate.[166] Yet, if Cavendish's report can be trusted, even Wolsey was scandalized by the idea that the naked

---

163. George Cavendish, "The Life and Death of Cardinal Wolsey," in *Two Early Tudor Lives*, ed. Richard S. Sylvester and Davis P. Harding (New Haven, Conn.: Yale University Press, 1962), 121.
164. Ibid., 122.
165. Ibid.
166. Ward, *Foundation Statutes*, xxvii.

redistribution of property to a better use would be equitable. Meanwhile, Cavendish reported, as was attested in other sources, that the men who received Wolsey's properties came seeking his "confirmation unto their grants," unsure that they had secure title.[167] There was an increasing need for clarity and surety in real property transfers of all kinds, and the questions of the strictness of purpose and the role of the patron in giving consent were inhibiting broader designs of both the state and the bishops.

167. Cavendish, "Life and Death," 129.

5

Gifts in the Continental Reformations

John Burcher, who was sent from England to Poland to promote the Reformation, wrote in 1557 to the Swiss reformer Heinrich Bullinger that the prince of Cracow "has [been] brought truly to acknowledge that the pope is antichrist." Burcher added, "Nor does any thing make him hesitate, except the misapplication of church property, and the right understanding of the Lord's supper. They will easily be brought to agree, that the property of the church shall be converted to pious uses."[1] Even if the pope was the antichrist, there were hesitations about redirecting the property under his control. The only good answer an evangelical could give, and one with great moral force, was the promise of new, truly pious uses.

The Reformation included an enormous turnover, or secularization, of ecclesiastical property, in which the problem of the relationship between the donor and the gift emerged repeatedly. Of course, the property of the church had never been inviolate, and in some respects only the scale and the scrupulosity of the Reformation were new.[2] Where late medieval critiques of endowments had focused

---

1. Letter CCCXXVIII (November 4, 1557) in *Original Letters Relative to the English Reformation*, ed. Hastings Robinson, vol. 2 (Cambridge: Cambridge University Press, 1847), 688.
2. G. G. Coulton, *Art and the Reformation* (New York: Alfred A. Knopf, 1928), 411–51.

on their effect on the church, Protestants emphasized their effect on the world: the current use was offensive to God, and the new uses would be socially better. Still, no unified doctrine emerged here, only a variety of explanations that demonstrated the cultural strength of the *ius commune*. Had there been a cy-près doctrine, it would surely have been brought out to explain the transfers, as so many other canonical principles were. After all, two favorite motifs of the reformers would be Ambrose's use of church plate to feed the poor in a time of emergency and the right of kings to use church property for defense. The canonical prohibition that gifts made to bad ends had to be returned to the family might even be one explanation for why reformers often insisted that there had once been some good intention in the gifts they redirected.[3] Meanwhile, the principle that *abusus non tollit usum* (abuse or disposal does not take away the use) would support the demand to reform an endowment rather than destroy it. The natural rights of the commons to property as well as the rights of the poor to their patrimony also resonated as themes. Eventually the Modestinus opinion emerged as an *ex post facto* justification for the redirection of property. Canonical restrictions on the treatment of gifts would thus inadvertently encourage a tendency to explain the secularizations as both not really a transition in use and yet also a better fulfillment of the donor's original intentions than the previous use—an anticipation of what would become cy-près's dual perspective on approximation.

The Reformation inaugurated a new concept of the free gift—a gift made gratuitously without the expectation of return—and it thus severed the ongoing relationship between giver and gift.[4] This understanding did not necessarily transform the social use of gifts,

3. This did not prevent reformers from using the accusation of fraud to justify other changes, as Speyer did in "demand[ing] that the payment of taxes to the church be abolished because the pious foundations had been 'fraudulently' established." See Bernd Moeller, *Imperial Cities and the Reformation; Three Essays*, trans. H. C. Erik Midelfort and Mark U. Edwards Jr. (Durham, N.C.: Labyrinth Press, 1972), 58.
4. Parry, "The Gift." Some Catholic humanists, including at times Erasmus, also upheld this new ideal. See, for example, Erasmus's letter to William Warham of June 1514: Erasmus, *Collected Works*, vol. 2, 291.

but it did weaken the material claims of the donor and his heirs. The new interpretation of gifts was necessary because of the emphatic belief, held across the Reformation, that God gave freely to humans, who could not give anything back to God but should imitate him in giving freely to man.[5] Luther explained, suggestively in the context of secularizations, why it was offensive to return a gift to its giver:

> If a prince were to allot his property to you and give you a written testament of his last will as a pledge, and he did this out of kindness and goodness because of your poverty, demanding nothing from you except that you love him and accept the testament with gratitude and joy and keep it intact; and if you were to go and offer the testament back to him, so as to increase his property and not your own, and you wished to be honored as a benefactor, while he would be disgraced by accepting something from you, a poor beggar: would you not be considered mad and foolish and lacking in understanding?[6]

To believe that it was possible to give or do anything for God was works-righteousness. As the 1530 Augsburg Confession declared, justification was a "free gift of a donor, [not] the reward due to the laborer."[7] William Tyndale, elaborating on works-righteousness in his 1528 *Parable of the Wicked Mammon*, explained the gospel promise of storing up treasure in heaven as a command to do good for its own sake, as a free gift to fellow man, this good being done out of brotherly love and with no thought of return. But if all men were al-

---

5. Ilana Krausman Ben-Amos, *The Culture of Giving: Informal Support and Gift-Exchange in Early Modern England* (Cambridge: Cambridge University Press, 2008).

6. Martin Luther, "The Misuse of the Mass," trans. Frederick C. Ahrens, in *Luther's Works* (hereafter: LW), vol. 36 (Philadelphia: Fortress Press, 1959), 170. Martin Luther, "Vom Missbrauch der Messen," in *D. Martin Luthers Werke* (hereafter WA), vol. 8 (Weimar: Hermann Böhlau, 1966), 512–13: "Wenn eyn Fürst dyr seyn gutt beschiede und gebe dyr tzu eym pfandt eyn geschrieben testament feyns letzten willen, und thett das auss seyner milde und gütte umb deyns armutts willen und foddert nichts von dyr, denn das du mit danck und fremden das testament annehmest, wol bewareft und yhn lieb hetteft, und du gingest hyn und opfferts das testament ym widder, auff das du feyn und nit dyn guetter merest, und *wölbest* als eyn geber ehre haben, und er tzuschanden wurdt, das er von dyr armen betteler ettwas nehme: wurdest du nicht fagen, das der toll und töricht were und gar nichts vernehme."

7. Article XX, from *Triglot Concordia: The Symbolical Books of the Evangelical Lutheran Church: German-Latin-English* (St. Louis: Concordia, 1921).

ready elect or reprobate, then they could not help each other in the most essential matters. Paradoxically, predestination increased the urgency to put gifts to useful worldly ends, because if they had no good secular effect, then they were entirely squandered.

This new model of giving rebuked the endowers of the church. Luther praised simple gifts, which were free gifts or acts of friendship, and criticized those who endowed the church for their motives in giving: "they seem vigorously in pursuit of glory, indeed not only of glory but of repayment both temporal and eternal, as is plain to see from the way they lay burdens on people obligated to them."[8] In his *De libertate Christiana (On the Freedom of a Christian)*, Luther spoke to the donor directly: "if, however, you wish to pray, fast, or establish a foundation in the church, I advise you to be careful not to do it in order to obtain some benefit, whether temporal or eternal.... Make your gifts freely and for no consideration."[9] The donor should sever his relationship to the gift in every sense—mentally, physically, and emotionally. Elsewhere Luther censured the specificity of gifts, which bound them: "they arrange for certain choir songs in such a way, as if they would not get their due if the choir were to sing less or in a different way."[10] In fact "I greatly fear that few or no colleges, monasteries, altars, and offices of the church are really Christian in our day" because "in all these we seek only our profit, thinking that through them our sins are purged away and that we find salvation in them."[11] By hoping to lay up treasure, the donors erred: "these people are double-minded. For they do not give in simplicity for the

---

8. Luther, *Scholia on Romans* 12:8, LW, vol. 25, 449; WA, vol. 56, 457: "Vehementer enim videntur gloriam querere, immo non tantum gloriam, sed retributionem tam temporalem quam aeternam, scilicet dum certis oneribus premunt obligatos."

9. LW, vol. 31, 370–71; WA, vol. 7, 68: "si quippiam voles orare, ieiunare aut in Ecclesiis fundare (ut vocant), cave facias eo fine, quo tibi aliquid commodi sive temporalis sive aeterni pares ... da, quod das, libere et gratis."

10. Luther, *Scholia on Romans* 12:8, LW, vol. 25, 450; WA, vol. 56, 457: "Sed cantus certos ita disponunt, quasi si aliter fierent vel minus, non satisfieret eis."

11. Luther, "The Freedom of a Christian," LW, vol. 31, 370; WA, vol. 7, 68: "ego vehementer metuo, pauca vel nulla collegia, monasteria, altaria, officia Ecclesiastica esse Christiana hodie ... dum arbitramur, per haec purgari peccata nostra et salutem inveniri."

glory of God but for the sake of their own future advantage in heaven." Consequently, the gift had no fruit: "[T]hey do not realize this but go smugly along as if they were absolutely certain of repayment for these gifts, not alert to the fact that they have already received their reward."[12] Since exchange had been corrupted by its similarity to commerce, Christians should strive instead for purely spiritual sacrifices, which they offered as members of the royal priesthood.[13] Later, with the rise of martyrdom, a resolute Protestant could sacrifice his or her life to God, a singular gift.[14]

Whereas prayers for the dead had once promised to allow all of the participants to lay up treasure, as effect of the gift was multiplied in a countergift, now they were only a waste—or worse. By breaking up the veneration of the saints, the Reformation similarly ended another network of gifts and countergifts. Prayers and donations had been offered to the saints and their shrines, with the expectation of return. The saints spent the treasure that they had amassed in heaven to help their clients on earth in another gift-countergift exchange that they presumably conducted with God. When the Reformation cut off these exchanges, the problem remained: what should be done with previous donations, given in error due to superstition, simplicity, or attempted manipulation? The donors had misunderstood what they were doing, and they had been defrauded by the church, but they had not given freely either.

Earthly exchange networks also drew criticism, especially those necessary to have petitions heard, receive indulgences, be successful in church courts, or obtain access to the sacraments.[15] The anony-

---

12. Luther, *Scholia on Romans* 12:8, LW, vol. 25, 450; WA, vol. 56, 457: "Verum et ipsi duplices sunt. Quia non pro gloria Dei simpliciter, sed pro commodo suo futuro in caelo, non tributori, nisi suum commodum sperarent. Sed frustra, quia duplices sunt. Neque hoc cogitant, sed secure incedunt tanquam pro iis certam habentes remunerationem, non attendentes, quod hic receperunt mercedem suam."

13. Luther, "Vom Missbrauch der Messen," WA, vol. 8, 492–93.

14. Brad Gregory, *Salvation at Stake: Christian Martyrdom in Early Modern Europe* (Cambridge, Mass.: Harvard University Press, 2001).

15. Johann Crotus, "Theologians in Council," trans. Erika Rummel, in *Scheming Papists and Lutheran Fools: Five Reformation Satires* (New York: Fordham University Press, 1993), 65; *Hutteni Opera omnia*, ed. Eduardus Böcking, vol. 4 (Leipzig:

mous early satire *Henno rusticus* cited Matthew 10:8, in which the apostles were instructed to give as freely as they had received, and it acerbically commented that "the order of the day is different in the church now than it was then."[16] The satire followed the travails of Henno, a poor farmer who wanted absolution for his only son, who had raped his cousin, and permission for the two to marry, since she was now pregnant. At every step of the process, everyone asked what gift Henno had brought. The papal legate ultimately condescended to take only one of Henno's two much-needed cows, a conclusion that perverted the gospel command that if you have two of anything, you should give the extra one to the poor. The Germans paid for the mercy that Christ gave freely, and when German money arrived in Italy, it served the poor only by being spent on poor Roman prostitutes.[17] The legate openly scoffed at the idea of helping Henno in order to accumulate treasure in heaven: "I've pocketed heaven a long time ago and can sell it off any day at my discretion."[18] The successors to the apostles, as the satirist described them, took their inheritance, the gift of the Holy Spirit, and sold it for whatever they could get. As this account of outrage suggests, implicit in much of Reformation thought was the concern that, although man could not give to God, he could still insult God and come close to frustrating His purposes. The church should perform repentance by casting off the goods it had sinfully received; indeed, many argued—in an echo of canonical restitution—that there could be no true reform without the return of ill-gotten goods.

In the Reformation, these long-running anxieties about the power of man to corrupt God's work and about the cleansing of church property remained paramount. Catholics accused Protestants of sacrilege, but the charge provoked little guilt in the early Reformation, when the need for reform seemed so pressing and trust in the re-

---

Teubner, 1860), 584: "Munera corrumpunt et obaecant etiam oculos sapientum."

16. Jacobus Sobius, "The Powers of the Romanists," trans. Erika Rummel, in *Scheming Papists and Lutheran Fools*, 17; *Hutteni Opera omnia*, vol. 4, 494: "alia olim, alia modo in ecclesia disciplina est."

17. Ibid., 14 and 21–22.

18. Ibid., 32.

form movement was high. And yet, although fear of sacrilege was not evident, the converse anxiety was quite apparent: that of pollution or blasphemy, through ignorance, superstition, and idolatry. Lee Palmer Wandel points out that in Zurich one of the first manifestations of iconoclastic piety was the notable shift from describing iconoclasm as blasphemy, punishable by death, to describing the icons themselves as blasphemous.[19] This led to the presumption that there was, as Ludwig Hätzer argued in Zurich in 1523, an absolute duty for a Christian to take down images or risk divine wrath.[20] Although man could not truly profane the holy, he could easily insult God by attempting to sacralize the profane.[21] In their earliest writings on images or the Eucharist, the initial position of many reformers was that these remnants were not necessarily harmful except for the superstitious worship that the ignorant might offer. But, since that trap seemed increasingly inescapable, their removal was necessitated. Bucer—who maintained some concept of the real presence of Christ in communion, at least for believers—wrote in frustration that other men were seeking to "seclude Christ our Saviour from our sacraments and holy assemblies, and confine him to his place in heaven."[22] But Bucer missed that the argument was not simply about the ability of Christ to be in heaven and on earth at the same time, but the desirability for Him to be so, given the vulnerability of the sacrament to profanation. And Bucer himself was aware of the risk in other contexts: "the godless use creation for the destruction of themselves and others, thus insulting and disgracing God."[23]

---

19. See Wandel's chapter on Zurich in *Voracious Idols and Violent Hands: Iconoclasm in Reformation Zurich, Strasbourg, and Basel* (Cambridge: Cambridge University Press, 1994).

20. *Ein urteil gottes unsers eegemahels wie man sich mit allen götzen und bildnussen halten sol, uss der heiligen geschrifft gezogen durch Ludwig Hätzer* (Zurich: Christoph Froschauer, 1523).

21. Carlos Eire, *War against the Idols: The Reformation of Worship from Erasmus to Calvin* (Cambridge: Cambridge University Press, 1986), 227.

22. Letter CCLIII (Whitsunday 1550), in *Original Letters Relative to the English Reformation*, vol. 2, 547.

23. Martin Bucer, *Instruction in Christian Love [1523]*, trans. Paul Traugott Fuhrmann (Eugene, Ore.: Wipf & Stock, 2008), 27; "Das ym Selbs niemant, sonder Anderen Leben Soll" in *Martin Bucers Deutsche Schriften*, vol. 1 (Gütersloh: Gerd

Concern about blasphemy was not the only element pushing for the redirection of offensive property to new uses. An equally unrelenting issue at the time was the sense of ever-mounting salvific debt to God combined with the seeming impracticality of reconciling apostolic Christian life with the demands of family and community. Paul had said that the Hebrew law was an impossible standard, but in the late Middle Ages the gospel demands to be perfect seemed to ask Christians to have nothing, love everyone, and set themselves against the world in order to follow Christ. What humanism, the Reformation, and the Catholic Reformation offered instead was that it was, in fact, possible, to be an ordinary Christian, no longer chastened by the ideal of living in voluntary poverty. There could be some tension here: the ideal of apostolic poverty still served as a powerful critique of the clergy, even as it lost its valence for the laity. Nicholas Manuel's *Totenfresser* openly avowed this double standard. But for the common man it was enough to serve one's brother in Christian love by means of one's property, earned through honorable work.[24] God would supply the rest. This was not so different from the aftermath of Trent, in which the Catholic Church would reemphasize the sacraments as vehicles for transcendent grace that enables heroic piety, but would also highlight the infinite opportunities for small works, in the manner of Francis de Sales's *Introduction à la vie dévote*, in which everyday life gives the ordinary Christian the chance to prepare for heaven by loaning his handkerchief to someone who needs it. All of the apparent worldly attachments of society were occasions to practice detachment. To have was the necessary first step before giving up the claim to have. Thus the demands of salvation were moderated and expectations were moved back to the compromise of superfluities, but the new requirement in turn was to set gifts free.[25] If man did not need to count the cost of heaven, to make the best possible use of his resources for spiritual and temporal purposes at the same time, then he

---

Mohn, 1960), 50: "der dann die gotlosen ynen und menigklich so vil n yn gelegen zu verderben und gott zur schmach brauchen."

24. Brad Gregory, *The Unintended Reformation: How a Religious Revolution Secularized Society* (Cambridge, Mass.: Harvard University Press, 2012), 262.

25. Luther advocated for the theory of superfluities in thesis 46 of the 95 theses: LW, vol. 31, 29; WA, vol. 1, 235.

likewise should not count the cost when making a gift, out of gratitude for his liberation and in imitation of God. For Protestants, and increasingly for Catholics as well, gifts should be made and forgotten about, not forever bound to the donor.

But this ideal of a free gift did not mean that no one should supervise the gifts. Donors were losing their moral claim for an ongoing relationship with the gift, but the secular powers were gaining a claim for increased oversight. Nor did the rise of the ideal of the free gift mean that older gifts should be treated unlawfully, turned to new uses without a good reason or without due appreciation of the legal and moral rights of the donor and his heirs. In this rather extraordinary situation, donors had given gifts for purposes that had truly become impossible according to the new theological dispositions. The solicitude that evangelicals would display for the rights of the donor, even in the face of their theological commitments to free gifts, is a remarkable demonstration of the power of the medieval idea, supported by the *ius commune*, that the donor retained an interest in his gift.

Any reform movement of the early sixteenth century needed to grapple with property, specifically the afterlife of gifts, in order to implement change.[26] Secularization originated from the long-standing critique of the endowed church, but it was not possible simply to leave the property of the church alone: many of the early leaders of the Reformation were themselves able to live only because they were supported by church property that allowed them to preach and to write; much of the property of the church was perceived as in some sense belonging to its community; and since endowments could corrupt those who had access to them, they could not be left to fester. The issue of licit, legal, and moral resolutions to property claims would be a theme over decades. To take one prominent example, Bucer spent much of his career living off of endowments and turning church property to new uses. After Bucer broke with the Catholic Church, Franz von Sickingen installed him in Landstuhl, where the knight had the rights of presentation.[27] He married a former nun

---

26. Euan Cameron, *The European Reformation*, 2d ed. (Oxford: Oxford University Press, 2012), 51 and 97.

27. Greschat, *Martin Bucer*, 40.

and then, twenty years later, fought for the return of the money that had accompanied her entrance to her former monastery—to which she had the legal right.[28] With Bucer's approval, the city of Strasbourg used monastic endowments to establish the distinguished Strasbourg Academy, housed in the former Dominican monastery, and to pay its schoolmasters with prebends' stipends.[29] Bucer subsequently fought the plan to compromise with Catholics in the aftermath of the Battle of Mühlberg by giving them back some church property.[30] Upon his arrival in England, Bucer was given the Regius Professorship at Cambridge, "created by Henry VIII with funds obtained from the confiscation of church property."[31] But despite all of this, Bucer would still defend the cause of a possessioner church, albeit on a smaller scale than before, and he would come to believe that the dispossessing of the English churches had in fact been a form of sacrilege.[32] The problem of the correct use of property ran throughout his life and writings, as was true for many evangelicals. Property issues were intertwined with the Reformation, which was funded in part by the benefices, endowments, and rents of church property. Andreas Osiander, and other Lutherans, obtained preaching positions in Nuremberg through endowed posts, just as Huldrych Zwingli did as *Leutpriester* in Zurich.[33] From the elector, Luther received as his residence the Augustinian monastery where he had previously lived as a monk.

Consequently, the question of what ought to be done with church property came almost immediately to the foreground of Reformation texts and debates; a Reformation that was insistent on setting the material aside found itself deeply engaged with material questions. This does not need to be evidence for a materialist explanation of the Reformation itself. Carlos Eire suggested that the Reformation was a dividing moment in which the utter mutual impenetrability of the spiri-

---

28. Ibid., 201.
29. Ibid., 80 and 147; Jeannine E. Olson, "Calvin and Social-Ethical Issues," in *The Cambridge Companion to Calvin*, ed. Donald K. McKim (Cambridge: Cambridge University Press, 2004), 156.
30. Greschat, *Martin Bucer*, 224.
31. Ibid., 234.
32. Ibid., 239.
33. Cameron, *European Reformation*, 110.

tual and the material was asserted. In the thought of the Reformation, a man, in order to ascend to the spiritual, must put aside the material.[34] A more prosaic difficulty would be how to demonstrate that the material had been properly set aside in an inescapably material world.

Luther's initial impulse would be to turn the property back.[35] Certainly this was what he believed the church ought to do. In thesis 83 of the 95 Theses, he suggested that the pope should return the money for masses for the dead to the donor or his heirs, since one should not keep praying for the saved—an inversion of the Lollard critique that one should stop praying for the damned. As a reformer he initially intended to apply the same standards in Wittenberg and the other municipalities he advised. The return of unused gifts seemed legally correct, assured clean hands, and provided a nice contrast to avaricious prelates. As for new gifts, Luther supported bequests for schools and scholarships, which he claimed would please God and keep children from hell.[36] If good bequests like this could be pleasing to God, then perhaps He might also approve of the redirection of foolish gifts, which could reconcile the intent of the testator and the needs of the common good. Still, Luther preferred that the purposes of these institutions should fade away: the gospel could empty them out through conversion by the Word, while secular law could forbid new entrants. Once they were void of purpose, then something better could be done with any unclaimed money. This was not very different from some techniques for suppression already employed in the late Middle Ages, and it obscured the problem of the transfer of use. Zwingli used a similar tactic in Zurich: he silenced the organs in 1524, but they remained in the churches, unused, until they were dismantled in 1527.[37]

Within the first year of reform, Luther abandoned his initial sug-

34. Eire, *War against the Idols*.

35. As Cohn notes, Philip of Hesse defended his actions during the secularizations by pointing out that he allowed heirs to retrieve the endowments donated by their ancestors. "Church Property in the German Protestant Principalities," in *Politics and Society in Reformation Europe: Essays for Sir Geoffrey Elton on his Sixty-Fifth Birthday*, ed. E. I. Kouri and Tom Scott (London: Palgrave, 1987), 167.

36. Luther, "A Sermon on Keeping Children in School," LW, vol. 46, 257; "Eine Predigt, dass man Kinder zur Schulen halten solle," WA, vol. 30, part II, 587.

37. Charles Garside, *Zwingli and the Arts* (New Haven, Conn.: Yale University Press, 1966), 61.

gestion of the simple return of donations to the donor and came instead to suggest that some more complicated interventions in church property were necessary. His 1520 *Long Sermon on Usury* claimed the church should follow the example of Ambrose and Paulinus and give the treasure of the church over to the poor. In the same year, his *To the Christian Nobility of the German Nation* demanded that pilgrimage shrines be destroyed so that funds would cease being collected from the gullible; that anniversary masses should be abolished or consolidated so that God might no longer be angered by avaricious and insincere prayer; and that the community and government had a duty to abolish anything that was harmful to man or offensive to God. But his uncertainty remained. Luther's monastery in Wittenberg stopped celebrating private masses by 1521; Luther supported this cessation in his *De abroganda missa privata* (*The Abrogation of the Private Mass*), translated into German by Luther as *Vom Missbrauch der Messe*, or *The Misuse of the Mass*, in which he encouraged the frustration of the purpose but was reluctant to specify how the endowments that paid for the private masses ought to be used.[38] He urged priests not to continue saying them "either out of a sense of duty to its endowment or otherwise for the sake of money." Rather, he reminded them to "scorn human endowments and ordinances."[39] But this did not necessarily mean the endowments should be seized; Luther left unsaid what ought to be done with the endowments that were to fund private masses, although he condemned the cantarists, who were "of no use to anyone" but who "deceive the foolish people and draw them into hell after themselves, and with their lives rob the people of their money and property."[40] The old use should be stopped, but what should be done with the vacant property was the question.

Luther suggested that endowments could be secularized as a local response to the foreign abuse of money, which was perhaps a new twist on canonical permission to use church property in the case of

38. WA, vol. 8, 411–76.
39. LW, vol. 36, 226; WA, vol. 8, 560: "auss pflicht yhrer stifftund oder sonst umb geldes willen ... menschen stifftung und satzung veracht."
40. LW, vol. 36, 178; WA, vol. 8, 520: "niemant neutze find ... thun nichts anders, denn das sie das herrische volck betriegen und mit yhn tzur helle tzihn, und beramben sie mit yhren leugen an gellt und gutt."

invasion. Italians had gobbled up the endowments and foundations that ought to provide for Germans, Luther wrote. Taking back the endowments would better honor German donors, who had meant to help local causes. Thus local claims to property were one means for Luther to become comfortable with more vigorous steps to secularize property without offering the right of return. The fact that mendicants had defrauded local donors then helped him arrive at a new understanding of what the original intentions of the donors had been when they gave and how these higher intentions could morally supersede the specific dictates of the testator's will. In many cases, Luther argued, it was not even the testator who had erred but the institutions that the testator had trusted. This was similar to an argument to transfer trustees on the grounds of mis-employment, drawn from canon law. Moreover, Luther claimed that there was a distinction between the old endowments, in which the nobility were providing a living for their children to study, and new endowments, which turned to private masses. All endowed masses ought thus to be abolished in order to return to the original form of endowments. Similarly, in a very popular 1530 defense of turning endowments to new uses, Luther argued—in an echo of a late medieval theme—that the first monasteries were originally schools, an opinion with which many other reformers agreed: "they were originally founded long ago by pious kings and lords precisely for this precious work of training such preachers and pastors. But now, sad to say, the devil has brought them to such a wretched state that they have become death traps, the very ramparts of hell, to the hurt and detriment of the church."[41] It was only just to return them to their original purpose, Luther argued: "perhaps if the world lasts a while longer and

41. LW, vol. 46, 225. See also his assertion on p. 231 that the revenues for monasteries were given to educate poor boys; WA, vol. 30, part II, 535: "sie vorzeiten und anfenglich von frumen konigen und herrn, all zu mal, zu diesem theuren werd gestifft sind, das man solche prediger und pfar herr drinnen erziehen sollte, nu aber leider durch den teuffel ynn den iamer geraten, das es morddas Gott wird unsere sterbliche leichnam aufferwecken umb seines geists willen, der inn uns wonet." Melanchthon signed on to Karlstadt's 1521 argument to the elector that monasteries were originally established as schools: see Christopher Ocker, *Church Robbers and Reformers in Germany, 1525–1547: Confiscation and Religious Purpose in the Holy Roman Empire* (Leiden: Brill, 2006), 82n and 141n.

God gives the princes and the cities grace to act, the property of the foundations and monasteries will be restored to the use for which [it] was originally intended."[42] It was a sensible solution—and one that evaded the legal problem of the donors' rights by honoring their true intent. Many Protestant cities embraced this idea, turning monastic property and endowments in particular over to the creation of new schools, like the cloister schools of Württemberg.[43]

On the issue of secularization, Luther was cautious and ultimately rather deferential to the law. Luther's father had served on his city council for a time, and Luther himself had briefly studied law, so the legal issues of patronage and donations were particularly clear to him. Consequently he recognized ongoing interests in donated property, and only with time could he find ways to justify turning the gifts over to new uses without the consent of the heirs. Other reformers of the time, even some more theologically radical than he was, agreed about the justice of returning at least some church property to its original donors. For example, when Zwingli prepared 67 theses to defend in Zurich in 1523, he began from the Pauline assertion that Christ was the head of the church. Since Christ rejected wealth, then the church ought to reject it as well.[44] Any property that had been wrongfully acquired, such as donations to a church that ought never to have become wealthy, should be returned, and only if the donor could not be found should it be given to the needy.[45] He allowed those who relied upon endowments but wanted to become evangelical to keep using the endowment as a source of income until their death, at which point it would be returned to the donor or given to the needy.[46] This honored the rights of all parties. And Zwingli's legal carefulness on this point extended even in challenging situations. He was asked by Oswald Myconius of Lucerne to

---

42. LW, vol. 46, 235; WA, vol. 30, part II, 551: "Villeicht, wo die welt lenger stehet, und Gott gnade gibt, das die Fursten und Stedte da zu thun, meugen der stifft und fleofter guter auch widder zu folchem brauch tomen, da zu gestifft find."

43. Cameron, *European Reformation*, 261.

44. Huldrych Zwingli, *Sämtliche Werke*, vol. 1 (Berlin: Schwetschke, 1905), thesis 23, pp. 460–61.

45. Ibid., thesis 33, p. 462.

46. Ibid., thesis 64, p. 465.

comment on a case in which a woman, regretting her superstitious idolatry, took back and destroyed an image that she herself had given. The local council ordered her to pay a fine and give a new image to replace the old, and she had paid the fine but refused to have another image made. Here Zwingli agreed that she must make financial restitution for the value of the statue but not arrange for it to be made, and he offered to pay on her behalf. A donor never kept a complete claim on a gift, especially not if the gift was made for a purpose and that purpose was being fulfilled.[47] And yet he also urged her to tell Lucerne that "she had ordered the statue to be made not at all from reasons of piety but from hypocrisy and worldly pride, even feminine instability."[48] This would give both moral and legal permission to Lucerne to take down the statue when they reformed themselves, since her intentions had been bad and she no longer wanted it to be used for its original purpose.

In thinking about property, Luther and Zwingli thus harkened back to the canonical ideal that no injury should be done in the pursuit of justice. It was unimaginable that any would suffer as a consequence of the Reformation, unless God wanted to chastise them, because the Word would work in the world without causing harm. The wealth of the church could be managed in a way that would be perfectly fair, as former monks would be pensioned off with more than they had given when they entered the order, priests would be maintained until their death, endowments would return to the family of the donor or, if that was impossible, be funneled into poor relief, and patrons would naturally choose to turn over their patronal churches to the evangelical cause. Indeed, Luther's sense that the Reformation could cause no harm may even help to explain his flirtation with psychopannychism, the belief in the sleep of the soul between death and the Resurrection and Last Judgment.[49] As the prayers for the dead fell silent under his inspiration, the dead did not even observe this redirection of their gifts and had no consciousness of it.

47. Garside, *Zwingli and the Arts*, 99–102.
48. Ibid., 100.
49. C. A. Patrides, "Psychopannychism in Renaissance Europe," *Studies in Philology* 60.2.1 (1963): 227–29.

Luther's more pragmatic follower Philip Melanchthon was not quite as idealistic as Luther in this regard, but he found his own solution to honor the donor while providing for the needs of the evangelical church. He advocated the return of property to the donor first—but not to his heirs—thus nodding in the direction of cy-près.[50] Melanchthon used the Modestinus opinion to support this transfer, and from this point it was picked up by other Protestant and humanist jurists. It may have been the discovery of the Modestinus passage that swayed Melanchthon away from his earlier position of granting the right of recovery to heirs and toward a far more radical stance. As he explained the text, it allowed the gift "to be transferred to another public use" and that as a consequence it was even more certain that "legacies to invalid ceremonies are transferred to another ecclesiastical use and not returned to the heirs."[51] This suited Melanchthon's understanding of human justice, which was a pedagogy that had to coerce the impious (*impii*).[52] Melanchthon, *Praeceptor Germaniae*, could with a good conscience pursue the transfer of church property to education or poor relief, both of which were arguably ecclesiastical uses, because the Romans would also have done it.

Anxiety over the diversion of ecclesiastical donations to new uses could also be assuaged by the justice of the new use for the property: to fund the spread of the Word; to pay for scholars and preachers; to support municipal poor relief; or to build up the commonwealth.[53] Andreas Karlstadt laid out such an agenda for Wittenberg in the second half of his 1522 pamphlet against images in church. If a city had beggars, he wrote, then it would seem that there were "no

50. C. Scott Dixon, *The Reformation and Rural Society: The Parishes of Brandenburg-Ansbach* (Cambridge: Cambridge University Press, 1996), 90.
51. "Legata ad spectacula lex vult non reddit haeredibus, si spectacula tempore mutentur, sed ad alios usus publicos transferri: ergo multo magis legata ad vitiosas ceremonias, transferenda sunt ad alios usus ecclesiasticos, et non reddenda haeredibus." Philip Melanchthon, *Opera quae supersunt omnia*, in Corpus Reformatorum, vol. 16, ed. Heinrich Ernst Bindseil (Halle: C. A. Schwetschke, 1850), 844.
52. Philip Melanchthon, *Epitome renovatae Ecclesiasticae doctrinae* (Marburg: C. L. Pfeil, 1860), 5. See also Ralph Keen, "Defending the Pious: Melanchthon and the Reformation in Albertine Saxony," *Church History* 60.2 (1991): 180–95; Guido Kisch, *Melanchthons Rechts- und Soziallehre* (Berlin: Walter de Gruyter, 1967).
53. Lee Palmer Wandel, *Always Among Us: Images of the Poor in Zwingli's Zurich* (Cambridge: Cambridge University Press, 1990).

Christians or else very few, dispirited ones" and the magistrates ought to supervise the common duty to care for the poor, since the ordinary Christian had a duty to care for his household first.[54] In order to establish this program, it was necessary first to ban begging, particularly by the mendicants, who "often cheat the poor and rich alike of their possessions ... [harming] the poor person with their demands of cheese, grain, bread, beer, wine, their last wills, and much more. They tear out of poor children's mouths what they themselves need."[55] Then a "common bag or box was to be set up in which to gather what would be collected from all the [religious] congregations [i.e., monastic communities that were dissolving]."[56] Money that "is dedicated and given here for masses" should be taken, because "this is a devilish thing and contrary to the character of the blessed sacrament [and] ... we have too many priests who refuse to serve either God or their neighbor." But even admittedly useless priests, "who do not wish to learn anything" still "should not be cut off from any moneys" since "it is unchristian to fight mendicancy while creating new beggars."[57] The intentions of the donors were irrelevant to Karlstadt's calculations, even though he had received a doctorate in *utriusque iuris*. All that mattered was how God perceived the usage of money: "God rates your lamps and lights, your howling and prayers rather low."[58]

---

54. Trans. E. J. Furcha, in *The Essential Carlstadt: Fifteen Tracts by Andreas Bodenstein (Carlstadt) from Karlstadt* (Scottdale, Penn.: Herald Press, 1995), 120; *Von Abtuhung der Bylder, und das Keyn Bedtler unther den Christen seyn sollen* (Wittenberg: n.p., 1522): "das keyne ader ye blode und wenig Christen."

55. *Essential Carlstadt*, 126; *Von Abtuhung:* "Betrigen offtmalss arme und reiche umb das ir. Und beschettigen den armen man an foderung. Der Keese, Korn, Broth, Buhr, Wein, Testamet und allerlen. Reissen den armen Kindern auss irem maul das sie selber bedurffen."

56. *Essential Carlstadt*, 126; *Von Abtuhung*: "Das man eyne gemeine Beutell oder Kasten solt auffrichten unddar eyn das eynkomen aller bruderschafften brengen."

57. *Essential Carlstadt*, 126–27; *Von Abtuhung*: "In betrachtung das vil lehen alhie auff Messe gewidebt und gestifft seind. Das dan ein teuffelich dingt ist. Und wider natur des heilige sacraments. Ungesehen auch das tzuvil pfaffen seind die weder got nach dem nehsten deinen mogen und wellen auch nicht lernen. Den pfaffen welche ietz leben wellen sie weder heller noch pfennig abbrechen oder nhemen. Dan sie wissen das unchristlich is tzo ymand betlerey weren wolt und wolt neuwe betler machen."

58. *Essential Carlstadt*, 127; *Von Abtuhung:* "Ewere lampeln und licht geheull und beten acht gott gar kleyn."

So the poor could offer a legitimate means to redirect property, especially if authorized by secular authorities. In January of 1522 Wittenberg adopted a program of poor relief written by Karlstadt.[59] This famous ordinance began with the seizure of endowments: "It is unanimously resolved that all income from the churches, all of the brotherhoods, and the guilds shall be collected together and brought into a common chest ... to provide for the poor people."[60] But a distinction was made in the second point, for these private communities and testamentary bequests were to be seized immediately, but the salaries of priests endowed by these bequests were not to be touched until the priest died, at which point the property would be transferred. The ordinance carried on: no begging would be allowed, no mendicants could stay in the city, the monks must work, the cloisters were to be inventoried, everyone was to contribute if the common chest is not sufficient to the needs of the poor, and the priests "shall encourage no one ... to make a testament to their advantage."[61]

At about the same time as Wittenberg's attempted ordinance, numerous other evangelical cities made similar reforms. The emphasis these efforts were given in the midst of so many other pressing political issues and threats speaks to the centrality of poor reform in the vision of the reformers. It also attests the conviction that in good faith the reformers should not stop private masses, forbid begging, and take over endowments without first putting in place a systematic social welfare policy. In Geneva one of the first initiatives after the city voted to reform itself was the replacement of its small hospitals with a single large hospital. A further initiative used ecclesiastical treasure to create a city mint. Both of these actions put into practice

---

59. The elector subsequently banned the program at the prodding of Luther, who disliked its dramatic reforms of worship.

60. "Order of the City of Wittenberg," trans. Carter H. Lindberg, in *Beyond Charity* (Minneapolis, Minn.: Augsburg Fortress, 1993), 200; Emil Sehling, ed., *Die evangelischen Kirchenordnung des 16. Jahrhundert*, vol. 1 (Leipzig: O. R. Reisland, 1902), 697: "Ernstlich ist einhelliglich beschlossen, das all zins der gotzheüser, all priesterschaften, und alle zins der gewerken, söllen zuhaufen geschlagen und in ain gemainen kasten gepracht werden ... damit arm leüt versehen söllen."

61. "Order of the City of Wittenberg," trans. Carter H. Lindberg, in *Beyond Charity*, 201; Sehling, ed., *Die evangelischen Kirchenordnung*, vol. 1, 597: "doch söllen sie niemant zu testamentarien bestellen noch halten."

another policy of the humanists and reformers alike, that social programs should be centralized and subject to unified planning and supervision by the state. This arrangement was expected to yield better results than the apparently more random and chaotic alms of Catholic donations.[62] The magistrates had the right to supervise these programs and could also take to themselves the power to redistribute property on their own authority, but with God's sanction, for the good of the poor or the commonwealth. Thus the problem of donors could be solved by an appeal to the lawful exercise of secular power in pursuit of the common good.

The most prominent official program for poor relief of the early Reformation was the 1523 Leisnig Fraternal Agreement, written with the advice of Luther himself.[63] Luther published the text of the ordinance with his own preface. The Leisnig community had taken back the appropriated patronage rights over the parish church from the abbot of the nearby monastery of Buch, as the town determined that it ought to be able to elect its own pastor.[64] Luther's immediate advice to Leisnig was to establish a community chest so that the pastor's salary would be paid directly from the tithe of the town, thus mitigating the issue of patronage rights. Leisnig asked Luther to explain the biblical basis by which the community might call and dismiss pastors, which he did, admitting that on this issue "one should not care at all about human statutes, law, old precedent, usage, custom, etc." because of the seriousness and eternal consequences of the care of souls.[65] The sheep, Luther wrote, have the right to judge the teachings of bishops and pastors (John 10:4–5), even though "all bishops, religious foundations, monasteries, universities, and everything belonging to them rage against this clear word of Christ."[66]

---

62. Olson, "Calvin and Social-Ethical Issues"; Eire, *War against the Idols,* 150.
63. LW, vol. 45, 159–94; WA, vol. 12, 11–30.
64. LW, vol. 45, 163.
65. "That a Christian Assembly or Congregation has the Right and Power to Judge All Teaching," LW, vol. 39, 306; "Das eyn Christliche versamlung odder gemyne recht und macht habe, alle lere tzu urtylen und lerer tzu beruffen," WA, vol. 11, 408: "mus man sich gar nichts keren an menschen gesetz, recht alltherkomen, brauch, gewonheyt, etc."
66. LW, vol. 39, 307; WA, vol. 11, 410: "wer sihet hie nu nicht, das alle Bis-

This was the problem of ecclesiastical property: it used its worldly power to try to inhibit the work of the Word. It convinced the sheep that they did not even have the authority to follow Christ. Still, Luther avoided calling for property rights to be unnecessarily stripped away. It would be better for Leisnig to fund its own pastor.

Leisnig did subsequently also take over "all church properties within the parish," but Luther's advice to the Leisnig magistrates was to be scrupulously careful about legal rights, including patronage rights, as they did so. In Leisnig, church property should be turned over to the common chest, from which the needs of the poor would be supplied. But although the service of the monks was "blasphemous and damnable," it would be unchristian to simply dismiss them. Rather, any who wanted to depart should be pensioned off, while those who wanted to stay should be given a "provision even more ample and generous than what they may have had before."[67] No new applicants should be admitted, so that the monasteries would dissolve of their own accord, without force or spoliation. Luther acknowledged that there would "be a mad scramble for the assets of such vacated foundations," and if the evangelicals were not careful, then "things will go from bad to worse, and on our deathbed we will be overwhelmed by terrible remorse."[68] And so to Leisnig, on the matter of the will of the donors, Luther wrote that the donors "erred and were misled when they gave this property to monasteries," since "their intention certainly was to give it for the glory and service of God; but their purpose was not realized."[69] The purpose was not accomplished for two reasons: monasteries were too corrupt to use their wealth for good ends, and man could never give to God. Indeed, all donors, to the

---

choff, stifft, kloester, hohen schulen mit alle yhrem corper widder dis helle wort Christi toben."

67. LW, vol. 45, 171; WA, vol. 12, 12–13: "keyn nutz und eyttel schedlich yrthum und verfuererey ist ... auch reichlicher und milder, denn sie villeicht vorhyn versorgt gewessen find."

68. LW, vol. 45, 170–71; WA, vol. 12, 11–12: "das soelcher ledige stiffte gutter.... Es wirt sonst ubel erger werden, und wirt am todbett gar eyn boesser rewling komen."

69. LW, vol. 45, 172; WA, vol. 12, 13: "denn wie wol sie geyrret und verfuret sind, das sie es zu kloestern geben haben, ist dennoch iah yrh meynung gewessen, gott zu ehren und zu dienst geben, und haben also gefeylet."

extent that they rested on works-righteousness, had harmed themselves by their gifts. The purpose of the bequests, Luther argued, was being frustrated, and the ultimate intentions of the testators could be better served by redirecting the gifts. This is the ostensible logic of cyprès *avant la lettre*.

As for patronage rights, it was wrong for the right of presentation to be kept from the entire community, so this right was to be dissolved and ignored. But to the extent that patronage represented a property right, Luther believed it should be carefully maintained, and he acknowledged the family's rights more generally:

If the heirs of the founder are impoverished and in want, however, it is fair and in harmony with Christian love that the foundation revert to them, at least a large portion of it, or the whole amount if their need be great enough to warrant it. It certainly was not the intention of their fathers—and should not have been—to take the bread out of the mouths of their children and heirs and bestow it elsewhere. And even if that was their intention, it is false and un-Christian, for fathers are in duty bound to provide for their own children first of all; that is the highest service they can render to God with their temporal goods.[70]

As Witte observed, Luther kept returning to canonical principles even as he tried to discard canon law.[71] The language of patronage, intentions, the right of return, and even pious uses was not suppressed but rather was deployed to justify the transfer of property. In fact, where donors did not want their property returned, the evangelicals

---

70. LW, vol. 45, 173; WA, vol. 12, 13–14: "Doch ist das auch billich unnd Christlicher liebe gemess, das wo der stiffter erben verarmet und noettig weren, das den selben solch stifftung widder heym salle yhe eyn gross teyl, und ales miteynander, wo die nott so gross were, denn freylich yhrer vetter meynung nicht gewesen ist, auch nicht hatt sollen seyn, yhren kindern und erben das brott aus dem maul nemen und andersswo hyn wenden, und ob die meynung so gewessen were, ist sie falsch une unchristlich, denn die vetter sind schuldig yhre kinder fur allen dingen zuversorgen. Das ist der hoehist gottis dienst, den sie mit zeyttlichem gutt thun muegen." Luther's efforts to separate out *zinss* contracts from simple donations to protect the church from contamination also echo, in a limited way, jurisprudence on how the church should manage gifts made of ill-gotten property: WA, vol. 13, 175.

71. John Witte, *Law and Protestantism: The Legal Teachings of the Lutheran Reformation* (Cambridge: Cambridge University Press, 2002). See also Kenneth Pennington, "Protestant Ecclesiastical Law and the Ius Commune," *Rivista internazionale di diritto comune* 26 (2015): 9–36.

were eager to draw on the rights of donors, since evangelical patrons turned their "own" properties over to the cause of the Reformation, which helped to eliminate some of the legal issues of the transfer.[72]

Leisnig's ultimate ordinance was a little more uncompromising than Luther's preface to it. As Luther had recommended, the priests did not lose their salary, although after their death the benefices would be turned over to the common chest. But the ordinance made no attempt to offer property back to the destitute families of donors and instead claimed the right of the parish to take all kind of property donations and turn them over to the common chest.[73] Donors' intentions were not irrelevant, but they were defined in a way to make the transfer of property easy. Future donations, taxes, and bequests would also be collected into the common chest, although the city cautioned pastors about soliciting gifts from people on the sickbed—it could be permitted, but only "if the prospective heirs give their approval and the patient is still in possession of his faculties."[74]

In the end, despite Luther's idealistic push, the transition to the new system was not smooth, as he complained to his good friend Georg Spalatin. But whatever the disappointments of these new efforts, they did not lead to anything like the popular resentment of the treatment of ecclesiastical property that would be felt in England after the seizures and dissolutions. In German lands, the property was still largely controlled locally and mostly put to local causes. The 1528 church ordinance of Braunschweig, for example, proposed to use church property to fund schools, appoint preachers, create a common chest for the poor, and also pay for church upkeep. The common chest would receive the money that had been left for prayers for the dead with no right of return. There was no defense of the right to appropriate the bequests except that they were useless and could not serve the dead in any way.[75] This was the same logic

72. Ocker, *Church Robbers*.
73. "Ordinance of a Common Chest," LW, vol. 45, 179–80; "Ordenung eyns gemeynen kastens," WA, vol. 12, 17.
74. LW, vol. 45, 182; WA, vol. 12, 20: "auch weyll die menschen bey vernunfft, am siechbette, mit verwilligunge der anwartenden erben, ynn ordentlichen sellen zuthun."
75. Emil Sehling, ed., *Die evangelischen Kirchenordnungen*, vol. 6/1 (Tübingen: Mohr, 1955), 348–455.

that George of Polentz, the first Lutheran bishop of Pomesania, offered in banning services for the dead: "they are of no use, and of no avail," and so he ordered brotherhoods and guilds to turn their endowments over to "the maintenance of the poor and other pious uses."[76] The use was the solution, and as the evangelicals emphasized the use of church property for the poor and for all, they, in some ways, honored the canonical tradition.[77]

Iconoclasm

Even iconoclasm, which was motivated by the belief that gifts were polluting the community, tended to maintain the traditional right of return to the heirs for unused gifts. In Nuremberg donors were given the right of return, even if that meant that the treasure would then leave the city with the donor.[78] In Strasbourg too, the initial inclination in 1523 was to allow the donors to take back the images, and when remaining images were taken down in 1529, the city council insisted not only that donors could still retrieve their gifts but also that coats-of-arms remain on the walls to mark past gifts.[79] Ulm (under Bucer's influence), Bern, and St. Gall all gave donors the first right to take back their donation.[80] Some surviving works of late medieval religious art exist today only because a donor exercised this right. Christensen gives the example of Hans Holbein the Younger's Oberried altarpiece, "apparently rescued by the donor."[81] The heirs of the sculptor Veit Stoss successfully retrieved a retable he had made and donated in Nuremberg.[82]

It was not only the authorities who arrived at this solution: other

---

76. B. J. Kidd, *Documents Illustrative of the Continental Reformation* (Oxford: Clarendon Press, 1911), 190–91.
77. For an extensive examination of Protestant arguments over which uses might be legitimate, see Ocker, *Church Robbers*.
78. Carl E. Christensen, *Art and the Reformation in Germany* (Athens: Ohio University Press, 1979), 71 and 77–78; Cameron, *European Reformation*, 253.
79. Christensen, *Art and the Reformation*, 80 and 89–91.
80. Ibid., 233n276.
81. Ibid., 234n291.
82. Joseph Leo Koerner, *Reformation of the Image* (Chicago: University of Chicago Press, 2003), 58.

citizens of Zurich often agreed with Zwingli's adherence to the right of return for an unused gift to the donor or his or her heirs. After a sermon in 1523 by the Zurich reformer Leo Jud calling for the removal of all "idols," a member of his parish took offense: "If another had paid something and had it made, [Jud] should allow it to stand or go back from whence he came.... [Jud] had given nothing for them and therefore should not knock them off."[83] Those who had not given should not take it upon themselves to redirect or destroy pious donations. In the narratives that remain of iconoclastic conversation, it seems that the push to give the remnants of idols to the poor was the legal argument made by iconoclasts in response to this desire to return gifts to their donors. Laurenz Mayer, an assistant at mass, was reported to have said that "it would please him very much if the chaplain would knock the idols off the altar with the candlesticks, because there were so many poor people who sat in front of the churches and in other places and had very little, but had to suffer great hunger and wretchedness, who could easily be helped with such decorations; for one can easily find in Ambrose that such decorations are food for the poor."[84] Ludwig Hätzer's popular pamphlet on images avoided the legal problem of how to take the images down, but offered that in the future, "if anyone here still wishes to decorate a temple, let him give diligently to the poor who are a living temple."[85]

The most fervent iconoclasts were reluctant to return to donors their "idolatrous" gifts that had threatened the entire community with the wrath of God. If turning the material over to the poor was legally sanctioned, then this could punish the donor while removing the offense. This was Klaus Hottinger's strategy in destroying the elaborate wooden crucifix erected near one of Zurich's outer gates. The donor, a wealthy shipbuilder, was known, but Hottinger preferred to "sell the wood and ... give the money got from it to the poor people who could best use it."[86] His act was illegal, and Hotting-

83. Garside, *Zwingli and the Arts*, 105.
84. Ibid., 108.
85. Ibid., 115.
86. Heinrich Bullinger, *Reformationsgeschichte*, ed., J. J. Holtinger and H. H. Vögeli, vol. 1, (Frauenfeld, Switzerland: Beyel, 1838), 127. Garside, *Zwingli and the Arts*, 119.

er was jailed, but his argument to give the gifts to the poor instead of the donor was gaining popular sympathy. In response, donors began taking their gifts away themselves, as Kaspar Liechte did by retrieving statues, "saying that they had been put there by him and his forebears." As Garside observes, this permission to allow donors to retrieve their own works was "soon to become a major policy for the removal of works of religious art from the Zurich churches."[87] It was legally conservative, but it rankled those who believed that images were offensive to God no matter where they were placed. In a disputation held in Zurich to settle the matter, Ludwig Hätzer argued that images were forbidden everywhere, both in the temple and in "secret," that is, in private dwellings.[88] One citizen rose to note that "Saint Martin has done charitable work. May one not then paint him in doing so, in order that he may encourage the giving of alms?"[89] This iconophile was trying to make the old images appeal to the new priorities. In response the iconophobes emphasized that images did not encourage charity but diverted it: "[E]xpense should be no longer wasted on images of wood and stone, but bestowed upon the living, needy images of God."[90] The decree of the council in May of 1524 ignored these nuances: donors had a week to remove their images; images that had been collectively purchased by a parish should be dealt with by the parish as a whole; no more images should be made and those that remained in the churches should be ignored; crucifixes in particular ought to be left alone.[91] By June, the compromise had failed, and though donors still had the right of retrieval, all images were to be taken down by appointed committees. The raw materials left over from smashed images were handed over to the poor—after some prodding by Zwingli.[92]

Churches on the eve of the Reformation had "increasingly numerous lay donors," who were well aware of their legal rights. They had put their coats-of-arms on their donations and treated them as

87. Garside, *Zwingli and the Arts*, 124.
88. Ibid., 132.
89. Ibid., 143 and 149.
90. Ibid., 144.
91. Ibid., 156–57.
92. Cameron, *European Reformation*, 253.

family memorials, and they were accustomed to engaging with municipal negotiations over their right to provide upkeep for old gifts that needed restoration.[93] Herman Heimpel's pithy observation that the "image donors" became the "image smashers" was intended to demonstrate how abrupt the Reformation was.[94] He was right insofar as the areas that had been the most vigorous in the production of images do seem to have embraced the Reformation with the greatest zealotry. Religious enthusiasm may be adaptable from one ideology to another, but while there are some prominent examples of image-donors subsequently repenting of their idolatry, in the vast majority of instances those who smashed the idols were destroying someone else's gift and violating the directions of their preachers and magistrates, who usually wanted an orderly removal of the images, in which legal issues might be carefully handled and the stinging accusation of plunder avoided.[95] As Carl Christensen has pointed out, often it was the members of the city council, or their families, who had donated the images, whereas it was the most radical members of the artisan guilds, and even some artists, who were most eager to destroy.[96] Bruce Gordon has found notable class conflict in the outbreak of iconoclasm in Basel, as Thomas Brady also discovered in Strasbourg.[97] Wealthy cities where the elite could afford to give lavishly to the church were particularly likely to have aggrieved proletarian guilds; it was understood that votive gifts to the church were donations made to accumulate private benefits to the donor and his family in place of alms to the poor.

On the other hand, because of the communal nature of the

---

93. Christensen, *Art and the Reformation*, 15 and 71–72.

94. Herman Heimpel, "Das Wesen des Deutschen Spätmittelalters," in *Der Mensche in Seiner Gegenwart: Sieben historische Essais* (Göttingen: Vandenhoeck & Ruprecht, 1954), 134. Cited by Eire in *War against the Idols*, 2, as well as by Ozment in his *The Reformation in the Cities: The Appeal of Protestantism to Sixteenth-Century Germany and Switzerland* (New Haven, Conn.: Yale University Press, 1980).

95. Christensen, *Art and the Reformation*, 100, citing Oecolampadius and Fridolin Ryff on Basel.

96. Ibid., 71, 95, and 103.

97. Bruce Gordon, *The Swiss Reformation* (Manchester, England: Manchester University Press, 2002), 110–11; Thomas A Brady, *Ruling Class, Regime and Reformation at Strasbourg, 1520–1555* (Leiden: Brill, 1978).

church, it was possible for everyone to believe they had a claim to its wealth and thus for iconoclasts to argue that they were destroying or dislodging what belonged to all—including the iconoclasts themselves. Diversion of the images could be a punishment for blasphemy or restitution for theft. As the Lollards had once argued, the donations of the images had "rob[bed] poor men of their due portion ... and when such offerings to dead images rob poor men, they rob Jesus Christ," since it is "the meek true poor man that is the true image of God."[98] The sixteenth-century iconoclasts had similar sentiments. As Lee Palmer Wandel has shown, the images were seen to be continuously consuming resources, using oil for lamps and receiving donations.[99] The donor had bound up resources that were not his to give and deprived the poor in multiple ways.

As iconoclasm gathered force, city councils proved loathe simply to let the objects disperse or be destroyed; instead, seeking to lay a general local claim, they reframed the donations as mistaken gifts by the community as a whole. This redrawing of the gifts would allow the community to decide together how to put them to a new use. Local families had given these items, which consequently ought to stay in the city and not leave as monastic orders were chased out. The Dominicans, for example, would leave Geneva without any of their treasure, and in many cities international orders were turned out without their property, on the grounds that they had defrauded local citizens by encouraging them to make erroneous gifts instead of supporting the local, deserving poor and common good.[100]

A charitable use, directed by the municipality, might instead give wood to the poor after the art had been smashed or smelt precious metals for municipal poor relief. On rare occasions, art might be sold and its profits used for the city.[101] It is difficult to determine how central the charitable act was to iconoclasm itself, but the iconoclasts do seem to have recognized the canonical principle that it is always

---

98. From the General Prologue to the second Lollard Bible, quoted in Aston, *England's Iconoclasts*, vol. 1: *Laws against Images* (Oxford: Oxford University Press, 1988), 125 and 118–19.
99. Wandel, *Voracious Idols*.
100. Eire, *War against the Idols*, 149.
101. Koerner, *Reformation of the Image*, 59.

safe to give church property to the poor. Eire argues that "an integral part of the iconoclastic crusade was the effort to turn the destruction of the cultic objects into a charitable and practical operation ... [such that they were] put to practical use once they were cast down."[102] This was the one point of agreement, generally, between the mob and the city council, that a gift of the remnants to the poor was appropriate.

In fact, the poor were the only biblically and canonically authenticated recipients of gifts that were too offensive to be returned to the donors.[103] Indeed, although reformers beginning with Karlstadt were unwilling to concede that images were the "Bible of the poor," the phrase nonetheless suggested that there might be a kind of return to a donor's original intention—if he had believed that he was giving the image for the instruction of the illiterate—in using their gifts truly to help the poor. But sometimes, as in Basel, plans to give to the poor turned instead into squabbling and destruction by fire to prevent further social unrest.[104] As Aston notes, punishing the idols by burning them was satisfying: it had the imprimatur of the Old Testament, and it also gave momentary warmth to the poor.[105] But Basel was temporarily demoralized by this outcome, in which greed ruined the plans for the good use of the materials. Erasmus left the city and moved to Catholic Freiburg im Breisgau to emphasize that this was not the reform he had been hoping for. The behavior of the iconoclasts had certainly not mirrored his expectations for the prudent disposition of church property.

Of course, some of the occasions of image-breaking are described by contemporary sources not as poor relief enterprises but rather as opportunities for joyful destruction, a chance to poke out the eyes of an idol, to destroy a painting, to feed wafers to animals, or to bathe in holy water. The smashing of lamps that hung in front of images or in front of the rood was common to many iconoclastic scenes, as

---

102. Eire, *War against the Idols*, 164.
103. Henricus Bohic, *Distinctiones in quinque Decretalium libros* (Venice: Heironymus Scotus, 1576), X. 5.40.13, p. 300; Gl. Ord. ad Extrav. Jo. XXII, 1.3.1.
104. Eire, *War against the Idols*, 118.
105. Aston, *England's Iconoclasts*, 135.

in Wittenberg, Münster, Strasbourg, Geneva, and Zurich.[106] This gesture motioned toward the endowments that lay behind the lamps, frustrating their purpose. But often even riotous acts turned materials toward a new use. At times the rioters appropriated materials for themselves, turning altars into washbasins in Geneva and joking in Wittenberg about using the altars as gallows.[107] Materials from the images could be used to build something new and to serve a new function.[108] This finding of a new use was a demonstration that the images had never been more than matter—more convincing, perhaps, than their total destruction, and in a peculiar way more defiant than mere smashing and burning. The iconoclast who was willing to walk on cobblestones made of images would daily affirm his own rectitude and make everyone who passed by a participant in trampling on the idols.

Iconoclasm also pushed against donated property at its weakest point, by portraying it as pollution, blasphemy, and idolatry that would destroy the community that allowed itself to be contaminated by idols. The argument that idols were offensive was much stronger than the argument against prayers for the dead—and more easily grounded in biblical text. Because the donors of the property had risked the lives of the community through their idolatry, they deserved nothing back. In this case there was no argument that the donors had an intention that ought to be carried through into a new purpose. At best, the donors had been badly mistaken and were lucky to have had their blasphemy cut short by good Christians. Thus Martin Bucer's treatise on images, translated into English and published in 1535 by William Marshall, explained both the theological offense of believing that these works could be done for God and the social offense of substituting the donation of these images for real works of charity.[109] They gave the Christian a "false confydence in merytes" that naturally led to a "lothfulnesse to exercyse charite

---

106. Although Luther allowed altar lamps in 1528: Christensen, *Art and the Reformation*, 38, 59, 81, 88, and 100; Eire, *War against the Idols*, 63, 80, and 139.

107. Eire, *War against the Idols*, 137.

108. Koerner, *Reformation of the Image*, 105.

109. Martin Bucer, *A Treatise declaryng [and] shewig dyuers causes take[n] out of the holy scriptur[es] of the sente[n]ces of holy faders [and] of the decrees of deuout emper-*

towardes our neybours."¹¹⁰ And yet, although Bucer emphasized that the images must absolutely be removed, for the "so gret offensyons and occasyons of evyls" that "come through pyctures and images," he also stressed the singular importance of their removal from public spaces being accomplished lawfully and by the temporal authorities: "it is nat laufull for any man but the hed offycer and ruler to caste them out, namely out of open and comen places."¹¹¹ He acknowledged that the iconoclastic mob was scripturally correct:

> if we were dysposed to take awaye images, after suche maner and facyon as scripture techeth and commaundeth, which facyon doutlesse must nedes be best: we ought to breke them, yea, and that all to pouder, that they might never be made whole agayne, nor be restored into so wycked an use in which we ought nat to have so gretly regarded the labour & craft of man.¹¹²

And yet it was, Bucer wrote, more important to avoid offending men, who were in fact made in the image of God, and so "all thynges be done charytably, of pure and perfyte love, and desyre to de profyte to all men," which meant legally and carefully, not "presumptuousely, nor outragyousely."¹¹³

And so the solution was again that secular authorities should use their lawful powers to resolve the dilemma, keeping the hands of the common man clean. In this sense the English Reformation differed from the magisterial Reformation in the scale and consequences of state intervention, but not in the need to resolve the legal problem of the diversion of property through the state. In Germany the locality did triumph, temporarily; indeed, for a time the locality in theory triumphed over the Holy Roman Empire itself.¹¹⁴ Property was more obviously in local control and could serve local, even communal interests. Even if lords had taken advantage of the chaos to seize

---

ours, that pyctures [and] other ymages which were wont be worshypped, ar [in] no wise to be suffred in the temples or churches of Christen men. (London: T. Godfrey for W. Marshall, 1535), f. 8v.
   110. Ibid., f. 11.
   111. Ibid., f. 45v.
   112. Ibid., f. 46v.
   113. Bucer, *A Treatise declaryng,* f. 47v.
   114. See, for example, Ozment, *Reformation in the Cities.*

some church property for themselves, at least they were, usually, one's own local lords, and when evangelical patrons turned over their churches to the cause of reform, the end result was usually that local jurisdiction was reinforced.[115] In some cases it is retrospectively remarkable to see how municipalities had previously lost oversight over local donations. Basel, for instance, had received both the cathedral and a golden altarpiece for it from Henry II. The cathedral came to be ruled by a rich chapter of canons who diverted the gift to themselves and began excluding native Baselers from joining their ranks in 1337, although they continued to extract money from the town and dominate its religious life, often while not even being in residence.[116] It is no wonder that in such a situation, the community might eventually demand that the property be returned to its control.

Communal Property in the Reformation

The initial secularization of church property in the Reformation did not, at least at the time, represent a move to a privatized understanding of property.[117] Both Luther and his more radical followers, drawing on a long tradition from Acts, the pseudo-Isidorian fifth letter of Clement of Rome (featured by Sebastian Franck in his *Geschichtsbibel*), Augustine, and the *Decretum*, agreed at first that property was in some sense common and ought to serve the common good. Peter Blickle has shown that the drive toward a communal reformation of society and religion was widespread and a significant part of the initial enthusiasm for reform.[118] "Common" typically meant local, serving the good of the immediate vicinity; the era of cosmopolitan Protestantism came later.[119]

---

115. Winifred Eberhard, "Bohemia, Moravia and Austria," and David P. Daniel, "Hungary," in *The Early Reformation in Europe*, ed. Andrew Pettegree (Cambridge: Cambridge University Press, 1992), 34, 54, and 64.
116. Wandel, *Voracious Idols*, 156–59.
117. Gregory, *Unintended Reformation*.
118. Peter Blickle, *Communal Reformation: The Quest for Salvation in Sixteenth-Century Germany*, trans. Thomas Dunlap (London: Humanities Press, 1992).
119. George Huntston Williams, *The Radical Reformation*, 3d ed. (Kirksville, Mo.: Truman State University Press, 2000); Ernst Troeltsch, *The Social Teaching*

When the peasants rose in armed revolt, they issued calls to adjust property rights and return to what they claimed were older customs. The anonymous pamphlet *An die Versammlung Gemeiner Bauernschaft* emphasized the common ownership of some goods, like wild animals, the hunting of which had been restricted by the secular rulers. Still, the pamphleteer warned his readers that this was a call not for upheaval and mass appropriations but only for the taking back of what was properly theirs. Of course what was properly theirs was an ongoing question. Balthasar Hubmaier, a radical reformer and Anabaptist, offered a string of paradoxes from the Bible in his *Vom Schwert*, showing the apparently contradictory demands that had been placed on believers to give all or to give only superfluities.[120] Since the scholastic and canonical resolutions to the dilemmas of property no longer had moral authority, radical reformers would have to seek a new solution to the question of property.

It was the Anabaptists who, notoriously, pushed most vigorously for communal property as this solution, and they subsequently became a major dividing line in the Reformation. For the magisterial Reformation, no good Christian ought to withhold alms, and the temporal authorities had the right to intervene in property matters, to tax, to create poor relief systems, and to requisition goods for common use when necessary. But with the outbreak of the Peasants' War and the subsequent 1536 proto-communist experiment in Münster, many early reformers who had agreed in theory that goods were by right common, made clear that they disliked, at the very least, the methods of the radicals. Luther himself admitted in his early responses to the German Peasants' Revolt that their positions were not so different from his own, even if he regarded them as *Schwärmer*, or fanatics.

And so a dramatic bifurcation emerged. When the rural communal movements of the early Reformation flared into open revolt—as they had done a handful of times in the fifteenth century as well—

---

of the Christian Churches, trans. Olive Wyon, 2 vols. (Louisville, Ky.: Westminster John Knox Press, 1992).

120. 2 Corinthians 8:13–14; Luke 3:10–11; 1 Corinthians 9; Luke 5:14; Philippians 4:15–16.

they provoked a process of confessionalization that pushed the two groups further apart.[121] The magisterial Protestants, even those more temperate than Luther, found themselves vigorously upholding not just the rule of law but also that, under the supervision of the state, property ought to be held in private and ministers should be given resources that were allocated to them for their work. The Anabaptists, meanwhile, arrived at conclusions that the magisterial Reformation would ultimately disavow: property should be held in common, the community of the elect should avoid the company of the reprobate, political authorities were to be avoided as much as possible and certainly not allied with the church, and oaths were forbidden.

But even as the magisterial Reformation renounced its communal focus, the remaining claims of the poor were not forgotten. None of the evangelicals or reformers backed away from the idea—a remnant of that early push toward the common good—of creating a state-supervised and state-sanctioned common chest, drawn from church endowments, charitable donations, and perhaps some combination of tithes, fees, and taxed contributions. Indeed, their survival might be understood as a gesture toward the theoretical commonality of goods, rejected as impractical for everyday life, but remaining as an ideal that demanded that, at the very least, the poor ought to be cared for by the community. In England this ideal would be partially served by cy-près, which was one means of serving common interests.

That there was potential for a greater reformation in property than just the shifting of church endowments to poor relief was clear at the time. Thomas More wrote in his 1529 *Supplication of Souls* that the move by the German peasants in the revolt from attacking prelates to attacking secular lords and broader issues of property was to have been expected.[122] Thomas Brady saw the subduing of communal inclinations as the elimination of a broader set of societal reforms that seemed possible in the early 1520s: "When, therefore, the rulers yielded to the argument that ecclesiastical property should be ad-

121. Cameron, *European Reformation*, 204–11.
122. More, *Four Last Things*, 109–10.

ministered for the public good regardless of historic rights and the intentions of donors, not far beyond this idea lay the position that all property should be so administered."[123]

As the magisterial Reformation tried to evade the consequences of this potential, and more far-reaching, conclusion to the initial secularizations, some branches of the "radical" Reformation embraced them. The Moravian Hutterites were particularly noted for using the community to solve the problem of Christian private property. In 1537 Ulrich Stadler explained the system in his *Eine liebe Unterrichtung*: the community was small and poor, the members profoundly equal, because to own anything was to reject Christ. Instead, as Bishop Peter Walpot explained it in his 1577 *Das grosse Artikelbuch*, the community made possible the state of total yieldedness (*Gelassenheit*). All goods were from God, who had commanded in Deuteronomy 15 that there should be no poor, and so no man was to keep anything back from the community. All must work, and all must deny themselves while serving each other. No one could pile up earthly riches and hope to disperse them upon death. Rather, the community itself could take over the problem of how to live and how to provide for one's family in posterity. The community would occupy the role of an endowment or perpetual trust, but it would do so without accumulating a corrupting mass of wealth held in reserve and yet while supplying the mutual security that endowments had falsely offered.

Consequently, community was, Walpot argued, the narrow gate, the only solution and the only way for a Christian to live. Walpot criticized all of the compromises that Catholics and magisterial Protestants had made in attempting to accommodate private property to the Christian life; he especially criticized the idea of giving from superfluities. Alms were only an excuse. Communal living with no property made it possible to live and to be assured of a living without keeping your property. It was a way to hate one's parents and one's children without actually making them destitute, since they would be cared for by the community. This was a common inheritance that

---

123. Brady, *Ruling Class, Regime and Reformation*, 234–35.

belonged to no one—but belonged to no one in a different way than the property held by Catholic corporate bodies on behalf of a religious community.

For Walpot, communal living honored the command from 1 Corinthians 7 that when Christians bought something, they should treat it as if they did not have it.[124] And so, in the Anabaptist inversion of the medieval and early modern compromises struck between Christianity and the world, it would be possible to buy and not have, and also to give and not hold on. There would be no more "giving-while-keeping" in the Anabaptist community, but only free gifts for the immediate use of the community. The Hutterites were innovating a new concept of the gift to God, via the community, with no possible return, no claim left with the original donor or his family except the claim to be part of the community, which demanded everything and gave everything.

The magisterial Reformation had initially wanted to maintain and strengthen the medieval understanding of property that could be simultaneously both yours and everyone's, that could have multiple interests and claims layered on top of it, so that it could flexibly serve both the common good and one's private needs. This was how Luther had described property in his early writings. In fact, most of the demands and articles made by the peasants during the revolt suggest much the same image of property, in which they would argue predominantly for the common good as expressed through local rights. This aspect of the "radical Reformation" was far less total in its embrace of communal solutions than the Anabaptists would be. Luther reacted to the German Peasants' Revolt, which threatened his political support among the princes of the empire, with his famous rejection of the peasants as robbers who deserved to be put down like dogs. Although he, as we have seen, did not deny that most of their claims echoed his own, he wanted the magistrates to supervise how church property would be distributed. When Luther ultimately retracted his initial support for the parish to choose its own preacher in

---

124. Peter Walpot, "True Yieldedness and the Christian Community of Goods," from *Das grosse Artikelbuch*, in *Early Anabaptist Spirituality: Selected Writings* (New York: Paulist Press, 1994), 166.

favor of a stronger position in defense of traditional patronage rights, this may have been done out of legal scruples or to appease his noble supporters, many of whom held these patronage rights. Through this retraction, Luther and the magisterial Reformation moved away from a local perspective that had such widespread appeal in the early Reformation and limited the claims of "Mr. Everybody" (in the phrase of the Soest church ordinance of 1532) in a perhaps reluctant defense of private property instead.[125]

But just as communal property empowered the community in order to maintain its reformed state, so private property in reformed cities would also require magistrates to be furthered empowered, so that they could bring order to the errors or miscalculations that private charitable giving might entail. Johannes Eisermann (Joann Montanus Ferrarius) would suggest this heightened supervision as he linked centralized administrative power and private property in his discussion of charity.[126] Likewise, in this period Johann Oldendorp would argue that private property was commanded in the Decalogue, but he would also emphasize the ongoing use of equity by judges in order to make property dispositions and legal rulings consonant with natural law.[127] The initial distaste manifested by Luther and other reformers for equity when it was used as a means of evading or relaxing law might have to be set aside if private property, the common good, and charity were all to thrive together in the new order.

The *Consilium de emendanda ecclesia* and Legal Innovation

It was clear to Catholic reformers that property was intimately connected to many aspects of the Protestant Reformation. In 1536 Paul III commissioned nine Catholic reformers to write a report on necessary reforms, the *Consilium delectorum cardinalium et aliorum prel-*

125. Quoted by Koerner, *Reformation of the Image*, 158.
126. Johannes Eisermann, *De republica bene instituenda* (Basel: Joannes Oporinus, 1556), 127.
127. Witte, *Law and Protestantism*, 154–75.

atorum de emendanda ecclesia, which summarized what it called the "abuses" in the church, most of which were linked to property. These Catholic reformers laid the origins of corruption in the idea—whispered by flatterers to previous popes—that the pope could sell or dispose of benefices (*beneficiorum*) as he liked without committing simony. From this fatal understanding, the license to treat church property as an opportunity for profit spread. Paul III's commission urged that the laws of the church should be honored strictly "save for a pressing and necessary reason."[128] No one should profit personally from "ecclesiastical properties" which were "kept in common for the benefit of all."[129] To guarantee this, the income assigned to a benefice ought to be linked to it just as "the body to the soul," the two working together toward their intended purpose.[130] The only exception was that income could be diverted to alms.

The authors recommended closing down conventual orders, "not however that injury be done to anyone, but by prohibiting the admission of novices."[131] The authors were suggesting a method of winnowing down the monasteries similar to that employed by evangelicals, with the exception that ultimately "good religious could be substituted for them." The plan was to revive the monasteries with an allocation of more rigorous monks just before the conventual monasteries expired completely.[132] Like many reformers, Catholic and Protestant, the authors urged that better care be taken of the poor, especially in Rome itself. The authors singled out some pardoners for condemnation but allowed for fines to be collected for sins and then given "to the pious causes to which your Holiness contributes." This

---

128. John C. Olin, trans., in *The Catholic Reformation: Savonarola to Ignatius Loyola* (New York: Fordham University Press, 1992), 188; *Consilium delectorum cardinalium, et aliorum praelatorum: de emendanda ecclesia* (N.p.: 1538), n.p.: "nisi urgenti de causa et necessaria."
129. Olin, trans., *Catholic Reformation*, 190; *Consilium*, n.p.: "ut res haec ecclesiastica servaretur communis bonorum omnium, non autem fieret privata cuiuspiam."
130. Olin, trans., *Catholic Reformation*, 189; *Consilium*, n.p.: "Nam redditus sunt annexi beneficio, ut corpus animae."
131. Olin, trans., *Catholic Reformation*, 193; *Consilium*, n.p.: "non tamen ut alicui fiat iniuria, sed prohibendo ne novos possint admittere."
132. Olin, trans., *Catholic Reformation*, 193; *Consilium*, n.p.: "boni religiosi eis substitui possent."

compromise, however repugnant to initial Protestant rhetoric, would later be fairly widely implemented in Protestant cities, which used fines for antisocial behaviors to help fund poor relief.[133]

But the most striking and relevant passage of the text for the question of cy-près is the last abuse that the authors addressed: "It has also been the custom to alter the last wills of testators who bequeath a sum of money for pious causes, which amount is transferred by the authority of your Holiness to an heir or legatee because of alleged poverty, etc., but actually because of greed." This was intolerable: "unless there has been a great change in the household affairs of an heir because of the death of the testator, so that it is likely that the testator would have altered his will in view of that situation, it is wicked to alter the wills of testators."[134] This complaint was the only instance in which the authors castigated the church for being reluctant to help itself to money. The reformers wanted to strip the heirs of rights to recover pious gifts in some circumstances. This was novel, and it points to the ways in which the Catholic Reformation had embraced many of the same social ideals as the Protestant Reformation. It may also have been an acknowledgment that, if the church wished to press for the recovery of property on the grounds of the pious wills of the donors, it might need to have a more straightforward treatment of wills, in which priority would be given to the will of the testator above almost all else.

The report was not supposed to be circulated outside of the curia, but copies leaked out and, naturally, were seized upon by Protestants as evidence that the Catholics admitted their own corruption. Martin Luther translated and published the report with his own preface and a gloss, in which he argued that the Catholic Church could nev-

133. Olin, trans., *Catholic Reformation*, 195; *Consilium*, n.p.: "deputari ad pios usus, in quibus facit sanctitas tua impensas."

134. Olin, trans., *Catholic Reformation*, 196; *Consilium*, n.p.: "Consuevere etiam mutari voluntates ultimae testatorum, qui ad pias causas legant quampiam pecuniae summam, quam auctoritate sanctitatis tuae transferunt ad heredem vel legatarium, ob praetensam paupertatem etc. idque ob lucrum. Certe, nisi facta sit magna mutatio in re familiari heredis per obitum testatoris, ita quod verisimile sit testatorem ob eam mutationem mutaturum fuisse voluntatem, voluntates testatorum mutari impium est: de lucro iam toties diximus, quare putamus omnino abstinendum."

er reform itself, not least because to admit that their popes had erred would, he wrote, undermine their entire ecclesiology. In his gloss Luther railed against every instance in which dispensations were allowed that bent the rule for a particular circumstance. This had long been a concern of his, and it came out in particular force on issues of property. On the word "dispensations" he glossed: "That is, one reforms what and as one wishes. As the saying goes, 'Ignore the noise; it is all a part of the trade.'"[135] He made a similar comment on the word "discretion": "Again reformed, but still doing what they wish. The reservation is always made that, although reformed, they yet remain unreformed."[136] This was the almost singular refrain of the gloss: "Yes, the pope can reserve the right to do anything."[137] On urgency as a justification for the alienation of church property, Luther wrote: "'urgent,' that is, when and where they want—that is urgent."[138] On the stipulation that vows should be honored and not commuted into "other good works unless the latter are equal in value to vows," Luther noted, "This value shall be determined by the pope's will, and the pope's will is to hear the pennies clink."[139] He dismissed the demand to treat testator's gifts to pious causes in the same way: he did not object to the proposed reform, but where the authors gave room for the pope to return money to the heirs if their situation had changed as an unexpected consequence of the testator's death, he added: "So that, after all, the pope's hands are not tied. Thus this reformation does no injury to the wicked rascals."[140] In other words, the demand to honor bequests strictly and to eliminate the possibility of return to poor heirs was fine—a telling shift from his earlier stance to try to return gifts to the heirs—but

    135. LW, vol. 34, 251; WA, vol. 50, 298: "(Dispensiret) Das ist: Man Reformirt, wie und was man will. Es heisst: Klippern gehört zum Handwerk."
    136. LW, vol. 34, 258; WA, vol. 50, 302: "(Willen) Ubermal Reformirt, doch thun was sie wollen, Es wird imer vor behalten, das sie Reformirt werden und doch unreformirt bleiben."
    137. LW, vol. 34, 262; WA, vol. 50, 305: "Ja der Papst mag alles vorbehalten zu thun."
    138. LW, vol. 34, 263; WA, vol. 50, 306: "(Dringenden) Das ist, Wo und wenn sie wolten, so heissts dringend."
    139. LW, vol. 34, 263; WA, vol. 50, 306: "(Werd) Solcher werd sol stehen im willen des Papsts, darnach der pfenning klinget."
    140. LW, vol. 34, 264; WA, vol. 50, 306: "Doch das dem Papst die hende nicht geschlossen sind, So thut die Reformatio nicht schaden den bösen Buben."

that the pope might reserve the right for flexibility in the treatment of gifts was offensive. Luther's point would seem to be in conflict with his agreement elsewhere that destitute heirs had a right to the property given by their ancestors, but Luther had also long been suspicious of the concept of equity, which seemed to partake of injustice and inequality. He was not alone in wanting a new, simple, rule that would govern pious bequests toward a good direction by honoring the donor above all else. After all, the reforming cardinals seemed mostly to agree with him on that point.

Johannes Sturm also replied to the report, in a more polite but ultimately equally hopeless epistle to the authors in which he chided them for focusing so much on issues of property rather than on the gospel. Catholics had abused what had been instituted by Christ, whose laws ought to be returned to. In matters of religion, a return to the original terms of the gift was required, in the treatment of the Eucharist or of images, for instance. It was an error to imagine that God's will changed with the times (*cum temporibus voluntatem Dei commutari*), just as it was an error to try superstitiously to coerce saints by giving money and legacies to their images. These donations defied the original purpose of the images to educate and inspire.[141] The same perversions of purpose had occurred with monasticism, which had been instituted by "our ancestors" (*maiores nostri*) in order to "be useful to the cities" (*ut civitatibus utilis esset*). Sturm called on Catholics to revert monasticism to its original purpose and use, the *usus coenobiorum*, for the good of the commonwealth; let the monastics no longer embrace solitude but service in the world.

God's will was inviolable and unchanging, but men's intentions could fluctuate and err. We will not contend with you for riches (*de opibus non pugnamus*), Sturm repeatedly told the Catholic reformers.[142] This may seem ironic, since in the same year that Sturm wrote this

---

141. Johannes Sturm, *Epistola de consilio de emendanda ecclesia*, in *De consilio de emendanda ecclesia* (Zürich: Heidegger, 1748), 59: "Parum honoris opinamur eis haberi, si ad illorum recordationem gemitus et lachrymas praebeamus, neque satis cupiditatibus nostris, nisi devotiones et pecuniarum donationes et haereditatum assignationes, ad eam immanitatem adiungantur."

142. For instance: Ibid., 58: "Non de opibus pugnamus, quas nunquam vobis invidimus, non contendimus."

epistle he also founded his Strasbourg Academy out of secularized church property. In a sense, though, he was being perfectly consistent, as he did not object to the pope having the power to care for the church by properly arranging its things and distributing them as necessary.[143] The pope did not have the power to alter laws, Sturm argued, but he could shift property within reasonable limits, just as, in an unexpressed analogy, Protestant powers could turn local church property over to a better purpose if that seemed prudent. Whereas Luther still hoped that strict rules could harm no one, Sturm, like Eisermann and Oldendorp, had embraced the necessity of giving power room to maneuver. The essential point was that possessions should be "converted to the growth of religion and the glory of Christ."[144] Sturm cautioned Catholics that any charge to take care of the poor, the orphans, and the widows, should not intrude on princely prerogatives or imperial powers, as dedicated to the protection of the weak by the *bannus*, nor should they take to themselves the right to interfere with private property. As to the problem of the rights of donors, which was not addressed in the *Emendanda* but was pressing on the minds of reformers, Sturm argued against those who would suggest that the descendants of donors ought to have places of privilege within the church or government. Although they were not to be excluded from these positions, it was also important that the governing powers—not the church —made sure that no one was in need and that everything was equitably distributed across ranks and degrees. The nobles should not take the goods of the church, as it was sacrilege not to give them to the poor, so Sturm proposed that the preachers and ministers of the church should be in charge of determining what to do with the property of the church. Sturm thus rejected the rights of donors and their heirs. The initial impulses of the Reformation to return property when possible was settling down into a more pragmatic, but also more innovative, attitude toward donations as they were set free of

---

143. Ibid., 53: "Etiam quod huic finitimum est prudentissime statuitis, non esse dominatum qui committitur Pontifici, sed curationem talem, qua Ecclesiarum munera suis ordinibus dispenset, atque distribuat." He repeated the point later.
144. Ibid., 58: "Ut ad amplificationem religionis, et ad gloriam Christi convertatis."

the multiple interests in them but also vested more formally under control from above, whether secular or spiritual.

As the examples of Luther's and Sturm's responses to the *Consilium* show, the Protestants never found one clear rule for the treatment of church property. Ironically, the secularizations went smoothly enough that it was not necessary to do so, despite the many pamphlets written about the topic and litigations pursued over legal claims to church property. Over the long run, continental Protestant jurists would embrace some alteration of use, would eliminate the rights of the heirs, and would vary in the importance they placed on consensus to change. Thanks in part to the interpretations of the Modestinus passage by Melanchthon and Cujas, covered in the last chapter, the opinion became a central text in thinking about superstitious bequests. Caspar Mauritius, in his 1658 *Exercitatio secularis de simonia*, used the Modestinus opinion to defend the stripping away of assets from a simonaical church, as did Samuel Stryck's 1684 *Disputatio juridica de jure privilegati contra privilegatum*. Justus Böhmer featured it heavily in his *Jus parochiale* (1701) and again in his *Jus ecclesiasticum protestantium* (1714) to justify the redirection of property in the Reformation—and presumably also to allow churches to redirect illegal bequests to legal, pious purposes. He framed this in the context of the curses placed in wills prohibiting the living from diverting pious gifts to profane purposes, and his conclusion was that to turn a superstitious gift to a profane use was not allowed, but turning it to another equally pious and nonsuperstitious use (*ad alium usum aeque pium et non superstitiosum*) would be acceptable with the consent of the parties (*de consensu partium*). In particular, Böhmer offered that the gift should be converted to a "similar work" (*ad opus simile*).[145] So while

145. Justus Böhmer, *Ius parochiale*, 2d ed. (Halle an der Saale: Orphanotropheum, 1716), 261: "Hoc casu illud certum esse puto talia bona REGULARITER in alios profanos usus a posteris licite converti non posse; vid. *cit. disp. n.39*. ast alia quaestio est, an non mutatis temporibus, et deficiente ob repurgatam ecclesiam usu, ad quem bona illa destinata sunt, illa ad alium usum aeque pium et non superstitiosum, adhiberi debeant, non obstantibus eiusmodi exsecrationibus? Veluti si certa bona ad missas legendas sint destinata: quae tamen in ecclesiis nostris recte sunt abolitae. Quod omnino asserendum reor, praesertim cum ex *l. legatum 16. D. de usu et usufr. et reditu etc.* legitime inferri possit, relictum ad opus illicitum, convertendum esse ad opus simile aeque licitum de consensu partium, quod ad

Böhmer kept the canonical ideal of *consensu partium*, he allowed for the larger change, the change of use, rather than just the smaller change, of kind. Böhmer found that the change from one pious use to another was smaller than a change from a pious use to a secular use. To return a pious gift to the heirs might have been one form of profanation, but Böhmer was obviously struggling against the claim of the state to turn superstitious gifts to secular purposes.

The Modestinus opinion became more helpful to the Protestant cause the more that it became unmoored from its *ius commune* interpretation. Protestant readings of the text, tending to emphasize the new use that could be made, set aside the language of the original text that called for *alio et licito genere* and explained instead that what had been granted was to put it *in alium usum*. For example, Johannis-Jacobi Wissenbach made this transition from kind to use, and in his commentary on the Modestinus passage, it was essential that the will of the testator should not be obeyed; the heirs need not even be consulted, much less consent to the change.[146] At an inaugural disputation given in 1699 on the Modestinus passage, the text was framed in terms of interpreting the will of the testator benignly, and the disputant suggested that either another spectacle or another thing (*rem*) would be possible, avoiding the language of use entirely.[147] The disputant granted that the heirs would be called in to consult, but as he moved into contemporary scenarios, he dropped that stipulation. The Modestinus opinion could be applied to Franciscan property, which they were forbidden to have, and it was used, the disputant pointed out, after the Reformation to transfer donations left for masses, monasteries, and other such illicit uses. The disputant drew on the treatment of pagan gifts to the temple in the Codex Theodosianus, whose

---

praesentem de causa pia casum applicat BRUNNEM. *ad cit. l. n.2.* MAURITIUS *de secularisat.* STRYK. *cit. disp. c.2. n.46."*

146. "Voluntati testatoris parendum non est: sed legatum in alium usum, per quem memoria defuncti conservetur, convertendum est." Johannis-Jacobi Wissenbach, Disputatio IV, Desumpta ex titulo I de annuis legatis et fideicommissis, et quatuor sequentibus libri XXXIII Pandectarum, in *Exercitationum ad L. Pandectarum libros pars posterior ... editio secunda* (Franeker: Gerard Schick, 1661), 37.

147. "in aliud licitum spectaculum, vel rem aliam licitam." Wilhelmus van Erpecum, *Disputatio iuridica inauguralis ad leg. XVI ff. de usu et usufruct* (Franeker: Johannes Gyzelaar, 1699), 25.

use was changed by the emperor.[148] Still, the disputant emphasized that the Modestinus opinion applied only to illicit gifts. For other pious gifts, he concluded by contrasting the Catholic Favre, who held that pious uses were unchangeable except by the pope, and the Lutheran Benedict Carpzovius, who, on the basis of the probable intention of the testator, allowed for equivalencies to be substituted without consulting the heirs.[149] Following Ulricus Huberus, the disputant suggested that in these cases the donor had a pious motivation (*usus ex mente testatoris pius erit*), and that the apparent closeness of the substituted spectacles in the Modestinus passage should not be followed (*non ad alium maxime similem usum applicandum sit*).[150] Implicitly, to honor this pious donor intent, the gift should be turned to something that was not the next closest option, and the heirs were irrelevant, unnecessary even for consultation.[151] The boldness of this assessment is due to the fact that, for the disputant, the Reformation was remembered with a clean conscience.[152] The disputant trusted in the magistrates to care for the local good, and consequently the disputant saw no need to suggest that illicit gifts should be turned to a new use that was as close as possible to the old one. In England the story would be different, and approximation would emerge as an apparent check on redistributive power.

148. Codex Theodosianus 16.10.19.2.
149. Benedict Carpzovius, *Definitiones forenses ad constitutiones* (Leipzig: Ritzschiana, 1663), Part II, Const. V, Definit. 8, 416–17.
150. Erpecum, *Disputatio*, 31.
151. Ibid., 31: "nihil hic ad heredes testatoris pertinere."
152. As Cohn has shown, imperial cities mostly used church properties for the common good, as they had claimed they would do, and had little social dissention afterward.

6

Charitable Uses in the English Reformation

A violation of the "will of the donor" was enforceable grounds to retrieve donated ancestral lands, which meant that late medieval English politics sometimes strategically deployed concern about protecting the *voluntatem fundatorum* from threats, real or invented. Monks who wanted to evade papal extractions could protest that these extra burdens would prevent the monastery from distributing the alms or holding the services that their foundations required. This failure to maintain the terms of the gift would then jeopardize the endowment by opening it up to legal action by the heirs of the donor.[1] The king, meanwhile, could use the rights of the founders as a pretext for meddling with church property, as Edward I did with the 1307 Statute of Carlisle, according to which, conversion of use and deprivation of the rights of the heirs were the legal basis for new regulations and appropriations.[2] Edward III used a similar line of reasoning in his Statute of Provisors, as did Richard II, in his Second Statute of Provisors.[3] It was a useful point, repeated in a variety of contexts, and so when Henry VIII began turning his attention

---

1. Farr, *John Wyclif as Legal Reformer*, 106–11; Susan Wood, *English Monasteries and Their Patrons in the Thirteenth Century* (London: Geoffrey Cumberlege, 1955).
2. 35 Edward 1, st. 1.
3. 13 Richard 2, st. 2.

to church property, he found himself potentially thwarted by the argument that had once served so well. The pope could be ignored; a prior could be frightened into surrender; monks could be pensioned off; but the legal and moral rights of a founder were more difficult to overcome.

This mattered because the Henrician Reformation was "carefully legal in its unfolding," as befits a country where, as Zaller describes, "the importance of the law ... was second only to that of religion."[4] Indeed both Henry VIII and Cromwell were personally inclined to pursue a legal Reformation.[5] Consider, for example, the preservation of parochial rights in the monasteries that were dissolved: where a community had the right to use the nave or aisle, it was left untouched even as the rest of the monastery was destroyed around it.[6] The English Reformation, and its attendant dissolutions and seizures, was thus accomplished largely by statute, not proclamation, because statutes entered common law and could deal with property ("the life, land, goods or inheritance") beyond the powers already expressly granted to the king.[7] The attention to law would pay off in the largely nonviolent turnover of ecclesiastical property that followed.[8]

But despite the attention to both law and order, the English Reformation was perhaps the least theologically clear of all the Reformations—a fact that did not subsequently stop a proud whiggish tra-

---

4. W. K. Jordan, *Edward VI: The Young King* (London: George Allen and Unwin, 1968), 17; J. J. Scarisbrick, *The Reformation and the English People* (Cambridge, Mass.: Basil Blackwell, 1984), 90; Robert Zaller, *The Discourse of Legitimacy in Early Modern England* (Stanford, Calif.: Stanford University Press, 2007), 267.

5. G. W. Bernard, *The King's Reformation: Henry VIII and the Remaking of the English Church* (New Haven, Conn.: Yale University Press, 2005).

6. John Phillips, *The Reformation of Images: Destruction of Art in England, 1535–1660* (Berkeley: University of California Press, 1973), 69.

7. R. W. Heinze, *The Proclamations of the Tudor Kings* (Cambridge: Cambridge University Press, 1976), 32 and 39; Jennifer Loach, *Parliament under the Tudors* (Oxford: Oxford University Press, 1991), 8.

8. Scarisbrick, *Reformation and the English People*, 90. On the other hand, the commons did assert its right to take back local gifts when their use was destroyed: Ethan Shagan, "Selling the Sacred: Reformation and Dissolution at the Abbey of Hailes" and "Resistance and Collaboration in the Dissolution of the Chantries," in *Popular Politics and the English Reformation* (Cambridge: Cambridge University Press, 2003), 162–96 and 235–69.

dition from defending its apparently modern tendencies. For decades during the early Reformation, it was not evident to the common man what exactly one was supposed to believe—as illustrated by the simultaneous executions of both Catholics and Protestants under Henry VIII, who squashed heresy rather than defining it. A draft proclamation by Cromwell chastised both sides unhelpfully: "the one is too rash and the other too dull."[9] As Henry VIII dissolved the chantries, he also imprisoned for heresy Edward Crome, who had praised the dissolution, and then freed him when he acknowledged the saving power of the mass.[10] Many of those in charge of the seizure of intercessory institutions or the repression of dissent left bequests for prayers in their wills—most famously Henry VIII, Burgoyne, and George Talbot, Earl of Shrewsbury.[11] Henry even founded a monastery just before he destroyed them all—although, as Gasquet pointed out, he tended to endow that which he was about to destroy. While Henry VIII never formally disavowed purgatory, his *King's Book* forbade the use of the word, effectively but temporarily ending the discussion about the fate of the dead.[12] In silence there could be no dissent from an unarticulated theology.

As a consequence, it is unclear precisely when Henry VIII determined to break free from the pope—or if he ever determined it at all. But even if the separation from Rome was not set upon by a steady course, there is a good case to be made that Henry VIII and Cromwell proceeded deliberately, strategically, and with a great deal of planning and foresight in relationship to prospective secularizations of property.[13] Neither Cromwell nor Henry VIII needed to have been planning a purposeful Reformation in order to have had their eye on church property, and finding a way to harvest at least some of the property of the church was an ongoing concern, inspired not just by

9. Heinze, *Proclamations*, 139.
10. Kreider, *English Chantries*, 175–76.
11. Scarisbrick, *Reformation and the English People*, 8–9; Kreider, *English Chantries*, 137–38; Christopher Haigh, *English Reformations: Religion, Politics and Society under the Tudors* (Oxford: Oxford University Press, 1993), 201.
12. Shagan, *Popular Politics*, 241.
13. Cf. G. R. Elton, *Reform and Reformation England, 1509–1558* (Cambridge, Mass.: Harvard University Press, 1977), 236.

the Reformation but also by the behavior of contemporary continental Catholic rulers. Cromwell's suggestion that he would make Henry VIII extremely wealthy indicates that he must have planned to tap the wealth of the church in some way, just as Henry's frank advice to Scotland on how to go about capturing ecclesiastical property tells us that at the very least he retrospectively cast his actions as deliberate.[14] Virginia Murphy has shown that as early as 1527, Henry VIII, aware of the political strength of his position given the travails of the papacy and the sack of Rome, was unprepared to make any concessions.[15] Bernard observes that Wolsey threatened the pope with schism in 1528 and that there is evidence that in 1529 Henry VIII was studying the German example of ecclesiastical seizures.[16] Also in 1529 multiple publications began to make the case for secularizations. *The Lamentation for the Decease of the Mass* celebrated the putting down of the mass in Strasbourg, where it was no longer true that the clergy "devowred the sustenaunce of the poore/Wastynge the goodes of people temporall" but rather "the goodes of the churche are taken awaye/ Geuen to povre folkes soffrynge indigence."[17] Simon Fish's *Supplication for the Beggars* estimated how much money was wasted by the church, and an abortive petition appeared asking for the dissolution of the monasteries so that their properties could be put to better public use.

Cromwell absorbed Wolsey's lessons and pushed back on the requirement for founders to consent to transitions of use as he suppressed Christchurch, Aldgate in 1532, which E. Jeffries Davis pointed out was a test case for the dissolutions to follow. The prior was forced to surrender the property, which was left vacant for two years in order to qualify for seizure on grounds that the founder's inten-

---

14. Scarisbrick, *Reformation and the English People*, 79, citing *Letters and Papers, Foreign and Domestic, of the Reign of Henry VIII*, ed. J. S. Brewer et al., vol. 15 (London: 1862–1932), document 136.

15. Virginia Murphy, "The Literature and Propaganda of Henry VIII's First Divorce," in *The Reign of Henry VIII: Politics, Policy and Piety*, ed. Diarmaid MacCulloch (Basingstoke: Palgrave Macmillan, 1995), 135–58.

16. Bernard, *King's Reformation*, 12 and 31.

17. "The [Mock] Lamentation [for the decrease of the Mass]," in Edward Arber, ed., *English Reprints*, vol. 14 (London: A. Murray, 1871), 33 and 36.

tions were not being honored, but then it escheated to the king in violation of the rights of the helpless patron himself. An act of Parliament in 1534 was necessary to ratify this reversion to the king against the will of the patron.[18] Subsequently in 1535 the English ambassadors to the Schmalkaldic League sponsored a disputation on private masses, with Luther as respondent, to shore up arguments for their suppression.[19] Hall, in his *Chronicle*, attested that the desire to dismantle the monasteries entirely was accepted by at least some in Parliament even from the first statute of 1536, which aimed only at the smaller convents.[20] Cromwell, meanwhile, in an unpublished draft proclamation that Heinze dates to 1538 or 1539, indicated that superstitious ceremonies would yet be destroyed, although patience was required.[21] In other words, there was a steady march toward secularization, but it was necessary to find a way to do it that did not require the consent of the patron.

The legal problem was in some ways more significant than social resistance to the dissolutions. Benjamin Thompson has found that one reason the dissolutions occurred with relatively little struggle was because over time there had been "a striking upward mobility of advowsons," such that "no monastery was in the hands of the lineage which founded it." The natural consequence was that "there was no direct duty incumbent on patrons to support the prayers for the first founders" and "two-thirds of [advowsons] were in the patronage of the crown or higher nobility," and thus more likely to support crown policy and to attempt to profit from it.[22] This consolidation of patronage relationships meant that several social factors that could have inhibited the dissolution did not stand in its way. Legally, however, several problems remained. Robert C. Palmer has argued that Henry VIII's maneuvers, first in the 1536 Statute of Uses and then in the 1540 Statute of Wills, which latter reversed some of

---

18. E. Jeffries Davis, "The Beginning of the Dissolution: Christchurch, Aldgate, 1532," *Transactions of the Royal Historical Society* 8 (1925): 127–50.

19. Rory McEntegart, *Henry VIII, the League of Schmalkalden, and the English Reformation* (Woodbridge, England: Boydell Press, 2011), 56.

20. Loach, *Parliament under the Tudors*, 71.

21. Heinze, *Proclamations*, 139.

22. Thompson, "Monasteries and Their Patrons."

the least popular aspects of the previous statute, were cleverly done, not solely for fiscal reasons, as they have been understood, but rather to liberate the monasteries from some of their legal entanglements in view of the seizures.[23]

In the end, the expropriations of intercessory institutions was part of a larger pattern of rapacity by a badly underfunded state in economically difficult times. The process began with the most distant institutions, with the dissolving of the monasteries in the 1530s, and then moved to the dead with the chantry acts of 1545 and 1547 (under Edward VI), and finally arrived in 1553 at the parish, whose goods had already been ominously inventoried. In the name of eradicating superstition, preventing local confiscation, and putting donations to better uses, the state took the furnishings, plate, and other goods that had been built up over centuries through pious gifts.[24] The last proceedings were to be against the bishoprics and cathedrals, where the most politically powerful would have resisted, and in the end generally only some forced exchanges of property were pushed onto these institutions. Three dioceses were dissolved or collapsed into each other.[25] We cannot know whether Henry VIII planned to requisition all of these forms of property, but the fact that he—apparently strategically—began by taking the property that was least politically protected, then afterwards, using that precedent, proceeded against better defended holdings explains the lasting popularity of John Foxe's apocryphal anecdote that Henry VIII set down Fish's treatise on the wealth of the church and commented that one need-

23. Robert Palmer, *Selling the Church: The English Parish and in Law, Commerce, and Religion, 1350–1550* (Chapel Hill: University of North Carolina Press, 2002), 228–37.

24. Scarisbrick, *Reformation and the English People*, 85–88; On the aftershocks of the parish seizures, see the work of Eamon Duffy, particularly *The Stripping of the Altars: Traditional Religion in England, c. 1400–1580* (New Haven, Conn.: Yale University Press, 1992), *The Voices of Morebath: Reformation and Rebellion in an English Village*, rev. ed. (New Haven, Conn.: Yale University Press, 2003), and *Saints, Sacrilege and Sedition*, 57.

25. Scarisbrick, *Reformation and the English People*, 88; Peter Marshall, *Reformation England, 1480–1642* (London: Bloomsbury Academic, 2012), 74. Elizabeth I subsequently revived the effort to force exchanges: Scarisbrick, *Reformation and the English People*, 135.

ed to be careful when dismantling an old wall to start at the top and not the bottom.

The legal developments can be traced across the statutes. The 1532 Act for Feoffment (23 Henry 8 c. 10) forbade feoffments to religious uses and decreed that any attempted feoffment would be "utterlie void." "Void" here meant "without effect," but it did not mean "taken by the king." The act was an anticipatory move to block attempts to evade what would follow. In 1535, 27 Henry 8 c. 28 suppressed the smaller monasteries, and the argument turned to houses that "nowe beyng spent spoyled and wasted for increace and mayntenance of synne, should be used and converted to better uses, and the unthryfty Relygyous persons soo spendyng the same to be compellyd to reforme ther lyves." This language drew on themes of the Reformation—making "an honest and charytable Reformation of suche unthrifty carnall and abhomynable lyvyng," but also harkened back to the traditional grounds for diverting monastic property to a new use—it was insufficient to the purpose, or, in the language of the bill, the property was "spoyle dystroye consume and utterly wast." Although new uses were promised, the property (and its ornaments, plate, jewels, and other moveables) was, for the moment, transferred to the king and his heirs. All property rights were to be conserved: the rents, advowsons, tithes, etc., were, according to the act, maintained, including all rights of the patrons and founders.[26] The act affirmed that the transfer of property would serve "the honor of God and the wealth of this Realme."[27]

This first suppression attempted to sidestep the issue of founders' rights by suggesting that the handing over of the monastery by the prior or abbot was the key moment in the resumption, as though the interested parties to the property were only the king and the prior. This theme was picked up in the second act for the dissolution of all monasteries in 1539, which simply ratified the transitions that had already been effected by the sweeping turnover of the land that had taken place "of their owne free and voluntarie myndes good

---

26. 28 Henry 8 c. 28 § 16.
27. 28 Henry 8 c. 28 § 7.

willes and assente, without constraynte coaction or compulsion of any manner of person or persons."[28] This second act also saved rights to founders, patrons, and donors—or, rather, as it stated more skeptically, to "suche as pretende to be founders patrons or donours."[29]

The language of pretended patrons was also used in Henry's 1545 chantry act (37 Henry 8 c. 4), where it cast doubt on whether there was any connection between the original donor and whoever was currently claiming to have moral rights to the property. Parliament was forced to act because many of these soi-disant founders "and divers other, of their avarouse and covetouse myndes and of their owne auctoritie without [the king's] gracious licence" had been revoking their gifts—in anticipation, of course, of imminent seizures. Likewise, the act continued, some of the priests, wardens, or other masters of the property have, "by the assent and consent of their Patrons donors foundors or suche other as have had intereste in the same" made arrangements to lease the property or dissolve it. These actions were not only "to the great contempte of your Majestie and of your auctoritie roiall" but also "contrarye to the willes myndes intens and purposes of the foundors donors or patrons." Within a paragraph, the act acknowledged that founders (a term that included founders' heirs) had an interest in the property, had been consensually rearranging their donations with the wardens in charge of their chantries, and yet were acting against the will of the founders. This convoluted critique that the founders were thwarting the founders was indicative of a new sentiment that favored the original donor over his descendants. The meaning of "founder" would increasingly be limited to the original donor and would ultimately restrict the ability of his successors to make changes to his donation.

The act gave Henry the right to take whatever chantries, colleges, hospitals, brotherhoods, or fraternities he pleased, in order to fund the wars with France and Scotland, which made the residual "interests" entirely without value. This act was more forthright than the early acts about the destruction of the rights of patrons and their

28. 31 Henry 8 c. 13.
29. 31 Henry 8 c. 13 § 4.

heirs and their inability to recover in the future.[30] After ten years of dissolutions, it had become possible to be more explicit. But the insistence that the property would go to better purposes—that were also in keeping with the donor's intent—also emerged as a more vivid theme in this statute, which claimed that the chantries "have been established ordeyned founded had or made by the saide Patrons donors or foundors for ever, to thentent that almes to the poore people and other good vertuouse and charitable deedes mought be made done and executed."[31] But, as "it is right well knowen," this had not happened: these chantries had not spent their rents and profits "in Almes and other deeds of charitie, according to suche vertuouse and godlie intentes and purposes." Thus the king would have the land "used and exercised to more godlie and vertuouse purposes, and to reduce and bringe them into a more decent and convenient order, for the commoditie and welthe of this his Realme and for the suertie of his Subjects of the same."[32]

Thus the First Chantry Act helped to lay the groundwork for the second, in which the theme of better, charitable purposes emerged even more clearly—and in distinction to the "superstition and error" that had been introduced through "devising and phantasinge vayne opynions of Purgatorye and Masses satisfactorye."[33] As with Henry's chantry act, Edward's act noted that all of the chantries had been created with the king's license, which gave him the right to revoke the entire gift unilaterally. Edward's act would famously insist that schools and alms would be maintained, even as the institutions that had supported them were dissolved. For chantries that belonged to protected colleges, the king reserved the right "to dispose to a better use, as to the relief of some poore men."[34] Meanwhile, no one was allowed to re-enter "for the non doing not naminge or none fyndinge of anny suche priest or preists of poore folkes as is aforesaide, obyte anniversarye light or lampe from hensfurthe to be founden or done." This stricture applied no matter what "remaynder use or

30. 31 Henry 8 c. 13 § 4–5.
31. 31 Henry 8 c. 13 § 6.
32. 31 Henry 8 c. 13 § 6.
33. 1 Edward 6 c. 14.
34. 1 Edward 6 c. 14 § 33.

condition" had been placed on the chantry.[35] This was necessary because so many of these gifts had been set up to allow for them to be taken back for nonperformance.

In the early years of the dissolutions, founders wrote to Cromwell in astonishment that their rights were not being upheld.[36] But they fell silent as they observed the treatment of priors who resisted Supremacy and the political pressure placed on priors to surrender the monasteries to the government of their own accord, such that almost all of the monasteries were swept up before the second act, which then justified that transfer *ex post facto*. This silence did not mean the founders were indifferent. The duke of Norfolk, who was the patron with the second greatest number of monasteries after Henry himself, was denied permission by Cromwell to buy back his most important foundation, Thetford, where his ancestors were buried. Cromwell's fall would be Norfolk's revenge.

Propaganda for Charitable Uses

But this treatment of Norfolk was a misstep for a man who had effectively propagandized the Reformation and its secularization of property from the start. A number of texts that were published before and during the seizures demonstrate, sometimes in subtle ways, the efforts to support a transformation of use of church property and to create a new category of use, charitable uses. For example, in 1530 Cromwell asked Stephen Vaughan to find a copy of the late fourteenth-century *Disputatio inter clericum et militem* and bring it back to England from Antwerp.[37] Cromwell commissioned an English translation that Berthelet published in 1533. Here we find the expression "charitable use": "For those gyftes that are gyuen to god the very same gyftes are dedicated to holy and charitable uses."[38] The text included the defense of the realm and the good of the common-

---

35. 1 Edward 6 c. 14 § 34.
36. Knowles, *Religious Orders*, Vol. 3, 292–93.
37. James Christopher Warner, *Henry VIII's Divorce: Literature and the Politics of the Printing Press* (Woodbridge, England: Boydell Press, 1998), 36.
38. *A Dialogue betwene a Knyght and a Clerke Concernynge the Power Spiritual and Temporall* (London: Thomas Berthelet, 1533).

wealth as charitable uses. The *Institution of a Christian Man* (1537) likewise reinforced the concept of the "charitable use" in its discussion of the eighth commandment, the prohibition against theft.

Cromwell's influence can probably also be found in the anonymous but officially commissioned translation of Lyndwood's *Provinciale* and the ecclesiastical laws of the papal legates Otho and Othobone that appeared in 1534, printed with a privilege.[39] The translation made every effort to be friendly to the cause of the reform of the church, and it translated one constitution in such a way that it appeared to advocate for the donation to the poor of frustrated bequests. In the context of priests who were increasingly unable to keep up with the demand for intercessory prayers and who were tempted to abridge or combine their prayers, Archbishop John Peckham, the Franciscan, had urged in a 1281 constitution at Lambeth that there should be a strict performance of the exact terms. If a negligent priest delayed the performance, then he should not only make up the masses but also give the money he had received to the poor, as a punishment to himself and a recompense to the donor, whose journey through purgatory had been slowed down by the priest's laxity but could be sped back up by the prayers of the grateful poor. If the priest failed on both accounts, then the ordinary should discipline him:

And we monish them who have accepted of stipends for celebrating annals, or anniversaries, and yet through malice, or carelessness, do not perform their obligations, that they make full satisfaction for their omissions; and give to the poor such profits as they have received in behalf of those souls, and if they willfully neglect both the one and the other, let them be sharply corrected by their ordinaries, as deceivers of the faithful.[40]

---

39. Diarmaid MacCulloch, *Thomas Cranmer* (New Haven, Conn.: Yale University Press, 1996), 121.

40. *A Collection of the Laws and Canons of the Church of England*, trans. John Johnson, vol. II (Oxford: John Henry Parker, 1851), 276: "Illos autem, qui pro Annalibus, vel Anniversariis celebrandis stipendia receperunt, nec ex certa malitia vel accidia satisfaciunt, ut tenentur, Monemus, ut omissa suppleant, et ad plenum satisfaciant in futurum. Et quandocunque id non fecerint, fructus taliter receptos pro Animabus illorum, qui eis talia contulerunt, erogent pauperibus. Aut si utrumque istorum sponte neglexerint, sicut fraudatores fidelium ab Ordinariis suis aspere corrigantur."

It was a difficult passage, but it was not suggesting that a donation for masses could be made up with alms to the poor, a fact that is particularly clear when the passage is read in its context, in which Peckham demands full and exact observance of requested masses. The gloss supported this interpretation, insisting that the stipulations of the gift could not be altered and that the offending priest could not keep the payment for a duty he had failed to perform on time.[41]

In the anonymous translation of the sixteenth century, however, a shift occurred to imply that in the frustration of the purpose of the gift, the money might legitimately be given to the poor instead:

> But as concernynge them that have receyved stypend to celebrate annualles and anniversaryes, and of euyll mynd or neglygens do not theyr duetye as they be bound, we monyshe them that they supplye the thynges omytted and make full satisfaction in tyme to come. And when so ever they it doo not, let them gyve to the pore suche fructes as they have receyued, for theyr soules that gyue it unto them, or if they neglecte wyllyngly bothe these thynges, let them be sharplely ponyshed of theyr ordinaryes as deceyuers of the faythful.[42]

It was a small but important shift. In the original text the priest ought to make up the masses and give the money to the poor; in the 1534 translation the priest might give to the poor in lieu of the masses. The intention was to allow the redirection of lapsed gifts that were unused for their original purposes, as had been done on the continent. It was the first tactic that Henry VIII would try.

Other official translations at the time were produced to support a transition of uses. William Marshall published the Ypres proposal in 1535, to show what might be possible. Craig Thompson argues that Cromwell commissioned the 1540 English translation of Erasmus's *Peregrinatio religionis ergo* to support the closures.[43] Erasmus criticized those shrines whose saints had been dedicated to helping the poor but whose guardians retained the revenues of the shrines instead of doing with them as the saint would have wished:

---

41. William Lyndwood, *Provinciale* (Oxford: Richard Davis, 1679), III.23, 228–30.
42. *Constitutions provincialles*, 60–61.
43. Craig R. Thompson, introduction to *A Pilgrimage for Religion's Sake*, in Erasmus, *Ten Colloquies* (New York: Macmillan, 1986), 56. The 1540 translation was entitled: *A Pilgrimage of Pure Devotion*.

Since, then, the saint was so liberal towards the needy, although he was still poor himself and lacked the money to provide for the necessities of life, don't you think he'd gladly consent, now that he's so rich and needs nothing, if some poor wretched woman with hungry children at home, or daughters in danger of losing their virtue because they have no money for dowries, or a husband sick in bed and penniless—if, after begging the saint's forgiveness, she carried off a bit of all this wealth to rescue her family, as though taking from one who wanted her to have it, either as a gift or a loan? ... I'm convinced the saint would even rejoice that in death, too, he could relieve the wants of the poor by his riches.[44]

The most difficult passage of the colloquy for the purposes of advancing the king's agenda came near the end, when Menedemus observed that in the past bishops sometimes sold church plate to succor the poor. In the original, the response was that they should be praised for this, but not imitated: *Laudantur et hodie, sed laudantur tantum, imitari nec licet, nec libet opinor.* The translator weakened Erasmus's limitation: "Thay be praysede also now in our tyme, but thay be praysed onely, to folow ther doynge (I suppose) thay may not, nor be any thynge dysposede."[45] Perhaps then it was the fault of the times that people could not follow their praiseworthy example.

The translation of Marsilius of Padua that Cromwell authorized was also a creative translation.[46] It interpolated new material, such as a novel conclusion that no one should be required to give sustenance to bishops and ministers that was "superfluouse" to their

---

44. Erasmus, *A Pilgrimage for Religion's Sake*, in *Collected Works*, vol. 39, 644. The 1540 edition had no significant differences in meaning. *Peregrinatio religionis ergo*, in *Opera Omnia*, vol. I-3 (1972): 489: "Cum igitur vir sanctissimus tam liberalis fuerit in egenos, cum adhuc pauper esset, et ipse praesidiis pecuniarum egeret ob corpusculi necessitatem; an non putas aequo animo laturum nunc, cum tam opulentus sit, nec ullius egeat, si qua mulier paupercula, domi habens liberos famelicos, aut filias ob dotis inopiam de pudicitia periclitantes, aut maritum morbo decumbentem, omnibusque praesidiis destitutum, precata veniam, detrahat ex his tantis opibus aliquam particulam sublevandae familiae, velut a volente sumens vel dono, vel mutuo? ... Ego, inquit, plane confido sanctissimum virum etiam gavisurum, quod mortuus quoque suis opibus sublevaret inopiam pauperum."

45. *A Dialoge or Communication of Two Persons, Devysyd and Set Forthe in the Late[n] Tonge, by the Noble and Famose Clarke Desiderius Erasmus Intituled [the] Pylgremage of Pure Devotyon. Newly Tra[n]slatyd into Englishe* (London: n.p., 1540).

46. Shelley Lockwood, "Marsilius of Padua and the Case for the Royal Ecclesiastical Supremacy: The Alexander Prize Essay," *Transactions of the Royal Historical Society* 1 (1991): 89–119.

needs, and left out other parts, such as the conclusion that evangelical perfection was to be found in keeping no real property except in order to send it to the poor.[47] It translated "ad pias causas" as "charytable uses," even though Marsilius had treated them separately in giving supervision of both *ad pias causas seu misericordiae opera* to the sovereign.[48] The translator translated "pious" as "charitable" whenever it related to the disposition of property. In the 21st conclusion (the 28th conclusion in the original text), the translator took *cuncta temporalia quae ad pias causas seu misericordiae opera statuta sunt* and translated it as "all temporalles, which are ordayned for charytable causes, and to almosse dedes and the workes of pytye." In other words, the translator created a higher category, which was "charytable causes," and drew on the multi-valence of pytye, which was a word that meant pity, but which in English had the connotation of piety as well. Cromwell's translator was carefully merging alms and pious uses into a category of "charitable" uses or causes. Although for the *Valor Ecclesiasticus* Cromwell would encourage the reporters to minimize what counted as "alms" in order to take as much monastic wealth as possible, here Cromwell negotiated for flexibility.

But even more was going on in this particular translated conclusion. The original text ran:

All temporal goods which have been set aside for religious purposes or for deeds of mercy, such as legacies bequeathed for overseas crossing to resist the infidels, or for the redemption of captives or for the support of the helpless poor, and for other similar purposes, are to be distributed only by the ruler in accordance with the designation of the legislator and the [determination (*determinationem*) of the testator or the] intention (*intentionem*) of the donor.[49]

---

47. Marsilius of Padua, *Defensor pacis*, trans. Alan Gewith (New York: Columbia University Press, 1956), 3.2.38; in the Cromwell edition: *The Defence of Peace* (London: William Marshall, 1535), 3.2.28.

48. *Defensor pacis*, 2.17 and 3.2.28; *Defence of Peace*, 3.2.21.

49. *Defensor pacis*, 429: "Cuncta temporalia quae ad pias causas seu misericordiae opera statuta sunt, ut quae testamentis legantur pro ultramarino transitu ad resistendum infidelibus, aut pro captivorum ab ipsis redemptione, vel pauperum impotentum sustentatione, ceterisque similibus, ad solum principantem secundum legislatoris determinationem ac legantis, vel aliter largientis intentionem, disponere pertinet: ubi supra immediate."

In the original, then, Marsilius was claiming that the prince, along with the legislator, had the power to supervise the distribution of temporal goods that were left for good causes. The intention of the donor was a limiting factor: presumably Marsilius meant that the donor could assign the general purpose to the gift, but that the prince and legislator would be empowered to direct how the gift would serve that purpose. In the translation authorized by Cromwell, the prince alone held this power, which was typical of a translation that upheld the solitary authority of the prince. But the translation further reworked the second half of the text to read that "to hym [the prince] onely it appertayneth, to ordre the sayd thynges, accordynge to the determynacion, intencyon, and mynde of the testator or otherwyse gyver." This translation merged the two kinds of donors (living and dead), and listed three ways that their will might be understood: their determination, intention, or mind. The exact honoring of the will was weakened rather than strengthened through the elaboration of multiple ways to conceive of that will.

Cromwell's propaganda campaign drew volunteers. Thomas Starkey, a promoter of the purity of civil law over the rudeness of the common law, wrote enthusiastically to Henry VIII on how to put monastic endowments to social and educational purposes.[50] This was a theme that he had taken up in his *Dialogue between Cardinal Pole and Thomas Lupset*, dated by Mayer between 1529 and 1532.[51] Starkey had diagnosed the diseases that afflicted the commonwealth, including dropsy (from idleness) and palsy (from wastefulness).[52] Starkey offered an array of humanist remedies: all young men should be trained in useful arts and forbidden from pursuing monasticism; superfluous wealth from the church should be given to the poor; excess

---

50. Sidney J. Herrtage, *England in the Reign of King Henry the Eighth*, Early English Text Society, Extra Series, vol. 32 (London: Early English Text Society, 1878), xlvii–lxii. Elton, *Reform and Reformation*, 166–68, 237–38, and 258.

51. Thomas Mayer, *Thomas Starkey and the Commonweal: Humanist Politics and Religion in the Reign of Henry VIII* (Cambridge: Cambridge University Press, 1989), 1 and 77. As R. W. Hoyle has shown in his article "The Origins of the Dissolution of the Monasteries," the topic of the diversion of assets was already being discussed in 1529.

52. Kathleen M. Burton, ed., *A Dialogue between Reginald Pole and Thomas Lupset* (London: Chatto and Windus, 1948).

monasteries should be turned into educational institutions where the nobility might learn discipline, rigor, and how to serve the commonwealth; the king and a small group of advisers should direct social and economic reform centrally, obviating the need for Parliament to meet. This concentrated group of advisers could ensure that everyone receive their due; that wealth and honors be distributed fairly and evenly; that a poor relief system be put together on the model of Ypres; and that strict mercantilist principles be enforced. Secular clergy should be allowed to marry, and the waste lands should be handed over for cultivation by the servants of great nobles, who could sustain their own families on the profits they would make.

Starkey was Henry's adviser and chaplain, but he feared a loss of position because of his inability to persuade his friend Reginald Pole to support Royal Supremacy. Meanwhile, Henry was garnering notable criticism for the first dissolutions. In his famous second call to redirect monastic endowments for secular purposes, Starkey then suggested, in a classic piece of cy-près reasoning (although not referring to the idea), that if the testators were alive today, they would acknowledge the right of the sovereign to use the money for the public good (for obedience was due to the sovereign even in death) and would even prefer to turn their money to new uses:

Many there be which are moved to judge plainly this Act of Suppression of certain abbeys both to be against the order of charity and injurious to them which be dead, because the founders thereof and the souls departed seem thereby to be defrauded of the benefit of prayer and almsdeeds there appointed to be done for their relief by their last will and testament; and also the common weal and politic order appeareth to be much hindered and troubled by the same, because many poor men thereby are like to be deprived of their living and quietness, wherein lieth, as they think, no small injury.... [And yet] though great respect ever hath been had of the last will of testators and much privilege granted thereto, specially when it pertained and tended to matters of religion, yet this I trow was never thought of any men of wisdom and prudence that all their posterity should be bounden of high necessity to the sure accomplishment and full observation of their wills prescribed in testament, and that by no means they might be changed and ordered to other purpose, for this is a sure truth that the will and deed of every private man for a common weal may be altered by the supreme authority in every country.... Foreasmuch as every man by the order of God is subject thereto and his will ever presupposed to be obedient to the same, insomuch that though he be either absent or dead yet it is always by reason thought that if he were present he would give his consent to all such things as be judged by common authority to be expedient to the public weal, to the which no private will may be lawfully repugnant. Wherefore albeit the last will of the testator's be by this Act altered with authority yet it is not broken with injury, because the consent of the testator is presupposed to be contained therein. Insomuch that it may surely be thought that if they were now living again and saw the present state of this world now in our days, how under the pretense of prayer much vice and idleness is nourished in these monasteries institute and founded of them, and how little learning and religion is taught in the same, yea, and how little Christian hospitality is used therein, they would peradventure cry out with one voice, saying after this manner to princes of the world, — "Alter these foundations which we of long time before did institute, and turn them to some better use and commodity."[53]

The consent of living, interested parties (who were writing letters of protest to Cromwell about the seizures) was dropped in favor of a fiction of consent by dead, but obedient, subjects.[54] Only the interests of the original donors mattered.

Starkey remarked that the duty to give to the poor was a biblical command, meaning that the testators had failed by not giving directly to them.[55] Since performance was irrelevant to salvation, "whether we pray or pray not they schal not be depryvyed of theyr reward." He went further, arguing that it would be of "grete comfort and releyffe to them to see theyr posteryte to have them in charytabul memory, the wych thyng ys to be requyryd of al men in every sort and degre."[56] The diversion of charitable gifts then, would, by Starkey's reasoning, provide comfort to the dead, potentially even improving the state of their souls in the afterlife. Starkey was so insistent on this point—and so aware how fundamental this issue was—that he repeated it several times. Indeed, Starkey affirmed purgatory's existence and that souls in that place "ther takyng releyffe

---

53. Joseph Robson Tanner, ed., *Tudor Constitutional Documents, A.D. 1485–1603* (Cambridge: Cambridge University Press, 1922), 86–87.
54. Herrtage, ed., *England in the Reign*, liv–lv.
55. Ibid., lvi.
56. Ibid.

and comfort of our prayerys made in faythful love and charyte, yet thys schal not folow of necessyte that by thys acte of suppressyon they suffur any wrong or iniurye."[57] Modifying gifts would help the dead.

Still, despite Starkey's admiration for the civil law, and despite Cromwell's well-known suggestions to Henry VIII that the civil law allowed the king to do whatever he pleased, Starkey did not indicate that there was a civil law precedent for the transition of uses, nor did he refer to any kind of cy-près doctrine that might justify the king's seizures, not even in his desperation to prove his worth. Starkey did not argue that religious bequests already had flexibility in civil law; rather, he criticized them for being too strictly observed. Instead, Starkey reached toward something new, a justification for the bending of a testator's will for the good of the testator himself, on the grounds of obedience and the king's prerogatives.

Use and Abuse

Thomas More, in his 1529 *Dialogue Concerning Heresies,* had his interlocutor defend pilgrimages, images, and shrines from the accusation of "abuse" and "misuse" on the grounds that all good things are prone to the occasional misuse. If the world were set up to prevent all misuse, then the prevalent good use too would be lost. But this missed the more pressing point—or at least the point that was more important to some of his peers—which was that many humanists and reformers alike were sure that better use could be made of the materials that were in the hands of the church. Not only did the church encourage misuse and abuse, it was claimed, but it was preventing better use, especially to support universities or poor relief. The argument could be made on Henry VIII's behalf that the needs of the king to provide for the defense of the realm, to avoid further debasing of the currency, to build loyalty, and to otherwise replenish the treasury were also good uses, relevant to the health of the commonwealth. But these were not the most anticipated new uses of the

57. Ibid., lix.

wealth of the church, and they were not the uses propagandized by Cromwell. Indeed, many of the king's intended uses for the property would be understood as a new abuse, not the expected better use.

Eric Ives has shown that Anne Boleyn, a sincere reformer in her own right, supported the dissolution of the monasteries only if their goods be put to an appropriate new use.[58] Shortly after the act dissolving the small monasteries, she arranged for her almoner John Skip to give a sermon that deplored the machinations of Haman to take the wealth of the Jews and directed the attention of the king to the plight of the universities, which could produce so much good for England through the restoration of learning. This was a diversion of use that Anne could support, derived from the humanist and reformist circles with which she had long associated.[59] Skip, who was subsequently admonished for his interference in civil matters in this sermon, argued that it was right to keep the little ceremonies of the church so long as "they be used for the purpas and intentt that they weyre furste ordened." But the king had an inescapable duty to prevent the abuse of these things: "The kynges office is to se thabuses taken awey and not the good thinges themselffes except hit so be that thabuses can nott be taken awey, as Ezechias toke awey the brason serpentt when he cowde nott take awey thabuse of hitt."[60] Thus it was righteous and necessary for Henry to put down the small monasteries, which not only seemed to be verging on decay (the usual explanation for suppression) but also were described in the statute—justly or not—as places where religion was particularly abused. This abuse demanded that the king bring reform, and Skip, following Boleyn's lead, pushed the universities as the appropriate recipient. Ives points out that Anne herself refounded a collegiate church into a "bible-based educational house offering a bursary

---

58. E. W. Ives, "Anne Boleyn and the Early Reformation in England: The Contemporary Evidence," *The Historical Journal* 37 (1994): 389–400.

59. Elizabeth Norton, *The Anne Boleyn Papers* (Stroud: Amberley, 2013), 325; *Letters and Papers of the Reign of Henry VIII*, vol. 10, ed. by J. S. Brewer et al. (London: 1862–1932), doc. 699.

60. Ives, "Anne Boleyn and the Early Reformation," 395; from PRO, SP6/1 f. 10.

to Cambridge."⁶¹ He further suggests, following the report of her biographer William Latymer, that it was on her instruction that Hugh Latimer gave a sermon to the king about using monastic wealth for "education and poor relief."⁶² Ives even proposes that it was this defiance of Cromwell's intentions for the profits of the monasteries that may have provoked her ultimate fall.

Cranmer agreed discreetly with Anne, although he believed that a good use of monastic wealth might be the enriching of the treasury to such an extent that that no new taxes would ever be required. It was a tantalizing thought, to endow the king and set the people free. Still, Cranmer could not approve of the use that was ultimately made of church property. After the seizures, in fact, Cranmer would be interested instead in finding methods to prevent the resultant "stark beggery" of the church, which would influence his work on canon law, including the 1553 *Reformatio legum ecclesiasticarum*, an attempted Protestant revision of canon law that will be discussed later in this chapter. Although Cranmer did not agree with Miles Wilson that the despoiling of schools and hospitals was sacrilegious, he could not agree with that spoliation either, even if he could not find quite the right word to describe it.⁶³ Cranmer would pointedly include X 3.26.17 (according to which, goods that had been left for pious causes should not be applied to another use) as part of his compilation of canon law.⁶⁴ The enthusiasm of reformers for new uses was tempered by the sense that there should be limits on what those new uses were.

Perhaps to dampen expectations, the original justifications for the seizures focused on abuse and misuse, not better use. The visitation of all of the monasteries in 1535–36, then again in 1538, produced a *Compendium compertorum* that detailed how badly managed most monasteries were.⁶⁵ At the visitations the monasteries were asked

---

61. Ives, "Anne Boleyn and the Early Reformation," 399.
62. Ibid., 400; citing William Latymer, "Cronickille of Anne Bulleyne," ed. M. Dowling, in *Camden miscellany* 30 (1990): 57.
63. Thomas Cranmer, *Memorials of Cranmer*, vol. 3, ed. John Strype (Oxford: Clarendon Press, 1854), 649–59.
64. Ibid., 849.
65. Knowles, *Religious Orders*, vol. 3; Anthony N. Shaw, "The Compendium

specifically about any deviation from the stipulations of their foundations; the responses laid the groundwork for the seizure of the monasteries in the name of honoring donor intent. Once the monasteries were dissolved and it became clear that intercessory institutions might be next, *ad hoc* local seizures increased—and ironically, as we have seen, were cited by Henry VIII's chantry act as his motivation to intervene, as he complained that the testators' wishes were being violated and that subjects were converting endowments "of their own authority."[66] Any foundation which had thus been dissipated since the dissolution of the monasteries was to be given to the king. Henry's act further complained that endowments were being mismanaged and abused, again thwarting the intent of the founders. Consequently Henry VIII's chantry act also claimed ownership—once again acting in the interests of the founders—of all foundations that were not being used as they were supposed to be and also promised, as we have seen, better uses to come.

The move beyond mere abuse or decay as justifications for the dissolutions to include the pledge of much desired better uses may have been politically necessary to pass the bill. Beyond donor intent, the theory behind the confiscations was that the king was the ultimate owner of all the land in his kingdom, could resume his gifts, and was, in fact, incapable of alienating realty. Nonetheless, the House of Commons passed Henry's chantry act only grudgingly; Petre suggests that it was an extraordinarily narrow victory.[67] After the passage of the act, Henry gave a speech that was recorded in Hall's *Chronicle*—although in the portion of the *Chronicle* that was finished by Hall's friend and literary executor Richard Grafton, a propagandist.[68] The speech as we have it, then, can only safely be regarded as the comments that Grafton would have liked for Henry to have said: he promised that he would "order [the property] to the glory of God and the profit of the commonwealth" such that there would be no

---

Compertorum and the Making of the Suppression Act of 1536" (Ph.D. dissertation, University of Warwick, 2003).

66. See Kreider's chapter on "Anticipatory Dissolutions" in *English Chantries*.
67. Scarisbrick, *Reformation and the English People*, 65–66.
68. E. J. Devereux, "Empty Tuns and Unfruitful Grafts: Richard Grafton's Historical Publications," *Sixteenth Century Journal* 21.1 (1990): 33–56.

loss to the ministry, learning, or the relief of poverty. "Doubt not," he emphasized, "but your expectation shall be served more godly and goodly than you will wish or desire."[69]

Kreider remarks that despite the language of better uses in both the Act and the king's speech, Henry VIII did not bother asking "the commissioners who surveyed the chantries and colleges in 1546 to make special note of their charitable functions."[70] Kreider points out that the need was real, largely due to the millions of pounds being spent on war: the king had already sold much of the monastic seizures, sold crown lands, raised taxes six times within the last six years, borrowed money at extortionate interest rates, and debased coinage.[71] And so no attempt was made by the act to maintain any of the social purposes being served by the chantries that were seized.

By the time of the next, more sweeping, Chantries Act in 1547, under the boy-king Edward VI, the justification for the seizures had changed to the question of use alone, so that the endowments could offer "better provision for the poor and needy."[72] The imperial ambassador, François Van der Delft, claimed it was believed the king was taking over all chantry property "unconditionally," with the gentry anticipating a windfall, but that the Parliament was advocating for half of the money to be given to poor relief.[73] Given Edward's donation of Bridewell to poor relief efforts, it is likely that the king was sincere in his desire to remedy poverty, but the pressures of the enclosure movement, in which common lands were walled off by wealthier landowners, sometimes with some recompense to the villagers who depended on them, were creating popular unrest and magnified the sense that reform aimed only to help the rich take possession of goods that belonged to all.[74]

The original second chantry bill was to include hospitals and all

---

69. Quoted in Kreider, *English Chantries*, 169.
70. Ibid., 174.
71. Ibid., 171–72.
72. Dickens, *English Reformation*, 230.
73. *Calendar of State Papers—Spain*, vol. 9 (1547–49), ed. Martin A. S. Hume and Royall Tyler, December 5, 1547, and December 12, 1547, pp. 222 and 230.
74. Diarmaid MacCulloch, *The Boy King: Edward VI and the Protestant Reformation* (Berkeley: University of California Press, 1999), 23.

secular guilds, but successful lobbying and legislative resistance limited the seizures to those connected with intercessory institutions.[75] Kreider documents the strong, but ultimately unsuccessful, revolt of the House of Commons against the Second Chantry Act—a revolt that did, however, force the government to make concessions to some of the localities such that they could keep their endowments rather than handing them over.[76] Local claims would be, in fact, a key source of resistance to the state takeover of church property now that the rights of the donors' families had been repeatedly set aside, since property with local connections, that served local needs, was being absorbed into the state. As MacCulloch points out, "[M]any knights and burgesses were angry at the prospect of losing community assets for no obvious gain ... [and] this was the only time in Edward's reign when any official measure of religious change ran into trouble in the Commons."[77]

About 4,000 chantries and colleges were seized in this second, much bigger, wave of chantry dissolutions, plus an untold number of lights, obits, and guilds. These seizures netted well over one hundred thousand pounds.[78] Reimbursement for any charitable functions served by chantries—hospitals, schools, almshouses, the upkeep of roads or sea walls—was supposed to be made, so that the public would not suffer from the dissolutions. Scarisbrick does note several instances in which gifts of prayer for the dead were taken by the crown while charitable donations to the poor were carefully protected.[79] Nonetheless, the implementation of these intentions was spotty: most schools were successfully refounded as grammar schools, but almshouses and hospitals, which were not supposed to have been liable for seizure but which were largely attached to intercessionary institutions, generally survived only if the town stepped in to refinance them and paid for a new license.[80]

75. Loach, *Parliament under the Tudors*, 80–81.
76. Kreider, *English Chantries*, 189–95.
77. MacCulloch, *Boy King*, 77.
78. Kreider, *English Chantries*, chapter 8.
79. Scarisbrick, *Reformation and the English People*, 113.
80. Dickens, *English Reformation*, 235–38; Scarisbrick, *Reformation and the English People*, 114; Kreider, *English Chantries*, 193 and 207.

Many were outraged by the seizures and at the use made of the property. But cy-près doctrine was not used as the basis of any known contemporary critique, not even by those like Boleyn or Cranmer who wanted to support some new uses but not others. Nor was cy-près itself cited by the men in charge of the dissolutions as a motivation for the attempt to maintain poor relief services. At this key moment, when cy-près would seem to be relevant, no one was talking about it, not even Henry VIII's legal counsellors or the statutes themselves. Moreover, as Alan Kreider points out, with one notable exception (the secretary of state, Thomas Smith), the civilian lawyers opposed the chantry acts. This suggests that they did not see them as congruous with the *ius commune* tradition, even though the acts took money left for what was becoming an illegal use and applied it, at least in theory, to a new good use.[81] For that matter, had cy-près been a known principle in Chancery, Henry could have saved considerable trouble by employing it from the beginning, that is, by decisively outlawing practices in order to redirect the endowments dedicated to them.

Christopher Saint German

As part of his method of legal Reformation, Henry VIII "ground[ed] the Reformation statutes in learned opinion."[82] One of Henry's propagandists, Christopher Saint German, had been a member of the Middle Temple and utter barrister before he retired in 1511. He was listed by Wolsey as a Master of Requests in 1528 when the first Latin edition of Saint German's *Doctor and Student* appeared, although Guy notes that this is very improbable. His influence on Henry VIII and on Henry's chancellor, Thomas Audley, apparent author of the 1536 act to dissolve the monasteries, is known.[83] For a few years, Saint

---

81. Kreider, *English Chantries*, 202–4.
82. Zaller, *Discourse of Legitimacy*, 488.
83. Elton, *Reform and Reformation*, 237. The initial view of Saint German was that he was a propagandist without political influence: Elton upholds this in *Reform and Reformation*, 159. The work of John Guy, however, has established that Saint German worked far more closely with the Tudor government than had been thought. See also Franklin Le Van Baumer, *The Early Tudor Theory of Kingship*

German had the king's ear on matters both legal and theological. At one point he received a reward from Cromwell, presumably for his service, although he was never officially sponsored and seems to have lost influence at the end of his life. It was Saint German who, as Zaller argues, first formulated the Royal Supremacy and "laid the basis for the national church," for which he drafted legislation.[84] He was the only non-theologian amongst the four men to whom Henry, or perhaps Cromwell, circulated the *Institution of a Christian Man*, also known as the Bishops' Book, and Henry studied his responses to it. The writings of Saint German became a symbol of religious controversy: the "Pilgrims" of the Pilgrimage of Grace in 1536, a movement of Catholic resistance, demanded their suppression along with books by Luther, Melanchthon, Hus, and other Reformation theologians.

Saint German's driving goals were to uphold conscience (a term increasingly conflated with equity, although as David Ibbitson notes, equity was "subordinated to conscience" for Saint German) as a legal principle and to allow common law to triumph over canon law.[85] He defended state sovereignty and the right of Parliament to redistribute property as it saw fit. Saint German had supported uses (although not entailed trusts, which he thought were the source of "gret inconvenyens" that "can not lyghtly be preventyd") as good common law, and he was aware of the escalating political battle over the legitimacy of "uses" (that is, trusts) that was being spearheaded by Henry VIII and Audley, who had given a reading in 1526 against

---

(Ann Arbor: University of Michigan, 1940), and the assessment by J. B. Trapp in his "Introduction" in *The Complete Works of St. Thomas More*, vol. 9: The Apology (New Haven, Conn.: Yale University Press, 1979), especially l–liv. See also Zaller, *Discourse of Legitimacy*, 274. Guy points out that Saint German was "the first Englishman to articulate the theory of the sovereignty of the King in Parliament." *The Complete Works of St. Thomas More*, vol. 10: *The Debellation of Salem and Bizance*, ed. John Guy, Clarence H. Miller, and Ralph Keen (New Haven, Conn.: Yale University Press, 1987), xxxix.

84. Zaller, *Discourse of Legitimacy*, 278–80.

85. David Ibbetson, "A House Built on Sand: Equity in Early Modern English Law," in *Law and Equity: Approaches in Roman Law and Common Law*, ed. E. Koops and W. J. Zwalve (Leiden: Brill, 2013), 58. On the history of the two concepts, see Mike Macnair, "Equity and Conscience," *Oxford Journal of Legal Studies* 27 (2007): 659–81.

the "use" and against conscience as a factor in law more generally.[86] Saint German supported equity in uses, and he also acknowledged that at times in complicated enfeoffments to uses, whose legal status was still being sorted out, it would be necessary to discern "how an use may be reservyd by ye law contrarye to the wordes."[87] Already in the struggles over uses and *Lord Dacre's Case,* English law had confronted the problem of undoing the work of the testator who had created the use, however fraudulently.

Saint German was particularly interested in wills. His *Treatise Concernynge Divers of the Constitucyons Provynciall and Legatines* argued that *praemunire* in the common law ought to prevent clerics from having any temporal authority at all, including probate of wills. He took aim at the practice of charging for prayers, which was a refusal to give freely from what had been received. He likewise criticized some of the canons for being "against the kynges laws [and] ... nat so charitable as they ought to have ben."[88] He may have been one of the authors of the Commons' Supplication in 1532, which formally complained to the king about a host of issues with the ecclesiastical courts.[89]

In 1531, just after he revised *Doctor and Student,* he drafted a case for Parliament to take over both the governance of the church and administration of poor relief systems, for priests to pray for all of the dead in their care without charging money for it, and for municipalities to put their beggars to work on infrastructure projects.[90] Dismissing canon law, he called for the king and Parliament to "advoyde all suche lawes, uses and custumes inducyd by the spirituall

---

86. J. A. Guy, *Christopher St German on Chancery and Statute,* Selden Society Supplementary Series, vol. 6 (London: Selden Society, 1985), 79 and 86.

87. Ibid., 85.

88. Christopher Saint German, "Introduction," *A Treatise Concernynge Diuers of the Constitucyons Prouynciall and Legatines* (London: Thomas Godfrey, 1535).

89. Arthur Irving Taft, in *The Apologye of Syr Thomas More, knyght* (London: Humphrey Milford, 1930), 293 and elsewhere; Pierre Janelle, *L'Angleterre catholique à la veille du schisme* (Paris: Beauchesne, 1935), 150. Cf. G. R. Elton, *Reform and Renewal: Thomas Cromwell and the Common Weal* (Cambridge: Cambridge University Press, 1973), 74–76.

90. Printed in Guy, *Christopher St German,* 127–35; Loach, *Parliament under the Tudors,* 85.

jurisdiccion as they shall thynke to be unresonable."[91] To eliminate the need to maintain endowments for perpetual prayer, Saint German suggested that a dirige and mass should be held by all clergymen once a month "specially for the soules departyd in that parissh, and for all crysten soules," and that similarly "all howses of relygyn within the kinges domynyon do lykewyse oonys yn every monethe, and to pray specyally for the kyng, the realme, for theyr founders, and for all cristen sowles" but that "the seid Curates, servyng prystes, ne chauntery prystes, ne howses of religyon not to receyve any reward, oblacions, gyftes nor offerynges for the seid dirige and masse." Saint German proposed that the statute of mortmain be reinforced and that only the king would be permitted to make new foundations in the future.[92] The draft forbade the church from treating "legacyes, tythes, and such other" in any manner that contradicted "the kynges lawes," and it exacted a triple penalty for violations.[93] The draft was not passed, and perhaps not even heard, although Cromwell must have seen it, as the manuscript copy exists in his papers.

Saint German published his *Treatise Concernynge the Division Betwene the Spirytualitie and Temporalitie* anonymously in 1532. Influenced by Marsilius of Padua, Saint German argued for the king's authority over spiritual matters. He stated, in relationship to the new mortuary statute, "It is holden by them that be lerned in the lawe of this royalme that the parlyamente hath an absolute power, as to the possession of all temporall thynges within this realme in whose handes so ever they be, spyrytualle or temporalle to take them from oone manne, and gyve theym to an nother withoute anye cause or consideration."[94] The canon law requirement that such acts be done only *ex causa* was here explicitly repudiated in favor of a new vision of state power. He had prepared the terrain for this argument about the authority of the King-in-Parliament over all goods in his influential *Doctor and Student*, whose extended English version appeared in

91. Guy, *Christopher St German*, 128.
92. Ibid., 129–30.
93. Ibid., 130.
94. Saint German, *Treatise Concernynge the Division*, 24. Cromwell, who supported Saint German's work, had *Defender of Peace* translated into English and published in 1534.

1530. *Doctor and Student* was set up in the form of a dialogue, with a doctor of divinity questioning and learning from the student of the laws of England. The book began from the premise that canon law had no better claim to equity, or conscience, than English law, and was no more divine. In many cases the questions posed in *Doctor and Student* are replies to Baptista de Salis (Trovamala)'s casuistic *Summa Rosella* from 1495, showing the correct answer given by English law. Thomas More, with whom Saint German tangled over the persecution of heresy in church courts, repeatedly ridiculed Saint German's knowledge of canon law, pointing to his frequent use of the *Summa Rosella* as an indicator of his amateurish understanding.[95]

Of particular relevance to the issue of cy-près is chapter 34 from the second dialogue of *Doctor and Student*. Drawing on the 12th article of *alienatio* in *Summa Rosella*, the question was asked "whether a gift made under a condition be void, if the sovereign only break the condition." The answer from canon law, Saint German argued, was that the gift was not void, "for that the dede of the prelate [i.e., the sovereign of the monastery] onely ought not to hurte the chyrche." This was in some sense correct, since canon law would require that the prelate make good the situation, but canon law had also allowed that gifts were sometimes revocable. Nonetheless, the *Summa Rosella* served as Saint German's foil, as he rejected this answer for English practice: "the sayd solucyon holdeth not in thys realme neyther in lawe nor conscyence." On the contrary, Saint German had the student of English laws rejoin, "yf the condycyon be broken yt is lawfull by the lawe of England for the feffoure to reentre & to take his lande agayne and to holde it as in his fyrst estate."[96] If a gift was made

---

95. *Complete Works of St. Thomas More*, vol. 9, 146. Helmholz has convincingly argued that Thomas More's depth of knowledge about the *ius commune* was limited and focused on the treatment of heretics. He seems to have been familiar, Helmholz shows, with the basic texts and glosses, along with some textbooks, but not with Bartolus or other learned doctors. R. H. Helmholz, "Thomas More and the Canon Law," in *Medieval Church Law and the Origins of the Western Legal Tradition: A Tribute to Kenneth Pennington*, ed. Wolfgang P. Müller and Mary E. Sommer (Washington, D.C.: The Catholic University of America Press, 2006), 375–88.

96. Christopher Saint German, *Doctor and Student*, ed. T. F. T. Plucknett and J. L. Barton, Selden Society Annual Series, vol. 91 (London: Selden Society, 1974), 251.

with a condition, and the condition was not carried out, then the gift should return to the giver: "thys that I have sayd ys to be holden in thys realme bothe in law and conscyence and that the decrees of the chyrche to the contrarye bynde not in thys case."[97] The writ of *cessavit* (or its variant for religious houses, the *cessavit de cantaria*) was useful here, in forcing the return of an unfulfilled conditional gift.[98] Given Saint German's work advising the king, he may well have been thinking of the king's plans to take back church property—for much of which he could claim to be the ultimate founder. And yet Saint German carved out one striking exception to this rule:

But yf landes be gyven to an abbot, and to hys covente, to the intente to fynde a lampe, or to gyve certayne almes to poore men; thoughe the intente be not in those cases fulfylled, yet the feoffour nor his heyres may not reentre for he reserved no reentre by expresse wordes: ne in the wordes whan he sayth to the entente to fynde a lampe, or to gyve almes, etc., ys ymplyed no reentre ne the feoffour nor his heyres shall have no remedye in suche cases, onlesse it be within the case of the statute of westmynstere the seconde that gyveth the Cessavit de cantaria.[99]

Gifts made with a condition should be returned to the giver or his heirs if the condition was not fulfilled; indeed, the giver or his heirs could immediately re-enter for the failure to perform. But Saint German denied that there was any implied right to re-entry for gifts given with the intent that something should be done, like finding a lamp or giving alms.[100] In those cases, where Saint German claimed there was no express reservation, the donor was protected only by statutory law. In an echo of Bracton's treatment of *causa* gifts, if the statute did not give them a writ, then the donor was helpless. It is not clear whether Saint German's history is correct: for example, in 1240, prior to the Second Statute of Westminster, Berkshire rectors

---

97. Ibid., 252.
98. Westminster 2 (13 Edward 1 st. 1), c. 21 and 41.
99. Saint German, *Doctor and Student*, 252.
100. Contemporary bequests frequently used the language that money should be used "to find" something. It is tempting to read "find" as "fund," but this chapter will use "find" because the term would become significant in subsequent case law, as judges made distinctions between finding and paying in the *Case of Pele's Will* and *Adams and Lambert's Case*: 4 Co. Rep. 113 and 115; Duke 95 and 90.

warned the pope that the patrons would resume their endowments if the rectors did not fulfill the stated intentions of the gifts.[101] As Joshua Getzler has observed, Saint German wrote as a theoretician of equity, not focusing on "the way in which equity lawyers actually thought."[102] He cannot necessarily be relied upon as an accurate reporter of contemporary equitable practice. Guy has pointed out that his writings were "part of the process by which new ideas were assimilated within traditional forms."[103] Similarly, Victoria Kahn has argued that Saint German was decisive in inventing the distinctively English concept of "consideration" in contracts.[104]

Despite his interest in merging law and conscience, Saint German did not think there was any equitable reason to protect the rights of the donors for property given with an intent to do something. By implication, if the statutes changed, then the treatment of these kinds of gifts would change too. This was not cy-près, but it was a passage that would seem supportive of cy-près in future readings of the text, in which the Edwardian chantry statutes had taken over the governance of many of these gifts and insisted on the right of the crown to supervise their disposition. Even in conscience, Saint German would appear to say, the donor had no recourse unless he or she had expressly reserved the right to re-entry. This determination of Saint German's is quite similar to how cy-près has been treated in modern times: unless there is an expression of what should be done when a charitable gift fails, the donation may be subject to a cy-près scheme.

Saint German offered a solution to the problem that the *ius patronatus* would normally require the patron's approval (or that of his heirs) in order to alienate property for a new purpose: now, the in-

---

101. Matthew of Paris, *Chronica majora*, ed. J. R. Luard, vol. 4 (London: Longmans, 1872–83), 41.
102. Joshua Getzler, "Patterns of Fusion," in *The Classification of Obligations*, ed. Peter Birks (Oxford: Oxford University Press, 1997), 157.
103. Guy, *Christopher St German*, 94.
104. Victoria Kahn, *Wayward Contracts: The Crisis of Political Obligation in England, 1640–1674* (Princeton, N.J.: Princeton University Press, 2004), 43–45; A. W. B. Simpson, "The Equitable Doctrine of Consideration and the Law of Uses," *The University of Toronto Law Journal* 16 (1965): 1–36.

tent of the donor would prevent his heirs from having any claim if the original purpose was not fulfilled. Implicitly, in those cases, the intent itself carried on despite its nonperformance, which was not unlike *ius commune* resolutions to find a new trustee for a trust that had lain fallow, and statutes could decide how to cope with them, either to allow the donor or his heirs to demand it back or to do something else with them, perhaps honoring the "intent" in some other way. It was a gesture toward a continuity of charitable intent, not conceived as such by Saint German, but certainly contributing to the legal defense of Henry and Cromwell's work to take over church property, through their denial that under common law there was an automatic right of re-entry to many of the ecclesiastical gifts.

Meanwhile, Saint German continued to be read through the centuries. *Doctor and Student*, which is still one of only a few legal treatises cited as "books of authority" in English courts, remained the standard introductory work on equity until Blackstone's *Commentaries* were published in the 1760s. The relevant passage from the 34th chapter of the second dialogue was repeated in a shortened form in the popular abridgement produced for students of the law: "But if the land had been given to the Abbot and Convent, to the intent to finde a lamp, or to give certain alms, reserving no re-entrie, and the words imply no re-entrie, the feoffor nor his heirs have no remedy, unlesse it be in case of the Statute of West. 2 which giveth the Cessavit de cantaria."[105]

So *Doctor and Student* laid the groundwork, within the theory of equity, for the state to take unfulfilled gifts for purposes and supervise their distribution by cutting off the right of return or right of consent to donors and heirs. Saint German did not try to ground this argument in either Roman or canon law, nor did he discuss an approximation of intent. The two different examples he used—giving alms to the poor or finding a lamp—would become emblematic of the two different kinds of cy-près: the first was an example of a charitable use that would be eligible for judicial cy-près, and the sec-

---

105. *St. Germans Book of the Grounds of the Laws of England and of Conscience, or, An Exact Abridgement of that Exquisite Treatise called Doctor and Student* (London: John More, 1630), II.34.

ond would be considered a superstitious use for which prerogative cy-près would be imposed. Intentionally or not, Saint German's text thus provided a justification for a continuity of "donor intent" toward new ends in either situation.

This understanding of Saint German is borne out in his other work. In his *Treatise Concernynge the Division Betwene the Spirytualitie and Temporalitie,* Saint German argued that eliminating purgatory could help to dispossess the church and elevate its moral standing.[106] The clergy wrongly promoted chantries, trentals, and pilgrimages rather than the works that were more important to the souls of the common man: "the payment of theyr dettes / to make restitutions for such wronges as they haue done / or to doo the werkes of mercye to theyr neyghboures, that be poore and nedye / and that sometyme be also in right extreme necessite."[107] Saint German did not believe in predestination, and he suggested that by learning how to give correctly, in the new model of the free gift, men might be saved: "yf they had bene well and charitably handeled, they myghte haue benne refourmed, and paraduenture saued in bodye and in soule."[108] The setting right of charitable intentions could have eternal consequences. At the same time, where it was convenient Saint German echoed the evangelical concern that gifts to the church were not being used as they ought: "it hathe benne noysed, that the money shulde be bestowed to somme charitable use, as uppon the buyldynge of sayncte Peters churche in Rome, or to suche other charitable vse: it hathe appered afterwarde euidently, that it hath nat ben disposed to that vse."[109] But even in this assessment that gifts were being misdirected, Saint German did not present the remedy that they might be returned to the donor or forcibly applied to their original purpose. Notably, he also conglomerated the intentions of the donor into a general "charitable use."

In his *An Answer to a Letter,* Saint German argued, not quite accurately, that canon law had decreed either specific restitution for

---

106. *Complete Works of St. Thomas More,* vol. 9, 178.
107. Ibid.
108. Ibid., 179.
109. Ibid., 197.

wrongs committed or, alternatively, the performance of a penance to be determined by the church, by way of a "dispensacyon from Rome."[110] Saint German rejected the dispensations: "if [a man] thought another use more charitable, he might, and yet may, dyspose it accordingly, if he wyll, and let the dyspensacyon alone."[111] The advice of the church might be for the man to give to uses that were "nat most charytable, as for syngynge of trentalles, kepynge of obyttes, fyndyng of scolars, or such other," but a man should trust his conscience and "he therfore that muste refuse that counsell, and dispose it to suche use as his conscience serveth him beste to, as percase to releve poore men in extreme necessytie, to make high wayes, or such other lyke."[112] Any general charitable use could discharge the spiritual debt of the donor, and Saint German recognized that this was not the perspective of canon law, although it was an anticipation of cy-près reasoning that charitable uses could be exchanged and upgraded.

Thomas More, replying to Saint German's treatise with his own *Apology*, picked up on some of these implications. More denied that any clergyman would suggest leaving money for masses if the testator had not already accounted for debts, restitution, and "dedys of almoyse and mercy to theyr neyghbours that are poore and nedy," although he avoided calling these posthumous works charitable since he clung to the older definition of charity, particularly in relationship to testamentary gifts.[113] More also noted the contradiction that critics of the church hoped to reduce her to a holy poverty—even though not all saints had been penniless—while embracing wealth for themselves.[114] It was unlikely the laity were of significantly higher moral caliber as potential trustees than the clergy, whose faults were only human, and he suspected that any attempt to transfer ecclesiastical property "but for yt in dyuysynge what way they shold be better bestowed, such ways as at the fyrste face semed very good, and for the comfort and helpe of pore folke very charytable, appered after up-

---

110. "An Answer to a Letter," Chapter Six: Of Restitution, in Guy, *Christopher St German*, 142.
111. Ibid.
112. *An Answer to a Letter*, 143.
113. *Complete Works of St. Thomas More*, vol. 9, 74.
114. Ibid., 78.

pon reasonynge, more likely within a while to make many beggers mo, then to releue them yt are all redy."¹¹⁵ Nor did More imagine other secular benefits would be attained, since these changes would not ultimately serve "to mow stande the realme in great stede, and be an increase of the kynges honour, wyth a great strength for the lande and a gret suerty for the prynce, and a great sparynge of the peoples charge / well appered after uppon farther reasonynge, to be the clene contrary, and of all other wayes the worste."¹¹⁶

More repeated his argument from *Supplication of Souls* that the logic of turning property over to a better use would not necessarily stop with the church's endowments: lots of men's property "myght be better vsed yf some other had it."¹¹⁷ More, the former chancellor, had warned Simon Fish that if the first step would be to take church assets, with the justification that they were not being used as intended or could be put to better use, then the next step would be to apply this question of use to everyone's property:

> Now, some landowners may perhaps suppose that their case will not seem the same as that of the clergy because they think that the clergy have their possessions given them for purposes which they do not fulfill, and that if their possessions happen to be taken from them, it will be done on that basis, and so the lay landowners are out of that danger because, they think, such a cause or basis or perception is lacking and cannot be found with respect to them and their inheritance. Certainly if anyone, whether priest or lay person, has lands in the giving of which has been attached any condition which he has not fulfilled, the giver may with good reason take such advantage of that as the law gives him. But on the other side, whoever would advise princes or lay people to take from the clergy their possessions on the basis of such general allegations as that they do not live as they should, or do not use their possessions well, and would claim that therefore it would be a good deed to take them by force and dispose of them better—we dare boldly say to whoever gives this argument, as now does this beggars' spokesman, that we would counsel you to take a good look at what would follow ... the despoilment and robbery of all who have anything.¹¹⁸

---

115. Ibid., 82–84.
116. Ibid., 84.
117. Ibid., 77.
118. More, *Four Last Things*, 109–10.

It is clear from this passage that More believed that donors or their families had remedies to retrieve gifts that were not being used for their purposes and that the new impulse would take that away, first from ecclesiastical gifts and then perhaps from all donors of any property. More was unaware of any other legal precedent that gave the right to divert gifts from one purpose to another one. In short, cy-près appeared, as of 1529, to be unknown, even in the court of Chancery, which had jurisdiction over uses. Neither More nor Saint German drew on it in their debate over the use of church property and of frustrated gifts.

Covetousness and Waste

The after-effects of the seizures were somber, as the new use of the "abused" endowments and donations did not live up to expectations. Cromwell's propaganda campaign had raised hopes that he had probably never intended to fulfill, and although the Edwardian chantry statute had promised to preserve and augment all benevolent aspects of chantry and guild property, it was not perceived to have been successful in doing that. As Dickens points out, "it can only have damaged the reputation of Protestantism whenever a Protestant government allowed any functioning almshouse to disappear, or to survive merely through local initiative."[119] Scarisbrick observes that the second dissolution of monasteries ultimately produced "nothing like the scale that could have been expected" of charitable, educational, and religious establishments—only six new sees, two colleges, and a few royal grammar schools that were charged with alms and highway repair in order to make good on some of the charitable works lost in the seizures.[120] Bucholz estimates that "half of the 500 or so pre-Reformation charitable institutions for the poor had been closed."[121] Additionally, as Kreider writes, "the dispo-

---

119. Dickens, *English Reformation*, 238.
120. J. J. Scarisbrick, "Henry VIII and the Dissolution of the Secular Colleges," in *Law and Government Under the Tudors: Essays Presented to Sir Geoffrey Elton Regius Professor of Modern History in the University of Cambridge on the Occasion of his Retirement*, ed. Claire Cross et al. (Cambridge: Cambridge University Press, 1988), 64–65.
121. Robert Bucholz and Newton Key, *Early Modern England, 1485–1714: A*

sition of the chantry properties heavily favored the new nobility and the upper gentry who had governmental connections," with the result that, "by mid-1548 [the government] appeared to have wholly forgotten its beneficent purposes."[122] The citizens were less forgetful. Fifty years later, when John Stowe produced his 1598 *Survey of the Cities of London and Westminster,* he included a comprehensive account of the hospitals, noting both those "that have been of old time" and those "now presently are." He listed their founders, their suppressions and re-endowments, and citizen involvement in rescuing them. A record was still being kept, and Stowe counted the dead founders and the destitute among the victims of the seizures.

Jordan, who generally sees the post-Reformation era as a time of generous secular philanthropy, observes that the loss of the chantries was "the most shattering and irreversible action of reformation in England."[123] Marshall remarks that the chantry acts were "the most traumatic and inordinate demand that the Reformation made on the psyche of the English nation,"[124] while Dickens considers it to have "impinged ... obviously and directly upon the spiritual and social life of the English people ... [and to have] tended to lower the cohesion and morale of the nation."[125] The overall result of the dissolution of the monasteries, the seizures of the intercessory institutions, and the stripping of the parishes, writ large, was an "atmosphere of disillusion."[126] Several municipalities spent years petitioning to have charitable endowments returned to charitable use.[127]

In these decades before cy-près made its formal appearance, a number of popular works were published that accused the English

---

Narrative, 2d ed. (London: Wiley-Blackwell, 2008), 103; Neil S. Rushton, "Monastic Charitable Provision in Tudor England," *Continuity and Change* 16 (2001): 9–44; Neil S. Rushton and Wendy Sige-Rushton, "Monastic Poor Relief in Sixteenth-Century England," *Journal of Interdisciplinary History* 32 (2001): 193–216; Kreider, *English Chantries,* 187.

122. Kreider, *English Chantries,* 201 and 206.
123. W. K. Jordan, *Edward VI: The Threshold of Power. The Dominance of the Duke of Northumberland* (Cambridge, Mass.: Harvard University Press, 1970), 181.
124. Marshall, *Reformation England,* 78.
125. Dickens, *English Reformation,* 240.
126. Ibid., 240–42.
127. Scarisbrick, *Reformation and the English People,* 115.

of being insatiably covetous and castigated their poor relief system. Among these were Philip Stubbes's *The Anatomie of Abuses* (1583), Thomas Lupton's *Too Good to Be True* (1580), Henry Arthington's *Provision for the Poore* (1597), and Robert Hitchcock's *A Pollitique Platt for the Honour of the Prince* (1580).[128] The criticism was not new; rather, it was embarrassingly old. Simon Fish's 1529 *Supplication for the Beggars* had suggested the tremendous benefits to the poor that might be had from the wealth of the church; it was reprinted in 1546 with a *Supplication on the Poor Commons* to reiterate the position. In 1585 a pointed reprint was issued of Richard Tracy's 1544 *Supplication to our Most Sovereign Lord King Henry the Eighth*, which had urged that the poor be cared for with the excess resources of the undeserving monastics.

Even those who had supported the original acts found themselves "betrayed" by the government's failure to live up to its stated motivations for the seizures.[129] Elton finds a "quickly growing disillusionment after the Dissolution ... within some two generations, the sight of these ruins helped to bring on feelings of deep regret and real fears of sacrilege, feelings of which at the time no trace manifested itself."[130] Margaret Aston and Eamon Duffy both observe that a nostalgic antiquarianism grew among conservative Anglicans not long after the property had been redistributed—more so even than amongst the recusants, who could imagine the events as a setback before the eventual triumph of the Militant Church. When John Donne converted from Catholicism to Anglicanism, he wrote of the Church of England as "robb'd and tore."[131] Michael Sherbrook thought that the social fabric of the commonwealth had decayed since the dissolutions, with more poverty and worse governance than before.[132] The Tudors had discredited themselves.

---

128. Philip Stubbes, *The Anatomie of Abuses*, ed. Margaret Jane Kidnie, Renaissance English Text Society, seventh series, vol. 27 (Tempe: Arizona Center for Medieval and Renaissance Studies, 2002), 167–77.
129. Ibid., 110–11.
130. Elton, *Reform and Reformation*, 240–43.
131. Cited in Duffy, *Saints, Sacrilege and Sedition*, 29, from Holy Sonnet XVIII; see also Duffy's chapter "Bare Ruin'd Choirs: Remembering Catholicism in Shakespeare's England" in *Saints, Sacrilege and Sedition*, 233–53.
132. Duffy, *Saints, Sacrilege and Sedition*, 249.

The complaints started early and lingered. In the 1537 examination of Robert Aske by Thomas Cromwell, Aske contended that the suppression of the monasteries had been "greatly to the decay of the comyn welth."[133] Prior to the Second Chantry Act, Henry Brinklow published his 1542 *Complaint of Roderick Mors unto the Parliament House of England* in which he argued that the assets of the church had not been used charitably, unlike in German lands. Robert Crowley concurred in 1550 in his *Epigrams*, such as "On Abbayes," in which he "mused on thynges that have in my time bene done by great kings," thinking of the abbeys, "which are nowe suppressed all by a lawe." He lamented: "what occasion was here, to provide for learninge, and make povertye chere." Instead, the people go "astraye" and the poor "famishe everye daye."[134]

Crowley was no Catholic; he blamed the failures of proper redistribution on the unworthiness of the people and ended by asking God to care for his "chosen sorte." He even more pointedly described the transfer of wealth from the care of the poor to the hands of the elite in "Of Almes Houses," in which a merchant returned to England after years away and could not find the local hospital he remembered. Instead he found "a lordely house" and he exclaimed with joy, "Is my contrey so wealthy, / That the verye beggers houses / Be builte so gorgiouslye?" No, a beggar replied, "We are all turned oute, / And ley and dye in corners, / Here and there aboute. / Men of greate riches / Have boughte our dwellinge place, / And whan we crave of them, / They turne awaye their face."[135]

Crowley promised God's vengeance on England because of her failure to use the resources of the church wisely. His 1548 *Informacion and Peticion Agaynst the Oppressours of the Poore Commons* claimed that the "possessioners" of the realm did not understand their role as "stewards" of their wealth—with the consequence that the Anabaptist solution to social problems was increasingly popular. Crowley

---

133. Mary Bateson and Thomas Cromwell, "Aske's Examination," *The English Historical Review* 5.19 (1890): 562.
134. Robert Crowley, *The Select Works of Robert Crowley*, ed. J. M. Cowper, Early English Text Society (London: N. Trübner, 1872), 7.
135. Ibid., 11–12.

agreed that the law of nature demanded that everyone had inherited from Adam equal rights to property, although, he added, "take me not here that I should go about by these words to persuade men to make all things common." Instead, those who refused to give alms were to blame: "And if any of them perish through your default, know then for certainty that the blood of them shall be required at your hands. If the impotent creatures perish for lack of necessaries, you are the murderers for you have their inheritance and do not minister unto them."[136] Canon law had warned: those who divert the alms left by testators are the murderers of the poor. In secularizing the property of the church, the patrimony of the poor, England had appropriated their inheritance and now the people, in refusing to give alms, would bear the curse.

In the midst of social unease over the effect of the dissolutions, those who joined in the assorted rebellions of 1549 demanded, along with an evangelical return to Henry's Six Articles, the recovery of chantry lands and the resumption of prayers for the dead.[137] In Cranmer's response to the Fifteen Articles of the rebels, he gave examples of how canon law undermined nations, using his own prepared compilation of "A Collection of Tenets Extracted from Canon Law, Shewing the Pretensions of the Church of Rome." He cited in particular the rules against alienation, which tied up property in the church, preventing it from being put to other uses, and what he claimed was the canon law principle "that none of the clergy may give any thing to the relief of the commonweal and necessity of their own realm, without the consent of the bishop of Rome."[138] This proved that canon law was not made "for the common weal of all realms" but rather "for the private weal of the bishop of Rome, and of his bishops and clergy."[139] It was a tellingly defensive move.

In his sermon in St. Paul's Cathedral in July of 1549 against the

---

136. Robert Crowley, "Information and Petition," in *The English Renaissance: An Anthology of Sources and Documents*, ed. Kate Aughterson (New York: Routledge, 2002), 156.

137. Scarisbrick, *Reformation and the English People*, 83; MacCulloch, *The Boy King*, 121.

138. Cranmer, *Memorials*, vol. 3, 167 and 72–73, quoting X 3.9.3.

139. Ibid.

rebels, Cranmer accused them of being focused on temporal things, disobedient to King and to Christ. As MacCulloch shows, Cranmer aimed the accusation of "covetousness" back against those who complained of it: it was the rebels themselves who thought only of the treasures of the earth rather than the treasures of heaven.[140] When Thomas Lever issued a blistering series of sermons in 1550 criticizing the use of the endowments, the response of the government was again to criticize those who had noticed the covetousness of the state as being covetous themselves. *Honi soit qui mal y pense.*

MacCulloch demonstrated that this theme of covetousness was widely embraced in the aftermath of the 1549 rebellion, and it was made "the centrepiece of a government-sponsored preaching campaign in July 1551" when, in the midst of a sweating sickness, the Privy Council "ordered the bishops to stir people to prayer, 'to refrain their greedy appetites from that insatiable serpent of covetousness, wherein most men are so infected, that it seemeth each one would devour another without charity or any godly respect to the poor, to their neighbours, or to the commonwealth.'"[141] The bishops were blamed for their impotence. To this accusation, Bishop Ridley retorted to John Cheke that it was difficult for the church to preach on these matters at a time when "either ungodly men, or unreasonable beasts, be suffered to pull away and devour the good and godly learned preachers' livings."[142]

Martin Bucer also perceived a pervasive spirit of covetousness, writing to Calvin and the Marquis of Dorset about the *pleonexia* afflicting England.[143] Bucer began to use the word "sacrilege" to describe the devouring of the church's resources by laymen.[144] In a letter to Hooper from 1550, in the midst of the vestments controversy, Bucer argued that it would be better to focus on the fact that church property was in a worse position than ever. Fundamentally,

---

140. MacCulloch, *The Boy King*, 151–52.
141. MacCulloch, *The Boy King*, 153.
142. Ibid.
143. Andrew Edward Harvey, ed., *Martin Bucer in England* (Marburg: Heinrich Bauer, 1906), 135.
144. Harvey, *Martin Bucer*, 137; Constantin Hopf, *Martin Bucer and the English Reformation* (London: Blackwell, 1946), 106.

"in the holy assembly there is no justice for the poor: the Church has no goods."[145] And yet, Bucer wrote, returning to the theme of vestments that Hooper had originally raised, "[T]o affirm that these Vestments abused by Antichrist, have become so contaminated, that they can be suffered in no Church, even though she knows her Christ and prizes her liberty in all things, is a proposition which I scruple to adopt."[146] Papist vestments could be allowed in the churches, despite their abuse by the Antichrist. There was coherence here between Bucer's view of vestments, which could be superstitiously treated yet still should be tolerated, and his view of gifts that had been made to superstitious ends. The gifts had not been so corrupted by their origins (donations for simoniacal prayers) that they could not be of good use. Neither God nor His church should be defeated by the imperfections of man, which would be manifold in a church that had to include the reprobate as well as the elect. To throw out anything touched with imperfections would risk sacrilege: "What Scripture is there which teaches, that power has been given, to the devil, or to bad men, to render bad or impious in itself, through their abuse, any good creature of God—good even in signification and suggestion?"[147] No, the testimony of the Bible (Romans 14, 1 Corinthians 8–9, and 1 Timothy 4) was clear that it is not possible "that the impious, by their abuse, so vitiate the good creatures of God, [that] they cannot subserve a pious use to any pious man."[148] A canon lawyer might have added: *abusus non tollit usum*.

145. George Cornelius Gorham, ed., *Gleanings of a Few Scattered Ears, during the Period of the Reformation in England* (London: Bell and Daldy, 1857), 201; Martin Bucer, *Martini Buceri Scripta Anglicana* (Basel: Pietro Perna, 1577), 706: "in sacro coetu nulla iusta cura pauperum geritur, Ecclesia nullum habet peculium."

146. Gorham, ed., *Gleanings of a Few Scattered Ears*, 203; Bucer, *Scripta Anglicana*, 707: "dicere, has vestes per Antichristi abusum sic esse contaminatas, ut nulli Ecclesiae, quantumvis aliqua Christum suum, et rerum omnium libertatem nosset et coleret, sint permittendae, religio sane mihi est."

147. Gorham, ed., *Gleanings of a Few Scattered Ears*, 203–4; Bucer, *Scripta Anglicana*, 707: "Quae Scriptura docet, diabolo, vel malis hominibus eam esse factam potestatem, ut abusu suo ullam queant Dei bonam creaturam, et bonam etiam significando, et admonendo per se malam facere, et impiam?"

148. Gorham, ed., *Gleanings of a Few Scattered Ears*, 206; Bucer, *Scripta Anglicana*, 709: "Aut posse impios abusu suo bonas dei [sic] creaturas per se ita vitiare, ut nemini pio ad pium usum queant deservire."

In a letter to Cranmer dated December 8 of 1550, Bucer began by acknowledging the problem of vestments, about which Cranmer had asked. But then his frustration showed with this particular English obsession:

> Vestments have given rise to superstition in some, and to pernicious contention in others—it would be far better to abolish them: nevertheless, in this order, and on this condition; that we should first abolish all sacrileges; false and impious doctrines; perverse, superstitious, and profane disciplines, and rites; and all spoliation of Churches ... that there should be an end of all Simony, all sacrileges, by which Parishes are at this day horribly despoiled, schools ruined, and Christ's poor starved. Let faithful and suitable ministers be sought for every Parish, and let there be given to them as much as is needed for the decent and pious maintenance of themselves and their ministry.... Let Schools, and endowments for the really needy, be restored. Let provision be made for the King's Majesty, for the State, for individuals, as far as is needful from legitimate sources ... Piously has the tyranny of the Roman Antichrist been banished from this kingdom; banished, also, be the methods which he introduced of despoiling Churches, subverting Schools, defrauding Christ's poor.[149]

When Parker reprinted much of Bucer's letter in a 1566 tract, he left out this trenchant criticism of the despoliation of church property and Bucer's suggestion that the seizures were the sacrilegious work of the Antichrist.

Meanwhile the people were haunted, and by a new kind of ghost. Keith Thomas notes that medieval ghosts tended to be concerned with unpaid tithes, whereas seventeenth-century English ghosts were fixated on the misappropriation of property.[150] Finucane finds only

---

149. Gorham, ed., *Gleanings of a Few Scattered Ears*, 219; Bucer, *Scripta Anglicana*, 683: "vestes has, esse occasioni aliis ad superstitionem, aliis ad perniciosam contentionem: praestare, eas tollere: verum hoc ordine et hac ratione, ut tollantur et aboleantur ante omnia cuncta sacrilegia, falsae et impiae doctrinae, perversae, superstitiosae, et prophanae disciplinae, ac rituum: denique omnis etiam Ecclesiarum despoliationis ... fac cessant omnis symonia, omnia sacrilegia, quibus Parochiae hodie horrendum in modum despoliantur, et scholae vastantur, pauperes Christi enecantur. Quaerantur singulis Parochiis fidi, et idonei ministri, et detur his quantum eis ad bene, pieque vivendum et ministrandum opus fuerit.... Restituantur scholae, et vere egentium procurationes. Quaeratur Regiae Mai. Reipub. privatis, quibus opus habent viis legitimis.... Pie exclusa est hoc Regno Antichristi Rom. tyrannis, excludantur et rationes quas ille invexit, despoliandi ecclesias, evertendi scholas, defraudandi pauperes Christi."

150. Keith Michael Thomas, *Religion and the Decline of Magic: Studies in Popular*

two medieval ghosts who came back from the dead to ask that their last wishes be carried out—but many medieval ghosts who needed the living to make amends on their behalf.[151] Jean-Claude Schmitt, surveying ghosts from Late Antiquity to the late Middle Ages, agrees; he did not find a single ghost who haunted the dead over anger about last wishes not being honored, but rather many who begged for suffrages.[152] Medieval ghosts had needed the help of the living to rectify mistakes that the ghosts had made in life; post-Reformation ghosts by contrast were more likely to blame the living for their negligence or to warn that their heirs were not receiving their due.[153] This change is probably symptomatic of anxious consciences. At times the link to the seizures was made explicit: Henry Spelman wrote a book of warnings in 1632, *The History and Fate of Sacrilege*, to show that everyone who had profited from church lands had later suffered for their greed. The topic was so sensitive that his book could not be published until 1698.[154]

This anxiety seems to have been particular to England, since the material and spiritual concerns of English ghosts differed from those of Reformed continental ghosts, who appeared in order to cast doubt on the elect status of the departed.[155] In England a new form of propitiation of the dead was the result, since, as Keith Thomas argues, the sixteenth and seventeenth centuries "saw an obsessive concern with the provision of physical memorials to the dead in place of the

---

Beliefs in Sixteenth and Seventeenth Century England (New York: Oxford University Press, 1997), 599.

151. Finucane, *Appearances of the Dead*, 86.

152. Jean-Claude Schmitt, *Ghosts in the Middle Ages: The Living and the Dead in Medieval Society*, trans. Teresa Lavender Fagan (Chicago: University of Chicago Press, 1999), 65.

153. Finucane, *Appearances of the Dead*, 129–33; cf. Schmitt, *Ghosts in the Middle Ages*, 82.

154. Scarisbrick, *Reformation and the English People*, 106. Gibson's *Life of Sir Henry Spelman* claimed that the text was considered too offensive to publish even in 1666.

155. Bruce Gordon, "Malevolent Ghosts and Ministering Angels: Apparitions and Pastoral Care in the Swiss Reformation," in *The Place of the Dead: Death and Remembrance in Late Medieval and Early Modern Europe*, ed. Bruce Gordon and Peter Marshall (Cambridge: Cambridge University Press, 2000), 87–109. Natalie Zemon Davis, *Society and Culture*, 96.

monasteries and chantries ... it was the great age of architectural tombs."[156] This was a new way to pay tribute to the dead, who were no longer cared for by the old commemorations. But Thomas points out that these new memorials also often boasted of the great philanthropic works of the deceased, another novelty. As it would turn out, this would be one function of cy-près: to preserve the works of the dead and their secular commemoration through the trusts and endowments they had left behind.

William Shakespeare and his collaborator John Fletcher reflected on these themes in the 1613 play *Henry VIII*. In a late scene, after Wolsey's fall and death, Griffith offered words of praise about Wolsey to Katherine, persuading her to "honor" the man she "most hated." Griffith made the Ipswich and Oxford endowments the centerpiece of Wolsey's life, as though it were his generosity that had enabled them:

> And though he were unsatisfied in getting
> (Which was a sin), yet in bestowing, madam,
> He was most princely. Ever witness for him
> Those twins of learning that he raised in you,
> Ipswich and Oxford; one of which fell with him,
> Unwilling to outlive the good that did it;
> The other, though unfinished, yet so famous,
> So excellent in art, and still so rising,
> That Christendom shall ever speak his virtue.[157]

These lines express humanist sentiments, both in their praise of learning and in their positing that money badly acquired could be put right through a charitable use. They implicitly call for Oxford to be protected through the vicissitudes of time, to make good Wolsey's legacy when the man, finally humbled, could not. These are all motives for a cy-près power, to allow the best parts of men to live on through endowments that might need to change but would never need to die. If Wolsey's noblest deeds faltered, then all that he would leave behind in this world would be the more vicious or pathetic aspects of his life.

---

156. Thomas, *Ends of Life*, 604; Finucane, *Appearances of the Dead*, 103–4.
157. *Henry VIII*, Act IV, scene II, lines 48–68, in William Shakespeare, *The Complete Works*, ed. Alfred Harbage (New York: Viking Penguin, 1969), 809.

This humanist sensibility flowered into a philanthropic ideal of the seventeenth century, an ideal that tried to offer succor to all in the foundations of great works that would live on and preserve the memory of the donor in perpetuity. These works redeemed the imperfect lives of their donors. Much later it would be possible to question whether someone like Cecil Rhodes should be allowed to have his memory honored through his scholarships, built as they were on colonial suffering. But for a time in the early modern world, it was possible to move away from anxiety about the irredeemability of works done from tainted money and toward a new model in which blood might come out in the wash and in which society had a positive duty to the dead to help them be made clean, making usurious profits work for everyone through charitable ventures. This was all the more necessary because the kinds of fortunes that were required for grand philanthropic ventures were unlikely to have been assembled without profiting from an economy that was, in medieval terms, increasingly usurious and bound to the routine use of credit and debt. Indeed, in the seventeenth and eighteenth centuries an economy of usury was almost impossible for even the middling classes to avoid. In the late middle ages, the taint of usury would drag down even innocent recipients of its proceeds. Cy-près rulings inadvertently carried this older idea—that the children of a usurer should not inherit his money, lest they be hurt by it—into a new era, keeping the heirs away from anything given with a charitable intent, except, at best, a small portion that the judge might reserve from the larger sum if the heirs were found to be poor.

More prosaically, the lingering charge of covetousness would apply pressure to the Tudors to make good the seizures by constructing and adequately funding a poor relief system and finding ways to support charitable enterprises. A similar pattern held in many areas on the continent where state confiscation had appropriated church property rather than turning it over to a poor relief system, with the consequence that the governing authorities often had to make some kind of recompense in order to prevent escalating resentments. Timothy Fehler has illustrated the path to poor relief systematization in Emden (in Saxony), where, starting in 1529, the local count responded to the Reformation by seizing most church property for himself, leaving only a Franciscan monastery, the funds of the brotherhoods, and lay poor relief works. Fehler details numerous complaints, made in the aftermath of the count's actions, about inadequate resources for poor relief and for the upkeep of the remaining churches. Stop-gap measures were applied: voluntary assessments, a lottery, and the application of half of all civil fines to poor relief efforts. Ultimately the Franciscan monastery was taken into custody and formally turned over to a new use, the brotherhoods applied their resources to the poor, and new, state-funded poor relief institutions were created.[158] The behavior of the count in taking church property was long remembered and criticized: decades after the Reformation, resentment toward the count for his greed and lack of concern for the common good remained.[159] A similar pattern seems to have held in other regions where church property ended up largely in the hands of the state, as in Sweden, where the appropriations helped spur nationalist sentiment and the rise of Pietism, or in the hands of the nobility in coordination with the monarchy, as in Denmark, where the state took a very early role in creating a new poor relief system to quell dissent.[160] The duchy of Württemberg, where Duke Ulrich had conducted notorious depredations of church assets only to enrich himself, was left embittered. Ulrich's son, Christoph, wisely invested in social and educational programs in order to restore trust in the dynasty.[161] In England, cy-près powers, to save superstitious gifts for good purposes and prevent charitable uses from floundering, would be one part of this enterprise to redeem the reputation of the monarchy.

---

158. Fehler, *Poor Relief and Protestantism*, 1, 78–80, 89, 98–99, 135, and 137–44.

159. Ibid., 81 and 145–46.

160. Lars Bo Kaspersen and Johannes Lindvall, "Why No Religious Politics? The Secularization of Poor Relief and Primary Education in Denmark and Sweden," *Archives Européennes de Sociologie* 49 (2008): 119–43.

161. Henry J. Cohn, "Church Property in the German Protestant Principalities," in *Politics and Society in Reformation Europe*, ed. E. I. Kouri and T. Scott (London: Palgrave, 1987).

Bucer, Bill, and the Bishops

The legitimacy of canon law in England was attacked repeatedly in the Reformation, by king, Parliament, and lawyers who wanted statutory and common law to triumph over foreign imports. The 1532 Submission of the Clergy gave to the king the power to make canon law, and the next year the Parliamentary Act in Restraint of Appeals set England free from universal canon law and from the pope's ultimate authority over religious matters in England. The study of canon law was formally (although as Helmholz has shown, not effectively) abolished in 1535. Further statutes followed prohibiting the use of any canon law that conflicted with common law, and there were repeated calls by statute in 1533, 1535, 1543, and 1549 to create a committee of thirty-two clergymen to "set in order and establish all such laws ecclesiastical as shall be thought by the King's Majesty and them convenient to be used."[162] Cromwell created a committee of four to draft English canon law in 1535, but the completed project was never enacted.[163] Gerald Bray observes that "it was not in Cromwell's interest to tie himself to a code which would have been much too conservative for his taste."[164] Indeed, the 1535 canons were not very novel and included nothing at all that resembled cy-près. They set forth only minimal requirements that executors carry out the will of the testator and that bishops supervise the disbursement of the intestate's goods to the wife, children, nearest relatives, and to pious uses.[165]

In 1551, a committee of thirty-two (eight bishops, eight civil lawyers, eight common lawyers, and eight theologians) were formally set to the task of writing a code of church law, the *Reformatio legum ecclesiasticarum*. Archbishop Cranmer, who was already working on

---

162. 35 Henry 8 c. 16.
163. F. D. Logan, "The Henrician Canons," *Bulletin of the Institute of Historical Research* 47 (1974): 99–103.
164. Gerald Bray, *Tudor Church Reform: The Henrician Canons of 1535 and the Reformatio Legum Ecclesiasticarum*, in the Church of England Record Society, vol. 8 (Woodbridge, England: Boydell Press, 2000), xxix.
165. Ibid., 31.15, 127. 31.4, and 131. 31.11.

the project, directed it.¹⁶⁶ But the new laws were blocked, first by an angry duke of Northumberland, regent for the young Edward VI, and then by Elizabeth I. There was one provision in particular in the canon law collection that may have provoked Northumberland. This was a limited cy-près power that the *Reformatio* gave to the bishops, and it appears to have been inspired by Martin Bucer.

After Martin Bucer was cast out of Strasbourg in 1549, he came to England at Cranmer's invitation and stayed with him at Lambeth and Croydon.¹⁶⁷ His arrival was, as Greschat notes, sponsored by John Hales, who was also a friend of Somerset, and Bucer arrived "at the very climax of a grave and all-encompassing crisis" due to inflation, enclosures, revolt, and "an explosive increas[e] in poverty."¹⁶⁸ In his earlier work Bucer had served as an expert on reform for German cities, where he had instituted poor relief systems, among other projects. He had found in that work that local magistrates were usually reluctant to embrace his vision of a powerful but reformed church that had its own disciplinary functions and was not merely subject to civil authority.¹⁶⁹ In fact, according to Bucer, civil authorities should be subject to the church in spiritual matters, if the church was reformed, although if the church was undisciplined, then the state ought to intervene.¹⁷⁰ Both were required to "see[k] a common good ... in loving-kindness and care for one's neighbours."¹⁷¹

---

166. Ibid., xli–liv. Sachs notes that Cranmer, despite producing a "Collection of Tenets from the Canon Law," generally "does not show a deep learning in canon law." Leslie Raymond Sachs, "Thomas Cranmer's *Reformatio Legum Ecclesiasticarum* of 1553 in the Context of English Church Law from the Later Middle Ages to the Canons of 1603" (Ph.D. diss., The Catholic University of America, 1982), 100; James C. Spalding, *The Reformation of the Ecclesiastical Laws of England, 1552* (Kirksville, Mo.: Sixteenth Century Journal Publishers, 1992).

167. Basil Hall, "Martin Bucer in England," in *Martin Bucer: Reforming Church and Society*, ed. D. F. Wright (Cambridge: Cambridge University Press, 1994), 144–60.

168. Greschat, *Martin Bucer,* 227–30.

169. Ibid., 108.

170. Martin Greschat, "The Relation between Church and Civil Community in Bucer's Reforming Work," trans. Penelope R. Hall, in *Martin Bucer: Reforming Church and Community*, ed. D. F. Wright (Cambridge: Cambridge University Press, 1994), 17–31.

171. Hall, "Martin Bucer in England," 155.

Bucer had consistently advocated for this pattern of mutual reform and was unusual among reformers in pushing back against secular power on behalf of the church's authority.

Bucer lived until 1551, during the lead up to the *Reformatio*, on which, as Sachs argues, he had a distinct influence. We know from the letters Bucer wrote while in England that the problem of church property was his highest concern. In late November or early December of 1550, he wrote a letter to an unknown recipient on the question of "the demolition of altars." He began by acknowledging that it would be better to have a table rather than an altar, but at the climax of the letter he turned instead to the problem of sacrilege:

> May God grant, however, that, not only the instruments of impiety, but the very impieties themselves of Antichrist, with their abetters and defenders, may be abolished ... and the promoters of these abominations, — sacrilegious men, despoilers and destroyers of Parochial property: so that the whole, pure doctrine of Christ, and firm discipline, may be restored; and that Parishes may be furnished with faithful Ministers, having sufficient maintenance for themselves, for schools, and for the poor.[172]

To turn church property over to secular uses, whether to the state or to the heirs of the donors, was sacrilegious. Instead, property should be reformed and kept. Bucer was asked specifically about this by William Bill in a letter of November 5, 1550. At the time, as Bucer acknowledged in a subsequent letter to Hooper, he was "fully engaged" in "these urgent occupations on behalf of the kingdom of Christ," a probable reference to the *De regno Christi* that he would give to Edward VI as a New Year's Day present.[173] It was only four months before Bucer's death, but despite his ill health he was working strenuously, translating the Bible and writing lectures and sermons in addition to other treatises. Bill, meanwhile, was at that time the Master of St. John's College in Cambridge.

Bill posed a question to Bucer that he described as a "controversy." Ecclesiastics were conducting a lively debate about what to do

---

172. The letter is published in Gorham, ed., *Gleanings of a Few Scattered Ears*, 212.
173. Gorham, ed., *Gleanings of a Few Scattered Ears*, 209; Bucer, *Scripta Anglicana*, 710: "quaeso condona urgentissimis negociis, quae me his diebus detinuerunt causa regni Christi."

with superstitious bequests. Should the "goods and possessions" that were being given (*donabantur*, implying an ongoing problem) "in a superstitious spirit" to ecclesiastical institutions be converted "to the private use of the King or something else."[174] Bill presented two sides of the controversy to Bucer and begged him to find a harmony between them. Bill appeared to believe that the law would return all donations to superstitious causes to the estate, but that Christian love would be better served by keeping gifts that were tainted by superstition—indeed, whose intention (*animus*) was superstitious—but, of course, not using them superstitiously. Bill did not spell out exactly how either option might work, and he described it as an open dispute between the two sides.

Bucer replied twelve days later. Although he devoted more than half of his letter to the vestments controversy, he claimed that the question of donations was "of far greater importance."[175] He acknowledged the general problem of wealth in the church: the clergy ought to live according to the gospel, and Christians ought to serve each other eagerly, giving to each other what they need. Instead, England had large numbers of orphans, widows, the sick, and the poor, along with a badly underfunded church and undereducated clergy. If "we desire to restore the kingdom of Christ," Bucer wrote, "we need to prepare great stores."[176] Those schools "that have survived" (*quae supersunt*) needed to be conserved, and since monasteries were originally schools, they too should be restored for that purpose. It is a sacrilege and embezzlement to use public things for anything other than public good.

Bucer then quoted from Nehemiah 13. Tobiah had appropriated and profaned tithes and temple property. For redemption, the items were thrown out of the room, the chambers cleansed, and then the

---

174. "Altera controversia est, an bona et possessiones quae olim corrupto iudicio aut supersticioso animo donabantur Coenobiis Collegiis aliisve ecclesijs, possint publica autoritate et consensu converti denuo in privatos usus Regis aut aliorum." Letter published in Constantin Hopf, *Martin Bucer and the English Reformation* (London: Blackwell, 1946), 168–69.

175. The letter is published in Harvey, *Martin Bucer in England*, 143–59.

176. Harvey, *Martin Bucer in England*, 155: "Si volumus regnum Christi restitutum, copia magna paranda est."

vessels brought in again with, it seems, some of the original offerings, and given correctly; new tithes, also, were sought out to be the portions for the Levites. In other words, the churches were not to be permanently emptied simply because superstitious offerings had been made. Goods could be thrown out and then almost immediately brought back as new, cleansed offerings. This was affirmed in Roman law too, that ecclesiastical property was sacred and should never be alienated but should rather be restored, as Jovian did after Julian's reign. The secularization of ecclesiastical property in England would provoke God and cause His wrath to pour out over the kingdom. And so, Bucer argued, it was essential that the goods of the church be returned to pious uses, such as the support of schools and universities in order to create suitable pastors, which Bucer thought was the single most pressing issue in England at the time (an opinion that was likely to be favorably received in Cambridge), or to provide for the relief of the deserving poor. No sacred goods should be turned to any other use, either public or private, unless in a time of emergency.

The real problem, Bucer pointed out, was the argument that, to protect the church, a gift made "with a corrupt judgment and superstitious intent" (*corrupto iudicio et superstitioso animo*) ought to be totally rejected. Bucer dismissed that way of looking at donations. That is, he was not suggesting a cy-près power in order to preserve donor intent; he was suggesting it in order to cleanse donor intent. A distinctively Protestant theology underlay this idea. The church was composed of the reprobate and the elect, and it needed to find ways to manage the works of the reprobate (which would inevitably tend toward corruption) so that everything in the world would serve the glory of God. But, Bucer wrote, if the wealth of the church grew too much from taking superstitious donations and applying them to a good use, then the king should have the power to transfer them to a new use, whether public or private, that could serve the salvation of the people. How this would be accomplished without the threat of sacrilege Bucer did not say, but apparently the Reformation might require perpetual correction to undo the works of the reprobate. Bucer was unafraid to call explicitly for "impious" (*nefas*) things to be converted (*convertere*) to any other use (*in ullum alium usum*).[177] He concluded his letter by noting that his argument was in danger of being misunderstood, but that he trusted Bill would know what he meant.

Bucer offered this analysis to a man who would subsequently have many opportunities to pass it on to others. Bill was, along with Edmund Grindal, future archbishop of York, one of the "chaplains ordinary" that Edward VI sent on preaching circuits around the country, visiting from one parish to another.[178] Moreover, Bill, although not on the committee for the *Reformatio*, would also be the lord high almoner for Elizabeth I, meaning that his opinion on charitable bequests would then be particularly likely to reach her ears. His appointment was one of the first acts of Elizabeth's reign, made at a time when she would have been confronted with the problem of what to do with wills made under Mary. The lord high almoner typically had a close relationship with the monarch and was charged with significant preaching responsibilities. In particular, Elizabeth I assigned to Bill the duty of giving the first sermon at Paul's Cross.[179] Additionally, as almoner, William Bill would receive the right to collect deodands (property that has been responsible for someone's death) and the property of *felos de se* (suicides), with the expectation that these items would then be distributed to the poor, and their association with evil thereby wiped clean through almsgiving, or, as Coke would describe it, "distributed in works of charity for the appeasing of God's wrath."[180] This precedent has been described as a forerunner of civil forfeiture; in practice deodands were sometimes offered as restitution to the victim or employed either locally or by the crown for its own purposes.[181] It was a suggestive precedent.

177. Harvey, *Martin Bucer in England*, 156.
178. Patrick Collinson, *Archbishop Grindal 1519–1583: The Struggle for a Reformed Church* (Berkeley: University of California Press, 1979), 60.
179. Mary Morrissey, *Politics and the Paul's Cross Sermons, 1558–1642* (Oxford: Oxford University Press, 2011), 70.
180. Edward Coke, *Institutes of the Laws of England*, vol. 3 (London: A. Crooke et al., 1669), 57.
181. Anna Pervukhin, "Deodands: A Study in the Creation of Common Law Rules," *American Journal of Legal History* 47 (2005): 237–56; Harry Smith, "From Deodand to Dependency," *American Journal of Legal History* 11 (1967): 389–403.

In his *De regno Christi*, Bucer, in sketching the ideal kingdom, elaborated on his idea about what to do with superstitious gifts; he also included answers to other questions that were being posed to him in his correspondence at the time.[182] In chapter 13, "The Fifth Law: Claiming Ecclesiastical Goods for Christ the Lord, and Their Pious Use," he drew on Digest 33.2.16, the Modestinus opinion.[183] Bucer argued:

Men of jurisprudence are of the opinion that donations made to communities hold force, even when given for profane use, so that if anyone bequeathes a legacy on any city for some impure spectacle, which that city is then unwilling to exhibit to its citizens because of Christ's religion, that legatee is not on this account obliged to yield it to the gain of the heir, but it remains in the public control of the city to which it was given: 'The principals of the city are to ignore the claims of the heirs, in regard to the way in which they should use the matter entrusted to them, where the memorial of the testator is celebrated in a manner other than licit, ff.' [*De ususfructu legatorum. l. Legatum.*] How much more, therefore, should the things donated to the churches of Christ be left in their control but converted to pious uses, even though the things donated have by the false clergy been destined for impious Masses and other false cults by error of the donors.[184]

---

182. Hopf, *Martin Bucer*, 104.

183. Bucer had, as Cornel Zwierlein has shown, cultivated the study of Roman law since the beginning of his involvement with the Reformation, as is evident among other places in his 1533 tract on divorce, *Von der Ehe und Ehescheidung aus göttlichem und kaiserlichem Recht*. Cornel Zwierlein, "Reformation als Rechtsreform. Bucers Hermeneutik der lex Dei und sein humanistischer Zugriff auf das römische Recht," in Strohm, ed., *Martin Bucer und das Recht. Beiträge zum internationalen Symposium vom 1. Bis 3. März 2001 in der Johannes a Lasco Bibliothek Emden* (Geneva: Librairie Droz, 2002), 29–81.

184. Martin Bucer, in *De regno Christi*, trans. Wilhelm Pauck, *Melanchthon and Bucer* (Philadelphia: The Westminster Press, 1969), 305; Bucer, *Scripta Anglicana*, 80: "Caeterum, eam censent iuris prudentes habere vim donationes factas rebuspublicis, etiam in usum profanum, ut si quis legasset aliquid civitati cuipiam, pro impuro aliquo spectaculo, quod iam ea civitas propter Christi religionem nolit suis civibus exhiberi, legatum tamen illud haud debere propterea cedere lucro haeredum, sed in iure manere publico civitatis, cui esset legatum: primatesque civitatis adhibitis haeredibus dispicere, in quam rem converti debeat fideicommissum, quo memoria testatoris alio, et licito genere celebretur. Quanto itaque magis, quae donata sunt Christi Ecclesiis, debent in earum relinqui iure, sed in pios usus converti: etiamsi pro impiis Missis, et aliis falsis cultibus, ex errore donantium, per pseudoclerum obtruso, sint Ecclesiis donata?"

It is notable that Bucer did not give the whole passage but focused on the sentence that explicitly eliminated the claim of the heirs. He cut out the argument that the heirs be consulted in the redirection of the gift, and he did not limit the redirection to a deviation in kind but left open any possible pious use.

His take on the redistribution of faulty bequests in *De regno Christi* is consistent with one of his earliest works, the 1523 *Das ym selbs niema[n]t, sonder anderen leben soll. Und wie der mensch da hyn kummen mög.* All things came from God as gifts and endowments and should thus be turned toward God's purposes, not as a countergift but in acknowledgment of God's original plan for society, in which each person would care only for everyone else and not at all for himself. Man was the trustee over the material trust that God had given him on behalf of mankind, and the civil and spiritual authorities were responsible to ensure that selfishness (a misuse of one's endowment for oneself) did not thrive. Bucer suggested that all animals except man lived for the common good. To redirect material objects to the original purpose of the common good was to restore the social harmony and universal welfare that God had intended for mankind. Since caring for each other was humanity's purpose in life, it could not possibly be wrong, by implication, to take a harmful bequest—for the seeking out of private masses and prayers for the dead was surely a "will to drag others with oneself to eternal damnation" and hence a "satanic undertaking"—and turn it to a loving purpose, helping the dead to act as they should have acted. After all, obedience to God ought to extend past death.[185] In contrast to the more tempered vision of Aquinas that a man needed to care for himself first so that he could care for others, under Bucer's vision a man should care nothing for himself—and, by that logic, even less for the goods he left behind when he died or for the goods that his father had disposed of contrary to the will of God.[186] There was certainly no harm to the testator or his heirs if these mistakes were corrected.

---

185. Bucer, *Instruction*, trans. Paul Fuhrmann, 34; "Das ym Sebs niemant," in *Martin Bucers Deutsche Schriften*, vol. 1, 54: "Das doch ye ein teüfelisch fürnemen ist, mit ym selb yederman begeren in ewig verderbnüss zu bringen."
186. Greschat, *Martin Bucer*, 43.

In *De regno Christi,* Bucer acknowledged Ambrose's claim that the wealth of the church had at times been used for charitable purposes. When that wealth was drawn upon in emergency situations, he argued, haste had always been made to return it so that sacrilege would not occur.[187] He repeated this claim in his section on poor relief, the Sixth Law, citing canon law to claim that a fourth of the church's wealth should be used for the poor, which was not sacrilegious.[188] On the other hand, the diversion of donations to serve masses, which originated from having "persuaded the common people that it was far better if these goods were expended on their godless cults," could be redeemed by taking whatever remained of the pious donations ("if, therefore, in the visitations of the churches any remains are found of funds given for the use of the poor") and "restor[ing] them to the use for which they were originally consecrated to the Lord."[189] It was not an entirely coherent argument: Bucer acknowledged that the donors had been "persuaded" to give property to pay for masses, and yet by turning the remains of English church property back to the church for its functions, including poor relief, the intentions of the donors would somehow be restored. But Bucer's suggestion was consistent with his earlier writings on church property while in Strasbourg, where he had stated in his 1539 *Vom Nürnbergischen fridestand* that it was the Catholic church that had violated the intentions of donors in its use of church property, not the Protestants, who had merely restored the property according to the donors' original wishes.[190] Even Bucer, willing to change the use, could not help but frame the redirection of use as being somehow consonant with the donor's intentions.

187. Bucer, *Melanchthon and Bucer,* trans. Pauck, 303, citing Ambrose's *De officiis,* II, chapter 28; Bucer, *Scripta Anglicana,* 78.
188. Bucer, *Melanchthon and Bucer,* trans. Pauck, 310; Bucer, *Scripta Anglicana,* 82.
189. Bucer, *Melanchthon and Bucer,* trans. Pauck, 310; Bucer, *Scripta Anglicana,* 83: "vulgoque hominibus persuaserant, per haec bona longe melius consuli et vivis et defunctis, si impenderentur in impios ipsorum cultus.... Si quid igitur in ecclesiarum visitationibus possit pervestigari, ex huiusmodi in usum pauperum institutis et donatis receptaculis atque facultatibus superesse ... in eos usus, ad quos sunt initio Domino consecrata, restituere."
190. Greschat, *Martin Bucer,* 172–73.

Thomas Sampson acknowledged the contemporaneous support of *De regno Christi* by many bishops: "[S]ince his death, in private talk, they have much approved his book."[191] Bucer was friends with many politically important men, the "Commonwealth men," some of whom would serve on the committee for the *Reformatio*.[192] Cheke, describing Bucer's funeral in Cambridge to the reformer Peter Martyr Vermigli, claimed that it had a crowd of 3000 mourners, an oration by Haddon, and a sermon by Parker.[193] *De regno Christi* was published in Basel in Latin in 1557, and in the same year the section on poor relief, the Sixth Law, was translated into English anonymously and published in England as "A Treatise, How by the Worde of God, Christian mens Almose ought to be distributed." The preface to this translation accused the new beneficiaries of seized church property of defrauding the poor:

> Some craftie Hypocrites, no Friers in coates, but more subtil then Friers in maners, under colour to relieve and mayntain Orphanes, poore wydowes, poore Scolers, and other, gather muche, but put all into their owne purses, or bestowe litle, and that after their owne Fantasie ... and so by all these meanes, and manie other, good mens charities be utterlie abused.[194]

The translator also emphasized the testators' intentions in the selection from Bucer, adding a phrase that was not in the original but that was congruent with Bucer's comments elsewhere: that by diverting the endowments to new uses, "thei passed neither of the Fownders good myndes, nor the lawes of Magistrates."[195]

Although Bucer died shortly before the *Reformatio* committee formally began work, his *De regno Christi* was studied, in a manuscript version, by many of the men on the committee, and a copy was sent to John Cheke, a member of the committee, who distributed Bucer's

---

191. Quoted in Edward VI, *Literary Remains of King Edward the Sixth*, ed. John Gough Nichols, vol. 2 (London: H. B. Nichols and Sons, 1857), 476n.

192. Milton's use of (admittedly select) passages from *De regno Christi* in his *Judgment of Martin Bucer Concerning Divorce* suggests that Bucer's work had an ongoing authority well into the seventeenth century.

193. Gorham, ed., *Gleanings of a Few Scattered Ears*, 238–41.

194. Martin Bucer, *A Treatise, How By the Worde of God, Christian mens Almose ought to be distributed* (1557), Short-Title Catalogue 3965.

195. Bucer, *A Treatise, How By the Worde of God*, 16.

works to those who were interested in them.[196] Edmund Grindal bought a copy of the 1557 edition and annotated it as he studied it.[197] Sachs points out three elements from the text that were particularly influential to the *Reformatio*: Bucer's acknowledgment of the king's headship of the church; his support for poor relief in an organized and unified form (rather than *ad hoc* or personalized giving, which he, like many reformers, detested); and his concern that ecclesiastical property ought to be returned to the church and the church's endowments left untouched by future kings.[198]

Sachs suggests that "Bucer's interest in the restoration of ecclesiastical goods to the church ... [was] not reflected in the *Reform*," but this is not precisely true.[199] Certainly, the authors of the *Reformatio* knew they could not hope to have the seizures returned; indeed, the Catholic Cardinal Reginald Pole would come to the same reluctant conclusion under a monarch much more inclined to re-endow the church.[200] But Bucer's scheme, reified in the *Reformatio*, was to permit a novel cy-près power—but not under that name—under the clerical control of the bishops in an attempt to rebuild the wealth of the church. In return, the church would be solely responsible for charitable work in the state, since all private almsgiving would be discouraged. Thus in this one regard—the re-endowing of the churches and their supervision of poor relief—the *Reformatio* defied the power of the king or of the lay magistracy in favor of ecclesiastical control of property.

The *Reformatio* varied from traditional canon law in a number of

---

196. Bray, *Tudor Church Reform*, lxxii; Greschat, *Martin Bucer*, 240 and 236; Gorham, ed., *Gleanings of a Few Scattered Ears*, 227.
197. Collinson, *Archbishop Grindal*, 56 and 66.
198. Sachs, "Thomas Cranmer's *Reformatio Legum Ecclesiasticarum*," 113–14.
199. Ibid., 116.
200. Henry Gee and William John Hardy, eds., *Documents Illustrative of English Church History* (London: Macmillan, 1896), 395; Loach, *Parliament under the Tudors*, 79. When Cardinal Reginald Pole put together his own set of canons, he did not suggest that gifts for preaching could be redirected to Catholic causes, even though he supported the centralization of church finances, and he seemed unaware of any flexibility on the treatment of pious or charitable gifts. *Reformatio Angliae, Ex Decretis Reginaldi Poli Cardinalis, Sedis Apostolicae Legati, Anno MDLVI* (Rome: Paulus Manutius, 1562).

ways. The freedom to make a will was denied to heretics, the condemned, and assorted categories of persistent and unrepentant sinners. (Canon law, by contrast, was usually more reluctant to declare someone *intestable*, or unable to make a will.)[201] Some who could not make a will, however, were allowed to leave money to "pious causes."[202] This was another inversion, since canon law had been more cautious about accepting into the church gifts that came from sinful activity. Pious causes in the *Reformatio* included the broad understanding of charity advocated by humanists and the Tudors: "towards the release of captives, to the rehabilitation of the poor, [to] the support of orphans, widows and distressed persons of all kinds, especially and above all when something is designated in a testament for the marriage of poor brides, for the clothing of scholars in the universities and for the repair of the public highways."[203] And the *Reformatio* gave a limited cy-près power to the bishop: "when something is left for superstitious rather than for godly reasons, the bishop shall intervene by his authority and ensure that the legacy is distributed to pious causes."[204] This articulation of cy-près is clearly formulated in the terms of the English Reformation, with its distrust of superstitious uses.

However, the rest of the *Reformatio* does not treat failing bequests for purposes in relationship to a broader, equitable cy-près power. Bequests with unfair or impious conditions would pass over to the legatee without the condition attached, as long as he or she swore not to honor the condition, but if the legatee refused to swear not to honor the condition, then the bishop should turn over the bequest

201. Bray, *Tudor Church Reform*, 27.7, 414–15: "Quibus liceat vel non liceat testamentum facere."
202. Ibid., 27.8, 414–17: "Quomodo qui communi iure testamentum condere non possunt, tamen ad pias causas legata relinqu[a/u]nt."
203. Ibid., 27.9, 416–17: "Quae sunt [piae] causae": "Ad pias autem causas hae adnumerantur; cum aliquid ad vinctorum levationem, ad pauperum recreationem, [ad] orphanorum, viduarum et afflictarum omnis generis personarum sustentationem confertur, nominatim et maxime cum ad puellarum tenuium nuptias, ad scholasticorum in academiis degentium nuditatem propellendam, ad publicarum viarum refectionem quippiam testamento designatur."
204. Ibid., 27.9, 416–17: "Quae sunt [piae] causae": "Cum autem quicquam superstitiose potius quam pie legatum fuerit, episcopus auctoritatem suam interponat, ut legatum [in] pias causas distribuatur."

to pious causes. This seems like cy-près in the prerogative sense, but it seeks not to honor charitable impulses, but to stamp out impious gifts. Impossible conditions attached to legacies were considered to be void, which preserved the rights of the legatee or the heirs to the property. No consideration of charitable intent was mentioned.[205] Meanwhile, "if there is no condition which applies to the legacy" or if the legacy gave property that no longer existed or if it was given to buildings that were "either falling down or are in ruins," then the bequest would vanish entirely.[206] Here again, there was no stipulation to consider the intentions of the testator and to weigh whether the condition that had been attached to the legacy represented a charitable or pious intent in some way. Rather than turning a gift to a dilapidated building toward the cost of its restoration, the gift was refused entirely. Instead of discerning a similar purpose for an impossible (because nonexistent) purpose, the legacy returned to the estate. The bishops, in other words, were concerned above all with preventing gifts to superstitious causes and gifts that might be used to build up ruined monasteries, but outside of the Reformation context, they manifested no larger sense of an equitable cy-près power that could transform and rescue charitable gifts.[207] Pious causes received no special treatment in the *Reformatio* except in serving as a destination for superstitious or impious gifts.

This was not because the writers of the *Reformatio* rejected the *ius commune* entirely. When defective wills were nullified, the judge should still "follow the pattern of the testator's will as far as possible," in keeping with "the humanity of the civil laws."[208] The *Reformatio*

205. Ibid., 27.15, 422–23.
206. Ibid., 27.28, 432–33: "Quando legata non valent": "Legata valere non possunt nec praestari debent, cum legatarius a testatoris proposito receda/it; aut si conditio non extiterit ad quam legatum referebatur; aut ipsa si legata quocunque casu vel fortuita calamitate [prius] effluent et colliquescant, quam haereditas adeatur; aut si legata fuerint quae aedificiis sunt coniuncta, nisi vel corruant vel diruantur aedificia."
207. They were, after all, unable even to compel performance of the original terms: *Stinkley v. Chamberlain* (1598), Owen 33. Cited in Jones, *History of the Law of Charity*, 6n.
208. Bray, *Tudor Church Reform*, 27.41, 438–39: "Quando testamentum pro nullo capitur et facultates distribuendae sunt ab administrat{or/ion}ibus, hoc a

closed its section on testaments with the warning that "the boundless greed of men tries to circumvent the will of the deceased." For anything not made clear in the *Reformatio* "recourse must be had concerning them to the authority of the law of Caesar" unless it was the case that Roman law affirmed something "which is either repugnant to these our ecclesiastical decrees or which differs from the common law of our realm."[209] Moreover, the *Reformatio* upheld the traditional rights of patronage, and the *Reformatio* insisted that any alienation, even if done for a necessary and licit reason, required the consent of both the patron and the bishop.[210] The same was true of exchanges.[211]

Gerald Bray observes that the section on testaments in the manuscript version of the *Reformatio* was written in an unknown, nonscribal hand (so, not by any of the most prominent members of the committee nor by a scribe) and was almost unaltered in the final version. This section was tacked on to the end of the manuscript, just after a scribal copy of the sections on the dilapidation of church property and the alienation of church property. It is entirely possible that these last four sections were put together by one person, presumably an expert in property issues, who lacked time to have a scribe recopy the longest and most difficult section on wills.[212] Within this section on testaments, Bray points to the introduction of the *legitim* and the author's use of civil law as the default for all laws that do not contradict statutory or common law as the grounds for supposing that the author was a "specialist in the field."[213] Still, Bray acknowledges, "to what extent it can be regarded as a statement of actual practice is un-

---

iudice debet summe provideri, tantam ut testatoris habeat voluntatis rationem, quant{a/o} omnino maxima esse potest. Quanquam enim legitimum non fuerit testamentum, tamen legum civilium humanitatem libenter sequimur, ut in propriis bonis ultimas hominum voluntates et iudicia nunquam ad se reditura (quantum fieri potest) firma et inviolate conservemus."

209. Ibid., 27.43, 440–41: "dum infinita virorum avaritia mortuorum voluntatem circumvenire molitur.... de illis ad iuris Caesarei auctoritatem confugiendum erit; cum hac tamen exceptione, nihil ut inde sumatur huiusmodi, quod vel cum decretis hisce nostris ecclesiasticis pugnet, vel a municipali iure regni nostri dissideat."

210. Ibid., 16.1 and 16.3, lxxxvi and 322–25.

211. Ibid., 13.1, 302–3.

212. Ibid., lix. Additionally, the author wrote the sections on elections.

213. Ibid., cxxxix.

clear."[214] These sections, in fact, seem to vary between surprising innovation and reliable tradition. Bray suggests that Cranmer may not have read the sections before the final version, but given the very minor textual corrections that were made on them, a more likely scenario is that these sections represented exactly what Cranmer had instructed the author to include and so required none of the more significant revisions that he made to other sections.

W. K. Jordan describes Northumberland's response to the *Reformatio* as "at once bitter and implacable—a view shared more mildly by the strongly entrenched group of common lawyers in the Lower House."[215] Significantly, the ambassador Jehan Scheyfve attested that Northumberland's rejection of the codification was focused on the problem of property, as Northumberland made "an ominous attack on the selfish opposition of certain bishops and clergy to the consideration being given to the goods and property of the Church."[216] Peter Marshall believes Northumberland was wary of "its implication of great autonomy for the ecclesiastical courts,"[217] while Sachs points out that Northumberland "specifically was concerned with clerical opposition to his plans for division and acquisition of church property,"[218] and that his "relations with the bishops and clergy were often strained, perhaps largely because of his interest in garnering wealth from the church."[219] The restrictions on alienation, which was still based on the consensus model, may have raised Northumberland's ire, but given the recent dissolutions and Northumberland's plans for more, he probably also resented the implication that a mere bishop would have the power to redistribute superstitious bequests.

No similar stipulation to the right to divert superstitious gifts was included in the attempted statement of church canons in 1604.[220] But this does not mean that the church had given up on the idea. The 1547 Injunctions issued by Edward VI in the first year of his

    214. Ibid.
    215. Jordan, *Edward VI: The Threshold of Power*, 359.
    216. Ibid.
    217. Marshall, *Reformation England*, 74.
    218. Sachs, "Thomas Cranmer's *Reformatio Legum Ecclesiasticarum*," 61.
    219. Ibid., 228.
    220. *The English Church Canons of 1604*, ed. Rev. C. H. Davis (London: H. Sweet, 1869).

reign under the advice of Somerset had already included new requirements that parishes stock themselves with a poor box, urge the dying to remember the poor, and use money left in wills for lights and other intercessions for the poor box or parish renovations instead.[221] Thus, prior to the Second Chantry Act, the injunctions had already made the diversion of superstitious bequests into a new rule for probate—an antecedent to cy-près doctrine. The bishops seem to have agreed in common that they did have this power to divert superstitious gifts, and they used the Modestinus text to support the idea that this right to divert was always inherent in the *ius commune*. Helmholz has found in a civilian's casebook from around 1600 the notation that "if it bee not possible to observe the saide use, then the ordinarie may convert the same to some other use," and he notes that this is only one such example of many others that he has found.[222] It is reasonable that this idea would have had broad purchase amongst the prelates of the impoverished church.[223] Moreover, this proposal for redistributive powers did not need to conflict with the preference not to commit disherision, because naturally Bill and the bishops would have assumed that these commemorative, superstitious gifts would have been drawn from the "soul's part." Although Elizabeth I would continue to raid superstitious property for the crown, she also allowed bishops to exert some power on their own behalf, especially but not exclusively in probate. Thus in 1571 Edmund Grindal could insist in his injunctions that altars and rood-lofts were to be taken down and the proceeds given "to the use of the Church."[224] The church had a motive to find ways to re-endow itself, especially since the populace understood that the church was an easy target for a predatory government and had become unwilling to give it any more money than the law required.[225]

221. Duffy, *Voices of Morebath*, 115–16; Kreider, *English Chantries*, 187.
222. Helmholz, "The Law of Charity," 119, from Civilian's Casebook c. 1600, Worcestershire Record Office, Worcester, ms. 794.093 BA 2470/B, f. 170v.
223. Christopher Hill, *Economic Problems of the Church: From Archbishop Whitgift to the Long Parliament* (Oxford: Oxford University Press, 1956).
224. Strype, John, ed. *History of the Life and Acts of Edm. Grindal*, vol. 1 (London: John Hartley, 1710), 167.
225. Marshall, *Reformation England*, 83 and 172; Attreed, "Preparation for Death," 52.

324   English Reformation

But even at the end of Elizabeth's reign, works that tried to align civil and common law did not suggest that there was a cy-près doctrine, either in approximation or in favorable treatment of charitable gifts *per se*. John Cowell's *Institutes of the Lawes of England* cited statutes to explain that trusts that were injurious to the lord or prince could be removed (*sustulerunt*) or significantly changed (*aut saltem magna ex parte mutaverunt*).[226] William Fulbecke, in his 1601 *Parallele* comparing civil, canon, and common law, found cy-près—not so named—to be absent from all three systems.[227] He held that civil law interpreted the terms of a grant strictly against the grantor, whose failure to "have expressed his meaning in more full, large, and manifest words" was taken as evidence of the limitations of what he did, in fact, mean.[228] Fulbecke held that common law voided pious gifts made to nonexistent institutions—a point that would be affirmed in ongoing cases.[229] Civil law tended in construction to favor the devisee, while Fulbecke thought that common law was "equally divided betwixt the advantage of the devisee, and the intent of the devisor," suggesting that the focus on donor intent was particular to English concerns.[230] Common law simply voided illegal devises, whether pious or not, honoring the rights of the heir when possible, but not amending them.[231] Fulbecke did not discover a cy-près doctrine in his discussions of either impossible conditions or the equitable construction of conditions.[232]

Henry Swinburne's 1590 *Briefe Treatise of Testaments and Last Wills* has been cited as evidence that the *ius commune* had a rule for the re-

---

226. John Cowell, *Institutiones iuris Anglicani* (Cambridge: Johannes Legat, 1605), 143. In the 1651 English edition: "those inventions of Uses being injurious to the Prince, and to the Lord of the Mannor, are by Acts of Parliament either wholly taken away, or at least for the most part altered." John Cowell, *Institutes of the Lawes of England* (London: Thomas Roycroft, 1651), 152.

227. William Fulbecke, *A Parallele or Conference of the Civill Law, the Canon Law, and the Common Law of this Realme of England* (London: Thomas Wight, 1601).

228. Ibid., 10v.

229. Ibid., 25v.

230. Ibid., 45v–46.

231. Ibid., 46v.

232. William Fulbecke, *The Second Part of the Parallele* (London: Thomas Wight, 1602), 65v–71.

direction of gifts. Swinburne, who was trained in civil law at Oxford before working in the ecclesiastical courts of York, did not use the term cy-près or discuss approximation. Swinburne agreed that deviations were permitted, although he did not use that term either: if a condition to a legacy to a pious cause could be fulfilled by some other means than that specified by the legator, this was allowed. Swinburne at one point contrasted this privilege to other legacies, which he claimed required precise observance of the condition, but later in the text he acknowledged that there were situations in which flexibility could be offered to ordinary, non-pious gifts.[233] Regardless, this is not the same as cy-près: a condition attached to a legacy is not necessarily the purpose that the gift is left to fulfill, and the alteration of a method (or mode) used to fulfill a condition may well leave the purpose untouched, as had been stipulated in the *ius commune*. Moreover, Swinburne gave an excellent, extended discussion of conditions in general and the many ways in which they might become impossible.[234] Sometimes, according to circumstances, they would then be treated as if they had not been written; in other situations they would void the entire gift. But for those "in favour of libertie, or *in favorem piae causae*, when the testator doth bequeath any thing to be imployed to godly uses, for then the condicion which he supposed possible is reiected, and the disposition availeable as pure and simple."[235] It would become an outright gift to the legatee or trustee.

For gifts to pious uses, Swinburne allowed that the condition, even if it was not impossible, could "be effected by other equivalent meanes, though not according to the precise literall forme of the condition," and he permitted similar deviations for non-pious gifts as well, in which conditions could be satisfied "by other meanes" rather than

233. Henry Swinburne, *A Briefe Treatise of Testaments and Last Wills* (London: John Windet, 1590), 31. See also folios 130–130v: "when that which is left conditionallie is to be distributed in *pios usus*: for in these two limitations [for pious uses or "in favour of libertie"] it is sufficient, that the condition be effected by other equivalent meanes, though not according to the precise literall forme of the condition." See generally folios 128v–130v for limitations on the strict application of conditions.
234. Ibid., 121–28.
235. Ibid., 125v.

strictly.[236] However, Swinburne thought that conversion of use was better than an outright gift in some cases: "when the condition cannot be performed in such manner as is prescribed in the condition: as for example, the testator giveth a summe of money if so manie sermons be made in such a church within such a time, during which time the church is interdicted, by occasion whereof the condition can not be accomplished. In this case the disposition is not absolutely void, but the monie maie be converted to some godlie use."[237] Swinburne changed the traditional *ius commune* example of masses to sermons, and he left out the suggestion that the conversion should be made with the consent of the interested parties. He cited the sixteenth-century jurist Simone de Praetis (many of Swinburne's sources were contemporary jurists) and also Digest 50.8.6(4), on diminishing the terms or changing the use of a gift that was insufficient to its end. He did not mention the Modestinus passage. Though Swinburne did not discuss consensus in that example, he did acknowledge elsewhere that the beneficiary of a gift could "consent that the same bee accomplished in other manner"; that is, the terms of the gift could be reworked through consensus even for cases in which the condition was not impossible.[238] This was certainly not the common law understanding that would develop alongside cy-près in the seventeenth century.

Swinburne revised the 1611 edition himself and included some English statutes. Neither the 1640 nor the 1677 edition had anything new on charitable bequests. By the 1793 seventh edition, however, several common law findings were added to the end of Swinburne's text, including the fact that a charitable intention expressed in a will would survive even if a will was invalid; that surplus funds should go to the charity itself (citing the *Case of Thetford School*, discussed in the next chapter); that "where a devise of charity was to the poor indefinitely, in such case Equity gives the Disposal thereof to the King; because the Word Poor extends to all the Poor in Great-Britain."[239] The

---

236. Ibid., 130.
237. Ibid., 130v. Swinburne also described the difference between a condition and a mode, 137v, but treated almost exclusively of conditions, probably because modal gifts passed much more easily, no matter what difficulty arose.
238. Ibid., 129v.
239. Henry Swinburne, *A Treatise of Testaments and Last Wills*, 7th ed., (Dublin: Elizabeth Lynch, 1793), I § 16 †70.

editor admitted that civil law would treat gifts to "the poor" differently. These common law additions included a requirement that the stipulations of a gift must be adhered to strictly. No heir could modify the terms of a gift, even by the request of the charity itself.[240] This dispossessing of the heir, which is key to the practice of cy-près, is treated as a feature of common law alone, not originating in the *ius commune*.

Statutes and Readings

When Elizabeth came to power, there were new "superstitious" gifts that had been made during the reign of Mary. These gifts could no longer be framed as given in some innocent state of error. Instead, they meant to "reduce this Realme" to "darkness and superstition" and to "decay" the possessions of the queen.[241] They were motivated by their obedience to foreign powers, but the queen, in taking this property, given to treacherous purposes, would employ it "to suche good profitable and godly purposes and uses," such as the public weal, the advancement of the true religion, and whatever "shall seme good." Privileged chantries that belonged to protected universities could be reformed by the queen to whatever "shalbe thought meete and convenient."[242] Elizabeth I sent her gentlemen-pensioners to look for suspicious property, armed with newly strengthened injunctions, issued upon her ascension, that forbade even private ownership of superstitious items within the house.[243] But she was also aware of the need to rescue what charitable gifts could be found and to enforce charitable measures to avert the widespread criticism of Tudor covetousness. It took until the 1580s to make up the loss in poor relief services that had been disrupted by the dissolutions, and the years of famine in the 1590s saw a noticeable decline in bequests.[244]

---

240. Ibid., I, § 16, †71.
241. 1 Elizabeth 1 c. 24.
242. 1 Elizabeth 1 c. 24 § 10.
243. 1559 Injunctions, Section 35, in Gee and Hardy, *Documents Illustrative*, 433.
244. Paul Slack, *Poverty and Policy in Tudor and Stuart England* (London: Longman, 1988), 13. Scarisbrick, *Reformation and the English People*, 187, suggests that it took until the 1630s. See also Ian W. Archer, *The Pursuit of Stability: Social Relations in Elizabethan London* (Cambridge: Cambridge University Press, 2003), 170–74.

Elizabeth I was sympathetic to the humanist revulsion at wasteful uses, as she made clear when she ridiculed monks who held candles in daylight: "Away with those torches! We can see well enough."[245] It was her two statutes on charitable uses that, by giving a structure for the supervision of charities, laid the scene for cy-près.[246] The first (39 Elizabeth 1, c. 6), of 1597, manifested her concern to establish a system to monitor already existing charitable endowments, to avoid fraud, waste, misuse, or unnecessary failure. The act set up commissioners to respond to complaints by any parishioners that an endowment was not working as it ought. The commissioners could then investigate the situation and issue a decree.

Although bishops were placed on the commissions to supervise local charities, these commissions were not given the authority to change the use of charitable property or even to alter the terms of the trust much, even though the statute claimed that nothing would be taken away from the powers and jurisdiction of the ordinary, which suggests that bishops were not thought to have the power to modify pious trusts. The statute allowed a wide reporting of problems. Steve Hindle finds that rate payers made many of the reports—that is, men who paid significant poor relief taxes and who hoped to find alternate sources with which to relieve the local indigent.[247] The entire community could take an interest in supervising the scrupulous performance of the trust and had standing to report problems. And yet, paradoxically, by virtue of the statute, the community would also lose the ability to solve local charitable problems on their own authority, although this fact was not immediately clear.[248] The pressure brought by the commissioners increased the likelihood that trustees would address potential failures as they occurred and seek decrees to remedy nascent problems. Gareth Jones has shown that from 1597 to 1649 there were 521 inquisitions, each of which might have produced de-

---

245. J. E. Neale, *Elizabeth I and Her Parliaments (1559–1581)*, vol. 2 (New York: St. Martin's Press, 1958), 42.

246. Steve Hindle, *On the Parish? The Micro-Politics of Poor Relief in Rural England c.1550–1750* (Oxford: Oxford University Press, 2004), 135–36.

247. Ibid., 139.

248. *Attorney-General v. Kell* (1742) 2 Beav. 575. See also *Attorney-General v. Bovill* (1840) 1 Ph. 762.

crees for multiple trusts, and from 1649 to 1688 there were 855.[249] In total these inquisitions produced 3860 decrees, each of which could be appealed to the lord chancellor.[250] This statute, then, created a new administrative oversight over trusts, beyond just the heirs and the trustees. It made the functioning of charitable trusts into the business of the state to an unprecedented degree, and in so doing it weakened the connection between the heirs and the gift.

Elizabeth's 1601 second statute on charitable uses was even more revolutionary.[251] It affirmed the structure of the first statute and famously elaborated on what kinds of gifts counted as a "charitable use," thereby putting all of them into a large legal category that would turn out to be useful in future cy-près decisions to show that any one charitable gift partook of a broader charitable category. The definitions would also be used to reprove customary uses of unspecified gifts, as in *Fisher v. Hill* (1612), in which feoffees were instructed to find good, charitable uses, because "this court does not allow that any of the profits of the said lands should be employed to maintain pastimes feasting of gentlemen or law causes neither for any other employments to ease the townsmen's purses nor to discharge them from contribution to the poor nor to give relief to maimed soldiers."[252] The case demonstrated that although trustees were the recipients of some of the older anti-clerical suspicion traditionally directed toward those who had access to endowments, the law now clearly rejected the similarly traditional understanding that trustees might legitimately benefit from the trust they supervised.[253]

The second statute also made it explicit that the decree of the commissioners could, on appeal, be changed by Chancery: "whiche Orders Judgements and Decrees, not beinge contrarie or repugnante to the Orders Statutes or Decrees of the Donors or Founders, shall by the Authoritie of this presente Parliamente stand firme and good

---

249. Jones, *History of the Law of Charity*, 251–52.
250. Jones, *History of the Law of Charity*, 23; Hindle, *On the Parish?* 136.
251. 43 Elizabeth 1 c. 4.
252. *Fisher v. Hill* (Ch. 1612), in *The Chancery Reports of John Herne and of George Duke 1599 to 1674*, ed. W. Hamilton Bryson (Buffalo, N.Y.: Hein, 2002), 27–32.
253. Robert L. McWilliams, "Consideration and the Law of Trusts," *California Law Review* 14 (1926): 188–97.

accordinge to the tenor and purporte thereof, and shalbe executed accordinglie, untill the same shalbe undon or altered by the Lorde Chauncellor of Englande or Lorde Keeper of the Great Seale of Englande, or the Chauncellor of the Countie Palatine of Lancaster."[254] And on these revisions that the chancellor might make, the statute further explained that these revisions could "dymynishe alter or enlarge the saide Orders Judgements and Decrees of the saide Commyssioners," as long as it "shalbe thoughte to stande withe Equitie and good Conscience, according to the true intente and meaninge of the Donors and Fownders thereof."[255] This new call for the chancellor to use equity and good conscience in order to align his ruling with the "true intente and meaning of the Donors" indicates a change in priorities. The previous statute had not made it clear to what extent the chancellor could modify the decree of the commissioners. The commissioners themselves were tightly bound to the terms of the donors, but now the chancellor was urged in statute to consider equity and good conscience, and to discern the "true intent and meaning" of the founder—this true intent, presumably, not necessarily being identical with the precise stipulations of the trust. It was perhaps an invitation to change the decree and the trust, as long as it was in line with this "true intent." Still, it would take time for a "true intent" to be disentangled from the terms of the gift. The Elizabethan statute was supported by the notable addition in the *Heads of the Statute of Charitable Uses* that donor intent was the "*lapis ductitius* (ductile stone), whereby the commissioners and chancellors must institute their course."[256] The Latin phrase referred to a Quintillian description of *ferrum ducticius*, malleable iron. Since stone, unlike iron, is not malleable, passage implied that the commissioners and chancellor would have to bend to the intent, not have the intent bend to them.

George Duke claimed in 1676 that the eminent Jacobean barris-

---

254. 43 Elizabeth 1 c. 4, in Jones, *History of the Law of Charity*, 225.
255. Ibid., 228.
256. Herne 16; 2 Inst. 712. Some early seventeenth-century cases also refer to the "mind" or, less prominently (and only in cases that do not relate to a transition of use) to the "will" of the donor, but intent dominates the discussion. For "mind," see, for example, Herne 87: *Hide v. Parishioners of Gillingham* (1628).

ter Francis Moore was the author of the second statute on charitable uses, but Gareth Jones has shown that this is very unlikely.[257] Meanwhile, Moore's reading on the second Elizabethan statute, which he gave in 1607, did not indicate that trusts could be altered much. He mostly anticipated the curing of mistakes, uncertainty, and problems of corporation by the statute. Moore emphasized the limitations placed on the commissioners established by Elizabeth's statute; they could not change the "use and intent, for which the thing was given" and were granted the power in their decrees only to narrow use, not to shift to a new use or to broaden the terms of the gift.[258] Moore assumed that heirs would still have a relationship to the terms imposed on trusts and could save them by agreeing to their modification.[259] Commissioners could transfer the trust from one person to another, as long as the use would be maintained. But Moore's general inclination was to prevent the commissioners from exerting any significant power to amend, not permitting them to change the numbers of poor served, the "sex, quality, nation, trade, or profession" of the recipients, or the parish served. The commissioners could transfer the property from one trustee to another, "one person to another."[260] They could enforce a charitable use on an heir who entered into property that had not been employed for its intended purpose, and they could increase the money given to beneficiaries, but not the number of beneficiaries.[261] They could not eliminate a use given by the donor, if there was more than one, and they could not transfer from one specified charitable object to another or from one location to another.[262] They could change some terms of the gift for necessity if the changes did not infringe on the rights of others

257. Jones, *History of the Law of Charity*, 232–34.
258. Duke (Moore) 155.
259. Jones, *History of the Law of Charity*, 249.
260. Duke (Moore) 155.
261. Duke (Moore) 157.
262. Duke (Moore) 158. The reluctance to change location, which was a mere commutation in the *ius commune*, would remain. In 1786, *Attorney-Bishop v. Bishop of Oxford*, Lord Kenyon asserted that it would not be possible to move a proposed church, unwanted by the bishop, without violating the intent of the donor. Jones, *History of the Law of Charity*, 144–45; *Corbyn v. French* (4 Ves. 482); 1 Bro. C.C. 444.

(to spend money sooner than it was supposed to be spent in order to save the bridge it was intended to repair, but not to collect rent money sooner than it was due for the same reason).[263] Still, there was considerable distance here from the *ius commune* idea that *quod omnes tangit ab omnibus approbari debet*.[264]

Moore did not give much more flexibility to the chancellor either. Moore held that he could alter the time in which something would be done, but he could not change specifics that were important to the donor's intent, such as the day of the feast in which alms would be distributed nor the location in which the charity would take place.[265] Unlike the *ius commune* understanding of the purpose of a gift as the predominant concern of the donor, Moore suggested that donor intent bound all of the terms. If the commissioners had taken a general gift and reduced it to a specific use, the chancellor was bound by the use that they chose. The chancellor could take a general gift and make it particular as well, and if the decree had chosen an object for a particular use, he could shift it from one object to another, as long as the use stayed the same. He could narrow use from what the commissioners specified: Moore thought that, if the donor said the money was to maintain a school and the commissioners said this could be for a grammar school, then the chancellor could narrow it still further to a writing school. The chancellor could interpret a gift to build a causeway to mean that the gift was for a passage and could be applied to a bridge, if this was more fit and convenient according to his discretion.[266] Only this last scenario presents an example of a cy-près motion: pulling the gift up into a higher category (here, passage; later, a "general" charitable intent) in order to explain its subsequent descent back into a new and more suitable

263. Duke (Moore) 159.
264. "That which touches all must be approved by all." Yves-M. Congar, "Quod omnes tangit ab omnibus tractari et approbari debet," *Revue historique de droit française et étranger* 35 (1958): 210–59.
265. See also *East-greensteds Case*, Herne 60, on preserving the intended places precisely.
266. Duke (Moore) 169. This drew on the language of the statute, which allowed the lord chancellor, lord keeper, or chancellor of the dutchie to execute decrees and judgments as "shall seem fit and convenient."

"imployment," as Moore phrased it. Moore, however, did not generalize from this significant precedent.

Gifts were considered within the categories of superstitious and charitable use, and Moore warned that whereas churches and church repair were charitable uses, chaplains and ministers were not, since religion was dependent on the whim of the king, which meant that all were liable to be held superstitious and taken.[267] Moore noted that a devise could be made void for being imperfectly created but could then have the charitable use still held good by the chancellor; some charitable uses, though, such as those established by children, lunatics, and femmes coverts, were void and were to be vacated by the chancellor.[268] Not all of Moore's treatment of charitable uses derived from the *ius commune*, such as his requirement to pay charitable legacies before debts, which is a rule that is difficult to understand unless we account for the urgent need to make up for charitable donations.[269] Moore also did not suggest that illegal gifts, or ones with "no good ground," could be saved.[270] Rather, they should be annulled and returned to the estate.

Moore noted that when a tenant in fee-simple made a feoffment on condition of a charitable use, then the use remained if his heirs entered because the condition was broken, but this was not the case for a tenant in tail, who could not give more than was his.[271] On the other hand, if a tenant made a charitable use and his lands escheated to the lord for lack of an heir, the lord would also remain bound by the charitable use, as would creditors who received the lands of a bankrupt. The king would not suffer, however, because "a charitable use must give place to the treasure of the crown."[272] Neither here nor elsewhere in the text is there the sense that all property given to charity must be maintained in a charitable purpose forever.

267. Duke (Moore) 133.
268. Ibid., 110. But see the *Dame Billingsleys Case*, Herne 80.
269. Duke (Moore) 186: assets in equity were to go to charitable uses first, before debts or legacies; assets in law would settle debts first, then charity, then legacies.
270. Ibid., 168.
271. Ibid., 160.
272. Ibid., 167.

The problems of when a charitable use survived a transfer of property and when it did not (for example, if a purchaser or rentor was not notified of the use), or when it could defeat common law or statutory prohibitions and when it could not (as with femmes coverts or with violations of an heir's right under the Statute of Wills), would continue to be hammered out in the courts in the seventeenth century, and it is notable that the decisions did not include as part of their reasoning a consideration of whether charitable property was perpetually put to charity, either when preserving the use or when destroying it.[273] For example, the 1602 case *Goffe v. Webb* preserved a distribution to 20 poor kindred, "notwithstanding it does not appear that he had any poor kindred."[274] Egerton and Popham did not determine that the charitable aspect of the gift demanded that it should, in fact, help the poor. No attempt to find an alternate set of recipients that would qualify as poor, in order to honor the charitable intent, was suggested. The statutes did provide "relief" by which privileges of charity could be observed, as is on display in cases beginning in the 1590s and moving forward into the seventeenth century. Defects in charitable gifts, particularly in the transfer of possession, were remedied in order to preserve the gift, as were problems like the wrong name given for the recipient, gifts of land to the poor made as if they were incorporated, or the failure to name a trustee.[275]

Francis Moore unknowingly pointed forward to the destruction of consent to remake gifts and the stripping away of the heirs from the gift in his *Reading*, as he commented on the abuse of consent, treating it with fraud and covin: it was tempting for the heir of the feoffor and the feoffee to collude to eradicate the charitable use by breaking the old condition, re-entering, and making a new feoffment with-

---

273. *Willoughby v. Weavers of Gloucester* (1674), Duke 51; *Case of Sutton Colefield* (1636), Herne 69; *Peacock v. Thewer* (1638), Herne 100, Toth. 33; *Inhabitants of Woodford Parish v. Parkhurst* (1640), Herne 74. On a femme covert who made a charitable devise even though she was disabled to do so, which was voided by decree, *Bramble v. Poor of Havering* (1639), Herne 102. A deprived heir had a charitable use voided in *Lord Edward Montague's Case* (1619), Herne 92.

274. *Goffe v. Webb* (1602), Herne 97, Toth. 30.

275. Richard Bridgman, *The Law of Charitable Uses* (London: W. Clarke, 1805), 354, 356, and 360–62.

out the charitable use attached.²⁷⁶ This was a more extreme example of the ways that consent had been a vehicle for each party to take a piece of a charitable gift. The prevention of fraud required, then, that if a feoffor re-entered for nonperformance or a broken condition, then the charitable use would be destroyed, but if his heir did the same, he was still bound by the condition.²⁷⁷

Moore also developed Bracton's treatment of gifts for causes and Saint German's understanding of intent, particularly in generally allowing a charitable use to survive if an heir re-entered into property for a broken condition. In 1592 the possibility of using intent to prevent even re-entrance had been affirmed in *Martindale v. Martin*, in which a devise "upon trust and confidence" to build a school out of profits from land could not be re-entered upon for non-performance, because "it was no condition; for the words being upon trust and confidence, shew that he reposed trust in them, and would not have the land return for non-performance of it; and there can be no more apt words to shew his intent, and not to tie the land with a condition."²⁷⁸ The issue here was not the charitableness or piety of the gift to build a school, which was not discussed in the case report except that the use was not superstitious, but simply the difference between a condition and intent. Although the original devise seems to have used both intent and condition to describe the gift, it was determined "it was never his intent to have it to be a condition"; this determination allowed the remaining executor to have the land with the intent attached to it.²⁷⁹ Here intent defeated condition. Thomas has traced this development—reinforced in the late seventeenth century with *Freak v. Lee*—to prevent absolute and unburdened rights from vesting in the trustee by treating purposeful gifts as trusts rather than conditional donations.²⁸⁰

Prior to the seventeenth century, there were a number of cases in

276. Duke (Moore) 179.
277. Bridgman, *Law of Charitable Uses*, 137.
278. Cro. Eliz. 288. See also *Gibbons v. Maltyard and Martin*, Pop. 6.
279. Pop. 8.
280. T. C. Thomas, "Conditions in Favour of Third Parties," *Cambridge Law Journal* 11 (1952): 240–57; *Freak v. Lee*, 2 Show. K.B. 36.

which superstitious gifts were simply given to the king.[281] As late as 1588 land could be given to the king if its devise was accompanied by requests for prayer.[282] The *Dean of St. Paul's Case*, early in Elizabeth's reign, was unusual in not having superstitious property be "given to the king"; in later cases where there was a greater attempt to separate out good and superstitious uses or to save gifts from the king, the *Dean of St. Paul's Case* would be cited as an early and unusual precedent.[283] In 1602 two cases moved toward increased distinctions. The *Case of Pele's Will* did not give money to the king if the gift was only to pay for a priest, rather than to find a priest.[284] This gift was simply void, neither forfeit nor redirected. *Adams and Lambert's Case* was a more famous and extended development of this parsing.[285] The 1431 will reproduced in Coke's Reports for the *Adams and Lambert's Case* makes it clear why more differentiations in the law were necessary: many ordinary devises had included some kind of "superstitious" condition attached to them and were bound up in long chains of reversions for nonperformance.[286] The queen could not reasonably take all of England to punish it for its former superstition.[287]

Considerable effort would thus be made to separate out funds that had "any charitable use intermixed with the superstitious use."[288] The general rule was that the two should be strictly divided, so that the king would take the superstitious portion and the courts the charitable portion, but many cases from the seventeenth century add a confusion of exceptions. What was most important was that a precedent was set that allowed the charitable use to save the gift; at

---

281. In 1555: *Whetstone's Case*, Duke 89; in 1578: *Colborn v. Dale*, Duke 89, 4 Co. Rep. 116; in 1588: *Adams v. Stakes*, Duke 89, 4 Co. Rep. 116; in 1602: *Case on Sir John Tate's Will*, Duke 94, 4 Co. Rep. 113; in 1602: *Case of Walpole's Will*, Duke 95, 4 Co. Rep. 113.
282. Bridgman, *Law of Charitable Uses*, 356.
283. *Adams v. Stakes* (1588) Duke 89; 4 Col. Rep. 116; Bridgman 468.
284. 4 Co. Rep. 113; Duke 95.
285. 4 Co. Rep. 115; Duke 90.
286. 4 Co. Rep. 96b.
287. In expositions on the statute of Elizabeth, it was explained that the forfeiture of superstitious uses was intended as a "punishment." Bridgman 167.
288. Bridgman, *Law of Charitable Uses*, 350–60.

some points as long as the charitable use was the principal use, then the superstitious part could be left with the charitable portion. In 1629 this reasoning would protect Edward VI from having his own donations taken by virtue of his statute, because the charitable use was in fact "the principall intent" and not the "accessary" of prayers.[289]

Coke's report of the *Adams and Lambert's Case* noted that land that was given to relatives with the intent that some of its proceeds should find a priest could well be understood as primarily passing land on to the family and only secondarily designating superstitious uses. If the transaction was interpreted in that way, then it would appear unjust to take the entire land and deprive the family. But, the report continued, "the person, be he of blood or not, single or corporate, or politic, to whom the land is devised or conveyed, is not to be respected, but all is one within the purview of this Act."[290] Heirs and relatives had no special claim to recover an illegal gift, just as they had no claim to recover lands seized for treason or felony. Although not directly relevant to the question of the rights of heirs to a legal but impossible charitable purpose, it was a small support toward the recasting of bequests and trusts as free gifts made by an individual whose intentions were paramount, while the interests of the heirs to the estate were limited or even foregone.

The *Adams and Lambert's Case* suggested that the ongoing forfeitures to the king were necessary in order to eradicate superstition entirely. In particular, the strength of devotion commanded by a trust to honor the purposes for which property was given was described in Coke's report as one reason why the property could not remain with the devisees. The devisor had expressed his "confidence" in their reliability, and they would be inclined not to "betray the trust," especially since, in their errors, they would conceive of such a betrayal as sacrilege.[291] Thus forfeiture was the only way to "extirpate out of men's minds these superstitious errors, and to take them utterly away."[292] Attachment to the use of the gift was reconceptualized as

---

289. *Henshaw v. Pye, Mayor of Morpeth* (1629), Herne 73.
290. 4 Co. Rep. 106b.
291. Ibid. 106a.
292. Ibid. 106b.

a form of superstition—admittedly here only for "superstitious" gifts, but the report excluded any other motivation that devisees might have to maintain the purpose of a gift or any broader legal or political reason why the court should be concerned with upholding designated uses in general even if they were not "good." The power of this attachment of the use was so great that there was no solution but to take the land away in order to destroy bad uses. A solution of approximation of use was not suggested, even though the case tried to save uses from forfeiture, which suggests that the cy-près solution was not available. Indeed, Neil Jones has gone through the entry books of decrees and orders for Chancery under Elizabeth and found no example of a cy-près alteration in the purpose of a charitable trust: reductions or deviations in terms or mitigations of strict law did appear in the sixteenth century, but not a change in the use.[293]

The secularization of property did not, then, immediately provide a legal precedent for the transition of use. However, it would have long-term legal effects in England. On the continent, in many cases, the fate of church possessions became a matter for peace treatises, as can be seen in the successive settlements of the Peace of Augsburg (1555), the Edict of Restitution (1629), and the Peace of Westphalia (1648), all of which attempted to draw a chronological line in the sand, limiting Protestant possessions to those acquired prior to a particular year. But there were also (largely ineffective) proceedings in the Imperial Chamber, against which the Schmalkaldic League took collective action, neither fully recognizing nor totally discarding the authority of the court, and many secularizations were settled only *de facto*, not *de iure*.[294] Ultimately, the secularizations left little legal trace, particularly since, as Cohn notes, the legal arguments made by Protestant realms in these disputes centered on the point that "church property was being used for religious and educational purposes in accordance with the intentions of their original endowments."[295]

---

293. Personal correspondence regarding his research into TNA Class C 33, from the 1540s to 1600.
294. Ocker, *Church Robbers and Reformers*.
295. Cohn, "Church Property in the German Protestant Principalities," 167.

In England, meanwhile, the sale of monastic and chantry possessions provided a chance for many to purchase land and became a memorable legal precedent for the future. The need to restrain this precedent was recognized: Edward Coke used the example of a dissolution to explain why legislation should be limited by having its purpose explicitly stated, lest it become grounds for unintended actions.[296] Plowden, similarly, used the 1547 Chantries Act as an example of a statute that needed to be tamed by equity so that it would not be used immoderately.[297] The seizures and dissolutions honored one set of rights—firm property rights—with reasonable scrupulosity: rents, advowsons, and other such claims laid on the dissolved property were to be maintained into their next use. It was claimed that patronage rights were also to be maintained, although clearly some would be lost. It would be hard to present a rector for, demand hospitality from, use a surplus for destitute heirs from, or install a corrody within a non-existent monastic house. Certainly the right to take custody during a (now permanent) vacancy was not honored. But for the story of cy-près what is more significant is the loss of the right to consent to changes in the gift.

While many continental Reformations brought the locality to the fore, in England the Reformation would mark a great centralization. That centralization is part of the more general effect of "concentration" or narrowing of "foci of authority" that Scarisbrick ascribes to the Reformation, and this was an impulse that lies behind cy-près.[298] The men who benefitted in England from the secularizations often were not tied to the local community from which the property was taken, and each wave of Reformation was made through centrally organized "visitations" that imposed a standardized vision of Reformation upon the locality. Meanwhile the enclosure movement, although not directly related, threatened any sense that the community could control property for the common good. Cy-près would

---

296. Hoyle, "Origins of the Dissolution of the Monasteries," 293; Lawrence Stone, "The Political Programme of Thomas Cromwell," *The Bulletin of the Institute of Historical Research* 24 (1951): 1–18.

297. See the discussion of 2 Plowden 466 in Ibbetson, "A House Built on Sand," 61.

298. Scarisbrick, *Reformation and the English People,* 131 and 170.

emerge in this context as an appealing compromise. It drew on some traditional understandings of property as serving the good of all, but it taxed the dead (and increasingly only the wealthy dead), whose interests were of little concern. Moreover, this "common" property was centrally controlled by the king's Sign Manual, Chancery, or the Court of the Exchequer. Cy-près could simultaneously appear to serve the common good, although not necessarily the local good, while also fostering the sovereign power of the king. And yet, conversely, it could limit the king's ability to plunder, and it might prevent another, similar reform being visited upon England by Puritans or other dissenters.

Cy-près would be the rainbow after the flood, a sign of regret, an acknowledgment of how the confiscations ought to have been handled, and a promise that what *had* happened would never happen again. Things that had been given with a purpose would have that intent honored, not mocked. Cy-près, consequently, has an ambivalent relationship to the Reformation. Without the radical changes and statutory precedent of the Reformation, cy-près would not have emerged in the seventeenth century, or at least not in the form in which it did. On the other hand, the more scrupulous treatment of purposes in canon law haunted the Reformation in England, where expectations about the secularization of church property were thwarted. So the *ius commune* is not irrelevant to the story of cy-près power. But the attempt to locate the origins of cy-près transitions of property in the *ius commune* tends to obscure and muddy the issues. The two systems have very different vocabularies and concerns; they have entirely different preoccupations with power and consent. There is indeed a relationship between the two: the precedents for cy-près power are laid down in defiance of some *ius commune* norms while they honor others. In many respects what happened was that cy-près performed a cy-près operation on *ius commune* treatment of gifts: it lifted legal norms up out of their intended purpose and directed them toward new ends, all the while trying to claim that the diversion was very close to the original intentions.

7

A Doctrine Is Born

The most natural explanation for cy-près power would be that it began from impossible gifts—impossible in law or in fact—and then expanded outward into impractical or wasteful gifts. But the earliest uses of the power to alter gifts in the seventeenth century all occurred in cases in which the gifts were undesirable or impractical. They were not clearly illegal or infeasible. Over the course of the seventeenth century, pragmatic motivations and a precedent-based understanding of equity would cobble cy-près together by drawing on tempered statutory and prerogative powers to cope with these difficult gifts. The ground for this development, perhaps surprisingly, was prepared by the ascension of James I to the throne of a country that was suspicious of Scottish impositions and fraught with ongoing religious dissention. James arrived with a famously unabashed vision of his rights, happily citing 1 Samuel 8 on the terrible predations of kings to explain that his dominion over the property of his subjects was unlimited. Moreover, none of the Stuarts would be particularly interested in consensus as a method of obtaining justice, since it was increasingly difficult to understand the requirement for consent as anything other than an abridgement of rights and an opportunity for obstruction or profit.

But James was also eager to distance the Stuarts, whose name he perceived to have been disgraced by his mother, from the charge of covetousness that had been laid against the Tudors. John Whitgift, the archbishop of Canterbury who crowned James and participated in the Hampton Court Conference with him, may well have repeated to James his ineffectual warning to Elizabeth that the seizure of church property infected monarchs with spiritual leprosy.[1] James's interest in dark forces—spirits, ghosts, and witches who wanted to murder him—would have made him a receptive audience for this admonishment. The Tudors had been wiped out by their sin; the Stuarts could instead be known for rectitude, beneficence, and liberality, an appealing idea for a king who liked to give. James referred to Korah (Numbers 16) several times in his speeches and writings, and Henry Spelman claimed in 1632 that the censers of Korah, which God had recalled to the temple because they were holy despite their use by the wicked, were an inspirational motif to James.[2] Spelman also quoted James that he would not have taken the monasteries down but would rather have reformed them: "not meaning to continue them in their superstitious uses, but to employ them, as Chorah's censers, to some godly purposes."[3] This would be a reformed Reformation that would perfect and purify, rather than seize.

James adopted for himself the role of an ecumenical peacemaker.[4] In his first speech to Parliament James indicated that he would bring peace and union by moderating religious policy. He wanted the Temple to be "purged and cleansed from corruption," not "downethrow[n]." The Roman church was still "our Mother Church," which he hoped to "meete in the middest, which is the Center and perfection of all things" where "all nouelties might be renounced on either side." And although he could not "permit the encrease and growing of their Religion," he also wanted to leave conscience alone and not "be thought a Persecuter." He wished in particular "to revise

1. Scarisbrick, *Reformation and the English People*, 91.
2. James I, *The Political Works of James I*, ed. Charles Howard McIlwain (Cambridge, Mass.: Harvard University Press, 1918), 114.
3. Henry Spelman, *The History and Fate of Sacrilege, Discover'd by Examples of Scripture, of Heathens, and of Christians; from the Beginning of the World Continually to this Day* (London: John Hartley, 1698), 192.
4. W. B. Patterson, *James VI and I and the Reunion of Christendom* (New York: Cambridge University Press, 1998).

and consider deeply upon the lawes made against them," which he thought "haue been in times past further, or more rigorously extended by Iudges, then the meaning of the Law was." James expressed concern for the ways that the laws "might tend to the hurt aswell of the innocent as of guiltie persons."[5] This must have meant the family of the recusant, who suffered through the penal laws or the seizure of superstitious property.[6]

Thus James seems to have reasoned that to take superstitious property, which had been intended as a gift to God, risked sacrilege, but to return it to the heirs did not. With his ascension, the pursuit of superstitious property diminished. The church canons of 1604, to which James I gave his assent, dealt with problems of probate, including jurisdictional conflicts, but were silent on the disposition of superstitious or illegal gifts. James I issued a proclamation on the problem of extortion and theft in the practices of the pursuivants.[7] For a time he even suspended the penal laws, in part because the crown was pursuing a policy of pacification with Catholic Spain. James I was not in fact bound by the Second Chantry Act to confiscate all goods that were for superstitious use, and he could choose how to understand the statute and whether or not to enforce it. Consequently, two cases at the beginning of his reign both resulted in property being returned to the heirs. In the first case, *Croft v. Jane Evetts* (1605), a recusant trust was declared "void" and returned to the Protestant heir.[8] The same result occurred in *Lady Egerton's Case* (1606), in which it was determined that because the intent had to be honored, and the intent "could be to no other than the relief of poor recusants," the land was given to the heir.[9] There was no thought to approximate this intent in some way to save its charitable aspects.

But if recusant trusts could be returned, especially to Protestant

---

5. James I, *Political Works*, 274–76.
6. *Wickham v. Wood* (Lane 113; Duke 95) in 1611 would allow property left to find a priest, which had been taken as given to superstitious uses, to stay with the heirs of the original feoffees, against the interests in property held by the man who had been rewarded with the property under Elizabeth.
7. Rymer, *Foedera*, vol. 7, part 3, 144.
8. Moo. K.B. 784; Bryson, ed., *Cases Concerning Equity*, Part I, 342.
9. Duke (Moore) 133; Moo. K.B. 551.

heirs, dissenting trusts were more difficult for James. Even before the Hampton Court Conference, James was suspicious of the political consequences of dissent. The "Puritanes and Novelists," he said, were not innovative in religion but rather "in their confused forme of Policie and Paritie, being euer discontented with the present gouernment, and impatient to suffer any superiority, which maketh their sect unable to be suffred in any wel gouerned Commonwealth."[10] Even in the aftermath of the 1605 Gunpowder Plot, James affirmed the obedience of most Catholics and turned again to the seditiousness of "Puritans" as a greater threat to his reign.

This judgment of his would be tested in 1607 and 1608 with the *Sara Venables Case*, in which an enormous fortune was to be distributed to non-conformist ministers. The gift was not superstitious, nor was it necessarily illegal, since dissenters were not forbidden from receiving distributions. Sara Venables's brothers and sisters suggested that she had changed her will without their knowledge near her death, when ministers had visited her—in this case, they claimed, it was dissenting ministers that apparently inspired the superstitious panic of the deathbed. They also reported that they had been told the property would be forfeit under civil law. There were many reasons why this might have happened, including the potential forfeiture to the fisc of illegal trusts, the goods of a traitor or felon, or property made out to an unworthy recipient.[11]

Sara Venables had left notable Puritans as executors, and her family, despite their protestations, were suspect, given the tendency of dissention to run in families and across social networks.[12] Robert Cecil, earl of Salisbury and the Lord High Treasurer, turned to the wills she had drawn up before the last one and claimed that these could be used to explain what her intentions had been before the problematic will was made. Since these earlier wills simply gave property to poor ministers, Cecil set up the new trust to do that, but he included

10. James I, *Political Works*, 274.
11. Code 6.35, Digest 34.9.10, Digest 34.9.1. or Digest 34.9.9.1. See the discussion in William Fulbecke, *The Pandectes of the Law of Nations* (London: Thomas Wight, 1602), 9–14v.
12. Nicholas Tyacke, *Aspects of English Protestantism c. 1530–1700* (Manchester: Manchester University Press, 2001).

the provision that children of dissenting and non-conforming ministers who had died since the writing of the last will could be included in the disbursements. This was, then, truly about as close to her intentions as could be allowed with convenience. The decree held that the court would not "infringe the true meaning of the deceased so far as shall not appear notoriously inconvenient only." However, since the will

> tend[ed] to the disgrace and contempt of the government and discipline of the church now established and to the animating of such obstinate ministers to persist in their perverse disobedience ... the inconvenience whereof this court was careful to prevent, yet willing (the abuse and inconvenience aforesaid only diverted and avoided) that the said bequests should be reduced *as near to the true meaning of the testatrix as might stand with [the] conveniency* [emphasis added] of the church state now established.[13]

Thus forfeiture was declined and the property reformed in its use. The family requested to receive some money from the will, at minimum for their expenditures on the case, and although they were ultimately awarded £100, this came not from the Venables estate but rather was to be supplied by the executors. The importance of the principle that this property was applied as closely as possible was not immediately recognized in other courts: the decree was sometimes in the next few years understood not as an approximation of the intent but as its thwarting, applying it to "contrary" ends.[14] In retrospect it would be considered the first known case of prerogative cy-près, and Cecil gave no precedent for his ruling. It had been a difficult case that had sat unresolved for many months in the files of the previous lord treasurer. Cecil must have discussed the decree with the king and his counsellors, which included Cecil's cousin, Francis Bacon.

---

13. Bryson, ed., *Cases Concerning Equity,* Part I, 353, from PRO E 126/1, f. 144v. Jones, *History of the Law of Charity,* 76–77; S. P. Dom. 14/37/113.

14. *The King against The Earl of Nottingham and Others* (Lane 44) claimed the Venables case as precedent that: "when a thing is disposed, to maintain contempt and disobedience in any, this ought to be ordered and disposed by the court to a contrary end and use."

As Near as May Be

As it turns out, to do things "as near as may be" was a leitmotif of James's reign, particularly with regard to both religious matters and the relationship between Scotland and England.[15] Canon 96 of the 1604 *Constitutions and Canons Ecclesiasticall* called for the jurisdictions of bishops to be "preserved (as neere as may be) entier and free from prejudice." This is a remarkable caveat; the bishops would not have included it on their own, absent James's influence. The phrase appears repeatedly in other religious documents. John Spottiswoode, upon ascending to be archbishop of St. Andrews, wrote out the articles "required for the service of the church of Scotland," presumably with the king's assent, in which the "publick Confessioun of Faith must be formed, agreing so neir as can be with the Confessioun of the Englische Churche."[16] Laud reported that the king had authorized the Scottish bishops to make their liturgy "as near that of England as might be."[17] In the 1620 "Orders to be putte in Execution for Repressing of Poperie" in Scotland, it was commanded that "Popish Ladies" in Scotland be treated "so neare as may be" as they were in England.[18] The instructions given to the translators of the King James Bible asked them to keep names "as near as may be, accordingly as they are vulgarly used."[19] James's use of this concept may have been influenced by Lancelot Andrewes, who participated in the Hampton Court Conference and would become his lord high almoner.[20] An-

---

15. Alan MacDonald points out that although James embraced the ideal of contiguity and, more importantly, ecumenical reunion, ultimately most of his reforms pulled Scotland toward "Anglican" practice: "James VI and I, the Church of Scotland, and British Ecclesiastical Convergence," *The Historical Journal* 48 (2005): 885–903.

16. *Original Letters Relating to the Ecclesiastical Affairs of Scotland*, vol. 2 (Edinburgh: J. Hughes, 1851), 445.

17. William Laud, *The History of the Troubles and Tryal of the Most Reverend Father in God William Laud* (London: Richard Chiswell, 1695), 75.

18. *Original Letters Relating to the Ecclesiastical Affairs of Scotland*, vol. 2, 637.

19. Ascribed to Richard Bancroft. See Andrew Hadfield, "The King James Bible," in *English Renaissance Translation Theory*, ed. Neil Rhodes et al. *Modern Humanities Research Association 9* (2013): 179.

20. The expression had other uses as well, for example in statutory law to indicate how divisions ought to be made of land or materials.

drewes sometimes used the expression to try to convey the gap between the spiritual and the earthly and the problem that even the sanctified could never entirely transcend the limitations of the fallen world.[21] More broadly, the phrase represented a general policy of trying to keep to the middle of the road, despite the relentless fractiousness of English religious identities, and to reconcile differences as close as possible to an ideal, while acknowledging that perfect conformity was not a realistic goal at that time.

This was a policy advocated by Francis Bacon, who advised James early in his reign to embrace moderation and the passage of time as the means to achieve his ends.[22] In his *Brief Discourse Touching the Happy Union of the Kingdoms of England and Scotland,* Bacon offered the natural cycles of change as a model. There should be no forced conversions of nature between England and Scotland but rather a gentle mingling, out of which eventually "a new form agreeable and convenient to the entire estate" would emerge.[23] This was a process of "fermentation and incorporation" in which "it must be left to Nature and Time to make that *continuum,* which was at first but *contiguum.*"[24] To draw the kingdoms together into *contiguum* was thus the first step. Moreover, the heavens "do not enrich themselves by the earth and the seas, nor keep no dead stock or untouched treasures of that they draw to them from below; but whatsoever moisture they do levy and take from both elements in vapours, they do spend and turn back again in showers; only holding and storing them up for a time, to the end to issue and distribute them in season."[25] This analogy of taking and redistributing Bacon compared to the forsaking of "particularities" in order to "uphold the public." It was a suggestive metaphor in relationship to property, especially given Bacon's dislike of the penal laws.

21. Lancelot Andrewes, *Sermons by the Right Honourable and Reverend Father in God, Lancelot Andrewes,* 2d ed. (London: Richard Badger, 1632), 330 and 689.

22. Lisa Jardine and Alan Stewart, *Hostage to Fortune: The Troubled Life of Francis Bacon* (New York: Hill and Wang, 1998), 274.

23. Francis Bacon, *The Letters and the Life of Francis Bacon,* ed. James Spedding, vol. 3 (London: Longmans, Green, Reader, and Dyer, 1868), 94.

24. Ibid., 98.

25. Ibid., 90–91.

When this first discourse was well received by James, Bacon sent a second one to him, *Certain Considerations Touching the Better Pacification and Edification of the Church of England*. He urged "golden mediocrity" to reform the "corrupt and decayed," unlike the radicals who had advocating removing the abuses entirely.[26] Renewal in the face of corruption during "the dregs of time" (for time would make new things and corrupt the old) was necessary for "all institutions and ordinances, be they never so pure."[27] Charities, laws, and ecclesiastical institutions alike would need to change with the times. Elsewhere Bacon urged that only the best ancient laws ought to be kept: he encouraged the regular pruning back of English laws, which were too abundant, and he concurred with James I, "that in all usages and precedents, the times be considered wherein they first began; which if they were weak or ignorant, it derogateth from the authority of the usage, and leaveth it for suspect."[28]

As a result, Bacon disliked canon law provisions to derogate from rules *ex causa* or for necessity, as with private baptisms by women. This was irregular and only a concession previously made *propter duritiem cordis* (on account of the hardness of the heart).[29] Since the necessity was only "supposed," it would be better to hold to the regular rule or create a new rule. Derogation for cause promoted irregularity, inefficiency, and stasis of the laws, which were not forced to change to meet the circumstances. Consequently, derogation because of necessity was to be avoided whenever possible, but utility and convenience were good grounds on which to rationalize the customs of the church. For the endowments of the church, too, Bacon thought that their arrangement should be "a question of convenience, but no question of precise necessity."[30] The return of impropriations would be "the most proper and natural endowment," supported also by "the ancient claim of the Church, and the inten-

---

26. Ibid., 104.
27. Ibid., 105.
28. Francis Bacon, *Advancement of Learning*, in *Works of Francis Bacon*, ed. James Spedding et al., vol. 4 (London: Longman, 1858), Book II, 288.
29. Bacon, *Letters and the Life*, vol. 3, 117.
30. Ibid., 125.

tion of the first givers," but impractical.[31] The church had moved from a state of "superfluity" to a state of "lack," and it was Parliament that should "do somewhat for the Church" to remedy the property that had been taken from it. James took Bacon's advice, recommending at Hampton Court that pluralities and non-residences should "be taken away, or at least made so few as possibly might be," and, alternately, that where double benefices were used to support preachers, they should "have their livings as near as may be the one to the other."[32] Drawing near, through the approach of *contiguum,* was the method to be employed.

Contiguum implied no diminishment of the king's authority, however. Lisa Jardine and Alan Stewart argued convincingly that Bacon was predominantly responsible for the "establishment of the king's prerogative."[33] Bacon celebrated the prerogative of the king in part because it could revitalize the moribund. Moreover, Bacon wanted the law and the state to interact: "it is an happy thing in a state, when kings and states do often consult with judges; and again, when judges do often consult with the king and state ... let no man weakly conceive, that just laws and true policy have any antipathy; for they are like the spirits and sinews, that one moves with the other."[34]

In addition, Bacon emphasized utility, not donor intent, with regard to gifts. In his 1612 *Essays,* Bacon included "On Riches," which distilled the traditional ambivalence toward property and deathbed alms into a humanist essay, novel but not new. Riches were only *impedimenta,* like "baggage to an Army."[35] They were impossible to do without ("cannot bee spared, nor left behinde; but it hindreth the March") and yet man never really had a true hold on them. There was no holy poverty: "they despise them that despair of them." And yet, "of great riches there is no reall use, except it be in the distribution." Man had "custody" of riches, "a power of Dole and donative

31. Ibid., 126.
32. Ibid., 129 and 131.
33. Jardine and Stewart, *Hostage to Fortune,* 357. On earlier discussions of the *prerogativa regis,* see Margaret McGlynn, *The Royal Prerogative and the Learning of the Inns of Court* (Cambridge: Cambridge University Press, 2003).
34. Francis Bacon, "Of Judicature," in *Essays,* 2d ed. (1612).
35. Francis Bacon, "Of Riches," in *Essays,* 2d ed. (1612).

of them, or a fame of them, but no solide use to the owner." Hence man should be almost indifferent to money: "use soberly, distribute cheerefully, and leave contentedly." At the end of life, "men leave their riches eyther to their kindred, or to the publike: and moderate portions prosper best in both. A great state left to an Heire, is as a lure to all the birds of prey round about to seize on him ... Likewise glorious gifts and foundations, are both the painted Sepulchers of *Almes,* which soone will putrifie and corrupt inwardly." Bacon urged charity in life, since "if a man weigh it rightly, he that doth [give in death], is rather liberall of another mans, then of his owne." Bacon expanded the essay in the 1625 edition, calling "glorious" charitable foundations "sacrifices without salt." He added that almost all of the ways that riches could be accumulated quickly were offensive to virtue. The essay cleared the way for the state to remedy the foolish decisions that men made about their property.

Ineffective charity wasted resources and, as sacrifices without salt, putrefied over time.[36] Bacon was particularly frank in his advice to James I in 1612 about Thomas Sutton's will, which had left almost all of Sutton's estate to charity, to fund, among other objects, a hospital at Charterhouse with a school and garden. In his advice, Bacon rejected the terms of Sutton's will as highly impractical: "a blaze of glory, that will but crackle a little in talk and quickly extinguish."[37] Bacon preferred to re-organize the gift entirely. He suggested that it would be possible to "observ[e] the *species* of Mr. Sutton's intent, although varying *in individuo.*"[38] Bacon could have drawn on the power of commutation, but he did not, nor did he reach for a principle of cy-près to give legal justification for the alterations, despite his unabashed embrace of the power to change gifts. If anyone could have provided a fixed cy-près principle to justify the proposed course of action for Sutton's estate, it would have been Bacon, a student of

---

36. Bacon did uphold in 1617 the principle that legacies to the poor should be paid out without abatement for debt over all other legacies. *Rolt v. Smith,* Ritchie 53.

37. Francis Bacon, "Advice to the King, Touching Sutton's Estate," in *An Account of the Life and Times of Francis Bacon,* ed. James Spedding, vol. 1 (London: Trübner and Co., 1878), 648.

38. Ibid., 648–49.

John Whitgift and Jean Hotman, learned in civil, canon, and common law alike. That he did not do so indicates that he did not have it available to him but, as it turned out, was rather helping to bring it into existence, grounded in a theory of the king's prerogative.

Bacon began his advice with the intention of the donor, which was the ruling principle in law: "God is not pleased with the body of a good intention, except it be seasoned with that spiritual wisdom and judgment, as it be not easily subject to be corrupted and perverted." The eternal God was pleased with gifts that could withstand the corruptions of time. Intention itself was not enough; Bacon's God also demanded prudence and wisdom. Sutton's will "ha[d] the materials of a good intention, but not powdered with any such ordinances and institutions as may preserve the same from turning corrupt, or at least from becoming unsavory and of little use." It was not suitable to offer "a building fit for a Prince's habitation" to beggars; this was a gift "apt to provoke a mis-employment ... it will in small time degenerate to be made a preferment of some great person to be master, and he to take all the sweet, and the poor to be stinted." The poor were the *propter quid* of the gift, but the hospitals of the realm, like the Catholic foundations of old, were "begun in vain glory and ostentation ... [and] end in corruption and abuse."[39]

Thus far Bacon's argument rested on the imprudent nature and anticipated abuse of the gift. Then he turned to the law. If, he wrote, the gift were "perfect and good in law," then he knew the king would not be willing to do anything that was "not grounded upon a right." Moreover, "if the defects be such as a court of equity may remedy and cure, then I wish that as St. Peter's shadow did cure diseases, so the very shadow of a good intention may cure defects of that nature." But he did not think that the shadow of a good intention could be resolved by courts of equity; they did not have, at this point, the means by which to reorganize an impractical bequest. Instead, Bacon suggested a more novel method by which to accomplish this goal: "if there be a right and birthright planted in the heir, and not remediable by courts of equity, and that right be submitted

39. Ibid., 647–48.

to your Majesty, whereby it is both in your power and grace what to do; then I do wish that this rude mass and chaos of a good deed were directed rather to a solid merit and durable charity."[40]

This was an unusual idea: the heir would win at the law and then submit to the king, who would redirect the property. It bore some similarity to Bacon's behavior in 1618 on Edward Allen's mortmain application, which would give £800 to create a hospital. Bacon wrote to the king that he had "stayed [the application] at the Seal" because of the "decay" it would cause in wardship revenues.[41] Bacon scoffed at hospitals, which "abound, and beggars abound never a whit less."[42] On the other hand, there was "great want" for lectureships at Oxford and Cambridge, and Bacon proposed that £500 should go to the proposed hospital, and £300 for lectureships. Allen was still alive, so this was not a case of rearranging the terms of a will, but it highlights one of Bacon's assumptions: the application for the mortmain license gave the king full rights to set the terms of the charity. Presumably it would also give him the right to alter the terms later, when convenient.

Bacon advised the king on how to transform the gift if his plan for Sutton's estate worked. Sutton had left money for the hospital, the school, and a preacher. These "individuals resort to these three general heads; relief of poor, advancement of learning, and propagation of religion."[43] Each aspect of the gift belonged to larger categories from which the king might select new particular ends. This was how the "species" would remain the same while the "individual" was changed. Bacon thought the money could be used to found many smaller, less corruptible hospitals in poor areas, because *bonum quo communius eo melius* (the good that is common is better). Moreover, hospitals with smaller endowments would depend on "free gifts, which gifts would be withheld if they appeared once to be perverted," which would motivate rectitude.[44] It would be even better to trans-

40. Ibid., 648.
41. Francis Bacon, *The Letters of Sir Francis Bacon*, ed. Robert Stephens (London: Benjamin Tooke, 1702), 233–34.
42. Ibid., 234; quoted in Stephen Porter, *The London Charterhouse: A History of Thomas Sutton's Charity* (Stroud: Amberley Publishing, 2009), 12.
43. Bacon, "Advice to the King," in *Account of the Life and Times*, vol. 1, 649.
44. Ibid., 650.

form hospitals into "houses of relief and correction," to enforce work, relieving the rate payer. Grammar schools overeducated the population, leaving them "unfit" for employment, and so Sutton's "intention [should be] exalted a degree" in order to support university salaries. Instead of preaching ministers, Bacon suggested more radical and targeted methods to advance Protestantism, both at home and abroad. Bacon ended by insulting the donor: "that mass of wealth, that was in the owner little better than a stack or heap of muck, may be spread over your kingdom to many fruitful purposes."[45]

Bacon then represented the nephew of Sutton, Simon Baxter, in his attempt to overturn the will at the Exchequer. For this case we have only the report of the hostile Coke, who suggested that Bacon's objections (built largely on faults in the corporation and foundation) "were not worthy to be moved at the bar, nor remembered at the bench."[46] But the court's ruling may have also been influenced by the tactic of the executors, who had offered the king that half of the £20,000 that was left to them for charitable uses could be given to him for the repair of Berwick Bridge on the river Tweed, to facilitate the union of the two kingdoms. Bacon had suggested a complicated plan to reorganize the £8000 left for the hospital, while the archbishops had offered the king a greater sum directly. Ultimately, the judges upheld "this great work of charity," citing the statute *De Templariis* to preserve pious wills exactly in perpetuity.[47] Bacon and Baxter lost the case, and Baxter subsequently wrote to the archbishop of Canterbury to complain that he had been "seduced by wicked counsel" into the loss of the money that had been left to him in the will (now forfeit) and was oppressed by the fees of his lawyers.[48] The archbishop petitioned the other executors on his behalf to restore his legacy.

---

45. Ibid., 654.
46. 10 Co. Rep. 24a–b. Coke's comments do include one unusual observation: "the Holy Ghost (which moved Sutton to this work of charity) in the scripture takes it." 10 Co. Rep. 26a.
47. 10 Co. Rep. 35a: "ita semper quod pia et celeberrima voluntas donatorum in omnibus teneatur et expleatur et perpetuo sanctissime perseveret."
48. William Frederick Taylor, *The Charterhouse of London: Monastery, Palace, and Thomas Sutton's Foundation* (London: J. M. Dent, 1912), 235–41.

Approximation and Intent

Although Bacon was adventurous in his political and moral opinions on the disposition of charitable gifts, as a judge he offered a tempered justification of approximation. He used the phrase "to come as near as might be to the will and meaning of the testator" in 1617, a year after the "triumph of equity," in his decision for *Emmanuel College, Cambridge v. English*. He cited impossibility and inconvenience in changing a trust for Emmanuel College to make it "as near as might be to the will and meaning of the testator" even while eliminating funding for fellows that had been part of the original trust.[49] This was not a change in use, but a more extreme form of deviation, since one part of the original provisions was eliminated but another part was augmented. Inflation had ruined the original terms of the bequest, in which £50 a year was to support two fellows at £10 a year and six scholars at £5 a year for each. The fellowships were too small, and the college asked to eliminate them and use the money instead for more scholarships, which Bacon duly increased, both in quantity (providing for nine scholars) and in quality (giving each £5 6s. 8 d. each year). Bacon probably did not stick as closely as possible to the intention of the testator as he could have, since the testator would likely have wanted to keep one fellow with a more generous fellowship. As Gareth Jones noted, he also gave a liberal treatment of impossibility. But although this case has been cited as an early example of judicial cy-près, this is only because it uses the phrase associated with it. As Ritchie's report of the case indicated:

Bacon, L.K., declared that he did not intend to alter anything concerning the disposition of the legacy contrary to the will, except it were in that which was impossible to be performed, which might prove a hindrance and inconvenience to the college; and also that, in that which was necessary to be altered in respect of impossibility and inconvenience as aforesaid, he desired to tie himself to come as near as might be to the will and meaning of the testator in the ordering and disposing thereof.[50]

---

49. *Emmanuel College, Cambridge v. English* (1617), Ritchie 27–28.
50. Ibid., 28.

Bacon is described in this report as voluntarily tying himself, suggesting that he could have done otherwise and ordered a more significant alteration. Bacon was doubtless aware that civil law might allow him to treat the impossible as if it were not written. But he was also drawing out a common law tendency to allow intention to survive imperfection. Common law had already allowed for a little flexibility on intent in non-charitable uses, suggesting that intent should be upheld by a close approximation rather than perfect performance. Littleton used the phrase "auxi près" in 1481 to discuss how closely the intentions laid down in regular, non-pious uses ought to be followed by the feoffee, and it was probably from this general principle in uses to affirm the necessity of closely following intentions that it would later develop into the specific doctrine on trusts that allowed changes in use to occur.[51]

In fact, approximation was not limited to charitable or pious gifts alone.[52] In 1514 Fitzherbert explained in his *La Graunde Abridgment* why a newborn son could be added as a receiver to the estate, which had long been permitted by canonists, but he offered the language of the fifteenth-century Chief Justice John Fortescue, who urged that conscience in the law was to attempt to get "cy procheine" to the "volunte de dieu ... come reason puit"—to get as near to the will of God (not the will of the testator) as reason would allow.[53] Edward Coke then picked up on Littleton's formulation for his commentary on Littleton, which appeared in print in 1628.[54] Cy-près appears, thus, to be used in its most earnest sense, "as close as possible" to the intentions of feoffors and testators in the fifteenth and early sixteenth centuries, without application to a constancy of a general charitable

---

51. Thomas Littleton, *His Treatise of Tenures, in French and English* (London: S. Sweet, 1841), Book III, 396, 398, 453, and 462.
52. William Cruise, *A Digest of the Laws of England Respecting Real Property*, vol. 6 (London: A. Strahan, 1806), Title XXXVIII, Chapter IX, § 18, 161.
53. Anthony Fitzherbert, *La Graunde Abridgement* (London: Richard Tottell, 1565), title: sub pena, f. 116v. In his *La Novelle Natura Brevium*, he affirmed the rights of donors to determine use and the rights of heirs to recover when the use was not being maintained in his entries on the writs for *cessavit* and *contra formam collationis*.
54. Co. Litt. 219 b–220 b.

intent.[55] In the 1588 *Justice Windham's Case* in the King's Bench, two rules of construction were affirmed to preserve the lease: *quod res non destruatur* (that a thing shall not be destroyed) and also that a grant "shall take effect as near as may be according to the intent of the parties."[56] Thus that nearness to the intent was good enough to preserve a lease or a grant was expressed in non-charitable cases.[57] Cy-près would be used in cases to allow for imperfect performance of conditions as well, although it was more prominently associated with intent.[58]

Early on during Charles I's reign, the case of *Eaton v. Butter*, on a non-charitable conveyance with a condition that had become impossible, upheld that "when an act of God prevents a condition from being strictly performed according to the letter, it will be performed as close to the intent of the parties as is possible."[59] This was not an inherited privilege of charity; it was a granting of flexibility within conveyances and preventing frivolous re-entry. Meanwhile, Plowden in his commentary on *Eyston v. Studd* (1573) had explained the power of equity to expand or analogize upon statutes in a novel fashion as an imagined conversation with the law-giver in order to understand "his intent and meaning" and to arrive at "such an answer as you imagine he would have done, if he had been present."[60] This exercise

55. It also seems to have been used to mean "as soon as" with regard to the moment when land could be re-entered. *Boydell v. Walthall,* Moo. K.B., 723; "void cy pres" in *Englefields Case,* Moo. K.B., 304. It is also used in reference to the judicial attempt to discern non-charitable intentions in conveyances. For example, in the 1590s case *Sir Henry Berkley v. Le Countee de Pembroke,* Moo. K.B. 707, in weighing whether a stipulation was a condition or a covenant: "Mes nul rule certaine fuit done pur expounder ceo lou come condition et lou come covenant forsque denuer l'entent des parties cy pres que poit estre collect par les parols."

56. 5 Co. Rep. 8a.

57. This had not always been the case: Y. B. 4 Edw. 4, fol. 8, Pasch., pl. 9.

58. *Tollett v. Tollett* (1753), Amb. 178.

59. Jones, W. 181: "quand un condition ne poet estre literalment performe per act de Dieu, il serra perform cy-pres l'entent del'parties come poet estre."

60. 2 Plowden 466–67, as cited in Georg Behrens, "Equity in the *Commentaries* of Edmund Plowden," *Journal of Legal History* 20 (1999): 32. The idea of imagining what the legislator would have ruled had he been aware of a particularly difficult case that could not be justly resolved with his statute as written can be traced back to Aristotle, *Nicomachean Ethics,* trans. Terence Irwin (Hackett: Indianapolis, Ind., 1999), 5.10.5, 83.

to conjure up the intent of the law-giver is not so different from the later exercise to figure out what the intent of the donor would have been in present circumstances.

Within charitable trusts, the notion of approximating intent would combine with the relief offered by the Elizabethan statute to create a broad power that would ultimately allow the substitution of purposes and objects. Within non-charitable trusts, no more than deviation would result; absent the ability to cure uncertainties, non-charitable trusts would be far more prone to fail outright and so would not create opportunities to reflect on what "coming as near as may be to the intent" might mean or how it could be used. On the other hand, consent of the interested parties would remain a vital issue in the modification of trusts in non-charitable trust law, even as it dropped away from charitable trusts, which were increasingly being explicitly construed to cut out the relationship with the heirs.[61]

Bacon also believed that intention could be honored without being perfected; in fact, Bacon would argue that intention could be perfected inexactly. In his work on the revocation of uses, Bacon argued that uses after Henry VIII's statute still retained a greater flexibility in their understanding of intent than would have been true under strict common law. In his *Case of Impeachment of Waste*, Bacon had cited Littleton's point that the feoffee should go, as Bacon read it, "as near the condition, and as near the intent of the condition as he may." But, Bacon pointed out, "to come near is not to reach."[62] Bacon did at times argue for the revocation of uses, but did so while noting that a use "ought to be construed more favourably according to the intent, and not literally or strictly," and that while "uses in point of operation are reduced to a kind of conformity with the rules of the common law, but that in point of exposition of words, they retain somewhat of their ancient nature, and are expounded more liberally according to the intent."[63] Littleton and Bacon would have

---

61. *Cudrington v. Stokes*, in *Lord Nottingham's Chancery Cases*, ed. D. E. C. Yale, vol. 1 (London: Selden Society, 1957), 29.
62. On Littleton in the *Case of Impeachment of Waste*, see Bacon, *Works*, vol. 7, 543.
63. Ibid., 562.

considerable influence on the treatment of conditions and intention in non-charitable trusts and estates. Consequently in the seventeenth century trust law would move toward compensation rather than forfeiture, and, as Yale noted, "where there was a condition, as distinct from a limitation, the quality of the condition was often ignored, or if not ignored was transmuted by treating what were on the wording of the disposition conditions precedent as subsequent."[64] This mattered because illegal or impossible conditions precedent would normally eliminate and make void the entire legacy (in common law, but usually not in civil), whereas illegal or impossible conditions subsequent would normally vanish, allowing the bequest to pass without burden (as in civil law).[65]

Bacon appreciated the utility of intent, if interpreted flexibly. In the 1621 case *Grant v. Huish* he performed what could be called an administrative deviation. The will of Richard Huish, or Hewish, had put onerous terms on the executors and governors for his hospital foundation. This was "found difficult to work, and it was alleged that there were defects in the terms of the will which prevented it from expressing the real intention of the testator."[66] Inconvenience could thwart intention. Bacon modified the trust and allowed the governors to meet wherever was convenient to them. This was not a derogation for cause, which Bacon disliked. Rather, he suggested that a nuanced understanding of intent could allow reasonable alterations to suit ever-changing circumstances. The difference is subtle, but Bacon had found a way to honor donor intent, as required, but not allow this intent to stifle itself. This was a little anomalous; other judges on charitable cases in the seventeenth century would interpret donor intent literally and not use it as a means for alteration, but

---

64. D. E. C. Yale, "An Essay on Mortgages and Trusts and Allied Topics in Equity," in *Lord Nottingham's Chancery Cases*, vol. 2 (London: Selden Society, 1961), 29.

65. Co. Litt. 206 b. ii. 19–24. Although many legacies were made with both the language of trust and the language of condition used, charitable legacies (or any in which the courts desired to protect the beneficiary's rights) were increasingly interpreted through trusts rather than conditions, as explained by Thomas, "Conditions in Favour of Third Parties," 240–57.

66. Ritchie 29.

in his cases Bacon was drawing the law near to where he hoped it would be, employing *contiguum*.[67]

Nonetheless, for Bacon, prerogative remained the fundamental principle on which to ground the redirection of property, with intent and approximation just tools to be used, or not, in its support. In 1619, he heard *Bloomfield v. Inhabitants of Stowmarket*.[68] He enforced a charitable devise that had included a quarter of the gift to be used to sing for the souls of the donor and her family. Bacon honored her other terms strictly, but he took the money for the prayers and dispersed it to a new use: half to the poor where the church was located, and half to the poor where the donor had lived. The heir had been claiming that the entire gift should revert to him. Bacon did not comment on why he rejected that claim or why he refused to send back the superstitious quarter. He must have believed that what he did was within his power as the representative of the king's prerogative. He did not request the Sign Manual, nor did he try to approximate donor intent. James I, now in difficult financial straits, was still avoiding sacrilege but could no longer afford to turn back superstitious gifts to the heir, nor would it have been wise to treat recusants better than dissenters.

Surpluses and the Feoffees for Impropriations

The 1609 *Case of Thetford School* was vital to the development of cy-près, even though it had nothing to do with changing use. Land income devised by a will to support a school, a preacher, and the maintenance of four poor people had grown. The court found that it was permissible to increase the stipend of the preacher and the schoolmaster, and that the surplus of value should be "expended for the maintenance of a greater number of Poor, etc. and nothing should be converted by the Devisees to their own uses." Similarly, "nothing should be converted to the private use of the Executors or

---

67. On the afterlife of Bacon's hopes for the reform of law, see: Barbara Shapiro, "Sir Francis Bacon and the Mid-Seventeenth Century Movement for Law Reform," *American Journal of Legal History* 24 (1980): 331–62.
68. Duke 40.

their heirs." The intention of the testator was cited: "he intended all should be imployed in works of Piety and Charity."[69] If there was a surplus residual from property that was left to charitable uses, then that surplus would be maintained "to purposes *ejusdem generis*," or of the same kind (a phrase not in Coke's report but later attributed to the case), as the original object, because: "the court of Chancery will construe [the donor's] intent imperatively to be not only in exclusion of his next of kin, but to the disinheriting of his heir at law." Thus a surplus of rents given to a school would be used for the same educational purpose as the original donation and not returned to the heir of the donor. The case could ultimately support a larger principle that charitable donations should not return to private uses. However, since the terms of the original gift specified sums of money to be given "out of the profits" of the land, it seems entirely possible that the donor's intent had been for the "executors," as they are described in *Gibbons v. Maltyard and Martin*, to have the rest, as compensation and a gift in itself, which had not been an unusual arrangement. By rejecting that model and instead appropriating all of the profits to the charity, the court may have intended to punish the negligent executors. But it was ultimately a move to simplify the relationships within charitable property: from one donor to a perpetual charity, without a web of connected interests around them.

The early Stuart kings did not renounce the alternate principle that the surplus might be theirs to redistribute.[70] It was claimed in the 1633 *Feoffees for Impropriations Case* that surplusage of a charitable trust belonged to the king, *ad opus nostrum*; a 1327 case in Chancery was cited in which an excess left over from a gift was used to pave Cambridge.[71] In the seventeenth century, following the *Case of*

69. 8 Co. Rep. 130b. This case was a followup to the cases *Martindale v. Martin* and *Gibbons v. Maltyard and Martin*. The idea that surplus residues for charitable gifts should be given to similar purposes would remain vital and would be considered a fundamental application of the concept of *ejusdem generis* and "as near as may be": *Attorney-General v. Earl of Winchelsea* (3 Bro. C.C. 373); *Attorney-General v. The Haberdashers' Company* (1 Ves. Jr. 295).

70. Both Luther and the Schmalkaldic League had argued that rulers had the right to determine the use of charitable surpluses as well: see Cohn, "Church Property in the German Protestant Principalities," 163–64, and Brady, *Protestant Politics*, 172–73. Bucer had disagreed.

71. Bryson, ed., *Cases Concerning Equity*, vol. 2, 644.

Thetford School, the heirs, trustees, and executors lost their potential claims to surplus, and in relinquishing charitable surpluses to charity (although not necessarily the same charity or the same purpose as originally designated), the king was relaxing his prerogative just as he had done with superstitious uses when he permitted their "reform" to be their return to the heirs. In 1629 and 1630, Thomas Coventry as Lord Keeper sent the surplusage of a charitable trust "to other charitable uses."[72] The report did not indicate what these uses were or whether they were near to the original gift, but in many of the initial cases involving charitable surpluses, the surpluses stuck to the same objects originally designated in the will. For example, in the 1634 *East-greensteds Case*, Lord Coventry found that charitable residues—even if drawn from rent across several counties—could not be applied, at least by commissioners' decree, to places other than that which had been designated by the donor.[73] By 1674 Heneage Finch, probably influenced by Bacon and citing the principle *bonum quo communius eo melius*, allowed for a surplus to be used not just for the poor of the original city but also those of a neighboring city, since "in charities the most extensive and liberal construction was the best."[74] This would turn out to be unusual; it would be more common to maintain the designated beneficiaries strictly while finding another way to increase the charity. Still, surpluses, the superfluities of superfluities, would prove to be one of the most dynamic ways in which cy-près would develop as a concept, because of the phrase *ejusdem generis* that was applied to their dispersal.[75]

Surpluses as evidence of the sovereign's prerogative over charity would also be an ancillary part of the argument for the infamous *Feoffees for Impropriations Case* (1633), in which donors had given money to Puritan feoffees, who used it to buy advowsons, impropriations, or pay for preaching ministers. It was difficult for the state to articulate exactly what the feoffees had done that was illegal, with the consequence that the arguments in the case tended to shift. The case began with an assertion that the feoffees had taken money giv-

72. Duke 32.
73. Herne 63.
74. *Lord Nottingham's Chancery Cases*, vol. 1, 135.
75. *Attorney-General v. Green* (1789), 2 Bro. C.C. 492.

en to them and used it for personal, private uses, but when the record books were produced in court, this charge faded away. That the feoffees had incorporated themselves without letters patent and had written ordinances that touched on ecclesiastical matters (and so might be called canons) was another charge—and the one that Matthew Hale would later claim "was the only ground that could in any probability be insisted upon in the great case in the exchequer chamber touching impropriations."[76] Occasionally during the trial their activities were portrayed as a conspiracy to destroy the church from within. On the whole, though, the state chose a different tactic: to accept that the feoffees were "honest men" and that the donors too had good intentions (although Lord Cottington, Chancellor of the Exchequer, pointed out that the intentions of the donors did not seem to be good and noted sarcastically what "ill luck" they had that their first presentation was for one "sentenced for Blasphemy").[77] We know that the king himself did not believe the feoffees were honest, because at the end of the case he asked, according to Rushworth, whether criminal proceedings might be possible.[78] In the midst of a prolonged struggle between Charles I and the "Puritans," both sides in this case attempted to avoid the question of dissention. The state did not want to stir outrage with outright confiscation; neither did it want the property returned. Nonetheless, the use of the donated money was still misemployed, the state contended—perhaps because the feoffees had, in their ordinances, written that they would purchase impropriations, but instead they had also bought advowsons and places for schoolmasters (a point on which the defense countered that the donors had consented to, or in some cases insisted upon, these alternative plans), or perhaps because they had used their money for "dative" preachers rather than for livings

76. Matthew Hale, *Prerogatives of the King*, ed. D. E. C. Yale, Selden Society Annual Series, vol. 92 (London: Bernard Quaritch, 1975), 240–41.

77. Isabel M. Calder, *Activities of the Puritan Faction of the Church of England, 1625–1633* (London: S.P.C.K., 1957), 122. This emphasis on the good intentions of the donors is similar to the rhetoric of gifts during the German Reformation, once again perhaps because a gift that had been intentionally made to a bad end was entirely void and should probably be returned.

78. John Rushworth, *Historical Collections*, vol. 2 (London: John Wright, 1680), 152.

for perpetual vicars, pulling these men into their control since they could attach conditions to their salaries. Although it was legal to support preachers rather than vicars, some arguments were offered that this was not the "best" use—but this contention dropped from the discussion and was not part of the eventual decree.

The most revealing aspect of the case, however, is the extent to which the feoffees themselves had an older understanding of gifts. That the donor or his or her heirs had an ongoing interest in the gift and ought to be consulted about its usage was apparent in both the internal dealings of the feoffees and their external presentation of their case. For example, one donor had given money for lectures that were being "disturbed by the encumbent," and so the feoffees asked the donor whether "then the alowance maie be diuerted thence to serue for the maintenance of like purposes elswhere."[79] This was not even necessarily a change in purpose, but the feoffees knew that the donor should be consulted and had assumed that the trustees and donors could make rearrangements amongst themselves; this power of rearrangement would be lost by the end of the century. In fact, the attorney general assumed such rearrangement was possible too; he cited the problem that the feoffees, even as "good honest men," might still "alter and change and revoke what they now doe … [and] cannot infuse their minds and qualities into their successors."[80] At the hearing on February 11, 1633, Robert Holborne, counsel for the feoffees, drew on the adage "*cuius est dare, cuius [huius] est disponere*" [if it is his to give, it is his to dispose] to defend the idea that the links between donor and gift allowed the feoffees to use charitable money for conditional purposes, such as the hiring and letting go of lecturers or schoolmasters.[81] Similarly, counsel for the defendants asked why the donors or their heirs had not been called in to the case, since they were also interested parties:

ffor the next avoydance which they haue they are not the Patron but he that hath the inheritance, And this concerning him he is not a party to the

---

79. Calder, *Activities*, 149.

80. Ibid., 53.

81. Ibid., 95. On the use of this phrase in Moore (f. 47v), see Jones, *History of the Law of Charity*, 71.

364   A Doctrine Is Born

suite, also the donours of the mony to theis vses, and of the leases, etc. are alive, and are not complained on with the Defendants, how far forth their estates without them can be disposed of, we submit to your Lordships, we humbly offer this to be considered that if the estates be taken away they wilbe discoraged from going on and others from giving To so charitable a work, and those that haue given will repent them of what they haue done, So we humbly leaue it to the Judgment of the Court desiring that the vses may stand and the estates remain in the parties trusted.[82]

The Venables case was cited by Attorney-General Noy in his information and also read aloud in court midway through the proceedings in order to give some direction to an otherwise unprecedented situation.[83] The counsel for the defendants urged the use of the Venables case as a precedent. They did so with the knowledge that the far more likely alternative was forfeiture. Since the case as it was developing tended on whole to support that the original intention of the donors was to give to good uses, the counsel urged that the uses be perfected, not destroyed:

Now theis being the vses, vnder fauor of the Court, we Conceiue, they are good and well created vses, We confess that if an vse be raised and made, which is against the lawe or to an vnlawfull end This is not lawfully created, and may be rectified, and this way hath bin heretofore obserued to fauor charitable vses, soe far as the vse and will of the Donor (As nigh as might be) might be obserued ffor the Will of Mrs Venables by which it was ordeyned that mony should be given to silenced ministers, this was an vnlawfull end, Yet the sentence of the Court goeth not to take away the vse altogether but ordereth that the mony shalbe ymploied (as neere to the vse as might be) to the benefit of poore ministers that did conforme and to the wives and Children of such inconformable ministers being dead.[84]

It was true that the attorney suggested that the "vses may stand and the estates remain in the parties trusted," but still the argument was set before the court that the defendants would prefer to have the uses altered somewhat rather than destroyed altogether.[85] On the other side, the attorney general also asked for "a better use of this

82. Calder, *Activities*, 99.
83. For the records of the case, Bryson, ed., *Cases Concerning Equity*, vol. 2, 643–57.
84. Calder, *Activities*, 97–98.
85. Ibid., 99.

nature," saying that "now that theis monys are given and purchases made to such uses I shall not move to have it imployed to any seculer use."[86] Although the counsels for the defendants cited many different sources for their arguments—medieval statutes and Latin adages among them—they offered nothing else to support this concept of shifting a use slightly, "as neere to the use as might be" except the Venables case. To the extent that cy-près, as it was coming to be, was considered equitable, it would be largely because it was a relief from the potential penalty of forfeiture.[87] In this case, the counsel was suggesting that corrections be made, but that the feoffees and donors retain their connection to the gifts, not anticipating that the Venables case would be taken as precedent to sever these links.

The attorney general also drew on the Venables case and on the idea of correcting or reforming the use. He suggested that the feoffees were secretive and used their power to harass ("to weary") incumbents and put them out.[88] This might be a misemployment. Moreover, Noy claimed that "if any thing given to good uses be misimployed; The king may take it all into his owne hands in his Court of Exchequer."[89] Apparently the king's prerogative meant that *abusus tollit usum.* Noy went on. The king had the right to surpluses of money given to a charitable end: "if any thing remaine of the monyes for such publique good uses collected, then the same belongeth to the king of right and to no other person or persons."[90] Noy extended this to the king's supervision concerning *pietatis operibus* in general and gave the example of the Byzantine emperor who had come to raise funds; money collected after he left was kept by the king: "for it was Charity and it was not to be paid back againe to the Contributors."[91] Here the king's prerogative could treat all charitable donations as a free gift, with no return to the donor even if it was not going to be used for its intended purpose. Any gift to charity might be "given" to the king. Noy was making an argument about the inherent qual-

86. Ibid., 53.
87. A penalty reinforced by the statute *De religiosis,* 7 Edward 1.
88. Calder, *Activities,* 54–55.
89. Ibid., 56.
90. Ibid., 57.
91. Ibid., 58–59.

ity of charity; that argument, should it be taken to be a rule, would make it virtually impossible for heirs or donors to contest, successfully, a failed gift. Weston, the Lord High Treasurer, had a simpler legal precedent to suggest: the civil law provided, he claimed, for "confiscation of goods [and] banishment" as a consequence "if any meet about causes of religion" without "commission."[92]

In elaborating on misemployment as a theme, the case would be settled by removing the feoffees from control of the property—without consulting with the donors, many of whom were still living. This result was significant in part because it was specifically these feoffees that had been entrusted; other feoffees (like Laud) were not within the intention of the donors. Moreover, the feoffees had been active and effective—too much so—and the argument that they had deceived the donors about the plans for their money was well refuted by the materials that the feoffees produced. This was not traditional misemployment. Their activities were not exactly illegal, but they were "inconvenient," as it was expressed at the time.[93] This case would thus reinforce the "as nigh as may be" explanation from the Venables case, and it would also cut away at the relationships between donor, trustee, and the gift. Additionally, the replacement of trustees would eventually merge into the substitution of charitable objects, as would become clear later.[94] If cy-près had been a fully developed doctrine at this point, then misemployment would not have been so necessary to the case; conversely, the use of misemployment as a justification helps to explain how cy-près would come to be linked to the preservation of a specifically charitable intention.

But Charles I certainly did not intend to open up a greater flexibility in the treatment of gifts more generally; nor did he mean to extend what he considered to be a prerogative power to others. In the 1636 canons sent to the archbishops and bishops of Scotland, Charles observed that there had been "too great liberty" in dealing with the property of "churches, colleges, schools, [and] hospitals,"

---

92. Bryson, ed., *Cases Concerning Equity*, vol. 2, 657.
93. Noy's information had argued from the beginning that the king had the right to regulate charities both for abuse and for inconvenience. Ibid., 643.
94. *Attorney-General v. Andrew* (1798), 3 Ves. 633.

which discouraged donations. Instead, there could be no "alteration made of the benefactor's will," but rather the will would "stand firm and be preserved to the use for which it was first appointed."[95] The canon added no caveat to permit the amendment of impossible, illegal, impractical, or inconvenient gifts in any way.

From Prerogative to Equity

The lord chancellor served at the pleasure of the king, and Chancery was broadly perceived to be a court where the king's wishes ruled and the chancellor was "practically uncontrolled."[96] When James I, a theoretician of absolutist rule, responded to Bacon's flattery that the Chancery was "the court of your absolute power" by dismissing Coke as chief justice and decreeing the supremacy of the Chancery, this could only add to the widespread perception that Chancery served the whims of the Stuart kings.[97] Chancery could "command the owner of property to do with that property as the Chancellor directed, on penalty of imprisonment for disobeying."[98] Stuart Prall has shown that apparent "subservience to the crown" as well as "lack of consistency" was one of the many criticisms of Chancery in the run up to the English Civil War.[99]

During the Restoration that followed the Civil War, lord chancellors hoped to preserve equitable remedies while making the court seem less arbitrary, responding to Selden's famous charge that conscience varied from person to person like the size of a foot, which made conscience "an uncertain measure."[100] A focus on systematiza-

95. "The Scottish Canons of 1636," canon 17, § 9, in Gerald Bray, ed., *The Anglican Canons 1529–1947* (Woodbridge, England: Boydell Press, 1998), 549.
96. William S. Holdsworth, *A History of English Law*, vol. 16 (London: Sweet and Maxwell, 1966), 217.
97. Francis Bacon, "Letter to the King's Most Excellent Majesty, Concerning the Praemunire in the King's Bench, against the Chancery," 21 Feb. 1616, *Letters and the Life*, vol. 5, 252.
98. John H. Langbein et al., *The History of the Common Law: The Development of Anglo-American Legal Institutions* (New York: Aspen, 2009), 316.
99. Stuart Prall, "Chancery Reform and the Puritan Revolution," *American Journal of Legal History* 6 (1962): 37.
100. John Selden, *Table Talk of John Selden*, ed. Frederick Pollock (London: Quaritch, 1927), 43.

tion meant that precedent gained ground in Chancery.[101] This effort toward regularization occurred at the same time as dwindling charitable receipts and pressure to use charitable resources more effectively to solve the social dislocations of the chaotic seventeenth century, so it is not surprising that a nascent cy-près doctrine would formalize.[102] Framing the treatment of failing charitable gifts in terms of donor intent was a way to uphold the common good without undermining the individual's right to property or echoing concepts that had now been tainted by association with Anabaptists, Levellers, and Diggers. If cy-près could reform an inconvenient use, out of which a good intention might be rescued, then this approximation of donor intent could easily be applied to less troublesome cases of charitable uses, whose intent was all the more meritorious and deserving. It was a new sense of regularized equity, not the same as was practiced in the *ius commune* model of interacting norms and circumstances, and in this drive to regularize equity, a doctrine would be formed to govern the power to redirect charitable gifts.

As Quentin Skinner found in *Liberty before Liberalism,* even words that are used only rhetorically in political discussion can come to bind the speaker, trapping him with his own manipulations. This phenomenon occurred at least twice in the development of cy-près power and its attendant doctrine. First, in the explanation of the good uses to which chantry property was to be put, the Edwardian statute not only laid down a precedent of the lawful transfer of

---

101. Plucknett, *Concise History of the Common Law,* 690–92; J. H. Baker, *An Introduction to English Legal History,* 4th ed. (Oxford: Oxford University Press, 2007), 109–11; W. H. D. Winder, "Precedent in Equity," *Law Quarterly Review* 57 (1941): 245–79. On the persistence of the problem, see Mike Macnair, "Arbitrary Chancellors and the Problem of Predictability," in *Law and Equity: Approaches in Roman Law and Common Law,* ed. E. Koops and W. J. Zwalve (Leiden: Brill, 2013), 79–104. On conscience as a rule in Protestant thought during the second half of the seventeenth century, see Klinck, *Conscience, Equity, and the Court of Chancery,* 193–6.

102. It was also a time of the revival of voluntarist thought derived from Ockham, as noted by Klinck and Tully, which could support the affirmation of the particular intentions of the donor. Klinck, *Conscience, Equity, and the Court of Chancery, 201–2;* James Tully, "Governing Conduct" in *Conscience and Casuistry in Early Modern Europe,* ed. Edmund Leites (Cambridge: Cambridge University Press, 1988), 12–71.

property given for one purpose to another, but helped to provide the grounds for restricting the precedent. Second, over time even the insistence in prerogative cy-près cases that the transitions of use for superstitious or inconvenient gifts would be made "as near as may be" could evolve into a tempered doctrine that, through a small shift to their use, legitimately did try to honor impossible gifts.

John Herne, writing on the law of charitable uses in 1660, used neither the term "cy-près" nor the phrase *ejusdem generis,* nor did he indicate that the use of a charitable gift could be changed. Herne ignored Bacon's case on Emmanuel College completely, probably because he did not see it as either heralding or reinforcing a broader principle. The case on Thetford School did appear, with its striking language about the intent of the donor to cut off the heirs and the claiming for charitable uses of all surpluses associated with the gift, but Herne did not suggest that charity could never fail.[103] Rather, his focus was on donor intent and the procedures associated with the supervision of charitable uses. Herne missed the evidence that the law of charitable uses was in the process of transformation because it had not yet arrived at a fully developed cy-près doctrine. The expanded edition by George Duke in 1676 also did not consider the alteration of uses except in the cases of mixed uses, where the good use could save a property that also had superstitious uses attached.

In the 1675 *Attorney-General v. Peacock,* Heneage Finch claimed in overruling the initial demurrer that "all charities which were not within the regulation of the statute of 43 Eliz." were under the king as *pater patriae,* "for he was so at Common Law before that statute." For an uncertain charity, then "the King by his prerogative may make the application to such of his poor subjects as he please."[104] The original gift, made early in Charles I's reign, had been "an award and settlement by consent of parties," which the king, "by advice of Archbishop Laud and Coventry" had authorized—and which left a substantial portion of the charitable gift to the heir. This was, in the 1630s, still predicated on a model of building a consensus that might involve compromise. But with the death of the original heir, who

103. Herne 100–101, on *Peacock v. Thewer,* with reference to earlier cases.
104. *Lord Nottingham's Chancery Cases,* vol. 1, 209. See also Finch 245.

had devised his portion to the defendant, there was a new push to make the entire estate over to charity. Finch disapproved of the entire proceedings from forty years earlier and considered that "the case was never in a proper course until now." In fact, he said, "the consent of executors or heirs to the diverting of the charity is not material." The only question was to see what "his Majesty's pleasure" would be—he imagined it might be to support the king's new foundation at Christ's Hospital.

When the case came back before Finch later that year, his ruling was more precise: "a general and indefinite charity may be so applied by the King as to become certain and particular, but then the application must ever be to a charity *ejusdem generis*."[105] The king could not turn a gift "to the poor to repair churches or bridges." On the other hand, if "the uses to which it is designed are illegal and void, it becomes at last a charity at large, that is, general and indefinite ... [but] the King may make it certain and particular again by applying it to good uses *ejusdem generis*," on which point Finch cited the Venables case in Lane's reports.[106] Consequently, since the original gift was "for the good of the poor," all aspects of the award that were for poor relief were maintained, while those that were not were eliminated, including the provision for the heir. Finch stated that it was not within the powers of Chancery "either to divert the charity or straighten the remedy of it."[107] This is a powerful suggestion that Finch did not think that there was a judicial cy-près power yet; everything rested on the king's prerogative, but even the king's prerogative was now bound by the *ejusdem generis* rule. Finch excluded any poor relations of the testator "because it must be a settlement to the poor in perpetuity."[108] Moreover, although Finch did not give a final disposition, because he awaited the king's pleasure, he noted the many corrections and misemployments that he believed had been made out of the estate, anticipating assorted fines that could include penalties to the executors for "the profits which [the heir] re-

---

105. *Lord Nottingham's Chancery Cases*, vol. 1, 305.
106. Ibid.
107. Ibid.
108. Ibid., 306.

ceived during his life under the colour of that award and in breach of the charity." This was an astonishing, vigorous defense of the rights of charity; it was no longer safe to rely on the consensus of interested parties in order to modify a failing gift.

In that same year Finch had already made a similar determination in *Attorney-General v. Platt*, on a devise for fellows and scholars at St. John's College in Cambridge, long delayed because it was devised to the wrong name and then interrupted by the Civil War.[109] The parties had reached their own agreement, which Finch rejected: "[T]he College ought to take the Charity as 'tis given, or to leave it to the right Heir, and have done neither, but have made a special Agreement with the Father of the Defendant, that Agreement must certainly be void." This was "in Abuse of the said Charity ... because it was contrary to the Will of the Testator."[110] The brokered terms were discarded, and the original gift upheld.

The principle of the renewal of altered gifts through the consent of interested parties was demonstrated to have fallen into desuetude by the 1682 *Attorney-General v. Margaret and Regius Professors*, in which the lord chancellor set aside an agreement between Peterhouse and the heir-at-law to alter the terms of a lectureship in order to make it easier to find a speaker: "they should be held to the letter of the charity, and ... the heir had no power to alter the disposition made by his ancestor."[111] It would remain the case that interested parties might attempt to settle on a compromise, which could be presented to the attorney general for his consent and then ratified with a de-

---

109. The header summaries for the reports in Finch on *Attorney-General v. Peacock* and *Attorney-General v. Platt* (Finch 222 and 245) both cite Domat to explain that in civil law a gift to the poor would go to the local hospital. This is not evidence that Domat was used in the case, since Domat was published in French in 1689 and in English in 1722.

110. Finch 222; *Lord Nottingham's Chancery Cases*, vol. 1, 160.

111. 1 Vern. 56; for a similar treatment of the attempt by beneficiaries to consent to an alteration in terms, see *Man v. Ballett* (1682), 1 Vern. 45. *Lord Nottingham's Chancery Cases*, vol. 1, 209: "the consent of executors or heirs to the diverting of the charity is not material," for *Attorney-General vs. Peacock* (1675). The case *Attorney-General at the relation of Peterhouse, College in Cambridge v. The Lady Margaret and Regius Professors of Divinity in the University of Cambridge* is covered in Jones, *History of the Law of Charity*, 75.

cree.[112] They could not reform the gift on their own authority, but needed the approval of both the attorney general and Chancery, for whom the primary consideration was supposed to be the intention of the donor, not the rights and interests of anyone else.

In 1678 Finch's report on *Attorney-General v. Combes* cited the Venables case in the margins as a precedent. Money was left for "godly preachers to be chosen by most voices ... all which hath been discontinued ever since 1660." They were to preach on Mondays, Wednesdays, and Saturdays in three locations. This was "a kind of factious institution" and "no allowable charity," but "the best pretence of it being for instruction of the people, that intent shall be preserved by applying it to catechising upon these days by persons to be nominated by the bishop of the diocese."[113] Still, Finch did not think that Chancery was required to make good any gift with a charitable intention.[114] By the 1670s, then, Chancery was increasingly confident that both charitable surpluses and superstitious/dissenting gifts ought to be applied *ejusdem generis* as the original gift. As suggested by Finch in 1675, this rule had come to impinge even on the prerogative powers of the king that had served as the initial justification for choosing new objects for uncertain or unworthy charities. The 1684 case of *Attorney-General v. Baxter*, which gave money to be distributed among sixty ejected ministers, was designated by Charles II to go to building Chelsea College, but the court intervened: "the practice had always been to apply charities *in eodem genere,* and this being intended for ejected ministers, ought to go amongst the clergy."[115] The lord keeper then designated it for a chaplain at Chelsea College instead—although, like other prominent seventeenth-century cases in the change of use, the decree was subsequently vacated and the original will upheld—as a consequence, in this case, of the 1688 Act of Toleration.[116]

---

112. For instance, *Andrew v. the Master and Warden of Merchant Taylors' Company, and the Attorney-General* (1802), 7 Ves. 223; this compromise, if decreed and consented to, was then binding, see *Strickland v. Aldridge*, 9 Ves. 516; on the consent of the Attorney-General, see *Attorney-General v. Hewitt* (1803), 9 Ves. 232.
113. *Lord Nottingham's Chancery Cases*, vol. 2, 704; 2 Freem. 40.
114. *Gwyn v. Parker*, in *Lord Nottingham's Chancery Cases*, vol. 2, 703.
115. 1 Vern. 251.
116. *Attorney-General v. Hughes*, 2 Vern. 105.

These vacated decrees indicated the ongoing judicial discomfort with changing the use of a gift (in *Attorney-General v. Baxter* a coherent agreement was reached: "there was a difference between the charity and the use; and that the use was void, and not the charity"), but the emergence of a rule about how to make these changes seems to have assuaged Chancery's anxieties. The rule limited the power and made it appropriate for judges to employ it. Subsequent attempts to distinguish between prerogative cy-près and judicial cy-près would suggest that prerogative cy-près could be used to solve religiously problematic gifts, to cure uncertainty, or to direct gifts not placed with trustees. But the historical progression seems to have been that the attachment of a rule for how prerogative changes in use would be done made it possible for the judiciary to employ it and to consider it a "doctrine." And most importantly, rather than allowing a judge to reach an equitable solution to the particular circumstances of a failed gift, cy-près doctrine would dictate specific considerations to prioritize. For this reason alone it is not entirely clear that cy-près was an equitable doctrine, except in the sense that it had initially served to mitigate strict law.[117] Notably, equitable principles do not normally provoke the revocation of decrees made in their honor, as cy-près sometimes did. Nor did the equity of cy-près or of Chancery set the judges free to follow the particular justice of a situation; this reality would be demonstrated in *Attorney-General v. Whorwood* (1750), in which a judge expressed regret that he could do very little for a widow whose estranged husband had attempted to defraud her of as much property as possible in the name of charity.[118]

But the ideal of the maintenance of property for its given use had lost much of its cultural power, even if it survived, approximately, in donor intent. In non-legal writings, the rejection of Aristotelianism often included an embrace of "new uses," as when Thomas Browne summarized Nathanael Carpenter's rejection of final causes in his 1621 *Philosophia libera triplici exercitationum decade proposita*: "a thing

117. On early modern English equity, see Mark Fortier, *The Culture of Equity*, and Dennis R. Klinck, *Conscience, Equity and the Court of Chancery in Early Modern England* (Burlington, Vt.: Ashgate, 2010).
118. 1 Ves. Sen. 534.

is often conserved, when it is frustrate of its due end, as when its converted to a new use and end."[119] Across the seventeenth century new uses began to have their own, unashamed appeal. Even uses that had been appointed by God might be revised—"God's old works have new use in all ages"[120]—and God's covenants renovated when "there was, in the Promise, new Ends and a new Use given unto it."[121] A 1642 translation of Giovanni Diodati's annotations on the Bible, ordered by the House of Commons, allowed that God made new uses, as with the rainbow: "a new use of remembrance."[122] John Stileman offered that Christ took Jewish ritual and "applied [it] to a new use, end, and signification."[123] Hugh Chamberlen, proposing the creation of bills of credit based on land, rejected the "naked enjoyment of Adam" which lacked "all known inventions, which now serves our necessities, conveniencies, and pleasures," and offered that his proposal was only "the application of an old known Subject, or material to a new use."[124] In medicine, too, it became common to speak of the new use that might be made of materials for better treatments.

But it was harder to embrace new uses in law or political philosophy. Gifts and inheritance had previously worked in tandem to affix social and material relationships both past and present. Cy-près is only one part of a broader story about the destruction of the power of gifts to bind the recipient with regard to their use. As the old binding fell apart, it was necessary to tie society together in a new way. Both republican and absolutist theorists relied on the state to determine the terms by which society would be held together, and both cast about for new justifications for both the right to rule others

119. Thomas Browne, *Religio medici* (London: Scot, Basset, Wright, and Chiswell, 1682), 212.
120. David Dickson, *A Brief Explication of the First Fifty Psalms* (London: Thomas Johnson, 1655), 272.
121. John Owen, *Exercitations Concerning the Name, Original, Use, and Continuance of a Day of Sacred Rest* (London: Nathaniel Ponder, 1671), 231 and 426.
122. Giovanni Diodati, *Pious Annotations, upon the Holy Bible Expounding the Difficult Places Thereof Learnedly, and Plainly* (London: Nicholas Fussel, 1643), 11.
123. John Stileman, *A Peace-Offering an Earnest and Passionate intreaty, for peace, unity, and obedience* (London: Thomas Pierrepont, 1662), 124.
124. Hugh Chamberlen, *A Few Proposals Humbly Recommending to the Serious Consideration of His Majesty's High Commissioner* (Edinburgh: n.p., 1700), 37.

and the private property held by individuals. One possibility was for inheritance alone to step into the breach: Filmer's *Patriarcha* would attempt to put all of the weight on inheritance, as if distributions could be explained only by descent, and as if inheritance could eliminate the problem of consent by making current dispositions of power and property nothing more than a legacy received. As long as inheritance and gifts had worked together, then society was entangled across groups. To ground social settlements in inheritance alone, though, narrowed society unbearably. In response, Locke tried to revive the social fabric through commercial exchange. In Locke's view, gifts were distant: the world was a gift to man, but private dominion was justified by the labor put into it. Thus a world of gifts was turned into a world of things that had been made—and that could then be sold, remade, resold, and perpetually cycled through innovative commerce, not perpetually bound to any particular use. But Locke did not abandon the revocability of the trust placed in government. As Skinner notes, Locke drew on "one of the most familiar legal analogies" in paragraph 149 of the *Second Treatise of Government*, where he explained that trusts were limited by the purpose given to them, such that if the purpose is not honored, it is forfeited and returned to the donor. For Locke, this traditional understanding of trusts could legitimize, or delegitimize, legislative power, but simple gifts could not perform the same role in defending the private property arrangements and social relationships of people.[125]

An alternative solution to the impotence of gifts would be the contract, which ought to maintain securely the original terms laid out in the agreement. The free gift, given and lost, had replaced the ideal of mutual gifts, kept for their original purpose or requiring the consent of interested parties to alter. Given this loss, the contract—which required consideration on both sides and demanded precision in its execution—could behave similarly to the older form of the gift. Consequently, social contract theory would reconfigure the world as built through self-interest, not benevolence. The impotence of gifts

---

125. Quentin Skinner, "Meaning and Understanding in the History of Ideas," *History and Theory* 8.1 (1969): 9.

was one motivation for Hobbes, exactly in the middle of the seventeenth century, to describe an almost unbreakable contract as the foundation for civil society.[126] Notably, Hobbes introduced the gift in the section where he defined the contract.[127] In that section, the problem of the new understanding of gifts as unilateral, rather than bound up in mutual exchange, emerged: "When the transferring of right is not mutual, but one of the parties transferreth in hope to gain thereby friendship or service from another (or from his friends), or in hope to gain the reputation of charity or magnanimity, or to deliver his mind from the pain of compassion, or in hope of reward in heaven, this is not contract, but gift, free-gift, grace, which words signify one and the same thing."[128] Contracts, on the other hand, were "mutual translation," in which if one party performed their side first, they were then "due" the performance of the other side.[129]

The problem for Hobbes was that gifts could no longer be sufficiently bound to their original purpose. And yet some of the old understanding of the treatment of gifts for purposes crept in through the one escape clause to the social contract. If the fundamental purpose for which the social contract was entered into was broken, then the contract itself shattered with it. It was Hobbes's hope to resurrect the inviolability of purpose in a world in which the gift could no longer hold, even in a theoretical sense. But Hobbes's proposed social contract left at least one unresolved issue: gifts had originally tied donors and recipients together across generations. Contracts did not.

Unfailing Charity

The King James Bible admonished that "charity never faileth," and sometimes cy-près has been defined as a principle by which

---

126. Felicity Heal, *The Power of Gifts: Gift Exchange in Early Modern England* (Oxford: Oxford University Press, 2015), 22–23; Harry Lieberson, *Return of the Gift: European History of a Global Idea* (Cambridge: Cambridge University Press, 2012), 29–31.
127. Thomas Hobbes, *Leviathan*, ed. Thomas Curley (Indianapolis: Hackett, 1994), Part I, chapter xiv, 79–88.
128. Ibid., Part I, chapter xiv, § 12, 82.
129. Ibid., Part I, chapter xiv, § 16–17, 83.

property given to charity would always remain in charity.[130] The ambition to create perpetual alms was an old one, but charity could, in fact, fail. As late as 1720 Parker gave leave to the parties to a contested will to apply back to the court if the charity school in dispute failed, acknowledging the objection laid before him that in that case the "charity ought to revert to the founder."[131] In 1721 a charitable devise with only two witnesses was voided.[132] *Attorney-General v. Gill* (1726) involved a devise to charity that turned on whether the testator had intended "heirs" to mean "heirs-at-law" or the more colloquial "issue." Rather than employing a benign interpretation, the lord chancellor held that it was simply void: "supposing it void if given to a common person, so shall it be also when given to a charity."[133]

Charity often attracts ambivalence. In his recent survey of comparative gift law, Richard Hyland noted with surprise what a hostile legal reception gifts have tended to receive.[134] Historians and anthropologists alike have found restrictions on gifts or the sense that a gift was a curse.[135] There is an enduring resentment aimed at all participants in charitable gifts, even among academics who depend on endowments to subsidize research that is unlikely to pay for itself. The donor gave too late, too little, in the wrong way, or aimed toward the wrong end; the trustee profits too much or steers the gift away from the donor's pure intentions; and the beneficiary fails to appreciate and fails to thrive in the ways that the donor might have hoped. There is, too, a long tradition of distrusting everyone involved in the testamentary process. Testators waited until the very end to dispose of their goods and left it to others to do; confessors urged last-minute donations; heirs were greedy and litigious; executors delayed doing their duty or embezzled the money entirely. It was only the pious last wishes and the prudent disposition of testa-

130. 1 Corinthians 13:8.
131. *Attorney-General v. Hudson*, 2 Eq. Ca. Abr. 192.
132. 2 P. Wms. 260.
133. 2 P. Wms. 370.
134. Richard Hyland, *Gifts: A Study in Comparative Law* (Oxford: Oxford University Press, 2009).
135. Gerald Moore, *Politics of the Gift: Exchanges in Poststructuralism* (Edinburgh: Edinburgh University Press, 2011).

ments that dignified them. These were the most palatable aspects of the whole unpleasant business.

Although suspicion of gifts is not unique to the eighteenth century, there were circumstances that made the eighteenth century particularly hostile to them. Increasingly, charitable gifts in the seventeenth and eighteenth centuries were associated with grand foundations, linked firmly to the donor alone, in commemoration. They were often made at death, so the living had to implement the wishes of the dead, who had possessed their wealth for as long as possible. The law seemed entirely focused on what the donor had intended, not what the living wanted. As philanthropy gained in currency and a more expansive economy tended to undermine the model of the family estate for all but a few, it would increasingly be possible for the wealthy to focus on benevolent ventures at the expense of their heirs, conceiving of their wealth as theirs alone. The trusts they created did not live up to the older ideal of public property, owned by no one and held for everyone, nor were they free gifts. They were not given and then forgotten, set free to be used in whatever way the recipient should choose. Rather, donors exercised the last remaining right of the patron to determine the use of the gift, and the heirs, the trustees, and the beneficiaries were considered in relationship to what the donor wanted.

Ben-Amos notes that there was increasing "self-assertion" on display in the use of charitable trusts throughout the seventeenth and eighteenth centuries. A "great desire to exercise control over the beneficiaries" extended to "precise objectives and the type and exact quantities of offerings ... [as well as] meticulous orders ... for the management and operation." Hindle has found the same trend, as over the course of the seventeenth and eighteenth centuries "endowments became progressively more restrictive."[136] The result was an "onerous" burden on the trustees, who kept the trusts separate from general institutional funds in order to demonstrate their integrity of administration but also increasingly sought a means to use funds "flexibly and applied or manoeuvred as they saw fit ... [apply-

---

136. Ben-Amos, *The Culture of Giving*, 184–85; Hindle, *On the Parish?* 147.

ing] them well beyond the original intention of the donors."[137] This was a scenario, of ever more particular donors and increasingly adventurous trustees, that would make charitable trusts ripe for scrutiny and, consequently, that would create a plethora of cy-près cases that would build on and affirm earlier precedents.[138] The sudden flourishing of cy-près law was also supported by the immemorial tendency of donors to leave their estate to their closest relative for life and then pass it over to charity, satisfying the impulse to benefit someone who was dear and who would remember the testator fondly, but also allowing the donor to anticipate perpetual charitable effects thereafter. This was a method to solve the ancient dilemma of whether to succor one's family or the poor by giving the same property to both, but in succession. However, in the span of time between the instrument and the effect, any number of complications could arise that would bring the case into Chancery, especially if the donor had been particular. Cy-près flourished in these conditions. Whereas John Herne had not addressed cy-près in the 1660s editions of the *Law of Charitable Uses*, nor had George Duke included it in his expanded 1676 edition of the same, Henry Bridgman devoted two chapters to it in the updated and final 1805 edition of the work.

Meanwhile, the 1736 Mortmain Act was a direct attack on land given "to charitable uses," in part because of the "public mischief ... by many large and improvident alienations or dispositions made by languishing or dying persons or by other persons, to uses called *charitable uses,* to take place after their deaths, to the disherison of their lawful heirs."[139] The act encouraged the free gift as a renewed ideal, that is, gifts made by the living and healthy of finite property with no residual claim of any sort: "without any power of revocation, reservation, trust, condition, limitation, clause, or agreement, whatsoever, for the benefit of the donor or grantor, or of any person or persons claiming under him." The act was specifically aimed not at mortmain in general, but at mortmain for charity.[140] As such

---

137. Ben-Amos, *The Culture of Giving,* 184–87.
138. Ibid., 191.
139. 9 George 2 c. 36.
140. *Corbyn v. French* (1799), 4 Ves. 427.

it naturally did not suggest that attempted charitable gifts that were voided by the statute should be made up in another way, but neither did it address any conflict with a larger equitable principle. It was an obvious attack on the growing power and meaning of cy-près, but the conflict and resolutions were left to the courts to determine. There was some chaos in the eighteenth century as a consequence, since some illegal gifts were rescued and some were not. Lord Hardwicke clarified in *Da Costa v. De Pas* that "when the devise is to a superstitious use, and made void by statute, or to a charity, and made void by statute of mortmain, there it should belong to the heir at law or next of kin; but where it is in itself a charity, but the mode in which it is to be disposed, is such that by the law of England it cannot take effect ... there the crown, by sign manual directed to the Attorney-General, may give orders in what charitable manner it shall be disposed."[141]

Support for the Mortmain Act was increased by the perception that more and more property was being bound up in perpetual use, in part because of the effect of cy-près in preserving failing gifts. Consequently cy-près would suffer some significant defeats in the courts throughout the eighteenth century. However, if cy-près was perceived to act to prevent charity from ever failing, as sometimes it has been described, then the authors of the Mortmain Act would have counteracted it directly or put more limits on gifts of personal property, which were exempt from the act. The fact that they did not tells us something about the still erratic operation of cy-près at the time.

It is important to note the direction of ideas here: cy-près did not necessarily arise from a belief that charity could never fail, but, once instituted, cy-près could create the impression that charity would not be allowed to fail. If cy-près were more than an occasional alteration of a gift but were tending toward something more regular, then it would as a consequence produce the rule that any property given to charity was given in perpetuity. The fact that charity became plausibly unfailing only on the cusp of the modern era seems

---

141. Amb. 228.

to suggest that cy-près was regularized and recognized as such only then. Occasional alteration of gifts would not produce a larger rule about charitable property, but an expected cy-près policy, used both on gifts that were failing *ab initio* and for floundering institutions alike, would naturally produce the rule that property given to charity could not fail, especially when considered in conjunction with the many remedies offered to imperfect charitable devises. If charitable intentions could jump from one object to another and one use to another, then it would in fact be almost impossible for charity to fail. In other words, the relatively late development of the idea that cy-près could be summarized through the indestructibility of charitable intention seems to be a strong piece of evidence that there was not previously a legal norm in favor of the necessary alteration of failing pious gifts. It was possible to alter their uses, yes, and to discuss how and when this might be done, but other norms and considerations might win the day, which would mean that charitable or pious gifts were capable of suffering legal defeat. If charity were implicitly perpetual, never failing, known to be resilient to all of the insults that might be slung at it by circumstance, then some form of cy-près that did not even require the consent of interested parties would be an expected consequence. But if, on the contrary, the alteration of gifts for purposes was a rare thing that became a regular principle only relatively late, then we would expect the discovery that charity was theoretically indestructible to follow in its wake. This discovery would happen by the end of the eighteenth century.

Blackstone and others considered the Mortmain Act as a strike against "superstition" and the effort to save oneself at the point of death.[142] Cy-près, which tried to rescue superstition, was thus superstitious by proxy. Although eleemosynary corporations had special rights with regard to visitation, all corporations, regardless of their character, should "revert to the person, or his heirs, who granted them to the corporation" if the corporation dissolved or the cause failed.[143] For this reason, even though Blackstone believed that the

---

142. For the superstition of the deathbed, see Blackstone, *Commentaries*, vol. 2, 273 and 375.

143. Ibid., vol. 1, 472.

monasteries had been largely created out of the profits of conquest, he regarded the statutes for the dissolution of the monasteries as "injurious ... to private as [well as] public rights."[144] As for the Elizabethan statutes on charitable uses, Blackstone was most struck by "the piety of the judges," which, in less enlightened times, "hath formerly carried them great lengths in supporting such charitable uses." In that era, the privileges of charity were thought, Blackstone claimed, to "suppl[y] all defects in assurances."[145] Blackstone did not discuss cy-près directly, but he suggested that, in the seventeenth century, Chancery had, for reasons of piety, stepped outside of common law in order to favor charitable uses in a variety of ways that more rational laws were now curbing.

Still, Blackstone supported the idea that "the construction [of a will or conveyance] be *favourable,* and as near the minds and apparent intents of the parties, as the rules of law will admit," citing *verba intentioni debent inservire* (words ought to serve the intention) and *benigne interpretamur chartas propter simplicitatem laicorum* (documents are interpreted benevolently on account of the ignorance of the common man).[146] This was a general rule for the construction of all intent. Likewise, "where the *intention* is clear, too minute a stress be not laid on the strict and precise signification of *words.*"[147] The supervision of charitable trusts and the rectification of their abuse belonged to the king and his chancellor, in equity and not through common law, but Blackstone did not suggest there was a principle to alter the purpose of trusts, and any "mistaken charities, as are given to the king by the statutes for suppressing superstitious uses" fell under the Court of Exchequer, not Chancery.[148]

So, if cy-près seemed to partake of residual superstitions, upheld by overly pious seventeenth-century judges, it would need to be defended on new grounds. One way to do that would be to deepen the historical precedent for it, making it appear ancient and unavoid-

144. Ibid.
145. Ibid., vol. 2, 376.
146. Ibid., 379.
147. Ibid.
148. Ibid., vol. 3, 428.

able, not recent or circumstantial. Early cy-près cases did not make many references to the *ius commune*, but over time some references to Roman law or Swinburne crept in, although not always to explain a change in purpose. For example, *Attorney-General v. Hudson* in 1720 claimed that "though the Romans preferred a pious or charitable legacy to others, yet our law does not."[149] But after the Act of Mortmain, judges also began to cite the *ius commune* as a reason for their employment of the doctrine, now known as cy-près. In *White v. White* (1778), Lord Chancellor Thurlow connected it to uncertain public uses: "The cases have proceeded upon notions adopted from the Roman and civil law, which are very favourable to charities, that legacies given to public uses not ascertained shall be applied to some proper object. From Swinburn, down to Lord Hardwicke's time, that would be the effect where the object is disappointed."[150]

Wilmot connected cy-près to the *ius commune* directly in the 1767 case *Attorney-General v. Lady Downing*, which involved little more than fixing a trust whose trustees had all died before the trust could be effected. In *ius commune* terms the order did nothing more than uphold the purpose of the settlor, but attached to it Wilmot gave an expansive definition of cy-près, linked to its religious origins, that would be more influential than the case itself. Wilmot's comments indicate the many considerations and ambiguities that continued to afflict cy-près. First Wilmot would apply an estate "*ejusdem generis*, and as near the testator's intention as the rules of law and equity will permit" only if the trust were "illegal and void, or of such a nature as not fit to be carried into execution."[151] He was reassured that this case was not one of "immediate disherision," bad temper, or deathbed panic, which put this trust in a "favourable light."[152] Lady Downing suffered no real loss as a result of the gift.[153] On the other hand, the

---

149. Bridgman, *Law of Charitable Uses*, 509; Similarly, W. David H. Sellar, "Succession Law in Scotland—a Historical Perspective," in *Exploring the Law of Succession: Studies National, Historical, and Comparative*, ed. Kenneth G. C. Reid et al. (Edinburgh: Edinburgh University Press, 2007), 64.
150. 1 Bro. C.C. 15.
151. Wilm. 8.
152. Ibid., 18–19.
153. Ibid., 35.

gift was intended for Cambridge: "the most meritorious charity that can be given ... [offering] benefactions to the whole community."[154] He defended the donor against the charge of "vain glory and ostentation," a common eighteenth-century complaint against philanthropists that "tend[ed] to a public wrong, because it deters and discourages them" and was unfair, for "[vanity] loses all its malignant qualities, when it is productive of good."[155]

Wilmot posited that scrutiny of motives was best left to the "casuists." For his part, he held up the "intrinsic merit or demerit" of the gift as the grounds for evaluation.[156] And yet, he moved on to the puzzle: "[I]n every other case, if the testator's intention in specie cannot take place, the heir at law takes the estate. And as the motive inducing the disherision in a charitable devise, is a passion for that particular charity which he has named, if that particular charity cannot take place, *cessante causa, cessaret effectus*."[157] From there Wilmot launched into his much-quoted assessment of the civil law origins of cy-près:

> The right of the heir at law seems to arise as naturally in this case as in any other; but instead of favouring him as in all other cases, the testator is made to disinherit him for a charity he never thought of; perhaps for a charity repugnant to the testator's intention, and which directly opposes and encounters the charity he meant to establish. But this doctrine is now so fully settled, that it cannot be departed from; and the reason upon which it is founded, seems to be this: The donation was considered as proceeding from a general principle of piety in the testator. Charity was an expiation of sin, and to be rewarded in another state; and therefore, if *political reasons* [emphasis added] negatived the particular charity given, this Court thought the merits of the charity ought not to be lost to the testator, nor to the public, and that they were carrying on his general pious intention; and they proceeded upon a presumption, that the principle, which produced one charity, would have been equally active in producing another, in case the testator had been told the particular charity he meditated could not take place. The Court thought one kind of charity would embalm his memory as well as another, and being equally meritorious, would entitle him to the same reward.[158]

154. Ibid., 25.
155. Ibid., 26.
156. Ibid.
157. If the cause comes to an end, so should the effect. Ibid., 32.
158. Ibid., 32–33.

Wilmot then cited the Modestinus passage, which he noted was pre-Christian, and he took it to mean only a change within purpose: "any other spectacle would as effectually answer that purpose [of memorialization]."[159] Still, although Wilmot found cultural reasons to explain cy-près in both Christian and pagan contexts, he believed the doctrine was fundamentally necessary for "political reasons." It was a solution to policy problems.

Older precedents for cy-près could justify it, but so would a new understanding of how it worked. Gareth Jones notes that it was Master of the Rolls Richard Pepper Arden who, toward the end of the eighteenth century, "popularis[ed] the phrase *general charitable intention*," doing so largely in relationship to the question of what to do with a surplus from a charitable gift and with reference to the case of the Thetford School.[160] After the strict emphasis in the seventeenth century on donor intent, followed by the eighteenth-century backlash of the Mortmain Act, a general charitable intention would be a way forward, since some general charitable intent could be found in most gifts and was not diminished by the donor's other qualities of vanity or superstition.[161] Likewise, a new tendency developed to describe a change as merely a change in mode.[162] If a gift could not be fulfilled according to the specified mode, then an alternative mode might be used.[163] In *Attorney-General v. Boultbee* (1794) Arden both justified changing a particular failing intention if there was a general charitable intention and also offered the judgment that the mode and manner of the gift could be varied as long as it was consistent with the general intent in substance: "another mode may be adopted consistent with his general intention, so as to execute it, though

---

159. Ibid., 32.
160. Jones, *History of the Law of Charity*, 144n. On the explicit connection between the general charitable purpose and the use of cy-près, see *Attorney-General v. Bowyer* in 1798 (3 Ves. 714).
161. In a development that is outside of the scope of this book, many common law jurisdictions have moved away from the finding of a general charitable intent as a requirement, tending to presume it, absent evidence to the contrary. Mulheron, *Modern Cy-Près Doctrine*, 119–22.
162. Glos. Ord. ad X 3.26.18.
163. For example, *Attorney-General v. Whitchurch* (1796), 3 Ves. 141.

not in mode, in substance."¹⁶⁴ He drew on prior cases in which the purpose of a gift had been sorted into the principal purpose and the accessary. This theme had developed from late Elizabethan cases on separating the charitable from the superstitious, from which it was possible to find a rule "to overlook small circumstances ... to promote the general intention."¹⁶⁵

Arden's ruling was, perhaps, in keeping with *ius commune* norms that might allow for a condition to a gift to be satisfied in another way or for specific terms to be commuted in order to honor the use. But in the English cases, mode became a method to change objects: each object was just a different mode to fulfill the intent, especially a general intent. Mode was a way to talk about significant changes to gifts without necessarily having to acknowledge a change in purpose. At the same time, the conviction arose that cy-près "was formerly pushed to a most extravagant length; but is now much restrained."¹⁶⁶

Lord Chancellor Eldon's decision in *Moggridge v. Thackwell* not only solidified the victory of cy-près but also merged the concept of mode and purpose in his much-quoted summary: "The testator's intention of charity was the principal intention; that he meant at all events some charity; that his unlawful purpose was a mode of disappointing it; and the mode therefore was out of the question; and the intention should be carried into effect by another mode." Normally, purpose would be higher than mode, but here that was not clearly so; purpose, mode, and object were all becoming indifferent, so that either purpose or object could be changed without attention being drawn to the change. The intention was good; the purpose was unlawful; but a change in the mode could fix the deficits of the purpose. There were "many institutions to which property may be applied as usefully as to enrich a spendthrift heir," and it was wrong to allow a purpose to fail just because vanity could be detected in it.¹⁶⁷ The donor

---

164. 2 Ves. Jr. 380, 387, 388; 3 Ves. 220.
165. 2 Ves. Jr. 388–89.
166. E.g., *Attorney-General v. Minshull* (4 Ves. 14), where the previous practices of cy-près are described as searching out new charitable recipients ("objects") to take if the original recipients cannot; Boyle, *Practical Treatise*, 147.
167. 7 Ves. 54. Saving the general charitable intention by changing the mode would also appear in *Morice v. Bishop of Durham* (1804), 9 Ves. 405.

would be indulged for the greater good and in honor of that flicker of charitable intent that had spurred the gift.

Attorney-General v. Whitchurch in 1796 would also rest on a general purpose that could be attained by changing the mode.[168] Arden aligned his ruling there with *Attorney-General v. Boultbee* and even the more hostile *Attorney-General v. Goulding*, in which Justice Buller had argued that personal funds attached to a void charitable gift should not be applied "to some other matter *ejusdem generis*." His argument was: "The Court has certainly thought it could vary the use, but the rule may be drawn from the cases, that wherever the Court had directed the sum given to be applied to a different use, there has been proper ground for the Court to say the use to which it has been applied is consistent with the use declared in the will."[169] Buller did not find this to be possible in that particular will, and Arden in *Attorney-General v. Whitchurch* seized on the essential point: the question was whether the testator had an intention that could be fulfilled by finding another charitable object or not. Thus if there was no general charitable intention, then a failing charitable gift would be allowed to fail—as it did in that case.[170] These compromises would make cy-près a workable solution going forward. The privileges of charity did not demand the rescue of all charitable gifts, but only of those that manifested a general charitable intention. Under these new compromises, cy-près rulings did not have to claim to vary the use, but only the mode, which allowed it to change the object.

A "general charitable intention" could be presumed behind many specific intentions, since the smaller naturally appears to belong to the larger, and so courts had come to reason that a specific purpose did not indicate the limits of the testator's charitable intent. Hesitancy and even regret can be found in the rulings, rarely over a perceived harm to the testator, who had caused the inconvenience in the first place, but rather over the deprivation of the heirs-at-law.

---

168. 3 Ves. 141.
169. 2 Bro. C.C. 430.
170. *Attorney-General v. Andrew* (3 Ves. 644) in 1798 drew on these same problems, whether an intention was specific or whether another object could satisfy a general intention in a new mode.

For a time, judges sometimes allowed poor relatives to receive a portion of a cy-près scheme, but a charitable gift could almost never be entirely void, as that would be inequitable to the donor. But the donor was eventually left behind too: today, the adherence to donor intent and the discovery of a general charitable intent is no longer essential in all jurisdictions.[171] As cy-près has expanded, it has tended, as Mulheron discovered, to cohere around the phenomenon of a legally authorized unilateral transfer of property, as directed by the judiciary, that is effected in order to solve practical problems. It has become a palatable modern method that allows the prince—more properly, the state—to redeploy property *ex causa*. It in some sense permits the free exercise of a medieval right—absent a number of other, competing rights and restrictions.

Over two centuries, common law had gone from the reasonable verdict in the Venables case, which did in fact enforce much of her intent, to an unexpressed but implicit charitable intent that could survive the destruction of its object. Judges sometimes lamented cy-près before they imposed it, as if equity were forcing their hand to do something they thought was inequitable, but the doctrine stood ready for the miseries of industrialization, philanthropists with disreputable fortunes to clean, and bourgeois socialists and progressives who wanted to reform the philanthropists themselves.

171. *Report of the Committee on the Law and Practice Relating to Charitable Trusts* (Nathan Committee Report, Cmd 8710) (1952), § 8710, 75.

Epilogue

Many nineteenth-century American courts initially rejected cy-près power as arbitrary, tyrannical, and dependent on the king's prerogative, as explained in the 1852 Connecticut case *White v. Fisk*, which disallowed a bequest that would have been perfectly acceptable to the medieval church.[1] Money set aside "for the support of indigent pious young men preparing for the ministry" was void due to uncertainty.[2] The origins and use of cy-près in expanding state power in the Reformation and beyond seemed indisputable to American judges, but given the difficulty of defining what cy-près was, and its historical links to many different charitable modifications, it was not clear what powers would be left if cy-près was rejected. The 1855 *Harvard College v. Society for Promoting Theological Education* disallowed the modification of a trust because to employ cy-près doctrine would "leav[e] the question of the management and supervision of our public charities to be the subject of change with every fluctuation of popular opinion as to what may be the more expedient and useful mode of administering them."[3] In *Methodist Church vs. Remington*, the Supreme Court of Pennsylvania ruled that cy-près was forbidden: "the original trust, though void, was not a superstitious one; nor if it were, would the property, as in England, revert to the State, for the purpose of being appropriated *in eodem genere*, as no

1. Austin Wakeman Scott and William F. Fratcher, *The Law of Trusts*, 4th ed. (Boston: Little Brown, 1987) § 348.2.
2. *White v. Fisk*, 22 Conn. 31 (1852).
3. 3 Gray 280 (Mass. 1855).

Court here possesses the specific power necessary to give effect to the principle of cy-pres, even were the principle itself not too grossly revolting to the public sense of justice to be tolerated in a country where there is no ecclesiastical establishment."[4]

The history of the power was brought into the debate. In the 1867 case of *Jackson v. Phillips,* the judge, writing specifically of prerogative cy-près, suggested that "no instance is reported, or has been discovered in the thorough investigations of the subject, of an exercise of this power in England before the reign of Charles II."[5] In *Vidal v. Girard* (1844) an elaborate history of the English charitable use was constructed to prove that charitable cases were heard in Chancery before the Elizabethan statutes.[6] *Russell v. Allen* in 1882 then relied on this case to allow a charitable gift where the recipient institution had not yet been founded at the time of the deaths of the testator and his trustee.[7] Just as in eighteenth-century England, increased powers of the court over trusts became more palatable if it appeared that the powers were more ancient.

This was true until *Minot v. Baker* (1888), for which Justice Holmes made use of *Moggridge v. Thackwell* to encourage American courts of equity to exercise a broad range of powers in altering charitable trusts.[8] It had seemed to Lord Eldon that historically the king held the power to direct any general charitable gift made without a specific object whereas Chancery had administration of trusts whose object or trustee had failed. Lord Eldon, however, consolidated power in Chancery, on the grounds that the king "exercis[ed] a discretion with reference to the intention" such that the king and Chancery would come to the same dispositions: "there would not be, as there ought not, any difference in the execution."[9] That is, both king and Chancery were bound by the same rule of proximity of intent, which allowed Eldon to vest unified powers in Chancery, a decision he made with "anxiety" but for the sake of efficiency and in the belief that cy-près's prec-

4. 1 Watts 227.
5. 14 Allen 539 (Mass. 1867).
6. 43 U.S. 127.
7. 107 U.S. 163.
8. 17 N. E. 839, 147 Mass. 348.
9. 7 Ves. 87.

edent was undeniably set in the seventeenth and eighteenth centuries. Holmes, eager to make common law more flexibly responsive to the times, agreed that cy-près was a useful doctrine—one that, he acknowledged, had at times been used with "no pretense, or only a pretense, of carrying out the directions of the testator."[10] Holmes's desire to import cy-près into American common law was not driven by the conviction that this was an immemorial principle. After all, this was a man who claimed that "[an] explanation of the early law is a matter of antiquarianism"[11] and that "continuity with the past is only a necessity and not a duty."[12] Although Holmes drew heavily on Lord Eldon's legal reasoning, he acknowledged that "we do not propose to inquire very curiously whether Lord Eldon's view in the latter case before him is historically accurate or not."

Holmes likewise made no attempt to link cy-près to some ancient theological concern, nor would he have, given his expressed desire to move law from its primitive obsession with morality to a contemporary concern for objective standards. The value of the common law, Holmes argued, derived from its relative Anglo-Saxon freedom from Roman law, particularly later German interpretations of Roman law, in which the right to singular, absolute possession became so vital.[13] Holmes, elaborating on the Roman definition of possession as both physical control and mental intent, explained: "A man's physical power over an object is protected because he has the will to make it his.... The will of the possessor being thus conceived as self-regarding, the intent with which he must hold is pretty clear: he must hold for his own benefit."[14] Common law, whose native conception of property was more diffuse, fortunately paid less attention to this self-oriented intent. If primitive ideas about property were ill suited

10. N. E. 846.
11. *Robinson v. Bird* (1893) 158 Mass. 257, 260.
12. Oliver Wendell Holmes Jr., "Law in Science and Science in Law," *Harvard Law Review* 12 (1899): 444, quoted in David Rabban, *Law's History: American Legal Thought and the Transatlantic Turn to History* (Cambridge: Cambridge University Press, 2013), 267.
13. Oliver Wendell Holmes Jr., "Misunderstandings of the Civil Law," *American Law Review* 6 (1871): 37–49.
14. Quoted in Rabban, *Law's History,* 255, from Oliver Wendell Holmes Jr., "Possession," *American Law Review* 12 (1878): 701.

to the modern economy, then the "fictitious identification between the deceased and his successor" could also be discarded.[15] Cy-près, which could be used to return property to the commons and to further weaken the claims of the successors, was useful in both regards.

As law developed, Holmes argued, the "survivals" of older law needed to be either reinterpreted or cast off. "Judicial legislation" was the means by which judges could revive the law, "bas[ing] their judgments upon broad considerations of policy."[16] Cy-près doctrine gave judges the power to align gifts with the needs of the modern era without prematurely formulating new legal principles to do so. As David Rabban has observed, Holmes's "fundamental belief [was] that most survivals have become functional through the invention of new policies that replaced their original justifications ... [such that] much human progress ... depends on the adjustment of 'old implements' to 'new uses.'"[17] Why should American courts be limited in this work by the absence of a king?[18]

Inspired by Holmes, Progressive-era jurists lauded cy-près because it allowed old trusts to be turned over to more socially useful purposes. As John Bradway argued in 1925, if the public, the recipient of a charity, rejected its terms, then the public could "remould" it for their own benefit.[19] The *Yale Law Journal* in 1939 praised "the highly desirable trend of the courts toward disregarding the specific fulfillment of the donor's design in favor of the interests of public welfare."[20] This temptation to expand the power of the court in order to serve the public better remains a theme of the current scholarly

15. Quoted in Rabban, *Law's History,* 238 and 246, from Oliver Wendell Holmes Jr., *The Common Law,* ed. Mark DeWolfe Howe (Cambridge, Mass.: Harvard University Press, 1963), 154.
16. Quoted in Rabban, *Law's History,* 241, from Oliver Wendell Holmes Jr., *The Common Law,* ed. Mark DeWolfe Howe (Cambridge, Mass.: Harvard University Press, 1963), 33.
17. Rabban, *Law's History,* 248.
18. 17 N. E. 847.
19. John S. Bradway, "Perpetuating the Spirit of Charitable Bequests for Children through the Assistance of the Courts," *Annals of the American Academy of Political and Social Science* 121 (1925): 75–84. See also Lewis M. Simes, *Public Policy and the Dead Hand* (Ann Arbor: University of Michigan Law School, 1955).
20. "A Revaluation of Cy Pres," *Yale Law Journal* 49 (1939): 322.

cy-près literature, which can be exasperated by judicial reluctance to extend the power for the common good.[21] The Uniform Trust Code has supported an expanded cy-près, applying it to trusts that were wasteful, and statutory law is increasingly allowing cy-près for inexpediency. Similarly, Richard Posner has argued that economic efficiency should be grounds for cy-près if the original donation creates "opportunity costs."[22] Cy-près has been used to modify discriminatory trusts to make them non-discriminatory, even if discrimination was central to the donor's stated intentions.[23] Moreover, cy-près encourages the overall expansion of charitable trust law and its influence on other realms, such as in conservation easements, class-action suits, or private trusts that have run up against the Rule against Perpetuities.[24] Once we recognize that cy-près may well have originated in an extension of state power in the context of early-modern state-building, the trend to expand cy-près, and its uncomfortable relationship to donor intent, becomes clearer and even unsurprising. Perhaps Vico was right that origins can speak to the nature of things.[25] But cy-près is also, in its apparent simplicity and common sense, a doctrine ripe to be applied in new ways.

Whatever freedom of testation is given to the living, in reality the dead do not control what happens to property after their death, nor is it socially useful to suggest that the dead might be able to have infinite control over property. As it is, the dead exert a surprising

21. Ilana H. Eisenstein, "Keeping Charity in Charitable Trust Law: The Barnes Foundation and the Case for Consideration of Public Interest in Administration of Charitable Trusts," *University of Pennsylvania Law Review* 151 (2002): 1747.
22. Richard Posner, *Economic Analysis of the Law*, 4th ed. (Boston: Little, Brown & Co., 1992), 509.
23. Roy Adams, "Racial and Religious Discrimination in Charitable Trusts," *Cleveland State Law Review* 25 (1976): 1–43.
24. Alexander R. Arpad, "Private Transactions, Public Benefits, and Perpetual Control over the Use of Real Property: Interpreting Conservation Easements as Charitable Trusts," *Real Property, Trust, and Estate Law Journal* 37 (2002): 91–149. At times legal scholars have urged a mandatory use of cy-près, following *Evans v. Newton*, 382 U.S. 296 (1966), which reverted a racially restrictive trust to the heirs, "Mandatory 'Cy Pres' and the Racially Restrictive Charitable Trust," *Columbia Law Review* 69 (1969): 1478–95.
25. Samuel Moyn, *Last Utopia: Human Rights in History* (Cambridge, Mass.: Belknap Press, 2012), 9.

amount of power, even in a world that considers itself modern.[26] Property has passed through their hands to the living; charitable institutions operate in their name and often according to their values; constitutions and social compacts were created by them and are still binding on their descendants. In law the dead dictate to us their terms—even, increasingly, through perpetual trusts, as though the world could function if the dead were allowed to manage it from beyond in perpetuity, with the living acting on their behalf as trustees.[27] Thomas Paine argued against the rights of the dead to structure laws for the living in *The Rights of Man*; Thomas Jefferson likewise posited that "as the earth belongs to the living, not to the dead, a living generation can bind itself only."[28] The living have found their own ways of escaping the grasp of the dead—political revolutions, religious reformations, and statutes of mortmain. But the wishes of the dead have long had cultural and emotional weight to them; the living are rarely eager to throw the dead aside entirely, even if the dead have sometimes laid down an impossible or unreasonable charge. Besides, as James Madison pointed out in response to Jefferson's suggestion that acts should expire after 19 years in order to prevent the dead from controlling the living, it would be impractical to live in a state of constant overthrow. To make his case, Madison reached back for the language of gifts and inheritances:

If the earth be the gift of nature to the living their title can extend to the earth in its natural State only. The improvements made by the dead form a charge against the living who take the benefit of them. This charge can no otherwise be satisfied than by executing the will of the dead accompanying the improvements.[29]

Cy-près splits the difference between Jefferson and Madison, allowing the living to receive the inheritance of the past and then negotiate its terms.

Sandra Raban pointed out the many good reasons why the En-

26. Simes, *Public Policy and the Dead Hand*, 140. Thomas Paine argued against the rights of the dead to structure laws for the living in *The Rights of Man*.
27. Madoff, *Immortality and the Law*.
28. Quoted in James Madison, *Selected Writings of James Madison*, ed. Ralph Ketcham (Indianapolis, Ind.: Hackett, 2006), 190.
29. Ibid.

glish government enacted mortmain legislation to limit property from being tied up, controlled in perpetuity by the church, and subject to lower taxes.[30] As the church accumulated property, the religious could appear to be freeloading on the rest of society while removing valuable resources from easy circulation and taxation. The temptation to prevent land from being given to religious bodies—or retrospectively, to take it back from the religious bodies—has recurred across time and over a variety of cultures. In Europe it is a particular feature of the early modern period, from the Reformation to enlightened despots like Joseph II or Catherine the Great to the nationalization of church property during the French Revolution. Given this recurrent demand to liberate property and to make institutions responsive to contemporary concerns, cy-près satisfies the desire to renew charitable trusts that have misjudged their purpose. Finding a new purpose for a testator's gift that is close to his or her intended charity is a good compromise and a check on what might otherwise turn into wholesale appropriation. The threat of cy-près being applied in unpleasant ways may encourage donors to give away money while they are alive and can see current needs clearly, just as patristic theologians once encouraged their flocks to do. Alternatively, institutions can be funded and simultaneously be given the power to modify their direction as times change, as Merton tried to do—but of course this path would require the settlor to trust the trustees.

The Reformation initiated a broad set of questions about the extent to which society must be bound to the laws and decisions of the past. As Europe moved toward an age of revolutions, it continued, as Hannah Arendt pointed out, to justify apparent innovations as a return to something older.[31] The rhetorical and legal appeal to antiquity remained compelling. Sovereigns did not always foster this search backwards—they were increasingly ambitious to use new ideals, like divine right, absolutism, or the republic, in order to justify new policies—but where precedent could be made to serve, it did, and their ministers collected legal-historical justifications from the past to be used for present purposes. The rise of interest in the seventeenth

30. Raban, *Mortmain Legislation*, 1–11.
31. Hannah Arendt, *On Revolution* (New York: Viking Press, 1963).

century in social contract theories that moved backwards in time to some primitive agreement was an attempt to take this tendency to its natural conclusion—in an imagined origin that could support the particular political agenda of the author. Succession was then a vital tool for the continued legitimation of an imagined older settlement of political terms and material distribution.

This system of legal-historical precedent seemed to collapse in France during their revolution, for the past was reconceptualized as little more than a burden, a story of oppression and corruption. The peasants of 1789 proved just as canny about the location of power and wealth as those of 1525: they set off in the first summer of the revolution to burn the papers in local *châteaux*, so that the old agreements and privileges would be gone. Edmund Burke, appalled at the enthusiasm for throwing off the past, urged Europeans, and particularly the English, to remember that the past was an "entailed inheritance" that conveyed liberty "without at all excluding a principle of improvement."[32] And that is the crux of the matter, because the law is itself one of the most significant inheritances, one of the most binding testaments, left by the past, and it is virtually impossible to refuse the inheritance in total, as even the most vigorous antinomian movements have found. This parallel between the law and inheritance is not new; one prominent critique of Roman law claimed that it was a *damnosa hereditas*, an inheritance that bankrupts the heir.[33] And yet, despite the political weight given to succession as a means of patriarchal care for the future through the orderly distribution of property, even Burke acknowledged the need for some alteration when he explained the Glorious Revolution as a "deviation" that left the original purpose intact, cured only the "peccant" part, and maintained "the sacredness of an hereditary principle of succession in our government with a power of change in its application in cases of extreme emergency."[34]

---

32. Edmund Burke, *Reflections on the Revolution in France* (Mineola, N.Y.: Dover, 2006), 31.
33. Francis de Zulueta, "The Science of Law," in *The Legacy of Rome*, ed. Cyril Bailey (Oxford: Clarendon Press, 1923), 173.
34. Burke, *Reflections*, 19.

But not every difficult inheritance should have its purpose honored. In some cases, it might be easiest to keep the law but allow it to be interpreted and used in new ways—exactly as Holmes recognized in his appreciation for the utility of "survivals." Cy-près is thus a metaphor for a strategy in legal interpretation: to uphold the past and maintain the law, indeed to claim to sustain its broader intentions, while gently changing its purpose. It is honored neither in the breach nor in the observance, but in its use. Moreover, it is applied only to the trusts that are recognized to be charitable, to serve the common good. The state declines to give charitable protection to trusts that allow the eccentric dead to enforce their will if the trust is not generally recognized for the common good in some way, as was the case with George Bernard Shaw's failed trust for a new phonetic alphabet.[35]

Augustine pointed out that funerals and sepulchers were done for the benefit for the living, not the dead, and scholars have observed that our treatment of the rights of the dead is always in some respect about the living.[36] It is painful for the living to exclude the dead from the community by ignoring their wishes.[37] It is also painful for the living to contemplate a loss of control over both body and belongings, even after death. Michel de Montaigne, the sixteenth-century essayist, observed when he attended public executions that the audience had a greater horror for the quartering of an already dead body than for the execution itself: "How much the people are frightened by the rigors exercised on dead bodies; for these people, who had appeared to feel nothing at seeing him strangled, at every blow that was given to cut him up cried out in a piteous voice."[38] Less vividly, the surprising resonance of estate taxes as an issue on the

35. Re Shaw, [1957] 1 All E.R. 745. Cf. *In re Girard's Estate*, 127 A.2d 290 (Pa. 1956).
36. Augustine, *De cura pro mortuis gerenda*, PL, vol. 41, 591–609.
37. P. Metcalf and R. Huntington, *Celebrations of Death: The Anthropology of the Mortuary Ritual* (Cambridge: Cambridge University Press, 1993); Clare Gittings, *Death, Burial, and the Individual in Early Modern England* (London: Croom Helm, 1984).
38. Michel de Montaigne, "Travel Journal," in *The Complete Works*, trans. Donald Frame (New York: Alfred A. Knopf, 2003), 1148–49; similarly "On Cruelty" (II.2) and "Our Emotions Get Carried Away Beyond Us" (I.3).

American political scene demonstrates the reluctance of the living to allow the state to interfere overtly with the dispersal of property after death.

Despite these social and psychological reasons to let the living comfort themselves with the belief that they will continue to control their things in death, Adam Smith observed the tendency by jurists to reach for supernatural explanations for the apparently irrational right of testation:

> There is no point more difficult to account for than the right we conceive men to have to dispose of their goods after their death.... What obligation is the community under to observe the directions he made concerning his goods now when he can have no will, nor is supposed to have any knowledge of the matter.... The difficulty is here so great that Puffendorff [sic] called in to his assistance the immortality of the soul.[39]

The reason for the observance of the will of the testator, Smith suggested was that "we enter as it were into his dead body, and conceive what our living souls would feel if they were joined with his body, and how much we would be distressed to see our last injunctions not performed."[40] Nevertheless, the living found it difficult not to transpose the intentions of the testator, even inadvertently:

> The advices, the commands, and even the very fooleries of the dying person have more effect on us than things of the same nature would have had at any other period. We have a great reverence for his commands at such a time; and after his death, we do not consider what he willd, but what if he was then alive would be his will.[41]

Cy-près often rests on this reverential re-imagining of what the testator would have willed. John Stuart Mill, writing on endowments in 1869, extended Smith's analysis of the superstitions that surrounded the disposition of the property of the dead: any attempt to create a perpetual trust with a "binding disposition" was a form of "superstition."[42] The superstition was not that fulfilled gifts would affect the

---

39. Adam Smith, *Lectures on Jurisprudence*, ed. R. L. Meek et al. (Oxford: Clarendon Press, 1978), Report of 1762–63, § 149–50.
40. Ibid., 1766, § 165.
41. Ibid., 1762–63, § 150–51.
42. John Stuart Mill, "Endowments," in *Dissertations and Discussions*, vol. 5 (New York: Henry Holt, 1875), 1.

afterlife, but that gifts could remain nearly untouched monuments back on earth in perpetuity. Cy-près saves that superstition.

There are more reasons to imagine links between cy-près and salvation, no matter how obviously intertwined with secular affairs it has been. For one, cy-près makes meddling with the terms of a man's last will into a pious, rather than an impious, act. For another, as long as almsgiving in life was a method of storing up treasure in heaven, the unexpressed question for a Christian was: your heirs or your eternal life? Since cy-près doctrine denied the rights of the heirs, it could be assumed that the stakes for the donor must have been extraordinarily high. Moreover, across the centuries, those who sought transformation of church property claimed that it would comfort and perhaps even help the donors to see their property more properly disposed.

But the latter-day theory that cy-près came into existence to save the souls of the donors is even more psychologically rich, because, as Smith noted, inadvertently echoing Vives and Starkey, the question in cy-près cases can easily become: what *would* the donor have wanted in current circumstances? Surely he or she would not have intended that an archaic gift be maintained when new priorities and ideologies have emerged. Indeed, a donor who lived today would quite reasonably have contemporary ideals; the intentions that can be discovered are often not the intentions of the donor in his or her own time but updated intentions transposed and modernized. This meant that the testator, or at least his or her earthly legacy, was thus *saved*, by cy-près, from his or her own prejudices and outmoded ideas. He or she was improved to meet present-day standards. His or her negative attributes were redeemed, sloughed off to reveal the true charitable intent underneath that might now shine through the ages in the renewed disposition made of his or her fortune. The most prominent modern cases of contested wills or trusts almost always bring the character of the settlor into the broader discussion of the case, as with Alfred Barnes, Leona Helmsley, and Wellington R. Burt. There is little sympathy for rich cranks and grumps who dictate unpopular terms to govern their worldly goods after their death, but cy-près can metaphorically redeem their grasping lives by applying their wealth to the common good. Surely, wherever these settlors may be, they approve, or ought to approve, or have at last reached, through either sanctification or oblivion, that most elevated state of indifference to material things. If we have the legal means to help them on that journey toward spiritual perfection by rearranging their donations, then who are we to refuse? Despite everything, cy-près will always have religious resonances, because it gives the court, *ex cathedra,* this power of absolution—to bind or to loose.

Bibliography

A Note on the Bibliography: There is very little literature directly about cyprès, but there is a lot of literature that relates to the use of gifts in law, culture, and religion during the late medieval and early modern period and the broader contextual changes. Consequently, this bibliography includes a wide range of materials that were consulted in the writing of this book and may be of interest to the reader.

The 1917 or Pio-Benedictine Code of Canon Law: in English Translation. Translated by Edward N. Peters. San Francisco: Ignatius Press, 2001.
Adams, Roy. "Racial and Religious Discrimination in Charitable Trusts." *Cleveland State Law Review* 25 (1976): 1–43.
Agamben, Giorgio. *The Highest Poverty: Monastic Rules and Form-of-Life.* Translated by Adam Kotsko. Stanford, Calif.: Stanford University Press, 2013.
Ambrose. *Opera omnia.* In Patrologia Latina. Edited by Jacques Paul Migne. Vol. 16. Paris: Vrayet, 1845.
———. *Select Works and Letters.* Translated by H. de Romestin. Grand Rapids, Mich.: W. B. Eerdmans, 1979.
Anderson, Gary A. "Redeem Your Sins by the Giving of Alms: Sin, Debt, and the 'Treasury of Merit' in Early Jewish and Christian Tradition." *Letter and Spirit* 3 (2007): 39–69.
Anderson, John. *Art Held Hostage: The Battle over the Barnes Collection.* New York: W. W. Norton, 2013.
Andrewes, Lancelot. *Sermons by the Right Honourable and Reverend Father in God, Lancelot Andrewes.* 2d ed. London: Richard Badger, 1632.
The Anglican Canons 1529–1947. Edited by Gerald Bray. Woodbridge, England: Boydell Press, 1998.
Anglo-Saxon Wills. Edited by Dorothy Whitelock. Cambridge: Cambridge University Press, 1930.
Archer, Ian W. *The Pursuit of Stability: Social Relations in Elizabethan London.* Cambridge: Cambridge University Press, 2003.
Arendt, Hannah. *On Revolution.* New York: Viking Press, 1963.
Ariès, Philippe. *The Hour of Our Death.* Translated by Helen Weaver. New York: Vintage, 1981.

Aristotle. *Nicomachean Ethics*. Translated by Terence Irwin. Indianapolis, Ind.: Hackett, 1999.

Arnade, Peter. *Beggars, Iconoclasts, and Civic Patriots: The Political Culture of the Dutch Revolt*. Ithaca, N.Y.: Cornell University Press, 2008.

Arnold, Jonathan A. "Profit and Piety: Thomas More, John Colet, and the London Mercery." *Reformation and Renaissance Review* 12 (2010): 127–53.

Arpad, Alexander R. "Private Transactions, Public Benefits, and Perpetual Control over the Use of Real Property: Interpreting Conservation Easements as Charitable Trusts." *Real Property, Trust, and Estate Law Journal* 37 (2002): 91–149.

Aston, Margaret. *England's Iconoclasts*. Vol. 1: *Laws Against Images*. Oxford: Oxford University Press, 1988.

———. *Lollards and Reformers: Images and Literacy in Late Medieval Religion*. London: Hambledon Press, 1984.

Atkinson, Rob. "The Low Road to Cy Pres Reform: Principled Practice to Remove Dead Hand Control of Charitable Assets." *Case Western Reserve Law Review* 58 (2007): 97–165.

———. "Reforming Cy Pres Reform." *Hasting Law Journal* 44 (1993): 1111–58.

Attreed, Lorraine C. "Preparation for Death in Sixteenth-Century Northern England." *Sixteenth Century Journal* 13.3 (1982): 37–66.

Aufréri, Étienne. *Decisiones capellae Tholosanae*. Frankfurt: Nicolas Bassaeius, 1575.

Augustine of Hippo. *Confessiones*. Corpus Scriptorum Ecclesiasticorum Latinorum. Vol. 33. Vienna: F. Tempsky, 1896.

———. *De cura pro mortuis gerenda*. Corpus Scriptorum Ecclesiasticorum Latinorum. Vol. 41, 621–60. Vienna: F. Tempsky, 1900.

———. *Sermons*. Vol. 3. Translated by Edmund Hill. Brooklyn, N.Y.: New City Press, 1991.

———. *St. Augustine on Marriage and Sexuality*. Edited by Elizabeth Clark. Washington, D.C.: The Catholic University of America Press, 1996.

Avila, Charles. *Ownership: Early Christian Teaching*. Eugene, Ore.: Wipf and Stock, 2004.

Ayton, John. *Constitutiones legitime seu legatine regionis Anglicane cum subtilissima interpretatione domini Johannis de Athon*. Paris: n.p., 1504.

Bacon, Francis. *An Account of the Life and Times of Francis Bacon*. Edited by James Spedding. 2 vols. London: Trübner and Co., 1878.

———. *Essays*. 2d ed. London: John Beale, 1612.

———. *Essays*. 3d ed. London: John Haviland, 1625.

———. *The Learned Reading of Sir Francis Bacon, one of Her Majesties learned counsell at law, upon the statute of uses*. London: Mathew Walbancke and Laurence Chapman, 1642.

———. *The Letters and the Life of Francis Bacon*. Edited by James Spedding. London: Longmans, Green, Reader, and Dyer, 1868.

———. *The Letters of Sir Francis Bacon*. Edited by Robert Stephens. London: Benjamin Tooke, 1702.

———. *The Works of Francis Bacon*. Edited by James Spedding, Robert Leslie Ellis, Douglas Denon Heath, and William Rawley. 15 vols. London: Longman, 1857–1874.

Bibliography 403

Baker, J. H. *Baker and Milsom: Sources of English Legal History. Private Law to 1760.* 2d ed. Oxford: Oxford University Press, 2010.
———. *An Introduction to English Legal History.* 4th ed. Oxford: Oxford University Press, 2007.
———. *The Law's Two Bodies: Some Evidential Problems in English Legal History.* Oxford: Oxford University Press, 2001.
———. *Manual of Law French.* 2d. ed. Burlington, Vt.: Ashgate, 1990.
———. *The Oxford History of the Laws of England.* Vol. 6: *1483–1558.* Oxford: Oxford University Press, 2003.
Baldus de Ubaldis. *Consiliorum, sive responsorum.* Vol. 4–5. Venice: Hieronymus Polus, 1575.
Ballerini, Antonio. *Opus theologicum morale.* Rome: Libraria Giachetti, 1890.
Barber, Malcolm. *The Trial of the Templars.* 2d ed. Cambridge: Cambridge University Press, 2012.
Barbosa, Agostinho. *Pastoralis solicitudinis, sive De officio, et potestate episcopi.* Lyon: Durand, 1628.
Baron, Hans. "Franciscan Poverty and Civic Wealth as Factors in the Rise of Humanistic Thought." *Speculum* 13 (1938): 1–37.
Barraclough, Geoffrey. *Papal Provisions: Aspects of Church History, Constitutional, Legal, and Administrative in the Later Middle Ages.* Oxford: Blackwell, 1935.
Bartlett, Robert. *Why Can the Dead Do Such Great Things?: Saints and Worshippers from the Martyrs to the Reformation.* Princeton, N.J.: Princeton University Press, 2013.
Bartolus de Saxoferrato. *Commentaria in secundum Infortiati.* Lyon: Mathias Bonhomme, 1557.
———. *In primam Digesti novi partem.* Lyon: Compagnie des libraires, 1581.
———. *Opera omnia.* Turin: Nicolai Bevilaquae, 1577.
———. *Opera omnia.* Venice: Iuntas, 1590–1615.
———. *Politica e diritto nel Trecento italiano. Il 'De tyranno' di Bartolo da Sassoferrato (1314–1357) con l'edizione critica dei trattati 'De Guelphis et Gebellinis,' 'De regimine civitatis' e 'De tyranno.'* Edited by Diego Quaglioni. Florence: Leo S. Olschiki, 1983.
Basil the Great. *On Social Justice.* Translated by C. Paul Schroeder. Crestwood, N.Y.: St. Vladimir's Seminary Press, 2009.
Bateson, Mary, and Thomas Cromwell. "Aske's Examination." *The English Historical Review* 5.19 (1890): 550–73.
Baumer, Franklin Le Van. *The Early Tudor Theory of Kingship.* Ann Arbor: University of Michigan, 1940.
Baylor, Michael G., ed. *The Radical Reformation.* Cambridge: Cambridge University Press, 1991.
Beaty, Nancy Lee. *The Craft of Dying: A Study in the Literary Tradition of the Ars Moriendi in England.* New Haven, Conn.: Yale University Press, 1970.
Beaumanoir, Philippe de. *The Coutumes de Beauvaisis of Philippe de Beaumanoir.* Translated by F. R. P. Akehurst. Philadelphia: University of Pennsylvania Press, 1992.
Beck, Andreas. *Der Untergang der Templer. Grösster Justizmord des Mittelalters?* Freiburg im Breisgau: Herder, 1993.

Becon, Thomas. "Displaying of the Popish Mass." In *Prayers and Other Pieces*, edited by J. Ayre, 276. Cambridge: Parker Society, 1844.
Behrens, Georg. "Equity in the *Commentaries* of Edmund Plowden." *Journal of Legal History* 20 (1999): 25–50.
Bellomo, Manlio. *The Common Legal Past of Europe: 1000–1800*. Translated by Lydia G. Cochrane. Studies in Medieval and Early Modern Canon Law. Washington, D.C.: The Catholic University of America Press, 1995.
Ben-Amos, Ilana Krausman. *The Culture of Giving: Informal Support and Gift-Exchange in Early Modern England*. Cambridge: Cambridge University Press, 2008.
Berman, Harold J. *Law and Revolution: The Formation of the Western Legal Tradition*. Cambridge, Mass.: Harvard University Press, 1983.
———. *Law and Revolution II: The Impact of the Protestant Reformations on the Western Legal Tradition*. Cambridge, Mass.: Harvard University Press, 2003.
———. "The Spiritualization of the Secular Law: The Impact of the Lutheran Reformation." *Journal of Law and Religion* 14.2 (1999): 313–49.
Bernard, G. W. *The King's Reformation: Henry VIII and the Remaking of the English Church*. New Haven, Conn.: Yale University Press, 2005.
Bijsterveld, Arnoud-Jan. *Do ut des: Gift Giving, Memoria, and Conflict Management in the Medieval Low Countries*. Hilversum: Verloren, 2007.
Blackstone, William. *Commentaries on the Laws of England*. A Facsimile of the First Edition of 1765–1769. Chicago: University of Chicago Press, 1979.
Blakiston, H. E. D. "Two More Medieval Ghost Stories." *English Historical Review* 38 (1923): 85–87.
Blickle, Peter. *Communal Reformation: The Quest for Salvation in Sixteenth-Century Germany*. Translated by Thomas Dunlap. London: Humanities Press, 1992.
The Blickling Homilies of the Tenth Century. Edited by Richard Morris. London: Early English Text Society, 1880.
Blumenthal, Uta-Renate. *The Investiture Controversy: Church and Monarchy from the Ninth to the Twelfth Century*. Philadelphia: University of Pennsylvania Press, 1988.
Böhmer, Justus. *Ius parochiale*. 2d ed. Halle an der Saale: Orphanotropheum, 1716.
Bogert, George. *Trusts and Trustees*. St. Paul, Minn.: West Publishing, 1935.
Boggis, Robert James Edmund. *Praying for the Dead: An Historical Review of the Practice*. New York: Longmans, Green, 1913.
Bohic, Henricus. *Distinctiones in quinque Decretalium libros*. Venice: Hieronymus Scotus, 1576.
Borough Customs. Edited by Mary Bateson. Vol. 2. London: Quaritch, 1906.
Bossy, John. *Christianity in the West, 1400–1700*. Oxford: Oxford University Press, 2004.
Bouchard, Constance Britton. *Those of My Blood: Creating Noble Families in Medieval Francia*. Philadelphia: University of Pennsylvania Press, 2001.
Bowersock, G. W. "Introduction." In *On the Donation of Constantine*, vii–xvi. Cambridge, Mass.: Harvard University Press, 2008.
Boyle, William Robert Augustus. *A Practical Treatise on the Law of Charities*. London: Saunders and Benning, 1837.

Bracton, Henrici de. *De legibus et consuetudinibus Angliae.* Translated by Samuel E. Thorne. 4 vols. Cambridge, Mass.: Harvard University Press, 1968.

Bradway, John S. "Perpetuating the Spirit of Charitable Bequests for Children through the Assistance of the Courts." *Annals of the American Academy of Political and Social Science* (1925): 75–84.

Brady, Thomas A. *German Histories in the Age of Reformations, 1400–1650.* Cambridge: Cambridge University Press, 2009.

———. *Protestant Politics: Jacob Sturm (1489–1553) and the German Reformation.* Boston: Humanities Press, 1995.

———. *Ruling Class, Regime and Reformation at Strasbourg, 1520–1555.* Leiden: Brill, 1978.

Branch, Thomas. *Principia legis et aequitatis.* London: Henry Lintot, 1753.

Brand, Paul, and Joshua Getzler, eds. *Judges and Judging in the History of the Common Law and Civil Law.* Cambridge: Cambridge University Press, 2012.

Bray, Gerald, ed. *Tudor Church Reform: The Henrician Canons of 1535 and the Reformatio Legum Ecclesiasticarum.* Church of England Record Society. Vol. 8. Woodbridge, England: Boydell Press, 2000.

Brayley, Edward Wedlake. *A Topographical History of Surrey.* Vol. 3. London: G. Willis, 1850.

Brejon, Jacques. *Un jurisconsulte de la Renaissance: André Tiraqueau (1488–1558).* Paris: Librairie du Recueil Sirey, 1937.

Bridgman, Richard Whalley. *The Law of Charitable Uses.* London: W. Clarke, 1805. A revised and updated edition of the 1660 and 1663 editions by John Herne and the 1676 edition by George Duke.

Brock, Stephen L. "What is the Use of *Usus* in Aquinas' Psychology of Action?" In *Moral and Political Philosophies in the Middle Ages.* Edited B. Carlos Bazán, Eduardo Andújar and Léonard G. Sbrocchi, vol. 2, 654–64. Ottawa: Legas, 1995.

Brooke, Z. N. *The English Church and the Papacy: From the Conquest to the Reign of John.* Cambridge: Cambridge University Press, 1931.

Brooks, Christopher W. *Law, Politics and Society in Early Modern England.* Cambridge: Cambridge University Press, 2008.

Brown, Edward. *Appendix ad fasculum rerum expetendarum et fugiendarum, prout ab Orthvino Gratio.* London: Richard Chiswell, 1690.

Brown, Elizabeth A. R. "The Tyranny of a Concept: Feudalism and Historians of Medieval Europe." *American Historical Review* 79.4 (1974): 1063–88.

Brown, Peter. *Augustine of Hippo: A Biography.* 2d ed. Berkeley: University of California Press, 2000.

———. *The Ransom of the Soul: Afterlife and Wealth in Early Western Christianity.* Cambridge, Mass.: Harvard University Press, 2015.

———. *Through the Eye of a Needle: Wealth, the Fall of Rome, and the Making of Christianity in the West, 350–550 AD.* Princeton, N.J.: Princeton University Press, 2012.

Browne, Thomas. *Religio medici.* London: Scot, Basset, Wright, and Chiswell, 1682.

Bruck, Eberhard F. *Kirchenväter und soziales Erbrecht. Wanderung religiöser Ideen durch die Rechte der östlichen und westlichen Welt.* Berlin: Springer-Verlag, 1956.

Brundage, James A. "The Cambridge Faculty of Canon Law and the Ecclesiastical Courts of Ely." In *Medieval Cambridge: Essays on the Pre-Reformation University*, edited by Patrick Zutshi, 21–46. Woodbridge, England: Boydell and Brewer, 1993.
———. *Medieval Canon Law*. London: Longman, 1995.
———. *Medieval Canon Law and the Crusader*. Madison: University of Wisconsin Press, 1969.
———. *The Medieval Origins of the Legal Profession: Canonists, Civilians, and Courts*. Chicago: University of Chicago Press, 2008.
Bryson, W. H., ed. *Cases Concerning Equity and the Courts of Equity 1550–1660*. 2 vols. Selden Society Annual Series. Vols. 117–18. London: Bernard Quaritch, 2000–2001.
———. *The Chancery Reports of John Herne and of George Duke 1599 to 1674*. Buffalo, N.Y.: Hein, 2002.
Bucer, Martin. *Instruction in Christian Love [1523]*. Translated by Paul Traugott Fuhrmann. Eugene, Ore.: Wipf and Stock, 2008.
———. *Martin Bucers Deutsche Schriften*. Vol. 1. Gütersloch, Gerd Mohn, 1960.
———. *Martini Buceri Scripta Anglicana*. Basel: Pietro Perna, 1577.
———. *De regno Christi*. In *Melanchthon and Bucer*, translated by Wilhelm Pauck with Paul Larkin. Philadelphia: The Westminster Press, 1969.
———. *A Treatise declaryng [and] shewig dyuers causes take[n] out of the holy scriptur[es] of the sente[n]ces of holy faders [and] of the decrees of deuout emperours, that pyctures [and] other ymages which were wont be worshypped, ar [in] no wise to be suffred in the temples or churches of Christen men*. London: T. Godfrey for W. Marshall, 1535.
———. *A Treatise, How By the Worde of God, Christian mens Almose ought to be distributed*. N.p.: 1557.
Bucholz, Robert and Newton Key. *Early Modern England, 1485–1714: A Narrative*. 2d ed. London: Wiley-Blackwell, 2008.
Buck, Lawrence P., and Jonathan W. Zophy, eds. *The Social History of the Reformation*. Columbus: Ohio State University Press, 1972.
Bullinger, Heinrich. *Reformationsgeschichte*. Edited by J. J. Holtinger and H. H Vögeli. Frauenfeld, Switzerland: Beyel, 1838.
Burgess, Clive. *Absolute Monarchy and the Stuart Constitution*. New Haven, Conn.: Yale University Press, 1996.
———. "'Longing to be prayed for': death and commemoration in an English parish in the later Middle Ages." In *The Place of the Dead: Death and Remembrance in Late Medieval and Early Modern Europe*, edited by Bruce Gordon and Peter Marshall, 44–65. Cambridge: Cambridge University Press, 2000.
Burke, Edmund. *Reflections on the Revolution in France*. Mineola, N.Y.: Dover, 2006.
Burns, J. H., ed. *The Cambridge History of Medieval Political Thought c. 350–c. 1450*. Cambridge: Cambridge University Press, 1988.
———. *The Cambridge History of Political Thought 1450–1700*. Cambridge: Cambridge University Press, 1991.
Burr, David. *The Spiritual Franciscans: From Protest to Persecution in the Century after Saint Francis*. University Park: Pennsylvania State University Press, 2001.

Burrage, Champlain. *Early English Dissenters in the Light of Recent Research (1550–1641)*. Cambridge: Cambridge University Press, 1912.
Burton, Kathleen M., ed. *A Dialogue between Reginald Pole and Thomas Lupset*. London: Chatto and Windus, 1948.
Butterfield, Herbert. *The Whig Interpretation of History*. New York: W. W. Norton, 1965.
Buttigrarius, Jacobus. *Lectura supra codice*. Paris: n.p., 1516.
Bynum, Caroline Walker. *Christian Materiality: An Essay on Religion in Late Medieval Europe*. New York: Zone Books, 2011.
——. *Holy Feast, Holy Fast: The Religious Significance of Food to Medieval Women*. Berkeley: University of California Press, 1987.
Calder, Isabel M. *Activities of the Puritan Faction of the Church of England, 1625–1633*. London: S.P.C.K., 1957.
Calderinus, Joannes, Gaspar Calderinus, and Dominicus de Sancto Germiniano. *Consilia Jo. Cal. et Gas. eius filii et Dominici de Sancto Geminiano*. Milan: Ulderic Scinzenzeler, 1497.
Calendar of State Papers, Domestic Series. 12 vols. London: Longman, Brown, Green, 1856–72.
Calendar of State Papers—Spain. London: Her Majesty's Stationery Office, 1862–1954.
Cameron, Euan. *The European Reformation*. 2d ed. Oxford: Oxford University Press, 2012.
Canning, Joseph. "Law, Sovereignty and Corporation Theory, 1300–1450." In *The Cambridge History of Medieval Political Thought, c. 350–1450*, edited by J. H. Burns, 454–76. Cambridge: Cambridge University Press, 1988.
——. *The Political Thought of Baldus de Ubaldis*. Cambridge: Cambridge University Press, 1987.
——, and Otto Gerhard Oexle, eds. *Political Thought and the Realities of Power in the Middle Ages*. Göttingen: Vandenhoeck and Ruprecht, 1998.
Carpzovius, Benedict. *Definitiones forenses ad Constitutiones*. Leipzig: Ritzschiana, 1663.
Cavendish, George. "The Life and Death of Cardinal Wolsey." In *Two Early Tudor Lives*, edited by Richard S. Sylvester and Davis P. Harding, 1–194. New Haven, Conn.: Yale University Press, 1962.
Cesar, Floriano Jonas. "Popular Autonomy and Imperial Power in Bartolus of Saxoferrato: An Intrinsic Connection." *Journal of the History of Ideas* 65 (2004): 369–81.
Chamberlen, Hugh. *A few Proposals Humbly Recommending to the Serious Consideration of His Majesty's High Commissioner*. Edinburgh: n.p., 1700.
Champlin, Edward. *Final Judgments: Duty and Emotion in Roman Wills 200 B.C.–A.D. 250*. Berkeley: University of California Press, 1991.
Chasin, Chris. "Modernizing Class Action Cy Pres Through Democratic Inputs: A Return to Cy Pres Comme Possible." *University of Pennsylvania Law Review* 163 (2015): 1463–95.
Chiffoleau, Jacques. *La Comptabilité de l'au-delà: Les hommes, la mort et la religion dans la région d'Avignon à la fin du Moyen Âge*. Paris: Albin Michel, 2011.

Childe, V. Gordon. "Directional Changes in Funerary Practices during 50,000 Years." *Man: A Record of Anthropological Science* 45 (1945): 13–19.
Christensen, Carl E. *Art and the Reformation in Germany.* Athens: Ohio University Press, 1979.
Chrysostom, John. *On Wealth and Poverty.* Translated by Catharine P. Roth. Crestwood, N.Y.: St. Vladimir's Seminary Press, 1981.
Clark, Francis. *The Pseudo-Gregorian Dialogues.* Leiden: Brill, 1987.
Clark, James G. "Monasteries and Secular Education in Late Medieval England." In *Monasteries and Society in the British Isles in the Later Middle Ages*, edited by Janet Burton and Karen Stöber, 145–67. Woodbridge, England: Boydell Press, 2008.
Clarke, Peter D. *The Interdict in the Thirteenth Century: A Question of Collective Guilt.* Oxford: Oxford University Press, 2007.
Code of Canon Law, Latin-English Edition. Prepared under the auspices of the Canon Law Society of America. Washington, D.C.: Canon Law Society of America, 1999.
Cohn, Henry J. "Church Property in the German Protestant Principalities." In *Politics and Society in Reformation Europe*, edited by E. I. Kouri and T. Scott, 158–87. London: Palgrave, 1987.
Cohn, Samuel K., Jr. *The Cult of Remembrance and the Black Death: Six Renaissance Cities in Central Italy.* Baltimore: Johns Hopkins University Press, 1992.
———. "Renaissance Attachment to Things: Material Culture in Last Wills and Testaments." *Economic History Review* 65.3 (2012): 984–1004.
Coke, Edward. *Institutes of the Laws of England.* London: Societie of Stationers, 1628–44.
———. *Institutes of the Laws of England.* Second, Third, and Fourth Parts. London: Andrew Crooke, 1669–71.
A Collection of the Laws and Canons of the Church of England. Translated by John Johnson. Vol. 2. Oxford: John Henry Parker, 1851.
A Collection of the Wills, Now Known to be Extant, of the Kings and Queens of England. London: J. Nichols, 1780.
Collinson, Patrick. *Archbishop Grindal 1519–1583: The Struggle for a Reformed Church.* Berkeley: University of California Press, 1979.
———. "Puritanism and the Poor." In *Pragmatic Utopias: Ideals and Communities, 1200–1630*, edited by Rosemary Horrox and Sarah Rees Jones, 242–58. Cambridge: Cambridge University Press, 2001.
Colvin, Howard. "The Origin of Chantries." *Journal of Medieval History* 26 (2000): 163–73.
Concilia Africae A345–A525. Edited by C. Munier. Corpus Christianorum Series Latina. Vol. 149. Turnhout: Brepols, 1974.
Concilia Galliae A345–352. Edited by C. Munier. Corpus Christianorum Series Latina. Vol. 148. Turnhout: Brepols, 1963.
Congar, Yves-M. "Quod omnes tangit ab omnibus tractari et approbari debet." *Revue historique de droit française et étranger* 35 (1958): 210–59.
Consilium delectorum cardinalium, et aliorum praelatorum: de emendanda ecclesia. N.p.: 1538.
Constable, Giles. *The Reformation of the Twelfth Century.* Cambridge: Cambridge University Press, 1996.

Constantelos, Demetrios J. *Byzantine Philanthropy and Social Welfare.* New Brunswick, N.J.: Rutgers, 1968.
Contarini, Gasparo. *The Office of a Bishop.* Translated by John Patrick Donnelly. Milwaukee, Wisc.: Marquette University Press, 2002.
Corpus iuris canonici. 3 vols. Rome: n.p., 1582.
Corpus iuris civilis. Edited by Theodor Mommsen and Paul Krueger. 3 vols. Berlin: Weidman, 1888.
Corro, Antonio del. *A Supplication exhibited to the most mightie Prince Philip king of Spain etc. Wherein is contained the summe of our Christian religion, for the profession whereof the Protestants in the lowe Countries of Flaunders, etc. doe suffer persecution.* London: Francis Coldocke and Henrie Bynneman, 1577.
Cortese, Ennio. *La norma giuridica: Spunti teorici nel diritto comune classico.* Milan: Giuffrè, 1962.
Cosin, Richard. *Ecclesiae Anglicanae politeia, in tabulas digesta.* London: Johannes Norton, 1604.
Coulton, G. G. *Art and the Reformation.* New York: Alfred A. Knopf, 1928.
Cowell, John. *Institutes of the Lawes of England.* London: Thomas Roycroft, 1651.
———. *Institutiones juris anglicani.* Cambridge: Johannis Legat, 1605.
Cranmer, Thomas. *Memorials of Cranmer.* Edited by John Strype. Vol. 3. Oxford: Clarendon Press, 1854.
Crowley, Robert. "Informacion and Petition." In *The English Renaissance: An Anthology of Sources and Documents,* edited by Kate Aughterson, 154–58. New York: Routledge, 2002.
———. *The Select Works of Robert Crowley.* Edited by J. M. Cowper. Early English Text Society. London: N. Trübner, 1872.
Cruise, William. *A Digest of the Laws of England Respecting Real Property.* London: A. Strahan, 1806.
Cujas, Jacques. *Opera omnia in decem tomo ... tomus septimus.* Naples: Michael Aloysius Mutius, 1722.
Cyprian. *Opera omnia.* In Patrologia Latina. Edited by Jacques Paul Migne. Vol. 4. Paris: Sirou, 1844.
Daniel, David P. "Hungary." In *The Early Reformation in Europe,* edited by Andrew Pettegree, 49–69. Cambridge: Cambridge University Press, 1992.
Davies, Wendy. *Acts of Giving: Individual, Community, and Church in Tenth-Century Christian Spain.* Oxford: Oxford University Press, 2007.
Davies, Wendy, and Paul Fouracre. *The Languages of Gift in the Early Middle Ages.* Cambridge: Cambridge University Press, 2010.
———. *Property and Power in the Early Middle Ages.* Cambridge: Cambridge University Press, 1995.
Davis, E. Jeffries. "The Beginning of the Dissolution: Christchurch, Aldgate, 1532." *Transactions of the Royal Historical Society* 8 (1925): 127–50.
Davis, Natalie Zemon. *The Gift in Sixteenth-Century France.* Madison: University of Wisconsin Press, 2000.
———. *Society and Culture in Early Modern France.* Stanford, Calif.: Stanford University Press, 1965.
Davis, Virginia. *William Waynflete: Bishop and Educationalist.* Woodbridge, England: Boydell Press, 1993.

Decock, Wim. *Theologians and Contract Law: The Moral Transformation of the Ius Commune (ca. 1500–1650)*. Leiden: Martinus Nijhoff, 2013.
Decrees of the Ecumenical Councils. Edited by Norman P. Tanner. 2 vols. London: Sheed and Ward, 1990.
Devereux, E. J. "Empty Tuns and Unfruitful Grafts: Richard Grafton's Historical Publications." *Sixteenth Century Journal* 21.1 (1990): 33–56.
Dewar, Mary. *Sir Thomas Smith: A Tudor Intellectual in Office*. London: Athlone Press, 1964.
Dhuoda, *Manuel pour mon fils*. Edited by Pierre Riché. In Sources Chrétiennes. Vol. 225. Paris: Editions du Cerf, 1975.
A Dialogue betwene a Knyght and a Clerke Concernynge the Power Spiritual and Temporall. London: Thomas Berthelet, 1533.
Dickens, A. G. *The English Reformation*. 2d ed. University Park: Pennsylvania State University Press, 1989.
———. "A Municipal Dissolution of Chantries at York, 1536." In *Reformation Studies*, 47–56. London: Hambledon Press, 1982.
Dickson, David. *A Brief Explication of the First Fifty Psalms*. London: Thomas Johnson, 1655.
Dinges, Martin. "Health Care and Poor Relief in Regional Southern France in the Counter-Reformation." In *Health Care and Poor Relief in Counter-Reformation Europe*, edited by Jon Arrizabalaga, Andrew Cunningham, and Ole Peter Grell, 239–78. London: Routledge, 2014.
Diodati, Giovanni. *Pious annotations, upon the Holy Bible expounding the difficult places thereof learnedly, and plainly*. London: Nicholas Fussel, 1643.
Dipple, Geoffrey. *Antifraternalism and Anticlericalism in the German Reformation: Johann Eberlin von Günzburg and the Campaign against the Friars*. Aldershot, England: Ashgate, 1996.
Dixon, C. Scott. *The Reformation and Rural Society: The Parishes of Brandenburg-Ansbach*. Cambridge: Cambridge University Press, 1996.
Dobson, Barrie, ed. *The Church, Politics and Patronage in the Fifteenth Century*. New York: St. Martin's Press, 1984.
Domat, Jean. *The Civil Law in Its Natural Order*. Translated by William Strahan. Vol. 2. Boston: Charles C. Little and James Brown, 1850.
———. *Les Loix civiles dans leur ordre naturel*. Vol. 1. Paris: Durand, 1777.
Drees, Clayton J. *Bishop Richard Fox of Winchester: Architect of the Tudor Age*. Jefferson: McFarland, 2014.
Dubois, Pierre. *The Recovery of the Holy Land*. Translated by Walther I. Brandt. New York: Columbia University Press, 1956.
Duby, Georges. *The Early Growth of the European Economy: Warriors and Peasants from the Seventh to the Twelfth Century*. Translated by Howard B. Clarke. Ithaca, N.Y.: Cornell University Press, 1973.
Duffy, Eamon. "Cranmer and Popular Religion." In *Thomas Cranmer: Churchman and Scholar*, edited by Paul Ayris and David Selwyn, 199–215. Woodbridge, England: Boydell Press, 1999.
———. *Fires of Faith: Catholic England under Mary Tudor*. New Haven, Conn.: Yale University Press, 2009.
———. *Saints, Sacrilege and Sedition: Religion and Conflict in the Tudor Reformations*. London: Bloomsbury Academic, 2012.

———. *The Stripping of the Altars: Traditional Religion in England, c.1400–c.1580.* New Haven, Conn.: Yale University Press, 1992.
———. *The Voices of Morebath: Reformation and Rebellion in an English Village.* Rev. ed. New Haven, Conn.: Yale University Press, 2003.
Duke, George. *The Law of Charitable Uses.* London: Henry Twyford, 1676. Revised and expanded edition of the same title by John Herne.
Dunkley, E. H. *The Reformation in Denmark.* London: S.P.C.K., 1948.
Durantis, Guillelmus. *Speculum iuris.* Venice: n.p., 1585.
Eberhard, Winfried. "Bohemia, Moravia and Austria." In *The Early Reformation in Europe,* edited by Andrew Pettegree, 23–48. Cambridge: Cambridge University Press, 1992.
Eden, Kathy. *Friends Hold All Things in Common: Tradition, Intellectual Property, and the Adages of Erasmus.* New Haven, Conn.: Yale University Press, 2001.
Edward VI. *Literary Remains of King Edward the Sixth.* Edited by John Gough Nichols. London: H. B. Nichols and Sons, 1857.
Eire, Carlos M. N. *From Madrid to Purgatory: The Art and Craft of Dying in Sixteenth-Century Spain.* Cambridge: Cambridge University Press, 1995.
———. *War Against the Idols: The Reformation of Worship from Erasmus to Calvin.* Cambridge: Cambridge University Press, 1986.
Eisenstein, Ilana H. "Keeping Charity in Charitable Trust Law: The Barnes Foundation and the Case for Consideration of Public Interest in Administration of Charitable Trusts." *University of Pennsylvania Law Review* 151 (2003): 1747–86.
Eisermann, Johannes. *De reipublica bene instituenda.* Basel: Joannes Oporinus, 1556.
Elton, G. R. *F. W. Maitland.* New Haven, Conn.: Yale University Press, 1985.
———. *Policy and Police: The Enforcement of the Reformation in the Age of Thomas Cromwell.* Cambridge: Cambridge University Press, 1972.
———. *Reform and Reformation England, 1509–1558.* Cambridge, Mass.: Harvard University Press, 1977.
———. *Reform and Renewal: Thomas Cromwell and the Common Weal.* Cambridge: Cambridge University Press, 1973.
———. *Studies in Tudor and Stuart Politics and Government.* 4 vols. Cambridge: Cambridge University Press, 2003.
Engel, Ludovicus. *Collegium universi iuris canonici.* Venice: Bartholomaeus Giavarina, 1723.
The English Church Canons of 1604. Edited by C. H. Davis. London: H. Sweet, 1869.
English Reports. 178 vols. London: Stevens and Sons, 1900–1930.
Erasmus, Desiderius. *The Adages of Erasmus.* 2d rev. ed. Edited by William Barker. Toronto: University of Toronto Press, 2001.
———. *Bellum Erasmi.* London: Thomas Berthelet, 1534.
———. *The Collected Works of Erasmus.* Toronto: University of Toronto Press, 1974–.
———. *A Dialoge or Communication of Two Persons, Devysyd and Set Forthe in the Late[n] Tonge, by the Noble and Famose Clarke Desiderius Erasmus intituled [the] Pylgremage of Pure Devotyon. Newly Tra[n]slatyd into Englishe.* 1540.

———. *Opera omnia Desiderii Erasmi Roterodami*. Amsterdam: Huygens Instituut/Brill, 1969–.

———. *Ten Colloquies*. Translated by Craig R. Thompson. New York: Macmillan, 1986.

Erickson, Norma N. "A Dispute Between a Priest and a Knight." *Proceedings of the American Philosophical Society* 111.5 (1967): 288–309.

Erler, Mary C. *Reading and Writing During the Dissolution: Monks, Friars, and Nuns 1530–1558*. Cambridge: Cambridge University Press, 2013.

Erpecum, Wilhelmus van. *Disputatio Juridica Inauguralis ad Leg. XVI ff. de Usu et Usufruct*. Franeker: Johannes Gyzelaar, 1699.

Ertman, Thomas. *Birth of the Leviathan: Building States and Regimes in Medieval and Early Modern Europe*. Cambridge: Cambridge University Press, 1997.

Evans, G. R. *Law and Theology in the Middle Ages*. London: Routledge, 2002.

Falco, Mario. *Le Disposizioni 'pro Animo' fondamenti dottrinali e forme giurdiche*. Turin: Fratelli Bocca, 1911.

Farr, William. *John Wyclif as Legal Reformer*. Leiden: Brill, 1974.

Favre, Antoine. *Codex Fabrianus definitionum forensium*. Leipzig: Thomas Fritsch, 1706.

Fehler, Timothy G. *Poor Relief and Protestantism: The Evolution of Social Welfare in Sixteenth-Century Emden*. Aldershot, England: Ashgate, 1999.

Ferguson, Arthur B. *The Articulate Citizen and the English Renaissance*. Durham, N.C.: Duke University Press, 1965.

Fernández-Santamaría, J. *The Theater of Man: J. L. Vives on Society*. Transactions of the American Philosophical Society. Vol. 88.2. Philadelphia: American Philosophical Society, 1998.

Filmer, Robert. *Patriarcha and Other Writings*. Edited by Johann P. Sommerville. Cambridge: Cambridge University Press, 1991.

Finch, Heneage. *Lord Nottingham's Chancery Cases*. Edited by D. E. C. Yale. 2 Vols. Selden Society Annual Series. Vol. 73 and 79. London: Bernard Quaritch, 1957–61.

Finke, Heinrich. *Papsttum und Untergang des Templerordens*. Vol. 2. Münster: Druck und Verlag der Aschendorffschen, 1907.

Finucane, R. C. *Appearances of the Dead: A Cultural History of Ghosts*. Buffalo, N.Y.: Prometheus Press, 1984.

Fisch, Edith L. "The Cy Pres Doctrine and Changing Philosophies." *Michigan Law Review* 51 (1953): 375–88.

———. *The Cy Pres Doctrine in the United States*. Albany, N.Y.: Matthew Bender, 1950.

Fisch, Edith L., Doris Freed, and Esther Schachter. *Charities and Charitable Foundations*. Pomona, N.Y.: Lond Publications, 1974.

Forma subventionis pauperum quae apud Hyperas Flandrorum urbem viget, universae Reipublicae Christianae longe utilissima. Antwerp: Martin Caesar, 1531.

Fortescue, John. *On the Laws and Governance of England*. Edited by Shelley Lockwood. Cambridge: Cambridge University Press, 1997.

Fortier, Mark. *The Culture of Equity in Early Modern England*. Aldershot, England: Ashgate, 2005.

Fouracre, Paul. *The Age of Charles Martel*. Harlow, England: Pearson, 2000.

Fox, Alistair, and John Guy. *Reassessing the Henrician Age: Humanism, Politics and Reform 1500–1550*. Oxford: Basil Blackwell, 1986.
Fox, Richard. *Letters of Richard Fox 1486–1527*. Edited by P.S. and H.M. Allen. Oxford: Clarendon Press, 1929.
Fremont-Smith, Marion. *Governing Nonprofit Organizations*. Cambridge, Mass.: Belknap Press, 2004.
Fubini, Riccardo. *Humanism and Secularization from Petrarch to Valla*. Translated by Martha King. Durham, N.C.: Duke University Press, 2003.
Fulbecke, William. *The Pandectes of the Law of Nations*. London: Thomas Wight, 1602.
———. *A Parallele or Conference of the Civill Law, the Canon Law, and the Common Law of this Realme of England*. London: Thomas Wight, 1601.
———. *The Second Part of the Parallele*. London: Thomas Wight, 1602.
Gardiner, Stephen. *Obedience in Church and State*. Edited by Pierre Janelle. Cambridge: Cambridge University Press, 1930.
Garnsey, Peter. *Thinking About Property: From Antiquity to the Age of Revolution*. Cambridge: Cambridge University Press, 2007.
Garside, Charles. *Zwingli and the Arts*. New Haven, Conn.: Yale University Press, 1966.
Gasparri, Pietro. *Codicis iuris canonici fontes*. 9 vols. Rome: Polyglottis Vaticanis, 1926–39.
Gasquet, Francis Aidan. *Henry VIII and the English Monasteries*. 6th ed. London: John Hodges, 1902.
Gaudemet, Jean. "Utilitas publica." *Revue historique de droit français et étranger* 29 (1951): 465–99.
Gay, J., ed. *Les Registres de Nicholas III (1277–1280)*. Paris: Albert Fontemoing, 1904.
Geary, Patrick J. *Furta Sacra: Theft of Relics in the Central Middle Ages*. Rev. ed. Princeton, N.J.: Princeton University Press, 2011.
———. *Living with the Dead in the Middle Ages*. Ithaca, N.Y.: Cornell University Press, 1994.
Gee, Henry, and William John Hardy, eds. *Documents Illustrative of English Church History*. London: Macmillan, 1896.
Gemmill, Elizabeth. *The Nobility and Ecclesiastical Patronage in Thirteenth-Century England*. Woodbridge, England: The Boydell Press, 2013.
Getzler, Joshua. "Morice v. Bishop of Durham (1805)." In *Landmark Cases in Equity*, edited by Charles Mitchell and Paul Mitchell, 157–202. Oxford: Oxford University Press, 2012.
———. "Patterns of Fusion." In *The Classification of Obligations*, edited by Peter Birks, 157–92. Oxford: Oxford University Press, 1997.
Gierke, Otto. *Political Theories of the Middle Age*. Boston: Beacon Press, 1958.
Giles of Rome. *On Ecclesiastical Power*. Translated by R. W. Dyson. New York: Columbia University Press, 2004.
Gilmore, Myron. *Humanists and Jurists: Six Studies in the Renaissance*. Cambridge, Mass.: Harvard University Press, 1963.
Gittings, Clare. *Death, Burial, and the Individual in Early Modern England*. London: Croom Helm, 1984.

Gleason, Elisabeth. *Gasparo Contarini: Venice, Rome, and Reform*. Berkeley: University of California Press, 1993.
Godfrey, John A. "The Right of Patronage According to the Code of Canon Law." Ph.D. Dissertation, The Catholic University of America, 1924.
Goffin, R. J. R. *The Testamentary Executor in England and Elsewhere*. London: C. J. Clay, 1901.
Goody, Jack. *Death, Property and the Ancestors: A Study of the Mortuary Customs of the LoDagaa of West Africa*. Stanford, Calif.: Stanford University Press, 1962.
Gordley, James. *The Jurists: A Cultural History*. Oxford: Oxford University Press, 2013.
Gordon, Bruce. "Malevolent Ghosts and Ministering Angels: Apparitions and Pastoral Care in the Swiss Reformation." In *The Place of the Dead: Death and Remembrance in Late Medieval and Early Modern Europe*, edited by Bruce Gordon and Peter Marshall, 87–109. Cambridge: Cambridge University Press, 2000.
———. *The Swiss Reformation*. Manchester: Manchester University Press, 2002.
Gordon, Robert W. "Paradoxical Property." In *Early Modern Conceptions of Property*, edited by John Brewer and Susan Staves, 95–110. New York: Routledge, 1996.
Gorham, George Cornelius, ed. *Gleanings of a Few Scattered Ears, during the Period of the Reformation in England*. London: Bell and Daldy, 1857.
Gratian. *Gratian's Tractatus de penitentia: A New Latin Edition with English Translation*. Edited and translated by Atria A. Larson. Studies in Medieval and Early Modern Canon Law. Washington, D.C.: The Catholic University of America Press, 2016.
———. *The Treatise on the Laws (Decretum DD. 1–20) with the Ordinary Gloss*. Translated by Augustine Thompson and James Gordley. Studies in Medieval and Early Modern Canon Law. Washington, D.C.: The Catholic University of America Press, 1993.
Gregory I. *Dialogues*. Translated by Odo John Zimmerman. Washington, D.C.: The Catholic University of America Press, 1959.
———. *Opera omnia*. In Patrologia Latina. Edited by Jacques Paul Migne. Vol. 77. Paris: Migne, 1849.
Gregory, Brad A. *Salvation at Stake: Christian Martyrdom in Early Modern Europe*. Cambridge, Mass.: Harvard University Press, 2001.
———. *The Unintended Reformation: How a Religious Reformation Secularized Society*. Cambridge, Mass.: Harvard University Press, 2012.
Grell, Ole Peter. "The Protestant Imperative of Christian Care and Neighbourly Love." In *Health Care and Poor Relief in Protestant Europe, 1500–1700*, edited by Andrew Cunningham and Ole Peter Grell, 42–63. London: Routledge, 1997.
Greschat, Martin. *Martin Bucer: A Reformer and His Times*. Translated by Stephen E. Buckwalter. Louisville, Ky.: Westminster John Knox Press, 2004.
———. "The Relation Between Church and Civil Community in Bucer's Reforming Work." Translated by Penelope R. Hall. In *Martin Bucer: Reforming Church and Community*, edited by D. F. Wright, 17–31. Cambridge: Cambridge University Press, 1994.

Gribben, Crawford. "Angels and Demons in Cromwellian and Restoration Ireland: Heresy and the Supernatural." *Huntington Library Quarterly* 76.3 (2013): 377–92.
Groebner, Valentin. *Liquid Assets, Dangerous Gifts: Presents and Politics at the End of the Middle Ages.* Translated by Pamela E. Selwyn. Philadelphia: University of Pennsylvania Press, 2002.
Grosso, Giuseppe. *I legati nel diritto romano.* 2d ed. Rome: Giappichelli, 1962.
Grundmann, Herbert. *Religious Movements in the Middle Ages.* Translated by Steven Rowan. Notre Dame, Ind.: University of Notre Dame Press, 1995.
Günzburg, Johann Eberlin von. *The Fifteen Confederates.* Translated by Geoffrey Dipple. Eugene, Ore.: Wipf and Stock, 2014.
Guido Papa. *Decisiones Guidonis Papae.* Frankfurt am Main: Petrus Fabricius, 1573.
Guy, J. A. *Christopher St German on Chancery and Statute.* Selden Society Supplementary Series. Vol. 6. London: Bernard Quaritch, 1985.
———. *Politics, Law and Counsel in Tudor and Early Stuart England.* Aldershot, England: Ashgate, 2000.
———. *The Public Career of Sir Thomas More.* Brighton, England: Harvester Press, 1980.
Hadfield, Andrew. "The King James Bible." In *English Renaissance Translation Theory.* Edited by Neil Rhodes, Gordon Kendal, and Louise Wilson. *Modern Humanities Research Association* 9 (2013): 179.
Hätzer, Ludwig. *Ein Urteil Gottes unsers Ehegemahl wie man sich mit allen Götzen und Bildnussen halten sol, uss der heiligen Geschrifft gezogen durch Ludwig Hätzer.* Zurich: Christoph Froschauer, 1523.
Haigh, Christopher, ed. *The English Reformation Revised.* Cambridge: Cambridge University Press, 1987.
———. *English Reformations: Religion, Politics and Society under the Tudors.* Oxford: Oxford University Press, 1993.
Hale, Matthew. *Prerogatives of the King.* Edited by D. E. C. Yale. Selden Society Annual Series. Vol. 92. London: Bernard Quaritch, 1975.
Hall, Basil. "Martin Bucer in England." In *Martin Bucer: Reforming Church and Society,* edited by D. F. Wright, 144–60. Cambridge: Cambridge University Press, 1994.
Hall, Edward. *The Lives of the Kings: Henry VIII.* Vol. 2. London: T. C. & E. C. Jack, 1904.
Halliwell, James, ed. *Foundation Documents of Merton College Collected by James Heywood.* London: William Pickering, 1843.
Hannan, Jerome Daniel. "The Canon Law of Wills: An Historical Synopsis and Commentary." J.C.D. Dissertation, The Catholic University of America, 1934.
Harding, Matthew. *Charity Law and the Liberal State.* Cambridge: Cambridge University Press, 2014.
Harper-Bill, Christopher. *Religious Belief and Ecclesiastical Careers in Late Medieval England.* Woodbridge, England: Boydell Press, 1991.
Harris, Troy L., ed. *Studies in Canon Law and Common Law in Honor of R. H. Helmholz.* Berkeley: Robbins Collection Publications, 2015.

Harrison, Robert Pogue. *The Dominion of the Dead*. Chicago: Chicago University Press, 2003.
Harvey, Andrew Edward., ed. *Martin Bucer in England*. Marburg, Germany: Heinrich Bauer, 1906.
Haskett, Timothy S. "The Medieval English Court of Chancery." *Law and History Review* 14 (1996): 245–313.
Heal, Felicity. *The Power of Gifts: Gift Exchange in Early Modern England*. Oxford: Oxford University Press, 2015.
Heers, Jacques. *L'Occident aux XIVe et XVe siècles*. Paris: Presses Universitaires de France, 1966.
Heimpel, Herman. "Das Wesen des Deutschen Spätmittelalters." In *Der Mensche in Seiner Gegenwart: Sieben historische Essais*, 109–35. Göttingen: Vandenhoeck & Ruprecht, 1954.
Heinze, R. W. *The Proclamations of the Tudor Kings*. Cambridge: Cambridge University Press, 1976.
Helmholz, R. H. "The Early Enforcement of Uses." *Columbia Law Review* 79 (1979): 1503–13.
———. "The Law of Charity and the English Ecclesiastical Courts." In *The Foundations of Medieval English Ecclesiastical History: Studies Presented to David Smith*, edited by Philippa Hoskin, Christopher Nugent, Lawrence Brooke, and Richard Barrie Dobson, 111–23. Woodbridge, England: Boydell Press, 2005.
———. "*Legitim* in English Legal History." *University of Illinois Law Review* (1984): 659–74.
———. *The Oxford History of the Laws of England*, Vol. 1: The Canon Law and Ecclesiastical Jurisdiction from 597 to the 1640s. Oxford: Oxford University Press, 2003.
———. *Roman Canon Law in Reformation England*. Cambridge: Cambridge University Press, 1990.
———. *The Spirit of Classical Canon Law*. Athens: University of Georgia Press, 1996.
———. "Thomas More and the Canon Law." In *Medieval Church Law and the Origins of the Western Legal Tradition: A Tribute to Kenneth Pennington*, edited by Wolfgang P. Müller and Mary E. Sommer, 375–88. Washington, D.C.: The Catholic University of America Press, 2006.
———, and Reinhard Zimmermann. *Itinera Fiduciae: Trust and Treuhand in Historical Perspective*. Berlin: Duncker and Humblot, 1998.
Heming, Carol Piper. *Protestants and the Cult of the Saints in German-Speaking Europe, 1517–1531*. Kirksville, Mo.: Truman State University Press, 2003.
Herne, John. *The Law of Charitable Uses*. London: Timothy Twyford, 1660.
Herrtage, Sidney J. *England in the Reign of King Henry the Eighth*. Early English Text Society, Extra Series. Vol. 32. London: Early English Text Society, 1878.
Hicks, Michael. *Bastard Feudalism*. London: Longman, 1995.
Hill, Christopher. *Economic Problems of the Church: From Archbishop Whitgift to the Long Parliament*. Oxford: Oxford University Press, 1956.
———. *The World Turned Upside Down: Radical Ideas during the English Revolution*. Harmondsworth: Penguin Books, 1972.

Bibliography 417

Hillner, Julia. "Families, Patronage, and the Titular Churches of Rome, c. 300–c. 600." In *Religion, Dynasty, and Patronage in Early Christian Rome, 300–900*, edited by Kate Cooper and Julia Hillner, 225–61. Cambridge: Cambridge University Press, 2007.

Hindle, Steve. *On the Parish? The Micro-Politics of Poor Relief in Rural England c.1550–1750.* Oxford: Oxford University Press, 2004.

Hobbes, Thomas. *Leviathan.* Edited by Edwin Curley. Indianapolis, Ind.: Hackett, 1994.

Hobsbawm, Eric, and Terence Ranger, eds. *The Invention of Tradition.* Cambridge: Cambridge University Press, 1983.

Hogue, Arthur R. *Origins of the Common Law.* Indianapolis, Ind.: Liberty Fund, 1986.

Holborn, Hajo. *A History of Modern Germany: The Reformation.* Princeton, N.J.: Princeton University Press, 1959.

Holdsworth, William S. *A History of English Law.* 16 vols. London: Sweet and Maxwell, 1922–66.

Holman, Susan R., ed. *Wealth and Poverty in Early Church and Society.* Grand Rapids, Mich.: Baker, 2008.

Holmes, Oliver Wendell, Jr. *The Common Law.* Edited by Mark DeWolfe Howe. Cambridge, Mass.: Harvard University Press, 1963.

———. *The Judicial Opinions of Oliver Wendell Holmes: Constitutional Opinions, Selected Excerpts, and Epigrams as Given in the Supreme Judicial Court of Massachusetts, 1885–1902.* Edited by Harry C. Shriver. Buffalo, N.Y.: Dennis, 1940.

———. "Law in Science and Science in Law." *Harvard Law Review* 12 (1899): 443–63.

———. "Misunderstandings of the Civil Law." *American Law Review* 6 (1871): 37–49.

Hopf, Constantin. *Martin Bucer and the English Reformation.* London: Blackwell, 1946.

Hornbeck, J. Patrick, II. *What Is a Lollard? Dissent and Belief in Late Medieval England.* Oxford: Oxford University Press, 2010.

———, Stephen E. Lahey, and Fiona Somerset. *Wycliffite Spirituality.* New York: Paulist Press, 2013.

Horne, Thomas A. *Property Rights and Poverty: Political Argument in Britain, 1605–1834.* Chapel Hill: University of North Carolina Press, 1990.

Hostiensis. *Summa.* Venice: Melchior Sessa, 1570.

Houlbrooke, Ralph. *Church Courts and the People During the English Reformation 1520–1570.* Oxford: Oxford University Press, 1979.

———. *Death, Religion and the Family in England, 1480–1750.* Oxford: Oxford University Press, 2000.

Howell, Margaret. *Commerce Before Capitalism in Europe, 1300–1600.* Cambridge: Cambridge University Press, 2010.

———. *Regalian Right in Medieval England.* London: Athlone Press, 1962.

Hoyle, R. W. "The Origins of the Dissolution of the Monasteries." *Historical Journal* 38 (1995): 275–305.

Hudleston, C. R. "Sir John Hudleston, Constable of Sudeley." *Transactions of the Bristol and Gloucestershire Archaeological Society* 48 (1926): 117–32.

Hudson, Anne, ed. *Selections from English Wycliffite Writings.* Toronto: University of Toronto Press, 1997.
Hume, David. *The History of England under the House of Tudor.* Vol. 3: *The History of England from the Invasion of Julius Caesar to the Revolution in 1688.* Indianapolis, Ind.: LibertyClassics, 1983.
Hutten, Ulrich von. *Opera omnia.* Edited by Eduardus Böcking. Vol. 4. Leipzig: Teubner, 1860.
Hyland, Richard. *Gifts: A Study in Comparative Law.* Oxford: Oxford University Press, 2009.
Ibbetson, David. "A House Built on Sand: Equity in Early Modern English Law." In *Law and Equity: Approaches in Roman Law and Common Law,* edited by E. Koops and W.J. Zwalve, 55–77. Leiden: Brill 2013.
Impallomeni, Giambattista. *Le manomissioni mortis causa: Studi sulle fonti autoritative romane.* Padua: CEDAM, 1963.
Innocent IV. *Commentaria super libros quinque Decretalium.* Frankfurt am Main: Sigmund Feyerabend, 1570.
Ives, E. W. "Anne Boleyn and the Early Reformation in England: The Contemporary Evidence." *Historical Journal* 37.3 (1994): 389–400.
———. "Henry VIII's Will: The Protectorate Provisions of 1546–7." *Historical Journal* 37.4 (1994): 901–14.
James I. *The Political Works of James I.* Edited by Charles Howard McIlwain. Cambridge, Mass.: Harvard University Press, 1918.
James, M. R. "Twelve Medieval Ghost-Stories." *English Historical Review* 37 (1922): 413–22.
Janelle, Pierre. *L'Angleterre catholique à la veille du schisme.* Paris: Beauchesne, 1935.
Jardine, Lisa. *Worldly Goods: A New History of the Renaissance.* London: Macmillan, 1996.
Jardine, Lisa, and Alan Stewart. *Hostage to Fortune: The Troubled Life of Francis Bacon.* New York: Hill and Wang, 1998.
Jerome. *Opera omnia.* In Patrologia Latina. Edited by Jacques Paul Migne. Vol. 22. Paris: Migne, 1845.
Joannes de Imola. *Super Clementinis.* Lyon: Joannes Moylin, 1525.
Johnston, David. "Munificience and Municipia: Bequests to Towns in Classical Roman Law." *Journal of Roman Studies* 75 (1985): 105–25.
———. *The Roman Law of Trusts.* Oxford: Clarendon Press, 1988.
Johnstone, Hilda. "Poor Relief in the Royal Households of Thirteenth-Century England." *Speculum* 4.2 (1929): 149–67.
Jolowicz, Herbert Felix. *Roman Foundations of Modern Law.* Oxford: Clarendon Press, 1957.
Jones, Gareth. "Francis Moore's Reading on the Statute of Charitable Uses." *Cambridge Law Journal* 25.2 (1967): 224–38.
———. *History of the Law of Charity, 1532–1827.* Cambridge: Cambridge University Press, 1969.
Jones, Norman. *The English Reformation: Religion and Cultural Adaptation.* Oxford: Blackwell, 2002.
Jones, W. J. *The Elizabethan Court of Chancery.* Oxford: Clarendon Press, 1967.

Jong, Mayke de. *In Samuel's Image: Child Oblation in the Early Medieval West.* Leiden: E. J. Brill, 1996.
Jordan, W.K. *Edward VI: The Threshold of Power. The Dominance of the Duke of Northumberland.* Cambridge, Mass.: Harvard University Press, 1970.
———. *Edward VI: The Young King.* London: George Allen and Unwin, 1968.
———. *Philanthropy in England, 1480–1660: A Study of the Changing Pattern of English Social Aspirations.* London: George Allen and Unwin, 1959.
Jütte, Robert. *Poverty and Deviance in Early Modern Europe.* Cambridge: Cambridge University Press, 1994.
Justinian. *The Digest of Justinian.* 4 vols. Edited by Alan Watson. Philadelphia: University of Pennsylvania Press, 1985.
Kahn, Victoria. *Wayward Contracts: The Crisis of Political Obligation in England, 1640–1674.* Princeton, N.J.: Princeton University Press, 2004.
Kantorowicz, Ernst H., *The King's Two Bodies: A Study in Medieval Political Theology.* Princeton, N.J.: Princeton University Press, 1957.
Kantorowicz, Ernst H., and W. W. Buckland. *Studies in the Glossators of the Roman Law.* Rev. ed. by Peter Weimar. Cambridge: Cambridge University Press, 1969.
Karlstadt, Andreas Rudolff-Bodenstein von. *The Essential Carlstadt: Fifteen Tracts by Andreas Bodenstein (Carlstadt) from Karlstadt.* Translated by E. J. Furcha. Scottdale, Penn.: Herald Press, 1995.
———. *Von abtuhung der Bylder, und das Keyn Bedtler unther den Christen seyn sollen.* Wittenberg: n.p., 1522.
Kaspersen, Lars Bo, and Johannes Lindvall. "Why No Religious Politics? The Secularization of Poor Relief and Primary Education in Denmark and Sweden." *Archives Européennes de Sociologie* 49.1 (2008): 119–43.
Keen, Ralph. "Defending the Pious: Melanchthon and the Reformation in Albertine Saxony." *Church History* 60.2 (1991): 180–95.
Kenny, Anthony, ed. *Wyclif in His Times.* Oxford: Clarendon Press, 1986.
Kent, Bonnie. *Virtues of the Will: The Transformation of Ethics in the Late Thirteenth Century.* Washington, D.C.: The Catholic University of America, 1995.
Keyser, Richard L. "'Agreement Supersedes Law, and Love Judgment': Legal Flexibility and Amicable Settlement in Anglo-Norman England." *Law and History Review* 30.1 (2012): 37–88.
Kidd, B. J. *Documents Illustrative of the Continental Reformation.* Oxford: Clarendon Press, 1911.
———. *The Later Medieval Doctrine of the Eucharistic Sacrifice.* London: S.P.C.K., 1958.
Kisch, Guido. *Melanchthons Rechts- und Soziallehre.* Berlin: Walter de Gruyter, 1967.
Kishlansky, Mark. *A Monarchy Transformed: Britain, 1603–1714.* London: Penguin, 1996.
Klinck, Dennis R. *Conscience, Equity and the Court of Chancery in Early Modern England.* Burlington, Vt.: Ashgate, 2010.
Knafla, Louis A. *Law and Politics in Jacobean England: The Tracts of Lord Chancellor Ellesmere.* Cambridge: Cambridge University Press, 1977.
Knowles, David. *The Religious Orders in England.* Vols. 2–3. Cambridge: Cambridge University Press, 1955–59.

Koerner, Joseph Leo. *Reformation of the Image*. Chicago: University of Chicago, 2003.
Koops, E., and W. J. Zwalve, eds. *Law and Equity: Approaches in Roman and Common Law*. Leiden: Brill, 2013.
Kreider, Alan. *English Chantries: The Road to Dissolution*. Cambridge, Mass.: Harvard University Press, 1979.
Kuttner, Stephan. *Kanonistische Schuldlehre von Gratian bis auf die Dekretalen Gregors IV: Systematisch auf Grund der handschriftlichen Quellen dargestellt*. Studi e testi. Vol. 64. Vatican City: Biblioteca Apostolica Vaticana, 1935.
Lahey, John Francis. "Faithful Fulfillment of the Pious Will: A Fundamental Principle of Church Law as Found in the 1983 Code of Canon Law." J.C.D. Dissertation, The Catholic University of America, 1987.
Landau, Peter. "'Aequitas' in the 'Corpus Iuris Canonici.'" *Syracuse Journal of International Law and Commerce* 20 (1994): 95–104.
———. *Ius Patronatus: Studien zur Entwicklung des Patronats im Dekretalenrecht und der Kanonistik des 12. Und 13. Jahrhunderts*. Cologne-Vienna: Böhlau Verlag, 1975.
Langbein, John H., Renée Lettow Lerner, and Bruce P. Smith. *The History of Common Law: The Development of Anglo-American Legal Institutions*. New York: Aspen, 2009.
Langland, William. *Piers Plowman*. Translated by A. V. C. Schmidt. Oxford: Oxford University Press, 1992.
Laqueur, Thomas W. *The Work of the Dead: A Cultural History of Mortal Remains*. Princeton, N.J.: Princeton University Press, 2015.
Larson, Atria. *Master of Penance: Gratian and the Development of Penitential Thought and Law in the Twelfth Century*. Studies in Medieval and Early Modern Canon Law. Washington, D.C.: The Catholic University of America Press, 2014.
Latymer, William. "Cronickille of Anne Bulleyne." Edited by M. Dowling. *Camden miscellany* 30 (1990): 23–65.
Laud, William. *The History of the Troubles and Tryal of the Most Reverend Father in God William Laud*. London: Richard Chiswell, 1695.
Lawrence, C. H. *The Friars: The Impact of the Early Mendicant Movement on Western Society*. London: Longman, 1994.
Lee, Wendy A. "Charitable Foundations and the Argument for Efficiency: Balancing Donor Intent with Practicable Solutions Through Expanded Use of Cy Pres." *Suffolk University Law Review* 34 (2000): 173–202.
Leges Alamannorum. Leges Nationum Germanicarum. Vol. 5. Part 1. Hanover: Hahn, 1888.
Le Goff, Jacques. *The Birth of Purgatory*. Translated by Arthur Goldhammer. Chicago: University of Chicago Press, 1984.
———. *Your Money or Your Life: Economy and Religion in the Middle Ages*. Translated by Patricia Ranum. New York: Zone Books, 1998.
Lehmberg, Stanford E. *The Reformation Parliament 1529–1536*. Cambridge: Cambridge University Press, 1970.
Leo the Great. *Opera omnia*. In Patrologia Latina. Edited by Jacques-Paul Migne. Vol. 54. Paris: Migne, 1846.

Leopold, Antony. *How to Recover the Holy Land: Crusade Proposals in the Late Thirteenth and Early Fourteenth Centuries.* Aldershot, England: Ashgate, 2000.

Letters and Papers of the Reign of Henry VIII. Edited by J. S. Brewer, James Gairdner, and R. H. Brodie. London: Stationery Office, 1862–1932.

Levison, Wilhelm. *England and the Continent in the Eighth Century.* Oxford: Clarendon Press, 1946.

Lewkenor, Lewis. *A Discourse of the Usage of the English Fugitives by the Spanish.* London: Thomas Scarlet for John Drawater, 1595.

Lieberson, Harry. *Return of the Gift: European History of a Global Idea.* Cambridge: Cambridge University Press, 2012.

Liguori, Alphonsus de. *Compendium theologiae moralis.* Ratisbon, Germany: G. Joseph Manz, 1851.

Lindberg, Carter H. *Beyond Charity.* Minneapolis, Minn.: Augsburg Fortress, 1993.

Little, Lester K. *Religious Poverty and the Profit Economy in Medieval Europe.* Ithaca, N.Y.: Cornell University Press, 1978.

Littleton, Thomas. *His Treatise of Tenures, in French and English.* London: S. Sweet, 1841.

Lizerand, Georges, ed. *Le Dossier de l'affaire des Templiers.* 4th ed. Paris: Les Belles Lettres, 2007.

Llewellyn, Nigel. *The Art of Death: Visual Culture in the English Death Ritual c. 1500–c. 1800.* London: Reaktion Books, 1991.

Loach, Jennifer. *Parliament under the Tudors.* Oxford: Oxford University Press, 1991.

Lockwood, Shelley. "Marsilius of Padua and the Case for the Royal Ecclesiastical Supremacy: The Alexander Prize Essay." *Transactions of the Royal Historical Society* Sixth Series. Vol. 1 (1991): 89–119.

Logan, F. Donald. "The Henrician Canons." *Bulletin of the Institute of Historical Research* 47 (1974): 99–103.

Luca, Giovanni Battista de. *Theatrum veritatis et iustitiae.* Venice: Typographia Balleoniana, 1734.

Ludovicus Pontanus. *Consilia sive Responsa.* Venice: Hieronymus Zenarum and Brothers, 1581.

———. *Repetitio de relictis ad pias causas.* Rome: Georg Lauer and Leonhard Pflugl, 1472.

Lugo, Juan de. *De iustitia et iure.* Lyon: Arnaud, 1670.

Lupoi, Maurizio. "Trust and Confidence." *Law Quarterly Review* 125 (2009): 253–87.

———. *Trusts: A Comparative Study.* Translated by Simon Dix. Cambridge: Cambridge University Press, 2000.

Lupton, Thomas. *Siuqila too good, to be true.* London: H. Bynneman, 1580.

Luther, Martin. *D. Martin Luthers Werke.* Weimar: Hermann Böhlau, 1833–2009.

———. *Luther's Works.* Edited by Helmut T. Lehmann and Jaroslav J. Pelikan. 55 vols. Philadelphia: Fortress Press, 1955–86; New Series, edited by Christopher Brown. 20 vols. Saint Louis, Mo.: Concordia Publishing, 2009–.

Luttrell, Anthony. "The Benedictines and Malta: 1363–1371." *Papers of the British School at Rome* 50 (1982): 146–65.

Lyndwood, William, and others. *Constitutions provincialles and of Otho and Octhobone Translated in to Englyshe.* London: R. Redman, 1534.

———. *Provinciale seu Constitutiones Angliae.* Oxford: Richard Davis, 1679.

Lytle, Guy Fitch, and Stephen Orgel, eds. *Patronage in the Renaissance.* Princeton, N.J.: Princeton University Press, 1981.

MacCulloch, Diarmaid. *The Boy King: Edward VI and the Protestant Reformation.* Berkeley: University of California Press, 1999.

———. *The Reformation: A History.* New York: Penguin, 2003.

———. *Thomas Cranmer.* New Haven, Conn.: Yale University Press, 1996.

MacDonald, Alan R. "James VI and I, the Church of Scotland, and British Ecclesiastical Convergence." *Historical Journal* 48 (2005): 885–903.

Macnair, Mike. "Arbitrary Chancellors and the Problem of Predictability." In *Law and Equity: Approaches in Roman Law and Common Law,* edited by E. Koops and W.J. Zwalve, 79–104. Leiden: Brill 2013.

———. "Equity and Conscience." *Oxford Journal of Legal Studies* 27 (2007): 659–681.

Macray, W. M., ed. *Calendar of Charters and Documents Relating to Selborne and Its Priory Preserved in the Muniment Room of Magdalen College Oxford.* London: Simpkin and Co., 1891.

Madison, James. *Selected Writings of James Madison.* Edited by Ralph Ketcham. Indianapolis, Ind.: Hackett, 2006.

Madoff, Ray. *Immortality and the Law: The Rising Power of the American Dead.* New Haven, Conn.: Yale University Press, 2010.

Mäkinen, Virpi. *Property Rights in the Late Medieval Discussion on Franciscan Poverty.* Leuven: Peeters, 2001.

Maitland, F. W. *Equity: A Course of Lectures.* Revised by John Brunyate. Cambridge: Cambridge University Press, 1969.

———. "The Origin of Uses." *Harvard Law Review* 8 (1894): 127–137.

———. *State, Trust and Corporation.* Edited by David Runciman and Magnus Ryan. Cambridge: Cambridge University Press, 2003.

"Mandatory 'Cy Pres' and the Racially Restrictive Charitable Trust." *Columbia Law Review* 69 (1969): 1478–1495.

Mansi, Giovanni Domenico. *Sacrorum conciliorum.* Vol. 25. Venice: Antonius Zatta, 1782.

Mantica, Franciscus. *Tractatus de coniecturis ultimarum voluntatum.* Geneva: Crispin, 1631.

Marius, Richard. *Martin Luther: The Christian Between God and Death.* Cambridge, Mass.: Harvard University Press, 2000.

Marshall, Peter. *Beliefs and the Dead in Reformation England.* Oxford: Oxford University Press, 2004.

———. *Reformation England 1480–1642.* London: Bloomsbury Academic, 2012.

Marsilius of Padua. *The Defence of Peace.* London: William Marshall, 1535.

———. *Defensor pacis.* Translated by Alan Gewith. New York: Columbia University Press, 1956.

Martène, Edmond, and Ursin Durand. *Thesaurus novus anecdotorum.* 5 vols. Paris: Delaulne, 1717.

Martin, Nick. "Liberal Neutrality and Charitable Purposes." *Political Studies* 60 (2012): 936–52.
Matthew of Paris. *Chronica majora*. Edited by Henry Richards Luard. London: Longmans, 1872–83.
Mauss, Marcel. *The Gift: The Form and Reason for Exchange in Archaic Societies*. Translated by W. D. Halls. New York: W. W. Norton, 1990.
Maximus of Turin. *The Sermons of St. Maximus of Turin*. Translated and annotated by Boniface Ramsey. Mahwah, N.J.: Paulist Press, 1989.
Mayer, Thomas. *Thomas Starkey and the Commonweal: Humanist Politics and Religion in the Reign of Henry VIII*. Cambridge: Cambridge University Press, 1989.
McCahill, Elizabeth. *Reviving the Eternal City: Rome and the Papal Court*. Cambridge, Mass.: Harvard University Press, 2013.
McEntegart, Rory. *Henry VIII, the League of Schmalkalden, and the English Reformation*. Woodbridge, England: Boydell Press, 2011.
McGlynn, Margaret. *The Royal Prerogative and the Learning of the Inns of Court*. Cambridge: Cambridge University Press, 2003.
McGovern, John F. "The Rise of New Economic Attitudes in Canon and Civil Law, A.D. 1200–1550." *The Jurist* 32 (1972): 39–50.
McGrade, Arthur Stephen. *The Political Thought of William of Ockham: Personal and Institutional Principles*. Cambridge: Cambridge University Press, 1974.
McIntosh, Marjorie Kenston. *Poor Relief in England, 1350–1600*. Cambridge: Cambridge University Press, 2012.
McKisack, May. *Medieval History in the Tudor Age*. Oxford: Clarendon Press, 1971.
McLaughlin, Megan. *Consorting with Saints: Prayer for the Dead in Early Medieval France*. Ithaca, N.Y.: Cornell University Press, 1994.
McVeigh, Terrence A. "Introduction." In *On Simony*. New York: Fordham University Press, 1992.
McWilliams, Robert L. "Consideration and the Law of Trusts." *California Law Review* 14 (1926): 188–97.
Meekings, C. A. F. *Studies in Thirteenth-Century Justice and Administration*. London: Hambledon Press, 1981.
Melanchthon, Philip. *Epitome renovatae ecclesiasticae doctrinae*. Marburg, Germany: C. L. Pfeil, 1860.
———. *Opera quae supersunt omnia*. In Corpus Reformatorum. Vol. 16. Halle, Germany: C. A. Schwetschke, 1850.
Menache, Sophia. *Clement V.* Cambridge: Cambridge University Press, 2003.
———. "Contemporary Attitudes Concerning the Templars' Affair: Propaganda's Fiasco?" *Journal of Medieval History* 8 (1982): 135–47.
Metcalf, P., and R. Huntington. *Celebrations of Death: The Anthropology of the Mortuary Ritual*. Cambridge: Cambridge University Press, 1993.
Mill, John Stuart. "Endowments." In *Dissertations and Discussions*. Vol. 5. New York: Henry Holt, 1875.
Miller, Maureen. "Donors, Their Gifts, and Religious Innovation in Medieval Verona." *Speculum* 66.1 (1991): 27–42.
Milsom, S. F. C. *Historical Foundations of the Common Law*. London: Butterworths, 1969.

———. "Law and Fact in Legal Development." *University of Toronto Law Journal* 17.1 (1967): 1–19.

———. *Natural History of the Common Law*. New York: Columbia University Press, 2003.

The [Mock] Lamentation [for the decrease of the Mass]. In English Reprints. Vol. 14. Edited by Edward Arber, 30–124. London: A. Murray, 1871.

Moeller, Bernd. *Imperial Cities and the Reformation: Three Essays*. Translated and edited by H. C. Erik Midelfort and Mark U. Edwards Jr. Durham, N.C.: Labyrinth Press, 1972.

Molina, Luis. *De iustitia et iure*. Vol. 1. Cologne: Tournes, 1759.

Mollat, Michel. *Les pauvres au moyen âge*. Paris: Hachette, 1978.

Monahan, Arthur P. *Consent, Coercion, and Limit: The Medieval Origins of Parliamentary Democracy*. Kingston, Canada: McGill-Queen's University Press, 1987.

Moneta, Johannes Petrus. *Tractatus de commutationibus ultimarum voluntatum*. Lyon: Cardon and Cavellat, 1624.

Montaigne, Michel de. *The Complete Works*. Translated by Donald Frame. New York: Alfred A. Knopf, 2003.

Monumenta iuris canonici. Series A: Corpus Glossatorum. 8 Vol. Vatican: Biblioteca, 1969–2014.

Moore, Gerald. *Politics of the Gift: Exchanges in Poststructuralism*. Edinburgh: Edinburgh University Press, 2011.

More, Thomas. *The Complete Works of St. Thomas More*. 15 vols. New Haven, Conn.: Yale University Press, 1963–97.

———. *The Four Last Things, The Supplication of Souls, A Dialogue on Conscience*. Edited by Mary Gottschalk. New York: Scepter Publishers, 2002.

Moreau, Jean-Pierre. *Rome ou L'Angleterre? Les Réactions politiques des catholiques anglais au moment du schisme (1529–1553)*. Paris: Presses Universitaires de France, 1984.

Morrissey, Mary. *Politics and the Paul's Cross Sermons, 1558–1642*. Oxford: Oxford University Press, 2011.

Mostazo, Francesco a. *De causis piis*. Lyon: Arnaud, 1686.

Moyn, Samuel. *The Last Utopia: Human Rights in History*. Cambridge, Mass.: Belknap Press, 2012.

Mulheron, Rachael P. *The Modern Cy-près Doctrine: Applications and Implications*. London: Cavendish Publishing, 2006.

Murphy, Virginia. "The Literature and Propaganda of Henry VIII's First Divorce." In *The Reign of Henry VIII: Politics, Policy and Piety*, edited by Diarmaid MacCulloch, 135–58. Basingstoke, England: Palgrave Macmillan, 1995.

Neale, J. E. *Elizabeth I and Her Parliaments (1559–1581)*. New York: St. Martin's Press, 1958.

Noble, Thomas F. X. "Paradoxes and Possibilities in the Sources for Roman Society in the Early Middle Ages." In *Medieval Rome and the Christian West: Essays in Honor of Donald A. Bullough*, edited by Julia M. H. Smith, 55–83. Leiden: Brill, 2000.

Nolf, J. *La Réforme de la bienfaisance publique à Ypres au XVIe siècle*. Ghent: E. van Goethem, 1915.

Bibliography 425

Norton, Elizabeth. *The Anne Boleyn Papers*. Stroud, England: Amberley, 2013.
Oakley, Francis. *The Conciliarist Tradition: Constitutionalism in the Catholic Church 1300–1870*. Oxford: Oxford University Press, 2003.
———. *The Mortgage of the Past: Reshaping the Ancient Political Inheritance (1050–1300)*. New Haven, Conn.: Yale University Press, 2012.
———. *Natural Law, Conciliarism and Consent in the Late Middle Ages: Studies in Ecclesiastical and Intellectual History*. London: Variorum, 1984.
Oberman, Heiko. *Masters of the Reformation: The Emergence of a New Intellectual Climate in Europe*. Translated by Dennis Martin. Cambridge: Cambridge University Press, 1981.
Ocker, Christopher. *Church Robbers and Reformers in Germany, 1525–1547: Confiscation and Religious Purpose in the Holy Roman Empire*. Leiden: Brill, 2006.
Ogle, Arthur. *The Canon Law in Mediaeval England: An Examination of William Lyndwood's "Provinciale," in Reply to the Late Professor F. W. Maitland*. London: John Murray, 1912.
Olin, John C., ed. *The Catholic Reformation: Savonarola to Ignatius Loyola*. New York: Fordham University Press, 1992.
Olson, Jeannine E. "Calvin and Social-Ethical Issues." In *The Cambridge Companion to Calvin*, edited by Donald K. McKim, 153–72. Cambridge: Cambridge University Press, 2004.
O'Malley, John W. *Trent: What Happened at the Council*. Cambridge, Mass.: Belknap Press, 2013.
Original Letters Relating to the Ecclesiastical Affairs of Scotland. 2 vols. Edinburgh: J. Hughes, 1851.
Original Letters Relative to the English Reformation. Edited by Hastings Robinson. Cambridge: Cambridge University Press, 1846.
Orme, Nicholas. *Education in the West of England 1066–1548*. Exeter: University of Exeter, 1976.
Orme, Nicholas, and Margaret Webster. *The English Hospital 1070–1570*. New Haven, Conn.: Yale University Press, 1995.
Owen, David. *English Philanthropy 1660–1960*. Cambridge, Mass.: Belknap Press, 1964.
Owen, John. *Exercitations Concerning the Name, Original, Use, and Continuance of a Day of Sacred Rest*. London: Nathaniel Ponder, 1671.
Ozment, Steven. *The Reformation in the Cities: The Appeal of Protestantism to Sixteenth-Century Germany and Switzerland*. New Haven, Conn.: Yale University Press, 1980.
Palmer, James T. *Anglo-Saxons in a Frankish World, 690–900*. Turnhout: Brepols, 2009.
Palmer, Robert C. *English Law in the Age of the Black Death, 1348–1381: A Transformation of Governance and Law*. Chapel Hill: University of North Carolina Press, 1993.
———. *Selling the Church: The English Parish and in Law, Commerce, and Religion, 1350–1550*. Chapel Hill: University of North Carolina Press, 2002.
Panormitanus. *Abbatis Panormitani commentaria in tertium Decretalium librum*. Vol. 6. Venice: Iuntas, 1588.
———. *Consilia tractatus, quaestiones, et practica*. Venice: n.p., 1571.

Parlopiano, Brandon T. "Madmen and Lawyers: The Development and Practice of the Jurisprudence of Insanity in the Middle Ages." Ph.D. Dissertation, The Catholic University of America, 2013.
Parry, Johnathan. "The Gift, the Indian Gift and the 'Indian Gift.'" *Man* 21.3 (1986): 453–73.
Parsons, Robert. *A Christian Directorie Guiding Men to their Salvation*. Rouen: n.p., 1585.
Pasquier, Étienne. *Le Catéchisme des Jesuites: ou Examen de leur doctrine*. Villefranche: Guillaume Grenier, 1602.
Paston Letters and Papers of the Fifteenth Century. Edited by Norman Davis. Oxford: Clarendon Press, 1971.
Patrides, C. A. "Psychopannychism in Renaissance Europe." *Studies in Philology* 60.2.1 (1963): 227–29.
Patterson, W. B. *James VI and I and the Reunion of Christendom*. New York: Cambridge University Press, 1998.
Paxton, Frederick S. *Christianizing Death: The Creation of a Ritual Process in Early Medieval Europe*. Ithaca, N.Y.: Cornell University Press, 1990.
Pearson, Eric G. "Reforming the Reform of the Cy Pres Doctrine: A Proposal to Protect Testator Intent." *Marquette Law Review* 90 (2006): 127–53.
Peck, Linda Levy. *Court Patronage and Corruption in Early Stuart England*. London: Routledge, 1993.
Pennington, Kenneth. *Pope and Bishops: The Papal Monarchy in the Twelfth and Thirteenth Centuries*. Philadelphia: University of Pennsylvania Press, 1984.
———. *The Prince and the Law, 1200–1600: Sovereignty and Rights in the Western Legal Tradition*. Berkeley: University of California Press, 1993.
———. "Protestant Ecclesiastical Law and the Ius Commune." *Rivista internazionale di diritto comune* 26 (2015): 9–36.
———. "Torture and Fear: Enemies of Justice." *Rivista internazionale di diritto comune* 19 (2008): 203–42.
Percival, Edward France, ed. *The Foundation Statutes of Merton College, Oxford*. London: William Pickering, 1847.
Pervukhin, Anna. "Deodands: A Study in the Creation of Common Law Rules." *American Journal of Legal History* 47.3 (2005): 237–56.
Petrus de Ubaldus. *Tractatus super canonia episcopali, et parochiali*. In *Tractatus universi iuris*. Tome XV, Pars II. Venice: Francesco Zilletti, 1584.
Phillips, John. *The Reformation of Images: The Destruction of Art in England, 1535–1660*. Berkeley: University of California Press, 1973.
Pierson, Christopher. *Just Property: A History in the Latin West*. Oxford: Oxford University Press, 2013.
Pietro d'Ancarano. *Super Clementinis facundissima commentaria*. Bologna: Societatis Typographiae Bononiae, 1580.
Pirhing, Henri. *Jus canonicum nova methodo explicatum*. Vol. 3. Venice: Remondiniana, 1759.
Plucknett, Theodore F. T. *A Concise History of the Common Law*. 5th ed. London: Butterworth, 1956.
Pocock, J. G. A. *The Ancient Constitution and the Feudal Law: A Study of English*

Historical Thought in the Seventeenth Century: A Reissue with a Retrospect. Cambridge: Cambridge University Press, 1987.
Pogson, Rex. "God's Law and Man's: Stephen Gardiner and the Problem of Loyalty." In *Law and Government Under the Tudors: Essays Presented to Sir Geoffrey Elton Regius Professor of Modern History in the University of Cambridge on the Occasion of his Retirement,* edited by Claire Cross, David Loades, and J. J. Scarisbrick, 67–89. Cambridge: Cambridge University Press, 1988.
Pole, Reginald. *Pole's Defense of the Unity of the Church.* Translated by Joseph G. Dwyer. Westminster, Md.: Newman Press, 1965.
———. *Reformatio Angliae, Ex Decretis Reginaldi Poli Cardinalis, Sedis Apostolicae Legati, Anno MDLVI.* Rome: Paulus Manutius, 1562.
Pollock, Sir Frederick, and Frederic William Maitland. *The History of English Law Before the Time of Edward I.* 2d ed. 2 vols. Cambridge: Cambridge University Press, 1968.
Ponte, Oldradus de. *Consilia, seu Responsa, et quaestiones aureae.* Venice: Franciscus Zilettus, 1571.
Poos, Laurence S., ed. *Lower Ecclesiastical Jurisdiction in Late-Medieval England: The Courts of the Dean and Chapter of Lincoln, 1336–1349, and the Deanery of Wisbech, 1458–1484.* Oxford: Oxford University Press, 2001.
Porter, Stephen. *The London Charterhouse: A History of Thomas Sutton's Charity.* Stroud, England: Amberley Publishing, 2009.
Posner, Richard. *Economic Analysis of the Law.* 4th ed. Boston: Little, Brown, & Co., 1992.
Possidius. "Sancti Augustini vita scripta a Possidio episcopo." Edited by Herbert T. Weiskotten. Ph.D. Dissertation, Princeton University, 1919.
Prall, Stuart E. "Chancery Reform and the Puritan Revolution." *American Journal of Legal History* 6 (1962): 28–44.
Prierias, Silvester. *Summae, nitori suo restitutae, Pars secunda.* Lyon: Mauricium Roy and Ludovicus Pefnot, 1555.
Pullan, Brian. *Rich and Poor in Renaissance Venice: The Social Institutions of a Catholic State, to 1620.* Oxford: Basil Blackwell, 1971.
Questier, Michael. *Conversion, Politics, and Religion in England, 1580–1625.* Cambridge: Cambridge University Press, 1996.
Raban, Sandra. *Mortmain Legislation and the English Church 1279–1500.* Cambridge: Cambridge University Press, 1982.
Rabban, David M. *Law's History: American Legal Thought and the Transatlantic Turn to History.* Cambridge: Cambridge University Press, 2013.
Raftis, James Ambrose. *A Small Town in Late Medieval England: Godmanchester, 1278–1400.* Toronto: Pontifical Institute of Mediaeval Studies, 1982.
Recueil des chartes de l'abbaye de Cluny. Edited by Auguste Bernard and Alexandre Bruel. Vol. 1. Paris: Imprimerie nationale, 1876.
Reiffenstuel, Anacletus. *Ius canonicum universum.* 6 vols. Paris: Vives, 1868.
Reinhold, Niebuhr. *The Contribution of Religion to Social Work.* New York: Columbia University Press, 1932.
Report of the Committee on the Law and Practice Relating to Charitable Trusts. Nathan Committee Report, Cmd 8710. London: H.M.S.O., 1952.
Restatement (Second) of Trusts. St. Paul, Minn.: American Law Institute, 1959.

Restatement (Third) of Trusts. St. Paul, Minn.: American Law Institute, 2003– .
"A Revaluation of Cy Pres." *Yale Law Journal* 49 (1939): 303–23.
Reynolds, Susan. *Before Eminent Domain: Toward a History of Expropriation of Land for the Common Good.* Chapel Hill: University of North Carolina Press, 2010.
———. *Fiefs and Vassals: The Medieval Evidence Reinterpreted.* Oxford: Oxford University Press, 1994.
———. *The Middle Ages without Feudalism: Essays in Criticism and Comparison on the Medieval West.* Burlington, Vt.: Ashgate, 2012.
Rhee, Helen. *Loving the Poor, Saving the Rich: Wealth, Poverty, and Early Christian Formation.* Grand Rapids, Mich.: Baker Academic, 2012.
Ritchie, John. *Reports of Cases Decided by Francis Bacon, Baron Verulam, Viscount St. Albans, Lord Chancellor of England, in the High Court of Chancery (1617–1621).* London: Sweet and Maxwell, 1932.
Robinson, Jonathan. *William of Ockham's Early Theory of Property Rights in Context.* Leiden: Brill, 2013.
Rosenthal, Joel T. *The Purchase of Paradise: The Social Function of Aristocratic Benevolence, 1307–1485.* London: Routledge and Kegan Paul, 1972.
Rosenwein, Barbara H. *To Be the Neighbor of Saint Peter: The Social Meaning of Cluny's Property, 909–1049.* Ithaca, N.Y.: Cornell University Press, 1989.
Rossi, Giovanni. *Incunaboli della modernità: Scienza giuridica e cultura umanistica in André Tiraqueau (1488–1558).* Turin: Giappichelli, 2007.
Rubin, Miri. *Charity and Community in Medieval Cambridge.* Cambridge: Cambridge University Press, 1987.
———. *Corpus Christi: The Eucharist in Late Medieval Culture.* Cambridge: Cambridge University Press, 1992.
Rudenstine, Neil L. *The House of Barnes: The Man, the Collection, and the Controversy.* Memoirs of the American Philosophical Society. Vol. 266. Philadelphia: American Philosophical Society, 2012.
Rudolph, Julia. *Common Law and Enlightenment in England, 1689–1750.* Woodbridge, England: Boydell Press, 2013.
Rummel, Erika. *Scheming Papists and Lutheran Fools: Five Reformation Satires.* New York: Fordham University Press, 1993.
Rushton, Neil S. "Monastic Charitable Provision in Tudor England." *Continuity and Change* 16 (2001): 9–44.
Rushton, Neil S., and Wendy Sige-Rushton. "Monastic Poor Relief in Sixteenth-Century England." *Journal of Interdisciplinary History* 32.2 (2001): 193–216.
Rushworth, John. *Historical Collections.* Vol. 2. London: John Wright, 1680.
Ryan, Magnus. "Bartolus of Sassoferrato and Free Cities." *Transactions of the Royal Historical Society* 10 (2000): 65–89.
———. "Succession to Fiefs: A Ius Commune Feudorum?" In *The Creation of the Ius Commune: From Casus to Regula.* Edinburgh: Edinburgh University Press, 2010.
Rymer, Thomas. *Rymer's Foedera.* Hague: Joannes Neulme: 1739–45.
Sachs, Leslie Raymond. "Thomas Cranmer's *Reformatio Legum Ecclesiasticarum* of 1553 in the Context of English Church Law from the Later Middle Ages to the Canons of 1603." Ph.D. Dissertation, The Catholic University of America, 1982.

Saint German, Christopher. *Doctor and Student*. Edited by T. F. T. Plucknett and J. L. Barton. Selden Society Annual Series. Vol. 91. London: Bernard Quaritch, 1974.

———. *St. Germans Book of the Grounds of the Laws of England and of Conscience, or, An Exact Abridgement of that Exquisite Treatise called Doctor and Student*. London: John More, 1630.

———. *A Treatise Concernynge Diuers of the Constitucyons Prouynciall and Legatines*. London: Thomas Godfrey, 1535.

Salter, F. R., ed. *Some Early Tracts on Poor Relief*. London: Methuen, 1926.

Salutati, Coluccio. *On the World and Religious Life*. Translated by Tina Marshall. Cambridge, Mass.: Harvard University Press, 2014.

Salvian. *Opera*. Corpus Scriptorum Ecclesiasticorum Latinorum. Vol. 8. Vienna: C. Geroldus, 1883.

———. *The Writings of Salvian, the Presbyter*. Translated by Jeremiah F. O'Sullivan. New York: Cima Publishing, 1947.

Sanchez, Tomás. *Consilia, seu Opuscula moralia tomus posterior*. Lyon: Jacobus and Petrus Prost, 1635.

Sare, John. "Art for Whose Sake? An Analysis of Restricted Gifts to Museums." *Columbia–VLA Journal of Law and the Arts* 13 (1988): 377–95.

Scarisbrick, J. J. *Henry VIII*. New Haven, Conn.: Yale University Press, 1969.

———. "Henry VIII and the Dissolution of the Secular Colleges." In *Law and Government Under the Tudors: Essays Presented to Sir Geoffrey Elton Regius Professor of Modern History in the University of Cambridge on the Occasion of His Retirement*, edited by Claire Cross, David Loades, and J. J. Scarisbrick, 51–66. Cambridge: Cambridge University Press, 1988.

———. "The Pardon of the Clergy, 1531." *Cambridge Historical Journal* 12.1 (1956): 22–39.

———. *The Reformation and the English People*. Cambridge, Mass.: Basil Blackwell, 1984.

Schmalzgrueber, Francis X. *Ius ecclesiasticum universum*. Rome: Camera Apostolicae, 1844.

Schmitt, Jean-Claude. *Ghosts in the Middle Ages: The Living and the Dead in Medieval Society*. Translated by Teresa Lavender Fagan. Chicago: University of Chicago Press, 1999.

Scott, Austin Wakeman, and William F. Fratcher. *The Law of Trusts*. 4th ed. Boston: Little, Brown, 1987.

Scott, Jonathan. *England's Troubles: Seventeenth-Century English Political Instability in European Context*. Cambridge: Cambridge University Press, 2000.

Sehling, Emil, ed. *Die evangelischen Kirchenordnung des 16. Jahrhundert*. Vol. 1. Leipzig: O. R. Reisland, 1902.

———. *Die evangelischen Kirchenordnung des 16. Jahrhundert*. Vol. 6/1. Tübingen: Mohr, 1955.

Selden, John. *Table Talk of John Selden*. Edited by Frederick Pollock. London: Quaritch, 1927.

Sellar, W. David H. "Succession Law in Scotland—a Historical Perspective." In *Exploring the Law of Succession: Studies National, Historical, and Comparative*,

edited by Kenneth G. C. Reid, Maurius J. de Waal, and Reinhard Zimmermann, 49–66. Edinburgh: Edinburgh University Press, 2007.
Seneca. *On Benefits*. Translated by John W. Basore. In *Moral Essays*. Vol. 3. Cambridge, Mass.: Harvard University Press, 1958.
Senis, Federicus Petruccius de. *Consilia, sive Mavis responsa, questiones, et placita*. Venice: Antonius Betranus, 1576.
Shagan, Ethan. *Popular Politics and the English Reformation*. Cambridge: Cambridge University Press, 2003.
Shakespeare, William. *The Complete Works*. Edited by Alfred Harbage. New York: Viking Penguin, 1969.
Shapiro, Barbara. "Sir Francis Bacon and the Mid-Seventeenth Century Movement for Law Reform." *American Journal of Legal History* 24 (1980): 331–62.
Shaw, Anthony N. "The Compendium Compertorum and the Making of the Suppression Act of 1536." Ph.D. Dissertation, University of Warwick, 2003.
Sheedy, Anna T. *Bartolus on Social Conditions in the Fourteenth Century*. New York: Columbia University Press, 1942.
Sheehan, Michael. "The Bequest of Land in England in the High Middle Ages: Testaments and the Law." In *Marriage, Family, and Law in Medieval Europe: Collected Studies*, edited by James K. Farge, 311–323. Toronto: University of Toronto Press, 1997.
———. "Canon Law and English Institutions: Some Notes on Current Research." In *Marriage, Family, and Law in Medieval Europe: Collected Studies*, edited by James K. Farge, 31–37. Toronto: University of Toronto Press, 1997.
———. "English Wills and the Records of the Ecclesiastical and Civil Jurisdictions." In *Marriage, Family, and Law in Medieval Europe: Collected Studies*, edited by James K. Farge, 199–210. Toronto: University of Toronto Press, 1997.
———. *The Will in Medieval England: From the Conversion of the Anglo-Saxons to the End of the Thirteenth Century*. Toronto: Pontifical Institute of Mediaeval Studies, 1963.
Sider, Ronald J., ed. *Karlstadt's Battle with Luther: Documents in a Liberal-Radical Debate*. Minneapolis, Minn.: Augsburg Fortress Press, 1978.
Sieglerschmidt, Jörn. *Territorialstaat und Kirchenregiment*. Cologne: Böhlau, 1987.
Las Siete Partidas. Edited by Robert I. Burns. Translated by Samuel Parsons Scott. 5 vols. Philadelphia: University of Pennsylvania Press, 2001.
Silber, Ilana F. "Gift-giving in the Great Traditions: The Case of Donations to Monasteries in the Medieval West." *Archives Européennes de Sociologie* 36.2 (1995): 209–43.
Simes, Lewis M. *Public Policy and the Dead Hand: Five Lectures*. Ann Arbor: University of Michigan Law School, 1955.
Simpson, A. W. B. "The Equitable Doctine of Consideration and the Law of Uses." *University of Tornoto Law Journal* 16 (1965): 1–36.
Sisson, Roger G. "Relaxing the Dead Hand's Grip: Charitable Efficiency and the Doctrine of Cy Pres." *Virginia Law Review* 73 (1988): 635–54.

Skinner, Quentin. *The Foundations of Modern Political Thought*. 2 vols. Cambridge: Cambridge University Press, 1978.
——. "Meaning and Understanding in the History of Ideas." *History and Theory* 8.1 (1969): 3–53.
Slack, Paul. *The English Poor Law, 1531–1782*. Cambridge: Cambridge University Press, 1990.
——. *Poverty and Policy in Tudor and Stuart England*. London: Longman, 1988.
Smith, Adam. *Lectures on Jurisprudence*. Edited by R. L. Meek, D. D. Raphael, and P.G. Stein. Oxford: Clarendon Press, 1978.
Smith, David Chan. *Sir Edward Coke and the Reformation of the Laws: Religion, Politics and Jurisprudence, 1578–1616*. Cambridge: Cambridge University Press, 2014.
Smith, Harry. "From Deodand to Dependency." *American Journal of Legal History* 11.4 (1967): 389–403.
Smith, Lionel, ed. *Re-imagining the Trust: Trusts in Civil Law*. Cambridge: Cambridge University Press, 2012.
Smith, R. J. *The Gothic Bequest: Medieval Institutions in British Thought, 1688–1863*. Cambridge: Cambridge University Press, 1987.
Smith, Thomas. *De Republica Anglorum*. Edited by Mary Dewar. Cambridge: Cambridge University Press, 1982.
Sobecki, Sebastian. *Unwritten Verities: The Making of England's Vernacular Culture, 1463–1549*. Notre Dame, Ind.: University of Notre Dame Press, 2015.
Somerset, Fiona, Jill C. Havens, and Derrick G. Pitard, eds. *Lollards and Their Influence in Late Medieval England*. Woodbridge, England: Boydell Press, 2003.
Spalding, James C. *The Reformation of the Ecclesiastical Laws of England, 1552*. Kirksville, Mo.: Sixteenth Century Journal Publishers, 1992.
Spelman, Henry. *The History and Fate of Sacrilege, Discover'd by Examples of Scripture, of Heathens, and of Christians; from the Beginning of the World Continually to this Day*. London: John Hartley, 1698.
Spinka, Matthew, ed. *Advocates of Reform*. Louisville, Ky.: Westminster Knox Press, 1953.
Stadtler, Ulrich. "Cherished Instructions." In *Spiritual and Anabaptist Writers*, edited by George H. Williams and Angel M. Mergal, 272–84. Louisville, Ky.: Westminster John Knox, 1957.
Stanhope, Arthur. *Episcopal Jurisdiction Asserted According to the Right Constitution Thereof*. Dublin: Benjamin Tooke, 1671.
The Statutes of the Realm. 11 vols. London: Dawsons of Pall Mall, 1810–28.
Stefano, Roberto di. "Lay Patronage and the Development of Ecclesiastical Property in Spanish America: The Case of Buenos Aires, 1700–1900." *Hispanic American Historical Review* 93.1 (2013): 67–98.
Stein, Peter. *Regulae Iuris: From Juristic Rules to Legal Maxims*. Edinburgh: Edinburgh University Press, 1966.
Steinbicker, Carl Richard. "Poor Relief in the Sixteenth Century." D.Th. Dissertation, The Catholic University of America, 1937.
Stephen of Ripon. *The Life of Bishop Wilfrid by Eddius Stephanus*. Translated by Bertram Colgrave. Cambridge: Cambridge University Press, 1985.

Stileman, John. *A Peace-Offering an Earnest and Passionate Intreaty, for Peace, Unity, and Obedience.* London: Thomas Pierrepont, 1662.
Stone, Lawrence. "The Political Programme of Thomas Cromwell." *The Bulletin of the Institute of Historical Research* 24 (1951): 1–18.
Story, Joanna. *Carolingian Connections: Anglo-Saxon England and Carolingian Francia, c. 750–870.* Aldershot, England: Ashgate, 2003.
Strauss, Gerald. *Law, Resistance, and the State: The Opposition to Roman Law in Reformation Germany.* Princeton, N.J.: Princeton University Press, 1986.
———, ed. *Pre-Reformation Germany.* London: Macmillan, 1972.
Strype, John, ed. *History of the Life and Acts of Edm. Grindal.* Vol. 1. London: John Hartley, 1710.
Stubbes, Philip. *The Anatomie of Abuses.* Edited by Margaret Jane Kidnie. Renaissance English Text Society. Seventh series. Vol. 27. Tempe: Arizona Center for Medieval and Renaissance Studies, 2002.
Sturm, Johannes. *The Epistle that Johan Sturmius, a Man of Great Lerninge and Jugement, Sent to the Cardynalles and Prelates, That were Chosen and Appointed by the Bysshop of Rome, to Serche out the Abuses of the Churche, Translated into Englysshe by Rychard Morysine.* London: Thomas Berthelet, 1538.
———. *Epistola de consilio de emendanda ecclesia.* In *De consilio de emendanda ecclesia.* Zurich: Heidegger, 1748.
Suetonius. *The Lives of the Caesars.* Translated by J. C. Rolfe. Vol. 1. Cambridge, Mass.: Harvard University Press, 1914.
Swanson, R. N. *Indulgences in Late Medieval England: Passports to Paradise?* Cambridge: Cambridge University Press, 2007.
———, ed. *Promissory Notes on the Treasury of Merits: Indulgences in Late Medieval Europe.* Leiden: Brill, 2006.
———. *Universities, Academics and the Great Schism.* Cambridge: Cambridge University Press, 1979.
Swinburne, Henry. *A Briefe Treatise of Testaments and Last Wills.* London: John Windet, 1590.
———. *A Treatise of Testaments and Last Wills.* Seventh Edition. Dublin: Elizabeth Lynch, 1793.
Taft, Arthur Irving, ed. *The Apologye of Syr Thomas More, Knyght.* London: Humphrey Milford, 1930.
Tanner, Joseph Robson, ed. *Tudor Constitutional Documents, A.D. 1485–1603.* Cambridge: Cambridge University Press, 1922.
Taylor, Nathaniel Lane. "The Will and Society in Medieval Catalonia and Languedoc, 800–1200." Ph.D. Dissertation, Harvard University, 1995.
Taylor, William Frederick. *The Charterhouse of London: Monastery, Palace, and Thomas Sutton's Foundation.* London: J. M. Dent, 1912.
The Templars: Selected Sources. Translated by Malcolm Barber and Keith Bate. Manchester, England: Manchester University Press, 2002.
Tentler, Thomas N. *Sin and Confession on the Eve of the Reformation.* Princeton, N.J.: Princeton University Press, 1977.
Thomas Aquinas. *Opera omnia.* Vol. 8. Rome: Polyglotta, 1895.
Thomas, Keith Michael. *The Ends of Life: Roads to Fulfillment in Early Modern England.* Oxford: Oxford University Press, 2009.

———. *Religion and the Decline of Magic: Studies in Popular Beliefs in Sixteenth and Seventeenth Century England*. New York: Oxford University Press, 1997.

Thomas, T. C. "Conditions in Favour of Third Parties." *Cambridge Law Journal* 11 (1952): 240–57.

Thompson, Benjamin. "Monasteries and Their Patrons at Foundation and Dissolution: The Alexander Prize Essay, Proxime Accessit." *Transactions of the Royal Historical Society*. Sixth Series. Vol. 4 (1994): 103–25.

———. "Prelates and the Alien Priories." In *The Prelate in England and Europe, 1300–1560*, edited by Martin Heale, 50–75. Rochester, N.Y.: York Medieval Press, 2014.

Thomson, John A. F. *Popes and Princes, 1417–1517*. London: George Allen and Unwin, 1980.

Throop, Palmer A. *Criticism of the Crusade: A Study of Public Opinion and Crusade Propaganda*. Amsterdam: N. V. Swets and Zeitlinger, 1940.

Tierney, Brian. "The Decretists and the 'Deserving Poor.'" *Comparative Studies in Society and History* 1.4 (1959): 360–73.

———. "Hierarchy, Consent, and the 'Western Tradition.'" *Political Theory* 15 (1987): 646–52.

———. *Medieval Poor Law: A Sketch of Canonical Theory and its Application in England*. Berkeley: University of California Press, 1959.

———. "'The Prince is not Bound by Law': Accursius and the Origins of the Modern State." *Comparative Studies in Society and History* 5 (1963): 378–400.

Tiraqueau, André. *De privilegiis piae causae tractatus*. Venice: Franciscus Laurentinus, 1561.

———. *Tractatus*. Lyon: Gulielmum Rouillium, 1559.

Toschi, Domenico. *Practicarum conclusionum*. Vol. 5. Rome: Stephanus Paulinus, 1606.

Tracy, James D. *Europe's Reformations, 1450–1650: Doctrine, Politics and Community*. Plymouth: Rowman and Littlefield, 2006.

Trexler, Richard C. *Church and Community 1200–1600*. Rome: Edizioni di Storia e Letteratura, 1987.

Triglot Concordia: The Symbolical Books of the Evangelical Lutheran Church: German-Latin-English. St. Louis: Concordia, 1921.

Troeltsch, Ernst. *The Social Teaching of the Christian Churches*. Translated by Olive Wyon. 2 vols. Louisville, Ky.: Westminster John Knox Press, 1992.

Tudor, Owen Davies. *Tudor on Charities: A Practical Treatise on the Law Relating to Gifts and Trusts for Charitable Purposes*. 5th ed. Edited by H. G. Carter and F. M. Crawshaw. London: Sweet and Maxwell, 1929.

Tully, James. "Governing Conduct." In *Conscience and Casuistry in Early Modern Europe*, edited by Edmund Leites, 12–71. Cambridge: Cambridge University Press, 1988.

"The Twelve Conclusions of the Lollards." *English Historical Review* 22 (1907): 292–304.

Tyacke, Nicholas. *Aspects of English Protestantism c. 1530–1700*. Manchester: Manchester University Press, 2001.

Valerianus of Cimiez. *Opera omnia*. In *Patrologia Latina*. Edited by Jacques Paul Migne. Vol. 52. Paris: Migne, 1846.

Valla, Lorenzo. *On the Donation of Constantine.* Translated by G. W. Bowersock. Cambridge, Mass.: Harvard University Press, 2008.

———. *The Profession of the Religious and Selections from the Falsely-Believed and Forged Donation of Constantine.* Translated by Olga Zorzi Pugliese. Toronto: Center for Reformation and Renaissance Studies, 1985.

———. *De professione religiosorum.* Translated by Mariarosa Cortei. Padua: Antenoreis, 1986.

Vitrano, F. Messina. "La convertiblità del modo eretto su legato o fedecommesso nel diritto romano classico e giustinianeo." *Studi Riccobono* 3 (1936): 97–110.

Vives, Juan Luis. *On Assistance to the Poor.* Translated by Alice Tobriner. Toronto: University of Toronto Press, 1999.

———. *The Origins of Modern Welfare: Juan Luis Vives, De Subventione Pauperum, and City of Ypres, Forma Subventionis Pauperum.* Translated by Paul Spicker. Bern: Peter Lang, 2010.

———. *De subventione pauperum libri II.* Lyon: Melchioris and Treschel, 1532.

Walpot, Peter. "True Yieldedness and the Christian Community of Goods." In *Early Anabaptist Spirituality: Selected Writings,* edited by Daniel Liechty, 138–96. New York: Paulist Press, 1994.

Wandel, Lee Palmer. *Always Among Us: Images of the Poor in Zwingli's Zurich.* Cambridge: Cambridge University Press, 1990.

———. *Voracious Idols and Violent Hands: Iconoclasm in Reformation Zurich, Strasbourg, and Basel.* Cambridge: Cambridge University Press, 1994.

Ward, G. R. M. *The Foundation Statutes of Bishop Fox for Corpus Christi College in the University of Oxford.* London: Longman, Brown, Green, and Longmans, 1843.

Warner, James Christopher. *Henry VIII's Divorce: Literature and the Politics of the Printing Press.* Woodbridge, England: Boydell Press, 1998.

Warren, Edward. *The Liturgy and Ritual of the Celtic Church.* Oxford: Clarendon Press, 1891.

Watson, Alan. "D.47.2.52.20: The Jackass, the Mares and 'Furtum.'" In *Studies in Roman Private Law.* London: Hambledon Press, 1991.

———. *Legal Transplants: An Approach to Comparative Law.* 2d ed. Athens: University of Georgia Press, 1993.

Watt, Tessa. *Cheap Print and Popular Piety 1550–1640.* Cambridge: Cambridge University Press, 1991.

Webb, Beatrice Potter. *English Local Government: English Poor Law History. Part I: The Old Poor Law.* London: Longmans, Green and Co., 1910.

Webster, Paul. *King John and Religion.* Woodbridge, England: Boydell Press, 2015.

Weever, John. *Antient Funeral Monuments, of Great-Britain, Ireland, and the Islands Adjacent.* London: W. Tooke, 1767.

Weiner, Annette B. *Inalienable Possessions: The Paradox of Keeping-While-Giving.* Berkeley: University of California Press, 1992.

Wells, B. W. "Eddius' Life of Wilfrid." *English Historical Review* 6 (1891): 535–50.

Whaley, D. *Later Medieval Europe.* London: Longmans, 1968.

White, Doug. *Abusing Donor Intent: The Robertson Family's Epic Lawsuit Against Princeton University.* St. Paul, Minn.: Paragon House, 2014.
White, Stephen D. *Custom, Kinship, and Gifts to Saints: The 'Laudatio Parentum' in Western France, 1050–1150.* Chapel Hill: The University of North Carolina Press, 1988.
———. "Inheritances and Legal Arguments in Western France, 1050–1150." *Traditio* 43 (1987): 55–103.
———. "'Pactum ... Legem Vincit et Amor Judicium'—The Settlement of Disputes by Compromise in Eleventh-Century Western France." *The American Journal of Legal History* 22.4 (1978): 281–308.
Whiting, Robert. *The Blind Devotion of the People: Popular Religion and the English Reformation.* Cambridge: Cambridge University Press, 1989.
Whitman, James Q. "The Lawyers Discover the Fall of Rome." *Law and History Review* 9.2 (1991): 191–220.
Wilks, Michael. *Wyclif: Political Ideas and Practice.* Oxford: Oxbow Books, 2000.
Willard, Joseph. "Illustrations of the Origin of 'cy près.'" *Harvard Law Review* 8.2 (1894): 69–92.
Williams, George Huntston. *The Radical Reformation.* 3d ed. Kirksville, Mo.: Truman State University Press, 2000.
Winder, W. H. D. "Precedent in Equity." *Law Quarterly Review* 57 (1941): 245–79.
Wissenbach, Johannis-Jacobi. *Exercitationum ad L. Pandectarum libros pars posterior.* 2d ed. Franeker: Gerard Schick, 1661.
Witte, John, Jr. *Law and Protestantism: The Legal Teachings of the Lutheran Reformation.* Cambridge: Cambridge University Press, 2002.
Wood, Susan. *English Monasteries and their Patrons in the Thirteenth Century.* London: Geoffrey Cumberlege, 1955.
———. *The Proprietary Church in the Medieval West.* Oxford: Oxford University Press, 2006.
Wood-Legh, Kathleen Louise. *Perpetual Chantries in Britain.* Cambridge: Cambridge University Press, 1965.
———. "Some Aspects of the History of Chantries in the Later Middle Ages." *Transactions of the Royal Historical Society.* Fourth series. Vol. 28 (1946): 26–50.
Woolf, Cecil Nathan Sidney. *Bartolus of Sassoferrato: His Position in the History of Medieval Political Thought.* Cambridge: Cambridge University Press, 1913.
Woolfson, Jonathan. "Bishop Fox's Bees and the Early English Renaissance." *Reformation and Renaissance Review* 5.1 (2003): 7–26.
Wright, Thomas. *Three Chapters of Letters Relating to the Suppression of the Monasteries.* London: Camden Society, 1843.
Wunderli, Richard. *London Church Courts and Society on the Eve of the Reformation.* Cambridge, Mass.: The Medieval Academy of America, 1981.
Wunderli, Richard, and Gerald Broce. "The Final Moment Before Death in Early Modern England." *Sixteenth Century Journal* 20.2 (1989): 259–75.
Wyclif, John. "On Civil Lordship." In *The Cambridge Translations of Medieval Philosophical Texts.* Vol. 2: *Ethics and Political Philosophy*, edited by Arthur

Stephen McGrade, John Kilcullen, and Matthew Kempshall, 587–654. Cambridge: Cambridge University Press, 2001.

———. *Select English Works of John Wyclif*. Edited by P. Arnold. 3 vols. Oxford: Clarendon Press, 1869.

———. *On Simony*. Translated by Terrence A. McVeigh. New York: Fordham University Press, 1992.

———. *Tractatus de civili dominio liber primus*. Edited by Reginald Lane Poole. London: Trübner, 1885.

———. *Tractatus de officio pastorali*. Edited by Gotthardus Victor Lechler. Leipzig: A. Edelmannum, 1863.

———. *Tractatus de simonia*. Edited by Herzberg-Fränkel and Michael Henry Dziewicki. London: Trübner, 1898.

———. *Trialogus*. Translated by Stephen E. Lahey. Cambridge: Cambridge University Press, 2013.

Yelverton, Henry. *The Reports of Attorney at Law Sir Henry Yelverton*. Andover, Mass.: Flagg and Gould, 1820.

Youings, Joyce. *The Dissolution of the Monasteries*. London: Allen and Unwin, 1971.

Zaller, Robert. *The Discourse of Legitimacy in Early Modern England*. Stanford, Calif.: Stanford University Press, 2007.

Zimmermann, Reinhard. "Cy-près." In *Iuris Professio: Festgabe für Max Kaser zum 80. Geburtstag*, edited by Hans-Peter Benöhr and Max Kaser, 395–415. Vienna: Böhlau, 1986.

———. *The Law of Obligations: Roman Foundations of the Civilian Tradition*. Oxford: Oxford University Press, 1996.

Zulueta, Francis de. "The Science of Law." In *The Legacy of Rome*, edited by Cyril Bailey, 173–206. Oxford: Clarendon Press, 1923.

Zwierlein, Cornel. "Reformation als Rechtsreform. Bucers Hermeneutik der lex Dei und sein humanistischer Zugriff auf das römische Recht." In *Martin Bucer und das Recht. Beiträge zum internationalen Symposium vom 1. Bis 3. März 2001 in der Johannes a Lasco Bibliothek Emden*, edited by Christopf Strohm, 29–81. Geneva: Librairie Droz, 2002.

Zwingli, Huldrych. *Sämtliche Werke*. Vol. 1. Berlin: Schwetschke, 1905.

Index

abbot, 42, 43, 151, 190, 191, 204, 236, 268, 290, 292
absolution, 55, 223, 400
absolutism, 21, 212, 395
abuse, 13, 62, 74, 77, 85–86, 174, 195, 219, 229, 254–55, 257, 279–82, 296, 298, 302, 317, 334, 345, 348, 351, 366, 371, 382
Acca, abbot, 42
accessary, 337, 386
Accursius, 62, 124, 138
Act for Feoffment, 268
Act in Restraint of Appeals, 308
act of Parliament, 188, 191, 266, 324n266
Act of Toleration, 372
Acts of Perpetua, 35
Adam, 300, 374
Adams and Lambert's Case, 290, 336–37
ademption, 14
advice, 37, 59, 113, 123, 128, 139, 155, 165, 194, 213, 236–37, 265, 323, 349–50, 352n43, 369, 398
advocate, 76, 86
advowson, 1, 76, 195, 266, 268, 339, 361–62
aedificatio, 73, 176, 190
Aelfgar, 44
afterlife, 35, 47, 55, 60, 103, 278, 399, 400. *See also* heaven; hell; purgatory; sanctification
Agatha, Council of, 28–29
Albert of Mainz, 49
Aldgate, 265
Alexander III, 73
Alexander of Hales, 48

alienation, 30, 50, 68, 70–72, 74, 76, 81, 86, 113, 145–47, 152, 166n166, 210, 212, 216, 256, 282, 289, 291, 300, 312, 321–22, 379, 395
Allen, Edward, 352
All Souls College, Oxford, 195
almoner, 280, 313, 346
alms, 11, 12, 24–26, 29, 31–39, 41, 43, 46, 50–54, 57–60, 65, 69, 79, 84, 94, 107, 111–14, 152, 172, 177, 180–81, 184–85, 187–89, 192–93, 204–5, 210, 236, 242, 243, 249, 251, 254, 262, 270, 273, 275, 277, 284, 290, 292, 296, 300, 313, 318, 332, 338, 349, 374, 377, 393, 399
almshouse, 51, 53, 57, 112, 152, 181, 188, 189, 204, 205, 284, 296
altar, 34, 64, 221, 241, 246, 310, 323
alteration, 5n11, 13, 15, 23, 62, 68, 69, 79, 87, 106, 120, 127, 138n65, 146, 169, 151, 152, 154, 158, 161, 181, 202–3, 205, 210, 211, 214n160, 259, 325, 338, 350, 355, 358, 367, 371n111, 381, 396. *See also* commutation; conversion; deviation; diversion
Ambrose, 27–28, 38, 61, 67, 131, 219, 229, 241, 316
Amicabilis concordia, 201
Anabaptism, 21, 249, 250, 252, 299, 368
Andreae, Johannes, 100
Andrewes, Lancelot, 346, 347
Anglo-Saxon, 41–45, 64n14, 391
Anselm of Canterbury, 40
Antichrist, 218, 302, 303–4
antiquarianism, 168, 391

437

Antwerp, 271
Apostolic See, 54, 87, 100, 151, 153, 155, 156, 161, 166
appropriation, 56, 88, 97, 98, 126n33, 154, 194, 195, 196, 236, 239, 246, 249, 262, 300, 303, 306–7, 311, 360, 389, 395
approximation, 2–4, 7, 9, 13, 15, 84, 98, 127, 129, 139, 145, 149, 152, 155, 157, 219, 261, 292, 324–25, 338, 343, 345, 349, 354–57, 359–61, 369, 373, 382–83, 390
Aquinas, 38, 47, 67n29, 93n113, 315
Aragon, 93, 96–97
Arden, Richard Pepper, 385–87
Arendt, Hannah, 395
Aristotle, 67n29, 174, 356n60, 373
Arthington, Henry, 298
as if it had not been written (*pro non scripto*), 80, 121, 123, 133, 325, 355
as near as, 1, 9–10, 345–46, 349, 354–57, 359, 360n69, 364–65, 369, 382–83. *See also* approximation; *aussi près que possible*; *auxi près*
Aske, Robert, 299
assent, 96, 269, 343, 346
Aston, Margaret, 111n169, 244n98, 245, 298
atonement, 40, 55
attorney general, 1, 3n5, 9n24, 10n28, 328n248, 331n262, 360n69, 361n75, 363, 365–66, 369, 371–73, 377, 380, 383, 385–87
Attorney-General v. Baxter, 373
Attorney-General v. Boultbee, 385, 387
Attorney-General v. Combes, 372
Attorney-General v. Downing, 9n24, 383–84
Attorney-General v. Gill, 377
Attorney-General v. Gouge, 1, 360–66
Attorney-General v. Goulding, 387
Attorney-General v. Hudson, 377n131, 383, *Attorney-General v. Ironmongers' Company*, 3n5
Attorney-General v. Kell, 3n5, 328n248
Attorney-General v. Margaret and Regius Professors, 371
Attorney-General v. Oglander, 3n5
Attorney-General v. Peacock, 369–71
Attorney-General v. Platt, 371
Attorney-General v. Tyndall, 10n28
Attorney-General v. Whitchurch, 385n163, 387

Attorney-General v. Whorwood, 373
Audley, Thomas, 285–86
Aufréri, Étienne, 146
Augsburg, Peace of, 338
Augsburg Confession, 220
Augustine, 27, 32–34, 37, 38, 61, 62, 72, 114, 169, 177, 248, 397
Augustinians, 109, 227
aussi près que possible, 4, 150
authorities: civil or secular, 22, 83–84, 94, 95, 120–21, 130, 179, 185, 194, 235–36, 240, 247, 250, 277, 288, 306, 309, 315, 329, 338–39, 349, 369, 372, 388; spiritual, 22, 82–83, 100, 141, 158, 159, 255, 287, 308, 310, 315, 319
Auxerre, Council of, 34
auxi près, 355
Avignon, 183
axiom of kinship, 40
Ayton, John, 76
Azo, 77

Bacon, Francis, 14n34, 345, 347–55, 357–59, 361, 367, 369
Baker, John, 16n43, 17, 368n101
Ballerini, Antonio, 163
bankruptcy, 333, 396
bannus, 258
Baptista de Salis, 289
Barbosa, Agostinho, 159–60, 163
Barnes, Alfred, 399
Barnes Foundation, 10, 393n21
Barozzi, Pietro, 186
Bartolus. *See* Saxoferrato, Bartolus de
Basel, 243, 245, 248, 317
Basil of Caesarea, 26–27, 36–37
Baxter, Simon, 353
Beaufort, Henry, Cardinal, 59
Beaufort, Margaret, 195, 206
Becket, Thomas, 76
Bede, 42–43
bede-roll, 52–53
begging: for alms, 87, 173, 181, 184, 220, 233–35, 265, 287, 295, 298–99, 351–52; for prayers or suffrages, 19, 55, 304
Ben-Amos, Ilana Krausman, 220n5, 378, 379n137
beneficiary, 5, 13, 26, 67, 110, 122, 126, 140, 149, 211, 317, 326, 331, 358, 361, 371, 377–78
bequest, 4, 6, 15, 26, 31, 33, 35–37, 40–42, 44, 48, 56–59, 64, 86, 99, 118,

Index   439

127, 136, 149, 151–52, 157, 159, 172–73, 177, 184, 186–87, 208, 228, 235, 256, 264, 275, 279, 290n100, 315, 326, 337, 354, 389; failed or frustrated, 11, 14, 150, 238–39, 272; illegal, 11, 121–22, 210, 358; impossible, 121, 320, 358; impractical, 11, 351; inconvenient, 345; infeasible, 1; pious, 25, 28, 38, 60, 137, 152, 166, 257, 325; superstititous or impious, 259, 311, 319, 322–23. *See also* legacy
Berenguer I, Ramon, Count, 41
Berkshire, 290
Bern, 240
Bernard, George W., 263n5, 265
Berthelet, Thomas, 175n24, 271
Berwick Bridge, 353
Bible, 26, 27, 34, 36, 101n133, 103n136, 223, 236, 244n98, 245, 249, 251, 280, 302, 310, 311, 341, 346, 374, 376, 377n130
Bill, William, 310–11, 313, 323
Biondo, Flavio, 168
bishop, 2, 4, 6, 32, 36, 42, 49, 61, 69–71, 78–82, 87, 95, 100, 105–6, 118, 127–29, 135, 137, 141, 145–46, 148, 151, 155–62, 165–66, 183, 185–87, 189, 191–203, 205–8, 215–17, 236, 240, 251, 267, 272, 274, 286, 300, 301, 308–9, 313, 317–23, 328, 331, 342, 346, 353, 366, 369, 372, 386. *See also* ordinary
bishopric, 186, 215, 267
Black Death, 125n31, 186
Blackstone, William, 21, 76n57, 292, 381–82
blasphemy, 112, 224–25, 237, 244, 246, 362
Blickle, Peter, 248
Blickling homilies, 41–42
Bloomfield v. Inhabitants of Stowmarket, 359
Bohic, Henricus, 68–69, 245n103
Böhmer, Justus, 259–60
Boleyn, Anne, 280–81, 285
Bologna, 122
Boniface, Saint, 35
Boniface VIII, 82, 147
bonum quo communius eo melius, 352, 361
Bossy, John, 17–18, 40
Bourchier, Thomas, 198
Bracciolini, Poggio, 168

Bracton, Henry de, 14n34, 39n75, 77–80, 129, 290, 335
Bradway, John, 392
Brady, Thomas, 243, 250, 251n123, 360n70
Bray, Gerald, 308, 318–22, 367n95
Brendan, Saint, 43
Bridewell, 283
bridge, 332, 353, 370
Bridgman, Richard, 334n275, 335n277, 336n282, 379, 383n149
Brinklow, Henry, 299
Broce, Gerald, 59
brotherhood, 52, 235, 240, 269, 307
Brown, Peter, 27n11, 28n15, 29, 31, 61n3
Browne, Thomas, 373
Brundage, James, 8n20, 70n37, 209
Bucer, Martin, 224, 226, 227, 240, 246, 47, 301–3, 308–18, 360n70
Buch, 236
Bucholz, Robert, 296
building, 70, 78, 120, 129–30, 165, 213–14, 320, 351, 372
Buller, Francis, 387
Bullinger, Heinrich, 218, 241n86
Burcher, John, 218
burden of performance, 78, 80, 104, 123–24, 129–30, 133, 135, 137–38, 151, 172, 221, 335, 358, 378. *See also* performance
Burgoyne, Robert, 264
Burr, David, 104n143, 105
Burt, Wellington R., 19, 399
Bynum, Caroline Walker, 49, 103n138
Byzantine, 35, 86, 365

caducum, 89, 12–25, 135, 134–36, 142, 147, 158n126. *See also* lapse
Caesar, 321
Caesarius of Arles, 41
Caister Castle, 198–200
Calvin, John, 301
Cambridge, 191, 195, 203, 205, 209, 281, 310, 312, 317, 352, 354, 360, 371, 384
candle, 52, 53, 328
canon (cleric), 248
canons, legal, 41, 165–67, 272, 287, 308, 318n200, 322, 343, 346, 362, 366, 367n95; of *1535*, 308; of *1604*, 322, 343, 346

Canons of Clovesho, 41
Canterbury, 40, 112, 195, 198, 342
Canterbury College, 112
captives, 61, 67, 141, 210, 275, 319
Caracalla, 124
cardinal, 19n53, 59, 70, 96, 105, 148, 216, 253, 257, 276, 318
caritas, 52, 84n85, 111n166, 174
Carmelites, 109
Carolingian, 64
Carpenter, Nathanael, 373
Carpzovius, Benedict, 261
Carthage: Council of, 34; Fourth Council of, 28
Carthusians, 173
Case of Impeachment of Waste, 357
Case of Pele's Will, 290n100, 336
Case of Robert Boyle's Charity, 3n5
Case of Thetford School, 326, 359–61, 369, 385
casus, 122–23
cathedral, 85, 88, 192, 248, 267, 300
cause, 77, 133, 136, 139, 211n149, 290, 384; for (*ex causa*), 67, 70, 167, 288, 348, 388; just and necessary, 151, 158; pious, 41, 70–72, 78–80, 82–83, 87, 95–97, 99, 106, 125, 130, 133–37, 139, 141–44, 147–48, 151–53, 155–60, 162–63, 166, 188, 210–13, 254–56, 275, 281, 319, 325. *See also* gifts, pious; uses, pious
causeway, 332
Cavendish, George, 215–17
Cecil, Robert, Earl of Salisbury, 344–45
cens, 96
censers, 342
centralization, 22, 184, 197, 236, 253, 318n200, 339
Ceolfrith, abbot, 43
cessante causa, cessat effectus, 147, 210, 384
cessavit, 14, 290, 355n53
cessavit de cantaria, 14, 76, 290, 292
chalice, 145
Chamberlen, Hugh, 374
chancellor, 2, 4, 16, 95, 195, 205, 208, 285, 295, 329, 330, 332–33, 362, 367, 371, 377, 382, 383, 386
Chancery, 2, 11, 15–17, 285, 296, 329, 338, 340, 367–68, 370, 372–73, 379, 382, 390
chantry, 49–52, 66, 159, 187, 188, 198, 201, 267, 269–71, 282–85, 291, 296–97, 299, 300, 323, 339, 343, 368
Chantry Act of *1545*, 267, 269–70
Chantry Act of *1547*, 188, 267, 283–84, 291, 339, 343
chapel, 138, 140, 144, 177, 196, 203
chaplain, 50, 51, 66, 187, 277, 313, 333, 372
charity, 7, 9, 11–12, 17–19, 34, 36, 57, 84, 105, 111, 113–14, 118, 174, 178–79, 181, 184–86, 242, 246, 253, 277, 294, 301, 313, 319, 326–27, 332–34, 350, 352–53, 356, 360–61, 365–66, 369–73, 376–77, 379–82, 384, 386–87, 392, 395; indiscriminate, 25, 48, 57, 60; unfailing, 3, 376–77, 380–81. *See also* failure; statute, of charitable uses; use, charitable
Charles I, 1–2, 356, 362, 366, 369
Charles II, 372, 390
Charles Martel, 67
Charterhouse, 350–53
Cheke, John, 301, 317
Chelsea College, 372
Chelsea synods, 41
chest: common, 183–84, 235–37, 239, 250; treasure, 88, 178
Chichele, Henry, 195, 201
Chiffoleau, Jacques, 183
childlessness, 75
Child of Bristowe, 54–55
children, 19, 30, 37, 52, 54–55, 64–65, 124, 176–77, 192, 228, 230, 234, 238, 251, 274, 306, 308, 345, 364; posthumous, 46, 71
chorister, 187, 192, 204
Christchurch, 265–66
Christensen, Carl, 240, 243, 246n106
Christian, ordinary, 35, 40, 104, 105, 225, 234
Christoph, Duke of Württemberg, 307
Chrysostom, John, 28, 34
church: Anglican, 1, 298, 346n15; endowed, 105, 171, 323; Established, 2, 390; parish, 52, 57, 149, 208, 213, 346; proprietary, 73
Cistercians, 76
city, 81, 122–23, 129, 130, 132, 134, 140–41, 168, 175–76, 180, 184, 227, 231, 233, 235, 239–40, 243–45, 314, 361. *See also* municipality
Civil War, 367, 371

Clare, Richard de, 192, 194
Clark, James, 193
class-action suits, 393
Claymond, John, 206
Clement V, 91–100
Clement of Alexandria, 32
Clement of Rome, 248
Clementine constitutions, 98, 138. *See also quia contingit*
clergy, 37, 59, 112, 155, 193, 206, 225, 288, 293–95, 300, 308, 311, 314, 322, 372
Clermont, 212
cloister, 231, 235
Cluny, 74–75
cobblestones, 246
Code of Canon Law (*1917*), 165–66
Code of Canon Law (*1983*), 166–67
codes of law, medieval, 25
Cohn, Henry, 228n35, 261n152, 307n161, 338, 360n70
Coignet, Pierre du, 212
Coke, Edward, 207, 313, 336–37, 339, 353, 355, 360, 367
college, 3, 112, 136, 154, 189, 191–97, 199–203, 206, 212, 214, 221, 269–70, 283–84, 296, 310, 354, 366, 369, 371–72, 389
collegium, 119, 136, 137
commemoration, 25, 34–35, 42, 47, 49, 52, 65, 122, 152, 188, 200–201, 305, 323, 378
commission, 192, 254, 283, 328; diocesan, 197
commissioners, 329–32, 361
commons, 21, 79, 132, 169, 172, 219, 263, 287, 298–99, 392
Commons, House of, 282, 284, 374
Commons' Supplication of *1532*, 287
commonwealth: 21, 83–84, 90, 169, 175, 179, 189, 193, 233, 236, 257, 276, 282, 298, 300, 301; men, 317
community, 51, 52, 65, 118n3, 120, 124–26, 169, 182, 225–26, 229, 236, 238, 240–41, 244, 246, 248, 250–53, 263, 328, 339, 384, 397–98
commutation, 6, 7, 64, 69, 97, 123, 127–28, 138, 142, 145–47, 149, 151, 154–67, 214n160, 256, 331n262, 350, 386. *See also* alteration; conversion; deviation; diversion
Compendium compertorum, 281

complaint, 36, 142, 148, 190, 214, 239, 255, 282, 287, 299, 301, 307, 328, 353, 364, 384
conciliarism, 137, 144, 212
condition, 44, 45, 51, 77–79, 81, 108, 134n58, 142, 150, 202–3, 205, 211, 271, 324–25, 333, 357–58, 363; broken or unfulfilled, 289, 290, 295, 333–35; changing the, 4n10, 326, 386; illegal, 123, 210; illicit, 122; impious or superstitious, 319, 336; impossible, 80, 121, 123–24, 128–30, 138, 320, 324, 356; precedent, 123n22, 358; subsequent, 123n22, 358
confession, 25, 31–34, 41, 43, 46, 56, 58, 91, 98
confidence, 335, 337
confiscation, 92, 94, 100, 212, 267, 282, 306, 340, 343, 366
Connecticut, 389
conscience in law, 95–96, 133, 151, 207, 214–16, 286–87, 289, 291–92, 294, 330, 342, 355, 367, 368n101
consensus, 5, 67, 82, 91, 97, 101, 107, 115–16, 138, 141, 149, 157–58, 163, 165, 193, 199, 200, 203, 205, 208, 259, 260, 322, 326, 341. *See also* consent
consent, 4n10, 6, 13, 15, 39, 62, 64, 69, 70, 71, 74, 77–81, 84, 90, 93, 94, 101, 102, 106, 115, 127–30, 134, 136, 139–41, 144–48, 155–56, 158–59, 161, 175, 187, 190–92, 194–97, 209, 213–15, 217, 231, 265–66, 269, 274, 278, 292, 300, 311n174, 321, 326, 334–35, 339, 340, 357, 362, 369–72, 375, 381. *See also* consensus
conservator, 77
consilium, 23, 127n34, 128n37, 138, 139n67, 141–43, 157–58
Constantine, 20n57, 109, 170n4
Constitutions of Clarendon, 76
Contarini, Gasparo, 185
contiguum, 347, 349, 359
continuum, 347
convenience, 17, 145, 162, 208, 209, 212, 270, 286, 308, 327, 332n266, 345, 348, 352, 354, 358, 366–69, 374
conversion of property, 6, 78–80, 99n129, 100n130, 106, 110n165, 118–21, 127–28, 130, 138–43, 147, 155–58, 160–61, 164, 169, 173, 188,

conversion of property (*cont.*)
  196, 210, 214, 218, 241, 258–60, 262, 268, 282, 298, 311, 313–14, 323, 326, 346, 356, 359, 366, 374. *See also* alteration; commutation; deviation; diversion
Cordis dolere, 82n79
corporation or incorporation: 252, 331, 334, 347, 353, 362; eleemosynary, 381
Corpus Christi College, Oxford, 176, 195, 196, 203, 205, 206
Corpus iuris civilis, code of, 9n25, 118, 119n9, 124, 125n28, 131n44, 142n82, 147n94, 150n101, 344n11
corrody, 111, 339
corruption, 28, 88, 90n104, 113, 168, 181, 196, 206, 222–23, 237, 251, 254–55, 302, 311n174, 312, 342, 348, 350–52, 396
coseigniory, 48
Cottington, Francis, 362
countergift, 46, 50, 54, 63, 178, 222, 315
Counter-Reformation, 56, 225
court, 74, 132, 186, 188n73, 334, 336, 338, 345, 358n65, 359, 362, 364, 372, 377, 380, 384, 387, 400; American, 389–92; Chancery, 2, 11, 15–17, 285, 296, 329, 338, 340, 360, 367–68, 370, 372–73, 379, 382, 390; common law, 16, 66, 194; ecclesiastical, 11, 15, 148–50, 208–9, 222, 287, 289, 322, 325; English, 6, 292; of equity, 2, 12, 207, 351, 367; Exchequer, 204–5, 340, 351, 365, 382; imperial, 151; papal, 80, 155, 214; royal, 76; Savoyard, 163; secular, 148
covenant, 356n55, 374
Coventry, Thomas, 361, 369
covetousness, 269, 296, 298, 301, 306, 327, 342
covin, 334
Cowell, John, 324
Cracow, 218
Crates, 172
creditor, 55, 333
Croft v. Jane Evetts, 343
Crome, Edward, 264
Cromwell, Thomas, 18, 83, 263–66, 271–76, 278–81, 286, 288, 292, 296, 299, 308
Crowley, Robert, 299–300

crown, 1, 212, 266, 283, 284, 291, 313, 323–33, 342–43, 367, 380
Croydon, 309
crucifix, 241–42
Crusades, 85–88, 91–93
cuius est dare, cuius est disponere, 66, 147, 363
Cujas, Jacques, 209
curia, 155, 255
currency, 279
custody, 339, 349
custom, 33, 34, 39, 62, 71, 81, 87, 88, 101, 127, 131, 176, 255, 329, 348
Cuthbert, 42–43
cy-près, 2–18, 20–24, 26, 41, 55, 57, 60–61, 68, 72, 74–75, 77, 81, 84, 89–90, 95, 100, 107, 115–16, 118–19, 126n33, 134, 136, 139, 143, 147–51, 157, 166–67, 177, 180, 188–89, 191–93, 205, 208, 210–13, 219, 233, 250, 255, 277, 279, 285, 289, 291–93, 296–97, 305–9, 312, 318–20, 323–29, 332, 338–41, 345, 350, 354–56, 359, 361, 365–66, 368–70, 373–74, 376, 379–95, 397–99; equitable or judicial, 2–3, 5, 10, 12, 292, 319, 320, 354, 365, 367, 370, 373, 392, 393; prerogative, 2, 5, 293, 320, 345, 369–70, 373, 390
Cyprian of Carthage, 26
Cyril of Alexandria, 36

Da Costa v. De Pas, 10, 380
damnation, 35, 43, 37, 56, 72, 84, 109, 110, 112, 228, 237, 315
damnosa hereditas, 396
D'Ancarano, Pietro, 136, 138, 211–12
danger, 67, 149, 274
Davis, E. Jeffries, 265, 266n18
Davis, Natalie Zemon, 183, 185, 304n155
Davis, Virginia, 148n97, 189n80, 191n85, 192–93, 196–97, 199–200, 201n119, 202n122
deacon, 171, 187
dead, the, 5, 10, 15, 19, 21, 25, 27, 31, 33–36, 41, 47–48, 51–52, 54–58, 60, 63, 72, 84, 100, 106n147, 107–8, 111, 151–52, 154, 167, 171, 177, 185, 187, 211n149, 222, 228, 232, 239–40, 244, 246, 264, 267, 276–79, 284, 287, 297, 300, 304–6, 315, 340, 347, 364, 378, 393, 394, 397, 398–400
dead hands, 108

Dean of St. Paul's Case, 336
deathbed, 3, 14–15, 19, 25–27, 29, 31–33, 38, 41–43, 45, 54, 56–61, 70, 171, 176, 237, 344, 349, 381, 383
debt, 14, 15, 54–55, 59, 196, 306, 333, 350n36; spiritual, 31, 40, 42, 44, 57, 165, 225, 294
Decalogue, 253, 272
decay: financial, 50, 186–87, 196, 282, 327, 352; moral, 298–99, 348
deception, 214
decree, 12, 28, 73n50, 87n88, 98n124, 100, 102, 151–52, 154, 155n118, 165n157, 212, 242, 246n109, 268, 290, 293, 321, 328–32, 338, 345, 361, 363, 367, 372–73
decretal, 68–70, 245n103
Decretum, 35, 47, 131n45, 248
defect, 11, 79, 81, 144, 210, 320, 334, 351, 358, 382
defense, 83, 86, 91–92, 95, 201, 219, 271, 279
De Jong, Mayke, 64, 65n16, 67
delay, 38, 45, 80, 114, 135, 148n97, 149, 181, 197, 272, 371, 377
De Liguori, Alphonsus, 160n136, 163
Denmark, 307
deodands, 5n11, 313
derogation, 23, 348, 358
destitution, 55, 71, 73, 148, 178, 239, 251, 257, 297, 339
desuetude, 371
detachment, interior, 36, 137, 225
De Templariis, 353
determination, 275–76
deviation, 7, 10, 11, 87, 97, 104, 121, 130, 136, 149–51, 154, 161 189, 190, 200, 201, 204, 282, 315, 325, 338, 354, 357–58, 396. *See also* alteration; commutation; conversion; diversion
devise, 326, 333–38, 359, 370–71, 377, 380–81, 384
devisee, 324, 337–38, 359
devisor, 324, 337
Dhuoda, 44
Dickens, A. G., 188, 283n72, 284n80, 296–97
difficulty, 129, 162, 358
Digest, 6, 62n5, 80n71, 87, 117n1, 118n3, 119n9, 120, 212n17, 121n18, 122, 124n25, 128n37, 130, 133n53, 136, 145, 210n144, 211, 314, 326, 344n11

Diggers, 368
diocese, 85, 100, 208, 267, 372
Diodati, Giovanni, 374
disherision, 14, 20, 323, 379, 383, 384
dispensation, 6, 23, 56, 67, 70, 100, 148, 187, 190, 196, 199, 256, 294
disposal, right of, 45, 66, 87, 147, 363
dispossession, 70, 107, 110, 112, 293
disputation, 160, 163n147, 242, 259–61, 266, 271
disputes: confessional, 56; about Franciscans, 104, 132; about gifts, legacies, inheritances, 61, 69, 93, 133, 194, 197–200, 377; about jurisdictions, 76, 83, 93, 94; about rules, 124; about titles to land, 193; about wealth of church, 125, 338
dissent, 2, 8, 264, 307, 340–41, 344–45, 359, 372
dissolution, 97, 100, 125, 188, 239, 263–66, 268, 270–71, 276n51, 277, 280, 282, 284–85, 296–98, 300, 322, 327, 339, 382. *See also* seizure; suppression
diversion, 9, 12–14, 56, 68, 71, 86, 92, 97, 148, 155, 164, 173, 178, 183, 185, 187–88, 216, 233, 242, 244, 247–48, 254, 259, 268, 276n51, 278, 280, 296, 300, 316–17, 322–23, 340, 345, 370–71. *See also* alteration; commutation; conversion; deviation
doctrine, legal, 2–6, 8–11, 13–15, 17, 20–23, 25–26, 46, 57–58, 60–61, 68, 79, 89, 100, 119, 144, 149, 166, 177, 188–89, 200, 219, 279, 285, 323–24, 355, 366, 368–69, 373, 383–85, 388–89, 391–93, 399
Domat, Jean, 212–13, 371
Dominicans, 85, 104, 227, 244
dominion, 20–21, 341
dominium, 108–9, 117, 126, 142
donation, 4, 11, 13, 15, 19–21, 27, 29, 32–33, 38–42, 44–45, 48, 50, 52–54, 58, 62–66, 68–74, 76–78, 81–82, 84, 87–88, 97, 100–101, 106–12, 114, 117, 126, 132, 135, 138, 142, 145–46, 148, 150, 156, 158, 166, 170, 178–79, 181, 190, 202, 208, 214, 222, 229, 231, 233, 236, 238–40, 242–44, 246, 248, 250, 257–58, 260, 269, 272–73, 283–84, 291, 296, 302, 311–12, 314, 316, 333, 335, 360, 365, 367, 377, 384, 393, 400

donatio post obitum, 45, 46, 162
Donatism, 169
Donne, John, 298
donor, 1, 12, 14, 19, 21, 26, 28, 30, 44–46, 48–53, 57–58, 61–66, 71–72, 75–79, 84–87, 89–91, 93–101, 106–7, 109–15, 125, 132–34, 139, 142, 146, 153, 155n117, 156, 159, 173–74, 180, 187, 188n73, 189, 197–98, 202, 207–8, 210, 218–22, 226, 229–34, 236–46, 252, 255, 257–58, 261–62, 269, 272, 278, 290–94, 296, 306, 314, 329, 331, 353, 355n53, 359, 361, 363, 365–66, 375–79, 384, 388, 395, 399; family or heirs of, 20, 26, 50, 52, 61–62, 66, 67, 111, 146, 167, 181, 220, 228, 236, 238, 241, 252, 278, 284, 292, 296, 310, 359, 363, 366, 369; intent of, 2, 3, 9–13, 18, 68, 90, 100, 107, 110, 112, 127, 136, 145, 149, 154, 173, 179–80, 182–83, 185–86, 201, 219, 231, 234, 237, 251, 270, 275–76, 282, 293, 312, 316, 324, 330, 332, 349, 351, 357–58, 360, 362, 364, 368–69, 372–73, 379, 384–86, 392–93, 399
Dorset, Marquis of, 301
dotatio, 73, 175
Douai, 183
Dubois, Pierre, 87–90
Duby, Georges, 39n74, 60, 63
Duffy, Eamon, 19n54, 47n105, 267n24, 298, 323n221
Duke, George, 5n10, 290n100, 329n252, 330, 331n258, 332n263, 333n267, 334n273, 335n276, 336n281, 343n6, 359n68, 361n72, 369, 379
Durantis, Guillelmus, 80, 124n26, 131n45

easements, conservation, 393
East-greensteds Case, 332n265, 361
Eaton v. Butter, 356
Ecdicia, 37
Edict of Restitution, 338
education, 10, 51, 87, 88, 90, 152, 189, 191–93, 195, 201, 203–5, 209, 214, 227–28, 230–31, 233, 239, 257, 270, 276–77, 280–81, 284, 294, 296, 303, 307, 310–12, 326, 332, 335, 350, 352–53, 359–63, 366, 369, 377, 385, 389. *See also* college; scholar; school; university

Edward I, 262, 271n35, 290n98, 365n87
Edward III, 262
Edward IV, 203
Edward VI, 267, 270, 283, 291, 296, 309, 313, 322, 337, 368
Edward, Lord Thurlow, 17, 383
Egerton, Thomas, 334
Egyptians, 161n137, 169
Eire, Carlos, 56, 224n21, 227, 228n34, 236n62, 243n94, 244n100, 245, 246n106
Eisermann, Johannes, 253, 258
ejusdem generis, 360, 361, 369–70, 372, 383, 387
Eldon, Lord. *See* Scott, John
elect, 221, 250, 302, 304, 312
Elham, 195
Elizabeth I, 267, 309, 313, 323–24, 327–31, 336, 338, 342, 343n6, 357, 382, 386, 390
Elton, G. R., 214n157, 264n13, 276n50, 285n83, 287n89, 298
Ely, 208
embezzlement, 50, 94, 100, 311, 377
Emden, 306
emergency, 67n29, 68, 312, 316, 396
Emmanuel College, Cambridge. v. English, 354, 369
emperor, 118, 120, 124, 130–31, 164, 261, 365
endowment, 4, 7, 49–50, 60, 74, 82, 88–90, 94, 108, 110–15, 121n16, 153–54, 156, 179, 181–89, 191–96, 198, 200, 203, 205–6, 214–15, 218–19, 221, 226–32, 235, 240, 246, 250–51, 262, 264, 276–77, 282–85, 288, 291, 295–97, 301, 303, 305, 315, 317–18, 328–29, 338, 348, 352, 377, 398
ends, 92; bad, 158, 219, 232, 362n77; unintended, 174
enfeoffment to uses, 287
Engel, Ludovico, 160
England, 4, 15, 23, 41, 44, 45, 51, 66, 75, 76, 79, 82, 95, 99n127, 112, 117, 154, 157, 180, 187, 192, 194, 207, 218, 227, 239, 250, 261, 271, 280, 289, 297–302, 304, 307–13, 317, 324, 330, 336, 338–40, 346, 347–48, 380, 389–90
equity, 2, 4–5, 10–11, 15, 16, 61, 62, 67, 79, 81, 96, 101, 128, 150–51, 157, 165, 167, 194, 201, 204–5, 207, 217,

253, 257–58, 286–87, 289, 291–92, 319–20, 324, 326, 330, 333, 339, 341, 351, 354, 356, 365, 367–68, 373, 380, 382–83, 388, 390
equivalence, 93, 98, 122, 156, 261, 325
Erasmus, Desiderius, 102, 161n137, 169n3, 171–75, 206, 219n4, 245, 273–74
Ermessend, 40
error, 98, 110, 210, 222, 253, 257, 270, 314, 327, 337
escheat, 95, 125, 266, 333
estate, 11, 13–14, 24, 30, 31, 42, 44, 54, 59, 79, 80, 118, 139, 147–48, 162–63, 172, 181, 198–200, 203–5, 207, 211, 216, 289, 311, 320, 333, 337, 347, 350, 352, 355, 358, 364, 370, 378–79, 383–84
Eton, 191, 201, 203
Eucharist, 34, 35, 103, 224, 257
evangelicals, 58, 152, 154, 183, 204, 218, 226–27, 231–32, 235, 237–40, 248, 250, 293, 300
excessive, 70, 81, 106, 178
exchange, 167, 222, 376; commercial, 375; of gifts, 49, 63, 65, 75, 172, 174, 181, 376; of gifts and prayers, 27, 44; precarial, 67; of property, 22, 79, 106, 111, 115, 145–47, 190, 216, 267, 294, 321; for social purposes, 118
Exchequer, court of, 204–5, 208, 340, 353, 362, 365, 382
execution of a will or gift, 150–51, 197, 375, 383
executor, 3, 12, 24, 25, 36, 58, 101, 159, 162, 166, 193–94, 197–98, 200, 203–4, 308, 335, 344–45, 353, 358–61, 370–71
Exeter, 206
Exiit qui seminat, 106, 133
Exivi de paradiso, 138
ex officio v. Kyng, 150
expropriation, 21, 67, 105, 110, 127, 131n42, 267
Eyston v. Studd, 356

faciendo stare rationabilem divisam, 14
Faculty Office, 187
failure, regarding gifts or trusts, 2–5, 9, 11–15, 17, 38, 40, 70–71, 76, 80–81, 89, 93, 95–96, 107, 118–19, 122, 124, 128, 130, 135–36, 138–39, 144, 146,

152, 155, 158, 162, 177, 187–91, 196, 198, 201–2, 211–12, 262, 272–73, 290–91, 319, 324, 328, 334, 357, 366, 368–69, 371, 373, 376–77, 380–81, 385–87, 390, 397
Falcidian fourth, 38, 118, 121, 130
Fall, the, 176, 347
famine, 67, 327
Farr, William, 108, 262n1
fasting, 35, 40, 103, 221
Fastolf, John, 194, 198–200
Favre, Antoine, 163, 261
Federicus Petruccius de Senis, 138–39
fee-simple, 333
Fehler, Timothy, 52n123, 181n45, 306–7
fellows, of a college, 202, 354, 371
femme covert, 333–34
feoffee, 197, 201, 329, 334, 343, 355, 357, 359–66
Feoffees for Impropriations, 1, 359–66
feoffment, 268, 333–34
feoffor, 15, 16, 292, 334–35, 355
feudum, 96
fideicommissum, 119, 120, 122, 124n26, 134, 136–37, 211, 314n184. *See also* trust
Fifteen Articles, 300
Filmer, Robert, 375
Finch, Heneage, Lord Nottingham, 361, 369–72
Finucane, Ronald, 34n50, 303, 304n151, 304n153, 305n156
fisc, 79, 119, 125n30
Fish, Simon, 58, 265, 267, 295, 298
Fisher, John, 195
Fisher v. Hill, 329
Fitzherbert, Anthony, 355
Fleming, Richard, 195
Fletcher, John, 305
flexibility, 7, 8, 14, 65, 69n34, 115, 117, 121, 145, 163, 201–3, 207–8, 252, 257, 275, 279, 318n200, 332, 356, 358, 378, 391
Florence, 137
foot, 367
forfeiture, 1, 2, 5, 9, 210, 215, 313, 336–38, 344–45, 353, 358, 364–65, 375
form, literal, 325
Fortescue, John, 11n30, 365
foundation, 10, 49, 50–52, 57–58, 66, 74–75, 88, 91, 97, 98, 103, 113, 153, 166, 180–82, 187, 189, 191–96, 198,

foundation, (*cont.*)
    200–203, 206, 214, 219n3, 221, 230–31, 236, 238, 262, 271, 278, 282, 288, 306, 350–51, 353, 358, 370, 376
founder, 50, 51, 66, 68, 73–75, 88, 90, 92, 94, 96, 107, 111–12, 166, 176, 179–80, 182, 184, 187–89, 191, 193–95, 197, 200–202, 204–5, 214, 238, 262–63, 265–66, 268–69, 271, 277, 282, 288, 290, 297, 329, 330, 377
founder's kin, 194
Fouracre, Paul, 67
Fox, Richard, 176, 195–96, 203, 205–7, 216
Foxe, John, 267
France, 82–95, 191, 212–13, 269, 396
Francesco a Mostazo, 162–63
Francis, Saint, 104, 171
Franciscan rule, 104, 106
Franciscans, 48, 102–7, 126–27, 132–34, 138–39, 143–44, 260, 272, 307
Franciscan testament, 104
Franck, Sebastian, 248
frankalmoin tenure, 50
fraternity, 119, 269
fraud, 28, 41, 46, 50, 58, 81, 82n79, 112, 219n3, 222, 230, 244, 272n40, 277, 287, 303, 317, 328, 334–35, 373
Freak v. Lee, 335
Fredol, Berenguer, Cardinal, 96
free alms, 50
freedom, grant of, 24, 80, 124, 141n80, 211. *See also* liberty
freehold ownership, 20
freeloading, 395
Freiburg im Breisgau, 245
friars, 102–7, 113, 129, 132–34, 143
friendship, 36, 53, 113, 119, 169, 172–73, 176, 317, 376
fruits, 29, 45, 56, 60, 105, 117, 201, 222, 353
frustration of purpose, 26, 58, 94, 100, 109, 125, 151, 199, 229, 238, 246, 272–73, 296, 374
Fulbecke, William, 324, 344n11
fundatio, 73, 153n112, 155n118, 175
Fursa, Saint, 43

Gaius, 122, 123n22
gallows, 246
Gardiner, Stephen, 192
Gargantua, 74
Gasquet, Francis Aidan, 214n160, 264
Geary, Patrick, 63–64
Geneva, 235, 244, 246
gentleman-pensioner, 327
gentlemen, 329
genus, 119, 161
George of Polenz, 240
German Peasants' Revolt, 249–50, 252
Germans, 223, 230
Getzler, Joshua, 291
ghosts, 55, 303–4, 342
Gibbons v. Maltyard and Martin, 335n278, 360
gift: *ad pias causas*, 71–72, 135, 143–44, 147, 159n134, 275, 319n202; binding society together, 88, 374, 394, 396; *causa mortis*, 44–45, 81; culture, 40, 62–67, 85; free, 18, 46, 63, 75, 79, 138–39, 178, 219–23, 225–26, 252, 258, 287, 293, 337, 352, 365, 375–76, 378–79; free alms, 50; general, 11–12, 159, 106, 332, 370, 390; *inter vivos*, 163, 166; irrevocable, 44–46, 65; outright, 44, 123, 325–26; perfected, 79, 81, 357, 364; personal, 39, 15, 51n119, 59, 184, 318, 387; pious, 19, 25, 28, 31, 35, 38, 60, 72, 82, 89, 96, 99–101, 107–9, 115–16, 124, 126–27, 129, 132–33, 137, 144, 147, 151, 153, 158–59, 166, 202, 219n3, 241, 259, 261, 267, 316, 318n200, 324, 353, 377, 381, 383–84; *post obit*, 45–46, 162; *pro anima*, 15, 25, 37n66, 42, 65, 134, 139n68, 143, 152n104, 157n120, 158n126, 182n49; returned, 61; specific, 9, 12–13, 15, 56, 63, 69, 72, 81, 118–19, 136–37, 142, 145, 158, 184, 194, 211, 221, 230, 325, 331–32, 350, 366, 386, 392. *See also* exchange; failure; intent, original; resumption; revocation
Giles of Rome, 108–9
Gilmore, Myron, 137, 212
gloss, 62, 68, 70, 76, 100, 118n2, 119, 122, 131n46, 135, 157, 193, 209, 255–56, 273, 289n95
glossators, 38
Godefroy, Denis, 128n35, 209
Godfrey, John, 77n60, 164, 165n160, 166n162
Godmanchester, custumal of, 123n24
Goffe v. Webb, 334

good, common, 21–22, 79, 83, 88, 131–32, 135, 201, 228, 244, 250, 252–53, 261n152, 307, 309, 315, 339, 352, 368, 393, 397, 400
Gordon, Bruce, 47n104, 243, 304n155
Gordon, Robert W., 21
Grafton, Richard, 282
grant, precarial, 66, 67
grant of confirmation, 76, 93, 217
Grant v. Huish, 358
Gratian, 33, 37–38, 45, 47, 131n45
gravatus, 137
Great Schism, 125
Gregory I (the Great), 9, 35, 67n29, 69
Gregory II, 35
Gregory VII, 73
Gregory IX, 72, 104
Gregory X, 86–87
Gregory of Tours, 39
Grell, Ole Peter, 183
Grey, William, 208–9
Griffith, 305
Grindal, Edmund, 313, 318, 323
guardian, 112, 273
Guarino da Verona, 208
guild, 522–53, 235, 240, 243, 284, 296
guilt, 30, 48, 91, 125, 178, 223, 343
Gunpowder Plot, 344
Guy, John, 285, 286n83, 287n86, 288n91, 291, 294n110

Haddon, Walter, 317
Hale, Matthew, 362
Hales, John, 309
Hall, Edward, 214, 266, 282
Hampton Court Conference, 342, 344, 346, 349
Harvard College v. Society for Promoting Theological Education, 389
Hätzer, Ludwig, 224, 241, 242
heaven, 26, 29, 33, 36, 41, 47, 53–55, 177, 182, 216, 220, 223–25, 301, 347, 376
Heers, Jacques, 55
Heimpel, Herman, 243
Heinze, R. W., 263n7, 264n9, 266
heir, 5, 9, 12–15, 20–21, 24–25, 28, 30, 34, 38, 40, 41, 45, 55, 62–63, 66, 68, 70, 72, 80, 118, 120–30, 132–37, 139–42, 144–46, 148–49, 156–58, 160–64, 172, 177, 187–89, 194, 200, 208–9, 212–13, 220, 228, 233, 241, 255, 257–62, 268, 270, 290, 292, 315, 320, 324, 327, 329, 333–35, 337, 343, 351–52, 355n53, 357, 359–61, 366, 370, 377–78, 380, 384, 386–87, 399
hell, 35, 41, 44, 46–47, 54, 56, 112, 228–30
Helmholz, Richard, 5n12, 6n14, 14–16, 22, 68n31, 70, 82n79, 148n97, 149n98, 161n139, 208, 289n95, 308, 323
Henno rusticus, 223
Henry II, Holy Roman Emperor, 248
Henry II, of England, 76
Henry VI, 191, 197
Henry VIII, 22, 214–16, 227, 262–73, 276–86, 292, 300, 305, 308n162, 357
heresy, 91, 98, 183, 264, 289
Herne, John, 329n252, 330n236, 332n265, 333n268, 334n273, 337n289, 361n73, 369, 379
Hewish, Richard. *See* Huish
Hezekiah, 101, 280
highway, 296, 319
Hincmar, 67
Hindle, Steve, 328, 329n250, 378
Hitchcock, Robert, 298
Hobbes, Thomas, 376
Holbein, Hans, the Younger, 240
Holborne, Robert, 363
Holmes, Oliver Wendell, Jr., 8, 390–92, 397
holocaust, 64
Holy Land, 87–99, 140
Hooper, John, 301, 302, 310
hospital, 3, 7, 10, 53, 56, 71, 80, 100, 118, 129, 146, 152, 154–55, 162, 181, 184, 188, 191–92, 196, 213, 235, 269, 271, 283–84, 297, 299, 351–53, 358, 366, 370, 371n109
hospitality, 73, 175, 189, 278, 339
Hospitallers, 87–88, 91–99
Hospital of St. James in the Fields, 191
Hospital of St. John the Baptist, 192
hostels, pilgrimage, 155
Hostiensis, 70, 73n48, 81, 82n80, 148n97
Hotman, Jean, 351
Hottinger, Klaus, 241
House of Commons, 282, 284, 374
Howard, Thomas. *See* Norfolk, Duke of
Hoyle, R. W., 188, 276n51, 339n296
Huberus, Ulricus, 261

448 Index

Hubmaier, Balthasar, 249
Huddleston, Joan, Lady, 203–5
Huish, Richard, 358
humanism, 17, 85, 89, 137, 138n64, 144, 160, 162, 168–217, 219n4, 225, 233, 236, 276, 279, 280, 305–6, 319, 328, 349
Humbert of Romans, 85–86
Humiliati, 103
Hus, Jan, 113–14, 181, 286
Hutterites, Moravian, 251–52
Hyland, Richard, 377

Ibbitson, David, 286
iconoclasm, 104, 224, 240–47
idleness, 112, 276, 278
idolatry, 224, 232, 241, 243, 245–46
illegality, 9, 11, 77, 71, 119, 121–23, 127, 129, 132, 136, 140, 147, 210, 213, 241, 259, 285, 324, 333, 337, 341, 343–44, 358, 361, 366, 370, 380, 383
image, 49, 52, 224, 232–33, 240–47, 257
Imola, Johannes de, 146
impiety, 20, 25, 36, 184, 233, 302–3, 310, 312, 314, 319–20, 339
impossibility, 2, 4, 11, 15, 69, 78, 80, 87, 121, 123–25, 127–30, 133, 136–40, 142, 145, 147, 150, 156–63, 166, 199, 205, 209–12, 226, 232, 320, 324–27, 341, 355, 358, 367, 369, 394; initial, 121, 128; third party, 78, 129, 199
impracticality, 2, 11, 15, 166, 205, 225, 250, 341, 349, 350–51, 367, 394
impropriation, 1, 194, 195, 359–66
improvement: of donor, 399–400; of gift, 63, 68, 145, 190, 394, 396
imprudence, 162, 175, 351
income, 41, 85, 108n152, 153, 186, 235, 254, 359
inconvenience. *See* convenience
indenture, 198, 204
indiscriminate, 25, 48, 57, 60
indulgence, 53–54, 206, 222
indult, 191
in eodem genere, 372, 389
in extremis, 33, 46
inflation, 309, 354
ingratitude, 72, 81, 119, 174
inheritance: 30, 34, 37, 40, 61, 65, 70, 85, 102, 107, 113, 168, 172, 177–78, 223, 251, 263, 295, 300, 363, 374–75, 394, 396–97; entailed, 286, 396. *See also* heir; succession
injunctions, 322–23, 327n243; power of, 16
injury, 16, 62, 127, 142, 144, 148n97, 232, 254, 256, 277, 278, 324
Innocent IV, 39n75
inquisition, 328–29
institutions, intercessory, 51, 54, 267, 282, 284, 297
insufficiency, 9, 69, 121, 129–30, 144, 205
intent or intention, 33, 71, 81, 92, 94, 96, 126n33, 179, 207, 219, 257, 311, 335, 337, 355, 357–60, 391, 399; charitable, 4, 5, 12, 13, 19, 20, 31, 79, 90, 191, 193, 200, 306, 320, 326, 334, 343, 381; donor or testator, 1–3, 9–13, 16, 18, 21, 68, 75, 84, 90, 99, 100, 107, 110–12, 114–15, 127, 134, 136, 139, 141, 145, 149, 153–54, 156–58, 163, 173–74, 178–80, 182–83, 185–86, 187, 194, 198, 200–203, 205, 219, 228, 230–32, 234, 237–38, 245–46, 251, 261, 270, 275–76, 282, 290–93, 312, 316–17, 324, 330–32, 338, 340, 343–45, 349–51, 357–60, 362, 364, 366, 368–69, 372–73, 377, 379, 382–86, 388, 392–93, 399; general charitable, 3, 12, 13, 72, 355–56, 385–88; original, 2, 10, 63, 75, 84, 88, 90, 100, 105, 107, 111–13, 115, 128, 140, 155, 161n137, 166, 182, 187, 190, 205, 219, 230–32, 245, 252, 257, 269, 278, 292–93, 315–16, 335, 338, 340, 354, 360–61, 364, 369–72, 375–76, 379, 389, 392–93, 396; pious, 129, 162
interdict, 125, 132, 326
interest, 62, 71, 77, 84, 107, 133, 139–40, 149, 158, 169, 179, 197, 226, 231, 247, 252, 259, 269, 282, 328, 340, 360, 372; financial, 54, 283; of heirs or family, 38, 63, 145n90, 337, 363; life, 45, 203; public, 392, 393n21; reversionary, 20, 76n57, 178, 204; usufructuary, 67
interested parties. *See* parties, interested
interests, reversionary, 12, 13, 20, 45, 50, 61, 76n57, 90, 141, 178, 203–4, 238, 266, 336, 359, 377, 381, 389, 393n24
interpretation: according to intention, 143, 179, 207, 357, 382; according to

mind, 71; benign, 80n72, 207, 260, 377, 382; favorable or liberal, 357, 361; *largissime*, 135; to not harm third parties, 148n97; strict, 68n32, 160, 324
invasion, 67, 230
inventory, 235, 267
Investiture Controversy, 73
Ipswich, 305
Israelites, 169
Italians, 230
ius commune, 4–8, 10–11, 13–16, 22, 62, 72, 76–77, 79, 89, 115–16, 118, 122–24, 138, 145–47, 150, 157, 161, 208, 210, 219, 226, 260, 285, 289n95, 292, 320, 323–27, 331–33, 340, 368, 383, 386
ius patronatus, 72, 73n49, 75, 76, 153n112, 165, 231. See also patronage, rights
ius praestandi, 73, 75, 76, 115, 226, 238, 362
ius proprium, 131
Ives, Eric, 280–81

Jackson v. Phillips, 390
Jacobites, 109
James I, 341–44, 346–50, 359, 367, 376
James II, of Aragon, 93, 96
Jardine, Lisa, 173n22, 347n22, 349
Jarrow, 43
Jefferson, Thomas, 394
Jerome, 37, 173
Jesuits, 155–57, 163, 212
Joash, 83
John XXII, 96, 102, 126
John of Burgundy, 93
Johnston, David, 118n3, 120, 121n16
Jolowicz, H. F., 5n12, 6, 119
Jones, Gareth, 4n10, 5n10, 17, 188n73, 320n207, 328, 329nn249–250, 330n254, 331, 345n13, 354, 363n81, 371n111, 385
Jones, Neil, 338
Jordan, W. K., 263n4, 297, 322
Joseph II, 164, 395
Jovian, 312
Jud, Leo, 241
judge, 3, 5, 8–10, 12–13, 16, 20, 81, 109, 126n33, 128, 134, 138, 147, 150, 157–58, 193, 197, 213, 236, 253, 277–78, 290, 306, 320, 329, 330, 349, 354–57, 373, 382, 383, 387–90, 392

Julian, 312
jurist, 8, 21, 23, 33, 66, 70, 91, 103, 107, 117n2, 123, 125, 127, 129, 135, 137–39, 144–45, 156, 160, 161–63, 167, 210, 212, 233, 239, 326, 392, 398
justice, 28, 43, 48, 62, 108, 111, 130–32, 215, 231–33, 257, 302, 341, 373, 390
Justice Windham's Case, 356
Justinian, 118, 123, 124
Justus, 35

Kahn, Victoria, 291
Karlstadt, Andreas, 230n41, 233–35, 245
keeping-while-giving, 66
Kidderminster, Richard, 240
king, 1–2, 11, 20, 76, 79, 83, 85, 90, 92–98, 101, 107–8, 110–12, 132, 164, 191–92, 195–96, 203, 212, 215–16, 219, 262–64, 266, 268–70, 274, 277, 279–83, 286–88, 290, 299, 301, 303, 308, 311, 318, 326, 333, 336–37, 340–42, 345–46, 349–53, 359–62, 365–67, 369–70, 372, 382, 389–90, 392
King-in-Parliament, 95, 288
King's Bench, 356
Kings College, Cambridge, 201
Korah, 342
Kreider, Alan, 47n105, 58n138, 187n70, 188n73, 264n10, 282n66, 283–85, 296, 297n121, 323n221
Kyng, John, 150

Lady Egerton's Case, 343
Lambeth, 49, 272
lamp, 234, 244–46, 270, 290, 292
Landau, Peter, 62n4, 73
Landstuhl, 226
Langland, William, 112–13
lapis ductitius, 330
lapse, 89, 124–25, 135, 143, 134–36, 142, 147, 158n126, 276. See also caducum
Las siete partidas, 79–80
Lateran V, 164, 165n157
Latimer, Hugh, 281
Latymer, William, 281
Laud, William, 2, 201, 346, 366, 369
laudatio parentum, 39
law: canon, 3, 4, 6–9, 11–12, 14–17, 22–23, 25, 29, 36–37, 39n75, 41, 45–49, 51–52, 56–57, 60, 67–77, 80–82, 85, 92, 103, 109, 114–15, 131, 137, 141,

law: canon, (*cont.*)
  148–67, 175, 186, 188, 204–5, 209, 213, 219, 223, 229–30, 232, 238, 240, 244–45, 249, 260, 272, 281, 286–89, 292–94, 300, 302, 308–9, 316, 318–19, 322, 324, 340, 343, 346, 348, 351, 355, 362, 366–67; civil, 6, 8n20, 9, 16–17, 68, 71–73, 79, 124–32, 135, 166, 276, 279, 285, 308, 320–21, 323–25, 327, 344, 351, 355, 358, 366, 383–84, 391; common, 3, 5, 7, 9, 14, 15–17, 21–22, 39, 47, 66, 108, 194, 204–5, 207, 214–16, 263, 276, 286–87, 292, 308, 321, 322, 324, 326–27, 334, 355, 357, 369, 382, 388, 391; Hebrew, 225; natural, 68, 79, 81, 125–26, 131, 178, 219, 253; private, 131; Roman, 6–7, 9, 16, 62, 70, 75, 80, 117–25, 129, 213, 292, 312, 321, 383, 391, 396; royal, 79; statutory, 291–92, 321, 340–41, 346n20, 393; penal, 343, 347. *See also ius commune*; statute
Lazarus, 33
legacy, 14, 29, 32, 34, 106, 120, 124, 129, 132, 134, 136–37, 141, 144, 157n122, 158, 163, 173, 211, 213, 288, 314, 319, 320, 353–54, 358, 375, 383, 399; conditional, 80, 121, 123, 142, 325; *sub modo*, 124
legality, appearance of, 91–94, 196–207, 263
legatee, 34, 121–23, 255, 319–20, 325
legislation, judicial, 392
legislator, 275–76, 356
legitim, 14n34, 321
Le Goff, Jacques, 33n48, 35n56, 47–48, 54n129
Leisnig, 236–37, 239
Le Maire, Guillaume, 100–101
Leopold, Anthony, 86, 87n89, 92
leprosy, 3, 107, 342
letters conservatory, 154
Levellers, 368
Lever, Thomas, 301
Leverington, 208
Levite, 312
Liber extra, 80, 135. *See also nos quidem*
liberty, 3, 24, 55, 65, 80, 124, 134, 165, 211, 221, 226, 267, 302, 325, 366, 368, 395, 396. *See also* freedom
Libri feudorum, 62

license, 46, 50, 126, 133, 143, 187, 191, 195–96, 199, 270, 284, 352
Liechte, Kaspar, 242
light, 522–53, 234, 270, 284, 323, 328
Lincoln College, Oxford, 195
Littleton, Thomas, 207, 355, 357
Lizerand, Georges, 91n108, 92n112, 93n113, 94
loans, 69, 101, 117, 225, 274
locality, 53, 149, 155, 189, 247, 284, 339
location, 62, 64, 69, 128–29, 134, 140–41, 154–55, 159, 167, 199, 202, 211, 254, 331–32
Locke, John, 375
Lollards, 112, 228, 244
Lombardo, Alessandro, 47
lord, 1, 2, 12, 16, 17, 37, 58, 79, 83, 86, 92, 95, 108–11, 114, 161n137, 162, 187, 194, 209, 218, 230, 247, 250, 287, 298–99, 313–14, 316, 324, 329–34, 344–46, 357–58, 361–62, 364, 366–67, 369–72, 377, 380, 383, 386, 390–91
Lord Dacre's Case, 287
lord high treasurer, 1, 209, 344–45, 366
lord keeper, 330, 332n266, 361, 372
Louis IX, 93
Lucerne, 231–32
Lull, Raymond, 90
lunatic, 333
Lupton, Thomas, 298
Luther, Martin, 220–22, 225n25, 228–33, 235n59, 236–39, 246n106, 248–50, 252–53, 255–57, 259, 266, 286, 360
Lutherans, 41, 184, 227, 240, 261
Lyndwood, William, 49n114, 70, 192, 193n89, 272, 273n41
Lyon, 183, 185; Council of, 46; Second Council of, 80, 85–86

MacCulloch, Diarmaid, 103, 104n140, 265n15, 272n39, 283n74, 284, 300n137, 301
Madison, James, 394
Magdeburg Centuries, 41
Magdalen Hall/College, Oxford, 148n97, 194–95, 202
magistrate, 184, 212, 235–37, 243, 252–53, 261, 317–18
maiden, 136

Index   451

Maitland, Frederic William, 3n7, 14n34, 39n76, 40, 44n92, 45, 73n47, 128n35
Maldon, 194
manner, 12, 78, 314, 326, 380, 385
Manuel, Nicholas, 225
Marshall, Peter, 19, 47n104, 267n25, 297, 304n155, 322, 323n225
Marshall, William, 246, 273, 275n47
Marsilius of Padua, 274–76, 288
Martin, Saint, 242
Martindale v. Martin, 335
martyrdom, 175n26, 222
Mary, Queen, 313, 327
mass, 19, 35, 39, 47–52, 54, 56–59, 65, 74, 88, 90, 106, 128–29, 132–33, 139, 140, 149–52, 154, 159, 165–66, 177–78, 185, 188, 203–4, 228–30, 234–35, 241, 260, 264–66, 270, 272–73, 288, 294, 314–16, 326
Mauritius, Caspar, 259, 260n145
Mauss, Marcel, 63
Mayer, Laurenz, 241
Mayer, Thomas, 276
means: to achieve an end, 45, 59, 108, 120, 125n30, 145, 177, 192, 201, 209, 230, 235, 250, 253, 347, 351, 358, 378, 392, 396; to help the dead, 35–36, 51, 54, 57, 60, 400; to obtain salvation, 15; other, 325; to perform charity, 3, 225
Medici, Cosimo de', 137
medicine, 374
mediocrity, golden, 348
Melanchthon, Philip, 209, 230n41, 233, 259, 286
memorial, 19, 25, 243, 304–5, 314, 385
memory, 36, 119, 120, 122, 129, 133, 182, 209, 278, 306, 384
mendicants, 53, 86, 88, 103–5, 134, 140, 170, 184, 230, 234–35, 324
Menedemus, 274
mens (mind), 71, 80, 186
mercantilism, 277
Merton, Walter de, 192–94, 201–2, 206, 395
Methodist Church v. Remington, 389
military, 50, 84, 88
Mill, John Stuart, 398
Mills v. Farmer, 12
mind, 71, 80, 139, 143, 172, 186, 276, 330n256, 337, 363, 382
Minorites, 109

Minot v. Baker, 390
mint, 235
misappropriation, 88, 303
misemployment, 86, 100, 123, 362, 365, 366, 370
misuse, 13, 220, 229, 279, 281, 315, 328
mode, 23, 77, 150, 161, 325, 380, 385–87, 389
Modestinus, 119, 121–23, 127–29, 131, 157, 209, 212–13, 219, 233, 259–61, 314, 323, 326, 385
modification, 9, 166, 279, 327, 328, 330, 371, 393, 395. *See also* alteration; cy-près; deviation
Moggridge v. Thackwell, 17n44, 386, 390
Molay, Jacques de, 91, 97
Molina, Luis, 162, 163n147
Mollat, Michel, 169, 183
monastery, 39, 42, 50, 51, 64–66, 68, 74, 82, 85, 92, 97, 89, 90, 103, 107, 109, 111, 128, 135, 138–40, 152, 159, 173, 189–97, 199, 204, 206, 214–16, 221, 227, 229–31, 234, 236–37, 244, 254, 257, 260, 262–68, 271, 275–78, 280–83, 285, 289, 296–99, 305, 307, 311, 320, 339, 382
monasticism, 169, 207
Moneta, Johannes Petrus, 161–62
money, 3, 7, 10, 13–14, 26–27, 30, 31, 34, 36–37, 45, 49, 52, 55–56, 58, 68, 83, 86, 88, 90–91, 97, 105–7, 110, 112–14, 118, 120, 124, 128–30, 133, 140–45, 150, 159–60, 164, 168, 170–74, 177–81, 185, 193, 200, 204–5, 208, 215, 227–29, 234, 239, 241, 248, 255, 257, 265, 272–74, 277, 283, 285, 287, 290, 293–94, 305–6, 323, 326, 331–32, 336, 345, 350, 352–54, 359, 361–63, 365–66, 372, 377, 389, 395
monk, 35, 37, 42, 45, 51, 74, 89, 91, 113–14, 169–70, 184, 214, 227, 232, 235, 237, 254, 262–63, 328
Mons, 183
Montaigne, Michel de, 397
Moore, Francis, 4, 5n10, 331–35, 343n9, 363n81
More, Thomas, 18, 53, 58, 169n2, 172n18, 173, 250, 279, 289, 294–96
Mors, Roderick, 299
mortmain, 14, 46, 50, 82, 195, 196, 198–99, 288, 352, 379–81, 383, 385, 394–95

Mortmain Act, 379–81, 383, 385
mortuaries, 22, 288
Moses, 101
motherhouse, 190
Mühlberg, Battle of, 227
Mulheron, Rachael, 8n23, 385n161, 388
municipality, 120–22, 176, 179–80, 183, 185, 187–88, 228, 233, 244, 248, 287, 297. *See also* city
Münster, 246, 249
Murphy, Virginia, 265
Myconius, Oswald, 231

nationalism, 307
necessity, 70, 121, 158–60, 209, 249, 254, 293–94, 300, 321, 331, 348, 374, 381, 385, 391; of consent, 102, 117n2, 128–29, 134, 146, 161, 163, 187, 190, 196, 261
negotiation, 96–97, 195, 197–98, 243, 394
New College, Oxford, 191, 195, 201
Nicholas III, 106
nobility, 44, 95, 113, 191, 229–30, 258, 266, 277, 297, 307
Nogaret, Guillaume de, 91–92
non-conformism, 2, 344–45
nonperformance, 58, 78, 80, 118n5, 150, 202, 271, 290, 292, 335–36, 398. *See also* burden of performance; performance
non-residence, 349
Norfolk, 200, 271; Duke of, 271
norm, 4, 22, 62, 63, 67, 77, 79, 127, 135, 139, 147, 148, 150, 215, 240, 368, 381, 386
Norman Conquest, 45
Northumberland, Duke of, 309, 322
nos quidem, 80, 135
Nottingham, Lord. *See* Finch, Heneage
Novels, 73, 145n89
Noy, William, 364–66
nullification, 64, 162, 320
Nuremberg, 227, 240

oath, 66, 76, 96, 202, 250
obedience, 170, 206n130, 277–79, 301, 315, 327, 344–45
Oberried, 240
obit, 52, 284
object, 3, 11, 15, 141, 160, 331, 332, 357, 360–61, 366, 372, 381, 383, 386–88, 390

oblation, 64–65
observance, exact or strict, 7, 9, 29, 68, 70, 71n43, 86, 98, 104, 118, 125, 133, 146n91, 150–51, 156, 160, 165, 202, 204, 207, 256, 258, 272–73, 276, 279, 325–27, 353, 356, 359. *See also* deviation
Ockham. *See* William of Ockham
Oldendorp, Johann, 253, 258
Oldham, Hugh, 206
Oldradus de Ponte. *See* Ponte
Onesiphorus, 33
ordinance, 184, 194, 201, 229, 235–36, 239, 253, 348, 362
ordinary, 11, 156, 161, 204, 272, 328. *See also* bishop
organs, 228
Origen, 169
Orme, Nicholas, 187n68, 201, 203n124, 204n127
orphan, 311, 317, 319
Osiander, Andreas, 227
Otho, 49n114, 272
Othobone, 49n114, 272
oversight, 76, 181, 226, 248, 329
Oxford, 191–92, 195–200, 203, 206, 208, 305, 325, 352

Padua, 186, 274–75, 288
Paine, Thomas, 394
Palmer, Robert C., 125n31, 266, 267n23
panic: deathbed, 383; superstitious, 49, 344
Panormitanus, 141–44, 155n116
Papinian, 211
parents, 20n57, 30, 34, 37, 44, 54–55, 64–65, 81, 108, 124, 176–77, 231, 238, 251, 315, 341–42, 371
Paris, University of, 92, 184, 212. *See also* Sorbonne
parish, 179, 237, 239, 241–42, 252, 267, 297, 303, 310, 313, 323, 331. *See also* church
parishioner, 328, 300n256, 334n273
Parker, Matthew, 201, 303, 317
Parker, Thomas, 377
Parliament, 95–96, 101, 187, 188, 191, 212, 266, 269, 277, 283, 286–88, 299, 308, 324n226, 329, 342, 349
parties, interested, 5–6, 13–14, 16, 62, 67, 69–70, 75–76, 78–80, 82, 96, 98, 101, 115–16, 123, 127–28, 130, 134,

136, 141, 144, 147–48, 161–63, 165, 189–91, 193, 198–99, 208, 215, 231, 268, 278, 326, 357, 363–64, 369, 371, 375, 377
Pasquier, Etienne, 212
Paston, John, I, 199
Paston, John, II, 198
pastor, 230, 236–37, 239, 312
patrimony, 30, 164; of the church, 90, 216; of the poor, 48, 219, 300
patristic, 26, 37, 171, 173, 395
patron, 73–77, 81, 86, 90, 93, 109–12, 114–15, 146, 151–52, 154, 164–65, 175, 180, 189, 191–92, 194, 196–97, 217, 232, 239, 248, 266, 268–71, 291, 363, 378. *See also* founder
patronage, 50–51, 68, 74–76, 94, 107, 110–12, 114, 119, 147, 156, 158, 164–67, 175–76, 194, 231; rights, 52, 61–116, 141, 151, 153, 165, 194, 236–38, 253, 268, 321, 339, 378
Paul, Saint, 33, 225, 231
Paul III, 253–54
Paul's Cross, 313
Paulinus, 229
Paxton, Frederick, 31, 32n37, 34n50, 47
peacemaking, 69, 80, 82–83, 87, 148, 174, 199, 338, 342
Peasants' War. *See* German Peasants' Revolt
Peckham, John, 49, 201, 272–73
Pembroke, 205
penitence, 29, 32–33, 46, 59, 65, 72
Pennington, Kenneth, 21, 22, 23n65, 118n2, 137n62, 138n66, 147n94
pension, 99, 144, 188, 196, 232, 237, 263
Pentecost, 35
perfection, 275, 400
performance, 4, 36, 56, 58, 96, 106, 112, 114, 124, 133, 152, 172, 272–73, 278, 290, 292, 354, 398; cy-près, 12, 340, 376; diligent, 152; imperfect, 9, 11, 202, 326, 355–56; of penance, 25, 32, 33; specific, 16, 320n207. *See also* burden of performance; nonperformance; observance; terms
perpetuity, 11, 14, 26, 49, 52, 62, 82, 84–85, 108, 113–14, 123, 165, 185, 203, 251, 288, 306, 312, 334, 353, 363, 370, 377, 379–81, 394, 389, 398
person, 161, 212n149, 331, 377;

contemplation of, 136; fictional, 114; specific, 15, 54–55, 78, 135, 137, 212n149; uncertain, 89
Peterhouse, Cambridge, 371
petition, 222, 353; for alteration of gift, 151, 189, 203, 208; to dissolve monasteries, 265; to God, 41; to heirs, 45; by an oblate, 65; of the poor, 51; to return charitable endowments, 297
Petre, William, 282
Petrus de Ubaldis, 139–41
philanthropy, 19, 27, 34, 55, 58, 180, 297, 305–6, 378, 384, 388
Philip IV, 82–83, 90–94, 98, 132
Pietism, 307
pignora, 63
pilgrimage, 42, 140, 150, 155, 229, 273–74, 279, 293
Pilgrimage of Grace, 286
Pirhing, Henri, 156–57
Pistoia, Cinus da, 131, 150
Pius II, 203
plague, 67, 186
plaintiff, 197
Plaisians, Guillaume de, 93–94
plate, church, 61, 67, 219, 267, 268, 274
pleonexia, 301
Plowden, Edmund, 24n1, 339, 356
plurality, 349
Pole, Reginald, 276, 277, 318
policy, 85, 115, 176, 184, 235–36, 242, 266, 342–43, 347, 349, 381, 385, 392
Pollock, Frederick, 3n7, 14n34, 39n76, 40, 44n92, 45, 73n47, 367n100
pollution, 240, 246
Pomesania, 240
Pontanus, Ludovicus, 144–45
Ponte, Oldradus de, 127
poor, 6–7, 9, 11–12, 15, 17, 18, 26–30, 37–39, 41–43, 48, 51–52, 55–56, 60–61, 68–70, 83–84, 87, 89–90, 95, 103–6, 108, 110–15, 118, 129, 132, 134, 136, 140, 146, 149, 152, 159, 169, 172, 174–86, 193, 198–99, 210–11, 219–20, 223, 229–30, 232–37, 239–45, 249–51, 254–56, 258, 265, 270, 272–79, 281, 283–85, 287, 290, 292–94, 296–303, 306–7, 309–13, 316–19, 323, 326–29, 331, 334, 343–44, 350–52, 359, 361, 364, 369–71, 379, 388
poor box, 179, 183, 234, 323
poor law, 183

poor relief, 17, 115, 179–81, 183–85, 232–33, 235–36, 244–45, 249–50, 255, 270, 277, 279, 281, 283–84, 287, 297–98, 300, 306–7, 309, 312, 316–18, 327–29, 334, 343, 352–53, 357, 370
Popham, John, 334
portion, 2, 42, 54, 133, 147, 187, 196, 238, 244, 306, 350, 369, 370; canonical, 141; charitable, 9, 184, 336–37; Falcidian, 38, 118, 121, 130; Levitical, 312; superstitious, 336–37
Posner, Richard, 393
possession, 31, 86, 171, 178, 283, 288, 299
possessions, 27, 42, 87, 93, 102, 194, 196, 202, 215, 258, 295, 299, 311, 327, 338
Possidius, 61
poverty: critique of, 102–5, 107, 225; holy, 294, 349; voluntary, 102, 225. *See also* poor
power: of bishop, 80, 155–57, 160–61, 207, 319, 320, 322–23, 328; of commissioners, 331; of commutation, 350; to convert, 70, 78–79, 87, 155, 160, 163, 214; cy-près, 2–7, 10, 15–16, 20, 81, 90, 118, 193, 213, 305, 307, 309, 312, 318–20, 341, 368, 373, 380, 389–90, 392–93, 400; of discovery, 149; of equity, 356; of executor, 197; to expropriate, 67; of feoffees, 365, 395; of founder, 189, 194; of heir, 371; of inquest, 149; ordinary, 12, 77, 100, 156, 161, 328; of pope, 70, 83, 87, 156, 159, 163, 190, 214, 258; of prince, king, or emperor, 121, 174, 216, 263, 308, 340, 359, 366–67, 372; redistributive, 70, 236, 261, 322–23; to reduce masses, 151, 154, 159, 166–67; specific performance, 16; of statute, 357; of supervision, 82, 226, 276; state or secular, 17, 76, 101, 126n33, 130, 174, 212, 226, 236, 247, 288, 310, 340, 389; to transfer, 70, 97; unilateral, 107, 109
praemunire, 215, 287, 367n97
Prall, Stuart, 367
prayer, 18, 37, 40, 49–50, 52–53, 73, 88, 90, 105, 113, 149, 154, 165–66, 171, 178, 187, 189, 234, 278, 287, 301–2, 337, 359; for the dead, 19, 30, 33, 41, 43–45, 52, 54, 112, 152, 203–4, 222, 229, 232, 239, 246, 264, 266, 277, 279, 284, 288, 300, 315, 336; intercessory, 189, 272, 323; kneeling, 35; in response to alms, 36, 51–52
preacher, 10, 129, 192, 230, 239, 243, 252, 258, 301, 352, 359, 362–63, 372
precarium, 30
precedent, 9, 17, 23, 83, 89, 189, 192, 203, 213, 236, 267, 279, 296, 313, 333, 336, 338–41, 345, 348, 365–66, 368–69, 372, 379, 382, 385, 395–96
precision: in fulfillment of wishes or gift, 71, 166, 192, 325, 330, 375; in signification, 382; in soteriology, 48–49, 53–54, 103. *See also* interpretation, strict; observance; terms
predestination, 59, 221, 293, 302, 312
prelate, 125, 191–92, 216, 228, 289, 323
prerogative, of king or prince, 215, 258, 279, 341, 349, 351, 359, 361, 362n76, 365–67, 370, 372
prescription, 146
presentation, right of, 73, 75–76, 115, 226, 238, 362
Prierias, Silvester, 145
priest, 3, 36, 43, 45, 49, 53, 56–58, 73, 83, 108–10, 125, 136, 165, 171, 185, 187–88, 193, 198–201, 222, 229, 232, 234–35, 239, 269–70, 272–73, 287, 295, 336–37, 343
prince, 67, 81, 83, 90, 92, 125, 130, 134, 138, 144, 165, 174, 211, 218, 220, 231, 252, 258, 276, 295, 324, 351, 388
Princeton University, 13
prior, 85, 192, 194, 263, 265, 268, 271
priories, 78, 88–90, 196–97, alien, 82, 190–91
privileges, 101, 122, 210, 258–59, 272, 277, 327, 396; of charity, 7, 9, 11–12, 118, 144, 210–13, 325, 334, 356, 382, 387; of deathbed, 32; papal, 148; of religion, 136
Privy Council, 301
probate, 6, 15, 206, 287, 323, 343, fees, 22
proclamation, 263–64, 266, 343
Proculians, 123n22
procurator, 125, 134, 185
profit, 244, 254, 266, 270, 272, 277, 281–82, 304, 306, 327, 329, 335, 341, 360, 370, 377, 382

Progressive era, 8, 388, 392
propaganda, 18, 84, 91–92, 271–79, 280, 282, 285, 296
property, 23–24, 54, 63, 67, 73, 75, 77–78, 93, 103, 107, 115, 119, 168–69, 171–74, 176, 178, 180–81, 192, 199, 206, 214–17, 220, 250–51, 254, 275, 286, 291, 320, 327, 328, 331, 333–45, 347, 350, 352, 359–60, 362, 366–69, 373, 377, 379–81, 386, 388–89, 391, 393–96, 398–99; church or ecclesiastical, 1n1, 5, 61, 67–68, 70–72, 74, 86, 88, 90–102, 108–11, 151–67, 174, 185–86, 189–91, 193–97, 203, 209–10, 212, 218–19, 220, 223, 225–33, 235–40, 244–48, 254–59, 262–65, 267–71, 281–86, 292, 294–96, 398, 300–301, 303, 306–7, 310–13, 316–18, 321–23, 349; common or communal, 17, 79, 131, 173, 248–53, 300, 392; familial, 39–44; Franciscan, 104–7, 126, 132–34; monastic, 152, 189, 193–95, 206–7, 216, 227, 234, 244, 268, 275, 277, 281, 283, 339; moveable, 145, 268; personal, 15, 125; private, 17, 20–21, 173, 176, 188, 250–51, 253, 375; public, 79, 251, 378. See also rights, property
propitiation, 25
proto-humanism, 137
proximior, 155, 157
proximity, 155, 157, 390
prudence, 43, 166n166, 169, 171, 258, 277, 351, 377
pseudo-Isidore, 248
psychopannychism, 232
purgatory, 18–19, 33, 35, 46–48, 53–54, 57–58, 152, 264, 270, 272, 293
Puritans, 1, 2, 340, 344, 361–62
purpose. *See* cause; ends; intent; use

quarter, of estate, 42, 118
quartering, 397
quia, 77
Quia contingit, 100, 138, 146, 159, 161, 212n150
Quiltillian, 330
quod omnes tangit ab omnibus debet approbari, 147, 332

Raban, Sandra, 46n103, 187n69, 189n79, 394, 395n30

Rabban, David, 391n12, 293
Rabelais, 74, 210
Ralph, Lord Cromwell, 194
rate payer, 328, 358
rationalization, 87, 90, 178, 197, 348
re-entry, 290–92, 335, 356
rebellions of *1549*, 300–301
recipient, noncompliant, 124
reciprocity, 66, 77, 109, 172
recovery: of health, 45, 81; of property, 72, 96, 122, 208, 233, 255, 270, 290, 337, 355n53
rector, 290, 291, 339
recusant, 343, 359
redirection, 2, 21, 25, 58, 100, 118, 173, 174, 180, 190–91, 195, 218–19, 225, 228, 232, 235, 238, 241, 259, 273, 285, 315–16, 318n200, 336, 352, 359, 368
redistribution, 8, 12, 108, 178, 191, 217, 236, 261, 298, 315, 322–23, 347, 360
reform, 62, 74–75, 85, 87–88, 90, 107, 109, 113, 148, 168, 175–76, 178–79, 182–83, 193, 206–7, 345, 348, 359n67, 365, 368, 372, 388
Reformatio legum ecclesiasticarum, 281, 308–9, 317–22
Reformation, 2, 5n11, 9, 17, 35, 56, 57, 59, 60, 89, 101, 103–4, 110, 151, 153–56, 164, 189, 212, 342, 389, 394–95; English, 18, 22, 53, 247, 262–340, 342; German, 104, 183, 218–61, 299, 309, 360n70, 362n77; Henrician, 203, 263; magisterial, 247, 249–53; radical, 231, 248–52, 348
reformers, 195, 218–19, 228, 230, 235–36, 241, 245, 249–50, 253–55, 257–58, 279–81, 310, 317–18, 338
refoundation, 74, 195, 202, 280, 284
Regensburg, 183
Regius professorship, 227, 371
Reiffenstuel, Anacletus, 163
relics, 63–64
remainder, 7n18, 106, 365
Renaissance, 137
rent, 45, 227, 268, 270, 332, 334, 339, 360–61
repairs, 68–69, 83, 120, 142, 145, 149–50, 159, 165, 296, 319, 332–33, 353, 370
repentance, 29, 32–34, 41, 43–44, 54, 59, 223, 243, 319, 364

reprobate, 221, 250, 302, 312
republicanism, 374, 395
reservation, 90, 290, 379
Restatement of Trusts: Second, 3; Third, 2–3
restitutio in integrum, 70
restitution, 14–15, 25, 48, 54–56, 70, 83, 110, 178, 223, 232, 244, 293–94, 313, 338
restoration: of church property, 190, 318; of learning, 280; of monarchy, 367; through repairs, 142, 243, 320
resumption, 39, 76, 90, 94, 100, 108, 190–91, 201, 203, 268. *See also* revocation
retrieval, right of, 14, 50, 71, 187, 228n35, 240, 242, 262, 296
revision, of gifts, legacies, foundations, 10, 74, 163, 164, 187, 330. *See also* alteration
revocation, 44–46, 65, 76, 81, 83, 126, 147, 174, 289, 357, 373, 375, 379. *See also* resumption
reward, 14, 27, 34, 65, 169, 220, 222, 278, 286, 343n6, 376, 384
Reynolds, Susan, 21, 22n62
Rhodes, Cecil, 306
Richard II, 262
Richard, Lord Weston, Earl of Portland, 1, 366
riches, 26, 28, 30, 42, 58, 161n137, 170–71, 177, 251, 257, 274, 299, 349–50
Ridley, Bishop, 301
rights, 139, 146, 148, 156, 174, 176, 202, 242, 251, 331, 341, 352, 371–72, 381, 388; of beneficiary, 358n65; of the commons, 219; of commutation, 159; of the dead, 394, 397; of donor, 62–65, 97, 113–15, 119, 180, 226, 231, 239, 258, 262–63, 266, 269, 271, 291, 355; of God, 30; of heirs or family, 9, 14–15, 66, 114, 122, 124, 140–41, 181, 188, 226, 255, 259, 284, 320, 324, 337, 399; hospitality, 175; individual, 21, of interested parties, 16, 62, 93, 127, 133–34, 144, 190, 194; of the legatee or trustee, 320, 335; local, 252; of the poor, 178; property, 54, 77, 126, 237, 249, 268, 300, 339; public, 382; of supervision, 76, 79, 111. *See also* parties, interested; patronage

Ritchie, John, 350n36, 354, 358n66
Robertson family, 13
Robinson, Jonathan, 126
Rochester, 15, 149, 195
Rogerius, 122
Rome, 42, 87, 108, 149, 168, 185, 248, 254, 264–65, 293, 294, 300
Rule Against Perpetuities, 19
Rushworth, John, 362
Russell v. Allen, 390

Sabinians, 123n22
Sachs, Leslie, 309n166, 310, 318, 322
sacraments, 43, 125, 222, 224–25, 234. *See also* baptism; confession; Eucharist; mass; repentance
Sacred Congregation of the Clergy, 155, 164
sacrifice, 24, 36, 41, 44–45, 56, 57, 64, 65, 178, 222; without salt, 350
sacrilege, 67, 72, 111, 112n170, 113, 153, 184, 224, 227, 258, 281, 298, 301–4, 310–12, 316, 337, 343, 359
saint, 25, 35, 37, 40, 42–44, 51, 63–64, 103–4, 114, 174, 242, 257, 273–74; veneration of, 52, 222
Saint Evroux, abbot of, 190
Saint German, Christopher, 58, 285–96, 335
Salazar, Juan de Talavera, 56
Sales, Francis de, 225
Salutati, Coluccio, 175
salvation, 3, 4, 15, 25–26, 29, 31, 33–34, 36, 38, 40–41, 48, 54, 56–58, 60, 71–72, 105, 110, 148, 152, 162–64, 221, 225, 278. *See also* heaven; hell; purgatory; soteriology
Salvian, 29–31, 33, 38, 177
Sampson, Thomas, 317
Sanchez, Tomás, 157–58, 163
sanctification, 19, 46, 48, 72, 347, 400
Santiago de Compostella, 150
Sarepta, 183
Satyrus, 27–28
Saxoferrato, Bartolus de, 80n71, 106n147, 126–42, 147, 209, 211n147, 212n149, 289n95
Saxony, 306
Scaevola, 121
Scheyfve, Jehan, 322
Schmalkaldic League, 266, 338, 360n70
Schmalzgrueber, Francis, 163

Schmitt, Jean-Claude, 304
scholar, 7, 170, 193, 233, 319, 354, 371; poor, 7, 192–93
scholarship, 192–92, 228, 306, 354
scholasticism, 38, 47, 92, 115, 193, 249
school, 10, 88, 90, 152, 189, 192, 204, 209, 214, 227–28, 230–31, 239, 270, 281, 284, 303, 310–12, 326, 332, 335, 350, 352, 359, 360–63, 366, 369, 377, 385; grammar, 203, 296, 332, 353; writing, 332
Scotland, 104, 265, 269, 346–47, 366
Scott, John, Lord Eldon, 12, 16–17, 386, 390, 391
scribe, 321
secularization, 5, 28, 72, 151, 203, 218–20, 229, 231, 248, 258, 260, 264–66, 271, 300, 312, 338–40
seizure, 4, 66, 105, 152, 154, 188, 190, 212, 229, 235, 239, 247, 263, 265, 267, 269, 271, 278–79, 281–85, 296–98, 303–4, 306–7, 317–18, 337, 339, 342–43, 350
Selborne Priory, 196–97
Selden, John, 367
Seneca, 119
sepulcher, 350, 397
sermon, 14, 27, 32n44, 37n65, 172, 228–29, 241, 280–81, 300–301, 310, 313, 317, 326, 347n21
services, liturgical, 51, 189, 196, 346
servitude, 78, 117, 369–70
settlement, 15, 157, 199–200, 338, 375, 396
Seymour, Edward. *See* Somerset, Duke of
shadow of St. Peter, 351
Shakespeare, William, 305
Shaw, George Bernard, 397
Sheehan, Michael, 4n8, 5, 6n13, 14n34, 16, 25n3, 27n11, 32n43, 33n45, 36n59, 38n68, 41, 43, 44n92, 45n95, 46n99
Sheen Priory, 190
Shelley, William, 215, 216
shrine, 155, 222, 229, 273, 279
si, 77
sick, the, 49, 51, 83, 155, 274, 301, 311
sickbed, 239
Sickingen, Franz von, 226
Silber, Ilana, 66, 82
Simone de Praetis, 326

simony, 56, 107, 110, 112–13, 115, 165, 259, 302–3
sin, 32, 46, 54, 107–8, 110, 114, 132, 171
Six Articles, 300
Sixtus IV, 48
Skinner, Quentin, 368, 375
Skip, John, 280
slave, 3, 24, 80, 124
Smith, Adam, 1, 398, 399
Smith, Thomas, 285
social contract theory, 375–76, 396
Soest, 253
Somerset, Duke of, 309, 323
Sorbonne, 184
soteriology, 4, 8, 26, 48
soul, 4, 14–15, 18–19, 25–26, 28–30, 34–39, 42–44, 48, 50–55, 58, 72, 84, 95, 109–12, 134, 136, 139, 143–44, 147–48, 151–52, 156–58, 162, 164, 198, 203–4, 232, 236, 250, 254, 272–73, 277–78, 288, 293, 295, 323, 359, 398–99; health of, 4, 42, 95, 133, 139, 143, 157; soul's part, 39, 147, 323
sovereign, 174, 275, 277, 286, 289, 340, 361, 395
Spain, 56, 57, 79, 343
Spalatin, Georg, 239
spectacle, 120–23, 128, 157, 209, 233n51, 260–61, 314, 385
Spelman, Henry, 304, 342
Spicker, Paul, 180
spirits, 342, 349
Spiritual Franciscans, 103, 105, 126
Spottiswoode, John, 346
St. Andrews, 346
St. Gall, 240
St. George's Chapel, 203
St. John's College, Cambridge, 310
St. Paul's Cathedral, 300
Stadler, Ulrich, 251
Stainswick, 194
Stapleton, Miles, 203
Starkey, Thomas, 276–9, 399
state, 17, 22, 82, 109, 119, 122, 164, 176, 180, 185, 209, 217, 236, 247, 250, 260, 267, 284, 286, 292, 301, 303, 306–7, 309–10, 318, 329, 349, 361–62, 374, 388–89, 397–98
statute, 4, 14, 46, 82, 95–96, 122, 183, 201–2, 206, 236, 262–63, 266–68, 270, 280, 285, 288, 290–92, 296, 308,

statute, (cont.)
  321, 326–32, 334, 336–37, 339, 340–41, 343, 346n20, 353, 356–57, 365, 368–69, 380, 382, 390, 393–94; on charitable uses, Elizabethan, 4n10, 328–31, 357, 382, 390
Statute of Carlisle, 262
Statute of Uses, 14n34, 266
Statute of Westminster, Second, 290
Statute of Wills, 266, 334
Statutes of Provisors, 262
Stein, Peter, 121
Stewart, Alan, 347n22, 349
Stileman, John, 374
stipend, 187, 227, 272, 359
Stoss, Veit, 240
Stowe, John, 297
Strahan, William, 213
Strasbourg, 227, 240, 243, 246, 258, 265, 309, 316
Strasbourg Academy, 258
Stryck, Samuel, 259
Stuarts, 341, 342, 360, 367
Stubbes, Philip, 298
Sturm, Johannes, 257–59
subdeacon, 187
subject, 83, 174, 270, 282, 369
Submission of the clergy, 308
substitution, 12, 40, 119, 135, 261, 357, 366
succession, 8n20, 28, 30, 68, 114, 216, 223, 269, 363, 379, 392, 396. *See also* heir; inheritance
Suetonius, 118
suicide, 313
Summa coloniensis, 47
Summa Rosella, 289
superfluity, 38, 41, 83, 85, 86, 92, 147, 225, 251, 274, 276, 349. *See also* surplus
superstition, 2, 8, 17, 49, 57, 101, 113, 173, 175, 188, 222, 224, 232, 257, 259–60, 266–67, 270, 293, 302–3, 307, 311–12, 314, 319, 320, 322–23, 327, 333, 335–38, 342–44, 359, 361, 369, 372, 380–82, 385–86, 389, 398–99
Supplication for the Beggars, 265, 298
Supplication of Souls, 18, 58, 250, 295
suppression, 195, 202, 214, 228, 266, 268, 277, 279–80, 297, 299, 382
supremacy, royal, 271, 277, 286

Supreme Court of Pennsylvania, 389
surplus, 5n11, 73, 90, 113, 144–45, 158, 208, 326, 339, 359–61, 365, 369, 372, 385
survivals, 392, 397
Sutton, Thomas, 350–53
Swinburne, Henry, 324–26, 383
systematization, 306, 367

Tacitus, 39
taking-while-leaving, 66
Talbot, George, Earl of Shrewsbury, 264
Tarragona, Council of, 106
taxation, 96, 101, 179, 219n3, 239, 249–50, 281, 283, 328, 395, 397
Templars, 87, 90–101, 125
temple: biblical, 83, 161n137, 241–42, 311, 342; in London, 95, 285; Roman, 136, 260; of Templars, 92, 95
Temple Guiting, 203
tenant, 30, 333
Tentler, Thomas, 32
terms, exact, 149, 194, 201–2, 204, 272, 359. *See also* interpretation, strict; observance
testation, freedom or right of, 39, 319, 393, 398
testator, 1, 3–4, 6, 8–10, 12, 14, 16, 18, 20–21, 24–25, 28–29, 31, 36, 42, 44–45, 51–52, 57, 59, 61, 70–71, 80, 82, 118–24, 129, 133, 136, 139–43, 145–46, 149–54, 156–58, 161–64, 166, 173–74, 184, 194, 198, 205, 207, 209, 211, 213, 228, 230, 238, 255–56, 260–61, 275–79, 282, 287, 300, 308, 314–15, 317, 320–21, 325–26, 354–55, 358, 360, 370–71, 377, 379, 383–84, 386–87, 390–91, 395, 398–400
theft, 14, 64, 117, 161, 177–78, 244, 272, 343
Thélème, abbey of, 74–75
Theodosian Code, 64n12, 260–61
Thetford, 271, 326, 359, 361, 369, 385
thief, 56, 178
Thomas, Keith, 19n56, 303–5
Thomas, T. C., 280, 358n65
Thomists, 103
Thompson, Benjamin, 51n121, 190–91, 266
Thompson, Craig, 173n23, 273
Thurlow, Lord. *See* Edward, Lord Thurlow

Tiberius, 118
Tierney, Brian, 38n71, 69n33, 115, 128n36, 138n66
Tiraqueau, André, 210–12
tithe, 1n1, 54, 184, 236, 250, 268, 303, 311, 312
Tobriner, Alice, 182
tomb, 19, 177, 305
Tormarton, 187
torture, 91, 138
Toschi, Domenico, 157n122, 160n136, 161
Toulouse, 146
Tracy, Richard, 298
Tracy, William, 204
transfer: to another cause, 133–34; back to or out of commons, 21, 132, 299; at death, 20n57, 24, 44, 45; of jurisdiction, 11, 22; of property, 79, 91, 93–97, 99, 137, 147, 159, 161, 189, 217, 219, 233, 238–39, 255, 260, 268, 271, 294, 299, 334, 388; of relics, 64; of rights, 76, 376; of supervision or trustees, 185, 230, 331; of use, 68, 70–71, 85–86, 101, 120, 141, 168, 188n73, 190–92, 208, 212, 228, 312, 368–69. *See also* alteration; commutation; conversion; deviation; diversion
translation, 83, 180, 213, 229, 246, 255, 271–76, 288n94, 310, 317, 346, 374
treasure: of crown, 1, 333; on earth, 30, 39, 60, 221, 240, 244, 301, 347; in heaven, 39, 40, 60, 220, 222–23, 399
treasury of merits, 48
Trent, Council of, 72, 73n50, 148, 151–55, 157–60, 164, 165n159, 225
trental, 35, 204, 293–94
trust and confidence, 99, 335, 337
trustee, 5, 9, 13, 16, 62, 67, 93, 99, 113, 114, 122–26, 134, 137, 149, 169, 181, 186, 194, 230, 292, 294, 315, 325, 328, 329, 331, 334–35, 361, 363, 366, 373, 377–79, 383, 390, 394–95. *See also gravatus*
trusts, 7, 11, 14, 16, 63, 87, 88, 107, 114, 117, 118–19, 122–25, 132–33, 137, 178–79, 199, 211, 213, 251, 186, 292, 305, 315, 324, 337, 343–44, 354–55, 357–58, 375, 378, 383, 389, 392, 394, 399; charitable, 2–3, 10, 12–13, 328–31, 338, 360, 379, 382, 390, 395, 397;

discriminatory, 393; entailed, 286; private or non-charitable, 7, 394, 398. *See also* endowment; uses
Tudor, 188, 285n83, 298, 306, 319, 327, 342
turpitude, 82
Tuscus, Vivianus, 122, 128
Tyndale, William, 220
tyranny, 131–32, 303, 389

Ubaldis, Baldus de, 138, 141
Ulm, 240
Ulrich, Duke of Württemberg, 307
uncertainty, in gifts, 11, 89, 135, 184, 210, 331, 357, 369, 373, 383, 389
Uniform Trust Code, 2n4, 393
unilateral, 5, 67, 77, 81–82, 109, 116, 127, 148, 192, 270, 376, 388
university, 13, 92, 187, 205–6, 212, 236, 279–80, 312, 319, 353, 371
unworthy, 119, 125, 176–77, 299, 344, 372
usage, as custom, 62, 117, 236, 348
use: alteration, 13, 15, 23, 62, 68, 79, 87, 120, 127, 138n65, 146, 158, 181n46, 203, 205, 210–11, 214n160, 259, 338, 350, 355, 358, 367, 381, 396; bad, 84, 168, 246, 302, 338; better (*melius*), 10, 21, 58, 83, 85, 88, 90, 93, 105, 145, 158, 168, 173, 189, 205, 214, 216–17, 219, 228, 230, 258, 265, 267–68, 270, 278, 279–83, 294–95, 352, 361, 364, 392; charitable, 2–3, 8–11, 14, 17–18, 100, 118, 149, 194, 198, 244, 271–79, 294, 297, 305, 307, 316, 328–37, 353, 355–60, 365, 369, 379, 382, 390, 393, 395, 397; *coenobiorum*, 257; honest, 128–29, 140, 158n126, 160, 268; human, 147; inviolable, 92, 101, 376; licit or illicit, 106, 120, 122–23, 127–28, 130, 138, 157, 209, 259n145, 260, 261, 314; new, 23, 80, 86, 101, 119, 126–37, 140–43, 148, 160, 187–88, 191, 206, 209, 219, 225–26, 230, 233, 244, 246, 260–61, 268, 277, 279–80, 296, 307, 312, 317, 331, 359, 374, 392; pious, 41, 64, 70–71, 78–80, 83, 87, 95, 97, 106, 125, 130, 133–36, 139, 141–43, 148, 152, 155, 157n122, 160, 162–64, 169n3, 173, 174n23, 188, 192, 210–13, 218, 230, 238, 240, 254–57, 259, 260–61, 275, 281, 302,

use: pious (cont.)
308, 312, 314–15, 319, 320, 325, 328, 355; of the poor, 316; principle of maintenance of, 23, 64, 85, 101, 102; private, 81, 311, 360, 362; public, 233, 265, 383; secular, 71, 90, 147, 191, 259, 310; superstitious, 8, 259–60, 293, 311, 314, 319, 320, 322–23, 327, 333, 335–38, 342, 359, 361, 369, 372, 380, 382, 386, 389; worldly, 71, 147, 259. See also ends; improvement; intent, original
usufruct, 30, 67, 117
usury, 14, 54–56, 229, 306
usus, 7, 70–71, 78, 83, 86n86, 87n88, 93n113, 95, 99n129, 117, 119–20, 126, 128n35, 139n69, 141n80, 152n104, 158n126, 160n135, 164n152, 171n13, 180n40, 181n46, 219, 233n51, 255n133, 257, 259, 261, 311, 314, 316, 325, 365
usus pauper, 102, 106n149
ut, 77
utility, 8–9, 17, 51, 103, 147, 152, 155, 160, 162–63, 188, 209, 213, 257, 348–49, 358, 397

vacancy, 1n1, 51, 75, 85, 99, 229, 265, 339
Vaison, Council of, 28
Valla, Lorenzo, 20n57, 169–71
Van der Delft, François, 283
variation, 121
Vaughan, Stephen, 271
Vauzelles, Jean de, 185
Venables, Sara, 344–45
Venables Case, 9n24, 157, 344–45, 364–66, 370, 388
Venice, 185
Vermigli, Peter Martyr, 317
vestments, 301–3, 311
viaticum, 34
vicar, 363
Vico, Giambattista, 393
Vidal v. Girard, 390
Vienne, Council of, 91, 98–100, 102
Villavicencio, Lorenzo de, 183
virtues, 19, 169–70
vita apostolica, 103
Vives, Juan Luis, 176–84, 399
void, 78, 121–24, 133, 140, 160, 178, 211, 228, 268, 289, 320, 324–26, 333, 334n273, 336, 343, 358, 370–71, 373, 377, 380, 383, 387–89
voluntarism, 126n33, 368n102
voluntatem fundatorum, 10, 95, 262. See also will
votive mass, 65, 243

Waldensians, 184
Walpot, Peter, 251–52
Wandel, Lee Palmer, 224, 233n53, 244, 248n116
war, 83, 91, 140, 175, 190–91, 283, 367
warden, 112, 149–50, 187, 201–2, 208, 269
Warham, William, 206, 219n4
waste, 17, 85, 59, 119, 152, 178, 222, 242, 265, 268, 296, 357
wastefulness, 2, 145, 162, 171, 173, 175, 276, 328, 341, 350, 393
Waynflete, William, 148n97, 189, 192–202, 209
wealth, 19, 20, 26, 28, 30, 38, 41, 48, 51–52, 54, 55–56, 60, 104, 168, 170, 177–78, 180, 187, 194, 198, 202, 231, 237, 241, 243, 251, 265, 268, 283, 299, 340, 353, 378, 396, 400; of the church, 27, 82, 94, 98, 103, 107, 125, 156, 171, 194, 227, 231–32, 244, 267, 274–75, 280, 293–94, 298, 311–12, 316, 318, 322, 338; monastic, 82, 85, 281. See also possessions; property; riches; superfluity; surplus
Weiner, Annette, 66
welfare, social, 83, 176, 184–85, 235, 315. See also poor relief
Westminster, 191
Weston, Richard, 1, 366
Westphalia, Peace of, 338
White v. Fisk, 389
White v. White, 9n24, 17, 383
Whitgift, John, 342, 351
widow, 258, 311, 319, 373
Wilfrid, Saint, 42–43
will (*voluntas*), 1, 10, 80, 94–96, 124, 134, 137n61, 142, 146n92, 151, 153, 156n119, 157n122, 159n130, 179, 182n49, 190, 207, 255n134, 260n146, 262, 268, 321n208, 353n47; broken, 8, 133, 278, canonical, 7–8, 45–46, God's, 257, 315, inviolable, 118, 174, 179–80, 183, 190, 321n208; motivating aspect

of soul, 126n33, 368n102. *See also* intent
will and testament, 3, 5–11, 15, 20, 22, 24, 28–30, 35–36, 47, 56–59, 80, 104, 106, 135, 143, 151, 154, 177, 179, 204, 207, 210, 235, 277, 294, 319, 321, 324–26, 377, 396
William of Aquitaine, 74–75
William of Ockham, 126, 127n33
Wilmot, John Eardley, 383–85
Wilson, Miles, 281
Winchcombe, 204–5
Winchester, bishop of, 191, 194, 195, 197
Winchester College, 191, 194, 201
wishes, last, 6, 9–10, 12, 15, 25, 28–29, 66, 71, 112, 145, 162, 180, 200, 282, 304, 316, 377, 378, 394, 397
Wissenbach, Johannis-Jacobi, 260
witches, 342
Witte, John, 22, 238, 253n127
Wittenberg, 228–29, 233, 235, 246
Wolsey, Thomas, 70, 176, 206, 214, 216–17, 265, 285, 305
Wood-Legh, K. L., 49, 50n117, 66, 74n52, 110n162, 152n105, 187n68
Woodrow Wilson School, 13
words (*verba*), 43, 124, 382
work (*opus*), 120, 128, 145, 259
works, 9, 19, 26–27, 31, 35–36, 40–42, 46, 48, 50, 56, 58–59, 71, 76, 84, 103, 106, 130, 147, 169, 184, 204, 213, 220, 225, 238, 246, 256, 293–94, 296, 305–7, 312–13, 360, 374
world, the, 25, 28, 30, 38, 47, 53, 55, 60, 64, 84–85, 88, 90, 102, 104–6, 110–11, 170–71, 174, 176, 178, 214, 219, 225, 228, 230, 252, 257, 278–79, 305, 312, 347
writ, 14, 76, 290
Wunderli, Richard, 16n40, 59
Württemberg, 231, 307
Wyclif, John, 107–15
Wycliffites, 184

Yale, D. E. C., 357n61, 358, 362n76
Yale Law Journal, 392
Yelverton, William, 198
yieldedness, 251
York, 216, 313, 325
Yorke, Philip, Earl of Hardwicke, 380, 383
York Place, 215–16
Yorkshire, 188
Ypres, 184, 273, 277

Zaller, Robert, 263, 285n82, 286
Zurich, 224, 227–28, 231, 241–42, 246
Zwingli, Huldrych, 227–28, 231–32, 241–42

Also in the Studies in Medieval and
Early Modern Canon Law Series

Kenneth Pennington, General Editor

Bonds of Wool: The Pallium and Papal Power in the Middle Ages
Steven A. Schoenig, SJ

Gratian the Theologian
John C. Wei

Liberty and Law: The Idea of Permissive Natural Law, 1100–1800
Brian Tierney

Gratian and the Development of Penitential Thought and Law in the Twelfth Century
Atria A. Larson

Marriage on Trial: Late Medieval German Couples at the Papal Court
Ludwig Schmugge
Translated by Atria A. Larson

Medieval Public Justice
Massimo Vallerani
Translated by Sarah Rubin Blanshei

A Sacred Kingdom: Bishops and the Rise of Frankish Kingship, 300–850
Michael Edward Moore

A Sip from the "Well of Grace": Medieval Texts from the Apostolic Penitentiary
Kirsi Salonen and Ludwig Schmugge

"A Pernicious Sort of Woman": Quasi-Religious Women and Canon Lawyers in the Later Middle Ages
Elizabeth Makowski

Canon Law and Cloistered Women: Periculoso and Its Commentators, 1298–1545
Elizabeth Makowski

The Common Legal Past of Europe, 1000–1800
Manlio Bellomo

Huguccio: The Life, Works, and Thought of a Twelfth-Century Jurist
Wolfgang P. Müller

www.ingramcontent.com/pod-product-compliance
Lightning Source LLC
Chambersburg PA
CBHW020856020526
44107CB00076B/1815